CASE STUDIES
IN MUSIC THERAPY

CASE STUDIES
IN MUSIC THERAPY

Edited by Kenneth E. Bruscia

Barcelona PUBLISHERS

Case Studies In Music Therapy

1st Printing 1991
2nd Printing 1996
3rd Printing 2006

ISBN 0-9624080-1-8
LC 91-072288

Distributed throughout the world by:
Barcelona Publishers
4 White Brook Road
Gilsum NH 03448
Tel: 603-357-0236 Fax: 603-357-2073
Website: www.barcelonapublishers.com
SAN 298-6299

Cover illustration taken from artwork of unknown origin
Cover design: © 1991 Frank McShane

Acknowledgements of other publishers
for permission to reprint copyrighted materials
may be found at the end of each case study.

ACKNOWLEDGEMENTS

With Deepest Gratitude

*To the individuals whose stories are told in these case studies.
Sincere thanks are extended for allowing the authors
to share with the readers personal obstacles and triumphs
encountered in music therapy.*

DEDICATION

This book is a testament of the generosity and love of the authors. As therapists, they have generously given themselves to their clients, providing them with loving and healing therapeutic relationships. As musicians, they have generously shared their talents and expertise, helping to bring the joys and healing powers of music to their clients. As writers, they have generously given of themselves to their profession---taking the risks of self-disclosure, and struggling with great determination to describe the many ineffable experiences of music therapy. And finally, as authors, they have generously contributed their case studies to the present book. In appreciation and respect for their generosity and love, this book is dedicated...

TO

THE AUTHORS

Jo Salas, David Gonzalez, Helen Shoemark, Tony Wigram,
Carol Robbins, Clive Robbins, Edith Lecourt, Fran Herman,
Kenneth Aigen, Kerry Burke, Pamela Bartram, Rebecca Loveszy,
Amelia Oldfield, Julie Hibben, Alice-Ann Darrow, Nicki Cohen,
Helen Henderson, Claire Lefebvre, Janice Dvorkin, Kenneth Aigen,
Benedikte Scheiby, Diane Austin, Rhonda Rinker, Marilyn Clark,
Carolyn Kenny, Elizabeth Moffitt, Rosemary Fischer, Ginger Clarkson,
Jose van den Hurk, Henk Smeijsters, Gabriella Perilli,
Helen Miller, Phyllis Boone, Paul Nolan, Marcia Murphy,
Georgia Smith, Eugenia Pickett, C. John Duey, Dianne Allison
Nancy McMaster, Denise Erdonmez, Alicia Clair,
Jane Whittall, Cheryl Beggs, and Jenny Martin.

PREFACE

This book presents 42 case histories, each describing the process of music therapy over an extended period of time. The cases include children, adolescents, and adults receiving individual or group therapy in educational, psychiatric, medical or private settings. Examples are given of a broad spectrum of methods, techniques, and theoretical orientations.

The authors are highly qualified music therapists, and as the cases clearly illustrate, each therapist has very unique skills and areas of expertise ---as musician and clinician. Authors from nine countries are represented: the United States, Canada, Great Britain, Australia, France, Republic of South Africa, Denmark, The Netherlands, and Italy.

The book is intended for students and professionals in music therapy and related disciplines. Hopefully, it will be useful as a reference, a training text, and an introduction to the field. The authors and editor have made every effort to make the material accessible to the widest readership--- through clear, organized writing and through the elimination of as much jargon as possible. Nevertheless, it is unavoidable that some cases will contain concepts or discussions that will challenge the reader. Given the complexity of clinical work, and the depth of certain procedures, there is no way to insure that all of the cases will be completely accessible to every reader, or that every reader will be able to achieve a full or mature understanding of every method, approach or subtlety of music therapy detailed in this book.

Thus, when used in introductory courses for students outside of the field, or when used as required course readings for music therapy students, the instructor would be well-advised to carefully select those cases that will be most accessible to their students.

Two features of the book are important to consider. First, there is a glossary at the end of every case study. These glossaries provide definitions of diagnostic or technical terms which are not explained in the narrative. In most cases, the terms pertain to clinical conditions, symptoms, therapeutic techniques, or theoretical concepts. All terms defined in the glossary are indicated in the narrative with bold italics.

Second, it was not possible to provide definitions of musical terms and concepts, either through individual glossaries or one for the entire book. The reason is that, a rather large music vocabulary has been used, at least in certain case studies; thus to attempt to define all of the terms would have necessitated writing an entire music dictionary. On the other hand, the majority of case studies do not require the reader to have any knowledge of musical terminology.

A special note is also in order with regard to general vocabulary and spelling. Given that the authors come from so many different countries, and that the English language is written, spoken and spelled quite differently from one country to the next (even where English is the native tongue), readers will undoubtedly find variations in the way words are used and spelled. Throughout the book, the original spellings of the authors have been honored by the editor. Thus, British readers will "recognise" that Americans do not put a "u" in behavior, as do the Canadians and South Africans; and that Australians, unlike Americans, prefer to spell "improvise" with a "z" rather than an "s," which is certainly contradictory for the Americans because they spell "realise" with a "z." "Whilst" this creates inconsistencies between case studies, it makes for greater consistency within cases, especially where such words appear in both narrative and quotations (which are unalterable). More importantly, it became quite clear that the way each author used and spelled words gave important clues to their unique perspectives on music therapy and their clients, and that to change these aspects of their writings was tantamount to ignoring their cultural, national, and regional identities. It is hoped that honoring the author's language will make readers more comfortable with case studies from their own countries, while also reminding them of differences in perspectives when reading those from other countries.

As for differences in actual vocabulary or word usage, adjustments were made by the editor only with the author's consent, and only when differences in meaning or usage might have caused misunderstanding or confusion among the readers.

As for how the book is organized, Unit One provides an overview of music therapy practice written by the editor. Its purpose is to introduce students and professionals in other disciplines to the basic parameters of clinical work in music therapy. The remaining units contain the case studies, which have been grouped according to the client's age and treatment setting. Unit Two contains case studies with children (up to 13 years); Unit Three contains cases with adolescents (13-18 years); Units Four, Five and Six are devoted to cases with adults in private, psychiatric, and medical settings, respectively.

The Appendices provide a directory to the case studies according to: diagnostic or clinical condition, treatment setting, music therapy method, and theoretical orientation. As such, they serve as an index to the book.

All of the case studies follow the same general format, yet each is organized according to the unique nature of the case material. Every study begins with a title page, which includes the name, credentials, affiliation, and location of the author, followed by an abstract of the entire case.

Some of the studies begin with an "Introduction" section which orients the reader to the approach, client, condition, or related literature. This is followed by "Background Information," a section which introduces the reader to the client or group by providing biographical data, diagnosis, treatment history, reason for referral to music therapy, etc..

In a few instances, separate sections are used to describe assessment and evaluation procedures; in most case however, this information is integrated into other sections. Information on methods and techniques may also be found in a separate section or integrated into various parts of the narrative.

Every case study includes a section entitled "Treatment Process," which provides a detailed description of what actually transpired in each session or period of treatment. This is where the reader will find chronological sequences in the therapist's interventions, along with descriptions of the process of change evidenced in the client(s). In many cases, details on assessment, treatment, and evaluation have been included this section.

The next section, which appears in every case study, is "Discussion and Conclusions." This is where the author analyzes how or why music therapy worked (or did not work) with the client(s), or discusses broader issues or principles illustrated by the case.

At the end of each study is an alphabetized glossary which defines terms appearing in bold italics in the narrative, and a list of references which includes only those sources which have been cited in the case study.

It is important to note that every author obtained permission from the subject of the case study (or legal guardian as necessary) to disclose and publish matters and records privy to their work and their confidential relationship as therapist-client. The authors also used fictitious names for their clients, and disguised all information from their records that would reveal their true identity.

The editor would like to thank the authors again for their enthusiastic cooperation in preparing this book. It has been a real pleasure being editor, and it has certainly been a valuable professional experience. I have learned immensely---not only from the case studies themselves, but also from the editorial process and the many interactions with the authors---and not only about music therapy, but also about writing, editing, and working with colleagues! Thank you!

Kenneth Bruscia
Editor
June 25, 1991

TABLE OF CONTENTS

Unit Four: Case Studies With Adults

Unit Six: Case Studies With Adults In Medical Treatment

Appendices

Unit One

Introduction

The Fundamentals Of
Music Therapy Practice

KENNETH E. BRUSCIA, Ph.D., CMT-BC
Professor of Music Therapy
Temple University
Philadelphia, Pennsylvania

Abstract. *This chapter introduces the reader to music therapy by providing a definition, a survey of clinical applications, and a description of various methods, techniques and orientations.*

DEFINITION

Music therapy is an interpersonal process in which the therapist uses music and all of its facets---physical, emotional, mental, social, aesthetic, and spiritual---to help clients to improve, restore or maintain health. In some instances, the client's needs are addressed directly through the elements of music; in others they are addressed through the interpersonal relationships that develop between client and therapist or group. The music used in therapy may be specially created by the therapist or client, or it may be drawn from the existing literature in various styles and periods.

CLINICAL APPLICATIONS

Music therapy is used with individuals of all ages with a wide variety of conditions, such as: medical illness, trauma, physical handicaps, sensorimotor impairments, psychiatric disorders, emotional or behavioral problems, addiction, communication disorders, dysfunctional relationships, abuse, disadvantage, mental retardation, learning disabilities, and aging. It is also used to promote self-actualization, to stimulate developmental growth, to expedite or improve learning, to facilitate relaxation and stress reduction, to manage pain, to assist in childbirth, to accompany physical exercise, to treat musical problems, and to supervise therapy students and professionals. (See Appendix A for case examples).

Music therapists work in general hospitals, medical centers, psychiatric hospitals and clinics, schools and developmental centers, prisons, community centers, training institutes, private practices, and universities. (See Appendix B for case examples).

THE TYPICAL SESSION

What makes music therapy different from every other form of therapy is its reliance on music. Thus, at the core of every session is a musical experience of some kind. Music therapist may engage the client in any number of musical experiences. The main ones are: improvising, re-creating, composing, and listening to music---each of which may also involve verbal processing, drawing, painting, expressive movement and dance, play, poetry, story-telling, or drama.

In those session which involve improvising, the client "makes up" music while playing or singing, extemporaneously creating a melody, rhythm, song, or instrumental piece. The client may improvise a "solo," or participate in a duet, trio or ensemble which also includes the therapist, relatives, or other clients. The client may use his/her voice, or any musical instrument of choice within his/her capability (e.g., drums, cymbal, xylophone, autoharp, melodica, piano). The therapist helps the client to improvise by: creating an ongoing musical accompaniment that stimulates or guides the client's sound productions; presenting the client with a musical theme or structure upon which to base the improvisation (e.g., a rhythm, melody, scale, form); or presenting a nonmusical idea to express through the improvisation (e.g., an image, feeling, story, movement, dramatic situation).

In those sessions that involve re-creating music, the therapist engages the client in vocal or instrumental tasks that involve reproducing music in some way. This may include: learning how to use the voice or produce sounds on an instrument; imitating melodies or rhythms; learning to sing by rote, learning to use musical notation, participating in a sing-along, rehearsing, taking music lessons, performing a song or instrumental piece from memory, working out the musical interpretation of a composition, performing in a musical show or drama, etc.

In those sessions which involve composing, the therapist helps the client to write songs, lyrics, or instrumental pieces, or to create any kind of musical product, such as music videos or audiotape programs. Usually, the therapist simplifies the process by engaging the client in the easier aspects of composing (e.g., generating a melody, or writing the lyrics of a song), and by taking responsibility for more technical aspects (e.g., harmonization, notation).

In those sessions which involve listening, the client takes in and reacts to live or recorded music. The listening experience may focus on physical, emotional, intellectual, aesthetic, or spiritual aspects of the music, and the client may respond through activities such as: relaxation or meditation, action sequences, structured or free movement, perceptual tasks, free-association, story-telling, drawing or painting, dramatizing, reminiscing, imaging, etc. The music used for such experiences may be live or recorded improvisations, performances or compositions by the client or therapist, or commercial recordings of music literature in various styles (e.g., classical, popular, rock, jazz, country, spiritual, new age, etc.).

Music therapy sessions may also include verbal discussions. The discussions may be part of or subsequent to the ongoing musical experience, or they may focus on specific issues, feelings, situations, or events that are pertinent to the client's therapy. While verbal communication is essential in working with certain clients, it can be ineffective or undesirable in working with clients who are nonverbal or verbally defended, and who relate better to the nonverbal aspects of music.

Because music often overlaps with other art forms, a music therapy session may also include elements of dance, drama, poetry, and the visual arts. Such "interrelated arts activities" may focus on either the music or the other art form. For example, clients may improvise music as background for a given drama, story, or dance (thus giving greater attention to musical aspects of the experience); or conversely, they may create a drama, story or dance based on a given musical background (thus giving greater attention to the other art form). Similarly, song-writing may proceed by creating a melody to fit a given poem, or by creating a poem to fit a given melody.

In the same vein, music therapy sessions may also involve various games or play activities which involve music, or which spontaneously arise from a musically playful situation. These kinds of activities are used most frequently with children who need variety, or who cannot sustain musical involvement for an entire session.

FACTORS IN DESIGNING THERAPY

Client Need

Several factors determine which musical experiences will be most effective from a therapeutic standpoint. First and foremost, the therapist has to select or design the musical experience according to the goals of therapy. This is done by relating the client's problems and needs to the basic characteristics or requirements of the musical experience, and its potential effects on the client. A few of the many therapeutic applications of music are given in the paragraphs below.

IMPROVISING. Primary candidates for improvisational methods are clients who need to develop: spontaneity, creativity, freedom of expression, playfulness, a sense of identity, or interpersonal skills---as these are basic characteristics of the improvising experience. In addition, improvisation is useful in helping the therapist to establish a medium of communication with the client, and enabling the client to express feelings which are difficult to express verbally. It also provides a safe means of experimenting with new behaviors, roles, or interactional patterns, while also developing the ability to make choices and decisions within established limits.

Many different client populations manifest these therapeutic needs: from obsessive-compulsive children to adults with borderline or narcissistic personality disorders; from autistic, nonverbal children to verbally aggressive adolescents; from impulsive, acting out children to inhibited, depressed adults; and from developmentally delayed or physically disabled children to children free of handicap.

RE-CREATING. Primary candidates for re-creative methods are clients who need to: develop sensorimotor skills, learn adaptive behaviors, maintain reality orientation, master different role behaviors, identify with the feelings and ideas of others, or work cooperatively towards common goals---as these are basic requirements of singing or playing pre-composed music.

For example, individual singing lessons can help individuals who have speech impairments to help improve their articulation or fluency. In contrast, group singing can build reality orientation in elderly individuals, or help mentally retarded people develop adaptive behavior; or build cohesiveness in a dysfunctional family or group.

Playing instruments can help physically disabled clients to develop gross and fine motor coordination. When combined with reading notation, playing instruments can help learning disabled children to develop auditory-motor or visual-motor integration. With emotionally disturbed children, instrumental ensembles can be used to overcome behavior problems and to control impulsivity. Instruments can also help mentally retarded individuals to better understand the world of objects.

COMPOSING. Primary candidates for compositional methods are clients who need to: organize their decision-making, learn selectivity and commitment, develop economy of means, identify and develop themes, document inner thoughts and feelings, or have tangible evidence of personal achievements---as these are some of the basic characteristics of composing.

Perhaps the best example is song-writing, the most commonly used of these methods. With hospitalized children, writing songs can be a means of expressing and understanding their fears, and then leaving them there---on the paper! Song-writing can also provide adults dying of cancer with a container for expressing their feelings---about life and death---while also serving as a parting gift to loved ones. Clients with drug or alcohol addictions often find group song-writing to be an excellent vehicle for examining irrational beliefs and fears, and for documenting their determination to change.

LISTENING. Primary candidates for listening methods are clients who need to be activated or soothed physically, emotionally, intellectually or spiritually---as these are the kinds of responses that music listening elicits. For example, hospitalized patients find music listening helpful in relaxing, reducing stress, managing pain, and regulating body functions such as heart rate, breathing. It can also be arousing, energizing, and reassuring.

With psychiatric patients, listening to songs invariably accesses ideas and thoughts that need to be examined and discussed, while also bringing to the surface feelings that need to be expressed and shared. With individuals in psychotherapy, music listening can be used to stimulate images, fantasies, associations, and memories, all of which contribute immeasurably to the process. And with elderly individuals, listening to music can facilitate structured reminiscence or a review of their lives.

With learning disabled and mentally retarded children, perceptual listening tasks can be used to build auditory processing skills. Listening to songs and following the lyrics can also help these children to learn and memorize colors, numbers, vocabulary, behavior sequences and a host of other academic subjects.

Finally, with all client populations music listening is of inimitable value in bringing about spiritual highs or peak experiences. Such experiences instill hope and courage, while reaffirming the beauty of life---and its struggles.

OTHER. As for the other methods used in music therapy, primary candidates for verbal methods are those clients who need to bridge verbal and nonverbal modes of expression and communication. Primary candidates for interrelated arts and play methods are those clients who need to explore self-expression and communication through cross-modal sensory experiences.

The subtle and wonderful thing about music therapy is that, in actuality, every musical experience can be adapted to meet a broad spectrum of client needs. For example, consider how: improvising can be adapted to explore experiences of structure as well as freedom: re-creating music can be adapted to encourage free self-expression as well as compliance with the score; composing can be adapted to require spontaneity as well as planned decision-making; and listening can be adapted to be active as well as passive, or physical as well as intellectual.

Client's Musical Capabilities

The second factor to consider in designing music therapy is the client's musical capabilities. Since many clients have not had previous musical training, music therapy sessions are always designed to take advantage of the innate tendencies of all human beings to make music at their own developmental levels.

Music therapists believe that all individuals, regardless of age or musical background, have a basic capacity for musical expression and/or appreciation. This basic capacity does not require the special talents or extensive training that highly accomplished musicians have, but rather stems from general learnings and achievements that occur during the normal process of human development. Put another way, the process of human development prepares everyone to be a music-maker and music-lover---at a basic (not necessarily professional) level. This basic or normal capacity for music includes the potential for learning to: sing, play simple instruments, move to music, react to the elements of music, perceive relationships between sounds, remember music, image to music, and ascribe meaning to musical experience.

Of course, in clinical situations, music therapists often encounter clients who have physical, emotional, or mental impairments that interefere with these basic musical potentials. In fact, much can be learned about the nature of the client's impairment by assessing which of the basic musical potentials are missing or inadequately developed. For example, a client with a communication disorder may be unable to: sing, articulate lyrics, reproduce rhythms or melodies, order sound sequences, or participate in a musical ensemble---depending upon the specific nature of the disorder.

Care is always taken to adapt music therapy experiences to the capabilities of the client and to avoid anything that might cause harm or unncessary pain of any kind. Music therapists also screen clients who may have adverse psychological or psychophysiological reactions to musical participation.

Client's Preferences

Music therapy at its best is a source of motivation for therapeutic change. To insure that this happens, it is important for the therapist to select and design the musical experiences according to the client's tastes, preferences, and requests.   Important considerations are the client's proclivities with regard to
    ---type of activity (e.g., musical or nonmusical),
    ---setting (e.g., solo, duet or ensemble),
    ---type of musical experience (e.g., improvising or listening),
    ---musical medium (e.g., vocal or instrumental),
    ---instrument (e.g., drum or marimba),
    ---role (e.g., leader or follower), and
    ---style (e.g., rock or classical).
Of course, it is also important to realize that the client's preferences may be a manifestation of his/her problem, and therefore in need of modification or expansion. For example, a client who always insists on making music alone may need to derive some pleasure from ensemble work; or a client who will only listen to fast, loud music may need to develop an appreciation for more soothing selections.

THE CLINICAL PROCESS

The process of music therapy involves three basic steps: assessment, treatment, and evaluation. In assessment, the therapist uses any or all of the musical experiences described above to study the client---his/her condition, therapeutic needs, musical capabilities and preferences. Ideally, assessment brings an understanding of the client that enables the therapist to formulate relevant goals and effective treatment plans. Music therapists have developed myriad approaches and procedures for assessment, often with a particular population in mind.

In treatment, the therapist uses music as a means of intervention---to induce specific changes in the client, condition, or state of health. This involves selecting the most relevant methods and techniques, designing the musical experiences, preparing the musical materials, planning the session, setting up the therapy environment, and then actually conducting the session.

In evaluation, the therapist determines how much progress the client is making as the result of treatment. Progress is usually evaluated by identifying what changes a client has made during the course of therapy, or by comparing the client's functioning level or status at the beginning of treatment with his/her current level or status. Assessment data often provide baselines or criteria for evaluating progress. If a client is not making any changes or improving, it may be due to the client, the therapist, or the ineffectiveness of the treatment strategy. Thus, evaluating client progress is inextricably linked to evaluating the effectiveness of various interventions and strategies.

Various approaches are taken to assessment, treatment and evaluation. Sometimes assessment is a prescribed set of procedures carried out in the first few sessions, at others it is a continuous process of observation intimately linked to treatment and evaluation. Treatment may be provided in individual or group settings, and may involve the client in active music-making, listening, or other music-related activities. Evaluation may be based on changes in the client's music and/or in nonmusical goal areas.

ORIENTATIONS

Music therapists practice within many different theoretical orientations. Depending upon the work setting and client, a music therapist may draw upon treatment theories from many different disciplines, including: psychology, psychotherapy, medicine, holistic health, human development, speech and language therapy, occupational or physical therapy, music, music education, special education, or other arts therapies, to name a few. (See Appendix D for specific theories and theorists cited in the case studies).

It is important to realize that a music therapist's theoretical orientation exerts a profound influence on his/her clinical work, in large part determining: the goals, approaches to assessment and evaluation, treatment strategies, the nature of the therapist-client relationship, the role of music, and the course of treatment.

QUALIFICATIONS OF MUSIC THERAPISTS

Qualification requirements for music therapists have been established by many countries throughout the world. In the USA, where there are the largest number of trained music therapists, minimum requirements for certification and registration include a bachelor's degree in music therapy and a supervised internship of 1,040 hours, or the equivalent education and practical training. In addition, a standardized national examination has been established for entry into the profession, and continuing education requirements have been instituted for those already certified and registered. There is also a trend towards requiring advanced studies at the master's or doctoral level for certain positions and clinical settings. Degree programs are currently offered by over seventy-five colleges and universities in the USA, and at various universities and institutes throughout the world.

Specific competencies needed to practice music therapy fall into three areas:

1) Musicianship (e.g., music theory, history, literature, composition, voice, guitar, piano, etc.);

2) Clinical expertise (client populations, development, psychotherapy,

group therapy, family therapy, medications, etc.); and

3)   Music therapy (foundations, methods, techniques, assessment, evaluation, etc.).

LEVELS OF CLINICAL PRACTICE

Music therapy may serve as a primary or adjunctive treatment modality, depending on the client's responsiveness to music, and the kinds of other services also available.   In some cases, a client responds better to music therapy than to any other modality; in others, the client's needs are better addressed through another treatment modality with music therapy serving in a supportive role. The reasons are manifold: some clients have difficulty with therapies that emphasize verbal communication; some clients have a special relationship to music, either because of previous training or special talents, or simply because they love music; some have used music as the main source of solace throughout their lives; some have attachments and associations to music that are inextricably linked to their therapeutic needs; some feel a special rapport with the music therapist, etc.

In an attempt to further clarify the role of music therapy in various settings, and to establish qualification requirements for the kinds of clinical responsibilities involved, the author has identified four levels of music therapy practice (Bruscia, 1989, p. 90). They are:

---Auxiliary level: all functional uses of music for nontherapeutic but related purposes.

---Augmentative level: any practice in which music or music therapy is used to enhance the efforts of other treatment modalities, and to make supportive contributions to the client's overall treatment program.

---Intensive level: any practice in which music therapy takes a central and independent role in addressing priority goals in the client's treatment plan, and as a result, induces significant changes in the client's current situation.

---Primary level: any practice in which music therapy takes an indispensable or singular role in meeting the main therapeutic needs of the client, and as a result, induces pervasive changes in the client's life.

ETHICS

Given the responsibilities inherent in all types and levels of clinical work, ethical standards have been established for the music therapy profession concerning: professional competence requirements; standards of clinical practice;   the nature of relationships with clients, colleagues and employers; responsibilities to the community and profession; research; fees, and commercial activities; and announcement of services (NAMT, 1988).

REFERENCES

Bruscia, K. (1989). Defining Music Therapy. Phoenixville, PA: Barcelona Publishers.

National Association for Music Therapy (NAMT). (1988). Code of Ethics. Music Therapy Perspectives, 5, 5-9.

Unit Two

Case Studies With Children

Like Singing With A Bird: Improvisational Music Therapy With A Blind Four-Year-Old

JO SALAS, M.A., CMT
Music Therapist
Ulster County BOCES
New Paltz, New York

and

DAVID GONZALEZ, M.A., CMT
Music Therapist, Private Practice
New York, New York

Abstract. *This case describes a 10-month period of music therapy with Gabriela, a four-year-old girl with osteopetrosis, bilateral optic atrophy, and resultant developmental delays. The dramatic changes in Gabriela's functioning while in music therapy sessions are discussed, along with musical, interpersonal, and archetypal elements which contributed to the effectiveness of the therapy.*

BACKGROUND INFORMATION

At the time of this study, Gabriela was a four year-old girl attending a full-time program at a child development center for visually and neurologically impaired children. She was diagnosed as having *osteopetrosis*---excessive calcification of the bones---which had caused *bilateral optic atrophy*. She was completely blind. Her head was disproportionately large, measuring above the 95th percentile for her age, while her height and weight were in the 5th percentile.

Gabriela showed mild to moderate deficits in physical, cognitive, and language areas, generally functioning as a 12- to 18-month-old child. She was able to walk with assistance, but seemed to experience disequilibrium, anxiety, and possibly physical discomfort with movement, in part due to her over-large head and decreased muscle tone. She preferred to be carried. Fine motor coordination was also delayed.

Gabriela had little spontaneous or purposeful speech. Her most frequent verbalizations were echolalic repetitions of phrases she had heard during the day. In a similar repetitive way, she often sang lines or whole verses of children's songs. She cried and screamed frequently in a high-pitched, penetrating voice. Occasionally she would say "No" or "Leave me alone" in an appropriate context.

Gabriela's receptive language ability was difficult to assess since her apparent comprehension varied widely, probably according to emotional and behavioral variables. The Vineland Adaptive Behavior Scales placed her communication skills at about the one-year four-month age level.

Overall, Gabriela was a seriously impaired child, unable to interact effectively with peers and staff, almost immobilized by her blindness and other physical abnormalities, insecure in her world.

At home, she was reported to be somewhat more relaxed and responsive. She lived with her parents, grandmother, older brother, and twin brother, who was born without abnormalities. Italian was spoken in the home. Gabriela's family was very caring, and supportive of her treatment at the center.

METHOD

Gabriela was seen in individual music therapy from October 1988 to July 1989. This case study focuses on the period from February to May, when David Gonzalez (who was already working with Gabriela) was joined by Jo Salas.

Weekly half-hour sessions took place in a comfortable, medium-sized room equipped with a piano, percussion instruments, and guitar. Child-sized furniture was stored along one wall, leaving the floor space open. A floor-to-ceiling window gave a view of the busy central hallway with its constant flow of children, toys, and helpers. The noise of children playing and crying was often loud in the music therapy room, accentuating by contrast the subtlety of Gabriela's music. We turned off the lights for these sessions, creating a restful, intimate semi-darkness, further setting off this space from the larger environment.

Our approach in this work, established by David in the initial phase of therapy, was based on clinical improvisation, *client-centeredness*, and an in-the-moment responsiveness to all musical, affective, and behavioral phenomena, to the degree that we were aware of them. This open-ended approach reflected a shared theoretical orientation, and was also particularly appropriate with this child, whose inner world was a mystery to us and her other helpers.

TREATMENT PROCESS

Phase One: October to January with David

During this time, Gabriela developed a familiarity with David, with the instruments---drum, cymbal, tambourine, piano and guitar---and with some of the forms and possibilities of music-making. Her musical affinity began to emerge in her readiness to participate and in her ability to play with rhythmic accuracy. Consistent with her characteristic remoteness in other contexts, her playing tended to be self-referential and self-stimulating rather than related or communicative. Vocalizing was minimal, although she did sometimes sing fragments of children's repertoire familiar from her classroom.

A strong rapport and affection developed between Gabriela and David, along with some ritual elements which were to remain significant throughout her therapy. Among these was the "name cadence theme," her name set to a minor 7th interval resolving down to a major 6th or up to the octave.

Phase Two: February to May with David and Jo

2/8/89. In my first meeting with Gabriela, David carries her into the darkened room. I notice her over-sized head, the fluffy red hair, the huge eyes, the blank expression. Standing near me, Gabriela nestling in his arms, David tells her who I am. He begins singing her name, playfully, quite assertively, reflecting the guttural sounds she makes in response. I join in and we improvise on her name in harmony, our voices spanning the range from bass to soprano. David moves to the piano, placing Gabriela in my lap. I sense her surprise, her caution, her absorption of tactile information about me. Her congested breathing is noisy. David plays the name cadence theme, then develops the music into a rhythmic improvisation. I sing with the piano. Gabriela taps the rhythm into the palm of my hand, audibly and accurately. This three-way collaboration continues for some time, with Gabriela responding readily to changes in tempo, occasionally falling silent, then resuming her tapping. Eventually David segues into a "goodbye" song. Pausing, he invites her to supply the missing word: "It's time to say..." She is silent. David and I sing goodbye in unison, very softly.

2/22/89. This time, I am playing the violin as David brings Gabriela into the room. She responds to this new sound with small birdlike calls. When I play her familiar name cadence theme, she immediately sings a sustained note in the chord. Her voice has an astonishing purity and sweetness. She continues to sing, weaving her voice with the violin. Her sense of pitch is as precise as her sense of rhythm. David sings too, mirroring and supporting her sounds. She initiates some rhythmic articulation. We follow her lead. She becomes increasingly animated and playful, clapping the rhythms as well as singing. The music develops in intensity, the themes changing and evolving.

I switch to singing. Now our three voices move together in harmony, David singing in falsetto to stay close to her pitch range. He sings her name. She echoes it. Then she echoes his name, and mine. I feel she is acknowledging our presence with her, and at the same time, her awareness of our separate identities. Gabriela listens to pizzicato on the violin, then sings again and claps in rhythm when, with the bow, I play her name cadence. I am struck with a sense of privilege. It is like singing with a bird, so delicate, elusive, and beautiful is her music. In the goodbye song, she is silent.

3/8/89. Gabriela comes in to the sound of the violin playing contemplatively. She sings immediately, effortlessly finding a related pitch, then introduces a playful rhythmic motif. In the space of the next few minutes, she initiates a series of new melodic and rhythmic themes, which David and I embrace with an answering musical playfulness. One of these new themes is "Skip to my Lou." She stops to listen to us singing the song, then sings it again when she hears me play it on the violin.

We launch into a musical exploration of this song. We try different tempi, timbres, dynamics, tonalities. Gabriela sings, she plays the tambourine and cymbal, she makes musical invitations and accepts ours. Her musical expression becomes ever more varied, confident, and full. David praises her in Italian: "Che cosa bella, Gabriela!" (How beautiful!).

3/22/89. In spite of the two-week gap since the last session, Gabriela has no difficulty establishing continuity. Hearing the violin playing her name cadence theme as she comes in, she begins vocalizing with explorative, explosive sounds. I reflect and interact with her on the violin. Then she sings "Skip to my Lou." Her voice is as full and strong as it was at the climax of the last session. It is an extraordinary voice for a tiny child; exquisitely focused and rich, confident and accurate in pitch. This time she articulates more of the lyrics: "Lost my partner, what'll I do?" Accompanying on the guitar, David amplifies the boisterous mood she has created. We improvise together, trying variations and new themes. At one point, David inserts our names: "Skip to my Lou, Gabriela," "Skip to my Lou, David," "Skip to my Lou, Jo." She echoes his name and her own, but not mine.

David plays suspended guitar chords, the pace slower now. I sing "Skip to my Lou, my baby." She echoes my phrase precisely, matching its tenderness and intimacy. We keep singing in a lyrical, rubato call and response. Her phrases answer mine, not mimicking, but musically and affectively related. I feel our music's pathos and beauty and the connection we have co-created.

David, listening and supporting on the guitar, begins to sing softly in a bossa nova style: "The music makes me feel so good, it makes me want to dance." But Gabriela is quiet for a long time. David and I keep playing, searching for her. Eventually she joins in with drum and cymbal.

When David begins the Goodbye song, she sings very clearly: "It's time to say goodbye," then falls silent again.

4/5/89. David carries Gabriela into the room. She is bubbling with merriment. Soon we are all caught up in wordless laughing. What's the joke? Somehow it's just hilarious to be together, to be laughing for no reason. Gabriela's laugh is the most joyful sound I have ever heard.

She starts making percussive mouth sounds in a rhythm which she emphasizes by clapping. She stops when we join her, coming in again a moment later when she hears the violin. We are now singing in three-part harmony. Gabriela sings half-notes while clapping perfectly coordinated eighth-notes. She sings with the violin when I play the name cadence, then she introduces "Skip to my Lou." The energy builds until she is laughing again.

I play a sustained D on the violin. Gabriela quickly comes in with an F#. Still playing, I sing lyrical phrases based on "Skip to my Lou," similar to last time. She echoes and intertwines her own phrases in response. Our music moves through different moods, different styles. There is a strong sense of excitement, musically embodied in the volume and syncopated rhythms. With David's help, Gabriela dances on her fragile little legs, amid more peals of laughter.

As we approach the end of the session, I play more contemplatively. The mood changes. In Gabriela's silence we feel her reluctance to leave this joyful space. We praise her and hug her and try to help her look forward to lunchtime.

4/12/89. Gabriela is rather subdued when she comes in for her session. David mentions that she has been upset this morning. Her participation is at first sporadic and quiet, becoming gradually more adventurous. She sings in unison with the violin, she brings in melodic and rhythmic motifs, she responds without hesitation to changes in style, tonality, and tempo. The session culminates in a piece with a rhythmic modal theme to which we chant her name. Gabriela plays the cymbal forcefully. In the goodbye song, she plays the drum but does not sing.

5/3/89. David plays the guitar while I sing. He introduces the name cadence theme. Gabriela is silent until I play it on the violin---instantly, she sings with us. Then she shows us a new theme, a half-sung, half-chanted phrase which we cannot quite master. For a while we all stumble around in search of a place to meet. Then, over a sustained D on the violin, Gabriela breaks into "Mockingbird," her voice stronger than ever. She even has a little vibrato, perhaps in imitation of the violin. We all sing, in a spontaneous four-part arrangement. As usual, it seems effortless for this four year-old to maintain a harmony part.

David changes the words of "Mockingbird" to "Everybody loves Gabriela." She picks this up, singing the words triumphantly. The improvisation continues in a collective composition with several related themes, articulated, interwoven, and restated with artistic intent and effect. As in any inspired improvisation, the leadership shifts imperceptibly between all three of us. It is Gabriela who concludes our piece with a full-blown reprise of "Everybody loves Gabriela."

5/10/89. This is to be my second to last session with Gabriela. David plays a meditative ostinato in a IV-I progression with a suspended bass in the key of A, while I sing quietly on the note E. In this setting we begin to improvise on her name. Gabriela in her very silence calls us deeper and deeper into the music. Staying with the same chords, David begins to emphasize the rhythm. Gabriela claps loudly, then vocalizes playfully as I start to add violin. I hint at "Mockingbird," and she immediately begins to sing it, soon changing the words to "Everybody loves Gabriela." The ostinato continues uninterrupted, with the suspended IVth chord modifying to become a VIIth chord. David plays arpeggiated chords while I sing a harmony line a third above her melody. There is a deep, gentle holding in the harmonic integrity and repetition of our music.

The music becomes louder, more rhythmic. David and Gabriela sing playful sounds on the offbeats. So far this session the harmonic foundation has been the IV-I or VII-I progression. Now David makes a change, introducing minor, dissonant chords in a swelling rhythm. Eventually he establishes a slow descending progression: C-Bb-Ab-G. I play, amplifying the solemnity of the music. Gabriela sings in chest tones, her voice somber and passionate. She finds an F to sing and holds it against the descending line, creating a cycle of harmony and dissonance.

David places her on his lap, tucking her between the guitar and his body. We all sing her name. She introduces the words "Everybody loves Gabriela," finding a new melody for this tonal setting. The music flows on. Sometimes Gabriela sings alone, sometimes our voices blend in harmony. Finally we end with an all-out reprise of the theme, loud, harmonically rich, passionate.

She does not sing in the goodbye song in spite of an extended pause on an unresolved chord. I am struggling with my own resistance to saying goodbye. Eventually I sing that I will see her one more time.

5/24/89. This session, my last, begins with a vigorous improvisation around a 7th chord, reminiscent of last week's theme, this time with a rock beat. Eventually Gabriela introduces more lyrical singing. The music evolves exploratively through varied themes and moods. I sing about leaving. She joins in, her voice dancing with the violin. The music keeps changing. David plays her name cadence theme. For the first time, she sings it herself without waiting for the violin or our voices.

Our music becomes rather slow and mournful. Now she is making half-vocalized sounds, blowing through her tongue and teeth. I play a farewell improvisation for her. She continues with her mouth sounds. To the melody of "Skip to my Lou, my baby" I sing about our time together. She is silent.

Third Phase: July with David

In the first session after Jo left, Gabriela was confused, anxious, and even frightened by her absence. It was as if without the violin and Jo's voice she were in a different and unknown space. This time together was devoted to re-establishing our one-to-one relationship, to moving through the feelings of fear and loss, and to finding new musical surfaces for contact.

Her initial expressions were crying, screeching, and bizarre rote counting in a pressed, high-pitched voice. Playing the songs that had been established with Jo seemed to make the situation worse. She became mute. After a long silence, she began to tap the guitar with her hands. This became the first area of contact for us in the session---a pulse---simple and primary. I sang a bright pentatonic melody over it, but she did not respond with her voice. She played the basic beat over and over again. After a long while, I changed the music to a more introspective chord progression with a flamenco feel. Still no vocal response came but her tapping increased in tempo. This was the first sign of musical responsiveness. It gave me hope. The music moved through a short, halting improvisation and then stopped.

At the end of the session, I was stunned as Gabriela spoke in an unusually appropriate fashion and asked for several songs that had been part of her repertoire with Jo and me. It was surprising to hear her speak with such clarity and directiveness. Though she was grieving for Jo, and still getting used to being alone with me again, she knew that this was her music place. She did not want to leave, she needed more.

The following session proved her need. She came into the room saying "Tickle, tickle, tickle" in a delightful bouncy voice. This became a word/tone improvisation in which we echoed and reflected each other's phrases and pitches. Her astute musicality was back and as playful as ever. After this she requested "Happy Birthday" which we blended with the "tickle" theme in a long improvisation.

Then she introduced a poignant new melody. I accompanied it with a slow descending bass over a D major chord, leading to a G minor 6th chord in the first inversion. There was an immediacy in it, an urgency and momentum like that of the earlier sessions, yet somehow different. Because it was just the two of us again the music felt very intimate, very precious. Once again we had opened again into new musical territory.

The significance of this renewed musical expressiveness was great. It indicated the depth from which her own inspiration emerged. She had made the adjustment to Jo's leaving. Clearly this had been a loss for her. But the willingness to reach out and play remained. The capacity to connect through the music was as strong as ever.

DISCUSSION AND CONCLUSIONS

Gabriela entered music therapy as a very disabled child, handicapped physically, poorly connected to the world around her, almost completely helpless, powerless, and vulnerable. In the context of a rich musical environment and our loving, consistent presence, she experienced herself very differently. Strengths were revealed that had been hidden by her disabilities. In place of impairment, she encountered her giftedness; in place of isolation, she experienced intimacy and interaction; in place of powerlessness, she found herself able to shape the events and circumstances around her.

Nordoff and Robbins (1977) speak of the "Music Child," a well-functioning and healthy aspect, realized in music, of an otherwise poorly developed or disturbed personality (p. 1). Gabriela embodied the Music Child. Her outstanding musical ability was the vehicle for her connection and interaction with us, for her unconstrained self-expression. Far from being simply a random talent without broader significance, Gabriela's gifts were superbly integrative and communicative. Music was the catalyst for the potential that lay within this child.

Our interventions were mostly in service to the creation of a safe, aesthetically rich world whose operating principles were acceptance, spontaneity, and creative freedom. In this world, Gabriela was able to actualize far more of her being than was usually possible for her. She was called by the music she heard. It awoke her own musicality. She found that her every initiative or response met with an immediate acceptance and an answering creativity. An ecological process developed, with each experience of creativity and interaction encouraging her to become yet more adventurous and assertive. Her singing grew increasingly strong, extraordinarily so for a four year-old child. She clearly felt quite free to introduce new musical elements and themes, as well as readily responding to the highly varied and often sophisticated offers made to her. Initially, our playing provided a context, a connective tissue for her fragments of expression. But as she grew in confidence, she was able to establish coherence herself, quite masterfully shaping our improvisations with the introduction, development and recapitulation of themes.

The musical coherence, artistry, and integrity of our collective music was rewarding not only to Gabriela but also to us. The kind of musical high point that we might experience from time to time with other clients was, with Gabriela, the domain of our musical contact. We often found ourselves surrendering to the music, following its calls and suggestions, leaping hand-in-hand into musical adventure.

This was at first rather disconcerting. Could this be therapy if it was so pleasurable? Were we irresponsible to let the therapist/client polarity fade, to be replaced by a sense of being fellow musicians? Our doubts were soon eased. Gabriela's flowering in these sessions made it very clear that whatever was happening was healing for her. We realized that indeed what we were experiencing was a rare fusion of the aesthetic and the therapeutic. Each musical step that suggested itself was also the right therapeutic step. Fluctuations and increments of expansiveness, intimacy, autonomy, and emotional expression were synchronous with the changing elements of the music. To address the issues of the therapy was to address the issues of the music, and the beauty belonged to both.

Gabriela, the epitome of musical expressiveness, paradoxically also embodied isolation and helplessness. Part of our response to her came from the presence of these feelings within ourselves, primal emotions perhaps from our own mute early life. Just as our shared music allowed Gabriela to open to a place inside herself where transformation was possible, so we also allowed ourselves to be deeply touched and changed. We felt vulnerable and exposed in these sessions, moved sometimes to tears---or to laughter. In the presence of such weakness and such strength as hers, there was an imperative to be as honest and as giving as we were capable of being.

Our encounter with Gabriela was an important and memorable experience for both of us, in part because of the uniqueness of this little girl, and of our musical experience with her. We have come to feel that that there was a further aspect of the therapy and the three-way interaction that was unusual and notable. This had to do with the presence of masculine and feminine archetypes embodied in our personalities and in the music itself. The masculine principle was inherent in David's physical presence, his voice, his interventions and general style, the instruments he used and the ways he used them. David generally supplied the musical elements of rhythm, increased tempo and volume, and vertical harmonies. He often initiated change and risk-taking. Jo's music was characteristically fluid, effecting changes through incremental modifications. She contributed linear rather than chordal harmonies. The timbre and register of her voice and violin communicated a feminine quality, reflected also in her style of interaction. (We realised after these sessions were over that Gabriela, blind as she was, would not have been able to picture Jo playing the violin. To her, this instrument was another animated presence in the room, to which she related with a particular affinity).

We consider that it was significantly the fulfillment of this dimension that allowed Gabriela to flourish as she did during the middle phase of her music therapy. Her musical expression, her whole mode of being, was qualitatively different in this archetypally complete context. And, in the third phase, although she was shaken to find that Jo---and the violin---were gone, she was able to re-establish her strength and expressiveness. The time with all of us had been an opening to which there would be no closing. We were recently told by her mother that, almost two years later, Gabriela continues to reach out triumphantly to her world through her music.

Gabriela was the quintessential Music Child. Music allowed her to access the magnificently functioning expressive and creative aspects of her personality. Perhaps we can see the Music Child as another archetype, when, as in this situation, the Child finds its Music Parents.

GLOSSARY

Bilateral Optic Atrophy: Irreversible damage to the optic nerves.

Client-centeredness: Therapeutic approach developed by Carl Rogers based on the belief that growth and healing will take place in the context of a loving, authentic, and nonjudgmental therapeutic relationship (Roger, 1951).

Osteopetrosis: Excessive calcification of the bones, making them brittle and subject to spontaneous fractures.

REFERENCES

Nordoff, P. and Robbins, C. (1977). Creative Music Therapy. New York: John Day.

Rogers, C. (1951). Client-centered Therapy. Boston: Houghton Mifflin.

The Use Of Piano Improvisation In Developing Interaction And Participation In A Blind Boy With Behavioral Disturbances

HELEN SHOEMARK, M.M.E., B.Mus, RMT
Tutor in Music Therapy
University of Melbourne
Melbourne, Victoria, Australia

Abstract. *This case describes music therapy in a school setting with Brian, an eight-year-old boy who was referred to music therapy because of an excellent sense of rhythm and the need to develop relationships which encouraged interaction and participation. The goal in his Individual Education Program (IEP) was to develop piano skills and the interactive behaviors necessary to do so. The method used was piano improvisation, based on the principles of "Creative Music Therapy" (Nordoff & Robbins, 1977) and the classroom philosophy of "Gentle Teaching" (McGee et al, 1987). Through music therapy, Brian developed several basic music skills, learned to spontaneously interact and participate with the therapist in making music, and increased his participation in classroom activities.*

INTRODUCTION

This case study took place in a residential education facility for children with multiple disabilities. The philosophy of the school embraces Individualized Education Programs (IEPs) for each student. Music therapy is well established, employing two part-time music therapists at the time of this study to serve 54 students. The music therapists work to accomplish aims of the IEP within a team approach. The main areas addressed in music therapy are communication and self-awareness.

BACKGROUND INFORMATION

Brian comes from a family of three children, two girls and Brian (the youngest). Upon admission to the school, Brian was 6 years old, and during the course of this study, he turned 8. The family lived in a country town, while Brian was in residential care at the school. He returned home during school vacation periods. Brian had attended the school for approximately 18 months at the commencement of this program.

Brian was born by normal birth at 27 weeks gestation. During the first few weeks after birth, he had persistent and severe bouts of apnoea (cessation or suspension of breathing) and bradycardia (slowness of the heartbeat), and was treated for prolonged periods with ventilation. The large doses of oxygen induced retrolental fibroplasia, which in Brian's case, manifested as detached retinas. As a result, Brian had no useful vision or light perception. His hearing tested as normal. Brian also evidenced seizures from the time of birth and has been taking Tegratol to control them.

At 6 years, Brian's pediatrician noted head-banging, no speech apart from clicking of tongue, rubbing of eyes with fists and continual crying at home. Upon admission to the school that year (and for many months thereafter), Brian presented as a developmentally delayed child, with the same characteristics observed when he was 6 years old.

His behavior also included vocal chanting which was often wailing in nature. The phrase was usually 4-6 notes, with certain phrases being used often, and others occuring only occasionally. He would persist with this wailing for periods of up to 45 minutes, and it was usually intensified if a caregiver tried to redirect him. Thus it was used as a form of communication to remove caregivers and to avoid engagement in activity (Donnellan et al, 1985). The only positive interaction in which he would engage was cuddling with staff during lunch-times. This was deemed inappropriate for a boy of 7, and was halted.

During the first 18 months at school, Brian participated in group music sessions with his class (4 other students). He showed obvious enthusiasm for musical instruments, playing any that he could find. He displayed a sense of rhythm, beating in a regulated fashion for as long as allowed. He enjoyed songs and was able to accurately produce the melody and lyrics of several lines and/or line endings from songs in his repertoire. He would not tolerate playing or singing with anyone else. He used no verbal communication. He was unable to cope with turn-taking, withdrawing into eye-poking and tongue-clicking for much of the session when not engaged.

RATIONALE FOR METHOD

At the beginning of the school year, Brian had been placed with a new teacher and new class. The teacher advocated that a "gentle teaching" approach be taken, as outlined by McGee et al (1987). Its basic goal is to teach bonding through three interactional stances: (1) that the care-giver's presence signals safety and security; (2) that the care-giver's words and contacts (e.g. looks, smiles, embraces, touch etc.) are inherently rewarding; and (3) that participation yields reward. This shift in philosophical orientation required agreement from all those working with Brian's class, along with additional training.

Brian's behavior showed that he had little trust for those around him, and yet he desparately needed positive input, as demonstrated by the acceptance of hugging in the play-ground. The classroom teacher encouraged all those working with Brian to adhere to the central concept of gentle teaching: that bonding is the center of all future complex human development, and punishment results in submission, "the antithesis of bonding" (McGee et al, 1987, p. 19). Staff were to create an environment of proactive rather than reactive teaching; using activites which would offer reward for participation and interaction. To this effect, music was considered to be a primary tool .

Brian did not use speech and language to communicate, whereas rhythm and melody (as evidenced in his chanting) already existed as avenues for self-expression and communication. In the classroom, Brian had produced on a drum the commonly known rhythm pattern: "ta...ti-ti..ta--ta.......ta--ta!" He expressed great delight (jumping and laughing) when the pattern was correctly completed by the teacher, and subsequently, the music therapist. His enjoyment of this participation with another person, and his sense of rhythm indicated that music may be a starting point for developing an equitable and rewarding relationship, in line with the "gentle teaching" approach. Given his need for involvement in positive relationships, and his interest in rhythm, it was agreed that the music therapy program could focus on interaction and participation through his already established uses of rhythm and melody.

The long-term goal specified for the IEP was to employ a range of basic piano techniques in musical improvisation with the music therapist. Specific short term objectives were designed to move Brian through a gradual sequence from passive acceptance of the music therapist's participation to more active initiation of musical interaction with her. They were: (1) To accept the music therapist's touch and manipulation of his hands when teaching Brian playing techniques; (2) To co-actively work with the music therapist to develop techniques, using some effort to move responsively with the therapist; (3) To co-operatively work with the music therapist to develop techniques, by anticipating movements and using equal efforts; (4)To independently achieve techniques after modelling without the need for physical contact; (5) To initiate techniques without being presented a model (i.e., without mention or example); (6) To respond to the music therapist's techniques with reflective techniques, by mirroring, extending, and contrasting what is presented by the therapist.

TREATMENT PROCESS

Brian's music therapy program can be divided into three main periods: the initial period (February through April); the exploration period (May through August); and the control period (September through November).

Initial Period

In the initial period, Brian received two sessions per week in the classroom, with another child participating. The sessions were scheduled for thirty minutes early in the day to maximize energy levels, however, sometimes the sessions were shortened due to the short concentration span of the two children. These classroom sessions provided a period of observation and rapport development. Each session was devoted to introducing songs that would be used later as formats for teaching communication and social skills as well as rhythmic improvization skills on the drum.

In the improvization work during the initial period, Brian and the therapist both played the same small, tunable drum. This was done to give Brian equal opportunities for creativity and participation.

The therapist responded to any patterns initiated by Brian with imitation or playing the patterns simultaneously. Brian's patterns usually consisted of straight quarter/eighth note patterns or combinations of dotted and straight notes. They were generally of 4 quarter beats' duration. The therapist would also initiate patterns, and Brian would immediately try to copy them. He was usually successful with straight, dotted and triplet rhythms.

During these improvization exercises, Brian was relaxed (smiling, at-ease posture) and attended the activity for periods of approximately 10 minutes. He used open-handed and closed-handed beating, scratching with finger-nails and rubbing with open-hand. He accepted the therapist's presence, and participation in turn-taking, but he did not enjoy playing simultaneously.

It became obvious in the period from February through March that Brian would benefit more from individual work in a place other than the classroom.

His rhythmic interplay with the therapist was beginning to be an important part of each session, and this needed to be extended and explored; however, Brian was often distracted by other activity in the classroom. It was therefore decided to remove Brian to the music room for individual sessions. This allowed the entire session to focus on his music-making, and provided the isolation to encourage full concentration.

Exploration Period

As sessions were transfered to the music room, the possibility of using the piano was introduced. Since Brian had enjoyed playing the piano with the therapist while in the classroom, it was hoped that the piano could be utilized within the individual setting to extend the scope of his improvizations beyond rhythm to include melody, and greater texture and dynamics. Sessions were held twice weekly?

Beginning with this period of therapy, improvisation was used as the primary modality, based in principle on the Creative Music Therapy model of Nordoff and Robbins (1977). As described in Bruscia (1987), each session involves three phases which occur spontaneously as the client's responses dictate. They are: (1) meeting the child musically, (2) evoking musical responses, and (3) developing musical skills, expressive freedom and interresponsiveness. The author had successfully used this model with similar children on earlier occasions.

The main approach taken in relating to Brian during this period consisted of: introducing new techniques for him to learn through modelling and co-operative practice; and playing in an alternating rather than simultaneous fashion.

When placed at the piano, Brian demonstrated enthusiasm in creating sounds, and craved to discover new ways to approach the keyboard. Several piano techniques were introduced, along with variations of them in speed, volume, and register. The techniques were:

> TONE CLUSTERS: Brian would produce these either with closed fist or open hand or full arm placed at a right angle to the keyboard. He would also slide from black to white keys.
>
> FINGERS: Brian would play two or three fingers together, or isolated fingers on black and white notes.
>
> GLISSANDI: Brian would slide his fingers or hands across the keys in ascending or descending motions.
>
> TRILLS: Brian would alternate quickly between the two index fingers or between whole-hand clusters.

Brian listened closely as each new technique was introduced, and immediately made attempts to copy the sound. Generally, he was unable to learn new techniques simply by listening, but required demonstration or physical intervention by the therapist. Since Brian was reluctant to accept physical intervention at the beginning, the learning of techniques had to be approached in stages, as described earlier.

Each technique was introduced to offer a new type of sound, while also offering a new hand shape and tactile sensation. Brian had spontaneously offered the closed-hand cluster, and this remained his "home-base" sound. When he felt insecure with a new sound or technique offered by the therapist, he would return to the cluster. Similarly, when he was angry, upset, or frustrated, he would play the closed-hand cluster continually, until the intensity of the emotion was dissipated. It most often appeared at the beginning of a session, when he was coming straight from the play-ground to the music room. Brian was still overwhelmed by the playground because he did not have the skills of orientation and communication he needed to play with the other children. He was often frustrated, and sometimes upset. The therapist would offer Brian the piano, and he would "attack" it with the clusters.

The second technique which Brian thoroughly internalized was the glissando. The therapist introduced this to Brian as a contrast to the clusters. It took him several sessions (over a period of approximately 6 weeks) to master the glissando. As the therapist moved her contact finger over the keys, she held Brian's hand behind her's with her thumb, thus exposing him to the action without the responsibility for producing the actual sound. For approximately four sessions, he needed modelling first and then co-operative work before he would achieve it independently. After this he would use the glissando to express happiness. He would often play a series of glissandi after the clusters, almost to indicate a finale to the expression of frustration.

Rather than developing new or more advanced hand actions, the next technique was aimed at further delineation of the keyboard. Brian was exposed to the black notes as distinct from the white notes, using open hand and arm clusters. The arm clusters often brought giggles and smiles. Brian discovered sliding down from black to white notes, and thereby demonstrated his understanding of their spatial relationship.

The use of isolated fingers to play isolated notes originated with the use of the children's nursery song "Hey-Di-Ho." It had been sung in the playground when the music therapist was pushing Brian on the swing. In the session it was used as a familiar activity to close the session. Brian would sing, while the therapist played it on the piano.

As the second period of therapy progressed, and Brian would sometimes arrive happy, he would request "Hey-Di-Ho" to open the session. He made the request by singing the first line. Then as the therapist played, Brian began to search out the notes, an octave above. The therapist put Brian's hand over her's, grasping his index finger with her thumb and third finger, directing it to the notes of the melody. This offered Brian the contact with the correct keys and the spatial interval between the keys in sequence, while receiving total support for the rhythm and continuity of the melody. Brian was thrilled, smiling and requesting it verbally with "More?". Brian did not achieve independence in playing "Hey-Di-Ho," but this was not a priority.

After playing the song a few times, Brian would sometimes initiate independent exploration of other notes on the keyboard. If the therapist played a single note he would seek out the note an octave higher, and match it, then move by tone or semitone either side to hear the contrast. He could sometimes happily settle on a note one tone apart.

The final technique to be introduced was the trill. This was introduced incidentally, as ornamentation of "Hey-Di-Ho." Brian's excited response encouraged the therapist to introduce it to him as a technique. The fine manipulation of two fingers on one hand to produce a trill was overcome by using the index fingers from each hand. This was introduced in the same way as use of isolated fingers, with the therapist holding the index fingers within her own fingers. Brian learned this within two sessions, initiating extensions of it independently. He used random intervals for the index finger trills, and then incorporated them into his cluster playing.

At this point, playing clusters became part of his happy repertoire too. He began to utilize speed in the trills. He began slowly, building speed as he continued. The control of this aspect gave him immense pleasure. The therapist also demonstrated the use of decreasing speed, and he incorporated this to produce lengthy passages of accelerating and decelerating cluster glissandi.

In the latter part of the exploration period, Brian began to arrive in a happy state on a consistent basis. This was due to increased communication and play skills for the playground. His increase in confidence was attributed to the "gentle teaching" approach and the acknowledged role of music within it. His exploration of the piano took on an independent nature, not requiring modelling, and initiating techniques he had learned. Brian accepted the therapist playing piano with him for periods of about 4 quarter-note beats at a time. The therapist's improvisation during these brief periods was usually restricted to a rhythmic underlay to support Brian's material, occasionally extended to reflect Brian's material such as the clusters. This step into simultaneous playing, saw the shift into the third period of the program.

Control Period

This was a period when Brian worked to bring all of his piano techniques under greater control---so that he could produce them as he wanted, and in any combination. He accepted the therapist's participation, often halting to listen and then rejoining her with the same sound or a contrast.

Brian had the tendency to increase volume as he became more engrossed in his playing. The therapist had until this point controlled that by offering a different technique, thus evoking a halt in Brian's playing, and then often matching the reduced volume and playing style. During the control period, Brian would still increase volume but would also respond to a diminished volume in the same playing style by the therapist, displaying greater cognitive control over his playing. The therapist controlled the volume of his playing only when it was considered that the forceful playing was withdrawing Brian into a self-stimulating situation.

Brian enjoyed the contrast of high and low notes. He played clusters in the bass region, using his whole body weight in an almost jumping style, and would glissandi up and down the length of the keyboard allowing the therapist to complete the glissando where his reach ended.

Late in this period, Brian enjoyed the simultaneous participation of the therapist. He was able to sustain his playing and listen to the shifts in the therapist's playing; responding sometimes with an answer, and at other times choosing to sustain his own material. He would initiate a "theme," and then either return to it for security, or insist on the therapist's recognition of his leadership capacity. His signature themes were the clusters and the glissandi (which never ceased to make him giggle).

Brian arrived upset for only one session in this period. He furiously bashed clusters and glissandi for ten minutes, and as the intensity of the anger subsided, the closed-hand clusters opened into flat-hand clusters. The fingers finally began to search out the notes of "Hey-Di-Ho," as Brian sang the lyrics. The therapist supported this with an approximate bass line (Brian's melody was not accurate) until Brian moved away to more general improvising, and the relationship became an equal one.

EVALUATION

Evaluation was conducted through observation by the therapist. Notes were taken with regard to aims being addressed, and the therapist's participation.

By the end of his music therapy program, Brian had achieved all of the IEP aims and maintained all of the skills he had developed. Brian accepted the therapist's manipulation of his hands in late July. He skipped working co-actively, moving directly to a co-operative mode for late-July and August. In early September (just before the school vacation), he began producing techniques after modelling and initiating techniques without any modelling. In late October, Brian began to respond to the therapist's techniques with reflective techniques.

The development of a relationship involving interaction and participation through rhythm and melody (the underlying 'gentle teaching' aim) was established when Brian first accepted the therapist's manipulation of his hands to achieve a technique. From this point, it was strengthened and deepened by the participation in the music.

DISCUSSION AND CONCLUSIONS

The three core phases of a Nordoff-Robbins session: meeting the child musically, evoking musical response, and developing musical skills, formed the ideal basis for Brian's therapy. The musical interaction this approach fosters, echoes the bonding that the 'gentle teaching' method so explicitly details for working with children with special needs. The emphasis was modified to meet the educational constraints of IEPs, with much time being spent on actually developing musical skills. Nonetheless, the philosphical stance of meeting the child musically and evoking responses was ever present in the therapist's manner.

The music therapy program provided Brian with an intensive period of success on a bi-weekly basis. This success in interaction and participation served to help raise his self-esteem. Evidence of the carry-over in self-esteem came from his classroom teacher's reports that his mood was consistently happy on returning from music therapy (singing to himself, moving through space confidently), and he had become quite co-operative in following instructions. The music therapy sessions helped him to work more efficiently and comfortably within the more difficult environment of the classroom.

After this program, the therapist left the facility. The ensuing music therapist continued the individual music therapy program with Brian. After a another school year, his musical accomplishments culminated in a high-powered and complex drum improvisation with the therapist, which he performed at the school Christmas concert to a rapturous audience of nearly 200 people!

REFERENCES

Bruscia, K. (1987). Improvisational Models of Music Therapy. Springfield: Charles C. Thomas.

Donnellan, A., Mirenda, P., Mesaros, R., & Fassbender, L. (1985). Analyzing the communicative functions of aberrant behavior. Journal of the Association of Persons with Severe Handicaps, 9 (3), 201-212.

McGee, J., Menolascino, F., Hobbs, D., Menousek, P. (1987). A non-averssive approach to helping persons with mental retardation. New York: Human Sciences Press Inc.

Nordoff, P. & Robbins, C. (1977). Creative Music Therapy. New York: The John Day Company.

CASE THREE

Music Therapy
For A Girl With Rett's Syndrome:
Balancing Structure And Freedom

TONY WIGRAM, B.A.(Hons), L.G.S.M.(Mt), R.M.Th.
Head Music Therapist
Harperbury Hospital and Harper House Children's Service
Research Psychologist
Royal Holloway & Bedford New College
London University, England

Abstract: *This case study describes the assessment of an eleven-year-old girl with Rett's Syndrome, and a period of therapy lasting twenty-two months, beginning with a structured, directive approach and ending with a free, more psychodynamic style of work. A variety of vocal and instrumental techniques are used in conjunction with games and playful interactions with the therapist.*

HISTORY AND DIAGNOSIS

Helen was born in South Africa on the 5th of May 1979. Delivery was by Caesarian section, and she weighed 3.2 kilograms. She has an older and a younger brother, both of whom were also delivered by Caesarian section, and developed normally. Helen was described as a "serious and sombre" baby, who was not very cuddly.

Her mother kept a detailed early history. She sat at 4 months, crawled at 6 months, stood at 12 months and walked at 16 months (with assistance). She babbled at 9 to 10 months; words followed shortly afterwards and sentences at 15 months. She would string her words together such as "Oh dear me," "Look at lights." She fed herself by 10 months. She had bladder (but not bowel) control by 3 years. By 4 years, she could partly dress herself.

As a young baby she had no major illnesses, injuries or hospitalizations. Her hearing and vision were tested when she was 4 years. The results showed normal vision, and a slight hearing loss in her left ear. She had reasonably normal sleep habits.

Helen's development had been very normal until she was 18 months old. At this time, she slowly started to withdraw. First, she stopped saying the few words she had learned, and then she began to cease making eye contact with members of her family. She retreated from the world around her, and for a year she did not utter a word or respond to approaches from her family.

At the age of 4, she underwent clinical assessment. At this time, she was of average height and build, had no eye contact, was hyperactive and at times banged her head or hit it with her fist. A diagnosis of autism was given, in that she showed four essential criteria of the illness: onset before three years; self-absorbed and detached behaviour; language disturbance; and persistent ritualistic and compulsive behaviours.

When 6 years old, Helen's family moved to England, where she was enrolled at a special school for children with learning difficulties. Meanwhile, still carrying the label of autism, Helen's parents sought for her to receive specialized education in a school for autistic children. A further assessment of her abilities was considered necessary, and she was referred to the Harper House Children's Service, which specializes in investigating children with specific disabilities that come within the autistic continuum (Wing, 1979, Wing, 1988). Many children present themselves with autistic features, and it is increasingly essential to unravel in detail some of the fine differences between children who have autistic disability, language and communication disabilities, and other identifiable pathological disorders (Wigram, 1989).

Upon completion of the first diagnostic assessment, the opinion was that Helen was not typical of autistic children, and that her disabilities might be attributable to another cause. The evidence in support of this was that, in spite of her autistic-like problems in communication and interaction, her development was normal until 18 months, and that it was afterwards that she began to suffer quite serious deterioration.

A diagnosis of Rett Syndrome was advanced, citing as evidence, Helen's early developmental history coupled with the hand stereotypies she was demonstrating. Children with Rett Syndrome can present as autistic children, and it is a disability which initially may closely parallel autism, although it does develop differently.

The first descriptions of the condition were made by Professor Andreas Rett (1966), but the more detailed studies undertaken to identify the girls who were suffering from this syndrome began to reach the literature in the early to middle 1980s (Hagberg, Aicardi, Dias & Ramos, 1983; Kerr & Stephensen, 1985; Kerr & Stephensen, 1986). The main diagnostic criteria for "classical" Rett Syndrome include: female child; normal development from the first 6-12 months; deceleration of head growth after 6 months; behavioural, social and psychomotor regression around 16-18 months; loss of acquired, purposeful hand skill; stereotypies of handwringing, lapping, hand-washing; gait problems; scoliosis; and hyperventilation. Autistic behaviour is not a diagnostic criterion, but is nonetheless a striking feature.

Professor Rett, the International Rett Syndrome Association, and the Rett Syndrome Association in the United Kingdom have long advocated the use of music therapy in meeting the challenges that the syndrome presents (Montague, 1988). Goodship (1987) also recommended the following: "Parents can discover areas of mutual enjoyment with their child; e.g. music of all kinds, swimming and water play, animals (especially domestic varieties), gardens and flowers. Music therapy should be experienced whenever possible, and every Rett's child seems to derive pleasure from watching other children at play".

It was this belief in music therapy which prompted Helens's referral for music therapy assessment, and subsequently music therapy treatment.

MUSIC THERAPY ASSESSMENT

Helen was initially assessed in September 1988 at Harper House by Louise Ridley, and subsequently in January 1989 by the author. The music therapy assessment at Harper House was developed in 1984, and now offers a process by which a careful and comprehensive look at the child's musical behaviour, by means of a free and structured approach, helps to identify factors and elements that contribute to a diagnosis, management and educational future for the child (Wigram, 1988, 1989, 1990). The assessment seeks to highlight what a child can do, and generate motivation, social responses and non-verbal communication that may have been either unsuspected or unseen in the child.

In any music therapy assessment, it is inevitable that one will see features of the disability, pathology, or disorder in the child's musical behaviour, and it is important to consider these in the light of all diagnostic conclusions. It is equally important to isolate and identify normal musical behaviour and skills that are inconsistent with diagnostic labels, and to write as accurately and eloquently about the abilities and responsiveness of a client as one does about their limitations.

The process of assessment that the author has developed and used consistently at Harper House does not involve a rigid or formal sequence of tests or events. The style is fairly free, using improvisation, and offering a range of opportunities for a child to present him/herself both in a musical and non-musical context. To obtain the necessary information, a number of different approaches may be taken during the course of the assessment. This may happen within one session, or may take two or three sessions. When attempting to differentiate disabilities within the autistic continuum, the author always explores in the assessment session the child's response to: close contact and interaction; distancing; structure; free environment with no direction; intrusive intervention and pressure; and an imitative, intensive interaction approach.

The author also includes some investigation into the child's response to conventional music-making (i.e., Nursery rhymes, musical games, television theme tunes or film theme tunes that the child may be familiar with, songs that the child is known to recognise (from information supplied by the parents).

Evidence can also be drawn from this assessment to investigate the child's responsiveness to sound generally, with consideration to any evidence of *hyperacousis, pseudohyperacousis, hypersensitivity* or auditory disability. The child's physical skills, including their ability to handle instruments and equipment, and also whether they have a purposeful use of musical equipment, can reveal much, and free vocal improvisation as well as imitating the child's sounds (in the case of more profoundly handicapped children) is used to assess the child's verbal and vocal responsiveness. There is also a part of the session where imitation of simple rhythms may be attempted. In addition, comprehension and cognitive skill are looked at in terms of the child's ability to follow a sequence of instructions.

The assessment covers four main areas:

---General Interaction and Response: Focus, attention, diverting behaviour, body awareness, response to physical contact, response to verbal contact, remoteness, excessive friendliness, response to direction, ability to initiate and direct, impaired sociability.

---Abnormal Communication and Behaviour: Language delay, *expressive and receptive dysphasia*, facial expression, rigid and inflexible thought process, resistance to suggestions, strange interaction, lack of awareness of the patterns of normal interaction, talking without listening talking without waiting for an answer, no desire to communicate, using people as objects.

---Musical Behaviour: No concept of rhythm and tempo, no concept of playing with therapist, no concept or limited awareness of turn-taking, using musical equipment inappropriately, transference of behaviours or features of pathology into musical behaviour: (1) Manneristic behaviour (twiddling, fiddling, twirling, plucking, spinning); (2) Obsessive behaviour: sequencing, orienting to specific sounds continuously, perseverating and organising therapist to respond in particular ways.

---Physical Behaviour and Activity: Balance, posture, dexterity, handling equipment, handedness, synchronicity, ambulation, clumsiness.

HELEN'S ASSESSMENTS

The preliminary music therapy assessment Helen had with Louise Ridley revealed some quite specific difficulties, as well as a responsiveness that was both unexpected and rewarding. Ridley recorded the pronounced hand sterotypies that are characteristic of Rett's Syndrome, and commented on the more or less continuous tapping together of her hands, predominantly right hand on left hand. She also found that Helen used her hands in constructive ways, such as: reaching out, holding, carrying, pushing away and returning certain instruments, toys, or objects; and allowing the therapist to use her hands to make sounds on the piano.

In the second assessment and during the course of the first period of therapy, many of these examples of intentional hand use became more clearly identifiable characteristics of Helen's personality, demonstrating elements of resistance as well as elements of obsessive and ritualistic behaviour.

Ridley also reported that Helen's vision seemed good, although quite often she made a series of short, fleeting glances. When she was particularly interested in some items, i.e. watching the cymbal or metallophone being played, she could focus and track. Her hearing seemed in no way impaired, although she showed a response in different ways to the sound source, sometimes becoming still, sometimes turning her head away from the sound source, and sometimes by vocalising. She was attracted by familiar tunes, and by some of the instruments already mentioned.

During the first assessment, she spent most of her time lying on the floor, or seated on a chair, and was not unduly active or restless. It was certainly pleasurable to gain her attention and her interest throughout this session.

Ridley did not observe any response to the use of Helen's name, and reported a variety of vocal sounds, including distressed whines when troubled, and attractive vowel sounds when she was pleased. She also heard the consonant "mm" towards the end of the session.

Helen came back for another assessment with the author in January of 1989, followed by a series of music therapy sessions over a period of four months. The second assessment looked in more detail at the way Helen was behaving in the sessions, and the potential value a period of music therapy may have.

This assessment showed that Helen's main areas of difficulty were in the constructive use of her hands, her attention and her communication skills. She presented as a strong-willed, active and excitable girl with "butterfly behaviour" (i.e., flitting from one thing to another). She lacked focus, had various types of diverting behaviour, and although she frequently approached and communicated in her own way with me, she also, at times, demonstrated a remoteness and a lack of ability to respond to conventional interaction.

From the first sessions, she was excited and engaged by the musical sounds that I was making, such as free vocal sounds, improvised piano, with cymbal and drum beats. It was apparent to me that we were going to be able to achieve a relationship through the musical elements, and that there were going to be elements in her character and pathology that would make the development of this relationship and her therapy difficult.

Particularly problemmatic behaviours and characteristics were: (1) Her continuous activity and moving round the room, settling only for short periods (unless contained); (2) Her collecting objects and depositing them with the therapist; (3) Throwing or discarding objects; (4) Hand plucking movements and flapping; (5) Lying on her back and hand plucking, or using her hands to stimulate the area round her mouth and cheeks; (6) Grabbing for things, including: items of clothing, glasses, cymbals and other instruments near at hand: (7) Smiling and giggling, especially when things go wrong or something she does causes a reaction; and (8) Provoking, teasing and resisting behaviors.

It became clearer that she had very little concept of the process of making sounds on the instruments or sustaining a musical activity. This made it extremely hard to build up a musical relationship at this stage. It was clear that Helen enjoyed music, but had difficulty in making music and understanding what could be done with the instruments.

It was against this background that a period of therapy began, which falls into two fairly specific periods: the first eight months following the second assessment, when the purpose was to engage and involve Helen through a structured and often quite directive approach; and a second and longer period, when some of the structure was sustained, but within a more psychodynamic framework which allowed Helen to channel her newly acquired awareness and skills into an expressive and interactive exchange.

TREATMENT PROCESS

First Stage: Establishing the Boundaries

The first stage consisted of twenty-five sessions, spanning the period of January to August 1989. I was essentially concerned with three important questions: (1) Can I build a relationship through music with Helen, either at an active or a receptive level? (2) Can Helen sustain some focus and attention, initially with prompting and persuasion, but ultimately through self-motivation? (3) Can Helen use her hands? During this quite difficult early period of therapy, the first two questions were answered as an outcome of all the energy that went into the third question.

Helen had individual therapy sessions once a week, each lasting 40-55 minutes. They were held in a large room, which was eventually equipped with a video system that allowed Helen's mother to watch the sessions in another room. Helen appeared unaware and unconcerned by the vide, and it was of tremendous value for the mother to see the sessions each week.

The sessions were quite structured and prescribed. Each contained the following activities performed in the same sequence.

--Hello Song: I played the piano and sang, offering Helen physical contact, but allowing her to be free to wander (3 minutes).

---Playing Drums and Cymbals: I helped Helen to beat drums and cymbals, using her hands or beaters. I had to encourage her to stay in the chair, and would often have to hold on to her to keep her beside me (4-5 minutes).

---Cymbal-Tamburine Game: I would follow Helen wandering around the room, while also presenting her with the cymbal and tamburine, and encouraging her to reach out for them (5 minutes).

---Piano-Cymbal Duet: I improvised at the piano, stimulating and supporting Helen who sporadically played the cymbal. I had to encourage her to stay in the chair, and would often had to hold her to keep her nearby (6-9 minutes).

---Distancing and Closeness: I would move towards and away from Helen, as she wandered about the room, while offering her musical material with voice, tambour, or metallaphone, and encouraging her to respond (4-6 minutes).

---Vocal Exchanges: Leading on from the previous activity, I would move near to Helen and focus predominantly on listening to her vocal output. She was free to wander around (2-3 minutes).

---Guitar/Autoharp/Piano: I would encourage her to sit, and then try to engage her in playing the piano, guitar, or autoharp, improvising supportive musical material (6-8 minutes).

---Goodbye Song: I would sing the same good-bye song every week, as Helen wandered around the room (5 minutes).

---Discussion with Mother: After the session with Helen ended, her mother would come into the room and talk to me about what transpired, as Helen was free to wander (5-10 minutes).

Specific boundaries were established for all sessions during this stage of therapy. These became very important in building mutual understanding with Helen, and with providing her with the means by which she could try to "break out" of a particularly confining series of obsessions and preoccupations. They were: (1) If Helen deliberately dropped the beater, I encouraged her and helped her to pick it up. (2) If Helen threw the beater or the instrument, I encouraged her and helped her to pick it up or retrieve it. (3) I encouraged Helen to stay within the area of the room in which we were working, although she had freedom of movement within that area. (4) For periods of the session, I prevented Helen from "hand-plucking."

Progress was slow at first, and for two or three weeks it seemed very unlikely that Helen would ever hold the instruments or beaters. Every time I handed her something, she allowed it to slip to the floor, or she pushed it away. Her hand-plucking stereotypy dominated. After four weeks, she was prepared to stay in a chair for a few minutes, but still consistently dropped sticks. I held one of her hands out of the way (usually her right), and for very short periods she would either pat a cymbal, grip it, or grip the stick and hit the cymbal. When she did use the stick to hit a cymbal or a drum, she would play sustained rhythmic beats.

The cymbal was undoubtedly her favourite instrument at this stage, and subsequently. I worried at times that she was showing an almost autistic preoccupation with it, and actually excluded it from sessions for two or three weeks. This was not successful, and I re-introduced the instrument as it had evoked the most response from her.

Vocally, there were some delightful exchanges, where she demonstrated potential for good eye contact, good imitative ability, and an appreciation of my vocal contributions, and a good sense of humour. Her vocal range was considerable, although quite often produced repetitive one syllable vowel or consonant sounds such as "ng, ng, ng," "mer, mer, mer," "go, go, go..."

In the vocal exchanges, she often showed a sense of humour which also came out in any games where I had to "chase her" round the room. Generally, she responded well to game-playing and "escaping." Attempts to contain her often met with considerable resistance, and although Helen did not become distressed (almost the opposite, she giggled a lot), it was seven or eight weeks before she could sit for more than one to two minutes without trying to get away.

Given the alternation between free and structured activities throughout each session, our relationship varied: it could be physically argumentative, frivolous, confronting, aloof, avoidant, affectionate and often humorous. Helen had (and still has) tremendous energy, and this came over very strongly in her music therapy sessions.

Several important achievements were made during this time. She learnt how to hold and retain instruments and beaters. She became much more focused, and was able to sit for periods of four to six minutes. The "freer" parts of the session became more productive, and we both learnt how to use games to interact. We came to unspoken agreements about periods of the session when we needed to "work," and periods when we could "play."

Although she still "hand-plucked," there were more sustained periods (one to one and a half minutes) when she would use her hands purposefully. She began to use her right hand. She became less "angry" and resistive to containment.

Toward the end of this stage, Helen began to realise the scope for expression through music, and her moods and feelings became more apparent both in the sounds she made, and the body language she used when she was making the sounds. For example, she could at times hit the cymbal with tremendous force, and occasionally "accidentally" hit me on the arms or hands when she appeared to miss the instruments. Alternately, with a smile and often a giggle, she could play the cymbal or tambourine with fast movements using a beater, and "dancing" as she sat in her chair.

Her response during the good-bye song has always been particularly significant. Quite often, even after a session in which Helen had been agitated, resistive, or very vocal, the moment I began playing the good-bye song, she would quieten, sit down on the floor or come and stand near me at the piano. Sometimes, she did not want to finish the session, and after I had left the room she would stay behind.

Harper House is five miles further on from the school she attends, and her mother noticed how on Monday morning (when she would come to me before school), she became excited and active when they passed the school, realizing that she was on the way to her session with me. Her mother felt the therapy session was something Helen very much looked forward to, and she commented on the rapport we had. She reported that Helen was beginning to show a generalisation of the skills and focus she was gaining in the session, for example in the increased use of her right hand. Following a summer break, we resolved to continue the therapy sessions indefinitely.

Second Stage: Freedom and Maturity

The second period of therapy lasted from October 1989 to November 1990. It began by building on the achievements of the previous eight months. By now, Helen had achieved a state where she could come and sit with me, without being "contained." This was perhaps the most solid achievement of the first stage, on which I could develop our musical and personal relationship. Because she was no longer discarding instruments and beaters, but actively seeking instruments and trying to play them, I realised that she had finally gained an awareness of the effect her music had on me, and my reactions to it. It was from this point that our sessions took on a more *psychodynamic* quality, where instead of making enormous efforts to initiate and sustain a musical interaction and thereby bypass or overcome her pathology, I was conscious of the amount of feeling and emotion that Helen was showing through her music.

Although we continued with some very practical activities to develop her tactile experiences, the use of her hands, and her ability to focus for longer periods of time, I also found myself increasingly respecting and responding to the unconscious material that was evident. Helen's moods could range from frivolous to furious, from happy to sad, from withdrawn to engaging, sometimes within the space of ten minutes. Like any child, she has a need to keep "testing" the adult and pushing at not only the boundaries we had established, but also my response to her emotional state. In this respect, the more recent sessions over the last nine months have shown not only an increasing state of trust, tolerance and understanding between us, but also an element of confusion in Helen. As I have relaxed my requirements on structure in the session, and begun to interact with her at the level she initiates contact with me, there have been times when she has almost given me the impression of recognising me as a "collaborating playmate." For example, in one session recently, we were making music "on the move," as we used the space in the room quite actively. She has a habit of moving away and expecting me to come to her on occasions, and on this occasion I hid behind the curtains and kept holding out a tambourine so that she could just run over and hit it. This was very amusing for her, as the role reversal allowed her to identify me as the "resistive and mischievous" person, and her as the person making an approach.

Initially, the format of the session did not change dramatically, but the structure began to decay, and the sections became blended together into a more continuous and overlappng series of musical engagements. The session still began with a hello song and contact was still offered. What happened after this depended very much on what Helen wanted to bring into the session, her mood and sometimes what we had been doing the previous week. A range of percussion instruments including a large metallophone, large drum, large cymbal, tunable tambour, rotary timpani, bongo drums and xylophone were always available, and also I kept to one side the guitar, the zither, a melodica and a pipe. I left many of the other small instruments out of sight, so as to remove the temptation for Helen to spend her time relocating instruments around the room. I placed the cymbal near to me, as Helen would frequently play it and also try and pick it up.

By the Christmas period, Helen was sustaining musical activity for long periods of the session, and holding beaters for periods of three to four minutes before sometimes asking me to take them or putting them down. Very rarely, she would throw a beater across the room, or drop it, and by this stage, I could ask her verbally to pick it up, and she would respond.

She particularly enjoyed hitting the cymbal either with a stick or with her hands, and moving around the room with me while playing together. I can hold it in different positions, and most recently in the last seven or eight sessions she has enjoyed seeing it held right up near the ceiling and then coming down for her to play. It is as if she relishes the instrument being presented for her to make a sound to me, and then watching it move up into the high part of the room again.

Her work with her left hand has become confident and sustained, even though she still plucks with her right hand onto her left wrist or palm. This does not stop her playing, and I have had parts of the session where, while she plays with her left hand, I allow her to fiddle with my fingers with her right hand as a substitute.

At first, it seemed almost impossible that Helen could start using her right hand, as it was the main instrument of her hand plucking activity. The first real break-through came when in the beginning of this second part of the therapy I once again started to hold her left hand whilst giving her a stick to use with her right hand. This time, it was as if her motivation was much stronger, and she would reach over and play an instrument either crossing the midline or playing to the right side of her body. She still wanted to swap the stick into her left hand, and would only do it for a short period to start, but she did show very clearly that she could use her right hand. This was most encouraging for her mother, who also saw a generalisation of this effect at home, whereby Helen could start to hold toys in one hand and manipulate them with her other hand. This was most noticeably developing in her use of a musical toy which you wind up. She held it with her left hand, and learnt to wind quite a tightly sprung knob with her right hand.

Another development during this period was our interaction through physical contact. A new game began, called "Can Helen push Tony over?" It developed from a pat-a-cake game, when she started to use both her hands to clap and touch my hands. From this, she generated the idea of pushing me, at which time I would rock backwards in my chair, shouting "Ooohh" as I did it. The impression she had was that she had pushed me backwards, and this gave her a great deal of pleasure! I transferred this on to using tambourines and tambours, having her push them or take them in her hands. This developed into working with Helen on alternative uses of her hands, which had benefits not only from a purely physical point of view for Helen, but also as a extension to her means of self expression.

Until this time, most of her hand movements and her handling of equipment had involved either plucking, slapping, pushing or flapping to date. These began to expand considerably, as a result of the games described in the previous paragraph. We began to work on the surface of a drum: stroking it, scratching it, tickling it. For brief periods, Helen stroked the drum instead of hitting it with the flat of her hand or plucking at it. We also worked on plucking the strings of a guitar or autoharp. This proved to be difficult because I had to hold her wrist in a loose finger circle near the instrument, so that she could learn to make the necessary movements with her wrist to brush or pluck the strings. If not channelled in this way, she would approach the guitar with plucking or slapping movements which did not produce an effective sound.

We have also started to play instruments cooperatively. For example, I may ask her to hold a tambourine or small drum while I play it. She will do this for short periods.

I have found that despite the more directive nature of this type of work, she is much more responsive to it now, and it is as if she has become aware of her potential to make different sounds. There is still a limit to the length of time she is prepared to be engaged in this, although one can generate the activity into something more active, moving round the room.

Helen's response to the good-bye song has remained constant throughout. She is still affected by and understands the significance of the words, and I feel it is an important ending to the therapy each week. When she has discharged a lot of energy and emotion in the session, and when she has been quite active, she needs to come down to a quieter, gentle state before leaving for school.

CONCLUSION

The approach to assessment and treatment outlined in this paper shows the importance of balancing structure and freedom when designing a music therapy program to meet the needs of a child like Helen, who has quite exclusive problems. Helen is unusual for a girl with Rett's syndrome in that she is quite active and energetic. The therapeutic approach has had to confront or work round some very deeply rooted, neurologically driven behaviours (e.g., hand plucking), while trying to motivate Helen to make the necessary changes. Because the medium of music can offer considerable influence, together with the personality of the therapist, this has resulted in some quite substantial developments:

(1) Awareness of music has sharpened and developed not only in a passive and a receptive form, but in Helen's active use of music as a vehicle for expression, feeling and interaction.

(2) Physical dexterity and hand use has improved to a great degree, allowing a much wider scope in the session.

(3) There is a very definite understanding of and response to the boundaries established in the session.

(4) Maturity and growth in Helen and in the relationship with me has resulted in a change in the session's direction, and in the effect and benefit of our work together.

For any parent or therapist to come to terms with a child who has Rett's syndrome, the biggest challenge must be to overcome purposeless and manneristic activity, and to rechannel natural energy and need for human contact into an engagement at a therapeutic level that is productive, dynamic and satisfying. This case study shows such a process taking place, and emphasises the tremendous necessity for flexibility and variety in the therapist's approach.

GLOSSARY

Dysphasia (Expressive): A disorder of the expression of language caused by brain damage.

Dysphasia (Receptive): A disorder of language comprehension cause by brain damage.

Hyperacousis: An extremely acute sense of hearing.

Pseudohyperacousis: Lack of attention to certain auditory stimuli without any hearing deficit; functional hearing loss.

Psychodynamic: A process where the therapist seeks to acknowledge, interpret and reflect---either musically or verbally---therapeutic issues that have particular relevance to the client. Through this process, the therapist helps the client to gain insight into the inner emotional world.

REFERENCES

Goodship, S. (1987). Stress in the family of the Rett's child. Brain and Development, 9: 539-42.

Hagberg, B., Aicardi, J., Dias, K., & Ramos, O. (1983). A progressive syndrome of autism, dementia, ataxia and loss of purposeful hand use in girls. Rett Syndrome: Report of 35 cases. Annals of Neurology, 14: 471-9.

Howlin, P. (1988). The differential diagnosis of autism and other handicaps associated with developmental language delays. Pamphlet published by The National Autistic Society, 276 Willeden Lane, London, England.

Kerr, A., & Stephensen, J. (1985) Rett syndrome in the west of Scotland. British Medical Journal, 291: 579-82.

Kerr, A. & Stephensen J. (1986) A study of the natural history of Rett syndrome in 23 girls. American Journal of Medical Genetics, 24: 77-83.

Montague, J. (1988). Music Therapy and the Treatment of Rett Syndrome. Pamphlet published by United Kingdom Rett Syndrome Association, Glasgow, England.

Rett, A. (1966) Uber ein cerebral atropisches Syndrome bei Hyper-ammonämie. Vienna: Brüder Hollinek.

Ricks, D. M. (1978). Making sense to make sensible sounds. In M. Bullowa (Ed.), Before Speech (pp. 245-269). Cambridge, UK: Cambridge University Press.

Ricks, D. M. (1975). Vocal communication in pre-verbal normal and autistic children. In N. O'Connor (Ed.), Language, Cognitive Deficits and Retardation. London: Butterworths.

Wigram, A. (1988). Music therapy developments in mental handicap. Psychology of Music: The Journal of the Society for Research in Psychology of Music and Music Education, 16 (1), 42-52.

Wigram, A. (1989). Processo De Diferenciacao Do Autismo E Outras Mentais. (The Significance of Musical Behaviour and Musical Responsiveness in the Process of Differential Diagnosis of Autism and Other Handicaps). Paper presented at the International Multidisciplinary Symposium on Music Therapy and the Effects of Sound. Sao Paulo, Brazil.

Wigram, A. (1990). Processes in Assessment and Diagnosis of Handicap in Children through the medium of Music Therapy" Paper presented at the annual conference of The Association for Professional Music Therapists, Severalls Hospital Colchester, England.

Wing, L. (1979). Differentiation of retardation and autism from specific communication disorders. Child: Care, Health and Development, 5: 57-68.

Wing, L. (1988). The Continuum of Autistic Characteristics. In E. Schopler and G. Mesibov (Eds.), Diagnosis and Assessment in Autism. New York: Plenum Publishing Company Limited.

CASE FOUR

Self-Communications In
Creative Music Therapy

CAROL M. ROBBINS, M.S., CMT/RMT-BC
CLIVE ROBBINS, D.M.M., CMT/RMT-BC
Professors and Co-directors
Nordoff-Robbins Music Therapy Clinic
New York University
New York, New York

Abstract: This case describes creative music therapy with Lyndal, a nine-year old Australian girl with multiple handicaps. Through individual and group work aimed at developing her musical expressivity and interresponsiveness, Lyndal was able to find and set free the "music child" within her. The effects of this release of potential on various aspects of self are described.

INTRODUCTION

In answering a question,
one communicates one's self.

This simple aphorism of Sufi thought (Corbin, 1969) captures the very essence of creative music therapy. Every time the therapist creates a musical idea, or offers a musical phrase, it is an invitation for the child to respond---a question for the child to answer; in repeating the child's motif, or extending the child's phrase, or complementing the child's timbre, or in leading the child into another tempo or dynamic range, the therapist is in effect posing musical questions; and the child---in responding spontaneously to the music, the therapist, and the situation---is continuously communicating his or her self, and the state of the self. In doing this the child also communicates the individuality of that self---the inner directive will, its capability to assert or express itself or communicate its potentials as they manifest, and its inherent proclivities. So that in the child's response we experience together with the self, the being-within-the-self. And it is in the being-within-the-self that the potential for creative development lies.

In creative music therapy, the child's self is developed from within--- using inner resources---the most important of which is the "music child." The "music child" is that part of the inner self in **every** child "which responds to musical experience, finds it meaningful and engaging, remembers music, and enjoys some form of musical experience" (Nordoff & Robbins, 1977, p. 1). This individualized musicality is inborn in every child, regardless of handicap, and reflects a universal sensitivity to music and its various elements. In order for the "music child" to function, the child must be open to experiencing himself, others and the world around him; for it is through these experiences that receptive, cognitive and expressive capabilities are developed. Thus, it is the "music child" that answers the questions posed by music, and in so doing, communicates the self.

When the child is disabled or handicapped in some way, the music child is encased within what we call the "condition child." The condition child denotes the child as it has come to be, through the number of years it has been living with a neurological deficiency or a physiological condition, with some form of handicapping condition. A child's personality develops in response to the life experience he or she can assimilate. Very often this development is limited, partialized, deformed and incomplete---the child's potential for development has not been released---a state represented symbolically in Figure 1 by an uneven, irregular form.

Figure 1

The Condition Child

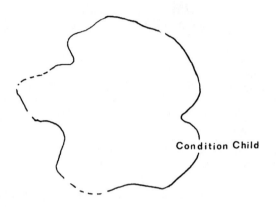

Condition Child

The condition child is obviously a self, the self that the child has been able to develop, or the present state of the child's self. Then we find that in music therapy we can reach the inherent, inborn musicality, which is so fundamental to human nature. We begin to reach the music child.

Figure 2

The Music Child

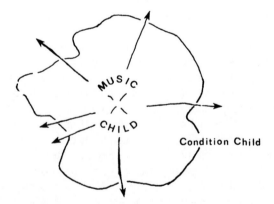

Condition Child

First, the therapist becomes aware of an inner growth of awareness. Perceptibly, if all goes well in the early sessions, the child's personality develops a new nucleus of selfhood which is formed in (or by) musical experience, through musical communication, through the beginnings of musical activity. This musical-personal nucleus then is nurtured, encouraged, challenged, supported, answered by the therapist and begins to take the individuality beyond the previous limits of its function, beyond the behavior barrier of the condition child.

Figure 3

The Old Self and New Self

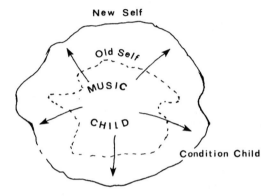

In the growing child-therapist inter-activity and inter-relationship the personality expands, a "new self" is formed, and the former condition child becomes the "old self." (See Figure 3 for symbolic representations). If a therapist is working with a child who is deeply neurotic, emotionally disturbed, or with what might be called a strong emotional overlay, you find that the old self remains, to some extent. Therapy then can lie in resolving the conflicts between the old and the new selves. The child is still going to be self-protective--an old mode of conduct--until it outgrows this need and old modes of life, reactions, habits or other limiting behaviors are replaced by new perceptions, a new sense of self, a new confidence in living.

METHOD

We would like to illustrate this process with excerpts from a course of creative music therapy with Lyndal, an Australian child. We worked with Lyndal over a period of 4 and 1/2 years, in both individual and group sessions. The individual sessions centered on interactive improvisation, and the group sessions involved Lyndal in a musical drama.

Creative music therapy involves two therapists working as a team, one at the piano and the other directly with the child or group. In individual work, musical improvisation is the predominant means of interaction with the child---it is the way that contact is established with the "music child":

...the therapist will find the essence of music as therapy
to lie in his improvisational creation of music as a
language of communication between him and an
individual child. The "words" of this language are the
components of music at his disposal, its expressive
content is carried by his use of them. In the clinical
situation he becomes the centre of musical responsiveness
himself; the music his fingers draw from the instrument
arises from his impressions of the child: facial
expression, glance, posture, behaviour, condition---all
express that presence his music will reflect and go out
to meet. The flexibility of his playing searches out the
region of contact for that child, creates the emotional
substances of the contact and sets the musical ground
for interactivity. The timing of his playing---its tempo,
its rhythms and pauses---attentively follows, leads and
follows the child's activity (Nordoff & Robbins, 1971,
143-144).

In group work, the predominant means of accessing the "music child" is
through learning, performing, and responding to specially composed songs,
instrumental pieces, and musical dramas, and to the developmental content of
such compositions.

BACKGROUND INFORMATION

We first met Lyndal in September, 1984; she was then 9 years old, and
had just become resident at "Warrah," a Rudolf Steiner special school in
Australia where we were working and living. She was brain injured, *mildly
microcephalic, hypertonic,* and with some unsteadiness of gait. She was
moderately mentally handicapped and emotionally unstable. Her behavior was
fearful, *stereotypic* and, possibly because of frustration and confusion, self-
injurious.

She reacted adversely to loud or unexpected sounds: dogs barking,
sirens, car horns, doors slamming, and so forth. Even radio and television at
normal listening levels provoked screaming tantrums and a self-injurious
reaction in which she would repeatedly strike her forehead against a wall or
other firm object. Beneath her bangs there was often a large contusion.

She was a much loved child, but life at home for her parents and two
brothers was constrained and muted. She had quite a bit of usable speech
and could make her wishes known; she often repeated phrases continuously
and inappropriately, apparently in the wish to make conversation.

Lyndal had attended a state school for some years and had made some
progress, although she remained on the sidelines in many school activities
because she was so fearful, self-protective and behaviorally unpredictable.

TREATMENT PROCESS

Don't Play the Piano!

Lyndal began weekly individual music therapy sessions shortly after being admitted to "Warrah". Very quickly her responses revealed a dichotomy, a split. She always came eagerly to the music room, she possessed considerable inherent sensitivity to music and enjoyed it immensely. She liked to sing---preferably something she could imitate---and had a good sense of pitch. She was also sensitive to rhythmic patterns and the melodic rhythms. But in beating the drum to piano and vocal improvisation she showed an instability that was linked to a disabling lack of self-control and confidence. At the drum she was over-vulnerable to musical stimulation and to the excitation of her own physical activity---and her beating always tended to break away into disorder. There was evidence that a drive to beat freely and strongly lived within her, but her reactions suggested that she was frightened of the power of her own impulsive energy and was repressing it. Whenever the music or her beating seemed on the verge of becoming too vigorous she would call out "Don't play the piano!" or interject "See you later!", her way of escaping the situation. She also developed a real anxiety about the large 16-inch cymbal, and it had to go out of sight behind the piano.

Gradually, in these sessions her responses took on some stability and it was apparent that---within limits she determined---she was beginning to place some trust in us and in herself, active in music.

Lyndal Takes A Role

After four sessions we temporarily suspended her individual therapy as rehearsals for a school play required schedule changes. We began working with the 35 children in the school on The Children's Christmas Play (Nordoff & Robbins, 1970). The girl who was to have played Mary became ill and we asked Lyndal to take the part. When her parents were told they were pessimistic: "We hope Lyndal doesn't spoil your play" was their concern. I assured them that this was play was for the children, and that if it was necessary for Clive to be beside her throughout the entire performance it would be perfectly fine. In the rehearsals she was initially scattered and giggly; she behaved well but did not seem to have any idea what it was all about. When the Angel brought Mary the doll that was the Christ Child, Lyndal took it carelessly with a complete lack of feeling, sometimes holding it upside down.

The turning point came in one rehearsal when, as the Angel approached Lyndal, seated in the stable, to present the baby, Clive made a big stretch upward with both hands, "Lyndal," he said, "reach up to Heaven where it's coming from!" The drama of the moment caught her, she imitated him---immediately attentive to the gesture---took the baby with much more awareness and held it as one would hold a child. We practiced this several times. Later that day, while Clive was walking outside, his and Lyndal's paths happened to cross and she came toward him raising her arms high in the same receiving gesture, smiling with pleasure and satisfaction. After this she became serious about the play and seemed to feel her role in it.

The play was performed to an applauding audience. Lyndal played her role securely, joined in singing the chorus parts, and sat attentively and quietly while other children acted out their roles. As the play approaches its ending, there is a rhythmic-speech chorus that builds to a climax on the words, "Hail King! Blessed is He! Joy! Joy! Joy!" These words are supported by strong chords on the piano, and as everyone bursts into the final chorus of "Christmas Bells," the hand cymbals enter with repeating dramatic crashes. We did not realize at the time the impression the experience must have made on Lyndal; the mood of this Handelian finale was one of celebration: bells were given out and more and more children rang them to build up the crescendo---through all of this loud, vigorous music, the hand cymbals and the large cymbal on the stand added to the jubilation. Bells and both cymbals finished with a sustained fortissimo tremolo. Lyndal showed no distress whatsoever at the very high dynamic level the music reached.

Lyndal's parents were deeply happy with their daughter's achievements. We received a Christmas card from them with the simple message: "Thank you for having faith in Lyndal."

Am I Going To Play The Cymbal?

Quite early in the new year, before school began and her individual therapy resumed, she would ask us whenever we met: "Am I going to play the cymbal today?" If we asked her in return: "Well, are you?" She would reply, softly but firmly, and perhaps a little wistfully: "No." It was obvious that the cymbal attracted her, obsessed her to a degree: to have had the freedom to let go and strike it forcefully with strength to produce a glorious crash, full of overtones and shimmer, would have been very important to this constrained child. The attainment of this freedom became one of the goals in our work with her.

Lyndal resumed individual therapy, and had one session weekly, lasting on an average 15-20 minutes. Her fifth session begins in a way that typifies her response at this time: she comes running in with a bright eagerness, happily sings her greeting song, loses control the moment she starts beating the drum, then, as the therapist accompanies her disorder, calls out "Stop!" and becomes anxious.

In this and the following session, Clive and I take our cue directly from her; we work to engage her perception of structure in music to stabilize her activity, develop her vocal and rhythmic skills, and build her confidence. Concurrently, we also gently lead her further into the area of freer beating where she becomes disordered; we want to explore her ability to acquire control over her reactions---and, at the same time, we work to familiarize her with this upsurging of emotional and physical energy in herself in the hope that she can come to enjoy using it self-expressively. We intuitively sense that in this deeper, eruptive region of reaction and disorder lies the source of Lyndal's self-injurious behavior, and that it could be therapeutic to engage this energy through improvisation and bring it into musical expression.

Lyndal's ambivalence continues, she is both drawn to the instrumental work and apprehensive of it. Carefully, she is led into using a very small cymbal (less than 6 inches in diameter) mounted on the cymbal stand. The trusting relationship develops as she requests activities and is secure in alternate moments in which we lead her into widening her areas of experience. She is always eager to show what she knows she can do---and at the same time very directly lets us know when she has had enough of a challenging activity. Gradually, a repertoire of shared music builds up and progressive connections are established, for example, the phrase she originally used as a means of self-protection, "See you later," becomes transformed into a much enjoyed song in tango rhythm:

Musical Excerpt 1

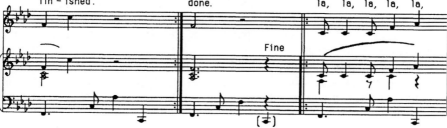

In tapping the melodic rhythm to this song on the drum, Lyndal spontaneously uses the small cymbal to punctuate the phrases. This results in warm approval from us and cheers of self-congratulation from Lyndal.

As a contrast in instrumental timbre, Lyndal plays resonator bells and is sensitive to the gentleness and lyric tonal quality of the music that is made with them: "Can You Sing To The Sun?" (Nordoff & Robbins, 1962). It is clear that in music her emotional life is being reached and engaged with an immediacy not possible in other areas of experience. Her powers of concentration are also being exercised by the clearly structured objectives of much of the work.

As the sessions proceed, her overall sphere of experience steadily deepens and widens, her attentiveness to rhythmic structure becomes more precise, and her ability to sustain focused work improves.

In the eighth session a medium-sized cymbal replaces the small one and through a quiet improvisation, she is eased into playing it. Later, she is intrigued by the Phrygian mode and is able to sustain a short but controlled crescendo on a timpani. When she does need to step aside from such a challenging activity she does it adroitly: using a beguiling tone of voice she diverts the therapists into a less threatening alternative, "Now! Carol, Clive, can we beat on the resonator bells?"--showing a more accomplished, healthier form of self-protection.

Although ambivalence shadowed her advances and each step forward was usually followed by nervous uncertainty, progress continued. Her confidence was steadily increasing, and this was fundamentally due to the nourishment her musicality was absorbing from the sessions. Her inborn musicality was such an important part of her personality that it was at the root of her personality development.

By the tenth session, Lyndal is smiling and confident playing the medium-sized cymbal. She plays it carefully yet in a relaxed manner. She is responding with trust, as we encourage her to sing freely as she beats to dramatic music.

In the fifteenth session, it is clear that much more was coming out by way of freedom and assertiveness. The work in this session sometimes sounds like a child making lots of noise, but it is Lyndal---a nine-year-old who always felt apprehensive, kept herself in, always suppressed, and always constrained, except when she banged her head on a wall in utter fear and frustration---now releasing this energy openly through the joy of music. How she needs a situation in which her feelings are accepted, enhanced and made communicative and self-expressive! In this session, Lyndal beats to forceful, serious music over a range of tempo. As she beats she raises her voice, and holds high tones. Then, to music in a Spanish idiom, she uses the cymbal with the same strength with which she is singing. Although she beats strongly, she moderates the cymbal's power by using it rather slowly, such as by beating on the first beats of measures. At no time in the session does she shrink from the intense coactivity.

Musical Excerpt 2

Free At Last

We had visitors observing the sixteenth session, and Lyndal seemed to have decided from the very first moment, and maybe because they were there, that this was the day to really let go. The session quickly built up to a high level of intensity and the dramatic discharge of energy overwhelmed the visitors. They were taken totally by surprise and sat in stunned immobility. Later they admitted that they were actually frightened by the power of the music and by Lyndal's unrestrained singing and use of the drum and cymbal-- so much so that they failed to see her rapturous beam of joy as she achieved the catharsis she had been seeking. The excerpt below shows the very vigorous compelling fortissimo music that was called for by Lyndal's forceful beating. I attempt to sing in a way that totally projects my energy into the room. Lyndal sings out freely as she is borne along by the drive of the penetrating rhythms and dissonances of the piano. At 160 beats per minute she can hardly control her beating. Our music-making together has an

intensity that borders on the maniacal, yet it has purpose and direction.
When I sing short dramatic phrases, Lyndal begins to use the cymbal---first
to punctuate them, then accent them.

Musical Excerpt 3

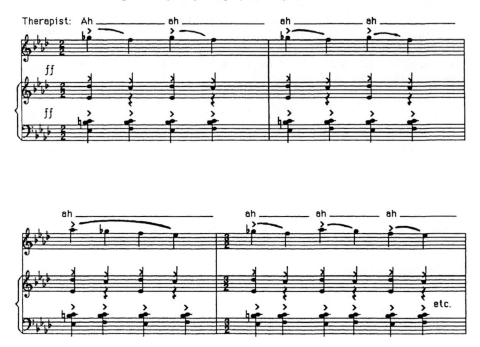

As the improvisation rises to a climax, Lyndal's cymbal beating becomes
continuous. She sustains a crescendo for over a minute, much of the time
beating as hard and as fast as she can. Her tempo attains 260 beats per
minute. The room rings with cymbal crashes, overtones, piano and voices.

Who would not love to do that, to be that free, that unrestrained, that
unconventional, that unlimited by the norms of behavior! And add to this
dynamic of experience what it must mean for Lyndal! Of course, our visitors
were in a state of shock; they had no way of knowing what was going on.
They knew nothing about Lyndal or where she was coming from, and this was
unlike any experience they had had. Where would they have heard music like
this unless in a very dramatic or adventurous film, or possibly an opera?

As the vigorous improvisation comes to a close, Lyndal calls out: "Now sing!" She sits beside me at the piano and joins in singing phrases antiphonally. I lead her into a world of music in total contrast to the preceding rhythmic percussion: the improvisation is in a moderately slow 3/4 and the experience is lyric and thoughtful; melody and harmony predominate.

Musical Excerpt 4

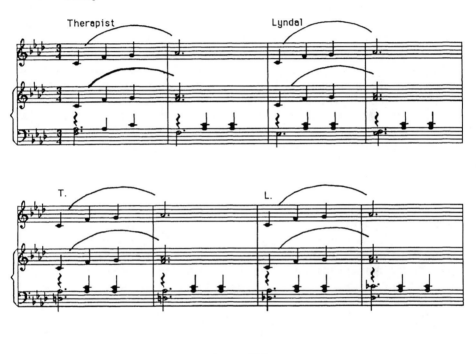

Lyndal is utterly attentive, she sings the melodic phrases accurately while responding to their rhythms on a drum with her hands. She anticipates repetitions of rhythmic structure and sensitively follows a ritardando and diminuendo. Then she asks for a reed horn and blows rhythmic patterns antiphonally with me. The session closes with Lyndal singing her good-bye song very freely, and bidding goodbye to the stunned, perplexed visitors.

After this session, Lyndal's parents reported that there was an immediate effect on her tolerance of "family" sound levels; she was no longer upset by louder or unexpected noises---all sounds at home could go up to normal levels. Reports from the school and residents at "Warrah" also indicated that the head-banging was diminishing and that the contusion on her forehead was healing.

It was absolutely necessary to generate this dramatic intensity of music-making to enable Lyndal to achieve her "break through." If one considers all of the great dramas, whether in theater or opera, they are essentially concerned with emotional disturbance and the conflict and pain this brings about---and perhaps the struggle toward resolution. So it can be in music therapy with emotionally disturbed children---they too can be in highly dramatic situations and making what for them are enormous steps. Such happenings are not little events! An achievement like this is a world-changing event! And it is wonderful that the power of music can support such developments---it nourishes the inner growth of these children.

Stage Two

After a transitional period in which Lyndal consolidated her new gains and confidence, we entered what was in effect "stage two" of music therapy with her. By this time, she sings and uses a variety of drums; the cymbal work now includes the two large cymbals in use in the regular group work.

In the thirtieth session, Lyndal's wish to use a large cymbal freely is well illustrated when she raises both mallets high above her head in time for the last note of a melodic phrase---apparently about to beat with great strength. Instead, she brings her arms down slowly with utter caution, makes contact with the cymbal gently and leaves the mallets resting on it to damp the sound.

Despite her caution, her use of the instruments develops steadily: her tempo range is widening, her control is improving and her movements are larger and smoother. She has acquired some poise and is becoming noticeably more graceful. Clive and I work directly for greater physical freedom---for with Lyndal, physical freedom promotes emotional freedom. There is a noticeable air of confidence about her that sustains a positive level of working relationship with us. She participates willingly in music and songs developed to widen her circle of experience.

During these sessions, Clive begins to raise both cymbals high to extend her reaching-beating movements. Her technique of cymbal playing, in which the beater simultaneously strikes and damps the instrument, is defeated by Clive playfully withdrawing the cymbal as she strikes it, so leaving its tone sounding freely. She sees the humor in what he is doing and goes along with it. Impulses to beat the large cymbal firmly progressively break through.

In her fortieth session, seated at the piano beside me, Lyndal participates in a creatively free vocal exploration that takes her up to the G above the staff. As she sings she often plays the piano freely, with an appropriate musical style. She is relaxed, smiling, confident, obviously enjoying the vocal competence she is discovering and the mutuality she shares in singing with us.

In these last weeks of our work with her she uses the cymbal proficiently, with decision, and no hesitancy whatsoever. She successfully masters a challenging part on a metallophone in the "Shaker Waltz," (Pinson, 1988), and works hard to sing "The Prayer of the Little Ducks" (Nordoff, 1983), which she then performs as a solo before the whole school---a new and important achievement for her.

DISCUSSION AND CONCLUSION

Lyndal's general development showed a rounded maturation: she had become quite a self-confident adolescent, she could hold conversations, could function better at home and had become the leader of her class at school. She had released and realized much of her potential. We experienced this at first hand on a visit to Australia in 1990, when we were asked to make a television videotape with her. After not seeing her for fourteen months, we found in our warm-up session that all her music was still alive within her. As she was filmed the following day in a twenty-five minute demonstration, she was radiant! It was so moving! She is such a self-possessed young lady now, and greets people with confidence. We have truly seen her changing in her personality, in her self, the self that she presents to other people, the self that she lives with. She now verbalizes her concerns and frustrations, and the self-injurious behavior has completely disappeared.

All through this work she has lived in a very supportive environment at "Warrah." This study of Lyndal shows well the effect of a central, focussed therapy, supported by several peripheral contributing therapies. What growth occurred in music would be taken up and developed in the environment; conversely, the security and courage she gained from the environment would play over into the music sessions---a very beneficial cycle of events.

In conclusion, let us look again at this concept of the "music child" present, not only in Lyndal, but in all children. If the "music child" is capable of changing the personality and changing it permanently---and of releasing developmental potentials to give the unfolding personality such a positive sense of identity---from where does it get the power to do this, to be a self-creating force within the self? In answer, we reintroduce a concept we considered earlier, one that will complete this working model: the "being within the self." We can term this the "being child," and find that it is contained within the music child.

Figure 4

The "Being Child" Within The "Music Child"

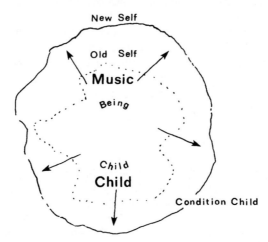

As the child develops, the "old self" disappears or dissolves, its remnants transformed and absorbed into the "new self." This process can be described in terms of the four major psychological orientations: behavioral, psychodynamic, humanistic, and transpersonal.

Quite often, as was evident in the work with the outer expressions of Lyndal, we are, to quite an extent, working behaviorally---we all must, of necessity, work with behavior. As you work to resolve, within developing children, the tensions that lie between the old self and the new self, you are also working psychodynamically, either on a practical level, where children's musical activities themselves symbolize inner needs or drives, or with clients who can articulate their inner lives verbally, in more traditional ways. In the centre of the diagram, in the region of being, music therapy is directly involved in self-actualization---which is the core of the humanistic force in psychology. Self-actualization in this context is also transpersonal insofar as we are, through creative music therapy, calling beings into existence that have not existed before. There has been the potential but it has not been actualized into existence before.

This may appear to be over-reaching, or presumptuous, but we are all working with the inner lives of children---and we are working for their futures, for every year of their lives to come. We are working to bring basic, fundamental changes to human beings. We are working at considerable depth, much greater depths than often we understand. This viewpoint is part

Figure 5

Orientations of the Self

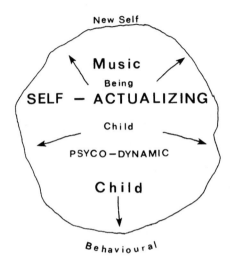

of the humility we should have in taking this art of music into therapy---because of all that's there in the music itself: music as it has been handed on to us through the whole of human evolution, through all that the great composers have evolved in their explorations of form, melody, harmony, rhythm and expression, through all that lives in the music we have inherited from all the folk of the earth.

As music therapists we have this glorious task, involving two glorious arts: the art of evolving a human personality out of itself through another art which enables us to communicate with all the dynamics that are potential there. One runs out of concepts and words eventually, in trying to put what music therapy is into words.

GLOSSARY

Hypertonic: Having excessive muscular tension.

Microcephalic: Having an abnormally small skull.

Moderately Mentally Handicapped: Generally denoting a person testing in an IQ range of 35-49.

Stereotypic: Having fixed, repetitive patterns of speech and behavior.

ACKNOWLEDGEMENT

The authors would like to thank the New Zealand Society for Music Therapy for its permission to revise and reprint this case study, which was originally published in the Society's Annual Journal (1990).

REFERENCES

Corbin, H. (1969). Creative Imagination in the Sufism of Ibn Arabi. Translated by R. Manheim. London: Routledge and Kegan Paul.

Nordoff P. (1983). Some Prayers from the Ark. Bryn Mawr, PA: Theodore Presser.

Nordoff, P. & Robbins, C. (1962). The First Book of Children's Playsongs. Bryn Mawr, PA: Theodore Presser.

Nordoff P., & Robbins C. (1970). The Children's Christmas Play. Bryn Mawr, PA: Theodore Presser.

Nordoff, P., & Robbins, C. (1971). Therapy in Music for Handicapped Children. New York: St. Martin's Press.

Nordoff P., & Robbins C. (1977). Creative Music Therapy. New York: John Day Co.

Pinson, J. (1988). Mallet Magic. Denton, TX: Home Church School Resources.

Off-Beat Music Therapy:
A Psychoanalytic Approach
To Autism

EDITH LECOURT, Ph.D.

Professor of Psychopathology
Head of the Research Center in Psychology
Secretary of the French Society of Music Therapy
University Louis Pasteur
Strasbourg, France.

English Translation by
ANGELA M. BREWER

Abstract: *This is a presentation of psychoanalytically based music therapy with an autistic, 4-year-old child. The process involved the progressive organization of the child's sound vocabulary within the dynamic of a transference relationship. A spatio-temporal structure was established through alternation paradigms, sensory integration, approach/avoidance mechanisms, principles of musical composition, and the development of an off-beat orientation to the world of music and speech.*

BACKGROUND INFORMATION

David is a four year-old boy whose physical development appears normal, but who shows signs of *autistic* behavior and does not speak. He was raised by his parents (Mr. and Mrs. D) until the age of six months, when they sought the help of a special teacher (Ms. E). Both parents felt they did not have the capacity to teach David, and they seemed to want some kind of guarantee that David would learn properly. The mother told me that they deliberately chose someone rather rigid for a teacher.

Shortly after hiring Ms. E, David's mother and father were divorced. It was at this time that Ms. E began to assume a central role within the family. It was she who made sure that the divorce settlement contained clauses stipulating that the child be removed from the influence of the father who was judged to be harmful.

The mother was awarded custody of David, and occasional visits with his father were authorized. Thus David has been brought up by his mother from the age of six months. His mother, about thirty years of age, lives alone with him, and is very absorbed by her work. She tends to be scattered and disorganized. Ms. E, about fifty years of age, is single, and continues to work for the mother.

Ms. E's domination of the child's education has hampered all outside intervention, and ruled out various kinds of treatment. When David began to show disturbances in psychomotor development at the age of nine months, he was taken for a neurological examination, however Ms. E has refused to take him to a pediatrician for routine child care. She feels that she is the only one who can understand and look after David.

The psychiatrist felt that psychotherapy would not be possible for David at this time, and when questioned by Mrs D, responded positively to the idea of David receiving music therapy. According to Mrs. D, she did not take him to music therapy immediately because Ms. E viewed it as "premature." In fact, Mrs. D had for some time been trying to investigate the possibility of music therapy for David, and after gaining some information in the press, came to me for consultation. Of course, Ms. E had already checked up on this information for herself.

David is very sensitive to music. Sometimes he hums spontaneously, and he has no trouble singing in tune and memorizing tunes he has heard; he can reproduce exactly what he hears. At home, David is particularly interested in listening to music, but both Mrs. D and Ms. E avoid this for fear that he become totally absorbed in it. He is also very sensitive to the noise of domestic appliances.

Although Mrs. D did not study music herself, as desired by her parents, she places most of her hopes for David in his musical abilities. It is worth mentioning that after the first few sessions I learned from colleagues that Mrs. D had continued to make inquiries amongst other music therapists. I took this as an indication of her anxiety and concern over David, as well as a manifestation of her escapist and scattered behavior.

Later, I discovered that another reason for Mrs. D's interest in music therapy was her concern over Ms. E's educational philosophy, and the tyranny that she exercised over both David and her.

David was presented to me as a child who has major feeding problems. He is never very hungry, shows no pleasure in eating, and meals are often like battles. He dribbles continuously, and refuses any oral contact with objects. David also has sleeping difficulties and is very often agitated during the night. He is not an aggressive child, but sometimes throws tantrums. He can show affection to Ms. E (who lets it be known that it is with the mother that things are difficult), but he has no relationships with other children of his own age. He never speaks.

For my part, I am most struck by his perpetual motion and state of tension. David seems incapable of relaxing or letting go, and does not allow himself to sit down. He also presents *stereotyped* gestures.

Ms. E's teaching is characterized by very rigid principles about the learning process and adult-child relationships. David's daytime schedule is programmed minute by minute. Within this context, it is interesting to note that Ms. E finds it difficult accepting our appointment schedule. I wondered if David's autistic behaviors were a means of self-protection against such a rigid context.

ASSESSMENT AND METHOD

From my first contacts with David's mother and Ms. E, I was most concerned about the relational problems that were apparent within this triangle. Thus, the objectives for the first few sessions were to observe all of the relationships, and to determine how David would react to my offer of a free space, and a place for free self-expression through sounds and music.

The sessions were held in a room in an arts center. The room is equipped with a piano, a table, chairs, low cupboards underneath bay windows, a tape recorder, and various musical instruments (small percussion instruments, bird calls, etc.). I immediately attempted to establish contact with David by using his spontaneous noise productions (whether deliberate, conscious or otherwise), and by using his reactions to the noise in his environment and to my presence. The sessions were always tape-recorded to permit a review of events, both in the session itself (i.e., playing back the sounds that David and I had just produced), and after the session (i.e., analyzing what happened in the session). In my research, I have found that prior to the establishment of sound codes (verbal or musical), it is very difficult for someone like David to remember the sound experience, and that if communication and relationships are to built through sound, auditory feedback is essential. Thus, by playing back and having David listen to the sounds, I am giving him an opportunity to become aware of, go over, remember, and make something of his spontaneous sound productions, and my responses to them. In this way, his sensory experiences are contained and made significant within our relationship.

I would have liked to have seen David twice a week because I felt that he needed it. This was not possible, however, because of the myriad problems it would cause Ms. E, who had to disrupt her minute-to-minute schedule in order to bring him to the sessions. So the sessions were limited to once a week, lasting from 45 to 60 minutes.

I had to insist on seeing David alone, since Ms. E had thought she should be present in order to receive some kind of training for herself. It was important, in this context, to stress that the child was being seen for himself, as an individual.

My psychoanalytical training led me to postulate that there was a link between David's autistic behavior and the problematic relationships involving those taking care of him. At this stage however, I was still unable to determine specific a priori causes and effects. In his relationship with Ms. E, David seemed like a kind of puppet whose strings she held; with his mother, he seemed engulfed in a relationship of fusion and tension. In addition, he was in the midst of constant fighting between the two women.

David's behaviors with regard to music and sound seemed to be examples of hyperexcitation, which made a breach in the *"protective shield"* combined with an *"adhesiveness"* (Meltzer et al, 1975). This provides some explanation of his musical abilities. He has perfect reproduction skills; he sings in tune; and he can immediately pick out on the piano any notes he hears. These behaviors should not be regarded as consciously developed skills, or replicable musical aptitudes but rather as evidence of David's fusion with the musical and sound environment.

1st Meeting: David and Mother

David's mother and I sit at the table, while David expresses his anxiety by running around us throughout the entire meeting, and trying to leave the room several times. He squints his eyes constantly, and avoids eye contact. He takes great interest and pleasure in sounds, and he continually returns to the resonance boxes which I played several times to beckon him. When I show him an animal call (which sounds like the bleating of a goat), he responds with both excitement and fear. His mother tells me that, as a baby, he was frightened by a similar toy, sounding like the mooing of a cow. He enjoys a metallic frog which makes a kind of "click clack" when it is pressed. I also notice that he is very attentive to outside noise, from the room next door, calling out several times as if to make contact. While running around, he often draws near to me, as if to have a closer look.

We discuss his learning program, and particularly his present toilet training. He is supposed to be put on the pot every thirty minutes; as it happens, however, my sessions last forty-five! I make no concessions on this point, and with this stance, my *"off-beat"* approach to working with David begins. (Translator's note: In French, the word "contretemps" means both "upset" and "off-beat").

2nd Meeting: David and Teacher

David literally rushes headlong into the room, accompanied this time by Ms. E. It is the first time she and I meet (after two phone calls). She remains very stiff and stays near the door. Only after some time does she come inside and sit down next to me at the table, still at quite a distance. From that moment onwards, Ms. E glances alternately at David and me, trying to be in control of everything at once.

David runs around the table throughout the whole session, still with his eyes squinted. Ms. E avoids speaking about David, but instead tries to interview me about music therapy. I have to make it clear that I am there to look after David, not to provide training to her. She seems defensive and uneasy. I also sense that she may have some guilt over David's state, as she is emphatic about how scrupulously she applies various educational and therapeutic concepts, and how voraciously she reads about them. She seems to "feed on" what she reads. Although she has had no musical training, she shows an interest in communicating with David through sound.

Ms. E categorically refuses to leave me alone with David for even a few minutes. I make it clear to her that all future sessions would take place without her being present. I realize that taking this firm position might be threatening to Ms. E, as an intrusion in her relationship with David, and despite the fact that I need her cooperation to bring David to my office on a regularly scheduled basis.

At this second meeting, David shows renewed interest in the sounds, and I attempt to answer him in the same sound vocabulary, while also escaping the clutches of Ms. E. He tries to control the bleating of the goat and to repeat the action with variations, and enjoys this very much. David reacts to the end of the session by pushing me into the corner, which seems like a kind of punishment he wants to give me. Since there is a curtain in the corner, I begin to play hide-and-seek with it, and I notice how important it is for him to escape being seen, which I associate with hiding from the inquisitional, terrorizing look of Ms. E (for both him and me!).

At the end of this meeting I become more aware of the complexity of the situation, and I recognize the limitations that I would have in obtaining positive results. I also begin to question who it is I should be treating, and further question David's diagnosis. I am taken by the pathological context of the relationships in which David finds himself, which are the same ones that will influence my work with him.

TREATMENT PROCESS

David was precisely 4 years and 2 months old when music therapy sessions began, and 6 years and 5 months old when it ended. Altogether, the treatment lasted for 2 years and 3 months, and David recieved a total of 88 sessions.

In the paragraphs that follow, I will begin by presenting a detailed description of the first ten sessions which will illustrate the way in which our relationship developed and the elements which I used in initially structuring our work. Then I shall go into greater detail in regard to those sessions and periods which constituted turning points or events of special interest in the relationship.

1st Session

David rushes into the room. Ms. E appears a few moments later, justifying her presence in the room by mentioning David's anxiety in the toilets before the session. She disappears a quarter of an hour later, leaving us alone.

David still tries to run away, and I make use of this in play in the following manner: I block the door with my body, making him drag me away (in this way making him play the role of the adult who usually has to drag him away). I describe the scene in sound, accentuating the difficulties vocally. This makes him laugh and he repeats the game. Apart from these moments he looks around anxiously, still squinting. I have set up an area in the room where he can take refuge (an overturned table which is like a hut). He goes back and forth without ever settling there. David clearly recognizes the instruments which have already been used. He has a clear preference for the resonance boxes and for the frog, which are both metallic timbres, one musical and the other noise-like. When I sing, accompanying the sounds he is producing, he watches my mouth, just as he looks at my feet when I tap them in imitation of his running around the room. He is thus showing an interest in the production of sounds by the body.

David is in a state of great excitation and motor agitation. He finds it very difficult to accept the end (I think of the "potty session" in store for him in the bathroom afterwards, with Ms. E). He discovers the tape recorder and gestures twice for me to start it up. When I play back the last part of the session, I do not know whether he connects what we are listening to with the noises he made.

At the end of this session I wonder how to structure a "sound space" for him and to provide a moment of relaxation.

2nd Session

David rushes into the room and runs around. This time Ms. E does not interrupt the session. He reverts to the vibraphone blocks, and I sing to accompany him. He introduces the idea of alternation in his play: noise (of his running around or dragging chairs) and musical sounds (the blocks, crystalline sounds). This time he enters more into visual contact, but most attempts are still evasive. He is more willing to allow me to interrupt his escape attempts, which I punctuate by saying "Hello there!" (which in French is an onomatopeia that sounds like "cou-cou"). At the end of the session, he reproduces the same sounds.

When he bumps into the table he comes to me to be comforted, which indicates a good prognosis for the development of our relationship. We play hide and seek with the tables and chairs. David then introduces, from under the table, a sound made with his mouth which I take as an imitation of a fart. I imitate his sound back to him, which surprises him greatly. He seems pleased and disapproving at the same time, and begins to plug his ears alternately and hide his face behind his arms as he continues to make the sound. He looks as if he is avoiding being punished. He repeats this sequence several times, obviously fascinated by my participation.

I record him using the frog toy (his favorite instrument), and let him listen to it immediately afterwards, trying to insure that he makes the connection between what he has just heard and what he had previously produced. His response is one of curiosity, pleasure and escape, showing once again how ambivalent he feels about sound. He wails like the whistle, as if wanting me to play it. Whenever he he wants an object, he reproduces their sounds vocally---and very precisely---as if he can make them appear by magic. He still refuses to put any object, even one producing sounds, to his mouth.

Some time during the session David makes me raise my arms, which I take as a request to carry him. I begin to respond but he quickly runs away. This time I notice that he has inhibited his own escape movements, and stops himself.

3rd Session

David arrives accompanied by his mother, and seems more relaxed. I have added a third vibraphone note to the two he was using previously. He notices this and plays with it for a long time, as I accompany him vocally and rhythmically. He is very attentive. In the course of this session, we review what is gradually becoming our sound vocabulary: single resonant boxes, the frog, foot tapping, and "fart" sounds which he makes while hiding. He alternates farts and the single notes. Once again he raises my arms but does not allow me to pick him up. David begins to show interest in listening to the recording. He takes me to the tape recorder for me to start it up, while at the same time seeming to be afraid of it. To listen, he goes to the other side of the room, again showing tremendous ambivalence.

For the first time he has been able to stay with me for an entire thirty minutes without attempting to run away. At the end of the session, Mrs. D, who has come to collect him, takes the opportunity to talk to me. Meanwhile, David produces lots of fart sounds.

She interprets these noises as David's attempts at kissing. In the course of the conversation I learn that David's toilet training schedule (every half-hour) has been going on for more than a year, and I indicate that it might perhaps be time to stop! Together we observe how difficult it is for him to leave the music room to undergo once again this very trying ritual in the washroom. Mrs. D decides to skip the ritual this time, and David gets into the pushchair with no difficulty. Mrs. D also tells me that after the sessions David produces many sounds and that he is calm.

4th Session

David's mother accompanies him to the session once again, and David rushes into the room and immediately launches a fart dialogue with me. At one point, he seems to want to dance, and begins to tap his feet for a few seconds. It is important to note that this happens when he is playing resonance boxes, and I am accompanying him vocally and rhythmically.

David shows interest in a mirror on the wall, and delights in seeing his own reflection. As he listens to the recording of our previous sounds, he places his forehead on the mirror. He repeats this routine many times during the session. On that day there is sunshine in the room, and David creates a game with his shadow; however, not wanting to play alone, he takes me by the hand, and we share the experience of seeing each other in our own shadows.

I ask Mrs. D about Davids's response to the mirror, and she tells me that she has never seen it before. I point out that he associates the visual feedback of the mirror with the sound feedback of the tape recorder and with my presence with him.

5th Session

Mrs. D brings David. We repeat our sound games, and he listens to each afterwards, again using the mirror as if trying to simultaneously find both sound and visual image. I introduce a new toy: little doll-whistles from India which have two little pipes with plastic doll heads attached to the top with a rubber balloon. When you blow into the pipes, the air fills the balloon and the doll heads take on all kinds of shapes. You can play one or both whistles at the same time, which makes them like puppets. This really fascinates David, and he cannot bear to tear himself away from them. He becomes fully involved (almost in spite of himself) in a lengthy vocal dialogue with the dolls, echoing their intonations. The sounds resemble laments or baby cries, which I imitate and vary somewhat. This is the first time that David finds himself in such a relationship of vocal dialogue.

6th Session

This is the first session in which I use the piano, which until now had remained closed in the room and had not attracted David's attention. This gradual introduction of sound objects, instruments and toys, was done intentionally, to observe how David reacts to and explores the world of sound.

David is accompanied by Ms. E, who this time excuses herself and leaves us alone with no difficulty. David is absorbed in exploring the piano and monopolizes the entire instrument, not allowing me to even touch it. He indicates a real enjoyment of certain very low notes such as G2. He asks to play with the dolls, and once again is very taken with their cries which he echoes, using the same modulations or making different ones. The farting game is also part of the session.

From this session onwards, the piano becomes David's instrument. He is interested above all in the black keys, and seeks to keep me at bay by "occupying" me with some other instrument which he asks me to play.

7th to 8th Sessions

David continues with the same sound activities (e.g., the farting game, the balloon dolls, the mirror, the shadow game and the piano). This time David expresses an interest in listening to the recording of himself playing the piano and then proceeds to improvise to it as background music. This game put him in the position of being his own echo.

At the eighth session David experiences a period of disorganization and anxiety. He drags me out of the room, and leads me around the halls to other offices, the elevator, and then to the washroom. We stay in the washroom for a while, and it makes me wonder if he wanted to show me where he goes before and after the sessions. In response, I invent a game using the lavatory flush (which frightens him). I imitate each of the sounds (taps, doors creaking, water gurgling in the pipes, etc.). He then introduces the fart sound and adds "ah-ah" (perhaps for "caca"). He repeats each of these situations many times, uttering high-pitched shrieks. We spend a long time there. I have to bring this very special session to a close: David resists, but then starts to hum.

I am very coldly received by Ms. E when she comes to collect him. She tells me that this washroom game will create problems at home where such things are forbidden. During this period she tries to alter both the duration and frequency of the sessions, giving David's potty training as the reason. I refuse, and remind her of the agreement we made earlier.

9th Session

David has been increasingly more active in what he produces: he himself operates the frog, the tape recorder and its control keys; and he sometimes allows an instant of his internal song to escape. When listening to the tapes he always displays ambivalence, either by rushing to the end of the room towards the mirror, or by remaining very close to the tape recorder where he makes mouth and lip movements as if he were taking the sounds into his mouth.

His expansive gesticulations at the piano makes me think of the way a conductor would direct an orchestra from the piano: he conducts with his left hand, plays with the right, and makes movements with his mouth, often with an authoritarian expression on his face. He seems caught up in an experience of omnipotence, and almost appears to be hallucinating.

I introduce the slide-whistle, and this captivates his interest. As with every other new instrument, he shows attentiveness and pleasure, and at the same time, plugs his ears or rushes off to the far corner of the room.

10th Session

David centers his attention on the piano, particularly on a few specific notes: E-flat 3 and some of the lowest notes. His conductor-like behavior is still evident.

Now there are four clearly distinguishable categories of sounds and sound patterns: (1) Body noises (farts) which are a sign in our relationship; (2) Voice-like noises (laments, chair scraping, door creaking, doll-whistles); (3) Crystalline noises (sounds of the resonance boxes, which I consider "celestial" because of the heavenward glance which he has when accompanying them); (4) Very low piano notes---at the other extreme.

11th to 17th Sessions

David invents a balanced movement on the piano using his whole body. With outstretched arms, he controls the entire surface of the instrument and plays, in alternation, the extremely low-pitched and high-pitched notes. He also improves his control and manipulation of other objects and instruments, which he greatly enjoys.

The game of opening and closing is used with the door, windows and piano. At the twelfth session he rediscovers, thanks to the sun, the game with our shadows which appear and disappear according to our movements. We also resume the game of "Hello there!" with the curtains. David returns to the slide-whistle, but since he is still unwilling to put it to his mouth, I have to blow it while he moves the slide. This gives him great pleasure. He shows total delight when I introduce the kazoo, and exhibits his usual pattern of surprise, pleasure, excitement, plugging his ears, and rushing towards the mirror. This instrument (which distorts the speech of adults) has a special attraction for him.

I notice that at each session he does a little more by himself. What he loses in the way of omnipotence and magic, he seems to gain in terms of the knowledge of objects and their manipulation.

David's mother informs me that, at home, he has become more attentive, that he expresses a preference for records of piano music, and that he often asks to listen to a playback of sounds he has produced. In our sessions, he seems to be comfortable with the space I give him in our relationship. He is clearly more at ease in it, is no longer squinting, is more able to meet my eyes, and he can remain in the room for the duration of the session.

At the seventeenth session, he arrives singing, and demands a great deal of corporal engagement on my part, but in a relaxed stated, with games such as hide-and-seek with the curtains. This time I experience the sharing of the true pleasure of a relationship between us.

The next session, however, was to be a painful one.

18th Session

This time David, accompanied by Ms. E, does not rush into the room. Ms. E has forbidden it and told him that he must learn how to behave like a big boy. He plays the piano and the rest of his games, and then discovers a new object: a paper blower which unfurls when you blow into it. This toy excites him and makes him laugh.

During the session we are disturbed by a lady who has come to look for something in the cupboards in my room. Nothing can now divert him from playing with the sliding doors on them. He seems uninterested in the content of the cupboards, and focuses only on the movement of the doors and the scraping noises they make. Since I cannot distract him from this, I accompany his game vocally by imitating the sounds. (This reminds of a composition by Pierre Henry, entitled "Concerto for a Door and a Sigh" which happens to be precisely about the modulations of a creaking door).

David cannot accept the fact that the session has ended, and when Ms. E arrives, he rushes off to slam the door in her face. I just manage to catch him before he does, and he proceeds to throw a grand tantrum. He pulls me, bites me and ends up exploding at the piano where his movements show remarkable vigor and fluency. He literally beats the piano with both hands. The moment is very striking and dramatic. I am very upset to think that he may feel that I have betrayed him by handing him over to Ms. E. I realize that his anger over this incident is a gauge of the level of his present commitment to our relationship.

This session is a turning point in my concern about his situation.

19th to 24th Sessions

The cupboard doors remain the focal point of David's activities for the succeeding sessions. He expends a great deal of energy on them, as if it is real work for him. He still resists any distraction. I then introduce the game "Open and Close" which we play while he slides the cupboard doors, and the "Goodbye" game which we play at the end of the session when it is time for him to leave. David then begins to alternate the noises made by the doors with his piano playing, and thereby incorporate them into his sound vocabulary. I accompany the door sound vocally, expanding them into a dialogue. This surprises David but he shows no displeasure.

After a few sessions, he begins to spontaneously inhibit some of his attention towards the game with the cupboard doors in order to play with the piano. I wonder if he is responding to Ms. E's reprimands.

In a later session, David and I discover that the cupboards have been inadvertently locked and I do not have the key. David is very disappointed but understands that there is nothing I can do about it. He takes refuge in the piano and is then attracted to a tall ashtray shaped like a metal tube. It has a very pleasing resonance. He is quite fascinated by it, and bends down to be nearer to the vibrations, and almost goes into a kind of ecstasy.

25th to 27th Sessions

Our relationship becomes closer, and this is most noticeable in our body contacts. David accepts and sometimes requires my presence at the piano. I play a few chords, and he sings and plays with both hands alternating low and high notes. He also allows me to guide his hands to play a broken chord.

During the following session he goes to hide himself for a few seconds in my fur jacket. Later on he becomes interested in my handbag and in the money which his mother gives me. He begins to express himself in the session using nonsense syllables and jargon.

When he arrives for the 27th session, Ms. E places David in front of me and tells him "This is Edith!" He looks me straight in the eye. I learn that he had said my name on the way to the session.

28th Session

This session takes place after a week's break for vacation. It seems to me that David is less well. He shows great interest when I make an off-beat vocal response to a note he played on the piano. He makes this into a game between us and asks for a repeat performance. He rapidly latches onto this game, and by the end of the session totally masters it: first he plays a note on the piano and then sings back the note off-beat. This syncopated echo becomes a new organizing factor in our relationship.

29th to 34th Session

In the course of these sessions, David consolidates his achievements. He now plays chords of thirds and begins to orchestrate the off-beat notes. First he plays the beat on a low note of the piano, then he sings a high note for one off-beat and asks me to blow the whistle on another off-beat. He continues to talk gibberish, particularly when asking for something--- this as an advancement over using body language alone. He is very disappointed with the mouth-organ because he is still unable to make mouth contact with objects.

35th to 42nd Sessions

I have brought along a key-holder which makes a repetitive high sound whenever its owner whistles. When I am unable to demonstrate how it works, David comes to my rescue by producing the corresponding sound. He is delighted at getting the response from the key-holder, as we whistle to a dog! I encourage him by saying, "Well done!" and lightly touch his shoulder. Afterwards, David asks me several times to repeat the gesture, which is awkward for me since I do not know what meaning this accidental gesture might have in our relationship. During the following sessions, he introduces several words like "Goodbye."

At the 38th session he is clearly seeking body contact. He again begins to raise my arm, wanting me to touch him on the shoulder. I notice that when he plays the tape recorder, manipulating the keys, he is always moving, encountering me as I stay in back. I realize that he is seeking back contact, as if he wants to be protected from behind. I make my presence behind him more specifically felt, which he appreciates.

Next he asks me to bend down to his level, and the allows himself to seek a proper "cuddle." He puts his head next to mine, very relaxed, and even brings his face near to mine as if to kiss me. It is a very moving moment.

In addition to introducing several new words, David continues his explorations of the piano, using successive and simultaneous intervals. Moments of affection recur in the sessions.

43rd Session

David introduces a different nuance into our relationship. He alternates moments of great closeness with moments of distance. He keeps me at arms' length when he is playing the piano. This allows him to show off and sing while I sit at the table watching him. Then he joins me at the table to play with the other instruments.

44th to 49th Sessions

During the last three sessions before the July-August vacation, David does a kind of review of his achievements in sound. As for our relationship, periods of keeping a distance alternate with moments of cuddling, at which time David displays increasingly more confidence. Now he curls up, leans on my body, allows himself to be carried, and so forth.

When the sessions resume in early September, we must temporarily change rooms and this causes David considerable anxiety. He hides his face in his arms and, to the amazement and admiration of his mother and myself, we hear him repeating after me: "It's this way!" (as a speaking boy).

He is still inclined to run away. He now demonstrates an entirely new behavior, putting instruments in his mouth and blowing them. One after the other, he puts into his mouth and blows the harmonica, the slide-whistle, and other whistles. He also resumes handling the tape-recorder and the call-response game with the key holder. Returning to the usual room, the following week, is clearly reassuring.

50th Session

For the first time, David shows an interest in notes which are next to one another (i.e., intervals of a second). He runs through all of the intervals on the piano: thirds, fifths, fourths, octaves, and now seconds.

When he tries once again to open the window, I instinctively accompany this behavior by a kind of improvised lullaby using the words "It's open... it's closed." He likes this game very much and for a moment I hear him speaking along with me, then answering "open." For the first time he says "goodbye" as he leaves.

51st to 57th Session

David resumes the game at the window and sings along with me. Now he calls himself "baby" and adds a few words to his vocabulary. Sometimes he comes to the session humming.

58th Session

As in every session, David spends some time "working" at the tape recorder as I remain close to him and try to understand what he is doing. When he encounters the table for the recorder has been removed, he finds a chair at the other end of the room, moves it next to the piano, and then places the recorder on top of it. I am delighted at his initiative. I notice that he is dribbling less, and that he seems to be in better control of his saliva since he has learned to play the wind instruments.

59th Session

We are interrupted by a pianist who has come to look at the piano before the concert which he is going to be giving at the arts center. I have to explain that the piano is David's territory and that it is very difficult for him to lend it to anyone. As the pianist is leaving, David leads me by the hand, indicating to call the pianist back. The pianist is willing to play along with David, and returns. He even performs a piano piece for David!

It is worth noting that in the course of this session, David takes hold of me from behind, placing his hands on my hips: he is thus able to reproduce on me, inverting the roles, the experience he had of my presence behind him and of the security and comfort he derived from it.

60th to 67th Session

During this period, I had moved my therapy room from the center to my own apartment. David does not display any panic, as he did the last time we changed rooms. He adapts very quickly to this new environment: a quiet room with a window overlooking the city. He explores the room, appreciates the feel of the new desk with a leather top, becomes absorbed in improvising on the mouth-organ, and rests his elbows on the desk while looking out the window, as if in a dream. He continues to use more words, and bits of sentences.

He introduces a game with the telephone: I am to take the receiver and to repeat after him "Who is it?...The piano!" He follows this game by playing the piano. He likes the mini-harp very much, and asks me to play chords as he goes to the window and hums along.

During this period, my relations with David's mother and Ms. E are rather strained. Ms. E would like to remove David from the influence of his mother (and perhaps mine as well). She goes so far as to develop a plan to bring David to stay at her new house. Meanwhile, David's mother is looking for a special school for him to attend.

68th Session

This is the first time David's mother brings him to the session since my move. During the session, a new game develops alternating the paper whistle and a note on the piano. This alternation becomes off-beat, then surprising, random and unpredictable. This causes a good hearty laugh and there is a real sense of complicity between the two of us. David awaits the "surprise" and exchanges understanding glances with me.

69th to 87th Session

This is a period of uncertainty and tension, as the conflict over David's future is being played out between Mrs. D and Ms. E. For this reason, David occasionally reverts to earlier behavior patterns: he has difficulty leaving; he returns to the cow toy and tries to master it as he had done earlier; and he resumes the farting game. In the course of the intervening sessions, David explores in great detail each new instrument, and introduces it in alternating sequence with already familiar sounds. He displays much emotion when investigating the guitar and how its strings vibrate. He wants me to be nearby and holds my hand.

He always tries to control sounds, and to combine or sequence them. On the tape recorder, he always uses his own sounds as background noise, and then adds all other kinds of sound effects, at which he is a true expert and which really give him a great thrill. What he produces using piano and tape recorder reminds me of contemporary musical composition techniques and of electro-acoustical music.

During these sessions there is talk of Mrs. D's plan to put David in a special school.

88th Session

This is the last session before the summer holidays. David uses the piano, the rattle (an instrument he has often used because of the loud noise it makes), and above all the guitar, still holding me by the hand. For the first time, David spontaneously sits down in the armchair which he has never allowed himself to do.

Ms. E informs me on the phone that David will probably not be coming back to the sessions because his mother has found a school for him. Ms. E has thus been dismissed, and eliminated from David's education. She is very upset at this.

Eight months later, David's mother telephones me to give me good news about David and herself. The situation seems much clearer. David is making progress and improving. He still speaks of me, and she is considering paying me a visit with David. David is now seven years old.

DISCUSSION AND CONCLUSIONS

Taking my work with David as a whole, I would like to make a number of points and place them in a descriptive, structural and psychodynamic context.

Alternation

Alternation was a key organizing principle in helping David to experience, explore, use, and relate to sounds. This itself presupposes that a certain of its basic components were already established. These include: repetition, regularity, differentiation, and categorization.

Repetition and regularity were established: through the sessions themselves (their scheduling, the way they were organized etc.), and within the sessions (echoing, sound feedback sequences, etc.).

Differentiation and categorization of sounds took place through comparisons of musical sounds and noise, and by contrasting "pleasant" and "unpleasant" (eg. the resonance boxes/scraping of chairs). As time went on, increasingly more refined contrasts were explored.

Alternation produces regularity and structuring in time, and requires both repetition and differentiation within a space that has two successive phases. Once it was established, David used this principle to organize the whole of his universe, including:

1) alternation of the people accompanying him and looking after him,
2) alternation of their presences and absences (repeated in the game with the shadows and in the hid-and-seek);
3) alternation within his spatial relationships: in front/behind himself (the fart moving from behind to in front through his oral reproduction of it); in front/behind me (contact from behind at the tape recorder to allowing him to cuddle me in front); near/far (with me at the table versus alone at the piano); closed/open (as with the door, window, piano and mouth);
4) alternation in his relationship to people and to things: same versus different, known versus unknown.

Alternation also helps to organize thinking. It gives each event predictability and anticipation: one thing follows another, one thing makes the other wait, one ushers in the other, etc.. This was the foundation of our first dialogues with the doll-whistles.

In David, the mastery of this structure peaked with the introduction of the unexpected, or what I called "the surprise element." The surprise eventually became a source of pleasure for David rather than panic. The unexpected takes place in time, on a beat, then off a beat, and finally, randomly.

Thus alternation came to be what Rosolato (1985) calls the "signifier of demarcation," that is to say, a "selection by means of perceptual repetition which brings into play a series of oppositions which are progressively explored by the child: presence/absence, good/bad, and especially pleasure/lack of pleasure and pain" (p. 30-31).

This signifier can also be linked to the alternation in which David finds himself between the two main figures in his life, his mother and Ms. E.

Linking Different Sensory Perceptions

The organizing principle of alternation makes it possible to link up the different sensory perceptions within a relationship, a notion also found in the work of Meltzer et al (1975). Examples of this are the situations which involved linking sounds (echo, recorded feedback) with visual perceptions (shadows, mirror images) with touches (my presence behind him). David was seeking simultaneity between sound production and visualization. But this could not provide satisfaction because of the necessary time lag between the sound production and its playback, and between the gesture of making sounds on the piano and the moment he looked after their image in the mirror (time lag and different spaces). Eventually however, he discovered something better: playing the piano while looking at his reflection in the varnished piano top. At long last, he was able to control both the sound production itself and its effects on his body. Then, after these links had been made, his relationship with me provided another context for exploring further connections. For a time, my presence behind him, our touching, and the visual control of his production that he exerted in the piano top compensated for his own lack of body organization. Then, David could produce sounds from in front, by discovering himself in the piano mirror, while at the same time being provided with my protection from behind. This served as a kind of substitute for his lack of *"psychic skin"* as described by Anzieu (1985, 1987).

Finally this function seems to be integrated when David introduces a distance between us. My visual holding becomes a sufficient support, a presence and awareness of the look of the other which leads him to collaborate in showing off: "I am being looked at," and "I enjoy being looked at."

Excitement and Control

From the outset, David's behavior in regard to sound was characterized by very strong excitation, of a kind which can easily lead, with certain timbres, to captivation, fascination, or entrancement (e.g., the doll-whistles, the tubular ashtray). These kinds of excitations and attractions to sound could lead to meaningful musical expression, but they also signify a breach in the "protective shield." This Freudian concept refers to a function and to an apparatus which supports it. "The function consists in protecting the organism against the stimuli coming from the outside world which, through their intensity, would risk destroying it. The apparatus is viewed as a surface layer covering the organism and passively filtering the stimuli" (Laplanche and Pontalis, 1968, p. 302). This body metaphor of the membrane is also used later by Anzieu (1976, 1985, 1987) in the form of *"Ego-Skin"* and *"Ego Envelopes."*

I have dealt with this particular form of excitation in an analysis of the myth of Pan (1991), the god of sound, who after his birth received neither care nor protection, and for whom excitation remained a permanent state in which he was capable of producing in the other person a true state of panic. Yet indeed, Bion (1962) stresses the point that "such hypersensitivity does not constitute a contact with reality" (p. 8). Sounds remain, in this case, "undigested facts," or *"beta-elements"* which are manipulated as things in themselves which cannot be represented.

David experienced sound stimuli with extreme ambivalence (attraction and fear), as demonstrated by the way he would block his ears and run to the far corner of the room while at the same time asking for the sound to be repeated and expressing pleasure and excitement when it was.

The way David used sounds to relate to objects and people was "magical" in the sense that he caused them to appear merely by calling them by their sounds. In fact, these sounds seem to be perceived at times as sound-objects, sound substances. This is reminiscent of an Australian magician-singer described by Schneider (1960): "During the many weeks he spends in solitude he strives to get to know the internal music of objects. Such an infiltration into the essence of cosmic life can only be achieved thanks to a feeling of solidarity which objects and complete identification of the man with nature by means of sound. The magician and his object have to become so steeped in one another that the limits between subject and object become blurred, which confers upon the magician the faculty of reproducing "with a true voice" the sounds which normally only belong to the objects which he is imitating" (p. 167).

But in the case of David there was no conscious awareness, solidarity or identification, but rather the contrary---alienation. He was functioning in a state of omnipotence. As the work continued, he gradually began to accept my interventions, and then eventually to ask for them. This happened particularly at the end, when he wanted to take possession of the sound gesture, and did so in the spirit of learning rather than omnipotence. This is the moment when he took possession of words as a new mediation and a new way of influencing his environment. Hence for example, he used my name outside of the sessions when he felt insecure, something that Ms. E found to be "incongruous," but which showed nevertheless that our relationship had been internalized and that David could use it when we were separated, and no longer only in a magical and alienating fusion.

A Work of Composition: A Thought in a Stereotyped Package

It is worth pointing out that David's interest in the universe of sound centered first on timbre and pitch, and then on composition and harmony. Thus we observed that when he applied alternation within the musical sphere, he followed a sequence according to what attracted him most. He began with comparing the different sound qualities of instruments. Then when he moved to the piano and alternated opposing registers, from the lowest to the highest notes, he gradually began to explore smaller and smaller extremes until intervals emerged. Eventually, alternation led to simultaneity of pitch, and of chords of two or more notes, and to an harmonic sensibility. Finally it brought David to discover notes which are next to one another on the scale. As far as rhythm is concerned, David moved straight from body rhythm directly to off-beats.

We cannot isolate David's musical products from the relationship developing between us. There was such a striking concordance between his musical exploration and the quality of our relating. He moved from maximum distance (in his attempts to run away from me so often at the beginning) to the relation between two successive sounds (two voices, two people), until finally daring to attempt simultaneity without getting lost in it, he discovered the harmony of "accord" and the cuddle. [Translator's note: the French word "accord" means both agreement or understanding and also refers to a musical "chord"]. At this moment, he took interest in codes---both musical (the scale) and verbal (the words).

If the work of a composer is to be found in all the associations and linkings attempted by David, it is in his behavior with the tape recorder that it appears in its most surprising form. Surprising indeed, since his behavior appeared to be consistent with standard descriptions of an autistic orientation towards such objects (i.e., a frenzied manipulation of mechanical things obsessive and stereotypic fashions).

David spent long periods manipulating the controls in a state of great excitement: alternating play and stop, varying sound levels and intensity, winding the tape forward and backward, obtaining and controlling various sound effects (e.g., the Larsen effect, wows, etc), and then improvising to the playback.

It was at the 46th session that my long waiting for finding some sense in, or understanding David's behavior with the tape recorder was rewarded. From the beginning of this treatment I looked at the frenzy and energy of David's sound explorations with the hypothesis that there was thinking behind the steretyped and compulsive gestures, and I stayed just behind him to show him my interest and research on this point.   In what he was doing at the piano, David was producing effects of contrasting intensity, as was his usual practice, which he then alternated with his off-beat game at the piano, returning to repeat vocally the off-beat game against the tape recorder playback, then with the piano, and so on. I finally perceived that what he was doing was playing off his own musical production in syncopation against itself, using the tape recorder as background to produce variations in loudness that created their own off-beats. I was extremely moved to have finally been able to make something of his activity and to realize just how long it had taken me to understand. In order to be able to communicate this understanding to David (who was still not using speech), I answered him vocally in the off-beats of the tape recorder.

The results of these manipulations of the tape recorder were on a par with a true work of musical composition, worthy of the investigations being carried out by contemporary composers of electro-acoustical music. As far as the organization of music and sounds was concerned, just as with his relationships, his behavior with the tape recorder was thus an extreme condensation of musical and relational meaning, which brought out a kind of overall stereotyped behavior pattern. (In fact, Ms. E and Mrs. D had reproached me several times for letting David keep his pathology or even on encouraging it!) Reference could be made, on this point, to my article (Lecourt, 1990).

The Anal Problem and the Off-Beat

It is not without importance that David should be interested in the off-beat and not the main beat. The disregarding of his physiological rhythms, of his physical needs (such as putting him on the pot every 1/2 hour, not allowing him to have a nap, etc.) all prevented his body from following its natural rhythms.

The whole question of toilet training was the first stumbling block and constituted the focal point of our relationship. My organization of the sessions disturbed his conditioning by "upsetting" the timing of his schedule. A 45-minute session does not fit into a 30-minute schedule. This upsetting of his toileting program was a constant reason for Ms. E to question the timing of the sessions.

But in fact, it was this very disruption that was central to his progress. For in this off-beat/upsetting of the schedule, a space was opened for therapy, a space for creativity in a world which was entirely controlled and managed. It was from this space that finally "surprise" was born, the unexpected, the random, which we could compare to the incongruous, the main characteristic of the fart, a body product, escaping from a behind which could neither be controlled nor planned. This somatic overflow from behind was a source of anxiety for David, and led to the need for protection. My body contact behind him created a sort of second skin (Bick, 1968). It was important for David to find ways of representing this (reproducing a fart, working with music). At the same time, David felt the other orifices as objects of fears and pleasures: mouth (controlling the saliva), ears (need to stop them with his hands). And finally, oral control was gained, first by playing with instruments and then, later, through speech.

In introducing the off-beat, I was also sharing something of this space of "upset" which David occupied in the conflicts of his parents, and then between the two maternal figures (Ms. E and Mrs. D).

In Conclusion: A Relationship in Suspense

Throughout these sessions my work was sustained by the purpose of discovering the thinking and the relationship behind the automaton who had been presented to me, and, in my dealings with Ms. E and Mrs. D, to get them to recognize this. As will have been noted, my role was essentially to provide attention, support, and backup. In going over the sessions once again I also note the importance of the playful element which I introduced right from the beginning and always maintained. I was also called upon to lend David a part of my body, to handle those instruments which he could not yet use himself (particularly the wind instruments which he could not use himself), as well as to provide "backup" protection for his back thereby enabling him to let go and find sufficient confidence and pleasure in his musical explorations.

As will have been noted, my description of this case has focused on the structuring of David's experience of sounds and relationships rather than on the analysis of the *transference* and *counter-transference reactions*. That is not to say that these were not important. Both reactions were projected and symbolized in the way David gradually related sounds (one sound with another) and in the final accord and musical composition of them.

The conclusion of the sessions and the end of this therapy was not decided upon in relation to the therapy itself but because a new path that been chosen for David---and new hopes awakened in Mrs. D that he could be placed in a special school using the *TEACCH* method. Unfortunately this is a a frequent occurrence in work with this kind of pathology: just as the child cathects the relationship and begins to speak, a brutal severing of the tie is brought about by the environment. In this case my feeling was one of a pseudo-failure. What was going to become of all this creativity within a new programming system? What use was it to the child to almost disentangle himself from one lot of conditioning only to be caught up in another? What room for thinking was going to be left to him?

However I do understand that the proponents of the TEACCH method might see in this a logical and very positive conclusion. Only the future will tell!

GLOSSARY

Adhesiveness: A term used by Meltzer et al (1975) to describe a relation with a high degree of a peculiar dependence on an external object---a dependence not only on its services but also its mental functions. It is found in certain kinds of autism.

Autistic: A pervasive developmental disorder characterized by impairments in social relationships, communication, and affect, oddities of motor movements, resistance to change, hypersensitivity, and self-injurious behaviors.

Beta-Elements: A term used by Bion (1962) for sensory perceptions that are experienced as material parts of the personality, as things, or as "undigested" facts. The perceptions are manipulated as things in themselves which cannot be represented. Thoughts are things and things are thoughts. This phenomenon is specific to psychotic processes.

Countertransference Reactions: In psychoanalysis, unconscious reactions of the analyst in the relation to his/her client, or to the client's transference.

Ego-Skin (Psychic Skin): A term used by Anzieu (1987): "The ego-skin's proper function--the libidinal recharge of psychic functioning and the maintenance of internal energetic tension and its unequal distribution among the psychic subsystems--corresponds to the skin as the sensorimotor tonus' permanent surface of stimulation by external excitations" (p. 21).

Off-beat or "Contretemps": This expression is first a musical one: to be off the beat, contra-tempo; but the French term has a broader meaning which is interesting in our situation---that of something which is a disappointment or inconvenience. And in everyday life, "a contretemps" means to come inopportunely (as does the fart).

Protective Shield: Freudian concept of a surface layer which covers an organism and passively filters stimuli from the outside world, which because of its intensity, may be destructive to the organism.

Ego Envelope (Psychic Envelope): Anzieu (1987) uses this term to describe frontier or boundary structures which serve the following functions: to insure protection against excessive excitations; to help define the psychic elements belonging to a given space (internal psychic space, perceptual space, other people's psychich space); to make connections between them. As complex and rich structures located on the boundaries of different individual psychic spaces, the ego envelope defines the ego space.

Stereotyped: Repetitive gestures made in a compulsive way, and apparently without consciousness or intention.

TEACCH: An educational method for autistic children wherein autism is regarded as an organic dysfunction of cognitive processes. The method offers a compartmentalized, pragmatic, and evaluative approach to education which makes it successful.

Transference Reactions: In psychoanalysis, the processes in which unconscious wishes are actualized in some objects (material object, human object, or part of an object) inside a specific relation (e.g., the client's transference on the psychoanalyst).

REFERENCES

Anzieu, D. (1976). L'enveloppe sonore du Soi. (The Sound Envelope of the Self). Nouvelle Revue de Psychanalyse, 13, 161-179.

Anzieu, D. (1985). Le Moi-Peau. (The Ego-Skin). Paris: Dunod.

Anzieu, D. (1987). Psychic Envelopes. (English Translation in 1990). London: Karnac Books.

Bick, E. (1968). The Experience of the Skin in Early Object Relations. International Journal of Psychoanalysis, 49, 484-486,

Bion, W.R. (1962). Learning from Experience. New York: Basic Books.

Lecourt, E. (1989). De l'echo à l'enregistrement audiophonique l'enfant autistique et le magnetophone. (From Echo to Sound Recording, the Autistic child and the tape Recorder). Bulletin de Psychologie, 395 (XLVIII), 7-13, 348-355.

Lecourt, E. (1990). The Musical Envelope. In D. Anzieu, Psychic Envelopes (English Translation), pp. 211-235. London: Karnac Books, 211-235.

Lecourt, E. (1991). Le dieu Pan, grand excité - excitateur: de la pulsion au psychique. (The god Pan, Aroused and Arousing: From the Physical to the Mental). Psychologie Medicale, 1991.

Meltzer, D., Bremmer, J., Weddell, D., Hoxter, S., & Wittenberg, I. (1975). Explorations in Autism. London: The Roland Harris Educational Trust.

Rosolato, G. (1985). Le signifiant de demarcation et la communication non verbale. (The Signifier of Demarcation and Non-Verbal Communciation). In Elements de I'interpretation, pp. 63-82. Paris: Gallimard.

Schneider, M. (1960). Le role de la musique dans la mythologie et les rites des civilisations non europeennes. (The Role of Music in the Mythology and Rituals of Non-European Civilisations). In M. Roland-Manuel, Histoire de la Musique, Volume 1, pp. 131-214. Paris: Gallimard.

The Boy that Nobody Wanted: Creative Experiences For A Boy With Severe Emotional Problems

FRAN HERMAN, M.T.A., C.C.W., R.M.T.
Director, Creative Arts Department
Hugh MacMillan Rehabilitation Centre
Toronto, Ontario, Canada

Abstract: This case describes weekly sessions over a fourteen month period with a nine-year-old boy with severe emotional problems. The approach combined music with play and creative experiences in the other arts, aimed at dealing with his depression, impulsivity and hyperactivity. By providing soothing media in concert with music, he was able to gain confidence from his own strengths, and to modify some of his destructive tendencies.

BACKGROUND INFORMATION

Robbie considered himself "The Boy That Nobody Wanted." He often wondered whether he would be better off as a government boy of the United States rather than a government boy of Canada. Given up at birth to be a ward of the Children's Aid Society by a teen-age mother, his history was dotted by transfers from one place to another with little opportunity for bonding, or for building relationships.

Robbie was nine years old when he first began his sessions in music therapy. He was a handsome, wiry, likeable little lad who had been through twelve foster homes and two treatment centres before his admittance to a children's psychiatric hospital. He was an aggressive "acting out" child who seemed unable to accept authority, and he had frequent temper tantrums where he would display destructive behaviour. He could neither read nor write and had never been able to stay in school despite many attempts and approaches. He lacked concentration due to his hyperactivity, exhibited frequent non-goal directed activities, appeared to have severe learning disabilities, was disruptive when other children were around, and had difficulty being compliant. He was an unhappy little boy who felt unloved and unwanted.

Robbie had been in the psychiatric hospital for ten months with little progress reported. School, occupational therapy, pottery, woodworking, swimming and other sports, as well as weekly visits to his psychiatrist were considered "tried and failed." Robbie had become resistant to doing anything, showed signs of deep depression and often refused to eat or get out of bed. He felt unable to face a new day, having given up hope of things ever changing for him. It might be said that Robbie lacked a sense of identity, often asking "Who am I?".

The need for an ordered life is universally important, whether or not this is understood consciously by the child. This search for an identity was a fundamental part of Robbie's difficulties. One day in rounds, when staff were feeling rather desperate about him, one team member commented, "The only new thing here that hasn't been tried is music therapy. Robbie always taps his toes when he hears music. Let's try it as a last resort." Everyone agreed and a few hours later Robbie was brought to the music room.

TREATMENT PROCESS

The Opening Wedge: Sessions 1 and 2

When Robbie first entered the music room he began racing around, plinking and plunking on the piano, banging on the drums, and tooting slide whistles and recorders. He circled several times in random fashion then spotted the autoharp on a small table in the middle of the room. He went to it and asked what it was. I explained the instrument and showed him how to strum it as I pressed down on the chord buttons. Robbie was intrigued. We then played some children's songs in this manner, and he sang and enjoyed our music making. He wanted to repeat the songs over and over again, until I finally told him the session was finished. He was reluctant to leave, but was invited to return the next morning after breakfast. His sessions were planned for that time as an attempt to get him out of bed to face his day.

At 8:05 the next morning, Robbie was there, bright and eager. He flitted around the room several times in the same manner as the previous day, and then once more settled down to playing the autoharp. We played the "Farmer in the Dell" several times, at which point Robbie requested that he press the chords and strum by himself. He proceeded to do this with the correct two chord changes and was very pleased. However, on the second playing he made a mistake, threw the pick on the floor and headed for the door saying, "I made a friggen 'Boob' and I'm going."

Robbie had demonstrated a pattern of leaving at the first sign of frustration and he never returned to a situation once he had abandoned it. Knowing it was essential to keep him there, I fell to the floor and began crawling around on my knees, smacking my lips, flicking my fingers, sniffing, looking under the radiator, peering into the piano bench, lifting up the mats on the floor, opening and closing the window, etc.. All of this was sufficiently bizarre to have stopped Robbie in his tracks. He began following me around the room asking repeatedly, "What are you doing.. hey ... what are you doing?" Finally I answered, "I'm looking for your Boob!". He was completely taken aback and muttered, "Hey Lady, are you crazy or something?" "No Robbie, I really am looking for your Boob!" I began to fire questions at him:

"I can't see it. Can you?"
"No."
"I can't touch it, can you?"
"No."
"I can't taste it or smell it, can you?"
"No."
"I can't even hear it anymore, can you?
"No!"

I continued: "And you know what kiddo, I think it just got away on us." But, the important thing is that you know you made a boob. Not many kids in this place would ever be able to do that. That means you are a very musical boy' indeed..." I went on to explain that musical mistakes don't matter because one cannot even remember them after a few seconds.

This was a very important concept for Robbie to understand. He had discernible problems with the permanence of drawings or modelling in plastic media. The visual impact of such efforts reminded him of how poorly he did things. "Music mistakes" that floated away became acceptable to him. For weeks afterwards he would deliberately make mistakes, then go through all the motions that I had previously made. Finally, he would declare, "Well, that's another one that got away."

For those of us working and caring for special children it is essential that we find ways of filling up their "metaphorical pots" as described by Virginia Satir (1988). They must be filled with creative experiences that are fulfilling and contribute to the child's growth. Specific techniques for helping expression through music therapy and the expressive arts are endless. Regardless of what activity you and the child choose to do at any specific time, the purpose remains the same---to nurture and help the child become aware of himself and his existence in this world.

Each therapist will find his or her own style of achieving this delicate balance between directing and guiding the child on the one hand and following the child's lead on the other. As nurturers, we know that change in children is a gradual evolving process. We delight in their smallest gains, knowing that they have been accomplished with considerable patience, support, energy and insight. What takes place inside the therapist and what goes on inside a child, is a gentle merging resulting in growth and change.

Once Robbie decided that I was a person that he could relate to and trust, his defensiveness lessened. It is important to realize that some children are resistant and defensive for good reasons. They do what they have to do to survive. They have learned from the chaotic worlds in which they live and from homes or institutions that are often harsh, uncaring and unseeing that they must do what they can to take care of themselves. They need to protect themselves from intrusion. As Robbie began to trust, he allowed himself to open up and to be a little more vulnerable. I had to move in easily and gently, always maintaining a sense of unconditional acceptance and an uncritical attitude.

Gaining Expressive Freedom: Sessions 3 to 24

Robbie's sessions were to be immediately after breakfast each week day. They were scheduled for thirty minutes, but the length varied depending on his moods and frustration level.

The first goal was to help Robbie sit still while focusing his attention on a specific activity. Sometimes music was in the background, at other times it was the focus of the activity. Mirroring, echo responses, moving and stopping to various cues were the techniques used, usually at the beginning of the session. These were followed by soothing materials for Robbie to explore; first water, then sand.

Robbie had never been allowed to play with water, and took much delight in simply pouring it from one vessel to another, using tubes, funnels, ladles and sprinklers. He revelled in squeezing sponges and playing with objects that float like ping-pong balls, corks, or boats made of styrofoam. At other times he would simply move his hands in warm water to the rhythm of the music playing in the background.

For the large sand table in the room I made several different sized combs by cutting plastic lids from margarine containers in half, then cutting the straight edge to make large or small tines, waves, and zig-zag patterns. Robbie was encouraged to make designs in the sand. As he took a comb and made a wavy pattern to the music, I would comment on the rhythm of his design. This was usually enough support to keep him trying out more and more elaborate patterns.

We also used water with sand so that he could make rivers, tunnels and castles. With buried sea shells and sea music playing in the background, Robbie would make all kinds of seascapes in the sand. He was beginning to take pleasure in moulding shapes and forms with his hands, creating his own miniature worlds. Often when he would create a scenario, I would improvise music to augment his need for movement. Using pieces of sheer blue nylon he would soar like a seagull, thrash around like waves in the sea, or roll unto the beach like a seashell.

Enjoying Self-Expression: Sessions 25 to 40

Leading Robbie to a slowly dawning appreciation of his own creativity was a long and tedious process. Early traumatization appeared to have produced a fateful block in many areas. Expressive activities which allowed him freedom of expression without involving the expectation of any end product became meaningful in the treatment process. Once Robbie became aware that there were no pre-conceived ideas of how these activities should turn out, he was released from the anxiety of facing failure.

At this point clay was introduced. Its flexibility and malleability suit it to a variety of ends. It can be messy, mushy, soft, sensuous or hard. The sensuousness of clay often provides a bridge between a child's senses and his feelings. Children like Robbie who are insecure and fearful, can feel a sense of control and mastery over clay. It is a medium that can be "erased" and it has no clear-cut, specific rules for its use. When Robbie had been exposed to clay before, he had rejected it. However, at this point in his therapy, with the success he was beginning to feel in his other efforts, he was able to accept this medium and use it to good effect.

Finger painting using paints, semi-jelled jello or chocolate pudding was also done to musical accompaniments. To Brahms' Lullaby, Robbie would make quiet undulating motions, which would change to straight lines in all directions when a march was played. Both finger painting and clay proved to be very valuable media for him. They lent themselves to many manipulations with their fluent and inviting textures. They were used at varying levels and to fill varying needs. In both media Robbie could explore the value of creating and expressing his feelings on a nonverbal level.

Slowly, but surely, Robbie's attention span was increasing so that he was able to stay with an activity and have some satisfaction from it. When he had difficulty focusing, I followed his quick changes by helping him experience what he was doing more fully. Returning his attention to task at hand was accomplished by speaking softly, touching his hands gently, giving him a hug, and by encouragement and praise for the smallest accomplishments.

Learning Structure: Sessions 41 to 70

Now that Robbie had begun to channel his own self-expression, he was ready for activities that would help him to pay attention and adhere to a structure. His inability to do so had greatly hampered his ability to learn several things, including how to read. Developing a child's ability to move his eyes from left to right, and to trace an idea from beginning to end can be helped by using a coloured note system of music. The concept of teaching piano using coloured notes is not new. However, in most of the prevailing books available on the subject, the cluttered quality of the page can deter a poor or non-reader from even attempting to follow the music. I therefore attempted to develop a simpler system.

In it, the three middle octaves are similarly coded with brightly coloured dots. To give the child an awareness of orientation, the middle octave remains plain while the upper octave is designated with a small black "V" on each note. The lower octave is marked with a small black "X." No more than three octaves should be used. In order to keep the music sheet as uncluttered as possible, a coloured stroke is used to designate a tonic chord, and a coloured stroke with a "7" under it is used for a dominant 7th chord.

The prime purpose of this system is to give the underachieving child a successful reading experience, with immediate satisfaction for his efforts and with the least amount of possible frustration. Fingering, phrasing, and note values are ignored, however barlines are used to provide an anchor point for the eye.

Using notation can be quite helpful in developing eye-hand coordination and directionality. For a child like Robbie who had problems with sustaining attention, this type of structured activity also provided him with training in concentration, patterning of work habits and motivation.

Robbie was intrigued with this new direction in his music sessions. He was determined to learn to chord to the melodic line. Since we were using folk songs which he knew, his musical ability came through once he was secure with the notes and he would play the piece in the appropriate rhythm. At all times his playing was referred to as "reading music" in an effort to emphasize to him that he was indeed able to read one language and soon would be able to read another. He was quite pleased and proud of the special book that we created of the songs we had color coded for him to read and play.

Being Himself with Others: Sessions 71 to 120

A child has to learn self-awareness and self-respect before s/he can learn how to be aware of and show respect for others.   As Robbie's tolerance for stress increased, his capacity to persevere at a task lengthened.   His "pot" was filling up.   He became more aware of and pleased with his accomplishments, and this prepared him for sharing his music experiences with other children.   Until this point, Robbie lacked social skills, and became belligerent at the slightest frustration.   He was unable to play with others and was too impulsive to wait his turn.

Membership in a group of peers is a matter of vital concern to most children.   Making friends and learning to set up satisfying relationships with others of the same age are important parts of growing up.   A group will begin to form when the children begin to feel, think and behave differently because they are members of the group.   The therapist must observe when children begin to "interact" with one another, and when their relationships begin to influence their behaviour.   As this takes place, a feeling of "bond" or a "we-feeling" will develop, and the group will emerge as a recognizable entity distinct from the members that comprise it.

A little girl whom Robbie liked was introduced to the sessions twice weekly.   When this began to work, two more youngsters were added. Through music games involving conducting, music bingo, reflection, drumming, rhythm work, mime, puppetry and dancing, Robbie began to develop greater tolerance, and to learn how to interact with his peers, both of which were basic life skills that he needed.

Just as there was progression in creative activities from the simple to the complex, as the children learned to tolerate frustrations and postpone satisfactions, so my role as group leader progressed from one in which I carried a great deal of responsibility for keeping the group together, to one in which I helped the group members assume responsibility for leadership of their own activities.

Robbie managed to weather this sometimes stormy period and emerged from it with a better ability to handle himself in a group situation.   Such skills were necessary as the time to enter school was approaching.

A remedial reading specialist was brought in, and together we collaborated in helping Robbie learn to read.   Eventually he was able to attend school for short periods of time, which increased as his tolerance level allowed.

Downs and Ups

Throughout the time that I worked with Robbie there were occasions when he entered the music room in a very despondent mood, wanting only to lie on the mat and curl himself into a cocoon with a sheet wrapped around him. His sheet provided a special space all his own---a space he could lie in, roll on, and fantasize with, and a space he could use to protect himself. At such time I would play quiet, lyrical music which nonverbally let him know that I understood, I was in his corner and that he was safe there.

Robbie often spoke about the music room being his "peace room," his "saferoom." As Robbie lay there, he had time to calm his inner turmoil until ready to rise up and move to a new energy within him. He was encouraged to dance to his own inner music which I followed on the piano. He created his own drama and his own dance as he twisted and twirled experiencing many sensations and emotions.

Afterwards he was sometimes able to articulate why he was upset and we could deal with it. At other times, he merely finished saying, "I'm okay now! See you kiddo!" Robbie was learning to cope with his anger, frustrations and anxieties in a more constructive way.

CONCLUSIONS

Robbie, a severely damaged little boy made significant gains in the combined modalities of music and related arts. The following summary of outcomes demonstrates his growth over the course of his music therapy sessions. It goes without saying that these changes were supported programmatically by other members of the team.

1) Before music therapy, Robbie had a short attention span and was easily distracted, he frequently failed to listen, and was unable to follow directions; afterwards, his attention span improved, he could stay on task up to 15 minutes without distraction, and he could follow most directions if presented clearly.

2) Before music therapy, he was physically disruptive, endangered his own safety, and required constant supervision; afterwards, his difficult behaviours decreased, he was able to stay with others in the room without disruptions, and he was more aware of safety considerations.

3) Before music therapy, he talked constantly, but was noncommunicative most of the time; afterwards his verbal communication improved in content and clarity.

4) Before therapy, he refused to take turns, verbally interrupted others when speaking, and displayed poor social judgment; afterwards he was able to wait for his turn without frustration, became more aware that each person needed space and time to communicate, and demonstrated better social skills.

5) Before he was easily frustrated when things did not go his way, and

had daily temper tantrums which required holding techniques; afterwards, he tolerated his frustrations more appropriately and his tantrums were reduced to a few times weekly.

6) Before he was so depressed that he often refused to get out of bed or eat; afterwards, his depression lessened, he no longer stayed in bed, and his eating problems disappeared.

7) Before he had very little self-esteem, and was considered so damaged that most of the staff felt he was unsalvageable; afterwards, his self-worth blossomed as his creative energy found alternative ways to construct his personal reality.

Robbie was adopted two years later.

REFERENCES

Satir, V. (1988). The New People-Making. Palo Alto, CA: Science and Behavior Books.

CASE SEVEN

Creative Fantasy,
Music and Lyric Improvisation
With A Gifted Acting-Out Boy

KENNETH AIGEN, D.A., CMT
Administrative Director
Creative Arts Rehabilitation Center, Inc.
Adjunct Faculty Member: New York University
New York, New York

Abstract: This case study details individual music therapy with Will, a musically and intellectually gifted, non-pathological, eight year-old boy who was brought to therapy for fighting in school.   Though Will engaged in a variety of musical forms during the course of therapy, the focus here is on his use of creative fantasy and music.   The entire year and one-half of therapy is discussed, and the lyric and musical content of one crucial session is examined in detail.   A psychological/developmental rationale is offered for the use of fantasy in personal transformation, and the role of music in enhancing the dynamic process is briefly discussed.

INTRODUCTION

In reading case studies, it often appears that treatment progresses according to a form common to works of art: in the beginning phase of treatment the participants become acquainted with each other and in some ways, the future course of the therapy is foreshadowed; this is followed by a deepening of the relationship and work---in other words, "the plot thickens;" then a climactic/cathartic session or series of sessions occurs involving significant insight or transformation on the client's part; treatment then concludes with a recapitulation of important themes and the mutual assent of both parties through a termination process of varying lengths of time.

This neat form, however, is not always achieved with clients who seek music therapy treatment for significant emotional difficulties. Often clients miss sessions, leave treatment prior to achieving their potential, evidence growth in a halting fashion, and in general, express their individuality in a way that defies a neat recounting of planned events unfolding to a desired end. In short, the therapeutic work with many of these clients does not make for "good" case studies, and their stories are rarely recounted in the published literature.

The present case study illustrates a therapeutic process that progressed in this latter form: the most significant session occurred relatively early in the treatment; there was no music for long stretches of time; and, there was no termination process of which to speak. Nonetheless, the therapy was considered successful as great progress was made in the problem identified as the most crucial one for this client. The value of this study then is to demonstrate that in spite of the lack of a neat, organic process of therapeutic development, important gains can still be accomplished.

BACKGROUND INFORMATION

Will is an unusually intelligent, creative and articulate eight-year-old with a sophisticated command of feelings and concepts. For example, in his initial music therapy session Will said that he felt "guilty" about knocking down another boy at school, and expressed surprise that we would be playing music because we were at a "clinic." Because his father abandoned the family when Will was three, Will has been without a significant male figure for most of the previous five years, living with his mother and sister. The once-annual visit from his father has proved to be a very damaging event to Will as the father tends to ignore Will and shower his sister with gifts.

A minority youth living in a quite dangerous, inner-city neighborhood, Will has been attending a predominantly white school for gifted children outside his neighborhood. His referral to music therapy indicated that Will was "antagonistic to other children in group situations, possessed poor self-awareness and listening skills, and demonstrated impulsive behaviors," leading him to frequently get in fights with other children. Since this fighting was jeopardizing his academic placement, this was judged to be the most important of his difficulties.

Within the music therapy sessions, Will demonstrates no signs of emotional difficulties or pathology, outside of a slight tendency to hyperactivity and a resistance to prolonged interpersonal contact. Though he often tests limits to determine what is acceptable in the session, Will normally responds favorably to these limits once they are firmly set.

MUSIC THERAPY ASSESSMENT

Although I did not employ a formal musical assessment procedure with Will, his significant abilities in this area played an important role in the course of his therapy and they warrant a separate discussion here. The wide variety of musical interests and skills that Will possessed was reflected in the activities he chose to engage in while in music therapy. These included: creating long blues and rap songs with improvised lyrics and harmonica playing; singing structured, pre-composed songs, ranging from the current pop repertoire to Gilbert and Sullivan songs he prepared for a school show; playing purely instrumental improvisations on the drums, piano, resonator bells or electric guitar; and lastly, weaving long and complex fantasies with musical accompaniment.

In all of these activities Will demonstrated: (1) a highly developed rhythmic sense, seen in his ability to maintain a constant rhythm while improvising as well as employ a variety of rhythmic phrases in an expressive and communicative manner; (2) a sophisticated sense of melody and pitch, singing in tune and improvising melodies in a variety of musical styles; (3) a strong aesthetic sense, seen primarily in his creative and flexible use of dynamics; and (4) a strong sense of musical form, seen in the ease with which he related through---and shifted among---call and response forms, rondo forms, and standard pop forms in his improvisations. More important than any of these skills, however, was Will's motivation toward creative self-expression. Combining this motivation with his skills made Will seem to be the ideal music therapy client.

METHOD

Will's weekly, 45-minute sessions, took place at the Creative Arts Rehabilitation Center, Inc. (CARC), an out-patient clinic devoted solely to the Creative Arts Therapies. Though providing a home to clinicians from a variety of theoretical perspectives, one binding element of the clinical work at CARC is strong sense of client-centeredness, where the client's individual needs, desires, perspective on their own difficulties, and pace of growth determine the course of therapy. This approach was particularly well-suited to Will's clinical needs for two reasons:

First, his intellectual and expressive capacity, combined with a strong, self-directed drive, left Will perfectly capable of deciding how to use his time in therapy. My willingness to allow him this flexibility demonstrated my respect for him, an essential component of any successful therapy. This strategy is not undertaken lightly, however, and, as will be seen in the following section, it led Will's treatment far afield of relating solely through music.

Second, with clients for whom impulse control is a problem (a problem indicated by Will's constant fighting), it is generally counter-therapeutic for the therapist to attempt to control the course and content of the therapy session. To attempt to exercise such control over the client---and a directive strategy is a controlling one---is to recreate the destructive dynamic that is proving so problematic to the client outside the therapy setting. The therapist's task is instead to musically contribute to the creation of an aesthetic context which will allow the problematic impulse to be transformed from pure, uncontrolled discharge into self-expression. Here, it is the aesthetic form---as opposed to social expectations of appropriate behavior or, in the therapy session, the therapist's limits--that functions as the resistance to the client's destructive impulse, and a client/therapist power struggle is thus avoided. Certainly Will's strong aesthetic sense contributed to the efficacy of this approach for him.

TREATMENT PROCESS

Will's treatment consisted of 48 sessions over a one and one-half year period, and he passed through three distinct phases during this time. For approximately the first six months, Will was very engaged in music and seemed to be a willing and motivated participant in his own therapy. This period was followed by three to four months where Will was, at times, totally disinterested in music and somewhat ambivalent about continuing in music therapy, and another three months where his interest fluctuated. In the last three months, Will seemed to reach a middle ground and was moderately engaged in music, though deeply involved in the sessions. Termination, though warranted given Will's progress and change in motivation, was unsatisfactory as a variety of factors contributed to Will ending treatment without the benefit of a termination process.

The Beginning: Music, Music, Music

In his initial sessions, Will introduced two structures that would be important components of his ongoing process. The first of these was his organization of the session as a musical show, with the two of us serving as the featured performers. This format is a common one that many younger children employ in music therapy. Additionally, Will created a brief story in his first session that was stimulated by the autoharp. Will commented that this instrument sounded like a "dream" and he told a story about a witch who was Dracula's wife. The witch was laughing at Will because she had turned him into a monkey. This mechanism of using music to stimulate fantasy material, particularly involving themes of transformation, was a crucial component throughout Will's therapy, and will be discussed later in greater detail.

During this time, Will often needed to control and orchestrate my musical contribution, much as a conductor controls an orchestra: he employed musical and visual cues that determined the timing and dynamic quality of my music. I went along with this need for two reasons: Since Will was treating his session as a "show" where he was the featured performer and I was his "back-up" band, accepting this structure (and hence Will's reality) meant that it was natural that the "leader" should have a primary, directive role. Second, though on one level Will was "controlling" me---and I do not mean to minimize the importance of providing a context for a child such as Will to exercise his need for control over others in a **positive** context---it is important to realize that he was **simultaneously controlling himself.** In flexibly employing various dynamic levels and planning my musical entrances and exits, Will employed his need for aesthetic expression to inhibit his destructive and aggressive impulses. In allowing Will to "control" me, I was allowing him the opportunity to channel these impulses and thus enhance his own impulse control.

In these first five sessions, Will sang popular songs, invented call and response "raps," and created a few stories with primarily aggressive and violent themes. Our level of contact varied from week to week, and Will was feeling out who I was and what was allowable in the session. Though Will was quite engaged in the music, in his sixth session I sensed that he was ambivalent about playing music. This was confirmed by Will, and he asked to end the session early to play video games.

This ambivalence served as precursor of a feeling that would dominate the second phase of Will's treatment. Yet, it also led to a discussion with Will's mother that provided some important information for me. Each day of the week Will was brought to a different after-school activity. It was apparent that Will needed more time to just be a child without being forced to meet the demands of some sort of structured activity. In an effort to care for him, his mother was actually **controlling** Will to an unhealthy extent that left him frustrated and without the resources to control himself.

Then, in session eight, Will requested the song "Twist and Shout." Playing this song became a regular part of the following few sessions, and was something that Will returned to later in his therapy. At first, Will just sang the song straight, without much embellishment or spontaneity. He soon began to use the section of the song containing an extended dominant seventh chord to scream at the top of his lungs. Here was an unbridled release, an unrestrained expression of Will's aggression occurring within, and elicited by, the safe musical context.

My clinical musical interventions were directed toward using the song structure, without getting caught up in the accurate performance of this structure as an end in and of itself. My goal was to tap the expressive potential typically associated with improvised music within the song form. Eventually, Will began using this song to express and explore all the extremes of his emotional life. In one session, for example, he sang "Twist and Shout" by alternating volume levels: between softer vocalizations of infantile babbling sounds, and shouted sections of "Shake it for me baby!" accompanied by macho posturing---quite surprising in a child of Will's age. It was this exploration of expressive extremes in an appropriate manner in therapy that I felt would decrease Will's need to gain mastery through destructive social interactions.

After Will's tenth session, his mother requested a meeting with me. Apparently, Will's fighting with other children was intensifying and she was finding him increasingly difficult to manage. Until this time, Will's relationship with me, and his use of the session time, had existed in a social vacuum of sorts, uncontaminated by the reality existing outside the session room. Yet it now seemed like I needed to discuss this problem with Will directly, if only to gain information about his perspective on the fighting issue.

From these talks I emerged with two contradictory senses of Will's self-image. On a more overt level, Will felt that he was being scapegoated by his teacher and classmates, and that none of the trouble in school resulted from his actions. On a deeper level, however, I felt that Will considered himself to be a "bad boy" and that he was stuck continually re-enacting behaviors (such as fighting) that would confirm this negative self-perception. It was this fixed, negative self-image that I felt was at the root of Will's difficulties, and any possibility of helping him would involve finding a way to transform how Will viewed himself. I determined that my clinical strategy should be: to support Will's transformative tendencies as they emerged; to facilitate his identification with "good" characters; while simultaneously allowing for the creative expression (and hopefully transformation) of his "bad" self.

Will's fourteenth session was the most significant one of his therapy, and I will discuss it in some detail. After briefly experimenting with the electric guitar and drums, Will settled on improvising a fantasy while I played the piano. He was completely involved in the lyric and verbal aspects of the fantasy and was not concerned with maintaining control over my musical input.

The fantasy grew out of an improvised song called "Monster Shout" that consisted of a very simple I-IV funky rock and roll chord progression. This song represented a familiar place to Will, and throughout the fantasy he regularly returned to it, using this song to end the session as well.   Will was dressed in a rather ghoulish halloween costume, which certainly influenced the theme of the session and supported his deep investment in it. What follows is a relatively detailed account of this session. Its significance for Will will be more fully articulated later in the "Discussion" section.

A Voyage to Trick Land

While singing the words "Monster Shout" over the I-IV progression, Will spontaneously says, "And now for the story of monster shout." I understand this as an indication that Will is ready to let go of the song structure and engage in his fantasy. I therefore change the' music to open-ended, suspended chords with a much lessened rhythmic impetus. Will begins his story, with my musical contribution helping to contain the narrative while deepening his investment in the fantasy:

> *Once upon a time in a far away land there was a friendly monster named "Trick or Treat." And if you went to his house he always let you play with his toys. But there was a bad witch after him. And there was a good pumpkin named "Pumpkinhead" who lived in a little cottage in a far away land called "Trick Land."*
>
> *And if you went there the monster would be there to greet you. But there was an old witch and an old wizard that ate little girls and little boys. So that's why they called this song "Monster Shout." And this story was far, far, far away in another world. The monster shout.*

Will returns to the song for a few refrains. I then ask him to tell me what happened when he came to Trick Land. He responds:

> *And in the far away land called Trick Land, when you went there, there was a nasty witch who also tried to kill pumpkin and get kids for her dinner and supper. But you don't want to be part of that, do you? I know you don't. You know why I know the story . . . because I was there. . . . She turned all the little boys and girls into toys and put them in the toy factory and she made masks out of their faces. . . . And she made other witches out of monsters.*

The locale of this story in a "far away land," and the unusual, magical music serving as a motif for this place, help Will to feel a sense of safety as the material is distanced from his personal experience. The theme of transformation---that I had previously decided to support---emerges as children are turned into toys. Will's conceptions about growth and change are also contained in his story. That witches can transform children by making masks out of their faces suggests that, for Will, change does not "bring" the self. That is, one loses one's identity through change (and, hence, through growth as a form of change) and, as such, change is discontinuous with the present self. Later on in the story Will says that:

> *The good fairy helped the children by when they were turned into toys, she made them into fairies and they could turn themselves back into little children. And they could turn themselves into whatever they wanted to be... and they could turn themselves back... into whatever thing they want to.*

Here, the possibility of a transformation which includes maintaining one's identity is introduced. One can be transformed and return to one's former self, thereby sustaining contact with the enduring self. Thus, the possibility of a fluid self-identity (another goal I wanted to support) has spontaneously arisen in Will's story.

Will appeared as a fountain of musical and lyrical creativity in this session. The session content was a spontaneously created opera, complete with arias, transitional musical passages and an epic theme. At one point in the story, Will began to sing the following lyrics in haunting and lyrical delicate tones that I accompanied with gentle alternated major and minor chords:

> *If you don't want to go to Mars*
> *You don't have to but you stay because.*
> *Anybody knows that you can be,*
>   *Anybody knows, Anybody knows.*
> *People think there is a big old wizard,*
> *People think there isn't a big old wizard.*
> *But I know there's bad wizards,*
>   *and I know there's good wizards.*
> *And I know . . . Anybody knows*

I sensed new possibilities from Will in this music. It contained neither the aggressive and murderous violence typical of much of his previous fantasy, nor the precocious "macho" posturing typical of his blues and rap lyrics. Here was the tender child coming through, whose young age left many possibilities open for development. And here was the child confused by adult conceptions of "good" and "bad" and struggling to differentiate between them through exploring their extreme manifestations.

Will's story then builds to a dramatic climax:

> *Do you want to kill people and turn them into toys or do you want to save people and turn them into happy little boys and girls? And the bad wizard said, "No longer am I a bad wizard. No longer will I turn little girls and boys into toys. I am a good wizard. Hocus-pocus."*

(The following with a triumphant musical accompaniment.)

> *Turn the bad wizard into dust,*
> *Turn the good wizard this you must.*
> *And let them live a happy life.*
> *. . . nobody should feel nice*
> *Everybody should feel nice.*
> *Nobody should have gripes*
> *And if you're not a nice wizard I'll turn you into dust.*
> *And all the good wizards, all be nice.*
> *All you have to do is be a nice wizard.*
> *And . . . they are dust.*

> *She was a nasty witch, but all of a sudden she found herself turning into dust. And getting smaller and smaller. But then she said: Hocus-pocus I am a good witch, and then the witch turned good, and she stomped on her . . . the dust stomped. And you know what happened? She became a good witch and lived a happy life. And they lived a happy life.*

Though it first seemed that the music and story were building to a dramatic triumphant climax, Will was not yet ready to end. The story and music take a sudden pensive and introspective turn. Descending chords that again alternate between major and minor provide a sense of recapitulating a shared odyssey. The power, beauty and sadness contained in Will's story---and by extension, his life---are contained in this short interlude that precedes the climactic transformation.

> *If I can live a happy life, and I'm a little kid. And nobody started dying. And I never died. There was a bad disease and nobody died.*

Because of me, when I was a little kid I promised myself,
I was a wizard. When I got to a teenager I thought I
could rule the world with my wizardness. And I started
to rule the world until the wizard of godness came. And
he taught me to be good--but I never listened to him.
Now I am listening to little boys and girls, to explain.
Why should I have to live a good life and everybody else
live a good/bad/good/bad life? Every girl and boy.

Then, with increasing dramatic urgency and tension, Will repeats the following four times:

Hocus-Pocus. Razzle-Dazzle.
Turn our toys into human beings and little girls.
Nobody should have to live a bad life.

The music and Will's story climax here, and then Will indicates that he wants to return to the initial song, the theme of this story: Monster Shout. We conclude after singing a few refrains of this song.

What is notable in this last, extended excerpt is that Will introduces the possibility of transformation between bad and good. Bad wizards and witches can turn into good ones and toys can be turned back into children. This was a very important theme as I felt that it was Will's inflexible sense of himself as "bad" that would inhibit his growth in therapy. In his fantasy, at least, he entertained other possibilities.

The many little transformations in the story act as a "rehearsal" for the big transformation at the end. Certainly this mirrors the pattern of normal emotional development and explains why children often need to repeat stories, songs and other activities in therapy, and why the therapist must not only endure but embrace this repetition: It is what provides the child with the security to move forward.

The fact that the transformation is a magical one (hocus-pocus, razzle-dazzle) is important in reflecting the child's view of the world. Will was not able to alter his fighting behavior, for example, from a deliberate effort on his part or by insight into the self-defeating aspects of these actions. Since to a child, change is magical and comes from without, engaging in this magical fantasy allowed Will to work on changing himself within the context of the magical thinking that defines his maturity level.

Lastly, it was quite important for Will to return to the "Monster Shout" at the end of the session. It was his way of "returning home" and returning to himself after a long adventure that involved experimenting with a variety of novel roles and forms of expression. After all, it was this song that served as Will's entry point to Trick Land, thus it was natural that he would need to return to it. This music allowed Will to close the circle of his journey and to re-establish contact with his enduring self after such a perilous voyage.

This was the beginning of the end of this period of Will's therapy. Though he did play some music in three out of the following four sessions, it appeared that he did so from a need to gradually ease out of the intensity of his "voyage."

In the session following this one, Will discussed an incident at school that began with another boy teasing him, and Will responding by pushing the boy. The other boy then attempted to kick Will, who grabbed the other lad's foot causing him to fall and injure his head requiring three stitches. As a result, Will was suspended from school. Obviously, the metamorphosis hinted at in Will's fantasy existed only as a possibility. Yet Will expressed feelings of shame at the incident in a manner that indicated---unlike previous expressions of guilt or shame---that he truly regretted this incident. This new response on his part indicated that Will was aware of a discrepancy between how he wanted to act and how he was actually acting. This awareness suggested that the change in Will's self-image that I was hoping to facilitate was, in fact, beginning.

The Middle: Where Did the Music Go?

For a period of three months (comprising sessions nineteen to twenty-seven) Will had very little interest in making music. During this time, we played ball, board games and engaged in fantasy stories without music. Themes of transformation involving intense violence and aggression dominated Will's stories. In one story Will and I scaled an enormous mountain where we encountered demons who were once humans and who were searching for an antidote to return them to human form. In these stories, Will created scenarios that required that I "kill" him or that he "kill" me. In the story with the demons, I had to "kill" Will so that he could return to being a demon and carry out a task that only a demon could accomplish. In the following session, Will and I were allies and had to kill the demon king who had stolen Will's gold treasure. In still another story, Will acted out violent fantasies toward me as he was a policeman who repeatedly shot me in a location that a Freudian analyst could only see as acting out a desire to castrate the father!

This period was particularly challenging to me as a music therapist. On one hand, I knew that it would not be fruitful to engage in a power struggle with Will by attempting to coerce his participation in music. It was important for him to know that I would be with him regardless of what he chose to do, and that my supportive and caring presence was not conditioned upon how he chose to use his time in therapy. Alternately, I felt that Will was coming to **music** therapy for a reason, that my expertise was working in music, and that if Will had no need of my skills in this area I questioned whether he should continue in therapy with me.

What I gradually came to understand was that musical interaction represented a certain kind of intimate contact to Will and that he needed to feel control over the depth and quality of this contact. Abstaining from music was one way for Will to control his environment and the relationship with me. I decided that this manner of expressing his need for control was a positive one and that my commitment to help Will transcended **my** desire to work in the music. After all, it was **Will's** need that was primary and it would be counter-therapeutic to demand that Will express himself or relate to me through music if he was choosing an alternate form of expression.

Midway through this stage, Will and I met with his mother and her therapist. Though Will was extremely resistant to this meeting, he used it to voice his feelings that he was being forced to engage in many after-school activities (gymnastics, guitar lessons, play therapy) that he was not interested in. At the end of the session the four of us engaged in a musical improvisation---Will's price for attending the meeting. Will enjoyed this playing so much that he actually requested that we meet as a group again! Actually "playing" with his mother was something that Will rarely did, and he seemed to take nourishment from the opportunity to just be a child with his mother.

Though Will engaged in some music during the second half of this stage of therapy, his interest level fluctuated and our contact was relatively superficial. In session thirty-eight (approximately nine months after the "Trick Land" session) I prepared Will for a six-week separation due to each of our summer vacations running contiguously. We played some music in this session. Will played the electronic keyboard and I played the drum set. I felt a significantly deeper contact with Will than I had felt in quite a long time. I realized then that regardless of all the other activities that we engaged in, our strongest bond was still in music. It also occurred to me that Will **was** abandoned by his father and that it must be very difficult for him to trust any males or to let our relationship grow past a certain point. Will's reluctance to engage in music became more intelligible to me seen in this light.

The Ending: A New Beginning for Will

In Will's thirty-ninth session, which took place after a six-week gap in his sessions, he appeared different and more mature. He was very interested in music again, though his tastes had changed. He was no longer interested in purely acoustic improvisations and wanted to recreate the heavy metal music he had been exposed to during his summer vacation. Will also wanted more autonomy in the music, expressing the wish that I should not "play the same song as him." In other words, my playing should be more **complementary** to his and not so nearly reflect the structural elements of his music.

Though Will was interested in electric music, in contrast to the previous stage, he was now using these instruments in an expressive way, creating sound "portraits" that reflected his then current feelings. He alternated between rapid, almost frantic, dissonant improvisations, and slower and more melodic ones. Also, though Will's testing behaviors emerged periodically throughout the first two stages of his therapy---primarily seen in his need to prolong the session or turn up the volume on the electric instruments to excruciatingly loud volumes---these behaviors had now dissipated. Will no longer needed to create interactions designed to put me in a position which would be experienced by him as rejecting.

This last stage, comprising nine sessions over a three-month period, was a transitional one for Will as he evidenced signs of growth and recapitulated elements of his year and a half in music therapy. In addition to his desire for increased autonomy, Will began to ask me what I wanted to do. He seemed interested in forging a more reciprocal relationship where I was not just an object for his fantasies, but a person in my own right.

These signs of growth were reflected outside Will's therapy, primarily at school. Fighting was no longer a problem and Will was not in danger of being expelled. Interestingly, his violent fantasies dissipated somewhat, though they still occupied a significant amount of his time in therapy. They primarily involved the killing of evil beings who became transformed through death. His need for this ritual, symbolic slaying as a precursor to personal transformation remained strong.

Unbeknownst to both of us at the time, Will's forty-eighth session was to be his last. He engaged in make-believe gun play using curtain rods and did not want any music. At the end of the session he had planned to sing "Twist and Shout," yet he abruptly changed his mind. Our last activity together was playing the song "Lean on Me."

Will's abrupt termination was due to a variety of factors: I needed to change his session time, and Will's mother was finding it difficult to arrange another time to bring him to the center; Will's mother was herself a client at the center and had ambivalent feelings about continuing her own therapy--Will's continuation became tied to her own; and lastly, Will himself seemed ready to let go of our connection.

Though he could have benefitted from more time, or at least a reasonable termination, Will had, in fact, outgrown and transcended some of the problematic behaviors that had plagued him. Not possessing any pathology but merely the victim of an unfortunate family situation, I could see that Will was ready to fruitfully engage life without the benefit of a therapist.

DISCUSSION

The Importance of Creative Fantasy

Having provided the reasons behind many of my specific clinical interventions in the previous section, I will briefly discuss my rationale for what was the most therapeutically salient elements of Will's treatment: his use of creative fantasy and music.

Bettelheim (1975) discusses the psychological significance of fantasy material (in the context of fairy tales) in a manner that demonstrates its relevance for normal development. Since the source of the characters and themes of fairy tales lies in the archetypal experience of childhood, we can see how the process of therapy can evoke the same themes discussed by Bettelheim, though their specific form will be determined by the individual child's personal experience. Thus, without having to accept Bettelheim's theories on the meaning of specific stories and symbols, we can still fruitfully make use of his rationale on the importance of fantasy for the young child. This involves not a thorough examination of Bettelheim's ideas on fairy tales, but merely a cursory look at what the elements of these fantasy stories tell us about the child's view of the world, which subsequently allows us to better understand the meaning and role of fantasy material in the music therapy milieu.

The characters in fairy tales have no moral ambivalence; they are either good or evil with no middle ground. Though not reflecting adult reality, this polarization reflects how children see the world. Thus, the creation of fantasy allows children to express their existential reality unfettered by (inappropriate) adult constraints on the nature of this reality. The child's subsequent moral development is dependent upon developing notions of morality through exploring their extreme manifestations. "Ambiguities must wait until a relatively firm personality has been established on the basis of positive identifications" (Bettelheim, 1975, p. 9).

The characters in all of Will's stories were either good or evil with no middle ground: no character ever possessed relative amounts of these qualities. It was important that I allow Will to enact his stories without trying to teach him finer points of morality and human nature. Will needed to explore moral **extremes**, to see pure good and pure evil, in order to begin to differentiate between the two and develop his own notion of morality. Providing him moral "instruction" (for example: "You see Will, you are not good or bad but contain relative amounts of these qualities as all people do") would not be appropriate for Will. His developmental level did not allow for this type of processing. As a therapist, my role was not to teach morality, but to facilitate the normal process of moral differentiation.

Bettelheim also believes that fairy tales represent the process of normal emotional development, and the solutions reached by the characters in the stories provide solutions to the child's own inner conflicts. Fairy tales do not teach in the sense that fables do, but instead encourage children to find their own meaning and solutions---their essence is necessarily interpretive.

This belief in the child's inner resources and ability to find solutions given a supportive, creative context, functions as a rationale for the client-centered use of fantasy material. I could diagnose what I believed was Will's need---such as developing a less static self-identity---I do not believe that I could directly provide this to him. Only by creating stories, themes, and characters that reflected his unique experience and conflicts could Will begin to work through these conflicts and find the solutions that made sense to him.

Just as "in a fairy tale, [where] internal processes are externalized and become comprehensible as represented by the figures of the story and its events," (Bettelheim, p. 25) creative fantasy in music therapy gave Will the opportunity to express the nature of his inner reality through an external form. His fantasy not only provided a manifestation of intangible inner processes in order to work with them, but also served an important function in externalizing the source of his difficulties. This distancing is important to children as the fantasy material must be seen as "something external . . . to gain any sort of mastery over it" (Bettelheim, p. 55).

Transformations

One consequent of the child's polarized view of people is that when alternate, "undesirable" character traits are expressed (such as anger or aggression), the child experiences the individual as transformed in some way. To Bettelheim, fantasy characters such as the evil step-mother serve an important function: they allow the child to pour all the anger and fear towards the real mother into an alternate form, thus preserving the real-life mother as a benevolent and nurturing presence. In the child's view, then, it is necessary to undergo a transformation in order to express that which would normally be repressed.

Now Will had no problem expressing his anger and aggression. Certainly his fighting in school was a testament to this. What was important for Will to do was to find a way to express his benevolent or "heroic" aspects, and this is what I attempted to provide in his music therapy sessions. It was not that Will needed to become "good" and that I was facilitating this type of actual transformation. This is an overly simplistic and concrete view of Will's process. Instead, I wanted to help Will to experience the potential of transformation between good and bad, so that he would not feel perpetually stuck in one end of this polarity. The only way to do this for Will was to actually experience this transformation as an active participant in his own fantasy. It was the **possibility** of transformation that I hoped Will would discover.

Because young children externalize inner dynamic forces by projecting them onto fantasy characters, their perspective on growth and change is that it results from the action of external forces, not by one's own conscious intent. It is wizards, fairy godmothers, and witches who facilitate growth and development through invoking their magical powers. Given this perspective, I decided not to focus on developing insight into the unconscious determinants of Will's conflictual behavior (fighting) because, in his world view, change would not come about through his own efforts---it was endowed from without. Instead, the fantasy material allowed Will to facilitate his own development through the metaphor of magical transformation as that which was developmentally appropriate.

Importance of the Music

Although it may not have always seemed obvious, this is a music therapy case study and the music had a few important functions in facilitating Will's ability to experience transformation. Though the role of music in accessing transformative processes in therapy is a broad (and too long neglected) area, I can only briefly describe those qualities that were specifically important to understanding Will's process.

Through my musical contribution, I was able to bring out the underlying feeling tone of Will's fantasies, increase his investment in them, and, in general, make them more real and thus enhance his participation. I wanted to help Will to actually experience his own transformative potential rather than remain a passive observer as one might when merely reading a story. By creating such individualized music, I was able to help Will to experience the story as his own; by providing Will's various characters with their own musical manifestation, I was able to deepen his identification with them.

Music also provided me with a field for interaction with Will that existed within his reality. In other words, I did not have to step outside of Will's fantasy to interact with him. This was important in allowing me to support, develop and comment upon the themes, such as examinations of the relationship between good and bad and movement between the two, that I felt would facilitate Will's therapy. Though not attempting to control the content of Will's sessions, I did use the music to comment upon and enhance the quality with which the emerging content was experienced. This was done through things like creating magical, other-worldly music for Trick Land, introducing triumphant music for the transformations, and alternately creating pensive or outgoing music to reflect Will's level of self-examination.

Another important function of the music was to provide a symbol for the enduring self that maintains itself through the dynamic changes represented by the voyage to Trick Land and the subsequent magical transformations. In the session previously described in detail, the tune

"Monster Shout" served this function. This deep-seated human need can be seen in the developmental realm---as when a young child playing independently needs to make periodic contact with the mother---and in the musical/aesthetic realm, in a rondo that alternates between melodic explorations and re-statements of the primary, enduring theme. Similarly, Will could go on a perilous, explorative journey as long as he could make this same periodic contact with that which represented his enduring identity and source of security and familiarity---the music.

This song also served as Will's dual-faceted entry point: it provided him with a transition from the "normal" reality of the session to the "magical" reality of the fantasy, while simultaneously performing the symbolic function of transporting Will to the "far-away" place represented by Trick Land. When engaging in this type of fantasy many children will use an actual vehicle, such as a bus, airplane, or rocket ship; Will's ability to live in, and be absorbed by, music is indicated by the manner in which music served this transportive function.

CONCLUSION

Emotional development and maturity has an attractive force because it holds the promise of a more rewarding life. Yet, to some extent, we all fear growth because it represents change and yielding to a process whose ultimate result we cannot foresee. The work with Will illustrates one of the most powerful functions of music in music therapy however, and this function is related to the fear of change. Music, for Will, reduced his fear of the unknown through associating novel experiences with the feelings of safety and security characteristic of that which is familiar. Will's familiar songs gave him the courage and empowerment to contact and engage the powerful, magical forces living in his fantasy, and by extension, his unconscious. To the extent that music represented that which was familiar, Will was able to use music to enter and explore this previously unknown and fearful realm.

REFERENCES

Bettelheim, Bruno. (1975). The Uses of Enchantment. New York: Vintage.

Music Therapy In
Working Through A Preschooler's Grief:
Expressing Rage And Confusion

KERRY BURKE, MTA
Professor of Music Therapy
Capilano College
Vancouver, Canada

Abstract. *Six months of music therapy helped four-year-old Adam express his rage and confusion at the death of his father. His aggressive behavior towards his peers and mother found another outlet when he played loud music and expressed his destructive rage.*

BACKGROUND INFORMATION

Adam's uneventful life changed when his father unexpectedly died playing golf. Four years old at the time, Adam was very close to his father and became aggressive towards other children in preschool and towards his mother, yet refused to leave her side without tantrums. After six months of increasingly disruptive behaviors, his mother brought Adam to me for weekly sessions. He saw no other therapist.

Adam's mother, who was also a therapist, selected music therapy because: "Adam, like his father, could not use words to work through his feelings." Also, the father had played the guitar which Adam liked to mimic.

ASSESSMENT

The mother described a child needing to express his anger towards his father for leaving him. Adam denied his anger and it became directed at other children and his mother, and his security had been threatened to the point where he did not wish to leave his mother's side.

Adam was able to express his sadness to his mother over the loss of his father with no difficulty. His mother, however, wished him to express and work through his anger and to have ongoing contact with a male authority figure.

For assessment, I asked Adam to improvise pieces entitled fear, happiness, sadness, frustration and anger, each in different intensities. He could not play loud anger, keeping it soft while reporting that it was louder. He played the other emotions both loud and soft. This assessment doubled as an activity to increase his range of expression which we called "the emotions."

When asked to draw while improvised various emotional states, Adam drew a grey picture with a solitary figure half smiling under the moon and stars.

The goals became for Adam to play loud, angry music; to stop aggressive acts towards others; to allow him to express whatever he wished through music and talk; and finally to provide weekly contact with a male figure, getting Adam to school and leaving his mother's side voluntarily.

After some sessions I talked with his mother and found out how things were going at home and school. After each session, I assessed progress towards these goals on an informal basis.

METHOD

Adam came to my house each week for an hour over a six month period. My equipment consists of piano, keyboards and guitars, xylophones, drums and percussion instruments of various sizes. Some sessions were recorded.

I admire aspects of the work of therapists Virginia Axline (1976), Carl Rogers (Rogers &Stevens, 1961) and Milton Erickson (Bandler and Grinder, 1978) suggesting that reflection can cure the client. In music therapy, reflection (Priestley, (1975), Nordoff and Robbins, (1977)) leads to creative techniques for each client while affirming each individuals needs. In my work with Adam, reflection meant that he was able to control the sessions to a large degree, by choosing activities and levels of intimacy. For example, Adam wanted "breaks" after each 20 minutes of playing so that he could play a video game, eat a peanut butter sandwich or play catch with a ball outside. Allowing him to do this led to a sharing of therapeutic power, a way in which I like to work.

On the other hand, I provided a loose structure. After a warm-up period during which Adam would play his choice of instruments, we would improvise "the emotions" trying to play louder than before. Sometimes I asked him to completed phrases such as:

I feel sad about.....	"being silly"
I feel silly about...	"school"
I feel happy about...	"coming here"
I feel angry about...	"having to leave"
I feel angry at......	"Mom"

Often we composed a song, and every week he drew a picture and often asked me to draw one too.

TREATMENT PROCESS

Initial Stage: Four Weeks

Sessions began with a discussion about what we could do. He warmed up by arranging percussion instruments and playing them in sequence. I encouraged him to play many instruments.

In this period we got to know each other. Adam became proficient at a variety of percussion instruments, copying my beats and asking me to copy his.

We tried to play songs on the guitar, using a half size guitar in open tuning, but it posed problems for Adam and was frustrating. However, together we prepared and played "Swing Low, Sweet Chariot." He asked me to sing and drum while he strummed.

The electronic keyboard was easier to play and he began composing pieces which we wrote down. The following week he asked about them when he came to the door.

Adam neither wanted to play his strong feelings nor talk about them. His approach was mental rather than emotional. I let him take his time.

Each week I modelled loud playing, challenging him to play louder than before, sometimes recording our playing to give him feedback. I made this fun and changed tactics when his interest flagged. He would not play louder despite my efforts.

A breakthrough occurred when he filled his page with black scribbling when asked to draw his feelings. Then he drew a dark crying face with big black tears. For the first time, he expressed his sadness and rage with intensity.

Middle Stage: Four Months

In this period, we found ways to express his feelings. He wrote a song for Halloween about monsters and we recorded it. Strumming an open chord on guitar, he wailed his song and a tape of it proudly went home to mother. He explored the piano, but never loudly. We worked on naming emotions as he experienced them during the day and set them to music.

We made pictures of his family tree and assigned feelings to each person. This led to pictures of the family tree divided between those in heaven and those on earth. In his weekly drawing, abstract collections of lines became "mazes" with a monster in the middle. Then came elaborate mazes with many monsters, underground rivers and secret spaces.

Maze 1

Adam played these mazes and monsters on various instruments but never loudly. This period ended as Adam began to play less music and asked for more breaks to play video games and eat sandwiches. It was time for a change.

Maze 2

Final Stage: Four Weeks

I developed two activities to encourage him to express his inner feelings. Spontaneously, I wrote a wiggly "score" for him to play on piano, as shown below. It incorporated loud and soft, fast and slow dynamics. Adam played it while my finger traced the wiggle. He loved it, turning it over and playing again, then turning it sideways. He made one for me to play. Suddenly, he played very loud, it was a breakthrough. The visual representation of loud and soft worked.

Wiggly Score 1

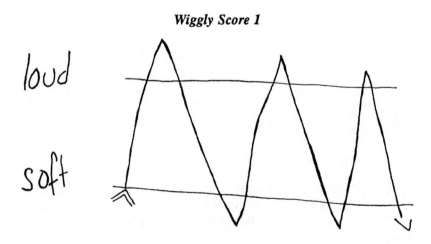

Wiggly Score 2

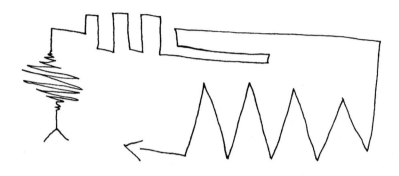

One day Adam noticed that a drumhead on a conga was starting to break. I invited him to finish breaking it. He wanted to but then held back, and this allowed his feelings to come into focus. He talked about how scared he was to break things. Then he began hitting the drum harder and harder, many times until it finally broke. It felt good and he discussed his fear that if he let his anger go, he could destroy people and objects.

The next week, I provided a cardboard box which Adam destroyed with a huge gong mallet. His mother provided boxes at home which he destroyed.

At the next session, Adam began to escape from his mazes, talking himself through it: "Keep to the side here and wait till the monster doesn't look here; the underground river has a bridge over it."

The following week, Adam did not arrive for his session. He had not bugged his mother to leave for music therapy and she had forgotten. She reported that he was going to school and was not clinging to her. His aggression had also stopped. We therefore agreed to end the sessions unless Adam brought the subject up again. The sessions ended.

DISCUSSION AND CONCLUSIONS

Adam's reaction to the death of his father was typical for a child of his age. What set Adam apart was his difficulty in describing his feelings, his closeness to his father which may have heightened his sense of loss, and his mother's sensitivity to his distress. He could experience sadness at the death of his father but not anger. However, with a male figure to help, along with our music-making, artwork, and games, Adam was able to express feelings and confusion over his father's death which he had difficulty talking about.

Reflection was easy with Adam. Each session, he came ready to work, usually to finish what we worked on the previous week. Thus, I felt confident giving him choices about how and what we would do each session. This indicated how completely Adam threw himself into the sessions.

Significant moments were first when he drew blackness and the crying face. His expression became intense at this point, which is an important indicator for me that therapeutic goals were being met. When we began to play wiggly lines, the volume of his playing increased dramatically, again indicating to me that his inner world was becoming involved.

Lastly, when he destroyed the drumhead and boxes, he could discuss his feelings of fear over the quantity of rage within himself. Ideally, these feelings would have been discussed in terms of the father, however, the sessions ended at this point. This destructive intervention developed by my noticing the way Adam's attention was drawn to the broken drumhead. He asked what would happen to it when it was broken and would I throw it away. After a number of questions, I asked him if he would like to break it. The violence in this action--and his enthusiasm for it--made me pause and consider the wisdom of encouraging Adam in this pursuit, and whether it may encourage him to act out. I decided that his interest in the drum indicated a symbolic representation of his inner conflict which seemed to be true from the results, and that it was safe to continue.

When his tremendous enthusiasm for the sessions vanished and he did not show for his session, it surprised me. No other client of mine has suddenly met the therapeutic goals in the way that Adam did, nor forgotten the sessions in a week. It seemed to indicate that his need for the sessions had ended for the moment and that to continue would provide closure for me, but not him.

Update

Adam now sees me twice a year. A year after sessions ended there was a message on my answering machine, "I need to see you, I can't escape from the maze again." There was a change in the family situation. With the mother's approval, Adam is allowed to set up appointments when he wishes.

These later sessions are more supportive than therapeutic: the emphasis is on peanut butter! He still draws pictures, but the maze has disappeared.

REFERENCES

Axline, V., (1976). Play therapy. New York: Ballantine Books.

Bandler, R., Grinder, J., (1975). Patterns of Hypnotic Techniques of Milton Erickson. Science and Technology Books.

Nordoff, P., & Robbins, C., (1977). Creative Music Therapy. New York: John Day.

Priestley, M., (1975). Music Therapy in Action. St. Louis: MMB.

Rogers, C. & Stevens, B., (1961). Person to Person. Boston: Houghton and Mifflin.

Improvisation And Play
In The Therapeutic Engagement
Of A Five-Year-Old Boy
With Physical And
Interpersonal Problems

PAMELA BARTRAM, M. Litt. Dip. Mus. Ther.
Music Therapist
London, England

Abstract: Tom is a five-year-old boy with a history of seizures, physical complaints and interpersonal problems, both at home and at school. In the 37 music therapy sessions which have been summarized, he engaged with the music therapist through musical improvisation and play.   Tom's plight is considered in the light of the material arising out of these interactions.

PROLOGUE

Tom: (*Talking to a puppet of Humpty Dumpty lying
          down). Oh Humpty, you're a very naughty
          boy....a very naughty boy.*

Pamela: *Because he keeps lying down all the time when
          it's in-time?*

Tom: (*Silence*)

Pamela: *He flops down dead.*

Tom: *He keeps going...flimp. Oh, now he
          won't...he's doing tricks. (Tom is holding
          Humpty by his two long legs and spinning him
          round and round).*

Pamela: *Oh no, poor Humpty, he's feeling sick with his
          upside-down tricks.*

Tom: *Oh whee, whee (spinning Humpty round).*

Pamela: *He's spinning around, spinning faster and
          faster. That's going to make him feel very
          sick, all that spinning.*

Tom: *Look....(laughing to Humpty). Look, you're
          tangled.*

Pamela: *Mmm...That's what spinning does. It makes
          you all tangled.*

Tom: (*Anxiously*) *How can this get back?*

In this dialogue, Tom and I (with the aid of Humpty) are exploring themes central to this study. There is the naughty boy, the boy who flops and flimps, or who spins around doing tricks. But the spinning tricks make him sick and tangled. How can he rediscover a better state of being?

Here we will have the opportunity to consider more fully Tom's state and the conditions which may have been instrumental in bringing it about. We will also consider issues raised by Tom's own question about how it may be possible for him to be something other than in a ball and sick or spinning, tricky or tangled.

For two reasons I will neither attempt to focus on changes through time in his behaviour, nor to make a case for improvement in his condition having arisen due to music therapy. These are: firstly, the way in which I structured my own contribution to the sessions changed as my understanding of his difficulties deepened under the influence of supervison and personal therapy (thus, I myself was a variable in our "equation"); secondly, it was clear that Tom associated his concurrent experiences in psychotherapy with those in music therapy. It was likely that processes prompted by his psychotherapy would bear fruit in the area of his creativity, both in general and in his musical material. It would be impossible therefore to judge music therapy events, and even less so, strictly musical events, as sole agents in any change process that might be identified.

My aim is therefore restricted to using session material to illustrate how it is possible: to know through music or through the mixing of musics (i.e., the therapist's with the patient's); to explore how such knowledge may be understood in relation to Tom's presenting difficulties; and to explore the meaning for him of moving in and out of musical material.

BACKGROUND

Tom, aged 5 1/2, was referred to me for music therapy by a clinical psychologist, both because he himself showed an interest in rhythm and musical instruments, and because she felt he needed to succeed in a non-competitive environment. At home he would sometimes sing rather than talk about his school day. Having met Tom for the first time, I had the impression that music therapy might indeed be a medium in which he could channel and creatively use his imagination and his physical energy. However, I also wondered to what extent a child as verbal and as scattered as he appeared to be, would actually take up and use the medium of improvised music-making.

Tom is the second child of financially comfortable upper middle-class parents. He has a younger sister who was born when Tom was three years old. Tom's development had been described by his pediatrician as "unusual" but not grossly delayed. When he was three years old, his parents took him to a Child Development Unit where they were told that he was retarded, hyperactive, and that he would "never earn his own living." On taking him for a second opinion, no doubt in a state of shock, they were told that Tom was well within the normal range of development. In the parents' minds, therefore, there has been confusion as to Tom's potential.

He was referred to speech therapy at three years three months, where he was described as having poor concentration, immature articulation and poor expressive language. A few months later, Tom was sent to a school run along formal academic lines, perhaps as a prepation for going to boarding school at seven years. Around this time, he began to suffer from recurrent attacks of headache and vomiting. There is a history of migraine in the family.

School described him as unable to concentrate, disobedient and failing to achieve, and he was often punished by, for example, being kept in to do school work at breaktime. He had no friends.

At four years eleven months he suffered a generalised convulsion in bed, and another almost a year later, also in bed. On the second occasion he went into *status epilepticus*, requiring intravenous valium. When he regained consciousness in hospital some hours later, he did not ask where he was or what had happened. Some weeks later however, he referred to the hospital as the place where he had had his headache.

CAT scans have shown no gross organic damage although there is a hypothesis of fetal distress during his delivery by Caesarean section, and a possible lack of oxygen having led to "minimal damage."

After the second convulsion, an *EEG* showed abnormal activity which might indicate that apart from the *generalized convulsions,* he may experience brief absenses or *petit mal seizures,* which go undetected. He has a history of eczema, allergies and a "droopy left eye" which becomes more pronounced when the nausea, headaches and vomiting prevail. He sometimes has a tic, a movement involving a head jerk back and slight roll of the eyes.

When Tom's mother first brought him to meet me, she referred to his difficulties primarily in terms of his vomiting, headaches and his short concentration span which was making him unsuccessful and unpopular at school. She said he ate well, although he always tended to regurgitate feeds as a baby. There was no disruption of sleep, in fact, she described how Tom loved to go to bed, fell asleep straight away, and slept soundly all night. He would often ask to be allowed to go to bed long before bedtime. I subsequently learned that he suffered from nightmares and bedwetting, which upset him considerably.

I also learned that he had a difficult relationship with his father; that he bullied his younger sister; that he was "disobedient" and without friends at school, and that there were difficulties in his relationship with his mother. Tom also had a tendency to be inappropriately friendly with adult strangers.

At the initial meeting with mother and son, I was struck by the contrast between them. She is a tall, elegant woman, softly spoken and with a gentle, dreamy, sometimes absent manner. (It has sometimes been difficult for her to remember Tom's appointments for music therapy). She described Tom (while he played outside) in bemused, slightly irritated and mildly ironic tones, as if he were a naughty boy and as if the situation was tiresome. Any anguish she might have felt was not expressed.

At that interview, Tom came into my office, a rather overweight, little boy, with angry red blotches on his face. He looked dishevelled, and his tic was noticeable. He spoke to me immediately, asking questions and then moving around the room without waiting for an answer, but helping himself to objects in the office and asking more questions. He spoke very loudly in what seemed to be a falsely sociable, apparently self-assured tone. Beside mother, who seemed so quiet and stylish, Tom looked a mess---and after a few minutes the office began to look a mess too. When I took him to meet a colleague who had agreed to occupy him, he did so willingly, running ahead of me without a goodbye between him and his mother, and then talking incessantly with my colleague. Tom gave a superficial first impression of being a "bit of a character." When I returned to the office, mother raised her eyebrows, smiled gently and gave a shrug.

Tom's father is a successful businessman, who on a later occasion, described how he arrives home tired in the evening with little patience for a naughty son. After Tom's second seizure, he was remorseful at the idea that he had sometimes disciplined Tom for bad behaviour which might have been related to his condition. At that time, both parents still tended to view Tom as a boy with medical problems, hitherto undetected, which had resulted in management problems. Thus, they assumed that once the medical problems were solved, the others would disappear.

In the case review a year after the initial referral, the pediatrician expressed the view that while Tom does have medical problems, possibly related to minimal damage at birth, his disposition and life events have interplayed with them to produce phenomena which cannot now be treated as medical problems, pure and simple.

A few months after beginning music therapy, Tom began anti-epileptic medication. Shortly after, he moved to a less academic local school, where he was at first excessively aggressive to other children, especially in the playground. This aggression subsequently diminished, however his difficulties in concentrating and in making relationships remained.

At the same time, Tom began weekly psychotherapy. Before offering him sessions, the psychotherapist contacted me, and after some discussion, we agreed that it would at least not be harmful for Tom to attend both psychotherapy and music therapy, and indeed together they might be useful.

TREATMENT PROCESS

From the first sessions Tom brought a mixture of musical and nonmusical materials, the latter often taking the form of nonmusical use of instruments and competitive games. The overall trend was away from music-making, although each session contained at least some musical material.

Although the organic development of session material cannot be sharply delineated as the following schema might suggest, the sessions can be conceived as falling into three sets. In the paragraphs that follow, an overview is given of what transpired in each set, and a more detailed transcript is given of the second session.

Sessions 1-8

The first eight sessions were characterized by a pervading atmosphere of anxiety, disorder, and brief, inconclusive engagements. Tom found it difficult to stay in the therapy room for the duration of the session. I had to discourage him from dismantling instruments and from bringing items such as food or toys into the room. Beginning and endings of sessions were abrupt and disordered.

Tom commanded and attempted to direct my musical and nonmusical activity. Musical material in which I had to imitate him was particularly significant. I tended to resist Tom's commands and to insist that I make my own choices. He often spoke in false voices, including a witch voice.

There was little sense of satisfaction, either individual or mutual. I felt resentful of his apparent communication that whatever I offered was not the right thing, and I also resented his attempts to help himself to something better.

Notes on Session Two

This session began with Tom racing me from the waiting room to the therapy room, and running into the therapy room alone. A variety of instruments are arranged as for the beginning of the first session with the addition of a reed horn which he had requested. He goes straight to the horn, picks it up and plays it briefly, then moves to the drum, playing with a bouncy body movement, and soon brings in the cymbal. I have closed the door and made my way to the piano where I sit, listening. Without stopping playing, Tom gesticulates for me to join in, but as this gesture is ambiguous, I have to talk over his playing to ask, does he mean for me to play. I begin to play, but after sharing only one full phrase length, he breaks off, saying that when he plays the drum, I must play the bells (which are small and tinkling). He tries to give them to me, but I am reluctant to change instruments at this point, and especially from the piano to the bells, given the force of his drum and cymbal playing. I say that we can each decide what we are going to play and I choose the piano. He returns the drum, though still appearing to instruct me in a lisping babyish voice. When he announces with stage-authority, "Off you go...the big drum," a duet begins with him on drum and cymbal and me on piano. This turns out to be an unusually sustained (six minutes or so) period of shared musical engagement.

During this *"episode of engagement"* (Stern, 1977), Tom changes his instrument several times (drum and cymbal, horn, drum, glockenspiel, piano, cymbal, drum and cymbal). Yet there is an overall sense of continuity, largely due to the rhythmicity of his playing, the recurrence of a tempo of 120 beats per minute, and the continuity of my own playing. Tom himself gesticulates and instructs me verbally to carry on playing during his changeovers, and I have an image of him trying to keep me going (like a machine) by conducting with one hand, while playing with the other.

He has a natural tendency to organise his percussive playing into a strong pulse which is regularly inflected and which contains rests that allow for the formation of repeated phrases. These features give a robust quality to his playing, and provides firm material for engagement. The volume and timbre give his playing a sturdy quality.

At the same time, his prevailing choice of percussive instruments limits his exploration of melodic qualities which might suggest to him contrasting dynamics, timbres or rhythmic forms. I try to play music which reflects and contains the strength of his playing, and which accommodates the changes in his tempo, rhythm, pitch and timbre. At one or two moments there is renegotiation of the elements after one player has introduced new material.

We play an intense "trembling" duet on the piano, but Tom abruptly breaks off and begins to spell out the piano brand name. Then giving one cymbal crash, he asks "How many minutes are we going to go?" I remind him of the length of the session and ask, "Does it feel like a long time to be away from Mummy?" He replies with an unexpectedly powerful and very loud cymbal crash. This leads into a few slow and deadly drum/cymbal beats, and then speeds up into strong pulse playing (126 beats per minute) which breaks off midphrase. Here my own playing becomes dissonant in response to the wilder character of his, nevertheless I am almost inaudible at times, as I struggle to judge the register and volume required to withstand the ferocity of his playing.

The final break which ends this episode of musical engagement occurs as did the previous two, midphrase, cutting across the musical phrase rather than arriving at a natural ending. Tom anxiously suggests, "Shall we go now?...or something?"

Even this short section of material reveals the extent and limits of Tom's creativity in musical and interpersonal relationships. His music is powerful and often has a recognisable form and organisation. It feels like a force to be reckoned with rather than, for example, a tentatively formed and executed music whose manifestations need to be awaited and delicately nurtured. Music such as Tom's might have a lot to contribute to a relationship.

On the other hand, he also seems to be struggling to create the illusion that he alone is starting, maintaining and ending our musical engagement, as well as largely determining its character. When I had refused his offer of the little bells, he acted as if he was the one determining the course of events, presuming to instruct me to do what in fact I was already doing. Rushing into the room and beginning to play without me, then conducting my playing while he changes instruments are perhaps other examples of this illusion-creating.

I sense that he feels responsible for my part, for my liveliness, as well as his own, and the energy he expends playing so strongly seems to serve the function of also keeping my part alive. It was unusual, but in retrospect understandable, that when Tom ended the episode, I suggested that he sit down and have a rest from playing. It was as if this illusion requires such energy to maintain, that Tom is left exhausted after only a short time; and there is a feeling of the impossibility of going on. In fact, there is no more sustained music until the last eight minutes of the session, when I remind Tom that it is near the end and ask whether he would like to play again.

We improvise a horn/voice duet. It has a jittery quality reminiscent of the "trembling" duet on the piano. There is a tense sharing of phrase lengths in antiphonal exchanges.

Antiphonal playing seems more tolerable to Tom than simultaneous playing, perhaps because it promotes a clearer demarcation of the separate parts. Tom further controlled even the antiphonal play by often insisting that I imitate him in this way, even more closely "keeping an eye" on my part.

Later in a drum duet, Tom divided the drums between us so that he had the bigger ones, and then proceeded to divide the musical material by insisting that I imitate him antiphonally, thus making my part dependent on his. As a leitmotif, he used the following rhythm in duple meter, that he introduced in the first session:

This sort of controlled duet could easily feel more like a mechanical test for me than a shared musical expression, nevertheless, we manage to enjoy a playful moment when I imitate his accidental stick-click, and he adopts it as part of our shared repertoire. Although Tom is laughing, the sound of his laughter has a tense, choking quality.

For some time I have resisted Tom's attempts to control my instrumentation and musical material, as this sort of domination feels entirely inappropriate within an art medium. The feelings evoked by being ordered, "Sing now!" or "Play like this!" painfully arrests the free inward ranging and suspension of disbelief so necessary to shared musical expression.

Here I was faced with a choice: either to satisfy the requirements of creative improvisation or satisfy the requirements of the anxious boy in the room with me. It now seems to me that to be helpful to Tom, I needed to be able to tolerate the feelings of being interrupted and cut-off, of being un-free, of being like a puppet, of being at best, a musician in his orchestra, playing his score...the feelings which he put into me. It was these considerations which led me to abandon some of my earlier structuring tactics, such as insisting that I choose my own instrumentation.

Tom's use of the chimes in this session and in later ones, illustrated his tendency to make primarily nonmusical use of instruments. A small table would be laboriously covered with a selection of musical instruments, usually fetched from the cupboard with my help. Tom and I would sit opposite each other, and he would repeatedly engage me in unnerving "tests" less related to the sound of the chimes than to their appearance. For example, he would play a phrase for me to copy which consisted of two small black bars and one large white one with a green dot. I was supposed to respond by playing two small black ones and one large white one with a yellow dot because I did not have a green dot. I would, of course often get this wrong, as I would be listening to the pitches rather than thinking about the color and size of the bars. Subsequently, Tom would change his criteria for correctness so that I seemed ever doomed to get it wrong and earn an irate reprobation. Thus

Tom effectively gave me a clear experience of what it is like to be on the wrong end of a learning difficulty.

Another chime game that developed was "Hey Pamela, Hey Tom." We would begin playing antiphonally or together, and then Tom would venture onto one of my chimes, at which time I would give a cry "Hey Tom!" Often I would be instructed as to when to play on one of his chimes so that he could then be indignant and cry "Hey Pamela!"

At other times our music games would require my imitation of his leitmotif. Sometimes these games began to move towards being truly musical, and short improvisations would "break out." Occasionally, waves of ringingly dissonant simultaneous chime playing would emerge briefly, which had a more abandoned quality than the robust and square playing of much of Tom's material.

In these episodes it seemed that the small sounds of the chimes made our shared engagement feel more manageable than did the larger instruments, although most often we soon had to return to more formally demarcated structures in order to be co-active. In one instance, Tom even halted the musical interaction with "Oh, I've got one point," as if we had been only scoring against each other rather than exposing ourselves in self-expression.

Sessions 9-18

Much of our work in sessions 9-18 was still characterised by disordered and interrupted exchanges, however Tom did begin to initiate and sustain some episodes of more prolonged and satisfying musical co-activity. I began to allow him limited access to the cupboards.

Particularly important in this period was that Tom began to find good objects (including the therapist) within the sessions, and began to communicate this. For example, he sings of one session, improvising "And it was good....and it worked..."

I continued to feel anxious, resentful and resistant to the unsatisfactory aspects of our relationship.

Sessions 19-37

From the 19th to the 37th session, some ordered, slower and calmer episodes occurred, along with some welcome silences. Our musical activity decreased, while nonmusical play and conversation increased. When musical activity did occur, brief moments of freer improvisation emerged within extended periods of playing together. Tom developed an increasingly important relationship with the gong. He was becoming more able to think about endings (e.g., of sessions and holiday breaks). I allowed him free access to the instrument cupboards, and allowed him to bring toys and other things into the room.

Tom spoke more in his own voice, and I became at times the wicked witch to whom he had earlier given voice.   He was also better able to take in what I said to him and to express his confusion verbally, thus allowing me to address it.

Eventually, Tom began to acknowledge me as a possible container, commenting for example at the end of Session 30, "I'll leave the mess in here." I began to feel more able to accept his plunderings and to tolerate my feelings of inadequacy.

DISCUSSION

Earlier it was mentioned that Tom would attempt to break away from an engagement by wanting to leave the room.   While this continued to be a feature in almost all sessions, it later developed in the form of his wish not to enter the therapy room at all but to dash into nearby rooms which might contain instruments, a television, or people whom Tom could try to engage in conversation.   Sometimes he expressed a wish to stay in the waiting room playing with toys rather than come to music.   Often during our half-hour sessions, he would run to the window banging and shouting to passers-by in witchy, authoritarian voice.

Tom's avoidance of the therapy situation turned out to be an important clue to understanding the feelings underneath all of his naughty, controlling, and tricky maneuvers.   It is therefore a fitting place to begin a more in-depth discussion of what Tom may have been revealing to me throughout these sessions.

Session 19 was of particular significance.   When our appointment time arrived, I found Tom sitting on the steps outside the building, sobbing and refusing to come in the main door. The sense of his fear and misery seemed more evident than they had previously been. The manner in which Tom had characteristically moved around in the therapy room, or expressed his wishes and dissatisfactions had always been similar to that described for our first meeting, and by his teachers, etc. He appeared confident, fussy and bossy, and his attempts to control me were irritating rather than expressive of fear and deep distress. On this occasion, when I asked Tom what he was afraid of, he was able to tell me through his tears: it was the gong in the therapy room---he was afraid of going into the room if it was there.

Tom's reluctance to enter the room;   his frequent requests to leave it; his wish to control my instrumentation;   his preference for antiphonal over simultaneous playing;   and his tendency to break away from musical improvisation seemed to be interrelated.   As in his fear of the gong, they may be viewed as aspects of a phenomenon in which Tom is terrified and distressed by something which is very big, whose resonances multiply set off by a single stroke, and which grow with an overwhelming effect of vibration and sonority, impacting on mind and body.   Perhaps the freedom of improvisation itself sets up these kinds of feelings within him. In fact, Tom developed an activity in which, standing together with him at the gong I must be ready to dampen it on his instruction, so that he could hit it very hard without its full resonance returning. Perhaps it is when that fearfulness, here elicited by the gong, is not fully conscious, that Tom has to adopt a range of maneuvers in relation to other people in order to keep it at bay. Maneuvers such as engaging in but prematurely breaking off interaction manifest as irritating, naughty and "tricky" behaviour and appear to be the result of poor concentration or sequencing problems, but in actuality may be defenses. It is easy to see that his relationships with family and peers would suffer as the result of such defensive maneuvers, as would his ability to take in and keep down learning.

Interaction with Tom often does feel tangled. It is difficult to sustain one activity with him without constantly expecting it to be broken off. In any setting where an adult had predetermined activity goals, I imagine that Tom would certainly be described as disobedient. It is as if Tom himself "gongs" around, as he did that first day in my office, a constant flow of physical and verbal activity, overturning and upsetting things, making sure that his "vibrations" disturb whatever is around him. Then, when he strikes the actual gong, it all comes back at him. Suddenly, all the unmanageability assaults him as if from outside---but magnified, amplified.

What elements of his disposition and early experiences might have contributed to his inner world being characterized by a fearfulness which seems to vibrate like the sound of the gong through his whole body? This image itself conjures up the frightening image of finding oneself taken over by a convulsion, which shakes one from the inside. We do know of at least two occasions on which Tom suffered from extreme forms of generalised convulsion. Conceivably, there may have been others, possibly nocturnal, which went undetected but were, nevertheless, experienced by Tom alone. His bed-wetting could have been seizure-related at times, and headache and nausea may have accompanied the seizures themselves, and be more easily alluded to by Tom than was the seizure itself. A family history of migraine might dispose him to experience these particular manifestations of illness.

While this vision should be borne in mind, I am also reminded of the contrast between Tom and his mother which suggested itself at our first meeting. Perhaps he has had a repeated experience of himself as somehow too big for her, too much to be "borne" by her. It may be that his frequent request to leave the sessions comes from a fear of being too much for me, of damaging me as he fears he has damaged his mother. For the child who experiences his mother as absent in some way, or not there for him, must attribute the cause of her absence to himself. Tom may also leave the therapy room in order to check that his actual mother is still accessible (although she in fact chose to leave the building during his therapy sessions). He may need to be physically close to her because psychically the safe inner mother seems absent, or not big enough to hold him safely.

These speculations seem to be confirmed by two themes in Tom's music therapy sessions: firstly, his preoccupation with broken objects, and an anxiety that he had broken or would break instruments; secondly, his preoccupation with big and little things, where he frequently tried to ensure that I have smaller instruments or beaters than his. The tragedy of this situation, or rather the tragedy of its internal meaning is that while he feels frightened that he is too big for the therapist, he is equally frightened that she is bigger than him: for what could be more frightening than to feel completely vulnerable with a big person who may not respond to your needs? In the moments when he breaks off our contact, he may be frightened that he is going to damage me with his bigness, or equally frightened that in being out of his control, I am going to damage him with mine.

In his rummaging in the cupboards, he seems to show that he needs to help himself to what he needs, rather than hope that together he and I can negotiate to fulfill his needs. If the carer is experienced as unable to contain the child's feelings, then the world feels intolerably unsafe, and the child feels unheld.

The spinning trickiness seems to result. Tom moves quickly from one thing to another, not managing to settle into a satisfying engagement. As in feeding, what food that is offered and taken in cannot be held down (vomiting), or feels as if it must come back up again (nausea). Tom feels ill, he rolls into a ball and asks to go to bed where at least the external spinning world recedes. But by lying down in a ball, he deprives himself of opportunites to take in, to learn, and to make real relationships rather than attach himself inappropriately to strangers.

Why might Tom experience himself as unheld and uncontained? Several factors may have contributed. Firstly, the dispositions of Tom and of his actual mother may have been in some way mismatched, so that if a slow and gently-moving mother has a fast-moving and extrovert baby, adjustments have to be made until they find possible ways of relating. Stern (1977) refers to such difficulties as the result of "mis-steps in the dance" of the mother-infant relationship.

The fact that Tom tended to regurgitate feeds as a baby might indicate that it was difficult for him to ingest the good things that were offered. The pace of feeding may have been a source of difficulty between them, and an optimal "balance of power" was perhaps not successfully achieved. Furthermore, if Tom did suffer minimal damage at birth, which is now related to his having both generalised and petit mal seizures, he may have had recurrent experiences of, as it were, the world dropping away from him. That is, constitutionally he may have been disposed to experience absences. In petit mal seizures, this would happen quite privately within Tom's world, unmitigated, therefore by observation and concerned explanation. When he awoke in hospital after his generalised convulsion, he may have had an experience not only of having dropped out of reality, but of reality itself having dropped away. This would easily integrate into an experience of a carer who seemed less than fully there, not quite "as large as life" as the child himself.

What has been described so far may well have been compounded by his experience of losing his mother to a sibling in his third year, and shortly afterwards being sent to a formal, academic school, thus losing his own time to be a playful child at home. While a hearing loss and an articulation problem may of course have an organic component, they may also externalise the child's experience of himself as not being able to take in and not able to make himself understood.

If Tom feels that he has to stop the world from disappearing from his frenetic activity, he must be in a state of pain and fear. Unfortunately, his "naughtiness" and "disobedience" make it harder to get and stay close enough to him to understand more about his real state. The "tricky" Tom is a draining child, and a drained carer has even less energy with which to try to understand him. A father, himself stretched by professional responsibilities, may avoid spending more time at home when his son is so frequently naughty and troublesome.

This study has in some ways focused on the tricky, tangled Tom, rather than on the sick and "in a ball" Tom who did not generally find a place in our sessions. One exception to this was the session following his hospitalisation, in which he made himself a bed on the floor and lay sadly hugging a small drum which he said was "the thunder in his bed."

Until now, I have perhaps not said enough about the well Tom, the hopeful Tom who engages with the therapist, bringing her not only his difficulties but also his resources. His playing, as we have seen, could be remarkably strong, sturdy, outwardly directed, self-organised, forward-moving, trembling, even randomly free. His break-off points were not due to a lack of sensitivity to my playing. On the contrary, it was his sensitive awareness of our being together in phrase, volume etc. which seemed to drive him to break off.

In his rummaging in the cupboards he often remarked as if to himself "Something might work..." His pun on the piano's brand name, substituting his own name for its second half, seemed both proprietal and celebratory, and became a repeated and much enjoyed point of shared understanding.

His present of a flower to me, with the remark that queens have flower, and brides do too...all these aspects of Tom seem to show that he has had good experiences, albeit incomplete or unfinished, and that he is hopeful of finding more or of "getting back." In one of our last sessions, Tom acknowledged that "Humpty needs a doctor...a lady doctor...the one he's pointing at" (Me).

The material in his sessions became less musical as time went on. In the last sessions before summer holiday, he very much wanted to play a game in which he repeatedly called me towards him, then sent me away again just as I drew near. When I related this to the holiday and the breaks between sessions, he was able to say solemnly and without "gonging" how much he would miss music.

It should be understood that when faced with the choice of committing myself to the medium of "pure" music versus trying to help Tom, I chose the latter. This did entail working beyond the medium in which I was originally trained, and was a responsibility which was not taken lightly. Though this did cause some anxiety, I came to accept less truly musical meaning in the sessions. Tom did surprise me in Session 35 by playing a free solo improvisation on the piano strings, an instrument he had previously anxiously avoided, fearing that it was broken. When he asked me if I liked what he played, I replied that I did and then asked him rather prosaically, "What did it say?" To this Tom replied, looking at me as if I should know better, "It didn't say anything, it was music." Perhaps my acceptance of all his material actually freed him to make musical explorations, which previously felt impossible because of his experience of my own resistance.

In the nursery rhyme, no one was able to put Humpty together again. This may have been at the back of Tom's mind when he asked anxiously, "How can this get back?" The answer is that he couldn't really get back, in the sense of putting back the clock and growing differently. However, my hope was that through the holding he experienced in therapy, he might find the ability to feel the pain and fear of his early losses fully, rather than being driven through current experiences under their power.

The role of improvised music-making in this process remains unclear. It may offer holding experiences, it may also reflect changes which have originated in nonmusical play. It may facilitate the surfacing of fear, although it cannot refer directly to its causes. It seems certain however, that therapeutic theory and technique must always adapt to the needs of the patient, rather than vice versa.

GLOSSARY

CAT Scan: Computerized Axial Tomography. A technique using computer technology to produce cross-sectional X-ray pictures of the body.

EEG: Electroencephalography. "A recording of the electrical activity of the brain as measured with the aid of electrodes attached to the scalp (Scott, 1969).

Episode of Engagement: "A sequence of social behaviours of variable length bounded by clear pausing time on either side" (Stern, 1977).

Generalized Convulsion: "A violent series of involuntary contractions of muscles, usually associated with complete loss of consciousness" (Scott, 1969).

Petit Mal Seizures: "A brief epileptic fit...not associated with convulsive movements but with a brief loss of consciousness" (Scott, 1969).

Status Epilepticus: "A serious condition in which one major fit follows another without consciousness being regained" (Scott, 1969).

REFERENCES

Scott, D. (1969). About Epilepsy. London: Duckworth.

Stern, D. (1977). The First Relationships: Infant and Mother.   London:
Open Books.

The Use Of Latin Music, Puppetry, And Visualization In Reducing The Physical And Emotional Pain Of A Child With Severe Burns

REBECCA LOVESZY, RMT-BC

Music Therapist,

Creative Arts Department,

Hugh Macmillan Rehabilitation Centre

Toronto, Ontario, Canada

Abstract: This study describes the use of music from a young boy's native culture - Honduras - to reduce his anxiety toward and resistance to painful treatment and to provide an avenue for the expression of feelings. It describes methods used to assist seven-year-old Eduardo through a grieving process while providing a sense of security and teaching methods for relaxation during painful treatment procedures. By enabling Eduardo to express himself in Spanish he was able to work through the various stages of grief and begin the healing process, internally and externally.

BACKGROUND INFORMATION

At the age of five, Eduardo was severely burned when his family's home, a grass hut, burned down. His younger sister died in the fire and his father was injured while attempting to rescue the children.

Eighty-percent of Eduardo's body was burned, all at the second and third degree levels. Initially, acute treatment occurred in a village hospital with minimal technical facilities; Eduardo was transferred to a general hospital in the Honduran capital, Tequcigalpa, after four months. His medical treatment continued for another twenty months by which time he had passed the critical stage; most of the burns were healing. However, because Honduran hospitals lacked facilities to adequately treat such burn patients, Eduardo had become immobilised because of *contractures* in his arms and legs. Facial deformities in the mouth and cheek area were also present.

Two years after the accident, the father and son travelled to a Shriner's Burn Hospital in the South-Central United States. There, Eduardo began the following medical treatments: skin graftings from his remaining healthy tissues; nine operations to release contractures; a course of antibiotics to reduce infection; up to three daily wrappings after each surgery; and the regular wearing of a *jobst garment.*

Within a week of admission, a multidisciplinary team was formed to address Eduardo's physical, emotional and educational needs. His treatment program included: physical, occupational, speech, music and child life therapies, as well as tutoring in English. As team members assessed Eduardo, they discovered that he had many ingrained fears. He was afraid of medical staff in white coats, people who wore masks and, understandably, anyone who inflicted pain. His father reported that Eduardo feared the unfamiliarity of being in a foreign country, and that the boy felt great distress at his inability to communicate in English. Spanish-speaking staff members were therefore included on the team.

Before each surgery, Eduardo cried continually, fighting the staff during dressing changes, the administering of medication and in physical and occupational therapy sessions. Such behaviour contrasted greatly with his father's description of the boy's personality before the fire. An even-tempered, gentle child, he had been protective of his sister and respectful of the elderly people in the village. He had been known to charm people with his great sense of humour and his love for singing and dancing. Deprived of all the things in life that had given him pleasure, Eduardo had become an alienated, uncooperative and angry patient.

Based on assessment and information from his father, the team's main goals for treatment were to minimize and to reduce the length of medical procedure. It was decided to emphasize music therapy in his treatment because of his love for music in the hope of addressing his level of anxiety.

MUSIC THERAPY ASSESSMENT

Eduardo was a likeable boy whose history included immersion in Latin Music through listening to his Uncle who played *"Bolero" guitar* during family gatherings. Family members sang a variety of Spanish songs on feast days, holy days and birthdays; as well as national songs during political holidays. Eduardo did not play an instrument but loved to sing with his sister.

During the initial assessment for music therapy, he attempted to smile when a birthday good morning song ("Las mananitas", which was very familiar to him) was sung to him. Throughout the assessment he was unable to move because of contractures and scarring. He had been right-handed, however the contractures prevented his use of either hand and precluded walking. He had limited arm movement and no use of his fingers. He was however, able to track visually and auditorally and to blow wind instruments held by the therapist. Cognitively, he was noted to initiate eye contact, and to use fairly clear speech (despite contractures of the mouth and cheek areas). His sentences in Spanish were well developed but slowly spoken with a breathy quality, always labouring to close consonants.

Eduardo was able to perform one-step tasks such as shaking a bell-tied to his wrist and responding appropriately to questions. He accepted touch but was unable to reach out. Because of hypersensitivity he asked to be touched very carefully. Hearing was normal and eye movements were controlled. He sang in Spanish - always folk or holiday songs. His attention was focused throughout the one hour assessment.

Affectively, Eduardo was noted to express sadness during a song about a butterfly, "Mariposa Linda;" he was visibly tearful. When asked about the song, Eduardo said he learned it from his uncle and had sung it with his sister. Eduardo was very fragile, emotionally. He was fearful and unable to trust. Often tearful when he spoke of his family in Honduras - especially his sister, he was unable to talk about the fire. His father could not explain how it had begun. During the birthday song, he managed a smile and told of his birthday in August.

Socially, Eduardo responded positively to the music therapist as well as the child life therapist entering the room as the assessment ended. When a nurse arrived, he screamed and cried, calming only when his father appeared.

Eduardo seemed to be a musical child with a pleasant singing voice and a good concept of rhythm. He liked to sing and was able to imitate rhythms played on the drum. This he did by making a clicking sound with his tongue; it was still too painful for him to use his hands. He loved to hear the guitar and wanted to play like his Uncle.

After the assessment it was recommended that music therapy take place before and during painful procedures such as dressing changes and physiotherapy sessions, as well as before and after surgeries.

METHOD OF TREATMENT

Phase I: 1-3 Months

Eduardo's first sessions took place at his bedside. Most of these were in conjunction with other therapies such as physical, occupational and speech or during dressing changes. This continued on a daily basis for three months. He felt comfortable with his native language, consequently Eduardo took part in fifteen-minute relaxation sessions, on a daily basis, one week preceeding each surgery. Sessions were in Spanish. Eduardo created his own music but also enjoyed traditional songs. The sessions were flexible, Eduardo controlling the music and the instruments.

Music therapy methods used were: guided imagery; progressive muscle relaxation; singing to strengthen lung capacity, express emotions, and provide familiarity; puppetry and music to express emotions and act out feelings; and adapted instruments to increase gross motor movement. Later, other instruments such as the guitar, were used to increase fine motor movement in the right hand and finger strength in the left. An effort was made to make most sessions relaxed in a dimly lit environment free from distractions of medical staff. This became easier when the sessions took place after lunch in the playroom during quiet time for other children.

It was during this phase that a strong rapport was building between Eduardo and the music therapist. A very playful atmosphere was created with music, and a puppet of a famous little mouse character from Mexico called "Topo Gigio." Topo Gigio spoke in a very high voice and liked to sing just like Eduardo. He found the puppet to be a friend whom he could laugh and sing with---and even yell at.

Eduardo and Topo Gigio learned how to relax together. Eduardo always mentioned that his puppet did not have legs and could not walk. Although Eduardo did have legs he was not yet able to walk. Eduardo's favourite piece to relax to was "Recuerdos de la Alhambra" by Tarrega. Only four minutes long, it was enough during the first month of learning to breathe deeply while thinking of his favourite place in Honduras. By the third month, he had added "Sevilla," a piece by I. Albeniz (transcribed by Andres Segovia) which was 4 minutes, 29 seconds. This additional time gave Eduardo the time to learn to tense muscles as well as relax them. This process was very difficult because of Eduardo's contracted skin; the muscles were very tight at this time.

The physical therapist joined the music therapy sessions during this time so that Eduardo would not hurt himself. The main focus was on breathing and expressing feelings. By guiding Eduardo through his strong emotions in a gentle, loving manner, he was able to begin to overcome a few obstacles, such as low tolerance for activity, deformities, and surgery.

Phase II: 3-6 Months

Eduardo became a favoured patient amongst the hospital staff and his peers on the ward.   The multidisciplinary team was beginning to catch glimpses of the pre-accident character his father had described.

There was something at the core of this little boy's heart that needed to be expressed but the time had not yet arrived. As a therapist one may, in fact, not see this occur within the treatment period.

Eduardo was preparing for his third surgery. He began to deal with pain by focusing on something pleasant. This he did by creating a simple guided imagery of his favourite place into which he introduced a strong, fearless animal. This favourite place at home was beneath a tree where he sat to look at animals passing by in the clouds. The lion was his favourite because it could roar so loudly. This particular animal was to prove a very strong image in later sessions.

Eduardo's lion remained constant. This was HIS animal, and when he needed to scream, he roared. Eduardo created a vision of being stalked in the jungle which required being quiet, attentive, and strong. He was then more able to cope with the injections he so greatly feared. One of the other children on the ward had introduced Eduardo to an English version of Kipling's "Jungle Book" with accompanying music. He requested this music each time he was to receive an injection. Eduardo knew that the playroom was his space for thirty minutes. He could do whatever he wanted, and for the three months, the first thing Eduardo did was to roar like a lion for five minutes. Then, he made noise however he could, mainly using his voice and instruments. Because Eduardo's hands were, at times, in splints, he used a mallet which could be velcroed to the splints as designed by occupational therapy. This ensured correct positioning while protecting his hands. It also gave him a means of ventilating frustration and anger, all the while increasing his range of motion. He always chose the larger drum with the deepest sound; hitting it as hard as he could, Eduardo would regularly work himself into a sweat. Slowly the sound became more musical until midway through the session he would ask the therapist to play "De Colores" when he would join in with the sounds of the animals in the song.

Although Eduardo's voice was still very breathy due to the scarring of his lungs, it was becoming stronger by the day and he was gaining more and more satisfaction from using it. The animal sound he was using was the Spanish sound for a hen: "ca ca ra ca ca". This was a good choice because he still had difficulty completely closing his lips. The Spanish sound for rooster, "qui qui ri qui qui," was also an excellent combination to practice. Eduardo also made the sound for baby chicks: "piu piu."   This was very difficult for him although his facial jobst garment facilitated the closure of his mouth. With time, Eduardo added more sounds with which he was successful. Each time it was a celebration.

Eduardo always chose to end his sessions by sitting or lying as close as he could to the guitar. He strummed it with an adapted pick made of a small plastic juice bottle, singing while the therapist chorded. The songs he chose depended on his current feelings. When he was happy he sang, "Hoy es un Gran dia" ("Today is a Great Day"). When he was in pain he sang, "Ay Que Dolor Vivir" ("Oh what a pain to live"). The session always ended in a positive way, even when he was not feeling well. The music was a soothing release for Eduardo.

Phase III: 6-9 Months

The signs of spring were all around: the earth was blooming and so was Eduardo. This was the turning point in his emotional healing at the hospital within his music therapy sessions. Eduardo's sessions were now very focused as well as increased in length. He was being seen for an hour, and each moment was of the utmost importance.

One of the Shriner Clowns who had heard of Eduardo's musical talents and his desire to learn guitar, gave him a first guitar, small enough to handle. Eduardo began to learn the "Slide Rule Method" of guitar playing; the instrument tuned to D major chord, the 6th string is D; 5th-A; 4th-D; 3rd-G; 2nd-B; 1st-E. It can be barred with an adapted steel or hard plastic tube or played with a finger. Eduardo used the hard plastic tube which enabled him to press the strings evenly. The first song he learned to play was the birthday song described earlier. Upon mastering the song, he celebrated for a week. Eduardo became the resident *"Mariachi."*

The joy that had been missing in this little boy's life slowly began returning after this first success. His repertoire of Spanish children's songs soon included: "Alla En El Rancho Grande", ("Over in the Large Ranch"), and "De Colores", ("Of the Colour"). A few of his own songs were also "El canto del Lion", ("The Song of the Lion") and "Il Titeri" ("The Puppet").

These two little songs led to a songwriting session which provided the staff and Eduardo's father the story of the fire. Eduardo called it "El Dia Que Muri" ("The Day I Died"). This emotional experience began when, with an adamant stride, Eduardo walked into the playroom saying, "Yo Quiero hacer un canto" ("I want to write a song"). Thinking he was going to write another song about his experiences and triumphs at the hospital, the usual routine was set up with guitar and piano. He promptly told the therapist, "No, no, no - quiero el tambor" ("No, no, no, - I want the drum").

Hitting the drum with fury, he said, "Tontos son los ninos quien juegan con lumbre", ("Bad are the children who play with fire").

He was not singing as he usually did - he was shouting. "Creen que pueden aprender el lumbre y apagar lo con un soplado" (They think they can light the fire and blow it out with one breath)

He continued to beat the drum with force - then he stopped - looked up, with tears in his eyes: "Se guemaron, se quemaron..." (They burned themselves, they burned themselves).

"Yo mate mi Hermanita" (I killed my little sister).

"Yo me queme" (I burned myself).

"Destruyi mi familia, y mi casa" (I destroyed my family and my home).

The therapist leaned over to hold Eduardo. At last he was able to release the guilt he carried. He and his little sister had been playing with matches. As an older sibling, he felt he was responsible for the accident. For a long time, Eduardo cried. This little boy had finally allowed himself to express his feelings through a song. It was information he might never have shared if he had not been provided a medium in which he felt comfortable, in a safe, non-judgemental environment. Eduardo was at last able to mourn for his sister through the music.

Eduardo truly began to "heal." He wrote several songs after this experience, one to his father for loving him, another in remembrance of his sister, and yet another about going home.

He was discharged nine months after arriving at the hospital. The Social Services Department was able to make connections in Honduras for community support. Eduardo returned for plastic surgery every six months for two years, then each year until puberty. He no longer lived in the village but in a city. He is reported to be well, continuing to sing and play his guitar, and living in a adobe home with his father.

EVALUATION

Eduardo's progress was evaluated on a weekly basis in the medical charts of the hospital in the progress note section using a subjective, objective, assessment and plan - S.O.A.P. format. This record helped to see Eduardo's progress from day one.

The interventions described were chosen by the music therapist after discussing goals with various team members working with Eduardo. The vocal intervention of "roaring" simply happened; Eduardo controlled this. The use of the puppet assisted him in speaking freely and in accepting his inability to use his legs. Eduardo's positive response was that at least he still had his legs - the puppet did not have legs. Eduardo's creativity played a strong part in his ability to write his own songs.

Songwriting, therefore, became the most obvious intervention. His continuing love for music and desire to play the guitar assured an outlet for his expression of feelings upon his return to Honduras.

DISCUSSION AND CONCLUSION

Prior to intervention Eduardo was a frightened little boy who did not speak English. He had experienced many losses in a short period: his physical identity; his beloved sister; and familiar surroundings. He also had to endure excruciating pain. His soul was crushed. Music, however, had remained intact for him; it had not changed and he loved it. Although the person who interacted with him using music had changed - the music itself had not.

It assisted him in ventilating his anger, sadness and guilt. After learning visualization, Eduardo was able to gain emotional strength and acquire "bravery," enabling him to undergo the daily injections. He had lost the sense of play but through puppetry it was regained.

Despite being physically immobile, through the use of adaptive instruments, he was motivated to work hard for the physical therapist. Eduardo's lungs were very weak but because of his singing he was able to increase breathing capacity, albeit with a reduced air volume.

Finally, the songwriting assisted Eduardo in expressing his deep sadness and guilt, both of which had initially hampered his emotional progress.

There was a strong trust between Eduardo and the music therapist. There was freedom in each session, with Eduardo given control, something which had been taken from him following the fire. He was not threatened by the therapy environment - it was "safe." Providing a very humanistic approach was important for Eduardo, and using music in his native language further enhanced the client-therapist bond.

GLOSSARY

Bolero Guitar: The playing of the guitar in 3/4 time for a Spanish dance characterized by sharp turns, stamping of feet and sudden pauses in a position with one arm arched over the head.

Contractures: A permanent shortening (as of muscle, tendon or scar tissue) producing deformity or distortion.

Jobst Garment: A garment made of nylon which fits tightly against the skin to reduce swelling and inflammation.

Mariachi: Lively music rooted in the cultural celebration of weddings. A mariachi is a person who play individually or in a group strolling from table to table in a festive setting, entertaining people.

Skin Grafting: The removal of healthy tissue to join or unite to burned tissue.

Preverbal Communication Through Music To Overcome A Child's Language Disorder

AMELIA OLDFIELD, *M.Phil.*, *R.M.Th.*
Music Therapist
Child Development Centre
Addenbrookes Hospital
Cambridge, Great Britain

Abstract.   This case describes two years of group and individual music therapy for a five-year old boy with a language disorder. A wide variety of music therapy techniques are used, all aimed at motivating Jamie to communicate, either nonverbally or verbally.

BACKGROUND INFORMATION

Jamie is the only child of very caring and capable parents. As a young child, he appeared somewhat smaller and slower than other children in his age group, and eye contact was often difficult. His mother reports that, as a baby, he did not babble at all, and used very few other non verbal means of communication, such as pointing. He was always a very quiet child, and only occasionally and inconsistently used words.

At two and a half, Jamie found mixing with other children very difficult, and would often appear to be in a world of his own. However, he did not present any major behaviour problems and was able to play by himself. At this stage, the pediatrician reassured his parents that Jamie's development was not necessarily abnormal. Nevertheless, both his parents and other professionals involved continued to be concerned. Jamie's health visitor wrote a report at this time describing him as: "rather worrying in a not altogether definable way."

When Jamie was three, he was assessed by a clinical psychologist who suggested that, although his overall intelligence was within the normal range, there were great discrepancies in his skills. He had high scores for manipulative skills, such as putting puzzles together, and marked problems with both comprehension and expressive language. Jamie's hearing was also tested at this stage as he seemed both oversensitive to some sounds and oblivious to others. It was found to be within the normal range.

Jamie was then referred to the Child Development Centre where he began having regular sessions with the speech therapist. He also started attending a small play therapy group of four children. This is a structured group run by a clinical psychologist where the emphasis is on encouraging social integration. She reports that, over a period of a year, Jamie took part in more group activities and managed to overcome some of his fears and obsessions. He became more able to tolerate the screaming of another child in the group, for example, which he had been terrified of at first.

When Jamie was four, he was assessed by the local specialist consultant in child psychiatry. He suggested that, although Jamie's language was very restricted, he was showing signs of imagination. In spite of his difficulties, Jamie seemed to be developing an understanding of the meaning of words; therefore, there seemed to be potential for the development of abstract thought. The psychiatrist felt that Jamie's social problems and occasional disturbed behaviour were the result of his great difficulties in understanding social practices. Thus, he diagnosed Jamie as having a specific language disorder. In his opinion, there was no evidence of autism or an autistic like disorder.

The term "language disorder" generally describes an atypical pattern of language acquisition and development. Unlike children whose language may be delayed but nevertheless following a normal pattern of acquisition, children with language disorders have both a delayed and deviant pattern of development (Webster & McConnell, 1987). Deviancy or disruption may occur in any or all aspects of speech and language: context, form or use; or as a result of a distorted interaction between them (Bloom & Lahey, 1978). Jamie had difficulties in all these aspects of language development, and particularly in the area of language use. This affected his ability to establish social relationships and to relate to the world around him.

A speech therapy report written a couple of months later agreed with this diagnosis. The speech therapist explained that Jamie had difficulties processing sentences in order to comply with a task. Although he responded to everyday instructions, he was reacting more to the context and the routine than to the actual meaning of the instruction. Jamie could say quite long sentences, but had difficulties learning when to use these sentences appropriately. He was mainly silent and only made occasional, spontaneous, self-generated comments.

From the age of four to the present, Jamie has been attending a small language unit for eight children with language disorders. The children in this class receive very specialised schooling, and the main focus of the work is on improving their language difficulties. The class is based in an ordinary school, and the children are integrated into other "normal" classes at times, as well as working together as a group at other times. Both the teacher from the unit and Jamie's parents are still unsure about Jamie's diagnosis, and suspect that he might have some autistic tendencies.

At five, Jamie was referred to me at the Child Development Centre by his language unit teacher. She had noticed that Jamie seemed to respond to words in songs more easily than spoken words. She hoped that I might devise some exercises for both her and Jamie's parents to use with him to improve his speech.

MUSIC THERAPY ASSESSMENT

I saw Jamie for three consecutive weekly, half hour music therapy assessment sessions. The purpose of these sessions was: (1) to determine whether music therapy would be a useful way of helping Jamie, and if so to roughly outline what kind of direction this treatment might take; (2) to see whether he responded to me in a different way through music and thus to shed new light on some of his difficulties; and (3) to suggest ways in which both his teacher and his parents could use music with him.

Jamie presented as a small, attractive looking boy with a serious and often puzzled expression. He had no difficulties separating from his mother, and showed no anxiety about coming into the music therapy room with me. He seemed to understand simple requests or comments such as: "Here is a chair for you, Jamie" or "Shall we finish this now?" He was able to point to me and to choose an instrument for me on request. He could listen to my playing and also play himself and was good at taking turns with me. He made very few verbal contributions or vocalisations, but at one point suddenly and surprisingly, made an appropriate comment about an instrument, saying in a very clear voice, "There's a ball inside."

Jamie particularly enjoyed activities where we teased one another, or where he could "control" me by, for example, making me jump when he played the drum. At these times, he would look straight at me and have a beautiful mischievous smile.

Jamie seemed pleased to listen to the music and the songs I improvised on the piano and the clarinet. He anticipated the ends of harmonic phrases by looking up at the appropriate moment, and showed that he knew and recognised a number of songs by occasionally filling in words when I left a gap. For example, I would sing: "London bridge is falling....," and Jamie would say: "Down!" Sometimes he would sing the words at the correct pitch to fit in with the song.

Jamie enjoyed playing the instruments, and would spontaneously explore various ways of playing them in a creative way. For example: he seemed to experiment with the different sounds the drumstick made on various parts of the drum, and played the cabasa in a number of ways, stroking and rattling the beads as well as shaking the whole instrument.

Jamie generally seemed to prefer the quieter instruments. He did not appear particularly frightened of loud sounds, but would blink slightly anxiously when they occurred. With a little encouragement, he could join in and enjoy both quiet and loud improvisations. He was able to follow dynamic changes when we improvised together, but had more difficulty following rhythmic changes. He appeared to be able to play in a regular pulse for short periods, but the pulse was hesitant and gave his playing a slightly tentative feeling.

Jamie found it difficult to move freely or spontaneously to music. His physical reactions were slow, and he needed encouragement to do things such as march or jump to the music.

Jamie seemed to be developing a positive relationship with me. He was at ease playing the musical instruments, and was able to both listen to and contribute musical ideas during our improvisations. I felt he would benefit from a situation where he could communicate with an adult without having either to understand spoken language or use words himself. The areas I thought we could work on were: increasing his motivation to communicate with another person; providing an opportunity for Jamie to vocalise freely and spontaneously; increasing Jamie's confidence and enabling him to speed up his reactions so they were more spontaneous. I therefore recommended that he should have weekly individual music therapy treatment for at least six months.

Jamie appeared to be more spontaneous in his communication with me during our sessions than he was with other adults. This was probably because far less speech was necessary in my sessions than in other situations. The fact that he was more at ease in this non verbal situation seemed to confirm the diagnosis of language disorder. After reading Jamie's notes, I had expected him to be more sensitive to loud sounds and was surprised when he did not seem to mind hitting the drum very loudly. On reflection, however, it became clear that it was unexpected and unexplained loud noises that particularly troubled Jamie, and not loud sounds that he knew were about to occur or sounds which he himself produced or controlled.

I did not think that it would be beneficial to give Jamie's parents or his teacher structured musical exercises to improve his speech. I felt the priority was to help Jamie feel at ease with a non verbal means of communication, so that he would eventually become more spontaneous in his efforts to communicate. I also thought that Jamie should be encouraged to enjoy making sounds and vocalising without the pressure of using the correct word or structure. Jamie had never babbled or experimented with sounds as a baby, and I thought that he needed to discover the fun of producing sounds. I therefore suggested that both his parents and his teacher should encourage Jamie to vocalise in any way, and that they should try to engage him in playful vocal dialogues. I also suggested they do "toddler" like rhymes such as "Incy Wincy Spider" or "Round and Round the Garden" with him, so that Jamie could laugh at them with an adult, and learn to enjoy communicating in a simple way.

TREATMENT PROCESS

Phase One: Introductory Group Work

Unfortunately, I did not have any spaces available to see Jamie for individual music therapy sessions immediately, and he was therefore put on a waiting list. As it happened, however, I had already arranged to see the group of children in the language unit that Jamie attended for a a twelve week period, starting four weeks after I had finished the assessment on Jamie. I was, therefore, able to observe and work with Jamie in a group setting before I started to work with him individually.

The group sessions occurred once a week, lasted approximately forty minutes and went on for one school term (twelve weeks). Both the teacher and the welfare assistant took part, and I reviewed our work with the teacher every week, directly after the session.

All eight children in the group were diagnosed as having language disorders. Jamie, however, was shyer and more withdrawn than the other children. The group sessions had two or three specific aims for each child. These were determined jointly by the teaching staff and myself after a couple of "exploratory" sessions. Generally, the goals were: to provide a different setting for the teaching staff to observe the children's strengths and difficulties, and to give the teaching staff ideas of musical activities to use in the classroom. Given my large case load, this is one of the only ways I can provide some input to a large number of children.

The musical material and the activities used in the group would vary from week to week, and was largely determined by the aims for individual children. Although suggestions for activities for the following week's session might be made when we reviewed our sessions, I would always remain flexible and would usually choose activities on the spur of the moment, based on the children's reactions and moods on any particular day. Nevertheless, I would always start off with a familiar greeting song and end with a "good bye" activity. Throughout the group I would often alternate between activities which involved the group as a whole and activities which involved one or two children playing on their own. An example of a general group activity would be: the whole group plays together on various percussion instruments led by improvised music I play on the piano. When the piano stops the children all move around and exchange instruments. Playing starts again when the piano begins. An example of an activity involving two children would be: two children sit back to back in the middle of the circle, each with a different instrument, and are asked to have a musical conversation. The rest of the group is encouraged to listen. I would also try to alternate between activities where the children were actively involved in playing instruments, singing or dancing, and activities which required concentrated listening without so much active involvement.

After observing Jamie within the group for two sessions it became clear that he was much more withdrawn in this setting than he had been with me on a one to one basis. We therefore decided that individual aims for Jamie would be: to help him concentrate and listen to instructions; to encourage him to communicate in any way with either adults or children; and to encourage him to make eye contact and to make any vocal sounds.

During the first five sessions, Jamie seemed to understand some but by no means all the instructions, and was able to take part in a few activities only. He seemed to enjoy choosing and playing instruments, but was unable to pass an instrument to another child. He did not understand the games involving drama where we pretended to put a tambourine to sleep, for example, and he needed help whenever any of the activities involved moving around the room. He made little eye contact, and only used a few sporadic single words. He often appeared to be in a world of his own, and made no efforts to communicate with either the children or the adults in the group.

During the sixth session, there was a marked change in Jamie. He suddenly appeared more at ease, smiling happily and looking straight at me when I played the clarinet. He was able to contribute some vocal noises to a song where all the children were suggesting different sounds, and even gave his instrument to another child when this was suggested to him. From this session onwards, Jamie continued to progress well. He learned how to "conduct" by pointing to other children and adults. He would listen to instructions better, and he began to take part in even quite complicated activities. He started using more words, both on request and spontaneously. Both Jamie's teacher and I were pleased with Jamie's progress within the group, however we felt that he would benefit even more from individual sessions.

Phase Two: Individual Sessions

Two weeks after the group finished, a space became available, and I started to see Jamie for regular weekly individual music therapy sessions. Although he had made some progress during the group sessions, the aims remained the same: to increase communication, eye contact, vocalization, and spontaneity. As Jamie's use of words had improved, I continued to keep a record of both spontaneous speech and the speech he used to answer direct questions. Nevertheless, I still did not want Jamie to feel that this was the focus of our sessions, or that I was putting pressure on him to talk.

The individual sessions lasted half an hour, and were held at the same time and in the same room every week. After each session, I would briefly discuss with Jamie's mother how he was progressing.

Like the group sessions I would start and end each session with familiar "hello" and "good bye" activities. In between, sessions would vary from week to week depending on Jamie's mood, on what had happened the previous week, and in what particular areas I felt I should be helping Jamie. In general, I would spend some time encouraging him to choose instruments or activities, and then attempt to follow and support his playing; at other times, I would make suggestions myself. For example, I might suggest that we take turns playing the glockenspiel, and pass each other the stick when our turn was finished; or I might encourage Jamie to play three different instruments that would make me jump, wave my arms or shake my head depending on which instrument he played; or I might suggest that we have a "noise" dialogue on the kazoos. I would always try to give each of our activities a structure with a clear ending. I would prepare Jamie for each ending by saying "One more turn each," or "Try to find a way to finish this off."

Jamie was at ease with me straight away, and was delighted with the familiar "hello" song on the guitar. This led to a sung "noise" dialogue accompanied by shared guitar strumming. Jamie initiated vocal sounds such as "Hey" with great delight, and would then laugh happily. He gradually added "funny" faces to these noises, particularly when I encouraged him by mirroring and extending his contributions. Jamie was clearly excited and pleased with these humorous exchanges, and I was able to keep them mischievous and creative rather than just silly. These vocal dialogues immediately followed my greeting to him, and became a regular part of our sessions. Sometimes Jamie would respond immediately, and at other times it seemed to take him a little time to relax and allow himself to enjoy this basic form of communication.

Over the first six months of treatment, Jamie continued to become more spontaneous in any familiar activities that we shared. However, he would revert to a blank, puzzled expression whenever I introduced anything new. I, therefore, made a conscious effort not to allow the sessions to become too stereotyped and, while always keeping some familiarity, tried to vary the way we played together, always introducing at least one new idea every week,

As Jamie became more able to make his own choices and contributions, he started to use more single words or two word phrases, both spontaneously and in answer to direct questions. In a conducting game, Jamie gradually managed to give me more and more complicated instructions, such as "Play the drum and the cymbal loudly." Nevertheless, his speech was still far from normal, and at times he would be unable to say something as simple as "Goodbye, Amelia" or tell me which day of the week he came for music therapy.

Jamie still found it difficult to move quickly or spontaneously. However, he started to enjoy and understand imaginative games where I pretended to fall asleep on the piano, or I hid from him in the room. At these times he could react quite fast to "Wake me up!" or "Find me!"

Jamie continued to enjoy experimenting with various ways of playing the instruments, and seemed to become more sensitive to various tone colours. He began to listen much more carefully to the sounds he produced. His sense of rhythm also improved. He would enjoy improvising on the piano and quickly became able to pick out tunes such as "Ba-Ba Black Sheep," "Happy Birthday To You" and "Puff the Magic Dragon." As he apparently wanted to learn more tunes, and enjoyed playing the piano, I arranged for him to start piano lessons with a teacher who had an interest in children with special needs. This also meant that there could be a clear separation between my work and more formal piano teaching.

As Jamie gradually became more spontaneous in his contributions, he also developed some slightly obsessive behaviours, such as repeating a tune fragment again and again, or insisting on holding the drumstick in a certain way. Nevertheless, he could be distracted from these obsessions relatively easily. As time went on, these rituals seemed to die away, and were replaced by ordinary "toddler like" naughtiness and rebelliousness. The only slightly strange behaviour that did occasionally creep back was that of Jamie "telling off" his right hand for misbehaving.

By the end of six months of individual music therapy sessions, Jamie had made great progress, and the aims set out at the beginning of our work together had been achieved. Progress had also been noticed at school, and at home Jamie's parents were delighted with his greater willingness and ability to communicate. However, they were also finding him a great deal naughtier and less easy to manage.

I therefore decided that, as I had developed such a good rapport with Jamie, I would continue to see him for another four months with a view to helping both Jamie and his parents to cope with these new "naughty" behaviours. I also thought that his communication skills could be further improved.

Phase Three: A Slightly New Direction

Aims for the last four months of treatment were: to diminish silly behaviours such as screaming or deliberately throwing objects; to encourage longer spontaneous and creative dialogues with me (nonverbal and verbal); and to help Jamie to answer questions appropriately (and not let him divert me from this).

When dealing with Jamie's "naughty" behaviours, I felt it was important to explain what I thought about these behaviours, and why I was responding in a particular way. I told him that we would work out ways of stopping his naughty behaviours together. At times, I would smile at him, and tell him in a "teasing" way that I thought he was trying to be naughty. At other times, I would suggest to him that it was easier to opt out of an activity and be naughty, than to continue our work. When he threw an object, I would take his hand and physically help him to pick it up again, saying that it was important for us both to make the naughty behaviour "better."

Occasionally he would get "stuck" when asked to do something and say "I can't." In this case I would either help him physically (and comment that I was giving him a "helping hand"), or I would say that perhaps what I had asked Jamie to do was too difficult. This approach seemed to work well. He remained mischievous but became more accepting of direction, and would allow himself to be diverted from whatever was causing a problem more easily.

During the last few sessions, Jamie sometimes became "moody," and on one occasion, he cried when he did not have time to play an instrument he had wanted to play. He seemed relieved to be told that there was nothing wrong with being sad and crying.

During the last four months, Jamie continued to make progress in his communication skills. By the end of my time with him he was able to hold ordinary conversations with me. He would initiate a conversation and ask appropriate questions. However, he would still sometimes need encouragement to answer questions.

Overall, the progress he made during that year was remarkable. From a quiet often mouse-like child, he had become a vocal, boisterous child, often full of mischief and fun.

DISCUSSION AND CONCLUSIONS

In the first instance, the musical instruments and our music-making interested Jamie, and motivated him to be actively involved with me. This enabled me to start building up a relationship with him which was initially based on shared enjoyment of the music and the musical activities. Jamie was able to maintain this positive relationship with me because I used very little speech in our assessment sessions. He could, therefore, relax and simply enjoy being with me. We were playing music together and communicating through sound, but very few specific words needed to be said or understood. It was the use of music as a means of communication which was essential at this point, and this could only have been achieved through music therapy.

For the first few group sessions, Jamie again became very shy and withdrawn. This was probably because far more speech was necessary in this situation to understand what was going on and what was expected of him. However, he was able to maintain an interest in the group because of his fascination for music. The familiar structure of the sessions gradually reassured him, and gave him the confidence he needed to take part with the other children and make his own contributions.

When I started working with Jamie individually, the familiar framework of a "hello" and "good bye" activity reassured him, and allowed him to start work with me straight away. In fact, it became clear that Jamie relied too heavily on familiar and predictable activities, and I had to start introducing "surprises" so that he did not become entirely dependent on this familiarity.

One of the most important things that we worked on throughout Jamie's individual sessions was vocalisation. As Jamie had never babbled as a baby, I felt that he needed to discover what fun it could be producing sounds and experimenting with different vocal noises. It is interesting to note that it was during these vocal exchanges that Jamie first started using his face in an expressive way, wrinkling his nose and making "funny" faces. This ability to encourage a child to have vocal sung dialogues which can be varied and made interesting through musical improvisation is unique to the music therapist.

Another important aspect of our work was the fact that I was able to put Jamie "in control" by encouraging him, for example, to conduct my playing. I think this was helpful in building up Jamie's confidence, as his language difficulties often made him feel confused and "out of control."

Slowly, and almost in spite of himself, Jamie discovered that it was not only easy to communicate with an adult, but that it could be fun and therefore worth the effort. This was my main aim with Jamie but it happened so gradually that I only realised how much progress he had made when I looked back at how little he had initially contributed.

Finally, it is interesting to note that as Jamie's abilities to communicate improved, he developed new "naughty" behaviours. The approach that I used to help him with these behaviours was based on explaining my actions very carefully, and making use of his new found language and comprehension skills. At this stage, I was also able to put more pressure on Jamie and be more demanding, something I would have avoided doing in the earlier stages. I think it was my relationship with Jamie which was crucial at this point, rather than the special skills that I have as a music therapist. Nevertheless, I had developed this relationship through our music-making, so it was important for me to continue and complete our work together.

When I recently telephoned Jamie's family one evening to find out whether they would be happy for me to write this case study, I heard a familiar voice in the background: "I don't want to go to bed!" Certainly, this is a well-known and unwelcome communication for any parent to receive from a child, but in this instance, I could not help feeling moved. I was reminded of the amount of progress Jamie had made since I first saw him two years previously, when he had hardly been able to use speech to communicate in any way at all.

Although I generally enjoy my work as a music therapist, I do sometimes wonder whether I am really achieving results, and whether the children could equally well be helped through means such as special teaching or play therapy. Cases like Jamie make up for the times when progress seems to be very slow or nonexistent, and help to maintain my belief that music therapy is a truly unique and invaluable form of treatment.

REFERENCES

Bloom, L., & Lahey, M. (1978). Language Development and Language Disorders. New York: John Wiley and Sons.

Webster, A., & McConnell. C. (1987). Children With Speech and Language Disorders. London: Cassel.

Group Music Therapy
With a Classroom of 6-8 Year-Old
Hyperactive-Learning Disabled Children

JULIE HIBBEN, M.Ed., CMT-BC
Director: Programs for Special Needs
Powers Music School

Music Therapy Faculty
Lesley Graduate School
Cambridge, Massachusetts

Abstract: In this case, the author recounts the progress toward group cohesion of an early elementary special education classroom. Most of the children are described as Attention-deficit Hyperactivity Disordered. In the twice-weekly sessions during the year, the therapist uses active music making and movement to engage the children in interactive play, and to develop intimacy and cohesion in the group. The instruments, props, and songs serve as objects which encourage and contain the children's action and feelings. Developmental stage theory provides a framework for anticipating and planning group interactions, and for evaluating individual progress. Group activities are described in terms of five dimensions: interaction, leadership, movement, rules, and competency.

BACKGROUND INFORMATION

The eight children in this self-contained classroom had chronological ages of 6-8 but in most cases they were academically at pre-first grade level. Many of the children had disruptive behavior disorders associated with *Attention-Deficit Hyperactivity Disorder (ADHD)* as well as *Learning Disabilities.* In some cases the children were at risk because of the severity of their anti-social behaviors and/or the lack of support from their family systems. Some of the children were on psychostimulant drugs such as Ritalin which controlled their hyperactivity to some extent. The children lacked developmental experiences such as nurturing play and spontaneous game playing with peers, either because of environmental deprivation or because of their learning or behavioral disorders. Their behaviors ran the gamut from excessive activity, interruptive talking, and physical aggression to negativism, lethargy, and introversion.

The brief description of the children below points up the diversity of their needs and behaviors:

Paul came from a special needs preschool, and at age 6.5, had just entered the classroom. He had no reading skills and had expressive and receptive language disabilities so severe that *auditory aphasia* was being considered as a diagnosis. Paul learned visually. Perceptual motor disabilities were apparent in his awkward maneuvers around the classroom. His relationship to his father was close and active.

Arnie had a history of depression and low self-esteem. His interaction during the music therapy assessment showed him to have ability (fluency, memory, originality) and confidence in expressing himself musically.

Al was moody and sulked a lot. Because of his lack of boundaries, he felt threatened by others in the group, even when the threat was not warranted. His voice was often raised in complaint.

Nathaniel had a history of passive aggressive behavior. He used his intelligence and verbal skills to manipulate those around him. Nathaniel, 8 years old, left the class after the first month.

Ken was dependent and passive, encouraged in this by his doting parents. He was medicated with Phenobarbital which slowed him down motorically. His thinking was very concrete. Ken was not able to verbalize his feelings, which often led to violent outbursts. His body was overweight and flaccid, and he showed signs of perceptual-motor disabilities.

Michael was anxious, hyperactive, and intelligent. During the middle of the year his cousin was taken to court for continually sexually abusing him.

Jose was humorous and friendly at times, and at other times was negative and depressed. During initial music therapy assessment, Jose was in control of the interaction, though he interacted only with expressive mime and eye contact. Jose left the classroom at mid-year.

Hattie (the only girl) was 6 years old. She was defiant, and deliberately annoyed others. Her behavior led to consideration of a diagnosis of *Oppositional Defiant Disorder* which was later withdrawn. She was quite seductive in her efforts to get attention.

Ted arrived in the class in mid-October, and buried his head in a book during his first music circle. He was the youngest in the class, and, notwithstanding his verbal intelligence, he did not read. Ted had a large body, and people mistook him for older than his 5.11 years. Ted loved to dance and play music with his family.

Daniel came to class in February from a period of hospitalization for depression and suicidal ideation. He was on anti-depression medication. He was very intelligent and quickly was recognized as having the highest academic ability in the class. He was 7 years old, and read at third grade level.

Individual music therapy assessments were conducted during the first week of classes by two music therapists, the author and a colleague also working at the school. The assessments involved one therapist observing while the other engaged each student in two play-like interactions using improvisation on simple percussion instruments. The students were rated on scales measuring interaction with the tester, self-control, self-expression in music, and motivation. Only three of the students described above were available for assessment on that day and all three showed no difficulty in any of the areas.

METHOD

The author worked with this classroom in half-hour music therapy sessions, held twice a week for a total of 59 sessions during the school year. The classroom space was very small. The children had two classroom teachers who attended the music therapy sessions. Both were well-versed in behavioral techniques needed to manage explosive behaviors. These included negative reinforcement (a progressive system of "time-outs" for inappropriate behaviors), and intermittent token economy or star systems for encouraging positive behaviors.   Although the primary role of the teachers was instructional in nature, they also supported the goals of the counseling staff in dealing with the children. All of the children were required to have individual counseling, and family counseling was available through a social worker. The progress of each child in meeting educational and therapeutic goals was monitored through *Individual Education Plans.* The music therapist attended regular team meetings and case conferences.

Several techniques were integrated into the therapeutic plan. Games were used to stimulate the children to spontaneously develop their own rules and variations (Orff, 1974).   Musical instruments and props were used to help the children express themselves. An adaptation of Dalcroze's techniques was used to encourage the children to express musical ideas through natural body movement (Hibben, 1984). Music was used to enhance, motivate, identify and contain the children's movement and play.   And in concert with the philosophy of the school, the therapist helped children identify their behaviors in the here-and-now, and conscientiously reinforced positive actions and interactions.

The children's histories showed a lack of stimulating or "good enough" environments (Winnicott, 1971), and in some cases, the ADHD disorder meant that normal or "good enough" mothering was not enough. The approach taken in music therapy, therefore was to use music (e.g., songs, instrument, stories and props) as *transitional objects* to help the children, through their play, to bridge their inner psychic experiences with the outer world.   In many of the sessions described below the song, story, instrument or prop became a container for action.   As the year progressed the children became better able to use these concrete objects or, in the case of songs and stories, predictable time-lines to experiment with and share ideas and feelings.

GOALS AND ORIENTATION

The goals of music therapy were different from classroom instructional goals. During classroom instruction, the children's behaviors were monitored on an individual basis, and interaction between children was discouraged; the children worked at individual desks with one-on-one instruction as much as possible.   During music therapy sessions, the children were encouraged to experience group play, and to work at developing play behaviors such as taking risks, tolerating ambiguity, using abstract thinking and sharing ideas.

The academic classroom can be thought of as a task oriented group in which there is submission of individual needs and styles to learning goals. The music therapy group sessions were intended to be different since the focus was on the reorientation of the children toward group awareness, intimacy, bonding, cooperation, and the problems of ego support and ego defense.

The music therapist also brought a different perspective to team meetings. Usually, team discussions focused on the individual child's progress, as manifested in short-term events and their specific impacts on the child's emotions and learning. The music therapist, although sharing concern about short-term events, looked at the long-term evolution of the group and evaluated the children's social and emotional growth in terms of expectations for the children relative to the stages of group development. From the music therapist's perspective, individual growth had to be viewed in terms of the norms for group behavior. Only the most needy children would continually resist or defy group consensus.

Group theorists describe the stages through which a group progresses in various ways (Garland & Jones & Kolodny, 1976; James & Freed, 1989; Lacoursiere, 1980; Schmuck & Schmuck, 1979; Siepker & Kandaras, 1985). All agree that the more cohesive a group becomes, the more possible it is to attain individual goals. A cohesive group is one in which the children trust each other enough to risk exposure, in which individual differences are accepted and where children can experiment with roles and alternate modes of behavior. The year long story of this classroom is one in which the children move from a group stage in which few are willing to risk exposure to one in which self-learning through action is possible and positive. The stages of group development proposed by Garland et al (1976) are used to describe the changes in this classroom.

TREATMENT PROCESS

Pre-Affiliation Stage

The Pre-Affiliation Stage is a time when children vacillate between approach and avoidance, and when they struggle to avoid pain and disappointment in the group. The therapist needs to allow distance, to invite trust, and to facilitate activities which do not have set rules that require interaction, competency, touching, or even eye contact.

On the first day, the class was calmly seated in a circle with Nancy, the teacher who had worked with most of them last year. The therapist began the session with a song that used the children's names, but slightly altered for rhyming purposes. The song, intended to identify and affirm everyone in the group, was ended prematurely: Arnie had disowned his name and said he wasn't going to stay in the circle. He had shown so much confidence in playing during the music therapy assessment, but he did not have the ego strength to be singled out in this group of peers. Ken's name brought teasing from several sources; Michael, guarding against psychic contact with his fellow, abruptly left the circle; Paul covered his ears. Fear and anxiety spread contagiously. Only Nathaniel, who had approached the music therapist on several previous occasions, handled his anxiety by allying with the therapist. In fact, Nathaniel, who seemed to have all the answers, used the therapist to help him keep distance from peers.

Approach/avoidance was normal for this stage of group development and thus the behaviors of the children (in retrospect) were understandable. This beginning pointed up the importance of using a theory of group development as a framework for planning activities and for identifying those variations from the norm that had diagnostic or evaluative significance for the team. For instance, in the first few weeks, Nathaniel's need to establish close identity with the music therapist to the exclusion of his peers was an interesting deviation from the norm, one which perhaps gave indication of a disordered personality.

Knowing now that the group was not, as it seemed with Nancy sitting at the helm, ready for sharing, the therapist came to the next session with a story song, "I had a Rooster." The song provided a safe container for the children since it did not require interaction, and it gave them time to develop some trust in the therapist. The therapist began with drawings of the various animals to incorporate in the song. "This is a baby song" someone said, but the group soon became mesmerized. They were safe. No participation or interaction was required, although guessing was encouraged. In the next two weeks, similar activities followed, allowing the children to engage in parallel play and to contribute to the group at their own rate.

At the end of September, Nathaniel was permanently moved to the next classroom to make room for a new student. At the same time, the children learned that Nancy, their teacher, was leaving in several weeks. The rooster song could now serve another important purpose. It could provide a vehicle for the children to talk about Nathaniel, to draw him, sing about him, and acknowledge ambivalent feelings at the loss. This time the need of the children to share feelings propelled them into a period of greater intimacy, which foreshadowed movement to the next stage of group development.

The last two weeks with Nancy were a like a honeymoon period for the group. The children brought to the music circle several sea creatures which they had picked up on a field trip. The name-rhyme song used on the first day provided the ideal structure for incorporating everyone's creature into a group activity, and the children responded so well that the song became their new opening ritual.

Nancy left in mid-October, about the same time as the arrival of a new student, Ted, and the new head teacher, Katherine. Katherine was faced with a regressed group, one in which each child was dealing with the threat, the hurt, and the insecurity of these changes. On the first day that Katherine had the class by herself, the music therapist observed the following: Ted was yelling and grabbing his toy from the nearest desk; Arnie was morose and not meeting the therapist's eyes; Hattie ran up and begged for permission to leave; Michael played compulsively at his desk with a few legos; Ken colored obliviously; and two others were in Timeout. No one greeted the therapist. Jose acknowledged, in disappointed tones, that he thought that it was lunch time.

How would it be possible to help these isolated individuals learn to express their anger and disappointment and to find, if not solace, at least common identity in each other? Was it possible to help these children, each so desperate for friends, to interact as a group? How could the therapist change the children's view of the classroom (and the world) as a hostile, threatening environment? In their minds and hearts, they fear they had been dumped because nobody cared about them and because they were dumb. Certainly time and consistent caring would help. The therapist hoped that, through playful activity under the umbrella of music, the children would release their anxiety and be more able to share their feelings and increase their sense of self-worth.

But this day, Arnie and Michael refused to come to the circle. The therapist put a big paper sheet on the easel and began the rooster song. Groans, fidgets and epithets of despair greeted the therapist's question about how they could talk about missing Nancy. The rooster song was Nancy's favorite, and now the therapist began to draw Nancy to elicit verses about her. Gradually the children got caught up in the tangible figure developing before their eyes. Each child took a crayon to draw what he/she remembered about Nancy: shoes, pencil, hair (drawn by Paul not near the head, but nobody criticized his contribution this time). Everyone sat dazed by the growing portrait and mesmerized by the guitar and singing, growing as it did with each contribution. Suddenly, Michael jumped up from his desk, overwhelmed by need, and pushing aside the last child, drew and drew and drew, unable to stop covering the page with undecipherable feelings about Nancy.

The children gradually began to accept the idea that their group would continue. But for several weeks the children could not be enticed into the circle, and if one did form, it would erupt into physical or verbal aggression. Interactions were either aggressive or non-existent. The therapist's attempts to give controls or leadership to the children through individual turns often backfired because the children would refuse to take any risks.

Power and Control Stage

By November, the children were no longer avoiding contact but were beginning to jockey for positions of power and status, both among themselves and with the therapist. The children in this stage were struggling with the need to form alliances for protection or aggression, and were not yet ready to try out new roles. The therapist planned songs and rules for turn-taking to provide the structure and safety in which the children could negotiate their power struggles and develop their ego strength and self-control.

Instruments and other concrete objects were used for the children to act upon. These objects became receptacles for the children's self expression. In a session worth describing, the therapist brought in combs and tissue paper, enough for everyone to make a kazoo (humming into the tissue) for accompanying one of Jose's favorite songs, "Turkey in the Straw." The activity became cacophonous as issues of power, control and scapegoating took over. "Why can't we have real instruments?" "Mine doesn't work." "Look at Arnie combing his greasy hair" "Who wants this song, anyway?" At least everyone was participating. Ted, who knew how to make his kazoo sound, began to help another. Before the end of the half-hour the song was sung many times with a wooden jumping jack (dancing Appalachian doll) and a washboard passed around the circle for added rhythmic flavor.

In this activity, the therapist gave controls to the children as much as possible. The children had to negotiate to keep the group together so that everyone would get a turn with the jumping jack, but the therapist had to protect individuals by establishing the order of turn-taking. The music acted as its own reward: if they did not play, the music would not be as good; if they did play, they would have a greater sense of pride in making their own music. The therapist purposely introduced the kazoos as a task requiring a moderate amount of competency, hoping to encourage positive leadership to emerge. The group tested the therapist's tolerance: Is it OK to reject the instruments she had provided? The therapist helped the children be aware of the impact their behaviors had on the group, and to sort out issues, such as: "It's OK to be angry, but it's not OK to hit Jose".

In the days before the December holidays, the children's anxiety reached new peaks. It was no longer safe or possible to go to the circle, as close proximity would trigger aggression. On one particular occasion, when Arnie and Ted were in an in-school suspension (out of the room) for inappropriate behaviors, the therapist played a tape for the children to draw to individually at their desks. This regression to the need for parallel rather than interactive play was not surprising during this stressful time before the holidays.

In January, the room had been rearranged and the circle of chairs was around a low table. The therapist encouraged the group to use the table as a bonding instrument, by introducing a chorus/verse song which had spaces in the chorus in which to "play" the table in what became known as "The Boom-boom Song." Although not everyone could coordinate this auditory/motor task, there was at once a feeling of being an ensemble: a metaphor, the therapist hoped, for the new year. Paul never got in synchrony with this rhythmic game, even after much encouragement from the group, and despite his interest and focus in trying to get it "right." The evaluation made from this highly motivated behavior was valuable for the team's treatment planning for Paul.

Intimacy Stage

During this stage, the children began to use the group session to practice and try out new behaviors. The children were ready to risk taking control and being a leader. Even if several children were not able to play by the rules, the whole group would not fall apart. The children now wanted others to know them, and were therefore more willing to show intimate feelings through their playing, moving and short verbal comments. The therapist's aim was to move the children to take more responsibility for the group activities, to urge them to make the rules, to be the leaders, and to share their intimate selves.

To raise the level of affective involvement in the group, the therapist now intentionally introduced activities which encouraged individual gross motor movement. The "Boom-boom Song" became the vehicle and the structure for a movement game. At first the therapist supplied a choice of hats to inspire the movement, but later the children did not need such inspiration. The music gave the children's movement both context and beauty, since the therapist, using guitar or drum and voice, matched the quality of the music to the physical and emotional quality of their movement. The returning chorus of the song (Boom- boom) helped focus the group. Each child used this game for his/her own needs, and indeed each child's needs became apparent in the process: Ted got to display his rap dance for all to admire; Arnie refused to take a turn but played an accompaniment throughout on the claves; Paul showed that he could dance backwards (It was Hattie's idea and Paul was successful only in short spurts); Michael got "crazy" in his dance, his hyperactivity spiraling, and had to be called back to the table; Ken didn't want a turn at first, fearing that he might be ridiculed for being fat, but later he put on an army hat and marched in and out of the desks, drawing a few positive comments from his peers. The children had taken control of the activity by choosing their movement and thus influencing the music. And, by confining their movement to the length of time of the song, they demonstrated remarkable self-control and an ability to sublimate their needs to those of the group. Only Michael had lacked the ability to self-regulate to which the therapist commented, "It looks like the movement brought up feelings which made you speed up your action out of control". Each child had discovered something new about him/herself and had been supported in that expression by the music and the group.

One day in early March, after Daniel had been in the room for two weeks, Katherine stopped the music therapist conspiratorially in the hall before class to say that the children were all hiding in the room, playing a hide-and-seek game. Upon entering the classroom, there was not a sound and the therapist had to search out each child---except for Hattie who stood up and said, "I'm over here." The children showed great strides in trust, risk taking and cooperation in this play, though the play was typical of much younger children. That day Ted brought his book, Frog Went A-Courtin', and let Hattie hold the book while the therapist sang and the others were caught up by the pictures. By teasing the therapist about the "ahummm, ahummm" at the end of each verse, the children showed that they were now viewing the therapist more intimately ("You remind me of my uncle") and were, in their new strength, no longer fearful that the therapist would desert or rebuke them. The classroom atmosphere was changing, although there were many setbacks as each child succumbed to the pressures and anxieties that arose. Katherine, their teacher, was also able to engage the group in learning games in which interaction was the stimulus. This was an important step in implementing a language based curriculum.

With time, the group began to develop its own agenda. In each session, one child or another would request a new "subject" for the opening riddle/song. Individual children would ask to lead the closing ritual. Some children brought in instruments or songbooks from home to share during the session. For the first time, the class asked what the other classes were doing during music, as though they suddenly were aware of themselves as an entity, possibly even a music group. They talked of taping a song for Jose (who had recently moved to the next class) so that they could share it with him at lunch time: "Yeh, Ted can use his keyboard thing and I'll get the congo" or "Yeh, man, we can show him our instruments".

During March and April the class developed a number of games that required cooperation, interaction and skill. In one bean bag tossing game, there was team play, pleasure, tolerance of frustration, and negotiating (pleading) for turns. A song was still there to keep the action going and to bond the group, while also lessening the anxiety of being unnoticed or unconnected. The song was a container for the group action as other songs had been before. Michael tried hard to sabotage this game by getting everyone to laugh at his acting out. For him the closeness of the group encouraged a negative bonding based on sexual inferences. Daniel (the new student) emerged as a leader and Ted, who wanted desperately to be a leader himself, regressed to struggles more typical of the previous stage of power and control.

At the beginning of May, the group created a drama that was a high point in their growth toward group cohesion. The drama was based on the story song, Frog Went A-Courtin'. Daniel, as the moth, laid out the table cloth and each child chose a part and danced the action using props he/she improvised from the room. They did the song in its entirety two times and when Ted, as the cat, came to disrupt Mister Frog's and Miss Mousie's wedding party, there was a chase. The children, responding to Ted's symbolic aggression or to the real fear of being caught, found hiding places. Of course, there was dissension and arguing and occasionally a need for the therapist to set limits, but there was also negotiation and new roles for just about everyone.

Although each child was able to try out new behaviors during this drama, the child's investment in defending his/her ego blotted out awareness of the action of others except when it was threatening. The group was not able to discuss or to mutually identify individual needs or actions. But the children experienced themselves in new roles, and were beginning a positive cycle toward development of feelings of self-worth. The school year ended before the group reached the Separation-Cohesion Stage (Garland et al, 1976). The children were too young and too needy as individuals to tolerate and accept individual differences and to support each other in the open forum of group play. In the next year they would develop individual ego strength that would allow them to mutually support their differences and to grow further.

DISCUSSION AND CONCLUSIONS

A major issue in music therapy group work with this population (as in all counseling work) was one of closeness and trust. In this group it was difficult to address individual goals without the emotional support and trust of the group. The therapist was concerned with accelerating the move toward intimacy (reaching group cohesion), and therefore planned interventions that encouraged growth in sharing and trying out of new roles. There was always a tension between the therapist's efforts to encourage intimacy and the groups readiness or stage of development.

A schema for thinking about the structure of music therapy activities was helpful (Hibben, 1991). The activities were thought of in terms of five dimensions: the amount of interaction required; the controls or leadership (how much control the children had); the level of movement; the rules; and the competency expectations (Vinter, 1974). During the year, the children progressed in their abilities to handle these various dimensions, and the therapist responded by gradually increasing the levels required in each dimension in order to achieve group cohesion and to facilitate individual growth.

During the first stage described above, the therapist (through the music) controlled the activity and the children were not able or expected to take leadership roles or to tolerate interaction, movement or complicated rules and skill requirements. In the next stage the therapist gave impetus to the move toward cohesion by encouraging interaction, responsibility, and leadership in activities such as the kazoo/instrumental improvisation. In the third stage the therapist planned an expanded movement dimension, encouraging the children to greater intimacy, sharing and expression of feelings. The children negotiated rules and roles and they took control of the games through their movement. The therapist purposely increased the competency dimension in the "Boom-boom Song" by requiring the booms to be played in the right spot. This served to challenge the children and to strengthen pride in accomplishment, a factor influencing group solidarity. The level of competency required was never so high that the children became task oriented in lieu of practicing social/interactional skills.

If the year had been longer, the children might have begun to interact with more intimacy, giving support to each other. Individual children might have begun to risk leadership roles such as planning or conducting a group improvisation. As it was, in May the children still needed the rules, structure, and controls inherent in songs or games to sustain their interactions. In terms of the activity dimensions, the interaction, movement and competency expectation dimensions were intermittently at high levels. The children's ability to lead or control the activities by deciding the rules was limited by the lack of ability to defer gratification of their own needs and by their inexperience with other play behaviors.

The music therapist used group developmental stage theory as a context for evaluating individual progress in social, emotional, cognitive, and perceptual-motor areas. As the year went on, the group music activities stimulated more actions and interactions that were in themselves corrective emotional experiences. These experiences were made possible by the children's ability to tolerate longer periods of closeness and by their ability to accept responsibility for their behaviors. The music helped move the group toward greater cohesion by holding the children together in its sound. Many times the music acted as structure for the group activity; the music provided boundaries in time such as repetition and closure, allowing the children to experiment safely within. The children entered into a kind of social contract through music-making and were rewarded by the music itself.

The music inspired the children in many ways, through: the movement of the beat, the associations with familiar songs, the metaphors for something funny, beautiful or lofty, and the messages within the lyrics.

GLOSSARY

Attention-Deficit Hyperactivity Disorder (ADHD): A disruptive behavior disorder, described in the DSM-IIIR, in which a person has developmentally inappropriate degrees of inattention, impulsiveness, and hyperactivity. Weisberg & Greenberg (1988) suggest that between 3-5% of school aged children have this disorder. These children do not put judgement between impulse and action, and tend not to feel responsible, because they do not believe they have the control that they do. The following features are associated with ADHD: emotional lability, low frustration tolerance, poor school performance, poor peer relationships, and low self-esteem.

Auditory Aphasia: An inability to understand spoken words due to a dysfunction of the brain centers.

Individual Education Plan (IEP): A requirement of Public Law 94-142 (Education for All Handicapped Children Act, 1977), the IEP is a written statement which includes annual goals, short term objectives and services for any handicapped child (up to age 22). IEPs are prepared jointly by the child's teachers, therapists, and parents under the supervision of the Public School Special Education Administrator.

Learning Disabilities: A general term indicating defects in the ability to learn basic school-taught skills such as reading, writing and mathematics. The diagnosis is found in the DSM-IIIR under Academic Skill Disorders (Specific Developmental Disorders, Axis 11). Children with learning disabilities may have normal intelligence but exhibit difficulty with sequencing, with symbol recognition, in attending to or isolating visual or auditory information, and with certain perceptual motor skills, all of which are necessary for academic achievement.

Oppositional Defiant Disorder: A disruptive behavior disorder described in the DSM-IIIR as showing a pattern of negativistic, argumentative, hostile and defiant behavior, but without serious violations of the rights of others.

Transitional Object: An object which can be used by the infant in place of or to simulate the comfort of the mother's breast (Winnicott, 1971). A child whose nurturing is constant and "good enough" is able to use the object (such as the thumb or, later, a song) as a replacement for or a bridge over to the desired object (the breast or the presence of the nurturer). With the transitional object the child moves from magical, passive control (cry and the food comes) to active manipulation. The development of the capacity to use an object in play as representation or replacement of something else depends on a facilitating environment, it is not inborn.

REFERENCES

Garland, J., Jones, H., & Kolodny, R.L. (1976). A model for stages of development in social work groups. In S. Bernstein (Ed.), Explorations in Group Work: Essays in Theory and Practice (pp. 17-71). Boston, MA: Charles River Books.

Hibben, J.K. (1984). Movement as musical expression in a music therapy setting. Music Therapy, 4, 91-98.

Hibben, J.K. (1991, in press). Identifying dimensions of music therapy activities appropriate for children at different stages of group development. Arts in Psychotherapy, 18.

James, M.R., & Freed, B.S. (1989). A sequential model for developing group cohesion in music therapy. Music Therapy Perspectives, 7, 28-34.

Lacoursiere, R.B. (1980). Life Cycle of Groups: Groups Development Stage Theory. NY: Human Sciences Press.

Orff, G. (1974). The Orff Music Therapy: Active Furthering of the Development of the Child. St. Louis, MO: MMB Music.

Schmuck, R.A., & Schmuck, P.A. (1979). Group Process in the Classroom. Dubuque, Iowa: W.M.C Brown.

Siepker, B.B., & Kandaras, C.S. (1985). Group Therapy with Children and Adolescents. NY: Human Sciences Press.

Vinter, R.D. (1974). Program activities: Their selection and use in a therapeutic milieu. In P. Glasser, R. Sarri & R. Vinter (Eds.), Individual Change through Small Broups (pp. 244-257). New York: The Free Press.

Weisberg, L.W., & Greenberg, R. (1988). When Acting Out Isn't Acting: Understanding Child and Adolescent Temper, Anger and Behavior Disorders. Washington, D.C.: The Psychiatric Institutes of America Press.

Winnicott, D.W. (1971). Playing and reality. New York: Tavistock Publications.

The Effect Of Programmed Pitch Practice And Private Instruction On The Vocal Reproduction Accuracy Of Hearing Impaired Children: Two Case Studies

ALICE-ANN DARROW, Ph.D., RMT-BC
Associate Professor of Music Education and Music Therapy
The University of Kansas

and

NICKI COHEN, Ph.D., RMT-BC
Instructor at Lockhaven University

Abstract: *Two case studies are presented showing the effect of programmed pitch practice via the PITCH MASTER and private vocal instruction on the ability of hearing impaired children to vocally reproduce pitches and pitch sequences. The first case is a 12-year-old girl with* **severe hearing loss** *who showed significant improvement after six weeks of daily practice; the second case is an 11-year-old girl with* **profound hearing loss** *who also showed significant improvement after three months of instruction.*

INTRODUCTION

The acquisition of singing skills is basically controlled by the ear. Young children learn to sing by imitating the sounds of others. Children with *hearing impairments* have the physical capacity to sing as well as any hearing child; however, due to limited aural access to the stimulus sounds made by others, their vocal skills develop more slowly and require supplementary instruction.

Since the mid 1800s, the majority of articles written about music for the deaf have described the development of instrumental music programs or the use of rhythm activities to improve speech production. Turner and Bartlett (1848) advocated the use of music as a source of "intellectual gratification and enjoyment" but felt that only instrumental music should be taught. Singing was used primarily for group recreation purposes (Solomon, 1980). In 1900, Jordon wrote an article that described singing as a means of controlling the vocal utterances of deaf children. Sandberg (1926) and Redfield (1927) made observations regarding the characteristics of deaf children's singing voice. More recent articles have advocated singing as a vehicle of self-expression (Rutkowski, 1985) or as a means of improving the speech and language development of the hearing impaired child (Darrow, 1989; Gfeller & Darrow, 1987).

The lack of attention given to the singing voice of hearing impaired children may be due to the fact that they are generally not considered singers---given the unusual voice quality which often accompanies a hearing loss. Children with *moderate to profound hearing losses* often have speech and voice characteristics that differ significantly from those of normal hearing children. Common characteristics of deaf speech include a higher *fundamental frequency* (Angelocci, Kopp, & Holbrook, 1964; Nickerson, 1975) and less variation in pitch (Hood & Dixon, 1969). The primary vocal characteristic of the severely hearing impaired is generally regarded as a high-pitched monotone.

Singing remains the primary means of performance in the elementary music classroom; because of this, vocal accuracy has often been a topic of discussion and investigation among music educators (Apfelstadt, 1986, 1988; Geringer, 1982; Sims, Moore & Kuhn, 1982; Small & McEachern, 1983). Because of aggressive mainstreaming policies, many hearing impaired children are now participating in vocal music programs. A number of suggestions for improving vocal accuracy have been proposed which are also applicable to the hearing impaired singer; such as early vocal training, use of appropriate models and feedback, structured practice, and consideration of the range of vocal material (Franklin & Franklin, 1988; Joyner, 1969). However, the vocal accuracy problems of hearing-impaired singers extend beyond those encountered in the regular classroom. Additional sources of assistance are required for the hearing impaired singer.

Few studies exist which specifically address the vocal skills of hearing impaired children. Darrow (1988) found the mean range of hearing impaired children's singing voice was significantly smaller and the midpoint significantly lower. This conflicts with common tonal characteristics of deaf speech which generally include a higher fundamental frequency than normal speech and frequently little variation in pitch. Darrow and Starmer (1986) found that vocal exercise can lower the fundamental frequency, and increase the frequency range of hearing impaired children's speech. Darrow (1990) evaluated the effect of *frequency adjustment* of a vocal stimulus on the ability to reproduce pitches. Stimulus frequencies were adjusted in accordance with subjects' *audiogram* via a standard stereo frequency band equalizer. Frequencies were amplified in relation to the subject's configuration and degree of loss. The data indicated stimulus frequency adjusted in accordance with the subject's audiogram may make auditory stimuli more accessible. The positive results of this study provided the impetus for the investigation of additional techniques which may improve the vocal intonation of hearing impaired singers.

One such technique is the use of the PITCH MASTER. Subjects sit at this electronic device and listen through headphones to a cassette tape at their most comfortable listening level (MCL). Following recorded instruction auditorially received or interpreted into sign, single pitches or pitch patterns are presented for the subject to sing back into a microphone. The device then measures the accuracy of the subject's response by tallying each quarter-second during which the pitch is sung correctly. The subject's numerical score is compared to a given acceptable score for each exercise.

The purpose of the present case studies was to examine the effect of programmed pitch practice via the PITCH MASTER and private voice instruction on the ability of two hearing impaired children to vocally reproduce pitches and pitch patterns.

CASE ONE

Assessment

Sara was a twelve-year old girl who had expressed a desire to sing in the junior high school chorus. Her musical background consisted of two years of piano, considerable family involvement in music activities, and participation in her elementary school music program. Her hearing loss is classified as *severe to profound* with a greater loss in the left ear. Her source of auditory amplification was an over-the-ear aide. Her method of communication was both oral and through sign.

A pre-test was given to assess Sara's vocal reproduction skills prior to treatment. A test tape specifically designed for the PITCH MASTER was used. Test stimuli consisted of twelve random pitches from the B flat below middle C to the B flat above. The results are shown in Table 1.

Treatment

A program of pitch practice was set up for the subject utilizing the vocalization tapes which accompany the PITCH MASTER. The program consisted of pitch matching exercises of increasing difficulty. Fourteen tapes were used.

Evaluation

The pretest was re-administered midway through the program and at the very end (See Table 1). In addition, daily data were recorded for each of the exercises on the fourteen practice tapes. Approximately six weeks of daily practice were required for Sara to meet proficiency criteria established by the program authors for the fourteen tapes.

A statistical analysis of the data was made by comparing pre- and post-test scores using the t-test. Results indicated an improvement, though not significant, in Sara's ability to reproduce a given pitch or pitch pattern between the pretest and midtest evaluation (t = 1.26, df = 11, p = .23); however, results did indicate a significant improvement in her ability to reproduce a given pitch or pitch pattern between the pre- and posttest evaluation (t = 2.14, df = 11, p = .05), indicating a need for program completion, or intense daily practice with the PITCH MASTER over a period of at least six weeks, in order for pitch accuracy improvement to occur.

Table 1

MEANS AND STANDARD DEVIATIONS (SD) FOR PRE, MID, AND POSTTESTS

TEST	MEAN	SD
Pretest	6.33	5.59
Midtest	7.75	4.51
Posttest	9.91	2.77

Data were recorded for exercises as they were completed in order to examine the difficulty of each exercise and the course of changing criteria for successfully completing each exercise. Considering the increasing difficulty of the practice tapes, recorded data revealed relatively similar vocal performance accuracy scores across all sessions, indicating a gradual chain of successive approximations to the terminal goal of pitch matching accuracy. These data also indicate no abrupt transitions in the course of changing criteria.

Figure 1

SARA: PERCENTAGES OF CORRECT RESPONSES
ON PRACTICE TAPES

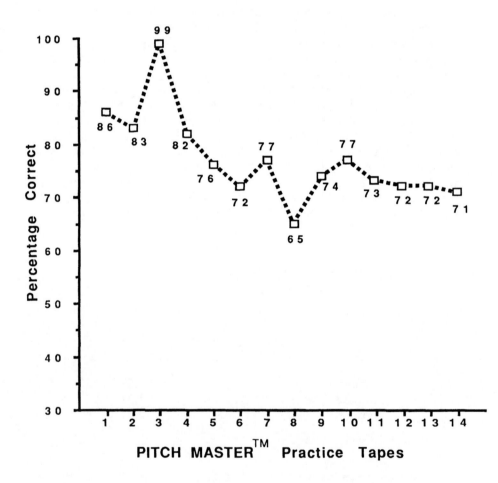

CASE TWO

Assessment

Adele was an eleven-year-old girl with an 80% hearing loss in her left ear and a 100% loss in her right ear. Adele had requested singing lessons so that she would be able to sing well enough to participate in the school chorus. Her family had considerable involvement with musical activities; particularly her father, who has a degree in music and had at one time, been a public school music teacher. Her source of auditory amplification was an over-the-ear aide. Her method of communication was oral only.

A pretest of Adele's ability to reproduce 20 pitches was administered at the first meeting. Results indicated that she vocally reproduced 64% of the pitches correctly on part one of the test and 45% of the pitches on part two of the test (See Figures 2 and 3). Adele was unable to reproduce any pitches consistently in 4:4 trials. The majority of her vocal tones were restricted to the chest register. Other vocal deficiencies included a strong nasality, a pushed, loud production when singing higher pitches, a *hypo-supported,* breathy vocal sound and poor diction.

A Toshiba portable stereo and Realistic audio cassette were used to record the test data. The researcher and another judge listened to the tape and evaluated it as nominal data, on or off the given pitch. Based on the results of the pretest and Adele's vocal deficiencies, an instructional strategy was developed. Goals formulated for improving her vocal technique were: 1) to strengthen *diaphragmatic and costal breathing*, 2) to develop a higher vocal register, 3) to create a kinaesthetic vocabulary that would correct vocal placement and improve intonation, and 4) to reinforce vocal flexibility and freedom.

Treatment

Weekly lessons were held in a room with a wooden floor to provide better vibratory feedback. Adele sat in a chair facing the piano with her knees touching the sound board. She was taught solfeggio syllables and hand signs to accompany vocal exercises. The solfeggio helped to give her a space-frame in which pitches could kinaesthetically be placed. Assignments were written out on manuscript paper and then recorded on cassette tape using the assigned pitches to be sung. Along with vocal exercises, Adele was given melodies in solfeggio notation. A discussion of rudimentary music theory accompanied the solfeggio instruction to assist her in developing a clearer sense of the pitch relationships, to identify harmonic intervals and to improve rhythmic accuracy.

After two months of vocal instruction, Adele began working on song literature, including: show songs such as "Do Re Mi" and "Sixteen Going on

Seventeen" (from <u>The Sound of Music</u>), popular songs such as "Out Here On My Own," and traditional songs such as "Oh What A Beautiful Morning." She was initially assigned songs with simple, diatonic melodies and relatively small ranges. In the piano accompaniment, no pedal was used and the melody was played with detached articulation in order to clarify the correct pitches. As her capacity to sing words and pitches improved, she was given repertoire with larger intervals, larger ranges and a faster rate of diction.

Evaluation

After three months of instruction, Adele was given the initial two-part pitch matching assessment. Part-one consisted of diatonic "mi- re- do" and part-two consisted of diatonic, descending "sol- fa- mi- re- do". Adele was able to correctly reproduce 85% of the pitches on part one and 75% on part two (See Figures 2 and 3).

Figure 2

ADELE: PERCENTAGES OF MATCHED PITCHES ON PART ONE

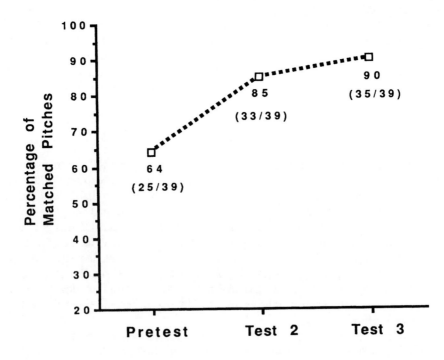

Seven pitches were matched consistently in 4:4 trials. Results of this test indicated a 21% improvement on part one and 30% improvement on part two. Five months later, the assessment instrument was again administered with Adele matching 90% accuracy on part one and 94% accuracy on part two. Fourteen pitches were matched consistently in 4:4 trials. When compared to pretest scores, the final figures represented a 26% improvement on part one and a 49% improvement on part two. A reliability check on data evaluation was conducted for all three tests. Interrater reliability was .88.

Figure 3

ADELE: PERCENTAGES OF MATCHED PITCHES ON PART TWO

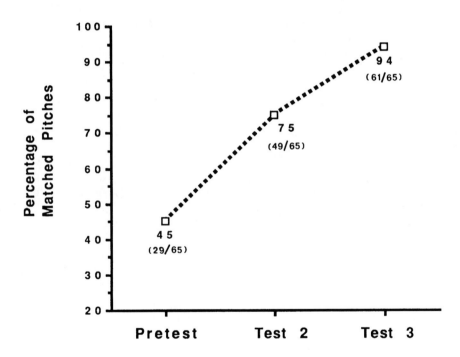

DISCUSSION

The purpose of the present studies was to examine the effect of programmed pitch practice via the PITCH MASTER and private voice instruction on the ability of two hearing impaired children to vocally reproduce given pitches and pitch patterns. Data indicated a significant improvement in their vocal reproduction accuracy between the pre- and posttest conditions, reinforcing the hypothesis that the singing voice of a hearing impaired child can significantly improve with the kind of focused attention usually given to hearing children. Both girls auditioned and were accepted into the school chorus where they continue to receive vocal instruction. The only special accommodations that were made to facilitate their participation in the school chorus were 1) to place both singers in the front where they have better visual access to the director, and 2) to place them next to other students with excellent vocal accuracy and to whom they feel comfortable asking questions when they are unable to understand verbal directions. Follow up conferences were held with the choral director who reported that both students were "valuable members of the school chorus." It should be noted too that both Sara and Adele have musical home environments where vocal activities are initiated and encouraged, thus providing additional reinforcement and support.

Sara had four items on the pretest and two on the midtest for which she received no points for vocal accuracy, accounting for the high standard deviation scores. She received points for vocal accuracy on all twelve items on the posttest. Testing for vocal accuracy maintenance without the intense daily exercise should reveal interesting data in the future. After vocal accuracy is stabilized, more attention can be directed toward vocal quality, an important factor with hearing impaired singers.

Anecdotal data with Sara revealed that she enjoyed singing the exercises with the PITCH MASTER, and particularly enjoyed singing into the microphone and watching the feedback provided. Observation during posttesting revealed Sara's ability to modulate her voice until the feedback indicated she was within the margin of acceptable vocal reproduction accuracy.

Adele asked to make an audiocassette recording of one of her songs during the third month of vocal instruction. After listening to the recording, she commented on her vocal nasality and poor diction. Adele then focused on improving these two area. Another recording was made a month later; at this time, she asked if she might give the recording to a family member as a present. Performance feedback is particularly important for the hearing impaired child who cannot always adequately monitor their own vocal production, particularly during the process of vocalization.

Both sets of vocal practice procedures described in these studies can be utilized with other hearing impaired children. The procedure used with Sara should be employed with students capable of independent practice, able to record their progress, and those whose major deficit is vocal accuracy rather than vocal quality. This procedure may also be useful for music therapists who are not well trained in methods of vocal pedagogy. The procedure used with Adele should prove more beneficial to hearing impaired students with limited ability to self monitor their own vocalizations, students whose vocal quality requires special attention, and to those students willing to commit to regular lessons over a number of months. This procedure requires that the music therapist have some background in vocal training. These procedures, used in combination, would be particularly useful in reinforcing independent practice, improving vocal quality, and increasing vocal repertoire.

Additional suggestions for improving the vocal accuracy of hearing impaired children might be: (1) spending additional time with daily vocal exercise, and other vocal activities such as participation in vocal ensembles; (2) working with level two of the PITCH MASTER program; (3) providing tactile and visual feedback regarding vocal accuracy; (4) extending vocal study over a period of several years; (5) using peer models for the vocal stimulus; (6) using instrumental accompaniment for pitch references; and (7) using hand signals (i.e., Kodaly) as a kinesthetic as well as visual reference.

If hearing impaired children are to remain and participate in public school music programs and/or music therapy programs, continued research in the vocal characteristics of these students is warranted. Further research is also needed to examine the effect of active vocal participation on the intonation and intelligibility of hearing impaired children's speech.

ACKNOWLEDGEMENT

The authors would like to thank Music Therapy Perspectives, a publication of the National Association for Music Therapy, Inc., for permission to revise and reprint this case study.

GLOSSARY

Audiogram: A visual graph on which are an individual's response to sounds at different frequencies and levels of intensity are recorded.

Costal breathing: An expansion of the ribs upon inhalation.

Diaphragmatic breathing - The effective coordination of the diaphragm and abdominal muscles in breathing.

Hearing Impairment:(Heward & Orlansky, 1988, pp. 259-260)

Mild hearing loss: (41 to 55 dB). Understands conversational speech at a distance of 3 to 5 feet. May miss as much as 50% of conversation if not face-to-face. May have limited vocabulary and speech irregularities.

Moderate hearing loss: (56 to 70 dB). Can understand loud conversation only. Will have difficulty in group discussions. Is likely to have impaired speech, limited vocabulary, and difficulty in language use and comprehension.

Severe hearing loss: (71 to 90 dB). May hear loud voices about 1 foot from ear. May be able to identify environmental sounds. May be able to discriminate vowels, but not consonants. Speech and language likely to be impaired or to deteriorate.

Profound hearing loss: (91 dB or more). More aware of vibrations than tonal patterns. Relies on vision rather than hearing as primary means of communication. Speech and language likely to be impaired or to deteriorate, and are unlikely to develop spontaneously if loss is prelingual.

Fundamental Frequency: The frequency at which the sound vibrates as a whole. This may be expressed also as the lowest pitch that the sound source is capable of producing.

Frequency adjustment: Adjusting stimulus frequencies in accordance with a subject's audiogram via a standard stereo frequency band equalizer. Frequencies are amplified in relation to the subject's configuration and degree of loss.

Hypo-supported sound: A vocal sound which is characterized by lack of correct breath support, a shallow thin sound.

REFERENCES

Angelocci, A.A., Kopp, G.A., & Holbrook, A. (1964). The vowel formats of deaf and normal hearing eleven- to fourteen-year-old boys. Journal of Speech and Hearing Disorders, 29, 159-170.

Apfelstadt, H. (1986). Perceptual learning modality and vocal accuracy among second graders. Update: The Application of Research in Music Education, 4 (2), 6-9.

Apfelstadt, H. (1988). What makes children sing well? Update: The Application of Research in Music Education, 7 (1), 27-32.

Darrow, A.A. (1988). A comparison of vocal ranges of hearing impaired and normal hearing children. (Unpublished manuscript, The University of Kansas).

Darrow, A.A. (1990). The effect of frequency adjustment on the vocal reproduction accuracy of hearing impaired children. Journal of Music Therapy, 27, 24-33.

Darrow, A.A. & Starmer, G.J. (1986). The effect of vocal training on the intonation and rate of hearing impaired children's speech. Journal of Music Therapy, 32, 194-201.

Franklin, E. & Franklin, A.D. (1988). The uncertain singer. Update: The Application of Research in Music Education, 7 (1), 7-10.

Geringer, J.M. (1982). The relationship of pitch-matching and pitch discrimination abilities of preschool and fourth-grade students. Journal of Research in Music Education, 30, 93-99.

Gfeller, K. & Darrow, A.A. (1987). Music as a remedial tool in language acquisition programs for hearing impaired children. The Arts In Psychotherapy, 14, 229-235.

Heward, W.L. & Orlansky, M.D. (1988). Exceptional Children. Columbus, OH: Merrill Publishing Co.

Hood, R.B. & Dixon, R.F. (1969). Physical characteristics of speech rhythm of deaf and normal speakers. Journal of Communication Disorders, 2, 20-28.

Jordon, S.A. (1900). Rhythm as an aid to voice training. The Association Review (now The Volta Review), 2 (1), 16.

Joyner, D. (1969). The monotone problem. Journal of Research in Music Education, 17, 115-123.

Nickerson, R.B. (1975). Characteristics of the speech of deaf persons. Volta Review, 77, 342-362.

Redfield, J. (1927). Teaching music to the deaf. Scientific American, 136, 310-311.

Rutkowski, J. (1985). The child voice: An historical perspective. The Bulletin of Historical Research in Music Education, 6, 1-15.

Sandberg, I. (1926). Rhythm. Volta Review, 28, 310-323.

Sims, W., Moore, R., & Kuhn. T. (1982). Effects of female and male vocal stimuli, tonal pattern length, and age on vocal pitch-matching abilities of young children from England and the United States. Psychology of Music, Special Issue, 104-108.

Small, A. & McEachern, F. (1983). The effect of male and female vocal modeling on pitch-matching accuracy of first-grade children. Journal of Research in Music Education, 31, 227-233.

Solomon, A. (1980). Music in special education before 1930: Hearing and speech development. Journal of Research in Music Education, 28, 236-242.

Turner, W. & Bartlett, D. (1848). Music among the deaf and dumb. American Annals of the Deaf and Dumb, 2, 1-6.

Unit Three

_____

Case Studies With Adolescents

Improvised Songs Stories In The Treatment Of A Thirteen-Year-Old Sexually Abused Girl From The Xhosa Tribe In South Africa

HELEN HENDERSON L.T.C.L., L.R.S.M., A.D.R.M.
Music Therapist: Child and Family Unit
Red Cross Children's Hospital
Rondebosch, Cape Town, South Africa

Abstract: This case describes transcultural music psychotherapy with Patricia, a 13-year-old girl who had been sexually abused by her father, and who had witnessed the murder of her sister by her mother. Patricia was born into the Xhosa tribe in South Africa, and has grown up in a tribal environment; however, for the major part of the past year she has lived at a Christian children's home. Therapy has involved song improvisations, play therapy and psychotherapeutic techniques based on Grinnell's model of "Developmental Therapeutic Process." It has also required helping Patricia integrate Xhosa culture and Christian traditions with regard to spiritual matters and the role of music in healing. As a result, Patricia has gradually become able to express, mostly in song, her dilemma. Therapy is ongoing.

BACKGROUND INFORMATION

Patricia is a 13-year-old girl from the Xhosa tribe, who lived at a Christian children's home prior to her admission to an in-patient unit of the Red Cross Children's Hospital. There she was diagnosed as having *post-traumatic stress disorder, borderline intelligence,* and moderate to severe impairment in general functioning (50-60%). It was also noted that she had suffered severe, *catastrophic psychosocial stress* prior to the onset of these symptoms. Patricia was referred to the hospital because of bizarre behaviors, bad dreams, poor scholastic progress, and sexually provocative behavior.

Patricia is the seventh child born to her parents. Four of her older siblings have died. She grew up under extremely poor socioeconomic circumstances. Her mother and father are presently living together in conflict, following a divorce during which the mother was imprisoned. There is no family history of physical or psychiatric illness.

Patricia was sexually abused by her father since the age of 4 years. When she was 12-years-old, she was admitted to a children's home. At the time, her mother had been imprisoned for fatally assaulting Patricia's older sister, who had also been sexually abused by the father. Patricia witnessed the mother's assault and the death of her sister.

Upon entering the in-patient unit, Patricia presented as a shy, reserved adolescent. She was *apsychotic* and *euthymic* with appropriate affect. She spoke Afrikaans and Xhosa equally well, but gave the impression of limited, intellectual ability. Therapy was conducted in Afrikaans.

Because she participated actively in musical programs at the in-patient unit, it was decided to refer her to music therapy. The information given to me at the time of referral was that Patricia's dreams and behavior were causing the staff great concern. Her dreams involved her father appearing in the form of a snake who kept calling her to him. She would become very afraid after the dreams. It had been reported that Patricia was taken to a traditional healer (diviner) by her father after the mother had been imprisoned, in order to rid her of "the sickness". The process involved her swallowing a small snake. Patricia's subsequent behavior suggested that this "healing" experience was an extremely frightening one for her.

Since her admission to the unit, Patricia seemed pre-occupied with survival guilt and depression. She also demonstrated extremely low self-esteem. It was clear that she was in a state of emotional shock, and due to her stressful situation, she frequently appeared psychically numbed to ongoing experiences. Her free floating anxiety state resulted in her not knowing what to do much of the time. As a result of all this, her general functioning and social interaction at the children's home were quite impaired. The older children found her behavior peculiar, and would often call her "mad" and run away from her. This created a vicious cycle and resulted in her on-going catastrophic stress.

METHOD

I use a combined approach of music therapy, play therapy and psychotherapy, based on the Developmental Therapeutic Process model originated by Barbara Grinnell (1970). Through this approach, Patricia has been able to express herself in whatever medium she feels safest, and because it is nondirective, she herself has chosen to use songs to express her thoughts and anxieties while I improvise with her. "Through improvisation, the therapist can give permission and support to the child to express feelings that the child perceives as forbidden, dangerous and overwhelming. The musical structure and context of the song make it safer for the child to experience feelings kept out of consciousness because of their threatening nature" (Bruscia, 1987, 378-379).

The therapy room is equipped with a piano, drum, percussion instruments, projective play materials (i.e. dolls, puppets, animals, drawing paper, paints and crayons), as well as a small selection of African instruments. The African drum is made by a specialist in this field. The skin is usually that of an animal which has been killed specifically for the purpose of drum-making.

I work under the supervision of a clinical psychologist, and am part of an in-patient team consisting of three psychiatrists, four psychiatric nurses, the psychologist and myself. The aim of the in-patient unit is to provide help for children with psychiatric disorders by providing the appropriate treatment for each problem and not the same treatment for all problems. Thus, the unit provides an individualized program within a range of interdisciplinary services.

As a music therapist in a transcultural, psychotherapeutic setting, it is important that total consideration be given to the patient's cultural beliefs. Failure to do so is tantamount to treating the patient as a fragment rather than a whole person, and is therefore quite anti-therapeutic (Buhrman, 1984). Although often very confusing, I needed at all times to understand the mingling of Patricia's Xhosa and Christian beliefs and traditions. It has been very important for me to reflect these in my musical improvisations and in the my attempts to understand Patricia.

The Xhosa people constitute one of South Africa's most populace Bantu tribes. In keeping with the pace of change in the whole country, they have rapidly embraced western civilization over the past few decades and have moved to the cities and towns in large numbers. However, with this exposure to western beliefs, the Xhosas find themselves in the throes of rapid sociocultural transition. There is a converging of traditional Xhosa and western Christian perspectives, and many Xhosas have found comfort in African indigensed Christianity, which retains some customs of the traditional rural society, and yet has incorporated religious and social values of the western world.

Within these transcultural settings, the emphasis is strongly placed on healing and wholeness. Music is part of the healing process, and although songs are sung in English, the rhythms are devised from traditional Xhosa divination. Drumming is the foundation for African rhythm, while singing, clapping, swaying and dancing are second nature, and all forms of music-making play a vital role in religious and healing services.

TREATMENT PROCESS

Patricia has been receiving music therapy on a once-weekly basis. What follows is a description of the 5 sessions conducted to date.

Session One

Patricia entered the music therapy room and immediately related to the drums and xylophones as instruments with which to praise and worship God. She generated spontaneous rhythms on the drum and sang songs of praise. The songs were in English, but her drum beating was distinctly in the Xhosa tradition. I accompanied her on the piano and supported the sounds she was making as if they were a by-product of rhythmical movement rather than sounds produced and organized for their own sake.

Eventually she moved away from the instruments toward the puppets, and I suggested that we make up a story and put it into song. Her story was as follows (English translation):

> *There is a mother puppet who has two daughters. The father is in bed. The mother tells both daughters to fetch water. They both decide not to go. However, the younger daughter tells the mother that it was the older sister who did not want to go. The mother kills the older sister. The surviving younger sister tries to call back the deceased sister. When she can't, she kills the mother.*

As we set the story to music, I improvise supportively, offering her the empathic contact which she needs. The music was improvised so as to reflect her mood (a deeply serious one), and to provide the necessary structure and support. Her guilt concerning her sister's death was evident, as was her anger towards her mother. In her story, both daughters were disobedient towards the mother, but TBesa (Patricia's elder sister) suffered the consequences of Patricia's deceit. She felt responsible and needed to take revenge on the mother. This displacement of the actual events leading to TBesa's death is a feature of post-traumatic stress.

Patricia's feelings of responsibility and guilt were further exacerbated by events immediately following her sister's death, when her father took her to his family saying that she was "bewitched." He claimed that she saw snakes that talked to her. It is a cultural belief that the snake is an evil creature sent by a witch. Moreover, anyone who has an untimely death (such as TBesa) is believed to have died because of an evil agent. As a result, Patricia has fears that she is a witch (the evil agent), and that she was responsible for her sister's death. These fears further intensify her ongoing state of anxiety resulting from her own personal traumas.

Session Two

Unlike the first session, Patricia did not begin in a religious manner but instead explored different instruments in a tentative way. She then began to create a song story, proceeding line by line and waiting for my acknowledgement of each:

> *There is a family of a mother, father and two daughters.*
> *Everybody, excepting the mother, dies. However, they*
> *all come alive again.*

A new story then emerged:

> *There are two daughters. One is murdered but nobody*
> *knows how this happened. The mother finds her. The*
> *father puts her in a box and takes her to where all the*
> *dead people are buried. (Patricia bursts out laughing.*
> *She says, however, that she is feeling very sad).*

Moving to the African drum, Patricia proceeded to have a "conversation" on it, beating with her hands rather than with beaters. She continued for quite a while, and I decided to stop improvising an accompaniment. She then had a lengthy "conversation" with the drum. When finished, she turned to me and said that the drum had spoken to her. Among the Xhosa, it is through drumming that a diviner "talks" to the ancestors, and then hears their reply (Hansen, 1981). Patricia interpreted her conversation on the drum:

> *The mother and daughter must love one another. The*
> *drum has spoken. Everybody must love everybody.*
> *Mother you must not do it. Mother you must not do it.*
> *We must all love one another.*

Before leaving, Patricia asked to borrow a recorder so that she could communicate with her deceased sister at night before going to sleep. It is customary for Xhosas to use certain instruments to communicate with the deceased, for it is believed that they will listen. It also occured to me that, since many Christian songs of praise that Patricia knows contain words about "the breath of life," she might also want to use the recorder to put "breath" back into her sister's life. I honored her request because, culturally, music is always associated with spiritual communication, and as such is always "good." For Xhosas, music never invites evil.

The psychiatric team in the ward also consented, and agreed that someone should be with her whenever she fulfilled this task before going to sleep at night. Not a night would pass without Patricia playing to TBesa, and each time she would wail and express her deep sadness at TBesa's death.

Session 3

Patricia brought the recorder with her to this session, and asked me to accompany her. The mood she presented was a very serious one, and she requested that I play Christian songs of praise. She sang two or three songs in Xhosa, followed by a period of prayer during which I would continue to play quietly. This procedure continued for quite a while. Her songs became deeply expressive, and eventually tears flowed freely down her face. The main themes of the songs were that Jesus loved her, and that He was all-powerful and could perform miracles. What was most noticeable was her complete involvement in the songs, emotionally, physically and vocally. At all times she clung to the recorder. Finally, she finished with a prayer, and in an emotionally exhausted state with eyes downcast, left the room still holding onto the recorder.

Session 4

Patricia entered and immediately moved towards the wind instruments (recorder, reed horns, etc.), all of which were associated with her deceased sister. She began to freely improvise a song which she seemed intent on revealing something to me. I therefore decided not to accompany her but to listen.

> *My family are all together,*
> *and mother sends TBesa away.*
> *She does not return.*
> *We look for her.*
> *She is in the hospital.*
> *But when we get there, she is dead.*
> *Patricia longs for TBesa.*

She hears me when I play for her.
She cannot speak, she's dead.
But when I sing I know she hears
Although I know she's dead.

Afterwards, Patricia moved away from the wind instruments and chose to play gently on the soprano glockenspiel. I interpreted her improvisation, which was in 6/8 time, as an expression of her need for comfort, and I began to improvise an African lullaby. Our interaction continued for quite a while and she finally whispered that she was scared. I kept supporting her musically, reflecting the mood she was projecting, and she then decided to join me at the piano. Before beginning to improvise, she said: "I feel very mixed-up." I suggested that she play on the black keys only, thus enabling me to accompany her using the Pentatonic scale. She sang the following, very softly:

I feel sad. TBesa cannot hear me.
I feel mixed up.
I am longing for my brothers.
I feel sad.

She changed to a song of praise

If you believe,
And I believe,
Then Africa will be saved.
The Holy Spirit must come down
And Patricia must be saved.

She left the piano and returned to the drum. In a more joyful mood she sang:

The Lord is oh so wonderful!
He saves us all from death,
and breathes into us life again.
Oh Lord be my shepherd until I die.

She sang the final line repeatedly, and it became clear to me that she was expressing her own fear of the punishment of death and sought solace from God in order to cope with the fear. I reflected this back to her in song while she listened attentively.

Session 5

She entered the room quite confidently and said that she had "worries". She took a very decided approach to communicate these to me. This time she verbalized only:

> *I want to be with my mother,*
> *But I can't get to her.*
> *I want to be with my father,*
> *But I am afraid of him.*
> *He has hurt Patricia (she generally avoids saying "me").*
>
> *Patricia worries over her brothers.*
> *Who will look after them?*
> *Patricia worries over her mother.*
> *These are my concerns.*
>
> *But God will help me to leave the home,*
> *In order to feed my family.*
> *God put me into the Children's home,*
> *Because I was sick.*
> *But now I'm getting better,*
> *And I need to go back home.*

She began to sing again.

> *One day I was left alone with my father.*
> *TBesa was still alive.*
> *But when she was killed,*
> *I was sent to the home.*

She asked me to hold her because she had a pain on her stomach. (It is customary in Christian Xhosas worship that the person appealing for healing is held by the Minister). I was aware that the pain was probably associated with the swallowing of the snake - which was intended to "eat the evil in her." I asked her what she thought the cause of the pain might be, and she replied in song that it had to do with TBesa's death. I spent at least twenty minutes holding and singing to her, reflecting back in song the pain she was experiencing and revealing to me in the session.

DISCUSSION AND CONCLUSIONS

Patricia has been able to use the supportive milieu of the in-patient unit and music therapy to deal with some of her anxieties, particularly those concerning her dreams and experiences with her father. This has allowed the team to begin working on other issues such as her self-concept, sexual identity and religious convictions, as well as her relationship with peers and adults. As a result, she does appear to be gaining confidence in herself and to show some assertiveness.

Music therapy has made some unique contributions to Patricia's treatment. Given her belief systems, the therapy room, with its African drums, xylophones, glockenspiels and woodwind instruments has provided Patricia with the tools a Xhosa Diviner uses for expelling evil and communicating with the deceased, while also enabling her to use music as a traditional Xhosa Christian form of worship. Healing in both of the above is always accompanied by music and in particular, drumming. In addition, as stated earlier, music is never associated with evil. Patricia, having been exposed to both forms of worship, can, through music therapy gradually reveal her experiences, albeit initially in a displaced form.

The techniques of a non-directive client-centered therapy where the child experiences empathic understanding, security and warmth (Axline, 1947), and an approach such as Grinnell's where the music serves to organize the session and give it form, have offered Patricia the structure she needs in order to be able to release her pent-up emotions. Using puppets, instruments or animals in projective musical stories has enabled Patricia to displace significant feelings while also helping her to work through them on a symbolic basis (Bruscia, 1987).

The process of transculturation is a stressful one. It is only through having understanding, acceptance and deeply communicative team work that we can begin to comprehend the extent of Patricia's dilemma, which resulted not only from the sexual abuse but also from the powerful superstitions of the Xhosa culture, and in many ways, the opposing Christian belief. It is an on-going learning experience for all of us.

GLOSSARY

Apsychotic: Does not suffer from a lack of contact with reality.

Borderline Intelligence: An IQ in the 71-84 range.

Catastrophic Psychosocial Stress: Out of the range of normal stress reactions for human (e.g., floods, rape).

Euthymic: A calm, relaxed state.

Post-traumatic Stress Disorder: A psychological disorder associated with serious traumatic events.

REFERENCES

Axline, V. (1983). Play Therapy. New York: Houghton-Mifflin Co.

Bruscia, K. (1987). Improvisational Models of Music Therapy. Springfield, IL: Charles C. Thomas.

Buhrmann, M. V. (1984). Living in Two Worlds. Cape Town, South Africa: Human & Rousseau,

Grinnell, B. (1970) The Developmental Therapeutic Process: A New Theory of Therapeutic Intervention. (Doctoral dissertation, Bryn Mawr College, Bryn Mawr, PA). Available from University Microfilms.

Hansen, D.D. (1981). The Music of the Xhosa Speaking People. Unpublished doctoral dissertation, University of the Witwatersrand, South Africa.

All Her "Yesterdays:"
An Adolescent's Search for
A Better Today Through Music

CLAIRE LEFEBVRE, M.A., MTA, RMT
Instructor of Music Therapy
Université du Québec à Montréal
Music Therapist: Montréal Children's Hospital
Montreal, Quebec

ABSTRACT: *This is the story of Melissa, a teenager who was admitted to an Adolescent Day Treatment Program due to a sudden onset of school phobia, combined with questions of drug abuse and unmanageable behavior at home. She received weekly individual music therapy throughout the school year. Active and receptive techniques were used to encourage emotional expression and to gain insight into affective components of her behavior. As a result, Melissa made progress in self-esteem, had more appropriate peer relations and could better organize aspects of her life where she previously experienced loss of control (school attendance, drug abuse, etc.).*

BACKGROUND INFORMATION

This case study is about a sixteen-year-old female, Melissa. She was referred to the Adolescent Treatment Program of the Children's Hospital by the family's social worker at the beginning of the school year. The reasons for referral were that Melissa had refused to attend school for the last half of the previous school year, and because her behavior was out of control and oppositional at home. Melissa states that she was referred to the program because she was also abusing drugs, including marijuana, LSD, and cocaine.

The Adolescent Treatment Program is unique in its multidisciplinary team approach. The team includes a psychiatrist, psychologist, social worker, teacher, coordinator and a full complement of creative arts therapists (Art, Movement, Drama, and Music Therapists). When the program receives a referral, a screening follows to determine if the client will be admitted, and to determine which of the arts therapies is best suited to meet the client's interests, needs, aptitudes, etc..

Upon admission, each adolescent must sign a contract in which they state goals they wish to work on during their stay. Melissa expressed two goals: to express more how she is feeling; and to overcome whatever it is that makes her stay away from school.

Records of her personal history show that Melissa has not had consistent parenting from infancy. Melissa's mother comes from a wealthy family of five children. She married when she finished high school, and she and her husband were reportedly very happy until they had their children. Melissa was the second of two daughters. Her mother describes her as a healthy baby who was a little shy and who cried a lot. Both sisters have a long history of psychiatric treatment: Melissa was referred at age three for self-abusive behaviour (e.g., severe hair pulling) and for exhibiting signs of depression. At the same time, her older sister (age five) was referred for inappropriate behaviour: she chewed things constantly, including the back seat of the car.

The family stayed together until Melissa was three years old, when her parents divorced. The mother then remarried, but the second marriage lasted only nine months. She remarried for the third time in 1982. Presently Melissa is living with her mother and stepfather, and does not get along with her stepfather. Her sister is staying with her natural father in another city. The family was seen in family therapy between 1984-87, and Melissa began individual psychotherapy last year.

Melissa is an attractive young female who is healthy except for mild asthma. She is a bright, personable girl. She has friends, some of whom are close, and she has been dating. Several months ago she went to live with her natural father, but left after a few weeks because of his violence in the home. Upon returning home, she felt rejected by her father and feared rejection by her mother. To avoid this, she stopped going to school so that she would not have to be away from her mother during the day.

After acceptance to the program, Melissa took an Academic Achievement Test and a Wide Range Achievement Test. Results showed that she was "high average" in reading and sight vocabulary, "superior" in spelling skill and "average" in arithmetic computation. Her scores placed her at the eleventh grade level, though she was in the ninth grade at the time.

Melissa was referred to music therapy because of a strong background and interest in music and also because she played piano.

TREATMENT PROCESS

Phase One: Assessment

The purpose of our first meeting was to introduce ourselves, and to familiarize Melissa with the music therapy room. I also explained to her some basic concepts of music therapy, and began asking her about herself. Although teenagers do not always respond well to verbal interviews, Melissa was intrigued by all the questions, and was particularly fascinated by how music is used in therapy.

According to Ivy (1981), taking a history of an individual's family background and involvement in music "may help diagnostically to decide the form of music therapy which might be most beneficial in treatment, and also the attitudes, values and feelings which may be influencing an individual's progress in Music Therapy" (p. 35). I began the second session by asking Melissa to do a family music tree. This is accomplished by filling in a genogram with information about the musical involvement of each of her family members (See Figure 1).

At first, Melissa said that her family was not very musical, except on her father's side. However, after talking with her mother, Melissa discovered that the maternal side of the family also enjoyed music. She was surprised to discover that her mother had studied piano for about 12 years, and that she and two of her aunts had been active in choirs. Sometime later, Melissa's mother remembered that in late adolescence, she composed her own "death march" in the styles of Debussy and Chopin. Apparently, music was "always" in her mother's household: Melissa's grandmother (who was of Irish descent) loved to sing, and whenever they had guests for dinner, classical music was played on the stereo. Melissa's mother sang lullabies to both of her daughters.

When asked about her own music background, Melissa said that her only formal musical training was in recorder, but that she did not remember any of it. She received her first radio when she was in the sixth grade, and really started to listen to music at that time. When she would go to her father's house, he would play piano and she would pick out various melodies by ear. In high school, he bought her an electric guitar, but it was stolen

Figure 1: MUSICAL GENOGRAM OF MELISSA

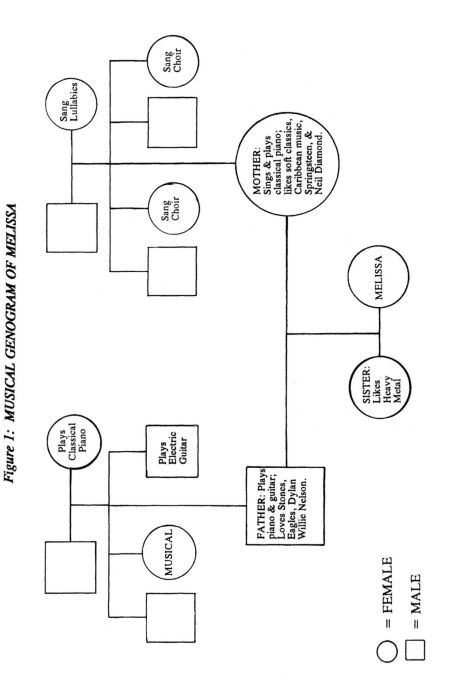

(or lost) one month later.

Melissa likes all musical styles except disco music. Her favourites are: the Stones, the Eagles, the Beatles, Bob Dylan, and as she would say, the "old stuff" such as Be-Bop, etc.. She also mentioned the group, "AC/DC" and a couple of heavy metal bands that she likes to play whenever she wants to get attention. She added that since she had gone to a French summer camp for five years, she knows many French "camp songs".

In the third session, Melissa was presented with various instruments and asked to experiment with them. I presented her the following: drum set with cymbals, piano, guitar, recorder, metallophone, and various small percussion instruments. Melissa did not show much interest in the percussion instruments. She tried the guitar, but felt that it was too complicated, and associated it with the one that had been lost. She liked the sound of the metallophone but preferred the piano. Melissa was very decisive in choosing her instrument. Throughout the year she played only the instrument she had initially chosen.

In the fourth and fifth sessions, Melissa was given the opportunity to do whatever activity pleased her most, as long as it related to music. Previously, I had encouraged her to bring her favorite tapes to the session. Melissa had two wishes: to play the piano, and to learn how to read music. Her first activity was playing the theme from "Star Wars" which was the first song her father had taught her on the piano. She enjoyed playing it very much. She also tried to play several traditional French songs that she had sung (e.g., Alouette, Ala Claire Fontaine, fire camp songs). Melissa was very conscious of her mistakes, and whenever she stumbled she would move on to the next song. Afterwards, I began to show Melissa the rudiments of music therapy. She was intrigued by how music was built---the melodies, rhythms, and combinations thereof. At the end of the lesson, she asked for homework, as if she was learning music in a regular classroom. Melissa and I agreed that for the next couple of weeks, each session would begin with a fifteen minute lesson in music theory.

Phase Two: "Pain and Pause"

When Melissa arrived on Monday morning, she had a bruised lip. She claimed that her mother had hit her. The agency for Youth Protection was then notified, and Melissa was taken to the Emergency Room for an examination. Upon her return to the unit, we started our music theory lesson at her request. Melissa seemed to enjoy visualizing what she could play by ear on the piano. She was intrigued by the different designs, what they stood for, and the general organization of music. She participated fully and asked questions.

After the theory lesson, she played the piano in a very unstable way. Whenever she made the slightest mistake she would automatically switch songs. When I pointed this out to her, she mentioned that she never could play them "perfectly anyway" and that it "bugged" her to start over. She seemed to want to keep up the image of showing only what was perfect in herself, thus masking her low self-esteem.

The following week, Melissa told me that she had given a piano lesson to another girl in the program. She was happy and excited about it, and seemed in a very good mood. She played the piano very softly, while explaining the different ranges of the instrument. Whenever she played an incorrect note, she would give a glance towards me and then start over without showing any signs of tension. When I complimented her on her perseverance, she smiled and turned her head in embarrassment. During that week, she did not attend the program for 3 days.

On her return the following Monday, she told me that she had not attended last week because she was angry at her mother, and because she did not want the staff to see her in this state of mind. I responded by asking Melissa if she wanted to express her anger on the piano. She refused, saying that the "piano should not be banged on" and that she "liked it too much to play it this way."

Since she had already started to learn Bach's Prelude # 1 from the Well-Tempered Clavier, she asked if we could continue working on it. We worked by rote, with her repeating each phrase after I played it. During the piano lesson, she sat very upright, facing the piano as she played in the middle range. At the end of the session, she said that she had not worked on the theory, because it was getting too complicated. Since she was "starting not to like it as much," we agreed to put it on hold.

From then on, Melissa showed more of the "dark" side of her personality. She was no longer the "perfect" teenager that she tried to portray. When playing the piano, she would play without energy or dynamics and at a very, very slow pace. When I reflected back the way she was playing, and expressed concern over her "state of mind," Melissa confided that she was worried about her mother's future and her own.

Her feelings about her mother were quite ambivalent. At times she enjoyed talking to her, and on other occasions, she would try to provoke her (by drinking, for example). Melissa liked to "test" her mother's limits, and then observe her reactions. On the other hand, Melissa talked about wanting to change her own name back to her mother's maiden name, so that she could pass it on to her children---whom she had already decided she would give the first names of "Payne" and "Pause." Melissa would not elaborate any further about these two names. I asked if they were related to her actual condition of suffering and her search for peace when she plays the piano very quietly. She said she did not know and changed the subject.

Melissa then asked me to play a quiet melody for her. I played "Jeux Interdits" (Forbidden Games). The melody has two distinct parts, one in a minor key and the second in a major key. Melissa loved this melody so much, that I asked her if she would like to put words to it at the next session. She agreed.

The following week Melissa had changed her mind. She said: "If a melody doesn't have words, it's because it was intended to be left as such." She also refused to play the piano or any other instruments. Instead, she complained throughout the entire session: about how tired she was; about how she did not like to go to the hospital to meet with her social worker; how the social worker's office is next to the psychiatric unit and that passing it by makes her uncomfortable. She wondered if the kids on the psychiatric unit were "weird" and if it was because of family problems. She added that one of her friends had tried to commit suicide because she had broken up with her boyfriend. After further discussion, Melissa realized that her friend's motives for attempting suicide were deeper than the boyfriend. In all likelihood, she had not sought the help she needed, or perhaps nobody heard her cry for help so she found another way to get attention.

Phase III: "Yesterday"

We were now at the beginning of December, and anxieties regarding the holidays were starting to show. Melissa was more engaged in the program and was expressing her anger verbally with both staff and peers. However in her music therapy sessions, she seemed to guard against anxiety attacks or any other kind of emotional crisis.

Melissa had been going through a piano book of "oldies," and she became interested in learning how to play songs by the Beatles. The first song she chose was "Yesterday". She memorised it without difficulty and played it well. She was very concentrated throughout the song and sat very straight. After the completion of the entire song, she became less talkative and was evasive. She refused to express feelings related to the song, said she did not know why she liked this song, except that she did.

Melissa never seemed to be interested by the faster songs of the Beatles, and in fact, stated that she preferred the quieter ones. The following week she started with "Hey Jude," and mentioned she was going to see her sister and father during the holidays. She was looking forward to the holidays and was also worried about how it would go. Her sister had told her friends that Melissa was "wild" (into drugs and liquor), and Melissa wondered how they would react to her now that she had changed.

Melissa then began talking about her first name, that it came from a character of a book that her mother was reading when she was pregnant. This girl was pretty and had several boyfriends (Melissa had difficulty maintaining a stable relationship).

I suggested that Melissa might benefit from trying to express all these different emotions through the piano, however she refused, explaining that when she plays the piano it makes her feel more peaceful and therefore better. I told her that what she was in fact doing was a form of "relaxation," and that there were other ways of relaxing with music. Melissa then told me that during the summer, in the movement therapy group, she had done some relaxation exercises using imagery, and that she would be willing to try again in January---"maybe."

Phase IV: "Star Wars"

Melissa returned three weeks later, after spending the Christmas holidays at her father's house. She was glad to be back in the program, but still felt that she was not ready to face school on the outside. She spoke of difficulties she had while with her father. Everything was not as great as she had expected. In fact, her sister had even asked for placement in a group home.

After returning to her mother, Melissa said that she was bored, and that she played a lot of piano because "there was nothing else to do." During the session she played "Star Wars" (the first song her father had taught her). She had not played it since the assessment.

The following week Melissa mentioned how tired she was and the difficulty she had sleeping. At home, she and her mother either fought or ignored each other, and tension was rapidly building up between them.

On the unit Melissa had become very provocative; she had started to sing very loudly whenever she was angry at her peers. They, in turn, reacted by becoming angry at her. She said she was ready for relaxation.

Phase V: Depression

We moved to a quieter, more comfortable room for the relaxation sessions. Melissa started giggling immediately, explaining that she was nervous and felt as if she had to move. So, we started off by standing up and shaking the different parts of the body. We then began breathing exercises, followed by "tension-release" exercises starting from the head down. Melissa followed the instructions and "tried hard" to relax.

After a very slow relaxation induction, Melissa eventually settled down on the floor and proceeded to hide her whole body, including her face, underneath the blanket. I had her listen to an excerpt from "Escale 84" by Claude Léveillée, a piano solo with orchestra and nature sounds. Melissa had a positive experience and was able to talk about it afterwards.

The following week, Melissa was again using her provocative "voice" on the unit. She admitted that she was "hyper." During the session, she did an imitation of Bob Dylan but in a high pitched, squeaky, female voice. While doing this, she sat in a slouched position, and ate her own hair. She then moved to the piano, and did a mocking version of "Greensleeves," emphasizing the words "Winter is here and the leaves are gone."

Phase VI: Abandonment

Melissa's relationships with her mother and stepfather were worsening, and the team recommended that she be placed in a shelter while continuing to attend the program on the unit. At the same time, I had to cancel our music therapy sessions for an extended period, due to a prolonged illness.

Melissa and I did not see each other for two months. Resuming sessions after such a long absence was very difficult---for both of us. The rapport that I had established was now on very shaky grounds, and Melissa's confidence had diminished. Melissa spent the first session only wanting to talk and reconnect loose ends.

Phase VII: Relaxation

At about the time that Melissa was placed in the shelter, and music therapy sessions were resumed, a change was noticed in her behaviour: outbursts on the unit occurred less frequently, and instead Melissa would often go to the music room and play piano.

We resumed the relaxation training, and by this time, Melissa was better able to pay attention throughout the entire relaxation process. The induction I used was a "Ball of Energy" moving through her body. Melissa reported that she felt the warmth of this ball, especially as it touched her stomach. She also reported that whenever she experiences stress or tension, she feels it as a knot in her stomach.

Melissa had now returned to live with her mother, and her behaviour was more appropriate both at home and with peers on the unit. Her mother had promised her a piano, if she proved and maintained her interest in it for two months consecutively.

As the program was drawing to a close for the summer, Melissa began to sever links with everyone she had known on the unit throughout the past school year. Relaxation also became more difficult as the time for termination approached. At first, Melissa seemed to be able to reach her "favourite place" (a meadow with a lot of horses), however her reflection and discussion afterwards were meagre. Then she began to refer to relaxation as "time to go to sleep," and would become oppositional about imaging her favorite place, saying that she did not want to go to there anymore, and that she did not want to think about anything.

Phase VIII: "Today"

At this session, Melissa tried to evade the piano. She talked about taking piano lessons once she left the program, so that she would not feel lonely and act out. During the week, Melissa had heard "The Rose" and started to play the song. She did not want to talk about the sadness, however.

In the next session, Melissa tried to cut herself off from all emotions. She did not feel like doing anything. She eventually played the piano in a very detached way; rapidly (which she never did), and playing through everything she knew. She played only in the upper register of the piano, and did not use any contrast. At the end of her recital, she said she was looking forward to the summer and she was hoping she and her mother would get along.

At Melissa's request, I brought piano books so that she could select a couple of songs for her to learn over the summer. At the end of the session, Melissa mentioned she had learned things about herself, and concluded: "It's up to me now as to how things are going to be from now on".

DISCUSSION AND CONCLUSIONS

The music therapy assessment was significant in Melissa's treatment process for several reasons: it gave a clear picture of her family's past and present living situations; it revealed that music had always been part of Melissa's upbringing; and that, although she never realized the importance it had in her life, Melissa used music to provoke others, to get attention, and to soothe and relax herself.

Music therapy provided opportunities for Melissa to express her feelings, and to gain some insight into how her emotions affected her behavior. As a result of this, and other aspects of the program, Melissa made progress in self-esteem, had more appropriate peer relations and could better organize aspects of her life where she previously experienced loss of control (school attendance, drug abuse, etc.).

Considering Melissa's unstable upbringing since infancy, it is amazing that she was able to show this kind of progress in such a short amount of time, and especially if one considers the unavoidable interruption in her music therapy sessions. Undoubtedly, the staff working as a team provided the stability that Melissa needed during my absence. Being in a safe and supportive environment was also crucial to Melissa's personal growth.

After working with teenagers for a certain amount of years, and witnessing the ups and downs of Melissa's therapeutic process, I have discovered how important the following points are for effective music therapy with adolescents:

1)   Listen, Listen, Listen! Adolescents need adults who will hear what they are trying to say. As music therapists, we should be particularly sensitive to a client's need to be heard.

2)   Know your client musically. It is important to know their musical

past, their current preferences and orientations, and their musical goals for the future. A thorough assessment which combines both active and receptive techniques is essential.   As when assessing anyone else, it is important to respect limits that a teenager places on self-disclosure.

3)   Teenagers have to take an active part in their treatment plan. It is important for them to set goals for themselves, and to evaluate their progress as they go along.

4)   Begin every session with something the teenager wants to do. Teenagers need to be motivated by activities that are relevant to their interests and needs.

5)   Be flexible. Teenagers are so unpredictable, and their lives are often in such upheaval, that it is unreasonable for a therapist to stick to a single plan or use the same approach regardless of what happens.

6)   Know clinically and musically when it is time to empathize and when it is time to challenge them to forge ahead in their therapeutic process. This means that the music therapist has to be aware of the usual ploys of adolescents at manipulation.

7)   Time can work for or against the therapist, the client, and the process. It has to be used to greatest advantage.

8)   "It's up to her now!" It is important for music therapists to give responsibility to the teenager for his/her life, and to trust in both the therapeutic process and the teenager.

Despite the interruptions in Melissa's music therapy, these eight points provided a framework for helping her to search for a better today and tomorrow. In a follow-up contact, I learned that, during the last several years, Melissa has completed high school and is now involved in career education.

REFERENCES

Ivy, V. (1981). The Music of your family Tree: Insights for Music Therapist and Music Therapy Practice. Proceedings of the Eighth Annual Conference of the Canadian Association for Music Therapy, Woodstock, Ontario.

Creative Music Therapy
In Bringing Order,
Change and Communicativeness
To the Life of
A Brain-Injured Adolescent

CLIVE E. ROBBINS, D.M.M., CMT/RMT-BC
CAROL M. ROBBINS, M.S., CMT/RMT-BC
Professors and Co-Directors
Nordoff-Robbins Music Therapy Clinic
New York University
New York, New York

Abstract. *Two therapists work as a team, using improvised music to engage Hilary, an acting-out adolescent girl with brain injury. Through the creative process, Hilary learns to channel her natural impulses into musical expression and interaction. As this occurs, she is able to bring order, change, and communicativeness into other aspects of her life.*

INTRODUCTION

Music is above all a means for bringing about changes: changes of mood, changes in relationship, changes of attitude, changes in attentiveness. One has only to consider how, in a lively, enthusiastic group sing-along, songs in various moods directly influence the participation of the singers. As an agent for the transmission of energy, stimulation, joy, warmth--and order--music is unique. In contrast to the melodic-conceptual experience of singing, consider moving to music, as, for example, responding to the compelling impact of tribal African drumming. How physically animating the beat and polyrhythmns are! How the timbres of the drums speak the rhythms directly into our bodies! And yet how directional such drumming is, what purpose it has! How it communicates the power of the body's need to move rhythmically!

In considering the kinds of changes that we work to bring about in a client in therapy, it is important to realize that sometimes our wish to bring about a particular change can be misplaced. We can only change what is inherent in the functional possibilities of the organism--to the extent that these make changes possible. Should the damage or the disturbance be extensive, such changes as may be achievable must lie within these possibilities. However, we must not underestimate what changes could become possible through a creative approach, especially when the explorative nature of music therapy based on improvisation discloses areas of ability and sensitivity which would otherwise remain undiscovered.

The all-important area in which we can bring about change, is personality development. Here we can, through music, often bypass some of the organically-based dysfunctions that hinder competent functioning in life. This is where improvised music can play such a vital role in treatment. In working interactively with a client, a therapist can improvise ways around the barriers, around the difficulties, to reach the living sensitivities, then work into the problem areas, where creative work has the possibility of releasing potentials for resolution and development.

Let us consider the act of creation or creativity, which is so intrinsic to the level of clinical musicianship we are considering. Those who consume music passively tend to think of creativity as something ephemeral, arbitrary, perhaps haphazard and undependable, and lacking in substantial reality. But a glance at the world of music will quickly demonstrate that the products of creativity are anything but insubstantial. Every piece of music that is important to us, that we are swept along by, enjoy in a particular personal way, has been created. Before it existed it was inconceivable. But some musician, or group of musicians, has a musical idea, and then begins the process of creation. It might last three minutes, it might last three years, but through this process an experience is realized that becomes part of the very fabric of life. Recognize that once all the music we respond to did not exist, and then through countless acts of musical creation, came into existence. And from being nothing before, now it exists. Realize how firmly it stands in our consciousness: how we carry it around with us, what a vehicle it is for us to share in, what strength it has in our emotional lives, our mental lives, our spiritual lives. It is extraordinary! The rich musical furniture of our lives, everything from folk music to film music, Scott Joplin to Bartok, all has come into being through this process of creation.

The potential impact of musical creativity transfers directly into the processes of music therapy. When a therapist works individually with a client through improvisation, he or she will be called upon to create, or adapt, in response to clinical situations, themes with which that individual comes to identify positively. These themes then become sources of nourishment for individuation, express much of the content of the client-therapist relationship, and provide significant opportunities for interaction and intercommunication. Such music, generated spontaneously in response to clinical events and needs, becomes uniquely substantial to the person in therapy.

METHOD

This clinical narrative provides an illustration of "Creative Music Therapy," an approach originally developed for handicapped children in 1959 by Paul Nordoff and Clive Robbins (1977). In its individual application, the approach involves two therapists working as a team with a single child, with improvisation as the focus of the creative therapy process. One therapist improvises at the piano, creating music to engage the child in a therapeutic experience, while the other works directly with the child, helping him or her to respond, either instrumentally or vocally, to the improvised music and to the clinical intentions of the therapist at the piano. The therapists work as partners with clearly defined and equal roles and responsibilities.

Each session involves creating an individualized musical repertoire for the child--one that capitalizes on the child's innate musicality and reflects the child's unique personality. This musical repertoire is created by the therapist cumulatively, session by session, motif by motif, line by line. Several basic concepts are involved.

First and foremost, the therapist improvises music which accepts and meets the child's emotional state, while also matching, accompanying, and enhancing how the child is expressing it. It is important for the therapist to respond to the child from moment to moment, often supporting every musical response the child makes, no matter how fleeting or incipient, and musically seizing upon every opportunity to explore its expressive possibilities. The therapist works to evoke either a vocal or instrumental response, depending on the natural propensities of the child. As the child formulates each response, the therapist creates musical situations and activities that encourage the child to further develop the response--to gain some measure of mastery over the music. In doing so, the therapist motivates the child to acquire musical skills needed to participate more fully.

Through improvisation the therapist is constantly "sounding out" the character and extent of the child's responsiveness, and stimulating, answering or stabilizing the child's activities as clinically appropriate. With the acquisition of each skill, the child is musically guided to discover new expressive options and choices that the skill has made possible. In the process of discovering musical possibilities and gaining musical skills, the therapist also engages the child in communicative dialogues, thereby showing the many ways that the child can relate his/her musical expression to that of another person. The child, increasingly confident in personal musical expression, learns how to be inter-responsive.

It is essential to the practice of this approach that each session be fully documented with the aid of an audio or video recording, thus ensuring continuity of clinical technique and a clear perception of all phenomena pertinent to the child's response process. This gives essential clinical guidance for subsequent sessions. Any improvised music that has been important is transcribed so that it can return as an ongoing theme in therapy.

We would like to illustrate creative music therapy by describing our work with a sixteen-year-old girl at "Inala", a Rudolf Steiner special school in Sydney, Australia. ("Inala" is an Aboriginal word for "peace"). To know this young lady, and the severity of her disabilities, is to realize that the only way you can do anything for her--apart from entertain her and perhaps lighten her mood--the only way you might bring about a significant change is through improvisation. This means a leap into the unknown from the first moment of the first session, to find out what responses music can stimulate-- and then support to foster and advance communication. How will a therapist achieve musical interaction with her? She is a multihandicapped person--it quickly became evident that how she manifested in music was symptomatic of her condition.

BACKGROUND INFORMATION

We want to introduce Hilary not as a "case study" but as a human being who is following a path. And we, as her therapists, are about to find and take a new path with her. We cannot know where the bends will be, where that path will lead us. When working with improvisation, working creatively, there is no recipe--as that would remove the spontaneity, the livingness, the creativity, and the wonderful unexpected moments of unfolding and discovery.

When we first began working with her, we did ask for case material, but inquired only about relevant medical problems, such as severe epilepsy. We wanted to meet her as she would be in music with us--to form and work freely from our own uninfluenced perceptions. Once our independent clinical assessment was made, then would be the time to study her case material.

Hilary was born in 1966. She was very much a wanted child as a long series of miscarriages and misfortunes preceded her birth. Pregnancy was difficult, birth was induced, and delivery was instrumental. Though difficult to diagnose with any certainty in infancy, it was later to be evident that Hilary had sustained brain damage. There were early breathing problems. Abnormality was noted at fifteen months, and all the developmental milestones were late. She did not develop speech. There were some physical disabilities: she had poor balance and was unsteady on her feet, walking in little shuffling steps a good deal of the time. She was frightened of heights and stairs. Generally, she was placid but overreacted to loud noises. When she was three, she began to react adversely toward other children and became withdrawn for long periods. She first attended Inala School as a day student. As she got older, her behavior problems worsened with tantrums and the pulling of other children's hair. At six her parents requested that she become resident at the school. Her behavior problems continued.

When Hilary was sixteen, her future became uncertain. She was uncooperative, stubborn and disruptive in the classroom. Her behavior was threatening to prevent her admittance to the Activity Therapy Centre (a sheltered workshop for moderately to profoundly disabled adolescents and adults) and she faced the real possibility of institutionalization. At this time we were asked to take her in the hope that music therapy could effect a positive change. Once weekly sessions were scheduled. We will describe the first four sessions in some detail, because this is where the major changes began to take place.

TREATMENT PROCESS

First Session

Hilary comes willingly to her first session, but is very tense; Carol repeats a "Good Morning Hilary" phrase to her, trying to put her more at ease. I notice her fingers trembling, and when I give her drumsticks, there are short bursts of fast, tense beating, most of it around 260 beats per minute (bpm). On the cymbal she beats forcefully at 190-220 bpm, drowning out the music that Carol is improvising to meet her.

As part of the exploration, I sit Hilary on the piano bench. She touches the piano keys twice then attacks Carol, grabbing her hair, pulling her head down. Carol goes with the pull, singing gently while undoing Hilary's grip. Hilary then grabs at Carol's skirt and knees. She is strong.

She yells once as we try to calm her. I return her to her chair, near the piano but not close to it. She listens quietly as music is played and sung to her. Her agitation diminishes over the next several minutes and she is calm when taken back to her classroom.

We noted in detail all aspects of Hilary's reaction and response. Most of the music had been improvised to meet her disturbed state, but because this did not recur (she never attacked Carol again) and the music was not appropriate to the coactivity that subsequently developed, it was not used again. However, the melodic phrase with which Carol greeted her at the beginning of the session did become part of her repertoire, becoming extended in later sessions. It was in a Mixolydian mode:

Musical Excerpt 1

Second Session

Hilary is noticeably happy to come to the session with me. She still shows much tension, but I also see a spark of anticipation. I bring her to the drum as in the first session and again she beats in a fast, driven tempo, 200-260 beats per minute (bpm). She is aware of Carol's improvising, and her beating becomes responsive to the music at times, as when she stops beating at the ends of phrases.

It appears that Hilary gains support from the music, she beats more confidently when the music is stronger--and often stops when the music is soft. She is obviously intent on having Carol make music for and with her. She makes a sound of pleasure when Carol begins to sing. We perceive her sensitivity.   Experimentally, I place a large timpani before her. At first, to encourage her listening, Carol plays gently using arpeggiated chords. Hilary impresses us with her self-restraint as she holds back her beating to this soft music. After a minute or so Carol introduces vigorous, forceful music to release Hilary into free strong beating. She needs to do this and

Musical Excerpt 2

seizes the opportunity immediately, beating the timpani energetically in the tempo of Carol's bass octaves at 200 bpm. (See middle of Excerpt 2).

As Carol brings the vigorous music to a close and returns to softer music, Hilary finishes her beating with a flourish which contains a clear, rapid triplet. It seems to originate unconsciously, but it tells us that rhythmic ability is latent within her. She is keen to continue and chuckles as she beats.

Late in the session she spontaneously beats to soft music at 200 bpm and follows a ritardando to 170 bpm. In an improvised "Goodbye song" her beating shows her sensitivity to dynamics. She smiles a number of times.

After the session ends, I escort her to the girl's toilet and, while waiting outside, I hear her screaming. Questions leap into my mind: Why, after such a promising session? Was she angry that she had to leave the music room? Could it be that in the improvised music and in beating with it, Hilary had experienced a special kind of release and freedom that carried over into this letting go of some of her feelings? The kind of liveliness of contact that she felt in the music was definitely unattainable in her daily life--where else in the normal circle of her life could she be this activated-- even though she was in a fine school? She must have found the session stimulating and satisfying; perhaps then, the screaming arose as a way of readjusting to the norm. It occurred to me that there was something quite positive about Hilary finding a private place to scream! In a little while she returned quietly to the classroom.

Further insight can be gained from studying Hilary's way of making music against the background of a comprehensive examination of the clinical and experiential significance of tempo and dynamics. Figure 1 (See page 241) presents a "Tempo-Dynamics Schema" derived from studying the responses of over 200 variously handicapped children in improvisational individual music therapy (Nordoff & Robbins, 1977, p. 158-159). When a fast tempo is determined pathologically by the present condition of the child, one finds that it originates in nervousness, tenseness, hyperactivity, overexcitation, obsessiveness, or in resistiveness, in which the child is "running away" to avoid contact through the music with the therapist. For the improvisational therapist, these reactions are much more vividly real than the words can convey: there is a directness and clarity of emotional communication when the therapist is creating music with the child. There is an immediacy of understanding if one follows and lives in the child's sounds moment to moment.

In contrast to the pathology driven fastness is a fast tempo which originates in normal musical experience. The normal range of fast tempos can bring activation and alertness, buoyancy--and a host of qualities that can open up musical enjoyments such as joyfulness, gaiety, playfulness, happy excitement, and fervor. It is interesting to note how all of the pathological states associated with fast tempos are self-isolating, whereas the normal musical experiences of fast tempos bring sharing and uniting with others.

When seen in this way, the schema provides a map of musical terrains that can guide the therapist in bringing about change. Through the give-and-take of improvisation, changes in tempo can bring the condition that is on the pathological side over, as this is possible, into the area of normal musical experience: to take what the child is driven to do, and through putting music to it, make it a shared experience in which new, more satisfying emotional experiences can be generated.

The dynamics of music can be used in the same way. When a drum or any instrument is beaten loudly, and when this originates in a pathological state of being, one hears aggression, frustration or anger; or as so often observed in emotionally disturbed children, adolescents, and adults, the sounds reflect a lack of impulse control, emotional-motor discharge, nonresponsive assertiveness, and the resistiveness of "shutting the other person out." In contrast, the loud dynamic in normal musical experience conveys animation and eagerness, exuberance, assertive freedom--all very positive qualities--confidence, and climactic fulfillment.

The universal significance of musical tempo and dynamic is nicely illustrated by the true story of an African drummer from Zambia. Whenever he became burdened with a certain emotional disturbance, he would get up in the night, awaken his two wives (both of whom were competent drummers), and then work through his disturbance rhythmically. The drumming allowed him to discharge his emotional tensions with the empathic support of his musicianly wives, who alternately followed and led him through various modes of rhythmic experience: from fast to slow and back, and from loud to soft and back. In terms of the schema, the man needed an emotional-motor discharge, in which he could assert himself and determine his own course of action, while still being supported by others beating with him. This shared release helped his drumming to become expressive and communicative. He could somehow "objectify" his feelings and their transformations--and therein be healed.

In Hilary's first session, her loud cymbal beating had the character of aggression, even anger. In the second session, she moved into loud drum beating, which seemed to come more from frustration. But as Carol took it up with minor, purposeful music, you could hear animation and eagerness coming to expression in her beating. Already a change was beginning.

Third Session

Hilary is eager and excited as she enters, but inhibited at first, unable to respond freely. When I give her the drumsticks, they tremble rapidly in the air. Her initial beating comes about as she tentatively brings the trembling drumsticks into contact with the drum--it is soft and fast, 360 bpm. It suggests tenseness possibly compounded with fear. Carol plays to match

Figure 1

TEMPO AND DYNAMIC SCHEMA
IN CREATIVE MUSIC THERAPY

<u>*Pathologically Determined*</u>   <u>*Normal Musical Experience*</u>

FAST TEMPOS

Nervousness	*Activation*
Tenseness	*Alertness*
Hyperactivity	*Joyfulness*
Overexcitation	*Gaiety, Playfulness*
Obsessiveness, Unrestrained drive	*Happy excitement*
Resistiveness: running away	*Fervor*

SLOW TEMPOS

Insecurity, confusion	*Attentiveness*
Despondency	*Calmness, ease*
Lethargy	*Seriousness*
Slow functioning	*Thoughtfulness, earnestness*
Vacuity	*Deliberateness, certainty*
Lack of motor vigor, weak drive	*Affirmation, warmth*
Resistiveness: avoiding "activity-contact"	

LOUD DYNAMIC

Aggression	*Animation*
Frustration, anger	*Eagerness*
Lack of impulse control	*Exuberance*
Emotional motor-discharge	*Assertive freedom*
Nonresponsive assertiveness	*Confidence*
Resistiveness: shutting out therapist, music	*Climactic fulfillment*

SOFT DYNAMIC

Fear	*Lightness*
Inhibition	*Delicacy*
Apathy	*Gentleness*
Listlessness	*Carefulness*
Remoteness, unawareness	*Suspense*
Resistiveness: avoiding self-declaration	*Intentness*

and meet her mood, and when she begins to sing, Hilary makes a sound of pleasure--in the same key. After much encouragement, Hilary begins to beat with a little more intention at 285 bpm. Carol carefully improvises to support her, and Hilary's beating becomes sustained. Her face relaxes.

A lightness and delicacy emerge in the shared music. Hilary's tempo comes down to 250 bpm. When Hilary has found her confidence and Carol feels she is in secure contact with her, she improvises a song to bring in the experience of a slower beat (See Musical Excerpt 3). The song is in waltz time and begins at 90 bpm: "Let's play a song, Hilary's song, Let's play a song, together. Hilary can play a slow song, together, together, together."

Musical Excerpt 3

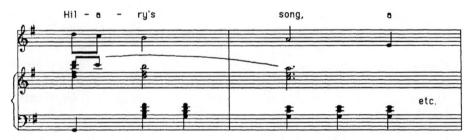

As the song is repeated Hilary beats the cymbal rapidly several times. Her beating impulses seem to begin in double tempo, two beats to Carol's one, but then quicken into cymbal tremolos. To give her an experience of beating in a slower tempo, Carol asks me to guide her, and adapts the song to include my name.

I take Hilary's left hand and beat with it to the song, now at 75 bpm; she makes an exclamation of pleasure. When I release her hand she accelerates until she is beating at 300 bpm--subdividing the beat exactly by four.

Hilary feels the pulse of the music, and is drawn to unite with it. Yet within her is tenseness that she can only discharge in fast tempi. But also within her is musical sensitivity and a sense of rhythm which, in a way we do not yet fully understand, somehow take over and order her "discharge" beating by bringing it into a 4:1 relationship with the slow tempo. She does not do this consciously by deciding: "Now I will beat four beats to one." Something much more primal takes place: as the internal pressure accelerates her beating toward the rapidity it needs for discharge, her hearing, musical feeling, and sense of rhythm bring about this concurrence, in this example through beating sixteenth notes. This ordering must happen at a subconscious level, but once it has happened she is able to hear and feel the concurrence, and so feel the release of the discharge within the secure pulse of the music. Carol's earlier improvising in the tempo of her fast beating must have given her a personal feeling of being accepted--while, at the same time, "making musical sense" of her need to beat fast. This imparting of musical meaning to the fast beating would have already contributed to the awakening of her musicality and so, to some extent, have prepared the ground for the beating of multiples of the basic beat. This now becomes part of her way of responding, it is just beginning; she will go on to do more of it.

As the session continues, I take her left arm again and beat to the song at 80 bpm; Hilary joins in with her right arm, beating in the same tempo. Clearly this is her beating impulse--I am only guiding. Again she enjoys the movement together and laughs. I let her arm go free and very steadily she accelerates to exactly two to the beat, stays with this for some moments, and then accelerates further. At the piano, Carol goes with the accelerated beating until a ritardando seems musically inevitable: as if it is the right segue into a repeat of the song. Hilary stops immediately--the ritardando heightens her awareness of the music. She waits as Carol's momentum unwinds to a natural conclusion, then recommences "a tempo," beating with the song at 85 bpm. She stays in the tempo to the end.

Hilary's control in the accelerando was remarkable! She was not letting herself simply "run away." When the music paused she stopped and waited until it continued. An inner control is beginning to show.

The session draws to a close with the "Goodbye Song," after which I experimentally invite Hilary to sing--something we have never heard her do.

As I sing freely, Hilary laughs in a musical voice.

Fourth Session

Hilary is very keen to come to music, and enters the room stamping her feet in excitement and humming with pleasure. Carol sings "Good morning" to her--this time introducing considerable rubato--Hilary watches and listens with total attention; the rubato brings the element of suspense into the song and she smiles as she receives the greeting.

It is so important in therapy to get out of a metronomic beat whenever it no longer serves its purpose--that of keeping the music or the music-makers together. Certainly a metronomic or fixed beat is absolutely necessary whenever rhythmic regularity is required or, for example, in group singing, when everyone has to know where they are in the music in order to stay together, similarly in movement to music. But the moment an improviser or performer brings in a pause, a fermata, or a ritardando, an expressive element is introduced. This arouses keener listening--one listens not because the music takes place on a predictable beat, but because a melodic statement is being made in its own time. The melody or musical statement does not have to move for any other reason than that the musician wants it that way. It is not driven by a beat, and this makes one much more attentive to it. This can add a living sense of immediacy to a song, especially when you are singing to a child. Thus, there are times in therapy when you need the predictability of the beat, and times when it is important to get away from it.

As the session continues, Hilary starts to beat confidently in tempo with the song, 120 bpm, then accelerates with impressive and steady control to 265 bpm. Carol accelerates all the way with her.

Hilary seems to be bridging something in herself. She made this measured accelerando from the tempo of Carol's music--in which she began because she is musically sensitive--to the fast beating which she still needs to do. What inner process is involved in this? This is the second time Hilary has presented this kind of response: she did not jump from one tempo to the other, but accelerated gradually across a range of tempos. She was linking her response to the music we were presenting with what she needed to do out of her state of self. She was connecting and integrating. There was something moderating at work--she was filling in a gap between sense impression and the tenseness and energy that comes to expression in fast beating.

Often, in this kind of work, it happens that a therapist has an intuition. At this moment, Carol decided not to go with Hilary's fast beating, but to hold a constant tempo and see what would happen. As Carol sets a tempo of 75 bpm, Hilary immediately beats multiples of the beat: 3:1 (225 bpm); a sequence follows in which she changes quickly from 3:1 to 2:1 and back to

3:1. When Carol sings and the tension of the music increases, Hilary's beating goes up to 4:1 (300 bpm):

Musical Excerpt 4

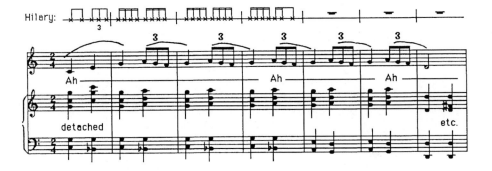

She stops, waits, recommences at 4:1, then drops to 3:1. She pauses again when Carol makes a diminuendo; as the dynamic is increased she beats again at 3:1. Carol now plays with her fast beating. This happens over a fifty-second period.

Carol decides to go further into structure by introducing an eight measure phrase in 3/4, in G minor, ending with a clear cadence. (See Musical Excerpt 5). We had heard Hilary stop beating many times at the ends of phrases--can we now use this perception deliberately in a short piece of rhythmic structure as a basis for work together?

Carol plays this phrase, stopping on the tonic and raising her hands off the keyboard in a clear visual signal to stimulate Hilary's control; Hilary beats in the tempo, 165 bpm, and stops five beats after Carol. To a repeat, she stops three beats after Carol. The third time she beats faster than the tempo and stops about two beats early--she looks cheekily at Carol as if to say "I made you stop this time!" We all laugh. The fourth time she again beats fast and deliberately continues long after the therapist has stopped, laughing in a spirit of devilment. The fifth time she "overbeats" by about six beats.

Later in the session when we come back to this activity, Hilary picks up the tempo more surely and responds attentively. This time Carol plays the phrase, and Hilary beats in tempo, 160 bpm, adding only two beats beyond the phrase. To a repetition, she beats three beats beyond the stop. The therapist takes this principle of coactivity into "Hilary's Song."

Hilary beats at 3:1 to the slow tempo. She stops one beat after the end of each of the first two phrases. She stops before the end of the next phrase--out of her keenness to participate, for she is watching Carol closely.

Musical Excerpt 5

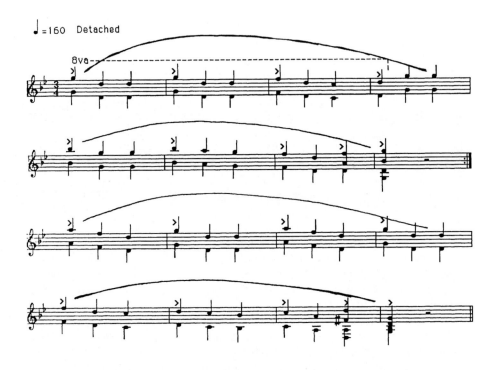

As the song leads into a climax Hilary beats vigorously; Carol accompanies her fast beating with the accompaniment while singing the song. Although she is animated, Hilary stops precisely at the end of the next phrase. Carol then begins the next phrase in a soft dynamic, Hilary beats quietly. The phrase is short but she is concentrating and stops exactly again. She laughs with recognition at the musical humor in what they are doing. She sustains her attentiveness.

I then stand behind Hilary and, holding her arms, guide her in beating at 55 bpm. She enjoys the assertiveness of the slow tempo and the accompanying music. As she beats, I move my hands up her arm until she is beating alone but can feel the support of my hands resting on her shoulders. She begins an extremely well controlled accelerando that reaches 125 bpm and holds it for eight measures. Her tempo then gradually rises to 210 bpm, where it stays for over 30 seconds. Throughout the accelerando she watches Carol keenly, obviously aware that they are making this musical adventure together--and enjoying the freedom of being a co-creator. The accelerando is led to its climax at 300 bpm, then Carol and I take her back to slow beating at 70 bpm.

As Carol begins the "Goodbye Song" Hilary joins in the singing. She does not have the language or the vocal control but the quality of her commitment is unmistakable. She sings through the first two phrases; her voice is soft and breathy but she sustains her tones and some are on pitch.

Musical Excerpt 6

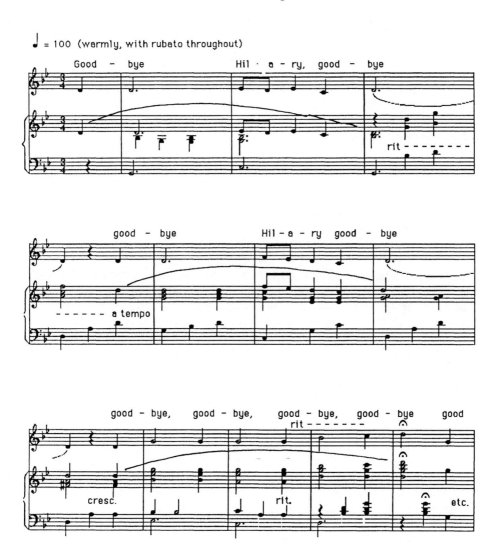

It was in this session that Hilary began to consolidate her involvement and abilities in music: she brought more control to bear on her urge to accelerate into faster beating; the compulsion to beat fast was becoming increasingly ordered by the rhythmic responsiveness of her multiple beating; she was gaining the control required to beat in a soft dynamic; slow and moderate tempos were coming into her tempo range; and she could participate closely with the therapist in a recognized goal in rhythmic structure.

As music was now such a uniquely important area of activity, experience and relationship for her, consolidation in musical participation would mean, in an intimately real sense, consolidation of self. It is not surprising that with this positive feeling of her own self, and her living pleasure in the music, Hilary should spontaneously attempt to sing--and sing a song to which she felt attached.

Subsequent Sessions

This brief singing apparently brought Hilary to the limit of her abilities. She did not sing again in music therapy until her thirteenth session, and then not until two years later, although vocal expressions of pleasure were numerous. Her individual sessions, averaging about 17 minutes in length, continued on a weekly basis.

On the afternoons of the days she had her individual sessions, she, together with several older girls, sat in on a group activity with a class of eight to ten-year-olds. These sessions brought her much enjoyment. She was included in greeting songs, and sometimes taken round to greet the children. She was gentle with them, and they were unafraid of her. While watching and listening to the singing games she could be seen hugging herself with pleasure. She was an ebullient "dancer" but, being unsteady on her feet, needed support. Even so, she could overwhelm her partner with the vigor of her movements. At this time, she also became an enthusiastic member of an adolescent music group.

Most of the effects of music therapy became evident in her school and hostel life by the twelfth session. She was lighter in mood, happier, more amenable and receptive. She seemed fulfilled, more complete as a person. It was noticed that she walked more purposefully. The aggressive behavior almost completely stopped, and only reappeared when she was unusually stressed or upset. Later it ceased entirely. Her teacher, an older woman with considerable experience with the handicapped, was outspoken about the positive changes in Hilary since beginning music therapy.

Her individual work continued to be essentially rhythmic. Her slowest tempo came down to 75 bpm, which made a wider range of musical experience possible. She spent about half her sessions at the piano, playing single tones in each hand with Carol's supportive, responsive improvisations. She reached a stage of freedom in her playing which, to any one who knew her line of progress in music, would be recognized as being creative. We continued taking her over the next two years as the staff of the school felt that her individual sessions were especially important to her. A year later, when she moved to the Activity Therapy Center, her sessions were reinstated for some months to support her during the transition. Altogether she had fifty-five sessions of individual therapy. She went on to join a music group of adults from the Activity Therapy Centre.

ACKNOWLEDGEMENT

The authors would like to thank the Australian Music Therapy Association for its permission to revise and reprint this case study, which was originally published in its proceedings of Thirteenth National Conference of the AMTA (1988).

REFERENCE

Nordoff, P & Robbins, C. (1977). Creative Music Therapy. New York: John Day.

Individual Music Therapy For An Adolescent With Borderline Personality Disorder: An Object Relations Approach

JANICE M. DVORKIN, M.A., M.S., CMT-BC
Music Therapist in Private Practice
New York City, New York

Abstract. *This study presents an object relations approach to music therapy with an adolescent on an inpatient unit, whose final diagnosis included Borderline Personality Disorder. Excerpts from eight months of individual work delineate the process of therapy and developmental issues integral to this population as described by Masterson (1985). Music therapy techniques include use of song as transitional object and improvisation as a basis for dialogue.*

BACKGROUND INFORMATION

Linda is a 17-year-old, Hispanic, bilingual female, who was seen during her first psychiatric admission. She was admitted for a suicide gesture (6 antibiotics and 2 birth control pills), and states she had made two previous attempts. Linda demonstrated Low Average Intelligence on the Wechsler Adult Intelligence Scale - Revised (WAIS-R). A complete psychological battery suggested a diagnosis of *Borderline Personality Disorder.* Her final Axis I diagnosis was *Adjustment Reaction,* and an Axis II diagnosis of Borderline Personality Disorder was added.

Linda lived with both parents until the age of two. At this time, her parents were divorced and she, and a younger sister, continued to live with her mother. Her mother placed Linda in foster care at the age of 11, due to her inability to manage her. There is a history of physical abuse. Her younger sister remained at home with her mother. Prior to this admission, she had run away from approximately 30 foster homes and, at times, had been living with "friends" or "on the street". She states that she was raped when 14 and 15 years old. Her remaining positive familial relationship was with her grandmother. She has a history of drug abuse, but denies use of alcohol.

Linda's initial behavior during her hospitalization on an adult unit was provocative, sullen, withdrawn (when upset), argumentative, rebellious, manipulative (*splitting* staff) and impulsively assaultive. Linda was frequently observed carrying security items with her, such as a blanket, pillow or food. She was morbidly obese and often looked unkempt. She was prescribed *Navane* (5 mg., T.I.D.) for six months of her eight month hospitalization.

She was referred for individual music therapy to increase her ability to tolerate feelings of anger and frustration. She was often observed singing and dancing to music on television and at parties. Linda enthusiastically attended the music therapy group, which was held three times a week. When the group's music or responses to it were on an emotionally superficial level, Linda would respond in ways similar to the rest of the group. However, when the music in the group became more intense, she would begin to take on the role of nurturer ("boss") to the group, in order to prevent her from experiencing the feelings which were being provoked.

Individual music therapy sessions were arranged at times that allowed for participation of her primary therapist; however, Linda would often remain in bed during the scheduled time. Efforts to help her reflect on the meaning of her withdrawal actions were continuous.

ASSESSMENT AND TREATMENT GOALS

Linda had demonstrated in her group work that she was open to using her voice and a variety of instruments to express her feelings and thoughts.

Therefore the function of the music was intended to be congruent with the phases of the therapy process:

(1) Music for the expression of feelings, supported by techniques of reflection;

(2) Music for the exploration of feelings, supported by techniques of working through; and

(3) Music for dealing with age-appropriate concerns and ideas.

Initially, Linda's depression and "pride" (a rigid demeanor meant to communicate a sensation of control and power in her environment) precluded her ability to focus on developmentally appropriate concerns. Her response to a request to divide up the keyboard of the piano and label the divisions was: Lowest range = death; Middle range = learning; Highest range = Blah. She resisted improvising on the keyboard, but divided up a set of resonator bells into "good" and "bad" significant others. Her grandmother was named as the only "good" bell.

As Linda began to demonstrate her frequent use of splitting and *projective identification* to defend against an *abandonment depression* (Masterson, 1985), I began to formulate the goals and method for treatment. Since Linda's sense of herself relied so heavily on the impression she made on others, the initial phase of therapy needed to emphasize my mirroring of her actions in music and then using that music to explore the meaning behind the action. The second phase would bring in composed music as a *transitional object*. Initially, songs would be used to bring her issues of abandonment and wish fulfillment to consciousness, while also enabling her to comfort herself and contain her rage. The song would provide a transitional object similar to a "child's blanket." Next, Linda would work on transforming the lyrics of the song in ways that would help her to work through these issues. Finally, Linda would be asked to bring her own selection of song material into the sessions in response to her emotional needs.

My goals for Linda in music therapy were:

---to connect her impulses to feelings;

---to regain control of expression of her feelings; and

---to accept reinforcement of her ego and autonomy of her self through a *"holding environment."*

To facilitate the accomplishment of these goals, my role as the therapist was:

---to reflect, absorb, transform and feed back Linda's responses;

---to maintain contact, concern and emotional availability (e.g., *"good enough mother"*);

---to set limits for her to help manage internal and external stimuli; and

---to accept her ambivalence with continued concern.

The model for my role as therapist is based on the theories of Winnicott (1989) and collected papers by Butler (1986).

TREATMENT PROCESS

Phase One: Testing

Linda began the testing phase by acting out, which consisted of entering the therapy room and lying down on a padded mat on the floor. According to Masterson (1985), this acting out is a means of "testing" whether the therapist can be relied on to "control" the behaviors, thus "enabling the patient to resume the work of mourning involved in separation" (p. 114). Initially, Linda also retreated to her bed when the time came for her session. This "testing to see if the therapist cares" (p.114) was met with verbal reflections of her actions and what words this behavior might be communicating. Many sessions were started by the therapist improvising music which matched the rhythm of her breathing and perceived mood. This music then became the basis for an ensuing dialogue which engaged Linda verbally and musically. The dialogues often focused on helping Linda to see how her acting out was a "vehicle for testing the therapist and a defense against feeling and remembering" (Masterson, 1985, p. 114). The suggestion of limited choices was offered to Linda, as it would be to a child at this developmental stage of *rapprochement.*

The following example demonstrates how the session proceeded from therapist-improvised music to improvised dialogue between Linda and me, to the use of composed music to explore her feelings and therapy issues.

SESSION ELEVEN. Linda is lying on the floor mat. Kay, her primary therapist is present. I am strumming the guitar with an Alberti-style accompaniment and humming the following melody repetitiously in a soft voice.

Janice:

Linda: *This is boring to me.*
Janice:

As I listen to this music, it feels so boring to me.

Janice: *What else?*
Linda: *Why do I always have to play music?   My*
          poem: The girl read it and she liked it.
Janice: *Could we finish this first?*
Janice:

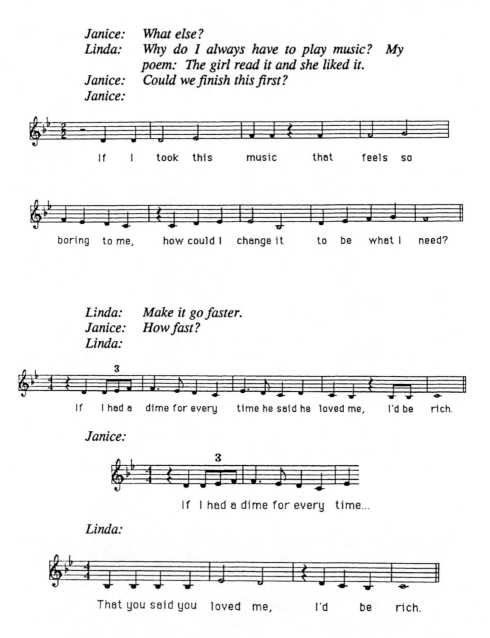

If I took this   music   that   feels so   boring to me,   how could I change it   to   be   what I   need?

Linda: *Make it go faster.*
Janice: *How fast?*
Linda:

If I had a dime for every   time he said he loved me,   I'd be   rich.

Janice:

If I had a dime for every   time...

Linda:

That you said you   loved   me,   I'd   be   rich.

The dialogue continued to explore Linda's perception of the concept of words versus action. She was able to verbalize, through the musical dialogue, her mistrust of the words that are spoken to her, as opposed to the actions that she observes others taking toward her. As my questions and responses were sung to Linda, she responded using an appropriate phrase of the music to match her verbal expression. This was supported by my continuing harmonic accompaniment and reflection of emotional content on the guitar. When her statements became more assertive, the strum changed to one that rhythmically mirrored the change in emotional tone. As she defended against the feelings of vulnerability that were beginning to surface, I was able to attempt to have her look at how she was defending herself and encourage her to continue exploring how she relates to others.

Janice:	*So you turned a boring melody into words to bolster yourself. When you say you're 'gonna get what you need', when you can't get it from anyone else. You're gonna say these things to keep yourself going when others aren't there to say that they care.*
Kay:	*Linda, when you said you wanted a dime for every time you loved, who did you mean?*
Linda:	*A boy, a girl.*
Janice:	*A mother?*
Linda:	*A father, a sister, not my grandmother, 'cause she loves me and I love her too. And I love Madonna (laugh).*
Kay:	*But you wish you had a family.*
Linda:	*So I'll make my own.*
Kay:	*With whom?*
Linda	*By myself!*
Janice:	*Alone?*
Linda:	*Alone. It's not a lonely word.*
Janice:	*(Singing chorus of song "Lonesome Valley"): You've got to walk this lonesome valley. You've got to walk it by yourself. Nobody else can walk it for you. You've got to walk it by yourself.*
Linda:	*You've got to cry, survive, lie, try, die by yourself*

The singing dialogue continued by having Linda complete the opening phrase of each line of the chorus (i.e., You've got to _____). Afterwards, Linda spontaneously switched to another song, and began to sing "Tomorrow."

Linda:	*The sun will come out tomorrow. Bet your bottom dollar that tomorrow, There'll be sun.*

This type of session was the prototype throughout most of the testing phase. As Linda began to bring to the sessions increasing attempts to address her present and past relationships with people, it became more evident that she was ready to begin to look at her abandonment/rejection and separation issues, and how they affected her relationships with people. Approximately one week after this session, the song "Maybe" was introduced to Linda, and the second phase of "working through" began.

Phase II: Working Through

According to Masterson (1985), the phase of "working through" is signalled by control over acting out, a consequent deepening of the depression, spontaneous recall of appropriate affect, and a detailed memory of the history of the environmental separation experience which precipitated the abandonment depression.

Linda's progression to the next phase began with the song "Maybe," which was introduced to help Linda begin to look at herself in realistic terms. Its introduction followed a session that ended with her saying "I don't care, everyone needs help but me." Her reaction to the song was: "It matches me perfect." Initially, it was used as a *paraverbal technique* to: facilitate the concrete expression, and identification of self; to heighten her awareness of her self perceptions and how this was inconsistent with reality; and to help her cathect feelings and increase her tolerance of her feelings concerning who and where she is.

The song structure provided organization for verbally expressing her feelings and repressed material (e.g., magical thinking, wishes, self perception) in her own words, and helped to increase her tolerance for her own words, ideas and feelings. The example of an adaptation of this song preceded the first time she would allow herself to express feelings about her good/bad mother and produced tears. Through this use of the song in the therapy process, Linda was able to allow repressed material to surface to a conscious level through imagery. The date that she refers to in her adaptation is the date of discharge.

Linda's version of "Maybe"

*There will come a day
When I will get my way.
I will be getting my parents
And I'll be getting a day (date).*

*Maybe in their house
Not hidden by a hill.
They'll be saying Linda
Won't you please stand still.*

Betcha they're young.
Betcha they're smart.
Bet they don't collect ashtrays and art.
Betcha they're good.
Why shouldn't they be?
They did the best thing
By finding me.

(ORIGINAL CHORUS)
So maybe now this prayer's
the last one of its kind.
Won't you please come get your baby, maybe.

The song was used as a transitional object in that it was able to absorb Linda's dangerous feelings and, in enabling her to communicate these feelings, comfort her. While the therapist is the transitional object in verbal therapy based on object relations theory, the use of the song in this manner freed my role in the therapy process and the way in which I could relate to Linda during the various stages of therapy. Buckley (1986) describes the transitional object, or "child's blanket", as an object which possesses attributes of its own, yet is not allowed to change unless changed by the child. It is used by the child - both loved and mutilated - and must survive both. It is not asked for help, but is symbolically placed in a protective shield between the child and the dangers of the outside world.

"Maybe" was further personalized and integrated in the therapy process by its use in improvised dialogues whose only musical accompaniment to the words was the music from the song. The example provided was improvised during the first session upon my return from vacation.

Arrangements were being made to have Linda discharged to a residential treatment facility outside of New York State. The staff was attempting to persuade her of its benefits in relation to her experience in the hospital. She was able to reflect on her present inappropriate behavior and need for further treatment, as opposed to her leaving the hospital with minimal follow-up care. The song offered her the opportunity to securely express her ambivalence concerning separation, in order to make a decision with which she was comfortable.

Following this dialogue, she was able to tolerate confrontation on her recent assaultive behavior and, during the following week, was able to ask for controls for her impulses. She was now able to use her own words, instead of using composed songs to symbolically express her therapy issues, e.g. "Hell Is For Children" and "Where Is Love?"

Singing Dialogue on the tune of "Maybe"

Janice: *Maybe I will leave.*
               I'm really glad to go.
               But there's a part that I'm feeling
Linda: *That doesn't want to go.*
Janice: *However, I will find*
               A place that I will be.
               They'll be a somebody
               I hope there for me.
               Maybe they're...
Linda: *Good.*
Janice: *Maybe they're...*
Linda: *Bad.*
Janice: *Maybe they're...*
Linda: *Strict as I thought they had. (laugh)*
Janice: *Maybe they're...*
Linda: *Fun.*
Janice: *Maybe they're...*
Linda: *Sad (laugh).*
Janice: *Don't really care as long as...*
Linda: *It's mine.*
Janice: *So maybe I will go...*
Linda: *As far as I can see.*
               I need the help for so long,
               And they're going to help me.
Janice: *You know they've helped me here,*
               Or so they tell me so.
               But you can see there's still problems
               Like putting on..
Both: *My clothes.*
Linda: *Maybe I don't want to get dressed today*
               Because there's nothing to do, and
               there's nothing to say
               Maybe I'm bad.
               Maybe I'm nice.
               Maybe I'm strict,
               As cold as the ice.
               Maybe I need a vacation.
               Don't really care, so long as...
Janice: *It's fun. So...*
Linda: *Maybe now it's time.*
               And maybe when I wake.
               I'll be going home sooner than I thought.

(Spoken Dialogue)

Janice: *You know you put in words like "Maybe I'm bad". Do you think you're bad?*

Linda: *No, a little hard-headed.*

Janice: *Did you feel hard-headed just now out there [on the unit]?*

Linda: *Who knows...David [a ward aide]*

(Singing Dialogue Resumes)

Janice: *When I leave this place,*
             my hard head goes with me.
             I don't leave it behind
             I goes with my body.
             There are other things I'll take

Linda: *Like my clothes.*
             But when am I just going to take me?
             Nobody really knows.
             Maybe I don't have the right words.
             Maybe I don't need the right words.

Janice: *What do you need?*

Linda: *Some peace of mind and a little love.*

Janice: *So, maybe at this place that I'll be going to*

Linda: *How long must I stay there?*
             As long as it's due.

Janice: *Maybe they'll have the love I'm looking for.*

Spoken Dialogue

Janice: *What does love look like?*

Linda: *What does it look like? You can't see what love looks like.*

Janice: *You can't?*

Linda: *Do you know what I mean?*

Janice: *Do you think people love you here?*

Linda: *Yeah.*

Janice: *How do you know?*

Linda: *(quietly) I know they love me.*

Janice: *What does it look like?*

Linda: *I've been good the past couple of days.*

Janice:	*That's not my question. How do you know?*
Linda:	*How do I know they love me?*
Janice:	*Yes.*
Linda:	*Because they take care of me.*
Janice:	*So, sometimes love looks like people taking care of each other. Right?*
Linda:	*Hm Hmmm.*
Janice:	*What else does love look like to you?*
Linda:	*Like a box of tissues.*
Janice:	*Like a box of tissues (laughs). That's a nice way to avoid. You say that you're looking for something. How do you know when you find it?*
Linda:	*Love is soft, it's sad, it hurts, it's joyful. It's full of love.*

(Singing Dialogue Resumes)

Janice:	*Maybe it's sad.*
	Maybe it hurts.
	Maybe it feels...
Linda:	*So unhurt.*
Janice:	*Maybe it feels as good as can be.*
Linda:	*But it's not good when you don't have a family.*
Both:	*So maybe now it's time*
	And maybe when I wake
Linda:	*I'll have a new family for me.*

Phase III: Separation

The last phase of "separation" focused on Linda's ability to tolerate and express her feelings about separations, in the present and from the past as suggested by Masterson (1985). She was able to work on this once more in reality, as Kay, her primary therapist, announced that she would be leaving before Linda. In addition to requesting that Kay consider adopting her, Linda indicated to us that she had developed significantly in her ability to maintain object constancy by working hard to terminate from her therapist in a healthy manner. Musically, she demonstrated this increase in ego functioning by announcing, during the start of the next to last session before Kay left, that she wanted to sing this song (recorded by Madonna).

Love Don't Live Here Anymore

Chorus: *You abandoned me.*
             Love don't live here anymore.
             Just a vacancy.
             Love don't live here anymore.

Verse 1:   *When you live inside of me,*
             There's nothing I could conceal that you
             wouldn't do for me.
             Trouble seemed so far away.
             You changed that right away, baby.

Chorus: *(Repeat)*

Verse 2:   *You're the windmill of my eyes.*
             Everyone can see the loneliness inside of me.
             Why'd you have to go away?
             Don't you know I miss you so and need your
             love.

Chorus: *(Repeat)*

By initiating the solo singing of this song, Linda communicated, this time, the true hurt and anger she was feeling regarding her separation from a surrogate mother. It enabled Kay, as her therapist, to openly help her find a way to resolve the feelings of betrayal and rejection. However, instead of defending against the intense feelings and displacing them into actions, Linda communicated them with words and the affective help of the musical structure.

In addition, by focusing on the issues of separation and perceived abandonment (and the resulting conflicts provoked in present relationships), Linda was able to learn to express her anger, rather than defend against it through internalization. Prior to her discharge, Linda was again asked to divide the keyboard. Her response indicated that she now could allow herself to tolerate a range of feelings, as well as verbally communicate what these feelings were. She divided up the piano into four sections: Low=terrible; Middle=good; Higher=exciting; and Highest=happy. She followed this by attempts to role play herself and her mother. She decided that her mother should be played at the "terrible" part of the piano. While she was able to reverse roles and participate in a non-verbal dialogue in the role of her mother, she was unable to play herself because "I start to get sad." It became evident that she had come far in looking realistically at her life and began to look at the choices available to her regarding change.

DISCUSSION AND CONCLUSIONS

Mahler (1975) defines the person with a borderline personality as someone who has experienced a disruption in *separation-individuation* (unable to complete the developmental phase entitled *"rapprochement"*), which often leads to stranger anxiety and a poor symbiotic experience.

Kernberg (1984) describes the borderline personality as having little capacity for realistic appraisal of others and, in the absence of a relationship, experiences others as distant objects to whom s/he can compliantly adapt.

It was through music therapy, that Linda was able to develop beyond her fixation in a stage of development which precluded her from forming relationships, for fear of the resulting abandonment. The music was able to reflect her moods in a way that words could not. She was then able to use this reflective music to expand and specifically communicate her experience. The therapist was then able to provide the empathic understanding that Linda sought.

The relationship was able to build further by removing the role of the therapist as the transitional object. Instead, all of Linda's feelings could be projected into the song, or by singing the song in different emotional tones. In this way, the therapist could be more supportive, as well as more confrontative, without leaving Linda with no reliable object of security. Once this structure had been used to help Linda "work through" or internalize her ability to express her ideas and feelings and maintain the relationship, the use of the song (as with the "child's blanket") was no longer needed. The sessions then moved onto other songs, other dialogues and other therapy issues.

The ability to separate from the primary care parent and to function autonomously is a major developmental milestone. In accomplishing this, Linda indicated that she had been able to make a move from the rapprochement to object constancy stage of separation/individuation (Mahler, 1975). Through the therapy process, she was being prepared to not only face and resolve her feelings about past emotional injuries regarding separation, but also to prepare for coping with future relationships. By looking to a musical structure, again a song by an age appropriate model, Linda was able to begin to experience and survive separations. In other words, she did not have to fear having relationships, because she was afraid of not surviving their ending.

GLOSSARY

Abandonment Depression: This is a term used by Masterson (1985) to describe the chronic appearance of depressive symptoms as a reaction to the borderline patient's inability to separate from the primary object; the patient therefore, remains developmentally delayed at this 1 1/2 to 2-year-old stage of emotional development. These separation problems are replicated in all relationships, including the therapeutic one. The patient unconsciously anticipates, and prepares for, his/her eventual loss through abandonment by the significant other in the relationship.

Adjustment reaction: According to the DSM IIIR (APA, 1987), the essential feature is a maladaptive reaction to an identifiable, psychosocial stressor, that occurs within three months after the onset of the stressor. The maladaptive nature of the reaction is indicated by either impairment in social or occupational functioning or symptoms that are in excess of a normal and expected reaction to the stressor. The disturbance is not merely one instance of a pattern of overreaction to a stressor or an exacerbation of one of the mental disorders previously described. It is assumed that the disturbance will eventually remit after the stressor ceases or, if the stressor persists, when a new level of adaptation is achieved.

Borderline Personality Disorder: According to the DSM IIIR (APA (1987), the essential feature is a personality disorder in which there is instability in a variety of areas, including interpersonal behavior, mood, and self-image. No single feature is invariably present. Interpersonal relations are often intense and unstable, with marked shifts of attitude over time. Frequently there is impulsive and unpredictable behavior that is potentially physically self-damaging. Mood is often unstable, with marked shifts from a normal mood to dysphoric mood or with inappropriate, intense anger or lack of control of anger. A profound identity disturbance may be manifested by uncertainty about several issues, such as self-image, gender-identity, or long-term goals or values. There may be problems tolerating being alone, and chronic feelings of emptiness or boredom.

"Good Enough Mother:" "A designation used to indicate a mother who offers a holding environment providing an optimal amount of constancy and comfort for the infant who is wholly dependent on her...She offers at the 'right time' instead of imposing her own timing and needs. Then, when the infant must face frustration, aggression and loss, she also provides support within a setting of ongoing basic empathy and holding" (Moore & Fine, 1990, p. 205).

Holding Environment: "A maternal provision that organizes a facilitative environment that the dependent infant needs. Holding refers to the natural skill and constancy of care of the 'good enough mother'" (Moore & Fine, 1990, p. 206) which is essential to healthy child development. The concept may also be applied to the nonspecific, supportive continuity of a therapist.

Paraverbal Technique: A therapeutic maneuver originated by Evelyn Heimlich, an example of which is the "metaphoric use of songs." In this type of paraverbal technique, "the therapist presents a song with lyrics pertinent to the client's life, feelings, or problems. The lyrics are considered therapeutic metaphors because they use imagery, symbols, and analogues to represent the client's experience, and because someone other than the client is a main character in the song" (Bruscia, 1987, p. 296).

Projective Identification: A term used by Melanie Klein to describe the process whereby "parts of the self and internal objects are split off and projected onto an external object, which then becomes identified with the split-off part as well as possessed and controlled by it. Its defensive purposes include: fusion with the external object in order to avoid separation; control of the destructive, so-called bad-object;...and preservation of good portions of the self by spltting them off and projectively identifying them in the therapist for safe-keeping" (Moore & Fine, 1990, p. 109).

Rapprochement: A subphase in Mahler's theory of separation-individuation "during which the child must resolve the intrapsychic crisis between the wish to remain with the mother (in symbiotic union) and the wish for autonomy that accompanies the awareness of the self as a separate individual" (Moore & Fine, 1990, p. 181).

Separation-Individuation: "Mahler's term referring to two complementary processes in the slowly unfolding intrapsychic stages and the psychological birth of the human infant. The term applies to a developmental theory, to a process and to a complex stage of development... Separation refers to those intrapsychic processes through which the child emerges from the symbiotic dual unity with the mother. It includes the development of object relationships, with the formation of a mental representation of the mother separate from the self. Individuation refers to those processes by which the child distinguishes his or her own individual characteristics, so that the self becomes differentiated from the object and is represented intrapsychically as a series of self representations" (Moore & Fine, 1990, p. 181).

Splitting: According to Masterson (1985): "one crucial dividend of a successful separation-individuation experience is a prerequisite for later interpersonal relations... this is the capacity to relate to others as individual whole objects, both good and bad, gratifying and frustrating, and to have this relationship persist despite frustration at the hands of the object...[However, in the borderline personality], there is a persistence of the primitive defense of object splitting. In other words, relating to objects as parts, either totally gratifying or totally frustrating, rather than as wholes" (p. 24).

Transitional Object: A term used by Winnicott to describe "the infant's first 'not me' possession, something inanimate but treasured, which the child uses in the course of emotional separation from the primary love object at times of stress, often on going to sleep. The transitional object often must have a characteristic odor and feeling thought to be reminiscent of the mother. It preserves the illusions of the comforting and soothing mother at times when the mother is unavailable; it promotes autonomy in the toddler, for the transitional object is under his or her control, whereas the mother is not... By displacement from the original love objects, these sounds or objects function in later life as transient...maternal substitutes (Moore & Fine, p. 207).

REFERENCES

American Psychiatric Association. (1987). Diagnostic and Statistical Manual of Mental Disorders - Third Edition Revised. Washington, DC: Authors.

Bruscia, K. (1987). Improvisational Models of Music Therapy. Springfield, IL: Charles C Thomas.

Buckley, P. (Ed.). (1986). Essential Papers on Object Relations. New York: New York University Press.

Kernberg, O. (1986). Severe Personality Disorders. New Haven: Yale University Press.

Mahler, M., Pine, F. & Bergman, A. (1975). The Psychological Birth of the Human Infant. New York: Basic Books.

Masterson, J. (1985). Treatment of the Borderline Adolescent: A Developmental Approach. New York: Brunner/Mazel.

Moore, B., & Fine, B. (Eds.). (1990). Psychoanalytic Terms and Concepts. New Haven: Yale University Press.

Stone, M. (1986). Essential Papers on Borderline Disorders. New York: New York University Press.

Winnicott, D. (1989). Psycho-Analytic Explorations. Cambridge, MA: Harvard University Press.

SONGS

"Hell Is For Children" (1980). Words and Music by Neil Geraldo, Pat Benatar and Roger Capps. Port Chester, NY: Cherry Lane Music Company

"Lonesome Valley" - Traditional Spiritual.

"Love Don't Live Here Anymore" (1978). Words and Music by Miles Gregory. Secaucus, NJ: Warner Tamberlane Publishing Corp.

"Maybe" (1977). Music by Charles Strouse, Lyrics by Martin Charnin. New York: Edwin H. Morris & Co.

"Tomorrow" (1977). Music by Charles Strouse, Lyrics by Martin Charnin. New York: Edwin H. Morris & Co.

"Where Is Love?" (1960). Music and Lyrics by Lionel Bart. New York: Hollis Music, Inc.

Unit Four

Case Studies With Adults

Mia's Fourteenth - The Symphony Of Fate: Psychodynamic Improvisation Therapy With A Music Therapy Student In Training

BENEDIKTE BARTH SCHEIBY, M.A. Diploma
Music Therapist in Private Practice
Professor of Music Therapy
Aalborg University
Copenhagen, Denmark

Abstract: *This psychodynamically based case study describes twenty-two individual music therapy sessions with Mia, a 27-year-old music therapy student in training. Free improvisations were used to facilitate her personal development while also imparting essential clinical skills. Mia's experience of the process is conveyed through excerpts from her diary, comments during sessions, and the therapist's notes.*

INTRODUCTION

This case study is unique because the client was a music therapy student in training, and because the therapy was provided as an integral part of her training program. The purposes of this kind of training-therapy are many: to enable the student to experience the deepest potential of music therapy in addressing childhood traumas and other formative experiences crucial to the development of the personality, as well as more current personal issues; to provide the student with a deep understanding of the meaning of a client-therapist relationship in music therapy; to help the student discover the different ways music can be used as a tool in therapy; to reveal "blind spots" in the students self-awareness; and to help the student develop his/her own musical language, along with a framework for making musical and verbal interventions.

This mode of training---practiced since 1982 at the four-year Master's program at Aalborg University in Denmark---is intended to provide an experience for the student that is as near as possible to the clinical reality outside the university. In the first year of training, students are offered sixteen sessions of music therapy in groups of five. Here they encounter self-experiential work in a music therapy group for the first time, and gain the preparation they need for the deeper work that follows. During the second year, all students are required to take a minimum of 20 individual, weekly sessions, and if they choose, they may extend the therapy for a longer period.

I have seen over eighty students in the eight years that I have been offering individual music therapy as part of academic training. I chose to write about Mia for several reasons. We both considered our work together successful; she was willing to share her notes on the experience, which are in the form of a diary; and the process that she underwent in therapy was fairly typical of music therapy students in training.

Having access to Mia's diary was important because I believe that what a client expresses verbally about the nature of their experience in therapy must have the highest priority in providing an adequate account of the therapeutic process. In the music therapy literature, we are usually only offered the therapist's interpretations, experiences and evaluations. This allows us to get only a glimpse at the therapeutic process and the music---and only through the therapist's eyes and ears. As a clinician, I have often noticed that the client's experience differs from mine, particularly with respect to how the music functions as a therapeutic agent. I therefore encourage all of my clients to write a diary after each session. Upon termination, they have the choice of whether or not to share it with me.

Mia decided to share her diary with me, and she also gave me permission to use the tapes from her sessions. I have purposely changed some of the biographical material to maintain her anonymity.

Since both Mia and I considered her therapy successful, I was most interested in analyzing how the work unfolded, and what implications I could gather for training purposes. I have deliberately used the word "unfold," as I noticed that the sessions unfolded like a lotus flower, each session leading to a new layer of Mia's inner life.

This particular work made a deep impression on me because of the manner in which the music: stimulated memories, images, and emotions related to her parents; tapped Mia's unconscious use of current relationships for continued parenting; and released a transformative process in her life.

METHOD

My clinical work is consonant with psychodynamic/psychoanalytic and humanistic theories, which reflects my own personal experiences in training-therapy. I am in debt to the inventor of *Analytical Music Therapy*, Mary Priestley (1980), with whom I trained and by whom my work is deeply influenced.

The form of music therapy that I practice involves the symbolic use of improvised and composed music by the client and the therapist for the purpose of transformation, integration, enhanced self-awareness and self-exploration. In my verbal processing, I attempt to relate the music to the client's present intrapersonal and interpersonal dynamic, to their emotional history, and to the reality outside the therapy room. I also believe that working with the music of the client's "inner child" (its traumas and resources) is essential. In addition, when desired or needed by the client and only because I have the necessary training, I may also combine music therapy with bioenergetic body work.

Many of my private clients, including adults and children with a wide variety of psychiatric diagnoses, demonstrate very little or no verbal abilities in the beginning of their therapy. By developing ways of communicating with them on a pre-verbal level, I have extended Priestley's approach further so that the musical and body communication can stand alone without the medium of words, if necessary.

I mention this aspect because Mia and I both felt that her transformations and deepest realizations tended to happen in those sessions characterized by an exclusive reliance on improvised musical communication. In one of those sessions (the 14th), Mia named the music "Mia's Symphony Of Fate," from which the title of this case study is derived. Her music was often based on programs such as this, and interestingly, I came to perceive every improvisation as separate movements in Mia's "Life Symphony."

Mia's weekly sessions lasted fifty minutes. The session room contained a large variety of instruments including: two pianos; gongs of different sizes and sound quality; orchestral string, wind, and percussion instruments; ethnic instruments from various cultures; and electric keyboards and guitars.

BACKGROUND INFORMATION

Mia is a 27-year-old woman, the youngest of three children. Her father committed suicide when she was five years old. Her mother is alive, and in describing their relationship Mia says: "She is a mystery to me." Mia lives with a boyfriend, Peter, with whom she became pregnant and then miscarried. She is currently under observation for cell changes in the uterus. Mia has been in massage therapy for two years before beginning her music therapy training. She experimented with different types of drugs when she was 21 years-old, but she is now trying to live a healthy life by meditating each day. She is often able to remember her nightly dreams.

Mia is functioning well in the academic milieu and is content with her life, except for problems in her relationship with Peter. When given a choice of which music therapist to have, Mia selected me because of the trust she had developed in me during our academic contacts prior to therapy.

TREATMENT PROCESS

In my approach, assessment and evaluation are not differentiated procedurely, but are an ongoing part of the treatment process. The sources of data include the client's improvisations, compositions, body language and verbalizations. My experience has shown that the content of a client's first session anticipates important themes and emotions that will be encountered later in the process. Therefore I have chosen to elaborate on Mia's first session as the first source of assessment data, and as the first step in the treatment process. Afterwards, I will describe (in similar detail) subsequent sessions leading to Mia's Symphony of Fate---a significant turning point in her process prior to termination.

1st Session: Warmth in My Sexual Organs

The session consists of a therapeutic interview that leads to a mutual improvisation. From the therapeutic interview---which consists of open-ended questions like: "What would you like me to know?"---I gathered all the information contained in the previous section, except for Mia's father's suicide, a fact which Mia chose not to mention at that time.

In this session, Mia states that her goal in therapy is to work with her sexuality, as it is a real problem for her in the relationship with her boyfriend. She feels that she cannot live out her sexuality, as he rejects her when she expresses her needs. Sometimes Mia feels like a nuclear bomb, whose impact her boyfriend is being forced to absorb. She would like to be able to contain her sexual feelings better and avoid pressuring him so much. She also would like to be able to cope with his rejection of her sexual overtures.

When she tells me this, I get an image of a little girl crying while her father walks away from her. I recognize this as a possible indication of my own *countertransference*.

Mia would like to integrate body and dream work in the music therapy, when it is relevant. When she says that, I notice that Mia has a fair amount of awareness of her body, some difficulties in maintaining eye contact, and a habit of sitting with one foot near her sexual organs. Her diary describes her feelings during the interview:

> *I gradually felt more safe with B and was happy that she asked why I had chosen her, so I could say that I felt confident about her. It is good to be asked about things, to be questioned. In the beginning, I became afraid/nervous when I talked about my problems with a therapist. I recognize that. It is getting close to me. I am looking forward to the "work!" I also noticed that I become nervous, when B makes it clear that what happens is up to me. MY RESPONSIBILITY !! I will determine what I am going to do with my own therapy. She doesn't want to be the mother that fixes and decides everything! Is never saying "good" or "bad!" Gives me room to finish my talking, and asks if I have something to ask about.*

Towards the end of the session, Mia says: "I would like to play together with you. I can feel warmth in my sexual organs. I would like to let that be the theme for our improvisation."

Mia chooses the following instruments: wind chimes, marimba, shaker, big Tibetan bowl, a metal rattle and her voice. I choose the grand piano, a Chinese bell tree and my voice. The latter two make it possible for me to acknowledge Mia by choosing instruments of the same sound quality as hers. I chose the piano because of its variety of timbres (keys, strings, wood, pedal echo), and overall versatility as a percussive, harmonic and melodic instrument.

I let Mia start the music, and she plays gentle sounds on the wind chimes, accompanied by breathy, pianissimo singing that contains an ascending and descending fourth from G to C and returning to G. While still singing, Mia changes to the marimba and plays a fast, running rhythm in C major. I join Mia with my voice on the C below hers, forming an octave accompaniment. On the piano I match her marimba rhythm. My intent is to create a holding environment that is not too intrusive. Through the quiet dynamic of the music, I get a feeling of withdrawn emotions. Images emerge for me from the music: of running water in a little stream, the wind blowing in the trees, and two people meeting and touching each other very gently and loving for the first time. Mia writes in her diary: *"I chose metal sounds--tones, a little like water. "*

   Now the music changes as Mia loudly and clearly introduces the following motif on the marimba in C minor:

   We begin to play together around this gestalt. In my right hand, I play the motif in different variations while providing a holding octave with my left hand. This continues for a long time and my image changes to a little girl who is all alone and sad, crying to be cared for. Mia leaves the marimba after a while and plays the metal rattle and the big Tibetan bowl, howling like a wolf in the high register of her voice. Here I sense an intensification in the sound quality of her voice, and I accompany Mia with dramatic tremolos in the bass. After this passage, Mia finishes by playing fine delicate sounds with the metal rattle and breathing aloud. When I look at her after a while she seems very relaxed in her whole body, and she breathes rhythmically. Mia says, "I feel all quiet now. Thank you!" Later, Mia writes this in her diary about the music:

> *I relaxed in the end, when we were finished - we*
> *ended in silence. I breathed!! And I felt relaxed in*

> *my neck and jaw. [Later] I am back home and I*
> *feel extremely well. Am enjoying the cat, the*
> *sunshine, the peace, the food. Thinking of B's*
> *responsibility as being good. When I later heard*
> *the tape of the music, I again got the warm feeling*
> *in the sexual organs. The music is carrying it in*
> *itself. B chooses instruments made of metal just*
> *like mine. She lets me start and finish the*
> *improvisation, and waits a long time before she*
> *looks at me again.*

I will let Mia's diary speak for itself and make just a few comments. Obviously, there is quite a lot of synchronicity between us, both in and outside the music. I think this is one of the reasons why the first session worked out so well.

I have often experienced that the shared improvisation bears many of the same qualities involved in different aspects of love, with the music offering sound patterns that phenomenologically resemble this human expression. In this improvisational meeting, at least four different aspects of love were present. First was the genital love of lovers, which is one of the biggest transformative forces in life. The music produced a warm feeling in Mia's sexual organs, and I had the image during the improvisation of two people making love to each other for the first time. Second, I noticed that most of the music in the section beginning with the motif in Example 1 had the quality of oral music---music that has the fusion and mutuality characteristic of the first phase of breast-feeding. I see this as a healthy element for Mia, and one that many clients experience at some point in their therapy. Third, the music seemed to help Mia love herself. Recall Mia's diary how she feels extremely well back at home enjoying everything around her. A fourth and very essential aspect of love that was evoked by the musical and verbal interaction was Mia's *transference* love for me, expressed in her very positive perception of me and the loving quality of Mia's music when we played together. This provided a basis for a strong therapeutic alliance.

The image of the little girl who is alone, sad, and cries to be taken care of, and that of the howling wolf, anticipated the manner in which Mia's feelings regarding her fathers suicide would emerge in several subsequent sessions.

The clinical technique that I utilized is one that Mary Priestley (1975) calls "Entering into Somatic Communication." It is used for exploring material when the client's emotions are manifested in physical symptoms which provide a means of keeping the underlying emotion outside awareness.

2nd Session: Fear of Losing Contact

Mia discusses the conflict with her boyfriend and how it makes her tired and tense in the shoulders and arms. Through bioenergetic body work which involves Mia letting her shoulders and arms "speak" to her, the theme "Fear of Losing Contact" emerges. She decides to explore this theme musically.

Mia plays the piano strings, hand cymbals and voice. I accompany her with my voice. She cries profusely while she dramatically and angrily tears the piano strings while holding down the sustaining pedal. I hear the voice of Mia's "inner child" saying, "I am afraid, alone and angry." Mia describes this music in her diary:

> *Desperate anger and emptiness---am swimming in a deep,*
> *black ocean. MISS MY FATHER. Fall down in a well*
> *and it gets dark. Something gets torn to pieces.*

After the end of the improvisation Mia speaks more about her relationship to her boyfriend, saying: "I don't want only half a heart." In her diary she writes:

> *Fear of losing contact--emptiness. I reach out and*
> *nobody is there. Fear and anger. But I can't stand it*
> *on the long run. It is weighing me down too much.*

I chose not to connect the "inner child" feelings to her early relationship to her father, as she does not mention her father in the session, and I feel that the timing is not right. Clearly, Mia seems to be getting in touch with how much she misses her father through the improvised music that evokes her longing and tears. It is interesting that she chose not to discuss these feelings in the session, but rather to write about them in the diary. It is probably too painful for her to speak about yet. However, she realizes what her needs are in the relationship with her boyfriend.

3rd Session: The Unspeakable

Mia wants to begin without a title today to see what will develop. She also wants me to play without any specific definition of my role. Mia chooses the following instruments: gongs of various pitches and sound quality, piano, chinese bell tree and voice. I choose the steel drum, kettledrum, Tibetan bowls, wind chimes, metal rattle and voice. The session falls into three parts.

PART I. Mia begins by fiercely hitting the Chinese bell tree and gongs and vocalizing in a deep and loud voice. This triggers images in me of ritual ceremonies in Bali, especially music that is played at funeral ceremonies. I

answer Mia by playing loudly on the Tibetan bowls, drumming in a quick
running rhythm held in pianissimo and using my voice in the same, masculine
manner. The music comes in big sound waves. Suddenly, Mia screams loudly
and hits the biggest gong very hard, as if to punctuate her musical
"sentence" with a period and provide a temporary stopping point. After this,
there is a very long period of silence. Mia writes in her diary about this
part of the session:

> *Music---the unspeakable---the thing that only can be*
> *whispered or hissed out with the breathing. DEATH.*
> *EMPTINESS, ABANDONED, ALONE. I DON'T WANT*
> *TO SPEAK ABOUT IT. I DON'T WANT TO HEAR*
> *ABOUT IT EITHER [Her father Tom's death]. FUNERAL*
> *--- Music for the dead --- TIBET --- Climax --- release,*
> *after that the sorrow, the silence. AS IF I SMASHED*
> *A WINDOW AND ENTERED THE ROOM OF SORROW.*
> *In this part of the music B was very supportive.*

PART II. While Mia cries silently, I breathe loudly and deeply like a
blowing wind. She responds with "Shhhh!" I stop my breath sound. Mia moves
to the piano and pulls violently on the strings. She writes about this phase:

> *I am shushing B with an S-sound. I want peace. Then I*
> *pull the strings---ANGER...DESPERATION. I wanted to*
> *get the pain out through the fingers, therefore I pulled*
> *the piano strings with the fingers.*

After this Mia plays atonal, dissonant passages with a melancholy color
on the piano. I play in the background on the steel drum, trying to
illustrate the tears, that are rolling down her cheeks. I allow Mia to finish
the improvisation. She ends by playing handfuls of clusters in the deep
register of the keys, letting the last cluster hang in the air. Mia writes
about this part:

> *Playing the keys - an attempt to do something about the*
> *condition - NO! - I DO NOT WANT TO! Nevertheless*
> *light sounds are sneaking in the piano improvisation. B.*
> *only played very little with me in the end. Perhaps she*
> *perceived that this time was about loneliness, emptiness*
> *- and therefore consciously stayed away. It had a*
> *reinforcing effect on my emotion. At one time I called*
> *to her and waited for her in the music and she did not*
> *come. Because of this, my situation or emotion became*
> *clearer.*

After the music Mia looks very unhappy, and I offer her my hands. She takes them and holds them very firmly during the whole conversation. She says: "There are some things, that one cannot talk about," and sobs very loud, "like when people are dying." There is a long break in the talking.

She resumes: "My father died, when I was five years old. He went into psychoanalysis and committed suicide. Then I got a stepfather who hit his dogs." She speaks about how she misses her father, what he was like, and says that her boyfriend reminds her of her father. Mia's voice gets gradually clearer and louder during this talk and she looks as if she is relieved. She writes about this verbal processing:

> *I became a little happy, when I had been speaking with B and told her about the circumstances under Tom's death. Peter is of course becoming the person that has to fill out the gaps after Tom, and therefore those enormously difficult situations arise, when he doesn't want to, or isn't able to fill up the hole.*

PART III. Mia asks me to play a piece of music for her on the grand piano while she lies on the mattress. I choose to improvise over the main theme from Chopin's "Nocturne in D Major," because I feel that it reflects her emotions, and also has a caring, holding quality. Mia looks satisfied when she leaves the room. In her diary, she writes that, in the session, "Time went so fast."

It also went fast for me, and I was very touched both by the intensity and ritual-like music in Part I, and by Mia's story and tears. She touched my own "inner child's" hurt and feelings of loss connected to my own father's suicide, which occurred when I was 3 months old.

I used the technique that Priestley (1975) calls "Subverbal Communication," where client and therapist improvise together without title, focus, or specific roles. It is used to share feelings, when words fail or become meaningless. It is meant to strengthen the ego.

4th and 5th Sessions: My Resources

In the fourth session, Mia makes a drawing that pictures her resources as she sees them. She does not want to improvise over the drawing, however. In the fifth session, Mia focuses on the feeling of not being good enough, and ends up improvising on the piano with the title "I am good!" I see this as a natural extension of the previous session.

6th and 7th Sessions: Mother-Daughter Projections

In the sixth session, Mia begins to work on a nightly dream in which she is trying to integrate the mother and the girl in herself, thus allowing her to be her own mother. She decides to compose a song from the little girl to the mother about how the girl feels when the drunken mother leaves the girl alone.

As a consequence of Mia coming in contact with her resources and benevolent side, she now has the strength to look at her own mother, take her in, and address the task of taking back the *"mother projection"* from me.

The seventh session begins with Mia singing and playing her composed "Song To Mother" on the piano. I accompany her on the accordion. The plea of the song's refrain is: "Stay by me, stay by me, because I love you."

Later I use Priestley's (1975) "Splitting Technique," which helps to explore experiences or situations that involve the exploration and integration of polarities. Mia improvises over the polarities of being a little girl versus being the mother. The musical sounds that Mia associated with being a little girl were "little, ugly, angry and hard." Sounds for being the mother were "big, soft, warm, and accepting."

8th Session: Interplay

Mia expresses a need to explore her interpersonal contact and relationship with me in a mutual improvisation without any title. This represents a progression in Mia's awareness of the process from an intrapersonal to an interpersonal level. Mia writes about this:

> *"The feeling in my chest area is changing. This hurt child is perhaps letting go, so that I can turn the energy outward."*

I sense Mia's *resistance* against verbalizing for the first time. I see it as a natural and important phenomenon in the therapeutic process. Here music serves as an excellent container and "waiting-platform," offering possibilities of intrapersonal and interpersonal dialogues at the same time. Mia expresses it in this way in her diary:

> *I am experiencing that I am losing some of the engagement in the therapy. Perhaps it is because the analyzing part of it doesn't offer me anything right now. Too much analysis, too little being. I prefer to experiment with the possibilities and depths of the music than dig into my own past. I want to play together with B because that is where something is happening - it is*

> *in the INTERPLAY.....[Later] As a therapist I, of course,*
> *have to be ready to contact on a deep level and stay*
> *there.*

It is my impression that in this session Mia starts the process of taking back her projection onto me as "the good mother." She now perceives me as a playing partner. I see it as a product of the former session where she worked on containing both the little girl and the mother. Later, Mia also has an important realization regarding the value of this improvisation for her training.

9th and 10th Sessions: Finding the Musical Self

We start out improvising together again without a title, and later listen to the taped music. In her diary, Mia describes this music as a crystallization of her needs: (1) to let go and give way to the unstructured, chaotic, and casual; (2) to meddle more directly in B's music, and be a little more confronting; and (3) to draw her boundaries. I sense, that Mia now is trying out her ability to say YES and NO with force and directness, as a part of integrating "the adult" in her.

The tenth session begins with Mia saying that she felt that her music contains many "redundant" tones. From that arose the theme for her solo improvisation: "Play One Tone, Wait and Listen, Until You Play the Next Relevant Tone."

This improvisation marks the beginning of a greater focus and concern on Mia's part for the musical material itself. This occurs naturally at certain stages in music therapy, when musical material takes precedence over emotional issues. I see this as a need to nourish the creative "composer" of the client, and also as an expression of a need to be on "neutral ground" for a time. It also represents a time when the client is reflecting upon and consolidating what has happened in the therapeutic process.

After the improvisation, we used the taped music for a guided imagery. Here is Mia's description:

> *The gongs were like healing. Their vibrations go deep*
> *inside the body. Became warm in stomach and sexual*
> *organs - combustion! I felt like under water for a time,*
> *while I listened to the music. It was very nice.*

11th sessions: Finding the Feminine Part of My Self

Mia wants to contact her feminine side through music. I take the role of an active listener. She begins on the piano, and searches for a long time. Mia writes:

> *I didn't like the keys. Couldn't use them. All the time*
> *I had to force the fingers to go on. The music became*
> *abrupt - a hard stroke. All the time an attempt to hit*
> *something. I didn't know if I just should stop it and say*
> *that I couldn't; but then I started playing on the strings,*
> *then it began to flow. It was very beautiful. I really*
> *liked the sound-board, that was there all the time. I*
> *didn't know, which tones I hit. I chose ONE TONE,*
> *THAT BECAME A BASIS. A very strong dissolution*
> *came and, after that, the music became much stronger*
> *and clearer. I see that I perhaps should pass old ideas*
> *and patterns to arrive at my feminine self.*

In processing the session, Mia says that she saw different types of female images in the end of the music. Mia realizes that she has to let go of old patterns to be able to truly be herself. The contact with the feminine parts of her Self, I see as a natural product of being in touch with her "inner mother." I also see this session as a beginning step of integration in that one of Mia's overall goals is to facilitate a balance between her feminine and masculine qualities. The first step in this process is to become aware of those qualities.

12th Session: Feelings Towards Peter

Mia speaks about not being able to express herself and her needs to her boyfriend. She wants to work with that. I begin by working with her body, using bio-energetic grounding and centering exercises aimed at helping her to "stand on her own two feet" without being overwhelmed by her emotions---in this case, tremendous anger. I then present a hand drum so that Mia can hit it while vocally expressing what she would like to tell Peter. It seems difficult in the beginning, but with my backing and re-inforcing on the drum, she finally manages to hit the drum fiercely, and with conviction in her voice. In the end, I take the role as Peter so that Mia can practice what she wants to say to him. About this session, Mia writes:

> *The doubt makes me weak! I loose my self when I flip*
> *out at home. I abandon my centering. I had to discover*
> *that! I practiced telling him what I wanted to say,*
> *clearly, unambiguously and convincingly. I have just*
> *done that and he said yes at once. I hadn't expected*
> *that. I have to work on staying clear and centered---*
> *to be in touch with my strength and sticking to my*
> *demands.*

In this session we used the technique of "Reality Rehearsal" (Priestley, 1975), where the client improvises how to take a needed step in her life, focusing on inner obstacles that are encountered---in this case the anger and fear of being rejected.

13th Session: Do I Want To Be Like My Mother?

Mia gives positive feedback on the last session, and recounts a dream from the night following this session. The dream provided her a symbolic representation of what had happened in the session and afterwards. A long pause in the session follows the discussion of Mia's dream. I notice that Mia looks irritated. She says that she does not feel like doing much today and I sense some resistance in the air. Silence occurs again.

She uses the rest of the session to speak about negative feelings about her mother (Anna), and makes one improvisational attempt to find out what she would like to own or take over from her and what not. I take a mirroring role. This exercise does not seem productive. One particular sentence lingers in the air: "I remember when I was little---even when she held me, she smelled badly."

I end the session by telling her that I sense that she is irritated, that she has some resistance towards working with her image of the mother, and that it is OK to feel like that. Mia writes about the session:

> *Bullshit! I was not able to get in touch with myself today. And I do not think that B offered me any help. I talked too much. I talked myself away. When I started thinking of Anna, I disappeared. I cannot use her femininity as a model. But I guess that's OK too.*

14th Session: The Symphony of Fate

Mia expresses her need to play with me without any predetermined theme. She chooses the synthesizer and I play the grand piano, kettle drum and cymbal. There is a quality of preparing for something fateful in Mia's broad, dissonant, and sustained sounds. I just listen. I get associations to programmatic or cinematic film music. Mia describes each part of the improvisation in her diary. Her descriptions are indicated below in italics.

Entrance: A door is opened.
>The chords become louder and have a threatening quality. I accompany Mia gently in the background, drumming on the kettle drum in a quick rhythm making dampened beats, as if a thunderstorm is heard in the distance and is coming nearer.

Dissolution: Violence, Anxiety.
Mia makes single tones jumping up and down the keyboard, and I answer them on the kettle drum and cymbal, as an offer to enter a dialogue. I hear that she is not answering me, but instead is self-absorbed in her own playing. I listen for a while without playing.
Emptiness: No orientation point.
The music consists of detached tones, atonality, and empty chords.

Then Mia uses the pitch modulator on the synthesizer to bend single tones. They sound like a little child screaming constantly. Tears are running down her cheeks. Through my atonal playing on the piano, I try to portray feelings of desperation, loneliness and unhappiness, while wailing in tremolo passages to underline the mood.

> *Lament---also angry---No! This last part is about my father's death. I could not bear that he should have died detested and unwanted by all people. Totally lonely - without any love. The music still makes me cry.*

This leads Mia to improvise a tonal elegy in a minor key, that I underline with a simple ostinato bass line. Mia's melody steps down note for note, like steps down a staircase, and ends on the deepest note of the synthesizer. I finish by allowing the A minor ostinato to slowly die out, repeating it more and more gently, like little sighs.

After the improvisation ends, there is a long pause. To further process the music, Mia takes a piece of paper and draws a picture of a long line that points downward, ending in a little spiral. She calls it "Sorrow." While she draws, I let the improvisation settle down into my consciousness, and I imagine that this music must have been about an important and dramatic part of Mia's "inner child." So important that, for now, it could not be expressed in words, but only on a symbolic level in music and drawing. Mia explains in her diary:

> *I could not talk - I just wanted to play. It was good to play. It became long. Mia's Symphony of Fate had a beginning and an ending with structure and melody. It was good that B was there and played together with me. She was backing up my expression. My teeth chattered. When I had been playing for a long time, I was able to think in mode, rhythm, and form without disappearing from the emotions in the music.*

Here Mia gets in touch with deeper feelings connected to her father: emptiness, lamenting, anger, sorrow. These feelings were also present as an undercurrent in the music of the first session.

The session causes "after-pains" six days later. In her diary, she describes the following image that arose during one of her meditations.

> *It was a big hole. I decided not to go in, but I wanted to light it up (there was a man next to the hole). It was a clammy cave. At the very end, a girl, twelve or thirteen years old, was sitting huddled up and bound. It was me who was being kept as a prisoner. I thought of entering the cave and picking her up, but was afraid of being caught myself. She became smaller and smaller. In the end she was a sack that got closed. The man had it (my father). That is the truth from that time. The fragile, sensitive girl that is kept as a prisoner, that has to be liberated, but does not know how - with warmth and love.*

15th Session: Entering the Cave

Mia says that her teeth were chattering in the last session and that she cried over the image just described. She also says that the music was also about her relationship to her mother and step-father, who moved into her home when she was twelve years old. She expresses that it is very difficult for her to share this with anybody. She feels as if she has lost the little girl, as if she has hidden herself in the cave far away.

I ask her about the connection to her daily life and Mia says that in her relationship with Peter, she sometimes becomes like the little girl in the cave, and he cannot handle that. It is also connected with a feeling of being unwanted, when she is too pushy and he rejects her.

I suggest that we improvise being in the cave together. Mia can then explore being the little girl and contact me if she wants. I encourage her to use her voice and facial sounds (as she had mentioned that her teeth were chattering in the previous session also). She prefers to have me outside the cave at the edge, so that we can communicate with each other, if she needs that.

I build a symbolic cave out of two quilts, and Mia takes the glockenspiel and triangle with her into the cave. I portray the cave on the grand piano with big hollow sounds made from pulling on the deep dampened strings while depressing the sustaining pedal. I take long breaks between each sound. I guide Mia into the cave through the music. I then hear Mia's voice from the distance. It is withdrawn yet wailing: "Oh-ya-ya....Ooohh...Mmmmmmmmm." I now support her voice by playing the same tones as her.

When I play louder, Mia's voice becomes louder and more twisting. She now beats the glockenspiel. It sounds like stamping. I stamp with her on a deep string as a drone. Then she plays the triangle gently while humming with her voice. Her diary describes the improvisation so far:

> *There were tears, but I also discovered other things. It was safe: I had chosen to go in the cave to protect myself. I liked communicating with B, then it became more joyful...I could play "princess music" in the cave and it could be heard outside. I felt like playing with this light music.*

As the improvisation continues, her voice glides up and down ending in various nasally aspirated sounds combined with facial grimaces. Suddenly, there is a big bang. Mia has thrown her instruments on the floor. I bang one time with the lid of the piano. It is over.

After the improvisation, Mia realizes that, today, the "cave part" of her also represents something positive--a place she can chose to go to of her own will. The existence of the playful "princess music" leads her to that realization. Mia can break out of her "inner prison" (the big bang), if that is what she needs to do.

Technically in this session, I used Mia's symbols (i.e., cave, little imprisoned girl) as a starting scene for a guided imagery to improvised music. Instead of guiding verbally, however I guided through my musical expression on the piano. This technique is used to explore unconscious material, and to find new solutions for persistent inner conflicts. Priestley (1975) states: "Symbols are accumulators and transformers of psychic energy. They have the relationship to ideas and action that an iceberg has to a waterfall. Using them, the therapist is dealing with the transformation of force" (p. 129).

In Mia's case, her musical exploration of the symbols opened her eyes to the positive aspects of contact with her "cave-part." It was a place where she could feel safe and protected, and where the playful and joyful side of her "inner child" could come forth.

Final Sessions

In the seventeenth session, Mia says that she has had a very positive dream about her father. In it, she was two years old, and he was sitting next to her. She was fascinated by him. She also had met him during a meditation where he had given her his love and held her, and afterwards had said good-bye to her. This experience had felt so real to her that Mia later wondered if it was something she was recalling from her childhood, or if it just came to her as an image. She says she is happy for the experience because it was an entrance--a channel--to get in touch with what she received from her father.

I see these phenomena as a result of the music's ability to establish contact with hidden emotions, memories, and experiences that are an important part of her existential being.

The music therapy continued for five more sessions and, interestingly, the music in these sessions did not contain undercurrents of melancholy, loneliness, wailing and solitude that were so characteristic of many of her earlier improvisations. In the very last session, the improvisation theme was "Goodbye," and it touched upon little sequences from most of the sessions, like a recapitulation or reprise.

In the verbal evaluation that took place upon her termination, Mia expressed that she was satisfied with the work because her sexuality was more in balance and the cell changes in her uterus were now minor and declining. However, she felt that she still had some work to do on accepting herself and not feeling compelled to live up to other people's expectations of her. I noticed that our musical and verbal contact was more of one adult to another, and that Mia was able to maintain eye contact as well as hold her own center. Her mood also seemed to have become more stable with less lability.

DISCUSSION AND CONCLUSIONS

How do I evaluate Mia's progress? First, her diary and her specific comments on the sessions represent clear evidence about what progress she made, and the effectiveness of various techniques and interventions. Certainly, Mia had addressed traumas of "the inner child" as well as more current personal issues, and showed an ability to work in the music with this difficult material.

Mia's growth as a therapist has also provided a testament to the productive nature of the work we did together. As I was Mia's clinical supervisor during the following half-year, I was able to closely observe her clinical development. She was able to establish therapeutic relationships through music, and one of her strengths was an ability to work effectively in both the verbal and musical realm. Mia was more aware of her own counter-transference and was thus able to avoid many of the pitfalls common to beginning therapists. She had developed her own musical language, and was able to tune her body as an instrument and use her voice as an important tool---on equal terms with the instruments. She also showed the courage to experiment with her own techniques.

Why did the music therapy work as it did? As I have previously discussed my methodological procedures and techniques, here I would like to offer my basic assumption concerning the structure in free improvisation, the technique used most prominently in this case. Any musical structure which a client presents in an improvisation is a mirror of the client's psychological organization and dominant function. By musical structure I mean melody, rhythm, timbre, pitch, dynamic, mode, pulse and tempo---in short, any parameter or element in music that organizes or is organized. This is a variation of Priestley's statement: "The musical structure as regards rhythm and pitch (less so timbre and dynamics which are more responsive to the mood of the moment) is governed by that mental institution [structure] or function which rules the patient's psyche at the time" (1980, p. 120). Thus, when describing each improvisation, I have placed particular emphasis upon those musical structures that seemed to have a significance in relation to Mia's psyche at the time.

A second important factor connected with the improvisations is their titles. Each one serves as a focus point for structuring the music, and certainly colors the content of the music. Naturally, our selection of the most relevant title for exploration is of central importance.

From this case, we can see that the act of improvising in itself offers possibilities for intrapersonal and interpersonal dialogues---dialogues which, as we have seen in Mia's case, can provide the basis for self-transformation and growth. The work with Mia also illustrates how music therapy, when used as part of training, can serve not only as a place for personal development but also as an experiential laboratory for gaining the insights and skills essential to becoming an effective music therapist.

GLOSSARY

Analytical Music Therapy: "The symbolic use of improvised music by the therapist and the client to explore the client's inner life and provide the proclivity for growth (Priestley, 1980, p. 18).

Countertransference: The therapist's unconscious reactions (in and outside of the music) to the client and his/her transference (Priestley, 1980, pp. 50-57).

Mother Projection: The client attributes aspects of her mother to the therapist, other person, or object.

Transference: "A process by which a patient attempts to relive with her therapist the unfinished business from former important relationships in her life. It can also be her attempt to come to terms with, or rid herself of, conflicting parts of her psyche by projecting them on to her therapist (Priestley, 1975, p. 238).

REFERENCES

Priestley, M. (1975). Music Therapy in Action. St. Louis: Magnamusic-Baton.

Priestley, M. (1980). The Herdecke Analytical Music Therapy Lectures. Translated into German by Brigitte Stein (1983). Stuttgart: Klett-Cotta.

The Musical Mirror:
Music Therapy For The
Narcissistically Injured

DIANE SNOW AUSTIN, M.A., C.M.T.
Adjunct Faculty Member, New York University
Music Therapist, Psychotherapist-Private Practice
Brooklyn Heights, New York

Abstract: *This study describes Jungian oriented analytic music therapy with a "narcissistically injured" woman in her mid-twenties, who at the time was studying to be a dance therapist. Through musical improvisation and the relationship that developed with the music therapist over a period of two and a half years, the woman began to uncover, explore and accept devalued parts of herself.*

INTRODUCTION

The word "narcissism" has entered our everyday speech as a pejorative term meaning extreme self-love and aloof impenetrability. The myth of Narcissus, however, implies something quite different. Narcissus was a beautiful youth who rejected all suitors for his love. To punish him, the goddess, Nemesis, made him fall in love with his own reflected image in a pool. Unable to possess the object of his love, he died in despair.

My psychological orientation is based on the work of Carl Jung (1968, 1969), and from this viewpoint, narcissism relates to the mystery of identity (Satinover, 1980; Schwartz-Salant, 1982; Kalshed, 1980). Narcissus falls in love with the reflected image of himself because he does not yet possess himself. He is alienated from his own being and longs for what he lacks. "The solution of the problem of Narcissus is the fulfillment of self-love rather than its renunciation" (Edinger, 1972, p. 161). This fulfillment or "union with the image in the depths, requires a descent into the unconscious, a symbolic death ... Narcissism, at least in its original mythological sense, is the way into the unconscious where one must go in quest of individuality" (Edinger, 1972, p. 162).

My clients are primarily artists (singers, actors, writers, art therapists, etc.) and the majority of them have been *narcissistically injured*. They cover a spectrum of narcissism in terms of the severity of woundedness as well as which aspects of the narcissistic character are highlighted. What they have in common is the need to be seen, heard and understood. They need to be valued for who they really are and not just for their special gifts or their ability to adapt to the needs of others. They each experience core feelings of loneliness and isolation from themselves and from others, and they each have a deep desire to find out who they are - to find the real self.

BACKGROUND INFORMATION

Sara is a very attractive, 25-year-old graduate student from California. She is presently attending New York University and majoring in dance therapy. She relates in a polite, soft-spoken manner and appears introspective, very bright but aloof and distanced from her feelings.

She is the oldest of three children, one boy and two girls. She describes her family as outgoing and financially comfortable. She indicates her parents were kind and understanding and gave her "a lot of space" while she was growing up. She feels she had too much freedom and that is why she never rebelled as a teenager.

Her relationships with boyfriends have been distant and painful, and she has a very dim awareness that perhaps she has a problem in her relationships with men. She had her first sexual experience at twenty; previously she had tried to have sex, but could not relax enough to let penetration occur.

Sara has had no previous therapy but fears she is becoming passive like her mother, and is aware that she feels constricted and distrustful of others. She is afraid that these qualities will get in the way of her professional training. She originally wanted to work with a dance therapist but the referring clinic was unable to connect her with one. She had studied piano briefly as a child and enjoyed it, and felt an experience in any of the creative arts therapies would be valuable.

METHOD

Therapy sessions took place once a week for an hour in a comfortable room. The client sat on a couch behind a table filled with various percussion instruments. I sat on a chair in front of the piano facing the client. Music was used in most, but not all of the sessions.

The Jungian perspective on Narcissism is that it is a stage of blocked development where the original personality still exists ready to unfold but is stuck at a grandiose - exhibitionistic level (six months to one and a half years of age). The *ego* is merged or identified with the *archetype* of the *Self*. This causes swings from inflation to deflation (Schwartz-Salant, 1982). Inflation is a false sense of integration; the client feels good or "high." However, when the ego's identification with the Self is broken (through criticism or a confrontation with self-limitations, etc.), deflation results. The center cannot hold. Clients have described this as an all or nothing feeling; a sensation of having no ground to stand on. There is a fragmentation of the personality which creates a lack of identity and self-worth as well as inner conflict. The psyche becomes dissociated into different parts wanting different things. The client feels divided between differing points of view or identifies with one of the fragments to focus the personality (Satinover, 1980).

I felt musical exploration of part-personalities would be an effective method of working with Sara. Music allows the image and associated feelings to be channelled into a concrete form, for example, "the needy part." The ego can then relate to a previously unknown aspect of the unconscious (Ulanov, 1971). The ability of music to evoke feelings directly would enable Sara to access the feelings associated with the different parts of her personality. The feelings could then be experienced and gradually accepted. This process would facilitate the integration of her personality.

I used the same approach when working with Sara's dreams. Dream images were looked at as parts of the psyche and were explored through musical improvisations.

All the musical activities Sara participated in were improvisational. My experience leads me to believe that music improvisation facilitates the engagement of the whole person; body, mind and spirit. Improvisation comes from a natural impulse. When that impulse is not blocked, but is allowed free expression, spontaneity is released (Spolin, 1963). Then the natural or real self can emerge.

Marion Woodman (1981, p. 78) wrote, "play constellates the unconscious in precisely the same way as does a dream" so that repressed and/or unknown psychic contents can come to consciousness through play. Winnicott (1971) wrote about the importance of play in the therapeutic process. He said there could be no healing until the client has learned to play. "It is in playing and only in playing that the individual child or adult is able to be creative and to use the whole personality, and it is only in being creative that the individual discovers the self" (Winnicott, 1971, p. 54).

Sara, like many who are narcissistically injured, grew up too fast. As a child she was a "little adult" who adapted to the needs of her parents. Now, she needed to learn how to play and to access her spontaneity. Music improvisation was the method I employed to meet this need.

The wound to the self that characterizes Narcissism occurs at a pre-verbal or pre-Oedipal stage of development. Music facilitates therapeutic regression because it more directly taps emotional rather than cognitive processes in the client. It also gives the client a language to express experiences they may have no words for.

In the early stages of therapy Sara often had no words and few memories of her childhood. There would be long pauses in which I felt it was difficult for her to speak. I later came to realize she often inhibited her self-expression for fear of judgment. Improvising at the piano together provided her with a safe avenue for expressing feelings. My playing with her provided support, encouragement and companionship.

In the later stages of therapy, music enabled Sara to bypass her intellectual defense system and reach her underlying feelings. The improvisations provided a container where she could actually have the experience in the moment instead of only talking about it.

The specific musical techniques I employed were "mirroring," "holding" and "dialoging." By "mirroring" I mean recreating important melodic phrases or motifs, chord progressions and/or rhythmic patterns that I heard in Sara's music. This technique seemed quite appropriate considering the chronic lack of mirroring (being seen, heard, empathized with and reflected uncritically) she received as a child.

By "holding" I mean creating a containing environment by sustaining chords that supported Sara's melodies and/or keeping a rhythm going once she had initiated it. My intention at these times was to gently support her musical statements without leading her or intruding my presence. Sara often spoke of feeling a lack of support from her parents and seemed to appreciate this form of musical accompaniment.

"Dialoguing" is more mutually interactive, like a spontaneous verbal exchange. Sara and I would take turns initiating and responding. Either of us could introduce new musical ideas. On one occasion, I reflected musically what I sensed she was feeling but not expressing in her music.   This technique can be very effective when combined with sung dialogue.

TREATMENT PROCESS

Beginning Phase

My initial impression of Sara was of someone asleep. The image that came to me quite often in the first few months of our working together was of "Sleeping Beauty." This very pretty and intelligent young woman seemed like a spirit, not yet embodied. I felt as if she had not yet entered life. As our work progressed, I often wondered what wicked fairy had put the curse of sleep on Sara and how could I break the spell and awaken her.

Her speaking voice was soft and flat, lacking in affect. She seemed depressed and got teary when speaking of feelings of loss. The loss seemed connected to her illusions about her parents. She was beginning to see them clearer and felt disappointment and sadness. They were not the ideal parents she wanted.   She was also feeling more separate from them because of choosing a career (dance therapy) to which they could not relate.

In the third session, Sara brought in a dream of "playing dead." A man and a woman were after her with knives and the best defense she had was to pretend to be dead. She had difficulty connecting to any feelings associated with the dream, so I suggested that we explore the dream musically. She agreed and chose the piano. I sat beside her on a separate chair and played the piano with her, using the mirroring and holding techniques. I played in the bass part of the piano.

Her music was very dissonant and she seemed surprised by how strong and rhythmically she was playing. As we continued to play, the music became slower, softer and centered on C minor.   She said it sounded "sad," "mournful," and "funereal."   She felt pressure on her heart. We did some breathing together and the pressure became a feeling of sadness.

After playing the piano, she was able to talk about how she "played dead" with her parents. The knives in the dream, she associated to a fear of being "knifed in the back." She felt she would be attacked if she dared to expose herself. This theme, fear of being seen and attacked, continued throughout the therapy.

Third Month

At this point in the therapy, Sara was concerned with her perfectionism and how it interfered with her ability to dance. She expected to be perfect the first time she tried to do anything and was fearful of making a mistake and "looking bad." She had little faith in the learning process and became very impatient with herself when creative ideas failed to come quickly or her body was unable to immediately obey her commands.

We decided to explore the "impatient part" of herself at the piano. She played a medium tempo marching rhythm. It had a driven quality to it. As she continued to play, she sped up the tempo and the music became louder and more dissonant with no particular key center. I supported her by mirroring and creating a holding environment. I felt the music had a relentless quality to it. This improvisation led to a discussion of the "critical part" of her psyche that always wants "more" and "better," and leaves her feeling that she will never measure up and be "good enough." An encounter with this "critical part" usually left her feeling insecure and depressed.

Sara talked about an experience she had in dance class a few days before. It was the first time she was able to be patient with herself and take into consideration the reality that she had been away from dance for several years, and that it would take time to get back into shape. This kinder attitude toward herself felt like a new part and I suggested we explore it together musically. My intention was to strengthen this part by focusing on it and increasing her awareness of it. In the music I could mirror and support her as she gave form to a more positive self attitude.

The music was consonant and in the key of C, with strong movement from the dominant to the root. The melodic line was flowing. The rhythm was light and somewhat playful with medium tempo and dynamics. Sara said the music felt "awkward," "new," "like emerging."

Resistance

In our sixth month of working together, Sara missed two sessions in a row. She had very good reasons but I suspected we were getting closer to feelings of loss and sadness and she might be experiencing some resistance. She was eventually able to talk about her difficulty trusting anyone, which made the prospect of depending on me very frightening. She could not really depend on her parents, in fact, her mother had depended on her emotionally. She was very much a "mother" to her parents and her younger siblings. She had to grow up quickly and be responsible from an early age. It seemed to me she had never been allowed to be a child. She was afraid that if she had needs she would be rejected. We decided to explore her fears of dependency at the piano.

The music was loud and dissonant with a strong, staccato rhythm. She played clusters of notes rapidly. There was no key center. She said she felt like she was behind a wall. She continued to play. She wanted to get through the wall. She said there were tears behind it. She stopped playing and cried. I felt that her pain was connected to the isolation she felt from her feelings and her real self. She said people were often attracted to her but not for who she really was. They did not really know her, and she was too afraid to let them in. When I asked how these feelings connected with her fear of depending on me, she said she wondered if I could really be interested in her for herself, with no "ulterior motive."

In the next session, I had difficulty listening to what she was saying. She seemed cut off from her feelings. She spoke vaguely and disconnectedly about "issues of perfectionism and control." She brought up a dream fragment and analyzed it herself. At one point I said to her, "You're doing all the work yourself and don't seem to need any help from me." I asked her what she was feeling and she said she did not know. She said she felt out of touch with her feelings. I suggested music and she once again chose the piano.

She began playing in F minor and stayed mainly with F minor, G minor and C_7 chords. The music was very rhythmic and melodic with a lot of energy and drive, very different from the "music" of our verbal exchange. At one point I felt we were connecting musically. Then her playing changed. It became slower and more dissonant. She left F minor. I could discern no key center. The rhythm was inconsistent and difficult to follow. I felt she was distancing from me.

When we discussed the improvisation, she said that she was aware of breaking the connection with me. She did not want to let me in anymore. She had met a man she was interested in but did not want to talk about it. I wondered out loud if she might fear I would do what her mother did, and pressure her to explain things before she was ready. She talked about her mother's intrusiveness. She said she felt pressured by her to always have to know what she was doing. She saw a connection between her mother's attitude and the way she inhibited her own spontaneity in the music. She told me she was enjoying the F minor section until she started analyzing the music. At that point she became distanced from her feelings and the music changed. She felt she was doing to herself what her mother did to her. I pointed out that we had a musical connection in the F minor section which was broken when the music changed. Her intellectual defense could have been mobilized to defend her against feelings of closeness with me. She said she felt more aware recently of judging the "needy part" of herself. If she allowed herself to feel close to me, this part might surface.

A few weeks later, she began the session by talking about the dance piece she had been creating. The theme of the dance was "The Struggle Against Resistance." We discussed her fear of coming out into the world with her authentic feelings and needs. She said: "In the beginning of the dance I felt like an unformed creature. When I opened my eyes, I felt like I was in a hostile world. My breathing stopped. I felt scared. I didn't want to move out into the environment. I wanted to curl back up inside myself."

I invited her to pick an instrument on which she could best describe her feelings when encountering this hostile world. She chose the claves. I supported her on the Syrian drum. Her playing was concentrated and loud. She hit the sticks together in a consistent rhythm that sounded mechanical and felt cold and relentless to me.

When we discussed the music, she said it felt "cold ... like icicles" and went on to say "danger" and finally "hate." She made associations to her mother's anger which felt cold and unrelated, and to her own difficulty in expressing anger. My association (which I did not share) was to Schwartz-Salant's (1982) work on Narcissism in which he describes the feelings of being "special" that a narcissistically injured child has. He believes the child remembers feeling special for his particular gifts, but represses the memory of feeling envied and hated by the parent (or parents).

Eighth Month

This session centered around feelings of abandonment brought on by her relationship with her supervisor at school. She felt she got no empathy or understanding from him. She felt he left her alone to take care of herself. She said she did express her needs to him, which was very difficult for her, but she got little response. She was afraid of being more direct with him. She felt he would experience her as demanding and then reject her.

We decided to explore the theme "no response" at the piano. She began and stayed in the key of A minor. I supported and held her by playing chords; mainly A minor to D minor. The music was slow and mournful. She played sparsely. Her melody was composed of small step- like movements. She began to cry as she played and soon stopped playing. She said she felt sad and abandoned. I asked her when she had felt this way before. She recalled the day her grandmother died. Her grandmother was living with her and her family because she was dying of cancer. Sara was twelve years old at the time. The day of her grandmother's death was the day she began menstruating. She was frightened and felt unprepared to "become a woman." She called to her mother for help and reassurance, but her mother was busy with her grandmother and could not come to her right away. When she finally did come, her manner was perfunctory and unsympathetic. When her grandmother died, a few hours later, Sara again needed comfort and support. She had been very close to her grandmother. It sounded as if Sara's mother dealt with her own loss by keeping herself busy and distracted. She was uncomfortable with her feelings and therefore unable to be emotionally available to her daughter.

Sara had told me this story before, but with no affect. This telling was very different. She was able to re-experience the trauma and feel companioned in her grief. She felt the sadness that she had not been able to feel in the past, and with it, compassion for the lonely little girl inside.

One Year

At this point in our work together, I noticed a change in Sara's music.

She played with "more feeling," her melodic lines were more flowing, and her musical ideas seemed more spontaneous and less cerebral. There was more musical interaction between the two of us, especially at the piano. Correspondingly, she seemed more aware of her feelings and more willing to express them.

One day she came in after being sick all week with the flu, and complained of being attacked by her "inner critic." I asked her if she could musically portray this critical voice. She came to the piano and played a loud, dissonant improvisation. She made staccato "jabbing" sounds by hitting clusters of notes rapidly. I was supporting her by reflecting and holding in the lower register of the piano. At one point in the music she flattened her hand against the keys and stopped playing. She then began again and stopped shortly afterwards. She said she felt "crowded out" by the "critical voice." I shared my association to the "jabbing" sounds, which was to her image from a previous session, of being stabbed in the back. She began to make associations which ended with memories of growing up and always feeling responsible for her mother's happiness. She felt that whatever she did it was "never enough" to please her mother.

I suggested that we play again. This time I played the "critical voice" and she played her feeling response. I repeated what she had played before and then, very gradually, began to blend in with the more consonant, melodic music she was now playing. We interacted and her music changed somewhat; mainly becoming louder and somewhat faster. I felt pleasure in this connection and used my feelings to gain some insight into what she might be feeling.

Afterwards, in our discussion of the music, she said that it felt wonderful when I became supportive. She said that she felt understood and responded to and that enabled her to express her feelings more fully and genuinely without fear of judgment and attack.

It was during this period that Sara expressed a desire to sing. She wanted some help in projecting her voice. Her speaking voice was soft and she often trailed off toward the end of sentences, becoming inaudible. Her breathing was shallow and she sometimes held her breath to control her feelings.

I gave her some basic vocal instruction and showed her how to breathe deeply and connect more to her body. Sara, like other women who lack a genuine bonding with their mothers, was not securely grounded in her own body and lived a lot "in her head." She was becoming more aware of this mind/body split, and realizing how difficult it was for her to get past her intellectual defense system to her underlying feelings.

We worked with open vowel sounds and she was gradually able to relax and open her throat. As she learned to breath deeply and allow the breath to support the tone, she was able to produce a fuller sound. We talked about her fears of projecting her voice so that it created a "bigger impression."

Singing had metaphoric implications for Sara, as it has for many people. To sing was to express herself freely; something she desired, yet feared. Would she be received, understood and accepted? Or would she once again be judged and found lacking? Did her voice (did "she") have to be perfect before she could send her sounds out into the world?

Emerging

It was now over a year and a half since Sara and I had begun working together. We had been "chipping away" at the idealization of her mother, and uncovering childhood feelings of sadness related to disappointment and loss. She felt she had to hide her own needs in order to take care of her mother. Her parent's marriage was not a happy one, and her mother turned to her for comfort and support. In many ways, Sara sacrificed her own childhood to become the caretaker for her mother and her siblings.

Sara had recently moved in with her boyfriend, Paul. This was the first time she had ever lived with a man and feelings were surfacing that surprised her. He reminded her of her father in the way he withdrew emotionally when upset. She felt a familiar disappointment when Paul was unable to reach out to her and unable to be supportive when she needed him. She saw her tendency to merge with Paul and lose herself; to take care of him and deny her own needs as she had done with her mother.

One day she arrived looking distressed. She complained of being unable to show the "weak and confused" parts of herself to Paul. She feared rejection and recognized the familiarity of these feelings. This is how she had felt with her parents. We explored further. She said she felt "scared and fragile ... new feelings to show anyone." She did not think Paul would be supportive and accepting of these feelings.

I suggested that she use music to express this "weak, scared part" of herself. She chose the piano and I played with her. I felt I could support her more effectively with music, and that the music would help her by giving form to and thus concretizing this aspect of herself. She could then relate to it while having some distance from it, with acceptance as an eventual goal.

She played softly and with one hand (right). The improvisation was in D minor, a sort of modal blues. I played mostly chords and mirrored and varied her theme while also creating a holding environment. At one point in the music she cried. She said she felt "like a small child, just growing up and fragile." She said she felt love for this part even though it was so weak.

Afterwards, she said she was afraid to play at first; "to realize it ... to give form to something so fragile." I responded by saying, "even though your playing was soft and involved only one hand, it had such clarity and depth of feeling that it conveyed a quiet strength and allowed space for me to connect with you." She took in my words and seemed reassured by them.

The thoughts that I did not share at this point, were about the "real self" (Miller, 1981) and how inadequate and inferior it feels when compared to the ideal self. The real self, once rejected by the parents, becomes a source of shame for the child. S/he rejects it as well, in favor of a "false self" (Winnicott, 1965) that meets with the parents' approval. The real self is hidden away. Hidden so well, in fact, that the child, and later "adult-child" loses access to his/her authentic feelings. Unable to trust and depend on his/her feelings for orientation, the narcissistically injured person is forced to look to others for a sense of identity.

Sara's false or adaptive self was closely related to her unconscious ideal of someone who was independent and self-sufficient. Her relationship with Paul, and her emerging feelings and dependency needs, were understandably causing her anxiety.

In the next few sessions, her music seemed to be more playful and spontaneous, less controlled. She would often stop playing even though she appeared to be enjoying the music. When I brought this up, she said: "I fear losing control and having no one there to catch me." We talked about our relationship. Would I let her down as her parents had? Could she really depend on me?

In the next few months, she often cried during sessions. She seemed to be mourning her unlived life. She was aware of years of denial and unexpressed feelings.

Two Years

Sara had to have an operation. She had a growth that could be cancerous. She was afraid to tell her parents; afraid they would not be there for her. She had a dream about a "mute little boy" that really touched her. We explored the image musically. She played the umbira and I supported her on a small xylophone. She played softly and slowly, and breathed deeply while releasing waves of sadness. She said: "He is fearful and sad but when he hides and shuts down I lose my life energy."

The next week she told me she had called her parents. She cried over the phone and told them she needed their support. Her mother seemed overwhelmed at first, but Sara stayed with her own feelings of need and eventually her mother was able to express genuine concern and caring. Sara was clearly encouraged and felt she was making progress.

The next few sessions focused on Sara's relationship with Paul. Things were not going well. The issues that were emerging were similar to her issues with her parents, in particular her mother. She felt unsupported by Paul, that he had no belief in her. He criticized her for being selfish and demanding, and she felt he was envious of her newly acquired confidence in her work and her increasing ability to assert herself.

One day, she arrived looking distraught and told me that she and Paul had separated. He was staying with a friend until he could find his own apartment. She said she felt "sad and abandoned" and longed to be "seen and accepted by someone." Paul had met some of her needs but not enough to make the relationship work. She confessed to also feeling relief that now she did not have to go deeper into "needy, dependent feelings."

She seemed distanced from me and from her feelings. She said she felt like hiding, and that when she was a child she would go off alone when she felt sad. She would not allow her mother to see her feelings for fear of disapproval. She said she often felt lonely and isolated as a result. I asked her if she wanted to try exploring the "hidden part" of herself with music. She said "No." So I offered art or movement as an alternative. She then showed some interest in playing the piano. We began by breathing together. During the breathing, I had the thought that I might be doing what her mother did to her; forcing her to reveal something before she felt ready to. I said, "You don't have to play the hidden part; you can play anything you feel like playing."

Her improvisation was D minor based but had no key center. It was very dissonant and had a strong driving rhythm. I supported and accented her rhythm by playing chords in the bass part of the piano. She interacted with me more than usual and looked directly at me several times.

When she stopped playing, she began to cry. She told me that it moved her when I said she could play anything. She felt that I was telling her she did not have to "confront" all the time and that I accepted her the way she was. She said, "I've probably always wanted to hear that."

Termination

Sara decided not to complete her dance therapy training here but to return home. She missed California and her friends and relatives. She also felt ready to confront her issues with her parents more directly. We had two months left in which to bring our work together to closure.

She was feeling unsure about her identity as a dance therapist, and was trying to give herself permission to live with this uncertainty. She did not want to have to know the answers anymore.

On this particular day, we began the session by playing the piano together. (The usual pattern was to talk for a while until an issue emerged that we would then explore musically). Sara's melody was beautiful. It was in the key of C, consonant and flowing. The melody was composed of whole octave jumps followed by small steps. It began softly, built in intensity and volume, and ended softly. I began by mirroring her in the bass and then "holding" by playing mainly C and F major seventh and ninth chords. At times we "dialogued" together. During these moments the music became more syncopated. I enjoyed this improvisation immensely.

Sara said the music felt "playful" and that it was new for her to stay so long in "such a playful place." She added that she felt "light," but grounded in her body and not a "bloodless spirit."

During the next session, she talked about being very responsible as a child; being a "little adult" who never got to play very much. She cried for the child that she was. She felt sad that she had never learned that it is alright to make mistakes, and that she was never taught that it is possible to enjoy the process of learning without having to worry so much about achieving a goal. She feared that she would not be loved unless she was achieving something "special" and being a "good girl," which we translated to mean being independent, and having no needs. She felt ready to take some risks but what if she "fell on her face?" Would she still be lovable? I talked about how she had internalized her rejecting mother but was beginning to experience another way of being with herself that was more accepting and compassionate. I observed that as she claimed her feelings and was able to express them, she felt better about herself. As she was able to honor her needs and find that they could be met, her self-esteem grew. Admiration for her achievements was not really "love" for her true self and she was beginning to feel the difference. As painful as this process was, it was liberating. She listened intently as I spoke, breathing deeply and nodding in agreement. She said she felt like hugging me but was too shy to do it.

The day of our last session arrived. We had been working together for almost two and a half years. In the previous two sessions, we focused on identifying her needs and exploring ways in which they could be met. Today she said she needed to play the piano with me. The improvisation was a driving, rhythmic one, very dissonant with many tri-tones in the melody. The musical key center was F Lydian Mode.

I supported by mirroring and holding techniques. At one point she slowed down and I followed her. She then stopped playing and appeared upset. She said that she did not want to stop but felt that I did, and that she did not want to go on alone. When she slowed down the tempo, she became aware of feeling lonely and scared. We discussed the symbolic meaning of her statement and how it related to her fear of separating from me and the support I had given her.

I suggested that she continue to play if she wanted to, and I would accompany her. She began again. This time her music was slower and had a tentative feel to it. She paused several times and then began again. Afterwards, she said that there was sadness in the pauses and that she could not continue playing until she felt the sadness. She had been rushing around all week, preparing to leave and she had not allowed herself "space to feel." She said she needed me "to help her feel and live more in her body," and that when I played the piano with her she felt "understood in a deep, non-verbal way."

We played "Sadness" again. This time the music was even slower. It was very dissonant and had no key center. I could sense her withdrawing deeper into herself, and her music reflected this. When we finished playing, we discussed ways in which she could "take me" with her. She could play the piano, work with her dreams, give herself time to breathe, to feel, to sit in the silence of herself and "just be." Her parting words were "Thank you for playing with me," and then "I need a hug!"

DISCUSSION AND CONCLUSIONS

Music therapy was an effective mode of treatment for Sara. The music helped to create a safe and playful environment for uncovering and exploring the hidden, devalued parts of herself. Music has the ability to directly access feelings. This was apparent in Sara's treatment process, time and again. The music was often able to penetrate the "wall" she constructed to protect herself against further injury. The music enabled her to become aware of what she was feeling, to give it a name, to learn to relate to the feeling and in the process of relating to accept more of herself. The creative play of musical improvisation was essential to this process. It was a particularly healing experience for her when she realized she could just "be" with herself and the music and did not have to "do" anything. When we played together, it was not her "products" or special talents that I was recognizing and affirming, but her spontaneous being as it emerged in the music.

In working with a narcissistically injured client, a great deal of the healing process has to do with mirroring the client's emerging real self; the feelings and qualities that make him/her unique so that these aspects of the personality become real. An ego-Self relationship can begin to form. The ego gains strength and a sense of growing power and effectiveness in the world as well as a realistic sense of ambition (Kalshed, 1980; Satinover, 1980).

Music has the ability to mirror one's inner state. So Sara had me, her therapist, as a mirroring self-object (Masterson, 1981), but she also had the music to accurately reflect the spontaneous sounds of the true self and give it an incarnation in life.

Music was valuable in helping to bring previously split-off parts of the self to consciousness. "The needy part," "the weak, scared part," "the mute little boy," "the critic" and "the playful child" were all brought to life and related to through musical improvisations. When a self-aspect is related to, it begins to transform. Sara's critic became less formidable as we worked to depotentiate it. As she began to musically and verbally explore and take a different attitude toward the weaker, needy parts of herself, she began to feel she had "a center, "a ground to stand on" and her own point of view. She had more energy available to her and she felt more confident.

Sara's music reflected her psychological process. In the beginning phase of our work, her music was often dissonant and disjointed and had a detached cerebral quality. There was little connection between the two of us. As the therapy progressed, her music became more melodic and flowing and her rhythms more syncopated. Now, whenever her music was dissonant, it seemed to be more connected to feelings and had more intensity. In the final phase of therapy, Sara's improvisations had more variety and at times a playful quality that felt new to her. She was also interacting with me more at the piano, sometimes making eye contact.

I was often moved and inspired when I witnessed Sara mourning the death of her illusions so that she could give birth to herself and move more fully into life. Healing the narcissistic wound is a long and difficult process that requires a lot of courage. The courage to face one's suffering and make it conscious; to find the meaning in the suffering so that the meaning can be restored to life.

GLOSSARY

Archetype: A symbolic concept. Archetypes are collective universal patterns or motifs. They are the basic content of mythologies, religion, and fairytales and emerge in individuals through dreams and visions (Perera, 1981).

Ego: The center of the conscious personality. It is a cluster of functions, affects, and images of the person and the world, all of which gather around the archetypal core of the Self. Throughout childhood, the ego gradually develops out of the unconscious. In order for a content to become conscious it must be connected with the ego (Ulanov, 1971).

Narcissistically Injured: An injury or wound to one's sense of self, self-image and identity which reduces the capacity to connect to authentic feelings and creates difficulties in regulating self-esteem. This injury is usually caused by a chronic lack of empathic mirroring. The child's primary need to be seen and valued as the person s/he is at any given time has not been met. The child is treated instead, as an extension of the parent(s). An adaptive or false self built on a compliance basis and focused on pleasing significant others to establish self-esteem is a predominant characteristic of a narcissistic injury (Miller, 1981; Kalshen, 1980).

Self: Self with a capital "S" refers to the central archetype or archetype of wholeness. It is the ordering and unifying center of the total psyche, conscious and unconscious. It is experienced as a transpersonal power which transcends the ego; for example, God (Edinger, 1972).

REFERENCES

Edinger, E. (1971). Ego and Archetype. New York: Penguin Books.

Jung, C. (1968). The Archetypes and the Collective Unconscious. (Volume 9 of Collected Works). Princeton, NJ: Princeton University Press.

Jung, C. (1969). The Structure and Dynamics of the Psyche. (Volume 8 of Collected Works). Princeton, NJ: Princeton University Press.

Kalshed, D. (1980). Narcissism and the Search for Interiority. Quadrant, 13 (2), 46-72.

Miller, A. (1981). The Drama of the Gifted Child. New York: Basic Books.

Masterson, J. (1981). The Narcissistic and Borderline Disorders. New York: Brunner Mazel, Inc.

Perera, S. (1981). Descent to the Goddess. Toronto, Canada: Inner City Books.

Satinover, J. (1980). Puer Aeternus: The Narcissistic Relation to the Self. Quadrant, 13 (2), 75-   108.

Schwartz-Salant, W. (1982). Narcissism and Character Transformation. Toronto, Canada: Inner City   Books.

Spolin, U. (1963). Improvisation for the Theater. Evanston, Illinois: Northwestern University Press.

Winnicott, D.W. (1965). The Maturational Processes and the Facilitating Environment. London: Hogarth Press.

Winnicott, D. W. (1971). Playing and Reality. London: Tavistock Publications.

Woodman, M. (1982). Addiction to Perfection. Toronto: Inner City Books.

Guided Imagery And Music (GIM): Healing The Wounded Healer

RHONDA LINEBURG RINKER, M.M., RMT-BC
Registered Music Therapist - Board Certified
Virginia Treatment Center for Children
Richmond, Virginia

Abstract. *A series of twelve GIM sessions was used to help a woman therapist heal emotional wounds of the past, and to bring resolution and closure to physical and emotional abuse that she had experienced. The safe, supported environment enabled her to work through and let go of the long standing pain from these experiences, and to emerge as a strong, self-assured individual capable of acknowledging herself as a worthwhile person.*

INTRODUCTION

"There is an inner urge in our own minds to grow, to expand, to break down the barriers of previous limitations and to ever widen our experience" (Holmes, 1990, p. 20). It is this "inner urge" that draws a person to Guided Imagery and Music (GIM). I became involved with GIM in an effort to take care of the "me" who spent much of my time taking care of other people.

Realizing the benefits of my own GIM experiences, I began offering workshops at the psychiatric facility in which I am employed, using guided imagery, relaxation, and imagery with music. The workshops were aimed at providing other mental health professionals opportunities to take the time needed to take care of themselves. Several of these professionals wanted to continue work with GIM on an individual basis. Lauren, the subject of this case study, was one of them.

BACKGROUND INFORMATION

Lauren is a woman in her mid-forties, with a master's degree in a mental health field. She was involved in clinical work when she chose to pursue GIM as part of her personal process work. Many mental health professionals have had experiences in their own lives that put them in the category of "wounded healer". Such was the case of Lauren.

She had grown up in an emotionally distant family. She did not recall a childhood with much warmth. There was little affection displayed by her parents to each other or to her and her brother. She reported that her current relationships with parents and brother were not close, and that she was very comfortable with that.

She is a divorced mother of four, with three children living at home. Her first marriage was at a reasonably young age and ended after four years. She separated from her husband prior to learning of her first pregnancy. Her son was approximately three years old when she married her second husband. He chose to adopt her son and this marriage lasted for over twelve years.

In this marriage, Lauren lived a reasonably affluent lifestyle with several opportunities for travel abroad. During her first pregnancy in this marriage, Lauren was physically and emotionally abused by her husband. She reported that her husband was not particularly interested in sexual intimacy except during her pregnancies. After a time, his interest then became somewhat abnormal and abusive. After the children were born, he began physically abusing her---pushing her around while she held the babies, shoving her and hitting her.

During the last year of this marriage, Lauren was hospitalized for five weeks for severe depression. She participated in individual therapy with a psychiatrist, and was treated with antidepressants. While in therapy, she was able to see the destructive situation in which she lived. Her self-esteem and self-confidence were seriously damaged. As part of treatment, she was discharged back to the same home situation. She reported drinking, for a time, as a way to avoid confronting the horrors of her marriage. She worked with a social worker and participated in group therapy. Eight months later, she made the decision to take her children and to leave her abusive marriage to begin a new life.

Life was not easy following her divorce. Her former husband provided minimal financial support. She put herself through graduate school while working part-time jobs and raising her children. She received no emotional or financial support from her parents. Her oldest son chose to live with her parents. Her remaining three children provided her the support and encouragement to complete graduate school.

At the time she came to pursue GIM, she was actively engaged as a clinician. She presented as a healthy, happy, articulate woman. She is very well read in psychology, social theory, counseling methods, and all areas related to mental health. She is also very interested in "holistic" approaches and was drawn to GIM for that reason.

Although Lauren's previous therapy had begun the process of inner exploration, and her career as a mental health clinician had introduced her to the benefits of personal relaxation and meditation exercises, she was aware that she still had emotional issues that were unresolved. For this reason, she decided to pursue GIM.

TREATMENT PROCESS

Lauren participated in twelve GIM sessions over a period of four months. Each session lasted from ninety minutes to two hours, and followed the same format. This included: a preliminary discussion, a relaxation induction, an imagery focus, imaging to music while dialoguing with the guide, a return to waking state, discussion and closure. As the guide, I had been trained in the Bonny Method of Guided Imagery and Music (1978), and I used the taped programs specially designed for GIM therapy.

In the first session, Lauren began to reveal some of the experiences encountered in her abusive marriage. She described them in various ways: being cornered and scared, needing to get away and make a change, not wanting to go back. She experienced sadness, anger, and fear very quietly, both in her body and in her words. Her imagery ended in a sandy, hot place where dust got in her throat and she was "not supposed to talk." She had apparently reached a point where her psyche realized the amount of material coming up.

During the verbal processing of these images, she noted the vast changes that had taken place in her life over the years. She was acutely aware of how deeply GIM had "probed" into her inner process and how relevant the images were to her life.

In this and the next few sessions, Lauren had an awareness of another person being there with her who did not reveal him/herself to her. She did not experience this person as frightening in any way, but rather as someone who was watching over her.

In the third session Lauren revealed her sense of how others frequently did not understand her, her different way of looking at things, and "where she was coming from." In fact, she was probably more enlightened and "in touch" with herself than most people she encountered. Apparently, her openness and honesty were very difficult for some people to accept. Lauren had experienced more pain than most people, and she had used it as an opportunity to grow, rather than as a weapon to hate and distrust others.

The next few sessions showed an emerging awareness of her growing self-confidence, and especially in the GIM process. She stretched freely in the sun and encouraged others to do the same; she felt like she could do anything or go anywhere she wanted. She began to shed external barriers, and to dig deeper into inner places, trusting the music to support her. Her body began resonating with her experiences, as she touched stone walls and felt their textures and as she described a warmth spreading through her body or tingling in her limbs.

Colors frequently appeared in her imagery: in flowers, in the colors of flowing robes, in bubbles and in rainbows. Several colors appeared in many sessions, pink, purple, turquoise and a royal "gold." These colors were important as they freqeuntly brought her healing experiences.

The fourth session brought deeper work. I used a face and head massage in the relaxation induction, while focusing Lauren on moving her breath throughout her body. This physical contact during the induction, from my experience, helps to connect the guide more closely with the subject and thereby facilitates deeper work to occur. I used a "Book of Life" as her beginning focus, and asked her to begin to look through the pages of her life as the music began. The music for this session was the taped program entitled, "Mostly Bach."

She immediately began describing her childhood home. It was "filled with all that I hate and love". It was "split like I felt split." Speaking of her parents, Lauren said: "they always made me do what I didn't want to do, and never acknowledged me for what I could do." As she recalled being a very small girl and being made to sing, "O Holy Night," she broke into tears. She talked about her grandmother as being the only person who really loved her and cared for her. I asked if she would like for her grandmother to hold her now. She did. I held her as her grandmother had many years before. While being held, she began to let go of some of her childhood: how her mother hated her for being unable to tell her that she was a good mother; how her mother resented Lauren's relationship with her grandmother, because it was the kind she should have had with her mother, but could not; how her mother disliked that she was a "pretty little girl with long blonde curls" and cut her hair off in an uneven, haphazard way. Lauren described her mother's house today as being cold, and "all clean waiting to die." She was glad not to live there anymore.

As she continued to cry, she had an image of herself having "golden tears surrounded by a rainbow of blues and purples." The tears were falling on her cheeks while the wind blew through her and took away all the "yuck." I began the following dialogue:

> "Are the tears cleaning out the dark places?"
> "Yes, the sun is trying to come out."
> "Do you want it to come out?"
> "I'm not sure."
> "You can stay in the dark or be in the sunlight. The choice is yours."

After a silence, a beautiful smile came over her face as she told me that she was lying in the sunlight thinking about all that she had done that was good.

After the healing images, Lauren had an awareness that the person who had been with her in the previous sessions was no longer there and she did not know why. I asked if the person knew that she had to do this on her own. She replied: "Yes... I had to do it myself. And I did...without falling either.... and no one laughed. It's a special gift I have." I added: "So the gift was in you all along."

This was a very moving session for Lauren because it allowed her to deal with her childhood and the pain associated with it. In our discussion afterwards, Lauren speculated that her grandmother had been the person who had been with her in the earlier sessions. She also had a sense that her grandmother continued to watch over her.

Most of the fifth session was spent healing herself in "medicine waters" and beautiful colors. However, near the end, she felt anger rising up "like a volcano inside me." I was prepared to shift tapes to use music that would support the release of this anger, but Lauren chose to do it in a quiet, focused way: "It's spitting mess everywhere all over my mother's house." She then took herself to a place of beauty where she could take care of herself. She used images from other session, such as healing water, bubbles of colors and so forth.

Following this session, we discussed her anger and her unwillingness to express it through stronger affect or behavior. Lauren stated that her mother had yelled at her so much as a child that she has no tolerance for loud noises, and especially yelling. In fact, Lauren would cover her ears in a session whenever sounds in her images became too loud or unpleasant. She chose to work with her anger in quiet ways throughout her GIM work.

According to Bonny (1978), "important breakthroughs seem to appear most frequently at the 5th, 8th and 10th sessions" (p.15). As will become evident, this held true for Lauren. Session 5 brought realization of all the pain that she had endured during a childhood in which she was never loved, acknowledged or appreciated for the person that she was.

This theme continued in the next two sessions. She returned to her childhood home, and spoke of a doll that had been taken away by "somebody big." She could not understand why her mother did not love her, and why she would say that Lauren "wasn't the right kind of little girl," and humiliate her in front of others. No wonder Lauren, the child, felt that she was a bad person. It was years later, and as an adult, that Lauren came to see her mother as the bad person.

Her father had made no attempts to change any of this. Her parents did not have a loving relationship with each other, then or now. When the death of her parents came up, she expressed sadness but no grief, describing them as "alive but already dead." She allowed herself to do some healing with colors and water.

Throughout this process, Lauren reported feeling physical changes. She began to lose weight after being overweight for some time. Her children began to tell her there was something "different" about her. They were not able to determine what was causing this change, but they felt that it was good. Randall McClellan (1988) pointed out that: "Changes take place within our physical bodies as a result of being exposed to both sound and music; these changes may take place whether we are consciously aware of them or not. Significantly, it may not be necessary that we maintain consciousness for these changes to occur or even that we give permission for those changes to take place" (p.137).

In guiding GIM sessions, one becomes very aware of the physical changes that are reported as part of the process: feelings of hot and cold, limbs trembling, body parts becoming numb, sweating, shaking, etc. The processing of the GIM experience does not stop at the end of the session but continues for some time after. These physical changes as part of this process may also continue for some time, consciously or unconsciously.

The eighth session was difficult for Lauren. It dealt with the failure of her marriage. I used a light/energy source moving through her body for the relaxation induction, and then focused her on allowing the light from her unconscious mind to come into her conscious mind with the music. The music for this session was the tape entitled "Grieving." Lauren began this journey at a church in France that she had visited with her former husband. She expressed a sense of sadness and loss: "I feel as though I have lost something, and don't know how to find it....like a series of people... or some kind of relationship... or sad pattern." I asked her where she felt the sadness, and she placed her hand over her chest/heart area. I followed with, "How does it feel to touch that sadness?" Lauren responded, "Warm... not as bad when you touch it... It feels really lonely... as if nobody else is alive... Wouldn't that be scary?... That's how I have felt all my life." Her parents had been physically there, but they were never there in a nurturing, emotionally supportive fashion. She did not have a close relationship with her brother. She had experienced two marriages that had failed. With the exception of her children, Lauren really felt unloved. She felt separate from other people, and did not let herself get very close to too many people for fear of being hurt again.

As the music progressed, Lauren contrasted two churches she had visited on that trip. The church in France recalled the sadness and stormy things that happened in her married life. Here she realized: "I'm there with the 'goon' who didn't love me." Her body felt heavy and angry, but not her head. I encouraged her to let go of the anger that she had been holding in her body for so long. Then an image came of herself as a little kid plucking out her mother's eyes with her fingernails, ripping off her hair. She spoke of how shocked her parents looked, but then said: "They don't even look real... They're sort of like dummies that have learned how to talk." In reality, their relationship with Lauren had been very artificial, and they had been more like mannekins than real parents.

Memories of her honeymoon then came with the music, and she lamented that "it could have been so perfect... I could have overlooked a lot if with the right person." Lauren described her marriage as "dreadful." Her husband blamed her for everything, just as her parents had always done. She became acutely aware of the hate she felt for her parents and her former husband, and then saw the lesson to be learned: "You don't have to punish yourself by trying to love people incapable of loving you!" She was loved by her children and no longer needed to punish or blame herself because others she had wanted to love had not been able to give that love to her.

The next session was healing and fulfilling for her. She allowed herself to be playful, to enjoy, and to re-experience her healing colors. She explored being out of her body after it had been "weighted down with rocks," and incapable of doing everything she wanted it to do," and she realized that she did not need it all of the time. She was more aware of the music and colors as they moved through her. Other people began floating with her but they were not discernible figures. The colors kept opening up over and over again, and she reported: " Each time I get more beautiful... Everybody sees it... and smiles... as if they're saying 'Yes, we're beautiful too'."

With each session, she had begun to open herself more, and in doing so, she was better able to see the beauty within herself. She had begun to acknowledge herself, and to permit others to do the same. Even when she had playful images, there was a real sense that Lauren was finally in touch with the essence of who she was and that she could enjoy that person and allow it to grow and emerge.

The tenth session provided Lauren the opportunity to "look" more closely at herself. There appeared an elderly, wise man who was looking at his own eye. He admonished her: "You can look anyway you want... and you are wise when you learn to look both ways." Lauren responded that she did know how. The man replied: "You have to be very brave... You must do what you think you have to do---even if others think it strange... You cannot skip over things you have to do."

Lauren had to look bravely at things that she had to do in her life. She had to grow up in a family that could not love her as she needed to be loved. She had to experience two marriages that were not right for her. She suffered terrible pain, physically and emotionally, in the second marriage prior to the realization that "she" was not doing anything wrong. And, she had to allow her parents to "die" in her imagery to permit the pain of her childhood to leave her.

In the last part of this session, the image returned of a volcano of anger raging inside her, and she realized that: "I have to stop being angry with myself for things other people do... I have to let it all go... It's floating away from my body... like really ugly black clouds." With this, she allowed herself to let go of all the anger, the disappointment and the sadness with the people in her life who had hurt her.

In the eleventh session, Lauren re-experienced images from earlier sessions, but this time as a strong, assertive person, capable of doing or accomplishing anything she wanted. She used the session to further strengthen and empower the person she had become. The image of herself as a little girl returned, and she allowed herself to nurture the little Lauren and teach her all the many things she knew. And at the end, she permitted herself to give something to that child part of herself that missed out on so many things while growing up.

The twelfth session was our final session. This decision came several days after the session had taken place. In this session, I used an induction image of a rainbow, with a color from it coming into her to relax her. At the end of the rainbow was a pool of healing waters. Lauren was cued to go into the pool, to enjoy its waters and to allow the music to share this experience with her. The music for this session was the tape entitled "Quiet Music." She immersed herself in the pool and allowed the waters to float through her body. It felt good and safe. She played with creatures who came from the nearby woods, and was surprised that they wanted to do what she wanted to do. The people in her life had never been able to do that. They had always told her what she had to do. She permitted snakes to go across the top of the water. They told her they were there to help her and not to scare her. There was a small stone hut at the edge of the pool as she came out of the water. This was a safe place. The sun was touching her all over and the animals all went to sleep.

In discussing this session, she talked about how she was not allowing herself to take things at surface value any more. Lauren appeared to re-integrate more slowly at the end of this session. Her body continued to feel a little strange, even after she had become fully alert and was moving around in the room.

We spoke a few days later and she reported still feeling a little strange and decided to stop sessions for awhile. Her body responded very acutely to the GIM process. It was telling her that it had reached a place of closure, that it needed time to integrate all that had transpired over the four months. She had re-experienced all the pain she suffered as a child. She had re-experienced the emotional and physical abuse that were parts of her childhood and her marriage. She experienced, again, the overwhelming sadness of never having felt truly loved throughout her life. All of this had transpired very quickly over a brief period of time.

Many people are unable to work with that much material in years of therapy. Her body and psyche had worked with all that it could. She felt very positive about her work with GIM. She related it to her individual therapy in saying that therapy had helped her to intellectually resolve these issues for herself. GIM had allowed her to touch the pain associated with these issues and to let go of it. In allowing herself to let go of the pain, she could go forward with her life with confidence and a growing appreciation for herself.

DISCUSSION

Lauren was an excellent subject for GIM. She was aware of issues in her life that traditional therapy had not adequately resolved. She was verbal, articulate and motivated to work. She had a healthy ego despite all of the emotional damage suffered during her life. She lacked some confidence in herself but made gains in that area as our work progressed. In conversations, long after her sessions had been completed, she felt very strongly that the GIM process had been the only method that allowed her to work with the pain of her life experiences. She felt safe and supported with the music and with me, and we developed a strong personal relationship during her work.

I believe that Lauren benefitted a great deal from GIM. In working with her, I have come to realize the need for the guide to determine the spacing of sessions. This process is a very powerful one, evoking many painful and pleasant associations that actively involve both body and psyche. Lauren had done twelve sessions over four months, and a great deal of highly emotional material came up. Time was now needed to allow her to process this material and integrate it into consciousness.

Lauren talks about coming back to do more sessions. I believe that she has completed her work, for now, with GIM. I see her as being a much stronger person now. She permitted herself to "trust the process," and in doing so, she made significant gains in her perceptions of herself. She has a healthier, more positive outlook on her life.

As a personal way of helping Lauren to integrate her GIM experiences and bring some closure to our time together, I wrote the following poem and gave it to her at our last session:

FOR LAUREN

Melodies, moving mysteriously and evocatively -
Touching places that have long been forgotten,
That may have been hurt and damaged,
Damaged to the point that I see myself as damaged
worthless;
Reliving all the pain and anger - crying those same
tears over and over again.
With the tears came the healing and the "letting go" of
those fearful places within me.
Beautiful colors appeared - golden images that told of
the Hidden beauty,
Beauty long since forgotten or felt -
overshadowed by the hurt and the "damaged" me.
All the while alive and still growing in me.
There is a re-birth process - a new person emerging
with beauty, confidence and love for itself.
There is a new rhythm in me, stirred by the varied
rhythms of the melodies.
I am a new song waiting to be played and
To be enjoyed by many.

From Rhonda

REFERENCES

Bonny, H. (1978) Facilitating Guided Imagery and Music Sessions, GIM
Monograph #1. Salina, KS: Bonny Foundation.

Holmes, E. (1990). The Eternal Path of Progress. Science of the Mind, 63 (10),
16-21.

McClellan, R. (1988). The Healing Forces of Music. New York: Amity House.

Emergence Of The Adult Self
In Guided Imagery And Music (GIM) Therapy

MARILYN F. CLARK, AMI Fellow
Private practice: Baltimore, MD
Adjunct Faculty in Music Therapy
Temple University, Philadelphia, PA

Abstract: *This case describes one year of GIM therapy with a young woman, who after undergoing an abortion, found a need to be healed emotionally on many levels. As a child, she had developed anorexic behaviors in response to a dysfunctional family system affected by alcoholism. Through GIM, the image of herself as a young female waif forced out on her own evolved into a mature woman seasoned in the trials of the world, able to care for herself and to create healthy relationships.*

BACKGROUND INFORMATION

At the time of therapy, Diane was a 35-year-old, white female who co-owned a small bookstore and had a private counseling practice. She was married, though not living with her husband, and she had no children. In appearance, she was quite petite, and had a childlike look about her.

She came from a large, upper middle-class family of six children: three boys and three girls. Her father, whom she idolized, was a successful businessman and an alcoholic; her mother, a housewife, was loving but regarded by Diane as weak. Her home life as a child was chaotic: with mother trying to keep things peaceful, and father appearing on the scene aggressive, bullying and mean when drunk.

Diane was a quiet, sensitive person buffeted about by circumstances. She felt neither in control nor protected, as her mother did not set boundaries for the family, nor did she chastise the father for his bullying behavior. Diane reacted by asserting control over her body with anorexic behavior when she was ten years old. Her mother noticed her weight loss over one summer and forced her to eat.

The eating disorder returned when Diane went to college. The summer before she started college she felt as though she were going insane. There was something inside of her, a negative force, telling her she was crazy and no good. She spoke of college as the worst time in her life, a nightmare. The eating disorder was never treated nor even recognized as a problem at the time.

As a child, she had sought the refuge of a dependent relationship with her mother. In college she met John, her future husband, and transferred her dependency to him. John, studying to become a lawyer, was a heroic figure to Diane. He was a man with a cause. He wanted to liberate the downtrodden, and he espoused radical politics. Diane saw him as someone who could save her too.

In their marriage, she gave him whatever he wanted. She was passive and had very low self-esteem. She felt as though he was the one who mattered, and that his decisions were important; whereas she was insignificant and a littly crazy. Their sexual relationship was not pleasurable for her. She felt it was something she had to do and often felt invaded. While he earned very good money as a lawyer, she was uncomfortable using his money and tried to live on the small income she made. This was another means of depriving herself in order to be in control of her life.

During college, Diane began to study psychology as an attempt to understand what was going on inside of her. She went into the counseling profession as a natural outgrowth of her studies; however, her primary interest was still in trying to heal her own pain. After a few years of marriage and work as a counselor, she opened a women's bookstore with a friend. In books she had found much support and affirmation of herself. The bookstore was probably the first major step she made towards her own expression in the world.

When Diane learned she was pregnant in her mid-thirties, she became very panicky. This was her second pregnancy. The first ended in an abortion. She became pregnant the second time when she and her husband were on vacation, although they had stopped living together at the time. She chose to terminate this pregnancy also, and John went along with her decision. Diane was not ready to have a baby. She feared the loss of control over her body, and feared becoming like her mother: lacking clear boundaries, having no control, and surrendering to another's will. She knew that her fourteen years of marriage had ended with the abortion. These losses precipitated the crisis which brought her into therapy soon afterwards.

Diane was present at a GIM demonstration which I did for a small group of therapists. She was very attracted to the method and felt an affinity for my style of working. She telephoned me soon after seeing the demonstration and asked to begin working with me.

She presented as a very articulate and aware person, who was highly motivated to work in therapy. In her first session, she demonstrated that she was particularly well-suited to GIM therapy: she worked extremely well with imagery processes, and was very responsive to the music.

METHOD

The method used throughout Diane's therapy was Guided Imagery and Music (GIM), as originated by Helen Bonny (1978). GIM is a method of self-exploration in which carefully selected musical pieces are used to elicit an internal response. Essentially, it involves imaging to music in a nonordinary (relaxed, altered) state of consciousness, assisted by a guide or therapist. Several basic steps are involved.

After building a solid rapport, the therapist guides the client through a physical relaxation and then focuses the client's imagination in preparation for listening to a specially designed tape of classical music selections. The client then shares with the therapist the various impressions, feelings, and images which arise spontaneously while listening to the music. Throughout the process, the therapist supports, amplifies, and resonates with the client's feelings and experiences through verbal and non-verbal techniques. When the music ends, the therapist assists the client to return to *waking consciousness*. A time of integration of new awarenesses follows, through discussions or the use of other expressive modalities.

Often the music imaging process stimulates experiences which were previously not available to conscious awareness. These experiences may be discussed or examined afterwards, or they may be allowed to remain in an imaginal state, so that they can inform the client's consciousness through a gradual process of integration.

My therapeutic orientation is client-centered, that is, I believe that individuals are capable of self-directed growth within the context of a therapeutic relationship. I regard GIM as an uncovering form of therapy, one which accesses unconscious material, and which requires in-depth work on the part of the client, and advanced, specialized training on the part of the therapist.

I view the psyche from a Jungian framework, and regard it as a rich source for healing. I also find that the *archetypes* identified by Jung are often helpful in understanding therapeutic movement in the GIM process.

TREATMENT PROCESS

Diane received GIM therapy for about a year. The sessions were 90 to 120 minutes long, and were scheduled according to the urgency of the process. Altogether she received 20 sessions.

The primary theme of Diane's therapy, the emergence of the adult self, can be understood through looking at her inner world of imagery. Summaries of each therapy session are presented below with emphasis on the imagery process as it evidences therapeutic growth.

Setting the Stage

SESSION 1: THE BASEMENT WITCH. Diane begins her imagery as a girlchild exploring a house. She finds a room with desks, and she says "I want to learn," showing her readiness to begin therapy. She then goes to the dark basement where a witch lives. The witch knows the story of the house. Diane confronts the witch, telling her: "Don't scare me! You're bad and you have no right to frighten a child. Stop it. You're taking advantage of me and I won't have it. When I ask you to come out, you come out. But I won't have you terrorize me. I'm not as big as you, but I have the power to say stop it!"

Diane begins to explore parts of the self which have lain in the *shadow* as depicted by the witch in the basement. She leaves the session feeling she has faced fears.

SESSION 2: THE MAGIC FOREST. Diane continues her exploration as a child in a magical forest, where she can understand the animals and were she is taken care of. She becomes a mature woman and dances. The forest is no longer enchanted. She is experiencing briefly the outcome of the therapy work. As gentle humming voices from Puccini's opera, "Madame Butterfly," accompany her, she becomes an adolescent and sneaks into a castle. She is exploring different times in her development through these shifts of the *imaging ego*. There is relief in being the adult self, but she cannot maintain that identification for long at this point.

SESSION 3: THE CASTLE VISIT. Diane encounters the King and

Queen of the castle and demands to be accepted on her own terms. The *archetypal* relationship to mother/father, female/male is further seen in images of the sun and the moon. She says to the sun, "Why won't you speak back to me? All I can do is breathe you in." The sun responds "I'm trying to reach you, too." With the moon she feels safe and able to speak the same language. The parental relationship is played out in this session in ways which feel safe and where she has control and respect.

SESSION 4: THE BEACH COTTAGE. Diane is an orphaned child who finds a homey beach cottage. A protective mother invites her in to share the family's meal. She is accepted by the father who takes a walk with her on the beach. The Pachelbel "Canon in D" gives grounded support as she integrates into the family making friends with the children. Diane is continuing to establish a safe space in which to work by populating her image world with a supportive family.

SESSION 5: DEATH/REBIRTH. Diane begins to surrender to the process of change in this session as she experiences images of being in a coffin. The Bach "Passacaglia and Fugue in C minor" with its strong descending patterns helps her to surrender to the inevitable ending of life and the reintegration into the earth. Images of spring and new life follow. She has a meeting with herself as a child. She promises to listen now to the little girl. The last images are of the funeral procession of the Queen. This theme of the death of the mother and birth of the child is key to her growth. These images set the stage for a more intense encounter later in her process.

SESSION 6: LEARNING TO TRUST. Diane is an adult feeling isolated, homeless, not knowing where she fits in. She does not yet feel confident in her adult self. A vaporous form takes human shape and communicates to her about trusting and patience. She is introduced through the music to many people. She sings with them while Vivaldi's "Et in Terra Pax" from the "Gloria" is heard on the tape. She makes a homey place for herself and gives herself permission to just be.

SESSION 7: THREE GENERATION DANCE. Carrying forward the positive feelings from the previous session, Diane begins this session at a dance feeling free and graceful. She heals a sick child by gently dancing with her. She meets an older woman whose dance shows the lessons of age. Once again Pachelbel's "Canon in D" helps to bring these three parts of herself together in a dance in which each one, the child, the adult, and the old woman are valued by the others.

SESSION 8: RAISING BABY BROTHER. Diane returns to the magical forest where she finds her baby brother. She is fiercely protective of him, and takes him to the city where she finds a gentle old man to help raise him. As with other elements of her personality, the young animus, or male part of her, must find a safe place in which to develop.

Integration

SESSION 9: THE FEMALE GUIDE. Diane meets a woman who counsels her to relax and trust. She tells Diane "I needed to take you on this lonely route so you could learn to love yourself." The imagery suggests a *transference* to the therapist. Diane admits that, though she still feels resistances, she feels her life is different than it has been for a long time. They dance together in celebration.

Confronting Family Patterns

SESSION 10: THE FAMILY SCENE. The first movement of Brahms' "Second Piano Concerto" helps to evoke the first look at Diane's chaotic childhood home. A quiet moment with her mother is interrupted by the family returning from a day at the beach. Father comes home and begins to put demands on Mother. Diane goes into a rage and threatens to attack anyone who does not show respect to her mother. She says, "See, Mother. This is what you needed...I'm your protector...I'm the best daughter you could want." In the imagery, she creates safe boundaries which were not present when she was a child, and she expresses anger at both parents.

Father

SESSION 11: FATHER GOD. Diane takes the struggle with Father to an archetypal level in this session. She becomes very angry when her devotion to a deep and powerful voice is not recognized. It's as if she has been pushed out of heaven. She finds a stream where she refreshes herself. The water shows her how to flow through life without caring. She feels as if she has aged. At the end of the session she reflects that this is the story of her life. She idolized her father, but he did not cherish her devotion.

SESSION 12: SLEEPING WITH THE STARS. Diane's psyche gives her a rest from the intensity of the previous sessions. She has images of sleeping. She floats among the stars in her sleep. This sleeping imagery is like a stop-action, giving her a break and a time to be nurtured by musical excerpts from Faure's "Requiem" and Wagner's "Lohengrin."

SESSION 13: FREEING THE KING'S HEART. Diane begins to integrate the work with Father in this *metaphorical fantasy*. She enters into a field in which a beating heart lies protected by barbed wire fences and daggers---poised to penetrate the heart if anyone invades the space. As she carefully makes her way to the heart, she wonders if this is a fetus, a reminder of the abortion. She learns this is the King's heart which he has put here and will protect at any cost. She teaches him about how to place the heart in his body where it naturally belongs. She says, "I thought he was a fierce, cruel, mean king. But he was just a lonely, empty man. This wouldn't have been possible if I hadn't taken the journey into the center of the heart."

SESSION 14: SHADOW MAN.   Diane continues to work with her animus, this time in its authoritative and competency aspects.   She begins with memories of a horseback ride with her father, where she proved her stamina.   Then to earlier memories and a fantasy of a mysterious military man who helps her discipline herself to not eat.   She wanted to be different from her mother whom she saw as a fat, weak person with no will of her own.   Diane felt she had a special purpose and was different from the women in her family.   The shadowy male figure is an aspect of her animus in its most negative, controlling aspects.

Integration

SESSION 15:   COMING HOME.   Diane returns to the fantasy style of imaging experienced in the first part of her therapy.   She enters into a land that is completely welcoming to her; all of nature is glad to have her there. She finds a loving woman there who wants to hear about all of her adventures.   Diane struggles to fully trust her until the woman reveals that she is a Goddess.   The Goddess tells her "You have to walk through the darkness and know it's a passing dream...Let your feelings play out...You're strong enough to pass through these times."   Her inner self is strengthening as she begins to find positive female images within her own psyche.

SESSION 16:   CELEBRATION.   Diane continues with the positive feelings experienced in the last session and has a *peak experience* which further reflects her inner strength.   In a spirit state, she meets the God and Goddess and dances for them.   She celebrates her expansive feelings while flying around the world with the accompaniment of Barber's "Adagio for Strings."   In the end, the Goddess appears to her in a rainbow, like the goddess *Iris* from Greek mythology.

Mother

SESSION 17:   DEATH-REBIRTH II.   Strengthened by the last two sessions, Diane moves into deep material once again.   Intense colors herald feelings needing to be explored which may be of a pre-verbal nature.   Colors give way to a fantasy scene observed by the two-year old Diane of a fawn massacred by a bear, and a witch running madly into the woods.   Diane, now older and surrounded by an aura of health and light, walks around her childhood home.   She feels evil coming from her mother's bedroom, perhaps indicating the confused messages she had received as a child about intimacy. She realizes her mother is dying and that she has killed her.   From her mother's body comes a young girl.   Diane brings the girl into her light to grow strong.   She tells the girl that she can grow up and be who she wants to be. It is interesting to note that the music played through this session was gentle and nurturing. The music provided a safe space in which this intense work could proceed.

Finding Herself

SESSION 18: INTEGRATION. Diane's *imaging ego* watches her double frantically riding horseback to no destination. The Goddess emerges from the woods and encircles both images of Diane, giving them a blessing. The two Dianes go to a land they can call home and where they can rest.

SESSION 19: EMERGING FROM THE OCEAN. With a dolphin as guide, Diane leaves the ocean and swims to a river. Once again she is back home. A woman comes out of the woods and is a channel for Diane's healing. The woman is connected to the moon, the archetypal feminine.

Closure

SESSION 20: THE DEATH OF THE QUEEN. Returning to an earlier theme, Diane returns to the castle where the queen is dying. This time, Diane appears as both a man and a woman: the man is a knight and the Queen's son who has returned home, the woman is the Queen's daughter and knight's sister. As the queen dies in peace, Diane (the son) vows to take care of his sister (Diane, the daughter). They move to the woods where he takes care of her by day, and she takes care of him by night. The Goddess helps Diane (the daughter) through the night and promises to be with her whenever she has need. This was the promise she wanted from her mother, but was never able to get. As her therapy reaches closure, she integrates the male and female, and is able to find a caring balance between the two.

DISCUSSION

Diane stated candidly in our first session that she had a clear feeling she could trust me. This enabled me to challenge her with some of the more intense musical selections in my tape collection. She was never frightened by the music and easily accepted it into her inner world. I was also able to encourage engagement and confrontation with the images as necessary. When working with scary and intense imagery episodes, she was always courageous. Her trust of me, the music, and the imagery were key to the success of GIM therapy for her.

Diane often preferred not to translate the imaging experiences into intellectual explanations. Yet, she was aware that on a deeper level, she was working through many feelings, and in the process, inner transformations were taking place. Throughout the course of therapy, she reported that she felt better, although she could not always explain why.

The first part of the series, Setting the Stage, was primarily metaphorical fantasy. Dramas were played out where Diane tested the safety of her inner world. She found places where she was accepted, where she could assert herself and where she could do as she pleased. She found friendly and loving companions. She protected the more vulnerable parts of herself. All of these experiences laid the foundation for the deep personal work which took place during the second part of her therapy.

In the second part of the series, Family Patterns (Father and Mother), Diane moved into the challenging and painful experiences from childhood with images of memories and fantasy bringing hidden parts of her personality into focus. Strong feelings of rage, frustration and anger flowed as she reenacted memories. She compensated for her powerlessness as a child through these images by bringing the help of her adult self. She also relied on the magical thinking of a child to make sense out of a chaotic environment. When particularly difficult work had been done, she took time to rest and to integrate what had happened. Her inner world presented nurturing and sometimes spiritually uplifting imagery at these rest times.

The imagery during this period suggested early traumas of which Diane had no conscious recall. The intensity of some of her imaging experiences led me to consider the possibility of childhood abuse. Upon reflection and conversation with her, it appears that what was being uncovered was emotional incest with her mother, brought about by the alcoholic behavior of her father. Her mother substituted emotional intimacy with Diane for sexual intimacy with her husband (Diane's father). This enmeshed relationship hampered Diane's ability to grow into the maturity of adulthood and to take on the responsibilities of developing authentic relationships with her husband and with herself.

The outcome of the work was a deep integration of the child, mother, and father into the adult self. From a homeless waif to the recipient of the Goddess' blessing was a journey marked by honest confrontation with fears and old patterns. The GIM process worked well for her as she was able to give clear voice to her inner world. She believed in it and acknowledged early in the course of therapy that she was feeling better and better. When the series was over, she took the advice of her guide, the Goddess, and gave herself time to rest. Her divorce was finalized, her share of the bookstore was sold. She took the opportunity to return to her family home for a visit and to get to know her parents from her adult perspective.

GLOSSARY

Animus: A Jungian archetype which represents the male or masculine experience within a female. It may be particularly apparent in authority and competence matters (Young-Eisendrath and Wiedemann, 1987).

Archetype: A universal pattern or motif which comes from the collective unconscious, and is the basic content of myths and fairytales. It may appear in visions and dreams (Hall, 1986).

Imaging ego: The ego as it is located in the imagery. In an image, it is that element which makes "I" statements (Clark, 1990).

Iris: In Greek myth, the goddess of the rainbow (Herzberg, 1954).

Metaphorical fantasy: One type of fantasy imagery which has a metaphorical meaning relevant to the imager's life (Clark, 1990).

Peak experience: Religious or spiritual experience of unity with nature or with one's understanding of the divine (Maslow, 1968).

Shadow: An unconscious part of the personality characterized by traits and attitudes which the conscious ego chooses to ignore. It may be positive or negative (Hall, 1986).

Transference: Projection onto the therapist of conscious or unconscious emotional connections to others (Hall, 1986)

Waking consciousness: Awareness in an alert, awake state; normal consciousness (Clark, 1990).

REFERENCES

Bonny, H. (1978). Facilitating Guided Imagery and Music Sessions. Salina, KS: Bonny Foundation.

Clark, M. (1990). Guided Imagery and Music. Unpublished lecture notes. Temple University, Philadelphia, PA.

Hall, J. (1986). The Jungian Experience. Toronto: Inner City Books.

Herzberg, M. (1954). Myths and their Meaning. New York: Allyn and Bacon.

Maslow, A. (1968). Toward a Psychology of Being. Princeton: D. Van Nostrand Co.

Young-Eisendrath, P., & Wiedermann, F. (1987). Female Authority. New York: The Guilford Press.

The Use of Musical Space
With An Adult In Psychotherapy

CAROLYN KENNY, Ph.D., RMT-BC, MTA
Associate Faculty: Antioch University - Santa Barbara
Music Therapist in Private Practice
Santa Barbara, California

Abstract.   Robyn came to music therapy after a long history of receiving standard verbal therapies. She was a psychologist who had been in private practice for seventeen years and was disenchanted with the verbal approach both for herself and her clients. She was involved in what she described as an addictive relationship and suffered a life long battle with two depressions per year. Over a three year period, between 1984 and 1987 she received 120 music therapy sessions. In these sessions a variety of techniques were employed in the category of "musical space." Methods included musical improvisation, authentic movement from silence, music imagery, music with art materials, etc. When this therapy ended, Robyn was depression-free, was able to leave the addictive relationship and reformulate a healthy friendship with her ex-partner, set a new direction for her personal and professional life, no longer needed the services of a therapist and continued her personal development through what she called her "women's circle". The author conducted a three-hour interview with this client five years after the therapy had ended. The italicized narrative are excerpts of the client's comments during this interview.

"ON MUSIC"

Music: you stranger. You feeling space, growing
away from us. The deepest thing in us, that,
rising above us, forces its way out...
a holy goodbye:
when the innermost point in us stands
outside, as amazing space, as the other side of the air:
pure,
immense,
not for us to live in now.

Excerpt from the poem
By Rainer Marie Rilke
Translated by Robert Bly

BACKGROUND INFORMATION

Robyn, a female client, was 44 at the initiation of her music therapy experience. She was raised in New York in a middle class working family. She described her parents as having an awful marriage. She was the older of two daughters. She reported that the most significant factor in her family experience was a complicated, competitive and ambivalent relationship with her mother. She described her mother as not present, neglectful, cruel, emotionally, physically and verbally abusive, and particularly mean to Robyn, as compared to her sister and father.

> *This colored everything in my life. The ambivalence was*
> *that she both wanted me to be all that she couldn't be,*
> *to grow and expand. And then when I would do it, she*
> *would batter me because I was doing it and not she.*
> *She would connect and merge and then she would*
> *separate and do it suddenly. The image is of being*
> *dropped out of the lap over and over again. That feels*
> *really connected to the work we did together (in music*
> *therapy). There was never a safe container in my*
> *childhood.*

Robyn had had a six and one-half year marriage to a male psychologist, then had lived alone for three years. When she came into music therapy, her romantic involvement was with a woman she had been living with for seven years.

> *There was a moment when I understood that I was in the middle of my primary experience and that it was a chance to go through it differently.*

TREATMENT PROCESS

Prelude

In our initial meeting, Robyn struck me as a highly verbal, warm and loving person who was in great distress. She seemed more comfortable giving than receiving. Although she was 44 years old, she reminded me of a very small and high-strung child---insecure, extremely bright, very anxious and intense. She was always very well-organized, yet seemed extremely vulnerable. My first goal was to introduce her to play, and to offer an atmosphere of unconditional acceptance in which she could experiment, break through and get to know herself within safe limits.

> *I never had permission not to crucify myself, so for me the biggest cyclic thing in my life were these once or twice a year deep depressions---like walking into a pit in which everything I said, did, or thought was a lie or an illusion, or a shredding. That was the place that was absolutely in full roar from the relationship that I was in at the time I came to you. I don't know how fully conscious I was then of what I am saying now. But there was a real recognition that there was a numinous moment. . . I heard about you from Sandy. I liked the thought of not using words. She told me about listening to music, drawing something, then shredding it. I had no way to describe in words what I felt. But somehow that she shredded it... It was all over the floor, and you didn't allow her to pick it up. She was to leave the mess, and you were to clean it up. That made me know in the deepest part of my being---I can feel it again, just when I'm talking [momentarily close to tears]. ---that I just had to go [to you]. This was the place. This was the space that I needed.*

It did not take long for Robyn to learn to trust the space. She seemed to know exactly what she wanted from the onset and had ways of providing me with adequate nonverbal or verbal cues so that I could design the ***musical*** *space* in ways that brought her to her own cutting edge emotionally, spiritually, cognitively. In the beginning, sessions lasted for one hour once a week, then progressed to two hours every other week. Toward the end, sessions tapered off to once a month. The method most commonly used was musical improvisation with instruments and/or voice, including *toning*. Sometimes Robyn would move to my musical improvisations on drums, gong or piano. Sometimes she would image to taped music or my musical improvisation at the piano. She also did *authentic movement*, moving organically out of the silence, with me as witness. Robyn and I both often created art forms after music listening or musical improvisation, sometimes listening to and interpreting taped improvisations immediately after they were played. Sometimes we used the *Runes*, as a projective method or *oracle*. We played with sand to music. Each session included an experience, a dialogue about the experience of the day and also carryover dialogue about issues which came up between sessions. Often I gave Robyn "homework" such as in the case of her art forms. I suggested that she display her drawings or clay structures in her home, in places where they could be easily seen, and to keep working with the images which she had created during the days between sessions.

> *The music-made space had images. That space and those images needed to be made visible. And, when they were made visible, they needed to be watched. Then I found things that had been coming from deeper places than I had been in touch with when I created them. By turning the images, they would keep on telling me more about myself, taking me through even more experiences. It's like a swirling that continued. I would say that the art, the making of my images, or clay forms, or manifesting the inner images was important because so much of my experience in life---and my language---has been to try to get what is inside out in some way that would communicate. The words always restricted and strained out a lot of the depth. There was a need to make manifest, not just to experience---and this is what the sounds always did for me. I needed not only to be in the experience, but also to make a symbol, to make it manifest in some way. Maybe that's because I have always been trying to articulate. The images were an incredibly powerful part of naming without words, giving myself an experience. How I feel about growing is that there is the immersion---you need not have words or brains. You need to go naked, just like a child, into the energy. Let the process carry you and have no ideas*

about how it ought to be or where it's leading or what it's about---really be able to have the trust. And I learned that in our work---to give up any hold on a conscious level, just immerse in the process. The sound was the carrier. But the art and movement were also carriers in a similar way. So there's a time for that, and then there's a time where it must be named in some way. The art gave me a way to name it without ossifying it, because the art then became another process that in its creation continued to show me things. I created a symbol. That image continued to feed me afterwards because it had the same quality as the sound. It was a process that was beyond anything that I experienced in the doing of it. There were layers and layers and more layers. I remember having art work around me in the house. From our sessions I would take the stuff and hang it on the kitchen walls like where a mother would have a child's drawings. They would always be in the periphery of my attention. It felt to me that I would suddenly one day know it was time to take one thing down. . . that I was done receiving from that. So the art was like the music, but it existed over time, in a different way than sound, the sound was in the moment. The sound stopped and the art became a way of moving sound into a space that let it continue over time.

Beyond the objective of creating a safe play container, a musical space, my selection of specific methods was totally intuitive. The night before a session, I would review Robyn's current situation in my mind, her burning questions, her feeling tone. Usually in the morning when I would awake, I had a very clear and simple plan for which methods would be appropriate for the day's work. The immediacy of our moments together seemed critical and I did not want to clutter them with unnecessary ideas. I wanted to be able to listen, in the moment. In this way, not only did I feel confident that I could be totally present, I also was able to interpret the needs of the client in the moment, i.e., need for emotional release, need for conflict, need for support, need for insight, as they would present. This seemed natural.

Robyn was learning to play.

It definitely was the space. The sound took place in a space that was already created. Maybe the kernel was created and the sound gave it more form. But the space was a wedge of time, a sector of time which became

infinite, expanded, separated from ordinary time, ordinary
reality. It was like crossing a threshold into the space,
and the nature of the space was, that whatever was, was
supposed to be. It was opening into this vastness that
didn't have any structure or form to constrict and bump
up against. But it was like a padded space because there
were boundaries. There's a difference between form and
boundary, and there was a sense of container. There
was a web around this or a basket around this. It was
loose, but it was really very much there within that
boundary...everything was infinite and there were no
forms to fit or fill. All that was asked was to be in
the middle of whatever was. I felt that you would bring
to the space 'a gift', that somehow in your reaching and
opening to my coming, you would hear something that
would guide you to provide the piece we would begin
with. I can't remember that it was ever wrong. It
never felt that if it didn't feel right, I couldn't say no
to it. There was always this sense of rightness,
whether we sat at the piano or played bells or drums or
toned, or if you had a tape to play that I could curl up
and dream to. It always felt like a blessing. It always
felt like that was the doorway.

Death

Robyn expressed a great deal of grief in her play---so much grief.
There was also loss and abandonment, as if she were truly a lost and sad
child. It was a deep pool of grief, ancient and enduring. She seemed so
fragile, so delicate. It felt like there was so much grief that she might die
from grief. I identified with grief. Perhaps it was not the same as Robyn's
grief. Yet I also knew grief. My aesthetic preferences were based on a deep
and authentic identification with feelings. My music, too, felt like swimming
in a dark pit. The music was so deep and dark and lonely, full of despair
and sadness, intense. In that pool of grief something did die.

When we started working I had a mother inside of me.
But I had a critical, hatchet lady who could just jump at
anything that I did and rip it to shreds; she cut under
any joyful or full-of-myself feelings that I had. The
only mother voice inside of me was this really brutal,
negative one. One of the women in my circle called her
the Nazi MauMau Mother, and that was the only mother
I knew...so I created another mother out of the dream of

what I wanted. The way I described the work we did to people was that I found someone who would be "Robyn" to me. In the work that we did, in the way that you created that space and that container, was that you provided me an external amplification of a voice that did exist in me, but that never had turned on to myself. The exact opposite is that it was a voice that I could never give to myself. I could give it away, but I couldn't give it to me until somebody gave it to me from the outside. I think that was a critical thing. I had never received that and you, by doing that "space-making," gave me a model of a loving permissive mother acting toward me. That was really the bridge, and when we stopped, or maybe even before we stopped, I was learning to talk differently to myself. I was learning how to still that other voice or talk to that other voice and ask it to step away---that Nazi MauMau voice. When we stopped working together, I continued parenting that part of myself, and more than parenting, it really feels like creating safety. When I no longer had the safe space I trusted you to create, I began to create that for myself and the language of it came later. But it began to be that when I would start with the [Nazi MauMau] voice, [a different] voice would come back and say over and over again: "That's not a good way to talk to yourself. It's really OK! It's OK to just be exactly where you are. It's really O.K. to just make sounds. They don't have to sound like anything. They are what they are and they are magic." That's the message of the sound work---that there's nothing right or wrong. There's just what there is at the moment. And it doesn't have to have words. It doesn't have to be defined. All that is asked is that you immerse yourself in it, and that in doing that, just being in the sound, making the sound or hearing the sound, becoming a resonance myself---that was both the method and the metaphor.

Birth

At a point along the way, a little creature began to appear in Robyn's drawings out of the music. She referred to her as "the little one." This little person was like an abstract representation of a baby. She was naked, joyful, free, innocent, zestful, delicate, capricious, and always flying, floating or dancing.

> *It feels to me like the work of the last five years was born in the work that we did together [in the three previous years]. That when we did the journey back and we found the little one, who was damaged, listening to "Lullabies from the Womb," the image it created was of bridging the pit---to go back to retrieve the little one from before. It was the first time in my life that I really felt that part of me had permission. I felt a safety to be with that part---to be with anybody with that part and that was the beginning of all the healing. It's so hard because in the years that have intervened, about seven years since we started, this volume of words like "the inner child" "the wounded child" [has developed]. Sometimes I feel like I want to puke from it. It's so many words and there's such a difference from the experience of that meeting. That was the piece that I was starting in that nonverbal space---the vision that came from that music. I remember being all curled up and covered under a comforter, listening to the sound and watching this little creature emerge who was lively and spontaneous and robust... full of life and mischief and just free... juicy, excited about life, full of herself, just fully alive, not wounded, not constricted, not constrained, not held back in any way. I can see the picture still in my mind of this little pink baby who was just dancing in the clouds and dancing in the greenery. That was the home, and that was remembering home; and what's come after is being able to walk to that place so that I could fully live there. That moment, in that session, I found home.*

The little one quite literally grew and developed over time, first in the sound making, then secondarily in the art and movement. She began to mature physically in the art. She began to develop affects and character which were audible and visible in melodies, rhythms, phrasing, expressions, body contours in movement expression and colors chosen to represent her movement and costumes. She was exciting and free and full of life. She was artistic and self-assured, strong, mysterious and illusive at times, compelling. She was fascinating.

Finale

As I visited and interviewed Robyn five years after we ended our music therapy work together, I was struck by her independence and autonomy, her lack of anxiety, the many musical instruments and art materials on her living room shelves, the playful nature of the decorating in her home, her graceful way of making me feel welcome in her home, not necessarily to constantly please, her insights as they had developed over the years about the value of the music therapy work, and the long-term results in her life, how it had changed her life. I was her last therapist, the one she had kept the longest in a series which stretched across the years. After we ended our work, she continued her development in a "women's circle," from which, after five years she had just separated and is re-grouping once again.

She had one question of me at the end: "Why did you end the work?" I had ended our work together, and I had a difficult time articulating the reasons, except that I knew that it was time for us to go our separate ways, for me to push Robyn out of the nest, to cut the cord. She said that she felt dropped, kind of like being dropped out of the lap. She said that this was the only thing in the entire three years of working together which felt like it had dishonored our experience together. This was another kind of death. I had been disenfranchised in her mind, in a sense.

At first, I felt confused as I tried to reconstruct that feeling I had had so many years ago, that it was time for Robyn to be free, for me to be free from her as well. As we talked, Robyn was very clear about expressing the fact that she had no bitter feelings, that she had trusted the process, even the ending. She indicated that this interview and being able to put the question to me had really created a beautiful closure for her of that container we had shared.

Although Robyn felt complete, I did not. I had to go away and reflect. Upon reflection, I realized that "the dropping" was the final test. Robyn was dropped by me, yet she had internalized the mother to such an extent, that she was not damaged. She only had a question. Robyn had managed to heal that deep wound at the core of her existence. She had internalized her ideal mother, given birth to her ideal child. When that child had developed to a degree that I intuitively felt she was strong enough "to fly" on her own, I cut the cord. And now after all of these years of incubation, the clarification of a question, the equalization of roles of therapist and client, the work is finally complete.

The last part of our interview/dialogue went like this:

> Robyn: "It feels to me like the female mode, and the way that the music therapist creates safety is that the music therapist is willing not to confine/constrain and give form, but that the music therapist is willing to

ride with the energy and be a companion in that space."

Carolyn: *"It feels very much like that to me. I can remember moments together with you and other clients where the intensity of emotion was horrifying. The anger went into such a scary place. I felt that my job was to take a deep breath and travel with them in that space and to take the risk of traveling with them, being a companion in that space and to be expressive with them. For example, drumming or playing the piano in an outrageous way. That was where a lot of the mastery was---to stay with the intensity, as opposed to cutting it off.*

Robyn: *That for me is really the critical difference between the two kinds of approaches (verbal and non-verbal), because in this therapy you don't have any handles. What you have to be willing to do is to be with that intensity, because if you can't be with that intensity inside of yourself, you can't work with anyone else.*

Carolyn: *Exactly.*

Robyn: *The other system (verbal) really beguiles you to believe that you can handle intensity because you have words and things, theories and frameworks that you can sort of use like robot arms handling hot stuff--- radioactive material. This is the heart of the matter.*

DISCUSSION AND CONCLUSIONS

In a sense, it is a phenomenological faux-pas to address theoretical issues. Yet it may be a more serious infraction to address these issues in fields in which there are well-grounded theories. Music therapy is no such field. Because of this, we may be easily "beguiled."

As music therapists we are intensely aware of the immediacy of our work, and thus equally aware that any theoretical structure is an overlay onto our experience, and thus runs the risk of coloring the descriptions of our experience in a way which may misrepresent the experience itself, the work itself.

Yet as human beings we need language. We need concepts. We need theories, if only to reassure us that we have a grasp on reality. Language and theory represent powerful and valuable control mechanisms, especially for the music therapist who deals with a daily paradox. The first part of the paradox is that often our patients and clients feel out-of-control and thus beg us for containment. The second part of the paradox is that music, by nature, is expansive.

It is so expansive, that perhaps the music therapist is sometimes afraid. And the set of controls which might assuage our fears is very different from those articulated in standard verbal psychological theories. It is different fundamentally, at least on two counts. First, it is nonverbal. Second, it is located in the aesthetic domain, i.e., dealing with aesthetic preferences and sensibilities, in its primary mode of engagement, music.

The music therapist puts her/himself at risk. In a sense, s/he is just as vulnerable as the patient or client because s/he also expresses authentically, thus becoming involved in the aesthetic process of selection, whether that be in musical improvisation, choice of music for imaging, choice of song for performance, or for that matter choice of word, phrasing of sentences, choice of techniques. Ontologically, these choices reflect something significant about the existence of the therapist. We do not own the process of the client; and in the end, if we do not disown it, perhaps the value of the therapy is diminished. Granted, the therapist often attempts to "walk in the moccasins of the client," but the therapist will never "be who the client is."

Together, they explore a field of existence through sound, a musical space. Together they create an experience in that space. This is the method and the metaphor. Our experience in music therapy is a constant reminder that existence is our primary concern because being fully alive, fully present, fully intense, fully expressive, fully vulnerable and immediate is what music therapy is all about.

GLOSSARY

Authentic Movement: A dance/movement therapy form initiated by Mary Whitehouse in which the person moves organically from silence, listening to the creative impulse to move from within rather than responding to outside stimuli.

Musical Space: The musical space is a contained space. It is an intimate and private field created in the relationship between therapist and client. It is a sacred space, a safe space, which becomes identified as "home base," a territory which is well known and secure. In early childhood development, it is similar to the space created between mother and child. Trauma necessitates the recovery of such a space for growth and change. It is a time when a person must reorganize and reintegrate him/herself, after trauma, a break in natural and healthy development. Initial entry into this space is gained when participants are motivated to make the first sound, a creative gesture, a risk, a self-motivated action from an intention to engage. In a sense, the space is "sealed off" or contained, when both participants have joined each other in these first sounds. They get to know each other in the territory. In this field of musical being and acting, the emerging process of delicate new beginnings in development is enacted in musical form (Kenny, 1989, p. 79).

Runes or oracles: The Runes are small stones imprinted with symbols which have meaning in Viking tradition. These were oracles which served as a vehicle for messages from the gods. These messages were interpreted to assist the seeker to improve the conditions of human life.

Toning: A form of vocal improvisation in which spontaneous sound-making with the voice is encouraged. This is not the form of toning initiated by Laurel Keyes, yet it is related.

REFERENCE

Kenny, C. (1989). The Field of Play: A Guide for the Theory and Practice of Music Therapy. Atascadero, CA: Ridgeview Publishing.

Improvisation And Guided Imagery And Music (GIM) With A Physically Disabled Woman: A Gestalt Approach

ELIZABETH MOFFITT, M.A., MTA
Coordinator of Music Therapy
Capilano College: Vancouver, Canada
Gestalt Therapist in Private Practice
Advanced GIM Training in Progress

Abstract. *This case describes music psychotherapy with a woman, paralyzed from the waist down, who had been traumatized from difficult hospitalizations. Gestalt verbal therapy was combined with musical improvisation and Guided Imagery and Music to enhance self-concept and to facilitate emotional expression.*

BACKGROUND

Jenny is a woman in her mid-twenties who has been physically handicapped from the waist down since birth, and has had repeated hospitalizations. She is intelligent, articulate, and a competent pianist. Jenny came to therapy saying that she wanted to match her internal feelings with her age. She felt she had been stunted in her emotional growth at an early age, and this was interfering with her life. She had the appearance of a sweet young girl, quiet and retiring. Jenny claimed that she was unable to speak up for herself to express her thoughts or needs, especially in a group situation. She was also clearly struggling to accept her body, as described in a poem she brought to our first session. Following are excerpts from it.

IN MY HEART A DANCER

She feels the people
closing in on her, closer and
closer, 'til she can no longer
breathe. She must leave
now, for not much longer can
she hold back the tears.......

Sadness
for what can never be, no
matter how much she may
wish or imagine, especially
since she never knew it to be
such a desire..................

You see, she
watched her friend dance
tonight. But unlike all
the other times when she
never gave it another thought,
tonight she watched from her
heart's eyes, and in her heart
lies a dancer..................

But her heart's joy is not
to be found, for her
body is not a vehicle.
Rather it seems more a
stone of unease and
embarrassment. Her body

ever remains for her heavy,
and awkward, painful and
clumsy, not at all a body for
the dancer inside who wishes
to be known, who yearns to
be free..........................

Jenny also brought a drawing which she had recently completed. Several bright colors were in one corner and all the remaining space was completely black.

Jenny then described a horrible series of circumstances at the age of 8, when she was taken from her country home to a city hospital. Her doctor wished to experiment with a procedure to stimulate growth in her legs by systematically breaking the bones as they were healing, hoping to thereby increase their length. When this did not work, the surgeon placed a steel rod from one thigh up to her hip. It seems that the surgeon measured the length of the rod incorrectly however, and unknown to the staff, it caused severe damage to her internal organs.

She became the bad girl on the ward, isolated and left alone, because every time the nurses came to change her dressings, she would scream and faint from the excruciating pain. An intern eventually spotted her greenish colour, and they rushed her to surgery to correct the size of the rod.

That particular time she remained in hospital for nine and a half months. She felt permanently damaged by this whole event. Jenny has rarely spoken about it, and has felt no permission or acceptance to express her depth of feelings regarding this traumatic experience. All this information was told to me in a very quiet, restrained voice.

I was personally moved and outraged, hearing Jenny's account. It appeared that she might require considerable support to explore ways to express herself, and specifically, to release the powerful emotions surrounding these events. It also seemed that she needed to find increased internal resources to sustain her as she worked to integrate the reality of her physical body with her hopes and dreams for a full life. Her obvious creative abilities and her courage would hopefully help with the work ahead.

METHOD

Based on Jenny's needs as initially presented, I chose to combine Gestalt verbal psychotherapy with musical improvisation. Gestalt therapy was originated by Fritz Perls (Perls et al, 1951) to assist the individual to become aware of, express, and reintegrate various aspects of the self. The first step is to develop awareness of both internal and external experiences (e.g., feelings, thoughts, physical sensations, spiritual desires, surrounding environment, degree of contact with that environment and the people within it). This awareness is approached with a spirit of discovery and curiosity, without judgement or evaluation. We wish to learn "what is, rather than what should be or what might have been. Thus, the person learns to trust [him/herself]" (Simkins, 1976).

The *two chair-technique* is one way in which the Gestalt therapist assists the client to explore, express and integrate various parts of the self. These parts are often conflicting thoughts, attitudes, and opinions, such as "shoulds" and "wants" (e.g., "I should write my paper" versus "I am exhausted and feel like sleeping"). The conflicts can also be contradictory internalized voices from parents or significant others in the past (e.g. "You have to work hard and be successful" versus "You must get enough rest"). By using the metaphor of changing positions with each side of an internal conflict by literally switching back and forth between two chairs, these internal splits are more easily brought to awareness. Once feelings and opinions are expressed from both sides, dialogue is possible. With dialogue comes the possibility of increased understanding of the functions of the opposing splits, and ultimately acceptance and integration of the self.

By focusing on present awareness, the Gestalt therapist believes that what is most important for the individual to experience in the moment will come to the foreground out of his background awareness. When the situation in focus is integrated, then it will naturally sink into the background, making space for the next situation to come into the foreground. This dance between fore- and background is seen as a life-long process.

Zinker (1978) describes the "Cycle of Awareness" as a creative process for dealing with any situation which may come to the foreground. Integration comes when the cycle is completed. The therapist works with any blocks or resistances which may occur anywhere within the cycle.

Figure 1

THE CYCLE OF AWARENESS

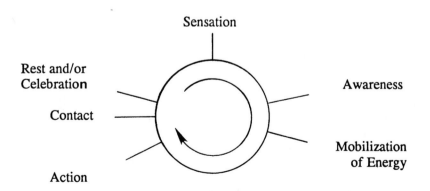

As the individual works to complete more and more of these cycles, increasingly integrating healthy aspects of him/herself, energy is freed to flow more smoothly. The person is more fully alive and creative, able to make healthy contacts with self and environment.

By its nature music is an expression of this moment in time. People can be immediately confronted with issues of being in contact or not, with self or others. This is especially clear in free musical improvisation. All the parameters of music, for example harmony, rhythm or intensity, can be seen as metaphors for the individual. Music is thus a stimulus to awareness, and also provides a creative, expressive medium to process this awareness. Through musical improvisation, a person can also eloquently express strengths and creative aspects of self which may have lain hidden and out of awareness. Music therapists who have worked with adults combining Gestalt therapy with clinical improvisation include Shelley Katsh, Carol Merle-Fishman, and Gillian Stephens (See Bruscia, 1987).

In later sessions with Jenny, I used Guided Imagery and Music (GIM) to access deeper levels of experience, to enhance further expression, and to facilitate contact with her inner psyche and the wisdom that resides therein.

The sessions lasted 90 minutes, and were held weekly. Towards the end of the therapy, GIM sessions were alternated with Gestalt sessions, so as to encourage her integration of imagery on a conscious level.

TREATMENT PROCESS

Phase One

In the first session, when Jenny had finished reporting about her hospital experience, she suddenly fell silent with head lowered. I asked her to focus her attention on her body and to report what she was experiencing internally. Jenny reported feeling a fire in her hip, warm and comfortable. When asked to focus more on it, she experienced the fire turning into burning rage within. During the rest of the sessions, Jenny was able to verbally express her anger, hatred, hurt and confusion, using the Gestalt two-chair technique, to everyone in the hospital including all of the doctors, nurses and aids. Everything was stated in a very quiet controlled voice. Jenny left this session feeling tired though peaceful.

Both sessions two and three began with free improvisation on the piano. Jenny felt she wanted to express more anger for the doctors, yet as she played in session two she was flooded with images of her family home, and being alone there. This led to some two-chair work with her mother, telling her how it was for the 8-year old Jenny to be left alone in the hospital. The session continued with this regression as Jenny cuddled up with pillows and blankets and asked me to sing her a hymn from childhood, "Jesus Loves Me."

In session three, Jenny played the piano in a very quiet, tonal fashion, in ABA form, even though she reported feeling extremely agitated inside. The resulting two-chair work in this session dealt with her relationship to her mother and her feelings about always having to control herself with a smiling face. Jenny expressed her resentments regarding this, again very quietly, but with clarity. By the end of the session she was able to integrate her mother's underlying caring without "selling herself out." In these two sessions, music stimulated important memories and accompanying feelings, provided emotional reassurance, and highlighted an outdated need to mask her true feelings.

In session four, Jenny brought in another drawing which showed progress from the first. Now the bright colours had grown in size, and the black had been broken into eight strips. She later related the strips to her age at the time of hospitalization. That day Jenny came in with her hands bandaged due to an inflammation caused by adjusting to a new wheelchair. She was unable to play the piano again until her return to therapy in the fall.

For this session and the next, Jenny worked on expressing her anger, and exploring how it had taken the form of physical pains, inflamed hands and severe headaches. Her body was always considered the enemy. She felt little attachment to living in it. Though never suicidal, she often wished to be moving on, free of her body, saying that she knew there was a pair of skates waiting for her in heaven.

In the remaining three sessions in this phase of treatment, Jenny was beginning to speak out for herself. The headaches began to disappear.

Phase Two

When Jenny returned for therapy after the summer, she talked of feeling lonely and isolated. Given these feelings, we began with an improvisation together at the piano. Her music had a plaintive quality with bursts of loud passages from which she retreated quickly. I supported her dynamic changes and at times invited more intensity by initiating louder playing. She then moved to the upper register and briefly played a motif similar to the Child's Tune (do, do, la, re, do, la). I imitated in the middle register of the keyboard.

Jenny associated this music with memories of being teased and tormented as a child, and silently ridiculed as an adult. On the keyboard she further explored the sounds of "The Tormentor," playing a loud rhythmic motif up and down the entire keyboard. She then improvised "The Tormented" using a soft, slow melody in the treble that had a strangely removed quality to it. We then took turns playing each role together.

I then suggested that Jenny experiment musically in the role of "The Tormented" to find other ways of handling "The Tormentor" which I played. At first she responded as if aloof, with spurts of frustration that would revert to more serene music, but as I persisted in the role of tormentor, her music became louder and more emphatic until she eventually established a beat so strong that I was drawn to follow it. Although there was much laughter at times during the improvisation, when it was over, Jenny felt very upset. To stop the tormentor, she had to change her way of playing (or being)---from serene and aloof to forceful and in contact. She also did not like to think of herself as capable of being the tormentor.

This was a very important session for Jenny, yet it was too revealing for her to improvise after this for several weeks to come. She said that she could not control what would be expressed in music as she could with words, and at that time, she needed some control.

The remaining ten sessions in the fall were spent working with poetry, drawing, and mental imagery. Through these experiences, we worked to help Jenny become more and more aware of her inner resources.

In the spring, Jenny started going for massages for the first time in her life. She came from one session feeling a tension in her abdomen as if there were sounds of grief and anger there. I asked her to express those sounds, and Jenny chose to improvise once again on the piano. She played a theme in the bass over and over, as if working into it in a trance-like fashion, going deeper and deeper into the lowest tones on the piano. Jenny described it as a "smokey blues saxophone tune" and imagined herself in a Southern bar listening to jazz. As she continued, she imagined hearing voices saying, "Who do you think you are?" It appeared that this new earthy form of expression was to be harshly judged by her internal voices from the past. Her "sax" music had sparked an awareness of herself as a sensuous human being, and this was unknown and forbidden territory for her.

As in the earlier session, I took the role of improvising the tormentor or judge on the piano, repeating the words "Who do you think you are?" This time Jenny quickly and completely responded with loud dissonant chords that silenced me.

After another massage, Jenny arrived feeling very grumpy. Instead of trying to banish the mood or cover it up, she decided to improvise music to learn more about it. Strong, directed music emerged with a rich bass emphasis. This was another new way of playing for Jenny. She described her music as strong, powerful and grounded. With her particular disability, Jenny had great difficulty feeling grounded.

We then proceeded to work with the Gestalt empty chair technique, where Jenny had an opportunity to express whatever she had left unsaid to significant people from her past, as she imagined each of them seated in the chair. We also used the technique to help Jenny to present herself to these people as a strong and powerful person. This was another important session in that Jenny was beginning to integrate her judge/tormentor/grumpy side, and use it to her advantage.

Phase Three

There was a long gap between the second and third phases of our work together due to summer holidays and a temporary move for Jenny. In this phase we saw each other less frequently and mainly dealt with issues related to a temporary job she had taken in a hospital setting. The job was a true test of her newfound ability to express herself, especially to medical personnel who represented so much pain from her past.

We then began to work with Guided Imagery and Music (GIM), a method originated by Helen Bonny (1980). In this method, the client (or traveller) listens to a tape of selections of classical music while in a relaxed state. The therapist (or guide) selects the tape based on the client's needs. The client is encouraged to give a running commentary on the images, sensations, or feelings that emerge while the music is playing. The therapist interacts with the client by witnessing, supporting, questioning for detail, and heightening significant images. Upon completion of the tape, the client discusses the experience and may draw a mandala to anchor images in a visual way.

GIM was used to access images that might help Jenny to integrate her physical body into her self-concept. Images came very easily to Jenny, as was already demonstrated in her piano improvisations, and her images became even clearer when listening to taped music in the GIM way. She experienced everything from being locked in a dungeon, to leaving familiar security and going on a raft, to becoming a warrior woman, healer and spiritual leader. At first she often imaged herself flying in the air. In time she saw herself more frequently walking on the ground (grounded). When Jenny needed to be nourished, she relived safe, loving family scenes or was replenished by her beloved forests and streams. In one session she allowed herself to completely enter a whirlpool in which there was only exquisite beauty and peace all around. Jenny later reported this to be a profound experience of transition, putting her in touch with a greater dimension.

Jenny was very upset in our last session after a confrontation with a doctor at work. She managed to clearly state her position to him, and indeed even challenge his actions. Yet it took its toll on her her, and she was feeling the need to retreat to a safe place for a while---literally under a blanket with all the lights off. After this, Jenny became physically ill with a flu, and went out of town to stay with family who could care for her.

A recent letter from Jenny states that she is well again, continuing to work with imaging to music on her own, and writing poetry. She reports a developing and sometimes surprising ability to make her own thoughts and feelings known, no matter what others might think! She states, "Now the feelings, previously unknown, have words and meanings from which I gain understanding."

CONCLUSIONS

Jenny and I have worked together for over two years. I regret that there has not been an opportunity to find closure to our work. Perhaps this remains for the future.

There are recurrent themes which run through the work with her. The little girl is becoming a woman, with strength and power, beginning to speak for herself, to comfort and advise herself, and to integrate various aspects. She is learning to access deep resources within herself giving meaning to her life.

The combination of improvisation, GIM, and Gestalt verbal work has proved effective, largely due to her high level of creativity and readiness to understand herself more and thereby move forward with her life. Within these methods are the freedom and support to proceed at one's own pace to find one's own wisdom. Jenny needed no more external pronouncements.

There is more work to be done. There always is! Jenny's internal dancer needs to be more integrated into everyday life. Living in Jenny's body is still a tremendous struggle. The more Jenny is aware of her emotions, and the more she can express them, especially the depth of her resentments from the past, the freer she becomes to be more fully alive in mind, spirit, and yes, even in body.

REFERENCES

Bruscia, K. (1987). Improvisational Models of Music Therapy. Springfield, IL: Charles C Thomas.

Bonny, H. (1980). GIM Therapy: Past, present and future implications. Salina, KS: Bonny Foundation.

Perls, F., Hefferline, R., & Goodman, R. (1951). Gestalt Therapy. New York: Dell.

Simkin, J. (1976). Gestalt Therapy Mini-Lectures. Millbrae, CA: Celestial Arts.

Zinker, J. (1978). Creative Process in Gestalt Therapy. New York: Brunner/Mazel.

Unit Five

Case Studies With Adults
In Psychiatric Treatment

Original Song Drawings In The Treatment Of A Developmentally Disabled, Autistic Young Man

DR. ROSEMARY G. FISCHER, RMT-BC, MTA

Director, Music Therapy

Wilfrid Laurier University

Waterloo, Ontario, Canada

Abstract: *This study describes the use of original songs and drawings in the treatment of a developmentally disabled autistic male. The sessions were conducted over a period of eleven months and are described in terms of three phases: 1) Food Song, elicitation of a preferential response, 2) Fear Song, reduction of irrational fears and, 3) Self Song, development of a positive self-concept.*

BACKGROUND INFORMATION

At the time of treatment, Albert was a 23-year-old *developmentally disabled, autistic* male living in a group home with four other similarly diagnosed males. His background was rural, and he came from a family consisting of both parents and a younger sister.

His receptive and expressive language skills were fairly good, given that his cognitive mental age was measured as six years on the Peabody Picture Vocabulary Test. He generally spoke in a flat monotone with an occasional sing-song quality. Albert's communication was limited to simple directions and exchanges of concrete information.

He had no apparent physical defects. His psychomotor skills were good, although he walked with a peculiar gait and exhibited bizarre mannerisms, such as walking on tip toe and flapping his arms.

Albert presented particular difficulties to the staff because of inappropriate sexual and verbal behaviors and occasional episodes of violence. When not agitated, he appeared lethargic and depressed. Throughout the eleven-month period, his medications included Stelazine, Lithium and Serentil. The characteristic most noticeable to the music therapist was his appearance of worry, confusion and general unhappiness.

The music therapist had been hired to work on group interaction and socialization skills with the five residents of the group home. Albert was referred for additional individual treatment to facilitate group goals, and to work specifically on disruptive behaviors which interfered with his functioning within the group home setting.

One of the most persistent of these behaviors was a repertoire of irrational fears which were expressed in rapid, verbal monologues to the staff, such as: "Will Albert get run over by a truck, get killed by spooks, dark closets afraid of haunted houses, is that true?" These monologues occurred without apparent provocation and were very disruptive. Contingency management was the most often used technique. Once begun, however, the monologues would continue unabated until Albert was reassured, at least temporarily, that these terrible things were not going to happen. This particular behavior was referred to by the staff as "ugly talk."

Other maladaptive behaviors included: sexually touching other residents, accusing others of touching him, inappropriate masturbation (termed by the staff as "hands in pants" behavior), following staff members and other residents to the bathroom, and exhibiting sexual arousal at the sound of a toilet flushing.

MUSIC THERAPY ASSESSMENT

Albert's limited communication skills and general apathy prohibited a formal initial assessment. Over a six-week period, in one 45-minute individual session and one 60-minute group session per week, observations revealed that he had the following range of musical skills:

1) Singing on pitch within a one-octave range, with the same flat quality as in his speech;

2) Strumming a beat on the ukelele, autoharp, and drum (though he was not encouraged to use percussion instruments because of his tendency to perseverate on them);

3) Responding by playing one of four different instruments when cued by a specific melody assigned to each instrument, i.e, he played the bells when the therapist played "Jingle Bells;"

4) Participating in a limited way in keyboard improvisations, repeating black key patterns in a stereotypical manner while the therapist improvised; and

5) Playing several instruments after hearing them without visual cues, although he could not repeat more than two in correct sequence.

Albert participated very little in group activities, and frequently interrupted both individual and group sessions with "ugly talk" and inappropriate sexual behaviors. When not responding directly to a simple instruction or engaging in the described inappropriate behaviors, he sat with his head down seemingly disinterested.

TREATMENT PROCESS

Phase One: The Food Song

The first priority was to establish a trusting relationship, and to elicit any preferential response that could be considered appropriate. Efforts to do this formed the basis of the entire methodological approach.

There was no way of knowing that where Albert's music therapy sessions were held would play such a key role in developing a method. All of his individual sessions were held in a common room open to the kitchen, and took place during meal preparation in the late afternoon. Thus the sounds and smells of the kitchen were part of the environment, and of considerable interest to Albert. Discussions about foods arose quite naturally, and the central question became "What does Albert like to eat?" His answer was: "Hamburgers, turnip greens, and bananas."

This was the first positive preferential response that Albert made in music therapy, and seemed ideal for making up a song about him. However, because he was unable to remember the items in sequence, it was difficult getting him to sing the song. The therapist then asked, "Could Albert draw hamburgers, turnip greens and bananas?" He certainly could! And he proceeded to do so. Figure 1 shows his first song-drawing. This drawing depicted the first verse of what was to become our "Food Song." It was significant that Albert regarded this drawing as his own form of musical notation. He would therefore use it to remember the correct sequence of foods when singing the song. To him, it was just like "reading" the music.

Figure 1

FIRST VERSE OF THE "FOOD SONG"

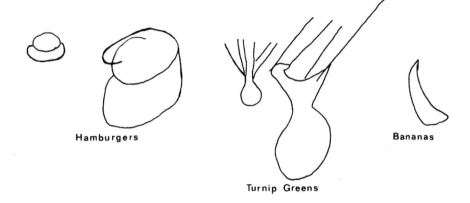

Hamburgers   Bananas

Turnip Greens

By this time, Albert was receiving both individual and group sessions once per week. Each individual session with Albert followed the same format. The three song-drawings were the primary focus of the music therapy interventions. Thirty minutes per session were allotted to them. The sessions also incorporated greeting and closure songs, and other activities and behavioral techniques to facilitate socialization. Thus, the central work was framed by peripheral activities which provided structure, and which allowed for the dissipation of feelings sometimes aroused by producing and performing the song-drawings.

In group sessions, the objectives were to help Albert and his peers to learn: turn-taking, delayed gratification, and risk-taking (e.g., performing one solo per week). Greeting and closure songs were also part of the format.

The idea of having Albert draw songs about himself became the cornerstone for the music therapy program that followed. It also helped to formuate the primary objectve for treatment: to reconstruct his disturbed sense of self through the use of auto-referential song-drawings.

By the third week of this initial phase of treatment, Albert had added two verses to complete the Food Song. As shown in Figure 2, the second verse included banana puddin', corn on the cob, and pig's feet; and the third verse had turkey salad, pizza, and raisin bran cereal. Albert continued to refer to the drawings as if they were actual music notation, and always reproduced the lyrics exactly as before.

Figure 2

COMPLETE LYRICS TO FOOD SONG

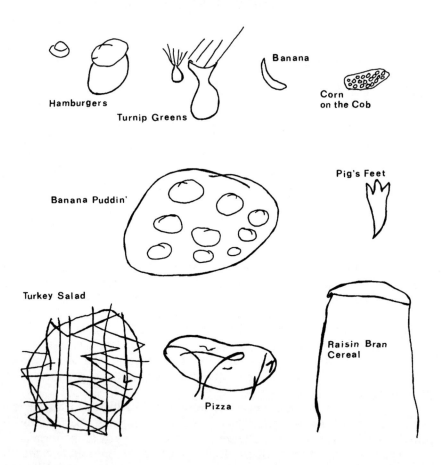

Figure 3 shows the melody of the song provided by the therapist. Albert altered the rhythm slightly by adding dotted notes at the beginning and end (rhythm for "Albert likes"), and he sang it the same way every time. He always sang pitches and intervals accurately, and he always started and finished in the key of "C" even when not given the starting pitch. This skill, an indication of perfect pitch, was demonstrated throughout the treatment period.

Figure 3

FOOD SONG MELODY

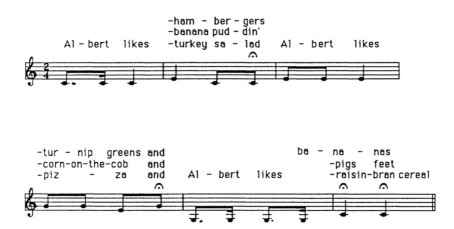

Albert quickly learned to accompany himself by strumming a baritone ukelele tuned to an open "C" chord, however he preferred to be accompanied by the therapist. This allowed him to stroke each object in the drawing as he sang, a tactile habit that continued throughout the sessions. The completed song became Albert's first solo contribution to the group sessions, and he always performed it accurately and with considerable musicality and expression. Other than this, his behavior in the group remained the same.

Phase Two: Fear Song

The second phase lasted 15 weeks, and was devoted to the reduction of disruptive "ugly talk" by producing a song-drawing that would allow him to express his fears openly and appropriately. The "ugly talk" did not appear to be related to attention-seeking, but rather a way of temporarily reducing the anxiety caused by fears that were very real to him. Some of these fears, such as "space men" and "rockets," reflected the content of popular television cartoons. Others, such as "dark closets" and "Cline's Chevrolet" (which could not be identified) seemed to stem from his past experience.

Drawing the verses for this song seemed to absorb Albert's total attention, and the intensity of his involvement was reflected in his posture and facial expressions. On occasion he would become very tense and agitated and would have to be directed to another activity. These drawings took much more time and showed much more attention to detail than the drawings for the Food Song. Based on Kellogg (1967), they are representative of the artwork of a five-year old child.

Figure 4 shows two verses of the Fear Song. It should be noted that after fifteen weeks, Albert had produced eight verses with one page of drawings per verse. The format of four fears per verse never varied.

Figure 4

TWO VERSES OF THE FEAR SONG

Figure 5 shows the melody of the Fear Song. It evolved from Albert's own chanting and improvising. Once finalized, the melody was always reproduced accurately, on pitch, and with evident feeling. He always gave a long plaintive rendition to the final recurring line, "and he's afraid of haunted houses." The habit of stroking the drawings continued while singing, and for this reason, he again preferred to be accompanied by the therapist. Each week the completed verses were performed for the group.

Figure 5

MELODY OF THE FEAR SONG

The most positive outcome of this phase, especially for the staff, was the discovery that the occurrence of "ugly talk" could be effectively reduced by a promise to sing the song later. The opportunity to share and express these fears openly apparently reduced their power over him, and channelled a disruptive behavior into an appropriate and acceptable outlet. In both the individual and group music therapy sessions, the "ugly talk" monologues were completely extinguished.

Phase Three: Self Song

During the 12 weeks of this phase, an attempt was made to build a positive self-concept by encouraging Albert to develop more positive attitudes about himself. This was difficult because he could only think of himself positively in terms of negative things he did not do.

The "Self Song" was designed by the therapist to give Albert an opportunity to fill in the blanks spontaneously. See Figure 6. Drawings were not used initially because he could only draw objects, and seemed not to understand the concept of drawing about "doing something," or, as it turned out, "not doing something."

Figure 6

THE SELF SONG

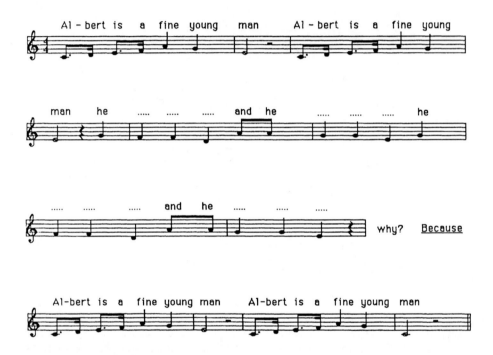

Filling-in-the-blanks worked, at least with regard to negative things he did not do. Each week brought new negatives. For example:

"He doesn't kill people,"
"He doesn't bite people,"
"He doesn't hurt Scruffy,"
"He doesn't run over people with a truck," etc.

When these possibilities were exhausted, Albert would repeat the previous verse, adding "He doesn't talk about" to the beginning of each line. For example:

"He doesn't talk about killing people,"
"He doesn't talk about biting people,"
"He doesn't talk about hurting Scruffy,"

"He doesn't talk about running over people with a truck," etc.

When positive topics were introduced such as "Albert helps wash dishes," or "is nice to Scruffy" (the group home dog), he would dutifully repeat whatever contributions were offered by the therapist with little, apparent understanding of the concept. The only contribution he made which was not "a bad thing he didn't do or talk about" was a thoughtful, and unprintable, suggestion of incest with his sister.

However, the statement, "Albert is a fine young man," eventually seemed to have a positive effect on him. He sang this line with enthusiasm and verve. The positive effect was reinforced by the other men in the weekly group sessions who had by this time shown considerable improvement in their ability to take turns. They not only listened, but also began to sing the chorus with him. Albert took great pleasure in this and would even stand up and conduct the performance.

An additional positive outcome of this song was the self-portrait that Albert drew of "a fine young man." See Figure 7.

DISCUSSION AND CONCLUSIONS

Unfortunately, the sessions were discontinued after eleven months because the therapist relocated. However, the methods utilized had effected positive changes by reducing disruptive verbal behaviors, and more importantly, by providing an enjoyable form of therapy. He appeared to look forward to both the individual and group sessions, and often interrupted the therapist's work with other clients to ask if it was his turn. A mild enthusiasm and lessening of observable depression were other positive indications. In addition to performing his songs for the group sessions, Albert was involved in two performances outside the group home. The final self-portrait, which he gave to the therapist as a goodbye gift, was seen as the beginning of a positive self concept.

Any therapy with a client of this level of disturbance with such limited communication skills has inherent limitations. The technique was not extended to deal with the inappropriate sexual behaviors, although this might have been possible had the sessions been continued. Two additional songs were attempted, "What would Albert Like to Be?" and "What would Albert Like for Christmas?" These attempts were unsuccessful, perhaps because Albert could not understand the concept of the future and could not conceive of himself as a separate entity with desires of obtaining or becoming. The only contribution he was able to make was a painstaking and realistic representation of a chocolate donut which was the sum total of his Christmas list (he did get donuts for Christmas).

Indications of a difficult past sometimes surfaced with Albert, including "dark closets," occasional references to the witches in the Fear Song as his mother, and several realistic drawings of his "father's belt" which were not

Figure 7

ALBERT'S SELF-PORTRAIT

included in any of the songs. There was also the sexual reference to his sister. Although he appeared to look forward to visits home, he often returned depressed and withdrawn. His cognitive and communicative deficits limited the possibility of dealing openly with these issues.

Albert will always be developmentally disabled and will always be autistic. He need not, however, remain locked into a totally negative sense of self. If continued over a longer period of time, the music therapy approach described here might have helped him to overcome permanently some of the negative effects of his past. It may have also continued to serve as the primary therapy.

The overall effectiveness of the therapy for this client was, in part, due to the combined use of three sensory modalities: visual, auditory and tactile (stroking of the drawings). The construction and rehearsal of the song-drawings also reinforced concepts that Albert needed to learn in order to build a better sense of self. The methodology was directed towards considering the underlying causes of his disturbance in modifying his maladaptive behaviors.

In conclusion, this approach is recommended as a practical alternative with individuals whose communicative and cognitive deficits preclude the use of conventional psychotherapy.

GLOSSARY

Developmentally Disabled: A person who is substantially handicapped by mental retardation, cerebral palsy, epilepsy, or neurological impairment which is present by the age of 18 and can be expected to continue.

Autistic: A pattern of early, severe withdrawal in children which leads to severe impairments in relationships and communication.

REFERENCE

Kellogg, R., (with O'Dell, S.), (1967). The Psychology of Children's Art. New York: Random House.

CASE TWENTY-FIVE

Music Therapy For A Nonverbal Autistic Adult

GINGER CLARKSON, M. A., RMT/CMT-BC
Music Therapist: Benhaven School
Consultant: Public Schools
Private Practice
New Haven, Connecticut

Abstract: *This case describes two years of music therapy with Jerry, a 22-year-old autistic man who is nonverbal and violent. The sessions involved improvised and structured instrumental and vocal activities, reading notation, and dancing to recorded music. Music therapy provided a creative outlet for self-expression, learning experiences that fostered self-worth, and opportunities to communicate and interact with others.*

BACKGROUND

At twenty-two years of age, Jerry is an *autistic* black male who is nonverbal and violent to himself and others. His mother, Nora, who is intimately involved in his treatment program, describes her pregnancy with him as normal until the third month when she was involved in a car accident that jolted her physically and emotionally. Shortly thereafter, she took a medical leave of absence from a strenuous job for the remainder of her pregnancy. In her eighth month, Nora began contractions and entered the hospital. Before delivering, the baby's heart slowed down and then stopped altogether. Emergency surgery was performed, but the baby was born "dead" from oxygen deprivation and the surgical team was barely able to revive him. Because the resuscitated infant was one month premature and weighed only three and a half pounds, he spent the first four weeks of his life in an incubator. Nora is certain that Jerry's autistic behavior stems from the brain damage he sustained before and during his birth.

Jerry is the second of Nora's three children by her first husband, and both siblings are normal. His father left home when Jerry was four, leaving Nora to raise the children alone. Her divorce was finalized two years later, and she did not remarry or deliver her fourth and last child until her autistic son had reached his mid-teens and was living in a residential program.

Nora recalls that although he never developed speech, Jerry responded positively at an early age to music he heard at home and at church. He was born into a highly musical family. Nora and several of her cousins enjoy singing and playing piano by ear, as did her father and his brothers. Jerry's older brother works as a disc jockey, and his younger sister is talented on the piano. According to Nora, Jerry rocked to music as soon as he could sit. After he learned to stand erect, Jerry spent many of his waking hours running and jumping up and down, laughing. If upset, he would wail "eeee" in a high pitched voice. His mother discovered that if she turned on a classical radio station just as he was starting to act distressed, Jerry would crawl onto a rocking chair and rock himself to sleep in rhythm with the music. Whenever she took him to church, from his toddler to teen years, he would sit quietly listening to the hymns and would even stay calm during the sermon in order to hear the closing music. At eleven years of age, Jerry amazed the guests at his uncle's wedding reception by jumping up and dancing spontaneously for hours to the band music. By the age of fourteen, he could play tunes on color-coded piano keys. Even though he was an obvious candidate for music therapy, he had to wait until he was eighteen before attending a school that employed a music therapist.

Jerry was evaluated at age three and was diagnosed as autistic. That same year he was enrolled in his first educational program at a church nursery school for special education students. From four to six years of age, he attended a public school for mentally retarded children; from six until seventeen, he attended special education classes run by a local agency. Although he learned enough sign language to communicate some of his needs, his behavior grew increasingly unmanageable. From eleven to thirteen years of age, Jerry had been prescribed Mellaril and Benadril, neither of which had significant effects.

By age thirteen, Jerry had virtually destroyed the family apartment during temper tantrums. Reluctantly, Nora permitted his social worker to place him for nine months at a residential institution for mentally retarded students, while continuing his schooling at the same day program. Due to crowded living conditions and little individual attention, Jerry's behavior deteriorated. By the time he was transferred to another living situation, he had become habitually withdrawn and frequently aggressive to anyone who interfered with his numerous compulsive behaviors. Other attempts were made at this time to control his behavior with various medications (e.g., Haldol, Thorazine, and Prolixin), but with very little success. At the time of this writing, he has taken no medications for about four and a half years.

When Jerry was seventeen, he was discharged from school for repeated incidents of aggression and bolting out of the classroom. Only after his mother sued the city of New Haven to provide her son with a day program were arrangements made for private tutoring. After two years of largely unproductive work, Jerry was admitted to a group home and a private school, both of which were more suitable to his needs. At last, his school teachers and his residential staff collaborated in reinforcing his use of sign language, teaching him some clerical and maintenance work skills, and employing behavioral management techniques to redirect his violent outbursts.

It was during this time that Jerry showed a real affinity for music and movement, and even learned some basic ballroom dancing steps. Thus, when I was hired at the school, Jerry was at the top of the list of candidates for music therapy.

Throughout his educational career, Jerry has been tested by numerous psychologists and psychiatrists on a variety of tests (e.g., Leiter Nonverbal Test, Peabody Picture Vocabulary Test, Goodenough-Harris Draw a Man Test, Vineland Test of Social Maturity). The results have been wildly contradictory: IQ scores have ranged from 39 to 79, Mental Age estimates from 2 to 8 eight years, and diagnoses from profound to mild levels of mental retardation. All of his examiners found Jerry's volatile and compulsive behavior to be a deterrent during testing.

When frustrated, Jerry tends to moan and howl, and either hits his ears and face with both hands or pounds his head against walls or floors until he draws blood. During such tantrums, he lashes out to hit or kick anyone who attempts to prevent his self-abuse, and he often does serious damage to property. Because he has repeatedly smashed a window, light fixtures, furniture, and appliances in his bedroom, the window has been covered with plywood, and all furniture has been removed except for his bed. Since Jerry is six feet tall and very powerful, it usually requires at least three trained staff to restrain his violent behavior. Witnesses of his explosive episodes report that Jerry has occasionally blurted out "No!" and "Sit down!" at the height of a crisis, and "Yes!" and "Get up!" when restrained. This "tantrum talk" is the only sign of intelligible speech to date.

When he first arrived at the present school four years ago, Jerry had tantrums daily, each lasting an hour or more; presently he averages only one every two weeks, lasting less than an hour. The latest outbursts have stemmed from his inability to bring himself to climax while masturbating, and from staff attempting to escort him to his room for more privacy. The overall decrease in aggressive outbursts appears to be due to a combination of quick interventions by trained staff and increased opportunities for creative expression through playing musical instruments, dancing, and doing arts and crafts. Although he destroys any glasses with prescription lenses designed to correct his severe myopia, Jerry spontaneously fashions his own spectacles and masks out of cardboard and cellophane. He intuitively knows that he can improve his vision by peeking through tiny peepholes in the center of his handcrafted glasses.

ASSESSMENT

In the fall of 1988, shortly after scheduling Jerry for weekly individual and group music therapy sessions, I gave him an adapted version of Boxill's assessment (1985). Under the category of "social awareness," Jerry was functioning at an independent level in: establishing eye contact when hearing his name in a song; using sign language to identify himself by name; waiting his turn during group activities; and shaking hands with designated members of the group. His "auditory localization" skills were highly developed; he could establish eye contact and reach towards the source of a musical sound. As for "attending skills," Jerry was able to match on bongo drums a steady rhythmic pulse at slow, moderate, and fast tempos, and to reflect both an acceleration and a deceleration in rhythmic pulse. Although he could reproduce loud sounds on the bongos, he needed assistance to reproduce soft sounds. His eye contact with me was sporadic; he tended to lower his head and gaze at his lap unless urged to "look at me." But Jerry was able to maintain eye-hand coordination on bongos throughout an entire song, beginning in time with the musical cue, but needing occasional verbal prompting to stop when the music stopped. Jerry's "auditory memory" was one of his strong points; he could imitate up to four beats of simple or complex rhythms, on both like and unlike timbres.

In the area of "receptive communication" skills, Jerry could follow one-step directions independently, but needed verbal cuing to follow two-step instructions, and appeared confused by complex directions. Under the category of "expressive communication," he did not vocalize randomly unless tantrumming, and he seemed incapable of imitating vowel or consonant sounds. Despite his ability to express with sign language isolated key words in songs, Jerry did not attempt to express short phrases, let alone the lyrics of entire songs.   In the area of "cognitive skills," he could identify six different instruments by pointing and two by signing. He could also recall a series of body movements, both within and between music sessions.

Under the category of "gross motor skills," Jerry demonstrated the ability to play bongo drums independently with simultaneously biltateral hands and with (awkwardly) alternating hands. Although his left hand was clearly dominant, he needed coaching to cross the midline. Under "fine motor skills," Jerry could independently hold and grasp a bell mallet, but he required assistance to relax his wrist enough to produce a ringing tone on resonator bells.   Shortly after the assessment, I discovered that Jerry could push designated buttons on an autoharp with one hand while using a guitar pick to strum the strings with his other hand. In spite of his myopia, he performed well under the category of "visual motor skills." Jerry could independently play a resonator bell while holding a beater in one hand and the bell in the other.   He had no trouble striking a bell, whether it was parallel or perpendicular to his beater, and he could just as easily play a series of bells when they were placed together as when they were placed apart.

Because he measured so much higher on musical skills than the three peers in his music therapy group, Jerry soon became the leader, demonstrating how to play a variety of instruments on cue and passing instruments to designated peers after completing his own turns. Unfortunately, due to changes in his schedule, he had to discontinue group sessions after one year.   The administration and his classroom teacher considered his individual music therapy sessions important enough to continue throughout his enrollment at the school.

Music therapy goals in 1988 for Jerry's half-hour individual sessions were: to increase direct eye contact to at least once per instrumental activity and throughout the duration of dance routines; to encourage the use of sign language to indicate "I want drum" or "I want to dance" before the start of each activity; to increase the incidence of choosing between two musical instruments through gestures or signs to at least twice per session; to increase the amount of physical contact tolerated in dancing and clapping games to at least five times per session; to encourage each session the initiation of at least one body movement pattern of his choice for me to imitate; and to increase the ability to discriminate on a drum between two or more rhythmic patterns initiated played at least four times per session. These goals focused on developing Jerry's interpersonal interaction and communication skills as well as on improving his innate sense of rhythm and melodic phrasing.

METHOD

In my work with Jerry, I use the improvisatory approach of Paul Nordoff and Clive Robbins (1977) combined with other standard music therapy techniques. My theoretical orientation is primarily psychodynamic, but I also utilize behavioral techniques such as positively reinforcing appropriate behaviors and ignoring negative behaviors that do not harm people or property. Although my primary instrument is the piano, I may also use guitar, autoharp, resonator bells, drums, or various percussion instruments, depending on Jerry's needs and moods.

Because he is autistic, Jerry requires predictability and careful preparation for any changes in routine. I therefore structure the sessions very clearly, beginning with a greeting song and ending with a farewell song (both by Nordoff and Robbins). Between these two songs, Jerry participates in beating rhythmic patterns on drums, playing accompaniments on a selection of melodic instruments, and dancing to recorded music. I believe strongly in the efficacy of using live music to encourage active participation, and therefore seldom use recorded music with my other clients. However, considering Jerry's history of dancing to radio and phonograph music, I decided to incorporate his favorite recordings into the sessions. At the end of each session, when we dance together, I concentrate on overcoming his autistic tendency to avoid human touch and eye contact.

During the rest of the session, I focus on enhancing Jerry's self-esteem and autonomy by developing his musical skills. After exposure to a variety of song materials and instruments, Jerry is expected to communicate preferences, to play accompaniments on cue, and to take responsibility for putting away whatever materials have been used. As much as possible, he is treated as a responsible adult. To keep him engaged, fun and easy tasks are interspersed with more challenging ones, as well as with new material. Since Jerry responds well to secondary positive reinforcement, I frequently praise him for making eye contact, for tackling new material, and for successfully completing difficult assignments. I use a combination of sign and spoken language to communicate with him, presenting him with increasing opportunities to initiate sign language. In response to Jerry's interest in art and visual stimuli, I have also incorporated simplified musical notation, using a color-coded system. During each session, I observe what songs and instruments appear to motivate him most, and then use those as a starting point in subsequent sessions.

TREATMENT PROCESS

Phase One

It took several months for me to earn Jerry's trust. During his initial session in March of 1988, he kept his head bowed down throughout most of the session until he was given an opportunity to dance. He did not use sign language spontaneously, and would not readily comply when asked to copy my signs. With gentle coaching, he watched warily as I sang a "Hello Song" and demonstrated an accompaniment on two resonator bells. Jerry grasped the mallet with his left hand, and made an attempt to imitate me. However, he would not let me touch his rigid wrist to help him rebound the mallet, and periodically he would interrupt his playing to lick his hands in a ritualistic manner. He appeared more relaxed while using two drumsticks to beat a standing drum. After only one runthrough, Jerry could beat in perfect rhythm to an imitative song and to an improvised piece that required him to switch from one to two hands on cue. Not only was he able to follow my changes in tempo and dynamics on the piano, but he anticipated phrase endings and cadences in the music. He tended to use simultaneous bilateral arm movements and to avoid crossing his body's midline. Surprisingly, for a man of his strength, his beating was quite timid and soft. When I introduced the challenging drumming game "Fun for Four Drums" by Nordoff and Robbins, Jerry initially beat an accompaniment with only one hand. Despite being able to copy a demonstration of alternating drumsticks, his arms moved slowly and awkwardly in this new motoric pattern, and he had trouble keeping up with the tempo of the piano. Since Jerry seemed to like the challenge of practicing the new musical skill, I slowed the piano part to match his tempo, and was careful to stop the activity before he became discouraged.

I then used sign language to prepare Jerry for a period of dancing to a recording of "La Bamba," one of his favorite songs. At this beginning stage of moving together, he stood facing me, watching carefully, from a distance of several yards. Whatever gesture or step I initiated, he copied, but he made no effort to add any motions of his own. Recognizing that his most fluid movements were above the waist, I began by moving only the upper body, and then just the lower body, slowly stepping to the back, front, and sides. As Jerry practiced and grew more confident about maintaining his balance, I experimented with combining upper and lower body movements, as well as stretching up on tiptoes, crouching down low, circling around, and twisting the torso. Although his legs and feet still lagged behind his arms, Jerry's body looked increasingly coordinated.

Once he had expanded his repertoire of movements by imitating me in this nonthreatening way, he was amenable to playing two resonator bells to accompany the "Goodbye Song." During his first attempt, he double-beat each bell, but after watching a second demonstration, he played the bells correctly, once each in sequence.

Jerry gradually grew accustomed to beginning each session with a greeting song and closing with a farewell song, but any change in routine disturbed him. One day after new folding chairs had just been installed in the music room, Jerry entered for his session. Without thinking, I folded one of the chairs to make room for dancing. In response to this break with the usual structure, Jerry threw himself on the floor and started moaning and hitting himself on his ears. His tantrum accelerated when I called for extra staff to help, and two hours passed before Jerry calmed down. In the aftermath of that episode, I was very careful to prepare him for any changes. To help him feel oriented in time, his classroom teacher instituted a daily picture schedule, using photos of different activities in the sequence in which he would be experiencing them. On "music day" he was guided to insert a photograph of me seated at the piano.

Phase Two

After six months of sessions, Jerry was making frequent eye contact and smiling whenever he successfully completed a rhythmic task. He would spontaneously sign "hello" and "goodbye," "dance," "more," and the numbers "one" through "ten." In addition, he would readily imitate signs for the colors tagged to specific resonator bells and bars of a Chimalong. Once I taught him to shake his left wrist to loosen it up, he could rebound a mallet to produce a clear, ringing tone on the melodic instruments. His memory for short melodic patterns learned in previous sessions was striking. While dancing, Jerry was increasingly comfortable with being touched. If I approached him slowly, offering my hands, he would hold hands with me for brief periods of time, twirl me around, walk next to me, and sway directly opposite me. Between dance numbers, Jerry often signed spontaneously "more" to continue dancing. No longer was he merely copying my movements. If I waited patiently, he would initiate a few of his own. During a movement game called "Head and Shoulders," Jerry would touch two different body parts to indicate his choice for each verse. Then I would follow his lead in touching the two body parts in a prescribed sequence.

After six months of practice, Jerry's drumming had improved as much as his dancing. He had learned to alternate drumsticks smoothly and rapidly. When participating in "Fun for Four Drums" by Nordoff and Robbins, he could differentiate among four different call and response rhythmic patterns, which is a demanding task for any student. Jerry learned the patterns, one by one, by listening and watching carefully as I modeled them on the drum. After he had practiced each rhythmic grouping numerous times in isolation, I started mixing cues for two distinct patterns. Jerry would concentrate very hard and smile each time he figured out which one was required. Once he had mastered differentiating between two patterns, it was a relatively easy task to add a third, and later a fourth. When I would correct his infrequent errors, he was tolerant and patiently revised the rhythm. He still needed encouragement to play with force and assertiveness.

Phase Three

Although the drum was his first preferred instrument during the initial six months of music therapy, Jerry began to show an interest in melodic instruments in the months that followed. He used pointing to indicate a choice among a Chimalong, an alto Orff xylophone, and a set of resonator bells. With very little practice, he was able to recall the sequence of tones to several melodies. At first he played slowly and cautiously, and he found it difficult to reverse direction on the bells. But after carefully watching me keep the mallet close to the surface of the bells to ensure accurate playing during rapid tempos, Jerry mastered a rapid accompaniment to a song in ABA form. He learned to reverse direction in the middle of playing the "A" theme, to rest patiently while I played the "B" theme on the piano, and to play on cue as soon as the "A" theme recurred. While playing bell accompaniments, he was so attentive that on one occasion he persevered while a workman was hammering nails in the hallway and a student was screaming in the next room.

It was during Jerry's second year of music therapy that he began to follow color-coded musical notation. I introduced him to the concept of notation by reviewing a bell accompaniment to a song that he knew well. I asked Jerry to sign the different colors of the dots marking each of the five bells he had just played. I then showed him a file card on which similarly colored dots were arranged in a sequence from left to right. As Jerry watched with obvious interest, I pointed to the dot on the first bell and then to the dot that was furthest left on the card, making certain that he understood that they matched. After I had pointed out the correlation between all the colored markers on the bells and those on the card, I asked Jerry to do the same. Once he successfully completed the task, I had him play the bells as I pointed to corresponding dots on the file card. His rapt attention and smiles indicated his excitement about comprehending a new approach to playing music.

Once he understood the concept of notation, Jerry was able to perform increasingly difficult bell accompaniments, including imitative ones that required distinguishing between two melodic lines. Because of his visual orientation, notation facilitated his memorization of a number of melodies. Even though he always reads the colored "notes" from left to right, Jerry can handle repetitions of notes and reversals of direction on the bells that correspond to the notation.

Phase Four

Jerry's progress in musical and social skills has continued until the time of this writing. Now his music therapy sessions are fifty minutes in length, and he is fully attentive throughout each session. Not only is he tolerant when rhythmic or melodic errors are pointed out to him, but he also learns quickly from his mistakes, seldom repeating the same one. Jerry rarely engages in the compulsive mannerisms that used to interrupt his performance, and he is responsible about putting away musical instruments. His drumming skills have improved to such a degree that he can accompany a waltz played on the piano. Through every measure of the lengthy piece, he steadily beats a drum once and a standing cymbal twice. Jerry's progress in following musical notation is so great that he recently tackled a complex bell accompaniment to a piano arrangement of J.S. Bach's "Jesu, Joy of Man's Desiring." Without any lyrics to guide him, he anticipates each recurrence of the opening melodic line, with which he plays contrapuntal harmony on six resonator bells.

During dance routines, Jerry takes pride in operating a cassette tape recorder. Between dance numbers, he spontaneously signs "more dancing." He is relaxed enough to initiate gestures and steps and to hold hands with me throughout entire songs. Not only does he twirl me in and out, but he also allows me to do the same to him. While dancing, Jerry's posture straightens, his eye contact is steady, and his expression is smiling. Despite wearing clumsy work boots, the movements of his feet are increasingly synchronized with the motions of his upper body, so that he dances more gracefully.

In recognition of how much he enjoys music therapy sessions, his supervisory team recently allotted money to purchase him some special dancing shoes. On one weekend outing, when he was given the opportunity to buy himself a present, he chose a Reggae tape, which he uses as background music for dancing.

At the end of his sessions, Jerry now regularly signs "Goodbye, Ginger." One day an observer took polaroid pictures while Jerry and I were dancing together and playing the "Goodbye Song." When he was shown the photos, Jerry pointed to himself and to me and smiled. In response to my signing "We are friends," he signed "Yes."

EVALUATION

To evaluate Jerry's progress, I write a summary immediately after each session. This helps me to keep track of which materials and approaches have worked effectively and which ones need to be revised or discarded. In his previous placement, I also wrote detailed semiannual progress reports, which were sent to Jerry's mother and to the team overseeing his vocational and residential programming. At the present placement, I arrange to have one of Jerry's music therapy sessions videotaped immediately before each of his quarterly team reviews, so the administration and staff can see evidence of his progress. At these quarterly meetings, I also submit copies of my weekly music therapy notes. In addition, if Jerry's mother is unable to attend a team review, I telephone to keep her abreast of the latest developments.

DISCUSSION AND CONCLUSIONS

Why has Jerry responded so positively to music therapy sessions? His lifelong love of music is a big factor. For eighteen years his musical soul was locked inside an isolated and frustrated body. It is tragic that Jerry had to wait so long before his musicality was developed systematically. One can imagine how different his life might have been if he had received music therapy as a young child. The predictable structure and carefully paced activities in his music sessions have provided him with enough security to meet and far surpass goals that were set in 1988.

Within his sessions, he has evolved from a passive and withdrawn person, prone to violent outbursts, into a self-respecting man who manifests confidence in dancing and playing various musical instruments. He has become assertive about indicating preferences, and he has begun to initiate sign language spontaneously. With the creative outlet that music provides, Jerry is less inclined to tantrum or to engage in ritualistic habits.

Underlying Jerry's autistic characteristics are a number of healthy attributes. Music therapy has tapped his strong sense of rhythm, his ability to dance, his innate sense of melodic phrasing, his excellent fine motor skills, his good short- and long-term memory, and his competent eye-hand motor coordination. Considering the speed at which he grasped the concept of notating songs, Jerry appears to be ready to learn traditional musical notation. He could practice with a large-scale notational staff on which the colors that he associates with individual bells are matched with corresponding notes on lines or spaces. Because he is so attentive to visual details, Jerry should be able to recognize different notes according to their placement on the staff. This skill would greatly enhance his independence in playing music outside of music therapy sessions.

To further develop Jerry's social interaction, I am now preparing him to dance with other partners. A female aide from his residence observed a recent music therapy session in order to learn some of his dance steps. At the end of the session, Jerry watched as I danced with her, teaching her some of the moves that he had just completed. When I asked him, "Do you want to dance with Lauren?" he signed "Yes."

To transfer his experience of creative interaction to other modalities, I have recommended that art therapy be provided. At the time of this writing, an artist on the residential staff has begun to provide Jerry with new experiences in arts and crafts and to transform his private pursuit of designing masks and glasses into a shared activity. Upon reviewing the extent of his progress in musical and social skills, Jerry's team is increasingly optimistic about his future. I feel honored to be a part of Jerry's development.

GLOSSARY

Autism: Creak et al (1961) described the classical criteria of infantile autism as: a striking inability from birth to form relationships with people; total unawareness of personal identity; innate failure to develop speech and language in order to communicate; obsessive insistence on preservation of monotony in behavior and sameness in the environment; extreme isolation with psychosexual fixation at the pre-oral level; persistent preoccupation with objects for repetitive movement; and good cognitive potentialities despite intellectual functioning at a retarded level.

REFERENCES

Boxill, E. (1985). Music Therapy for the Developmentally Disabled. Austin: Pro-Ed., Inc.

Creak, M., Cameron, K., Cowie, V., Ini, S., Mackeith R., Mitchell, G., O'Gorman, G., Orford, F., Rogers, W., Shapiro, A., Stone, F., Stroh, G., & Ydkin, S. (1961). Schizophrenic syndrome in childhood. British Medical Journal, 2, 889.

Nordoff, P., & Robbins, C. (1977). Creative Music Therapy. New York: John Day Company.

Nordoff, P., & Robbins, C. Fun For Four Drums. Bryn Mawr, PA: Theodore Presser.

Musical Improvisation In The Treatment Of A Man With Obsessive Compulsive Personality Disorder

JOSÉ VAN DEN HURK, R.M.T.
Music Therapist
Music Therapy Laboratory
Nijmegen, The Netherlands

and

DR. HENK SMEIJSTERS, PH.D.
Music Psychologist/Researcher
Music Therapy Laboratory
Nijmegen, The Netherlands

Abstract: *A 31-year-old man who was undergoing psychotherapy for feelings of doubt, unrest and panic was referred to music therapy to work through his emotional and interpersonal blocks. Musical improvisation was used as the primary method over the one year of treatment. The authors worked as a team, combining perspectives of therapist and researcher in assessing the client, formulating aims, designing treatment, and evaluating progress.*

BACKGROUND INFORMATION

At the time of this study, John was a 31-year-old man who had been referred to a psychotherapist by a general practitioner because of intense feelings of doubt, unrest and panic when making decisions. His problems with decisions were pervasive, involving important life choices such as not being able to choose between his wife and his girlfriend, and everyday tasks such as making an appointment to have his car serviced.

John had been referred to a psychotherapist before, but he did not continue with treatment after the first session. This time, however, his panic attacks were increasing in intensity, and the need for psychotherapy was more obvious to him.

John was living with his parents temporarily. He also worked with his father at the same company. John was very dependent on his father, and had, in fact, relied upon him for support while studying for his diploma. John looked to him as an authority figure, and the father, in turn, reacted strongly to his son, commenting regularly on his conduct and life. Being financially well-off was an important factor in John's life.

At work, John had occasional problems with his colleagues and supervisors, however he did function in a group of friends with whom he shared interests and hobbies.

There were no indications that John was using alcohol, drugs or medication at the time of treatment, although in the past, his alcohol consumption had been higher. When therapy began, John was also under the treatment of a dietician for high cholesterol levels.

John was referred to music therapy, because his current psychotherapist felt that music could help him to work through his rationalizations and emotional armors.

MUSIC THERAPY ASSESSMENT

Because music therapy was being used in tandem with verbal psychotherapy, and because the authors worked together in combining treatment and research (Smeijsters, 1990), information on the client's problem was gathered in several ways, including: (1) conversations with the psychotherapist previous to and during treatment; (2) a musical intake, consisting of 5 sessions in which both active and receptive forms of music therapy were used (e.g., improvisation, listening to music and looking at photographic materials, choosing preferred music, etc.); (3) short reports which the client wrote on request of the music therapist; and (4) continual communication between researcher and music therapist based on written clinical reports on each session.

Data from the first three of these sources gave an impression of John as an *obsessive neurotic character* (Cullberg, 1988; Kuiper, 1989). John did not dare to make decisions, and he constantly wanted validation for any decisions that he did make. He had a strong need for order, and was unable to cope with any deviations from rules. He was afraid of being overwhelmed by irregularities, and he avoided experimentation at all costs. John generally took an intellectualizing or controlling attitude, repeatedly asking whether he should behave in one way or another and why. He rarely admitted having any emotions, although some did surface in the musical intake on a few occasions. He felt uncomfortable in the presence of the female music therapist, and was meek and passive when interacting with her.

The music John produced during the intake was quite conventional, as if he were trying to adhere to musical norms or rules. It was characterised by fixed harmonies and diatonic melodies. He did not experiment. He chose large instruments, yet his playing was submissive. Motorically, his playing was restless, but the volume was rather flat. If rules were broken, he reacted strongly. On one occasion, he selected a piece of music that moved him to tears; on another, he selected a piece which was quite aggressive sounding.

John's intellectualizing attitude, his tendency to deal with problems and emotions in a rational, business-like fashion, his difficulties in accepting emotions, his rigid patterns of behavior, and his inability to be playful, all provided clear indications for music therapy (Schalkwijk & Luttikhuis, 1990) using an improvisational approach. By creating a safe atmosphere within the music therapy setting, and by using musical improvisation as a medium of self-expression, John would be able to learn how to make decisions, to be less concerned with rules and standards, to experiment with new behaviors, and to admit, express and vent his emotions.

METHOD

Music therapy sessions have been held once weekly over a one year period, and at the time of this writing, John is still enrolled in treatment. Sessions are one hour long, and are held in the rooms of the Music Therapy Laboratory in Nijmegen.

Although both active and receptive techniques were used in the intake, active participation in improvisation has been emphasized since then. The improvisations are based either on a musical theme (rhythm, melody, etc.) or on a verbal theme (idea, emotion, event, etc) related to the client's life. The improvisations are aimed at engaging John in decision-making and experimentation, while also providing a screen for projecting his emotions (Priestley, 1975; Hegi, 1986).

The approach to psychotherapy is based on several constructs, including:
    ---the *aesthetic illusion* (Kris, 1952) which by its protective
        function makes acting and feeling less threatening;
    ---the creative performance that brings healing (Klein, 1955;

Winnicott, 1971);

---the unblocking of emotions by evoking, reliving and physically discharging them (Lowen, 1969);

---Gestalt concepts like awareness, response-ability and experiment (Perls, 1969; Hegi, 1986; Frohne, 1990);

---client-centered, humanistic ideas on self-concept (Rogers, 1961);

---the role of mourning in working with the past (Kuiper, 1989).

Improvisational techniques used by the music therapist are derived from Bruscia (1987) (See Glossary).

TREATMENT PROCESS

Based on the assessment findings, the music therapist and researcher identified "focus points" for the treatment process. Focus points are problem areas of the client which have been identified as priorities for intervention. As such, they are goals that the therapist keeps in mind throughout each session.

Focus points are established through a spiralling process. Based on assessment, the most important areas of concern are identified for different stages of treatment. General aims and specific objectives are then formulated along with strategies for intervention. Then, based on what results are achieved with the client, these areas of concern, goals, objectives, and treatment strategies are constantly adjusted. In the present case, this process was carried out jointly by the therapist and researcher. Subsequently, the role of the therapist is to implement the actual work with the client, and the role of the researcher is to observe the reactions of the client to various therapeutic strategies, and to evaluate the client's progress in meeting the objectives. This cooperative approach helps to give the therapeutic work more accountability.

John's music therapy can be divided into three stages so far, each with its own set of focus points.

First Stage

After the musical intake of 5 sessions, the first stage of treatment lasted 10 sessions. This stage was defined by its own focus points, aims, treatment strategies, and expectations of progress.

FOCUS POINTS. Five focus points were established for the beginning stage of treatment. They were:

(1) John had an intense need for security, predictability and set rules. From the very first contact, it was obvious that John did not want to take any risks. He was afraid of the unknown. In musical improvisation, he demonstrated these fears by being passive, submissive, uncreative, and lacking in spontaneity. He selected instruments with which he was more or

less familiar, and he did not experiment with them. Whenever the music therapist did not conform to his rules or expectations with regard to music-making, John would become tense and irritated, demonstrating his inability to deal with unpredictable behavior in a flexible, creative way.

(2) John had feelings of inferiority which resulted from his inability to meet his own unrealistic aspirations and standards. He behaved very conservatively, and sometimes thought that he was useless. In music therapy, these characteristics were evident in John's self-criticism when attempting to play an existing piece perfectly, and in his comparisons of his improvisations with music of mentally deranged persons. In his personal life, his high aspirations were evident in the area of finance. Possessions, like a big car, served as compensation for feelings of inferiority. A vicious circle had come into being, in which standards and aspirations led to feelings of inferiority which had to be overcome by even higher standards and aspirations.

(3) John often doubted himself and needed validation, approval and reassurance. These could be regarded as symptoms of his inferiority feelings, and were particularly evident when making decisions. For John, making a decision was taking the risk that his choice would not meet with the approval of others. He therefore continually questioned others before deciding anything in order to insure their approval. This occurred when choosing musical instruments and in the comments he made about his own improvisations.

(4) John had an intellectual, non-emotional attitude. He talked a lot, but in a business-like fashion, constantly seeking rational explanations and suppressing any emotions. He played music mechanically, and reported experiencing no feelings or tensions. He would never expose or express his feelings in the sessions, and talked about feeling ashamed to do so. On those occasions when he could express his feelings, he admitted to being very sensitive. At the end of sessions, he always asked for explanations or interpretations of what he did. These attempts to rationalize and intellectualize his emotions can be taken as methods of defending and protecting himself against being hurt.

(5) John feared intimacy, and often behaved in a self-centered manner. This was clearly shown in his music-making. He would play without paying any attention to the therapist, and would not dare to make musical contact or have the experience of playing together. He would not try to match what the music therapist did, and he would quicky change his music if the therapist matched him. Musical contact was established only when the music therapist specifically asked for it. These ways of avoiding intimacy were particularly evident when the situation called for equality, and when there was no clear delineation of who was leader and follower.

AIMS. Given these focus points, the aims established for therapy were to help John: to abandon rigid patterns, to accept and react to unpredictable situations, to experiment and take risks, to take more initiative and responsibility, to make choices more freely, to enjoy his own music, to let go of his unrealistic expectations, to be less isolated and to allow greater intimacy in his music-making. It was decided that, only after a safe atmosphere could be established in music therapy, would aims related to his emotions be pursued.

ACTION PLAN. It was decided that the best way to accomplish these aims was to engage John in improvisatory situations that systematically varied the amount of risk and intimacy involved. The main variables were: whether John had to choose the instruments, whether the instruments were familiar to John, and how much distance the instrument created between John and the therapist. Several levels of risk and intimacy were identified for organizing each sessions:

(1) The music therapist selected two different but familiar instruments (e.g., guitar and percussion), one for John and one for herself. In this way, John did not have to make any decisions, and was permitted to play a familiar instrument that was distant from the therapist's in terms of timbre.

(2) The music therapist selected two identical, familiar instruments (e.g., two drums). Here John did not have to make choices or deal with anything familiar, but had to tolerate the closeness in sound of his instrument and the therapist's.

(3) The music therapist picked two unfamiliar instruments (different then identical). This allowed John to experiment with something new, first at a safe distance from the therapist, and then with increased closeness.

(4) The music therapist picked one instrument for both John and her to play, first a familiar one and then an unfamiliar one. Here John did not have to make a choice, but had to tolerate the intimacy of playing on the same instrument.

(5) John picked the instruments in the same order as described in 1-4 above. This added the challenge of decision-making, while allowing him to control familiarity and intimacy.

The improvisations were sequenced during the sessions according to the above levels. The musical improvisations following the combinations of freedom of choice, familiarity and intimacy formed the most important element of the plan of action. Daring to experiment, taking initiatives, making contacts and learning how to enjoy one's own spontaneous performance were worked on through the improvisations.

When improvising with John, the music therapist initially used *techniques of "empathy"* (e.g., imitating, synchronizing, pacing and reflecting), as defined by Bruscia (1987). Care was taken to offer enough distance, while also creating a safe place for John to begin taking the necessary risks.

After a safe atmosphere had been established, the music therapist began to use *techniques of "elicitation" and "redirection,"* such as repeating, making spaces, interjecting, introducing change (Bruscia, 1987), all aimed at encouraging John to experiment, take initiatives, and react spontaneously. To strengthen intimacy, she used *techniques of "intimacy"* (e.g., sharing instruments and sharing intensity of playing). See Glossary for definitions.

Verbal instructions were also helpful. For instance, the music therapist would say: "Let's try to make contact by reacting to one another's music," or "There is no need for you to prove yourself."

PROGRESS. During the first stage of music therapy, changes were observed in John's musical and verbal behaviour over a number of consecutive sessions. Changes could also be observed outside of the therapy situation, although it cannot be claimed with any certainty that these changes were caused by the music therapy, because John was also receiving psychotherapy concurrently. There was, however, a logical connection between focus points, therapy techniques and behaviour in and outside of music therapy.

During the first few sessions, there were only brief spells of playing together, at which time John would quickly change over to a different rhythm or musical instrument. When he took up the music therapist's rhythm he did not really make contact, but rather went his own way. John reacted to the music therapist's playing only when she demanded him to do so. He hardly paid attention to what she was doing, and was centered primarily on his own regulated, mechanical, technical and not very spontaneous ways of making music. The music therapist tried to get into feelings underlying the music, but found she could not.

John's verbal comments and written notes further underlined his musical behaviour: "I keep a distance, it seems like I am not there;" "I feel like I have to achieve something;" "I am afraid of exposing myself;" "I am insecure and I feel ashamed."

In later sessions of the first stage, these tendencies gradually changed. Playing the piano enabled him to pay more attention to the music therapist, because he could let go of his ambitions. This did not happen with the electrical guitar, which brought out his feelings of having to prove himself because he had studied the guitar. On the piano, this competitive spirit disappeared, and he was able to come out of his egocentric isolation and react to the music therapist. His music became more vital and dynamic, and it expressed more feeling, however spontaneity was still lacking. In subsequent sessions, John spontaneously picked the piano for his instrument. He increasingly dared to put more of himself into it, to respond to the therapist's music, and to experiment without fear. Playing the piano, close to one another, was initially experienced as threatening.

The fact that John abandoned his rigid, rule-oriented attitude was evident in statements like: "I increasingly experience the therapy situation as relaxed;" "I feel less like having to achieve something;" "The ensemble was more imaginative, less beautiful, but more enjoyable though;" "The performance is more intensive." These reactions showed that he still had a normative frame of reference ("less beautiful"), but that he was also learning to see the possibilities of non-normative, free self-expression. He felt more relaxed and liberated, and he discovered that through music, imagination and emotional intensity were possible.

John showed considerable insight into his own musical behavior. He wrote down, for example: "I find it difficult to take the lead when I am on unknown ground;" "I am afraid of setbacks;" "I only take the initiative when I feel quite sure about something;" and "When I am on unknown ground I wait and see what happens."

As for events outside of therapy, John indicated that he went for trips in his car without having to meticulously arrange and discuss everything in advance. Although he still had some difficulties with insecurity during these excursions, he had never dared taking such an uncertain step before. John was developing a new attitutde, one which was generally less rational and controlling, yet more self-assured. He said that now he knew what he wanted, what he was capable of doing, and what he felt. This was further evidenced by his intention to return to his wife, and the fact that he felt stronger with respect to his girlfriend.

Second Stage

As therapy continued, and John made more progress, the original focus points needed less and less emphasis, except for one. Up to this point, the acceptance of and dealing with emotions had only been touched upon indirectly. John had greater insight into his own behaviour, and had made changes in his behaviour both in and outside of music therapy, but he had not overcome his emotional blocks. Given his progress in the other areas, and his decision to end the relationship with his girlfriend, it seemed the appropriate time for him to pay more specific attention to working at the emotional side of things.

FOCUS POINTS. At the beginning of the second stage, which lasted for 8 sessions, the focus points were readjusted as follows in consultations with the client:

1) John had an indistinct personal identity. His concern for rules and norms, and his constant efforts to conform to other people's standards, had led to a self-concept in which there was no room for certain needs and feelings of his own. Because of this, John had lost touch with parts of himself, and had a weak identity, one that allowed for inaccurate self-evaluations, insecurity, indecisiveness and dependence.

2) John's emotions were repressed. Underlying his conforming, technical and rational attitudes were many emotions that had not been adequately ackowledged or expressed. In addition, after he split with his girlfriend, he had to adequately deal with his feelings of loss, and the

natural mourning process that ensues from ending such a relationship. Following the first step of making a decision comes a second one---living through the emotional consequences of the decision. John expressed a willingness to work on his feelings of grief.

AIMS.   These focus points were shaped into two aims: to help John discover his own identity, independent of confirmation and approval; and to enable him to relive repressed experiences and go on living emotionally.

ACTION PLAN.   In the routines used to strenghthen John's identity, all instruments in the room were used, so as to enhance the experimental character of the activities.   Initially, the music therapist and John together selected: what instruments would be used, how long they were to be used, when to switch to another instrument, and in what way the music should be played.   Making decisions together still retained an element of confirmation by the therapist.   Later, John would take on these responsibilities by himself. This would help him to focus more on his own desires, needs, and wishes, and thereby express his own identity.

Improvisational techniques employed by the music therapist during this stage were primarily in the "redirection" category (e.g., differentiating, intensifying, intervening).

The strategy for helping John to express emotions involved having him musically represent or depict a feeling. For instance: "Recall the atmosphere, the feeling of the past week;" "Play the times in which you feel good and the times in which you feel bad."   While John played these titled improvisations, the music therapist supported him with techniques of "empathy" (pacing, reflecting), *"referential" techniques* (projecting) and *techniques of "emotional exploration"* (holding).

PROGRESS.   The effects of these two strategies could be seen in changes in John's musical and verbal behaviours.   As a consequence of the first stage, John's fear of the unknown had been lessened.   He was able to choose unfamiliar instruments more readily, as illustrated by statements like: "I felt less restrained in changing instruments; I changed instruments out of curiosity, with the objective of improving the ensemble, and as a reaction to what the music therapist was doing."   Still the fear had not entirely disappeared, for John would still not dare, for example, to look into the covers of the recorders.

In the beginning, the client hardly offered any resistance to the music therapist; his musical identity was weak and he mostly let himself be guided by her.   After he had come out of his egocentric isolation and had made creative contact in the first stage, he still could not offer any resistance. When the music therapist cut straight through his performance, he avoided the confrontation and either let the music therapist have her way or switched to another instrument.   This way he could escape any "problems."   He did not yet have behavioural alternatives at his disposal with which he could display his own distinctive features.   Some irritation arose when the music therapist played the recorder, but John did not protest, but rather let it happen.

This passivity gradually diminished. In contrast to the superficiality of earlier sessions, John showed more and more concentration and force in his playing, focusing attentively on his improvising for long periods (at times as much as 45 minutes). He showed great self-assurance when using the kettle-drum, to him a symbol of strength and self-confidence, and on the vibraphone, he started to allow the notes to reverberate. At this time, the music therapist changed roles, and gave him the lead and herself took the supporting part. By doing this she achieved that his individuality was more stressed. A statement like "I liked having to take the initiative each time and being supported by the music therapist" indicated a reinforcement of the identity.

While doing the representational or referential improvisations, John was able to begin reliving past moments of grief. In selecting and playing the various instruments, he projected several emotions. He used the zither as an instrument of sadness, and played it in a grating way, sustained the notes. He expressed his hesitations and obstacles on the temple-blocks and other small percussion instruments. On the split drums he got into a trance, which provided him a moment of regression and flight from the present, but he used powerful strokes on the kettledrum to bring himself out of the trance and back to reality.

Feelings of sadness were sometimes accompanied by violent emotional release, as shown in the following example. John was depicting his sadness on the zither while the therapist supported him on the orchestra bells. His sadness was expressed mostly in low, soft and whining sounds which he transferred from the zither to the vibraphone. As the improvisation continued, he started playing louder and louder, with two sticks at a time. Then he switched to the kettledrums, and his movements and the sounds got fiercer and louder. Finally a sturdy, cheerful and powerful sound arose from the drums. Through this musical process, John went through the stages of a mourning process, characterised by grief, anger and illumination. His verbal comments afterwards verified this: "By playing the vibraphone, the kettledrum and the drums I finally achieved complete relaxation," "I got out of it and I feel indestructable," "I impressed upon myself that I was doing what was best for me." He said he wanted to hang the zither on the wall, as a symbol of grief overcome, but in reality, it took considerably more time to adequately deal with his grief.

Undoubtedly, the most important event outside of music therapy was John's acting out his decision to return to his wife and end the relationship with his girlfriend. John knew what he wanted now, and he openly admitted it. In his work situation, he acted more self-assured and he was capable of doing things without the confirmation of others. What he did made him feel "good." He said he generally felt well, and that he was no longer unhappy.

Another event illustrated John's new way of coping with difficult situations. He reported an incident in which he was trapped in an elevator for five hours. Throughout the entire time, he did not panic, but instead remained calm and self-assured.

Third Stage

The third stage began after John had adequately dealt with and expressed the various emotions involved in splitting with his girlfriend. Lasting only two session, this stage can be regarded as a consolidation of previous accomplishments in therapy. Its main focus was trying to find a balance between distance and proximity, which involved the integration of several of the old focus points (taking decisions, making choices, intimacy, emotional response, identity). During the improvisations, John could lead the ensemble into a certain direction by means of rhythm and dynamics, without needing confirmation for this kind of behaviour any longer. The music therapist supported him. Where previously she had always had to take the initiative, the client's resolute manner now made it difficult for her to do so.

The client's relation with his wife was still strenuous, though, especially where sex was concerned. This problem was closely related to the focus point on intimacy. It was decided that the individual therapy is to be followed by relation therapy. The relation therapy will not be taken into consideration here.

DISCUSSION AND CONCLUSIONS

It is striking to see that, consistent with the anticipated indications of music therapy, this approach to treatment was extremely well-suited to John. Problems in his daily life found a direct translation into the music therapy setting. Furthermore, John himself was fully capable of making links between his behaviour in and outside of music therapy. For example, John did not dare to take responsibility in his normal life, and he did not do so in his musical improvisations either. In his relationships with others, he hardly offered any resistance, and in musical improvisation he could not confront the music therapist's challenges.

On the whole, John underwent a sequence of changes which can be directly related to stages of treatment. John strengthened his identity through a number of steps. During the first sessions of the first stage, he was completely self-centered. As a result, there was hardly any contact with others initially, and there was little possibility for experimentation and reactions within the improvisations.

By creating a safe environment, and offering new possibilities within it, the music therapist helped John to let go of unrealistic expectations and standards, and to achieve a freer and more sharing kind of music-making. Out of his normative egocentrism, John came to discover new possiblities in himself: the ability to perceive and react to others. As he discovered himself, he was able to discover the other, and vice versa.

In the beginning of the second stage this led to a more flexible but nevertheless submissive musical stance. John did not offer any resistance, and had no clear musical identity as compared to the music therapist. He only found his identity after the music therapist gave him the leading role in the improvisations. In the third stage, John was so strong that he wanted to keep the leadership role. In summary, John went from having no contact to having experimental but subordinate contact, to having a contact in which he developed his own identity. In the end, John was able to communicate and interact with another person without losing himself in the process.

Acknowledging and dealing with emotions also took John through several steps. Initially emotions arose, incidentally or accidentally. Experimenting with different behaviours and learning to enjoy this new way of playing, both of which occurred during the first stage, developed a further dimension in the second stage when he learned to accept emotions. That the two coincided showed in John's verbal reactions. He once commented that being less open to pleasure took away from some of the pleasure to be sure, but it also lessened the sensitivity to pain. John had the idea that not being able to enjoy things is the price one must pay to rid oneself of pain. With the increase of pleasure during the first stage, feelings of grief were allowed to enter during the second stage.

Acknowledging the importance of emotions was preceded by greater freedom and pleasure in social interactions. Thus, the second stage can be regarded as a "deepening" of the first stage. There, John actively sought for a musical equivalent of his emotions and he found a suitable musical vent for his feelings of anger. Where the first and third stage focused on musical interaction, the second stage focused on the symbolic meanings of the musical instruments and on the musical utterances which made reliving emotions possible.

What happened in music therapy was a close analogy of what happened in reality, outside of the therapy situation. However, there was one large difference: musical improvisation was no more than playing, without any actual, negative consequenses. This shielded situation helped John to cross a threshold. The non-verbal and non-rational nature of music therapy was responsible for getting him away from old patterns of behaviour. The music provided him with a situation that was unfamiliar to him, with unregimented and limitless possibilities for playing, all with physical and emotional appeal. It was also important that John did not have to prove himself, and that in the therapy situation, the process of making contact through music was given more importance than the artistic quality of the musical product itself.

Upon reflection of how the focus points shifted, one finds that music therapy proceeded in a spiral pattern. Primary problems and the therapeutic objectives derived from them were exchanged for others; realizing certain aims followed only upon accomplishment of others. This made the music therapist continually aware of the possible effects of her actions. If music therapy is effective and leads to changes in behaviour, these changes in consequence influence the further course of the treatment. Thus, therapy is a continual and spiralling process of readjusting the focus points, aims, and plans of actions. Thus, treatment methods are not established a priori.

During this case study, the music therapist and researcher worked in close cooperation. The researcher took the part of the critical partner in this, the one who was constantly asking questions like "What is the problem?", "Is the problem still the same?", "Why are certain objectives selected?", "Why is an objective being changed?", "Why do you take this plan of action, this method?", "What do we do if actual events cross the treatment?". He also organized the rough data and fed it back to the music therapist.

The music therapist's part constantly changed along the continuum of leading versus following. Sometimes she followed the client, in those cases where creating a safe atmosphere or the supporting of expressions of emotions were concerned. At other times she took the active, leading part, because the client needed structure, or because the client needed a certain challenge, or because the client needed someone in opposition. Thus the participating role of the music therapist, one of the features of music therapy, can be described in terms of several gradations of activity.

GLOSSARY

Aesthetic illusion: a situation of play and fantasy in art that is not dangerous or forbidden because it is not real.

Obsessive Neurotic Character: individuals who regard thoughts as more important than feelings, and who have a strong need for orderliness and an incapability of making decisions.

Techniques of Elicitation: (Bruscia, 1987)

> **Interjecting** - filling in spaces in the client's music.
> **Making spaces** - leaving spaces in one's music for the client to fill.
> **Repeating** - reiterating the same rhythms, melodies, lyrics, movement
>   patterns, etc. either continuously or intermittently.

Techniques of Emotional Exploration: (Bruscia, 1987)

> **Holding** - as the client improvises, the therapist provides a musical
>   background that resonates the client's feelings while containing
>   them.

Techniques of Empathy: (Bruscia, 1987)

> **Imitating** - echoing or reproducing a client's response, after the response has been completed.
> **Pacing** - matching the client's energy level.
> **Reflecting** - matching the client's moods, attitudes, and feelings.
> **Synchronizing** - doing the same thing as the client at the same time.

Techniques of Redirection: (Bruscia, 1987)

> **Differentiating** - simultaneously improvising music that is separate, distinct, and independent of, yet compatible with, the client's music.
> **Intensifying** - increasing dynamics, tempo, rhythmic and/or melodic tensions.
> **Intervening** - interrupting, de-stabilizing, or redirecting fixations, perseverations, or stereotypes of the client.
> **Introducing change** - initiating new thematic material and taking the improvisation into a different direction.

Techniques - Referential: (Bruscia, 1987)

> **Projecting** - having the client improvise music that depicts a real situation, feeling, event, relationship, etc.

REFERENCES

Bruscia, K. E. (1987). Improvisational Models of Music Therapy. Springfield, IL: Charles C Thomas Publisher.

Cullberg, J. (1988). Moderne Psychiatrie. Baarn: Ambo.

Frohne-Hagemann, I. (Ed.). (1990). Musik und Gestalt. Paderborn: Junfermann-Verlag.

Hegi, F. (1986). Improvisation und Musiktherapie. Paderborn: Junfermann-Verlag.

Klein, M. (1955). The Psychoanalytic Play Technique: Its History and Significance. In P. Heimann (Ed.), New Directions in Psychoanalysis. London: Tavistock.

Kris, E. (1952). Psychoanalytic Explorations in Art. New York: International Universities Press.

Kuiper, P. C. (1989). Nieuwe Neurosenleer. Deventer: Van Loghum Slaterus.

Lowen, A. (1969). The Betrayal of the Body. New York: Collier Books.

Orlinsky, D. E., Howard, K. I. (1986). Process and outcome in psychotherapy. In S. L. Garfield and A. E. Bergin (Ed.), Handbook of Psychotherapy and Behavior Change. New York: John Wiley & Sons.

Perls, F. S. (1969). Gestalt Therapy Verbatim. Lafayette: Real People Press.

Priestley, M. (1975). Music Therapy in Action. London: Constable.

Rogers, C. (1961). On Becoming a Person. Boston: Houghton Miflin.

Schalkwijk, F., Luttikhuis, C. (1990). Opstellen over Kreatieve Therapie. Nijmegen: Hogeschool Nijmegen.

Smeijsters, H. (1990). Methoden van Onderzoek in Muziektherapie en Andere Kreatieve Therapieën. Nijmegen: Hogeschool Nijmegen.

Smeijsters, H. (1991). Muziektherapie als Psychotherapie. Assen/Maastricht: Van Gorcum.

Winnicott, D. (1971). Playing and Reality. London: Tavistock.

Integrated Music Therapy
With A Schizophrenic Woman

GABRIELLA GIORDANELLA PERILLI
Psychotherapist - Music Therapist
Secretary: Italian Society of Music Therapy
Rome, Italy

Abstract: *A comprehensive approach to music therapy was taken with a 20-year old woman diagnosed as residual schizophrenic. The 18-month treatment period was divided into four developmental stages in order to formulate goals and develop the most effective strategies. Techniques include: singing and playing pre-composed pieces, action songs, improvisation, song-writing, and projective listening experiences.*

BACKGROUND INFORMATION

At the time of therapy, Mary was twenty years old, and had been diagnosed as having *residual schizophrenia* in remission, with no organic damage. She was taking a minimum dosage of Serenase, a *neuroleptic drug*.

Mary was her mother's fourth child, and her father's first. Her mother had already had three sons from a previous marriage; her mother's first husband had died. Mary was born fifteen years after her three brothers.

As a child, Mary had disturbing dreams which caused her great anxiety. She also had early eating disorders. At school, she demonstrated several problems, including deficits in attention and memory, and hyperactive behavior. When she was three years old, she broke one leg while playing with another little girl. This turned out to be quite a significant event, not only because it frightened her so much, but also because she did not grow or gain weight for one full year.

Her family were both overprotective and critical of her at the same time. They were also of the opinion that it was impossible to cure Mary's mental illness, or to modify her disruptive behavior.

At the time Mary was referred to music therapy, she lacked many adapative, self-help and social skills, and had poor contact with reality. She had been in verbal psychotherapy for eight months, receiving three session per week. Nevertheless, her condition seemed to worsen, and her psychiatrist and parents decided to refer her to music therapy to see if a nonverbal approach might have an effect.

Mary demonstrated various forms of thought disorder, including *delusions*, fantasies, *loosening of associations*, poor reality-testing, and difficulties in concentrating, thinking, and remembering. She was unable to stay on-task for sufficient periods, and shifted topics of conversation from one moment to the next. Generally speaking, any kind of ordered behavior posed a challenge. Mary also had difficulty making decisions, not only because of her disturbed thinking, but also because she lacked interest and motivation. She was filled with ambivalence, and she rarely derived pleasure from anything she did. Her affect and mood ranged from *dysphoria*, depression and anxiety, to agitation and hyperactivity. She cried frequently. Mary also had disturbing nightmares, and a decreased need for sleep. Her sense of self was also disturbed. She felt worthless, and she often yelled out self-criticisms. She was generally withdrawn from others, and avoided interpersonal contact. She often exhibited hostility and anger towards others.

METHOD

Given the wide variety of problems that Mary presented, and the etiological complexities of schizophrenia, it became essential for me to clarify my own theoretical position and methodological approach as I began to work with her. We know that the schizophrenic process distorts the person's entire reality system, and disrupts important links between the ego and outside world (Andreasen, 1985). We also know that one of the most devastating symptoms is the deterioration or inadequate development of basic psychological functions, including those pertaining to thinking, affect and interpersonal relationships (APA, 1987).

I have found that many of these psychological functions can be approached in an integrated fashion through cognitive methods of psychotherapy. The works of Ellis (1962) and Kelly (1955) are particularly relevant. Taking Ellis' perspective, Mary presented two irrational beliefs or dysfunctional ideas: (1) "I am an incompetent person," which leads to feelings of inadequacy, depression, and lack of pleasure; and (2) "I cannot bear it," which leads to anger, hostility, aggression and inactivity. Taking Kelly's perspective, Mary does not have an adequate *"personal construct system"* for adapting to the world and changes therein; she therefore has an ongoing dread of what the future may bring.

From a cognitive point of view, Mary's problems formed a vicious circle: (1) She was terrified by demands from the environment, such as "You must be good in order to satisfy others," or "You must go to school and do well." (2) This led her to react with anxiety and self-deprecation: "I have no control over what happens to me;" "I can't do what everyone expects;" "I am incompetent, no good;" "I hate myself." (3) With these ideas, she would fall into depression: "What's the use, why bother to do anything?" "Life is miserable and meaningless;" "I can't enjoy anything." (4) The depression then led to blame and hostility towards others: "It's not my fault, it's yours;" "You are bad and incompetent." "I am angry at you, leave me alone." (5) Then, suffering the consequence of her inadequate behavior and the reproaches of her parents, Mary would feel punished and powerless: "I cannot do anything to stop what is happening to me." (6) This completed the circle in that she now would become terrifed by demands being placed upon her.

When I work with psychotic patients, I divide the therapy process into four stages. With Mary, these stages helped me to formulate goals and to devise appropriate therapeutic interventions. The first and second stages are considered *rehabilitative* in nature, and third and fourth are *reconstructive*. The main priority for the first stage is to establish contact and to gain rapport with the patient. The second stage is aimed at stabilizing current adaptive functioning while also restoring previous levels. In the third stage, specific problems are targeted for resolution. In the final stage, efforts are made to restructure the personality so that therapeutic gains can be maintained, and some degree of independence can be established.

Because my aims in therapy address the whole person, and integrate cognitive, affective, physical and interpersonal functions, I use a variety of music therapy techniques, as also recommended in Unkefer (1990). In my work, I integrate active and receptive techniques and use both structured and free musical experiences. Some are creative and some are re-creative. Some require perception, others require projection. I also shift the amount of interaction that is required. For these reasons, I call my approach integrated.

Using the full gamut of music therapy in this way allows me to gear the techniques to each stage of therapy and its corresponding goals. In this way, the client's needs are kept in the forefront. The following are the main techniques I used (and modified at the different stages) with Mary: playing and singing pre-composed music, action songs, improvisation, song-writing, and projective listening activities.

TREATMENT PROCESS

Stage One: Contact

For the first three months, I met Mary four or five times per week, each session lasting one hour or more. I felt that we needed to have frequent contact because of her disintegrated state. The sessions were held in my private office, a room large enough to accommodate Mary, my assistants (a musician and a social worker) and myself, and one that would permit free body movement. Most of the sessions were tape-recorded.

Establishing contact and gaining rapport with Mary was quite difficult. She did not like her previous (verbal) therapist, and in fact, described him as "awful." She experienced him as being very frightenining and intrusive, and even had nightmares and fantasies in which she imagined that the therapist was threatening to terrorize or kill her.

So at the beginning, I tried to approach Mary on neutral ground and on equal terms. I wanted to lower her anxiety level by respecting her deep inner space, and by not asking her questions about her maladaptive behavior, her past life, or her present life problems. I avoided any talk about her small stature and how it made her feel, her particular behavior towards people, and her hostility at home. In musical experiences, I was very accepting and nonjudgmental of everything that she did, and I found that this approach greatly increased her willingness to work on her own problems.

In our improvisations, my role was: to mirror her musical behavior, to give her feedback so that she could hear her own music, to help her stabilize and control the various musical elements, to encourage her to reproduce patterns, and to help her to express her negative feelings through music. I also improvised or composed songs with lyrics aimed at giving her an opportunity to become more aware and accepting of her body (e.g., I'm playing the drum, while touching my head, I'm playing the triangle while touching my arms, I'm playing the harp while moving my body, etc.).

We often had rhythmic dialogues. Mary often entered the room confused, agitated, and anxious. On one occasion, after finishing the welcome song, I asked her to play a duet on the drum. I began to play very ordered rhythms in 4/4 meter, and Mary responded with incoherent and disorganized beats. I let this continue for about three minutes, and then suggested that we take turns leading and following. She agreed, and as we went back and forth, her playing became stronger, more ordered and responsive. Patterns began to appear. Whenever we would match each other accurately, Mary smiled, and this seemed to relieved her tension a great deal. We ended with calming rhythms, and then listened to the tape-recording of our duet. I asked Mary what she thought about it, and she said that she was satisfied. We then talked about the process of making music, and I pointed out that first comes confusion, then attention to what is happening, then organization of ideas, and finally interaction. By this time, Mary was much more relaxed and was able to not only understand what I said but also repeat it.

Mary also did solo improvisations on various themes. In one particular session during this stage, Mary improvised two very different pieces on the piano. The first one was organized and coherent, and after hearing it, she said that its theme was "The Death of My Piano Teacher." During the improvisation, she demonstrated very good concentration, and was in contact with her ongoing feelings of sadness and discomfort. The improvisation was a study of the relationship between the various music elements: the use of the rest as a moment of reflection and an opportunity for progressing and developing her ideas in a logical and consistent manner; collaboration and integration between the right hand and the left hand; the use of regular rhythmic accents; and a perfect synthesis of thoughts and feelings within musical creativity.

The second improvisation was characterized by a lack of organization and coherence. This theme she decided in advance: "The Happy Country Woman." In this one, there was an absence of awareness and reflection; the music was confused and she made little effort to relate ongoing ideas to previous ones. Her concentration was poor and she did not pay attention to details such as accents, meter, rhythmic patterning; there was no unifying idea or sound quality; there was no homogeneity in the expressive material, and as a result there was no emotional coherence; momentarily, Mary would express her obsessive thoughts and anxious feelings through perseverative playing; there were no moments of rest or relief; and when dissonances occurred Mary seemed not to know how to resolve them. Overall, the improvisation sounded like a spasmodic search for something unknown which eventually began to bore her.

Based on the feelings that I experienced as I listened to Mary's improvisation, combined with a cognitive analysis of the musical structures themselves and Mary's verbal self-deprecations (I am stupid, I do not have any ability, etc.), I came to a better understanding of her inner state. Coexisting were intense feelings of depression and a pervasive confusion due to ego anxiety. These feelings of depression and confusion formed the basis for planning sessions for the next stage. I wanted to organize her personal construct system, lower her anxiety, and let her experience positive emotional states.

Stage Two: Stabilization and Rehabilitation

Goals for this stage were: to help Mary to focus her attention, and especially in tasks requiring perception and memory; to lengthen her in-task behavior and attention; to increase goal-directed behavior and perseverance; and to help Mary gain greater awareness and acceptance of her body.

To accomplish these goals, I used a variety of structured listening and imitative tasks. These included: having Mary compare two musical patterns and describe how they were similar or dissimilar; having her imitate rhythmic and melodic patterns that I presented; having her vary the same patterns in systematic ways (e.g., louder/softer, faster/slower, louder and faster, etc.). Two kinds of improvisations were used: ones that focused on here-and-now experiences, and those that explored a particular feeling or issue. Mary also told stories and drew to different pieces of music and made connections between them. Finally, we played a musical game which combined singing and matching instruments to various body parts.

The following is a transcript of a session which typifies this stage of therapy.

> *Mary arrives complaining that she is unable to think. She feels terrible because this prevents her from being able to understand when people talk to her. She also gets confused about how to do things. Her face shows how tense and upset she is.*
>
> *Given her state, I try to comfort and calm her through a listening activity. I ask Mary to tell a story, and she begins: Laura is a young woman who lives in a castle; she is in the garden taking care of the flowers. There are animals and birds in the garden. She is somewhat uncomfortable there because it is not as orderly and calm as she would like it to be.*
>
> *Two Princes arrive, and Laura joins them in the castle. She tries to explain to them how desperate she feels because she cannot take care of the flowers by herself. They quarrel. The Princes are eventually persuaded to cooperate with her, and they prepare lunch and all eat together. I help Mary to finish the story, and then wonder to myself whether I should proceed in a structured or unstructured way.*

I decide to invite her to select instruments to describe the main elements of the story. After making her choices, she begins to improvise on the drum (representing the castle) and plays a strong, steady beat. She then goes to the cymbal and sistrum (representing the Princes) which she plays in a loud and confused way. Changing to the autoharp (representing Laura), Mary begins to play soft, delicate arpeggios, followed by a steady beat on the hand-drum (representing animals), a simple rhythm on the triangle (representing birds), and scales on the xylophone (representing flowers). She then returns to the cymbal and sistrum and resumes playing in a loud and confused way (Princes). I then took up the autoharp (Laura), and accompanied her with the delicate arpeggios until she ended.

I then asked: What is happening to Laura now? Mary replied: "She feels happy, but still worried that she will not be able to find herself." Surprised by how personal this statement is, I asked Mary what she could do to help Laura. Mary answers: "Sing a song." She begins the lyrics with "Laura is unable to take care of the flowers." I then question her, "Will these words help Laura?" Mary replies negatively, and I ask "What would be more helpful to tell Laura?" Mary begins again and sings: "Laura is able to take care of the flowers." Feeling more comfortable with this solution, I begin to sing the same words with her, and as we repeat the verse over and over, I ask her to dance together.

As we finish, I ask Mary what she thinks about her song, and she replies, "Nice!" I then ask her how Laura feels, and Mary says: "Happy... because she now understands that it is her task to take care of the garden." I then ask if Laura will be able to find herself doing that, and Mary replies, "Yes, I think so."

I then invite Mary to play Laura's instrument (autoharp) and accompany herself singing the song. She decides that it is not the right instrument, and selects the xylophone instead. We sing the song again, with Mary playing a xylophone accompaniment. When I ask about it, Mary says that she is pleased with the instrument change. I ask her why and she says that she thought the autoharp was sad. I answer: "Sometimes I feel like that: the autoharp seems sad and quiet at times; it seemed more suitable to Laura when she was talking to the quarrelling Princes, but when Laura is working, she is lively and strong." Mary agrees, and I comment: "Mary, you have thought about and understood what has happened to Laura in a very clear way. As you can see, when you decide to focus your attention, you can do it...you can think very clearly." Mary says, "Yes, I am really OK."

I then begin to summarize: "You understand that Laura, the most important person in your story, was sad because she did not realize what she was capable of doing, but when she did, she became...." Mary inserted: "Happy, because she took care of the garden." I continued: Yes, she felt more self-confident because your song told her that she was able to do what she wanted." Mary agrees, and I ask her "Is it possible for you to say that you are able to do something?" Mary: "Yes, I am able to do something!" I ask her for an example, and Mary says that she can play something. I then ask her to say the full sentence, and she does: "I, Mary, am able to play the piano." As the session ends, I ask how she feels, and Mary smiles with the reply: "Better than before!"

Stage Three: Problem Solving

By the third stage, Mary was more present in the here-and-now, and her cognitive functioning was much better. The goals were: to decrease her distractibility, to build problem-solving skills and logical thinking processes, to help her become more aware of her feelings in different situations, and to help her formulate some goals that she would like to accomplish with regard to herself (e.g., self-management).

Each session began with a welcome song, and after a discussion of whatever Mary presented that day, we went into either song-writing or tellings stories with background music. After this activity always followed a review and discussion of what she had done, and how she felt about it. I would then give her homework assignments which made her practice and put into effect things we had worked on during this session. (Prior to this stage, she was not ready for these homework assignments). The sessions always ended with a summary of everything she had accomplished and explored, and a good-bye song.

As evidence of her increased cognitive abilities, she worked on the same story over several sessions. It was called "The Vegetable Garden." When she finally completed the various chapters, Mary exclaimed: "This is my life !"

Stage Four: Reconstruction

In the fourth stage, the main concerns were: changing some of her irrational beliefs, improving her coping and social skills, clarifying her interests and needs, and trying to integrate various aspects of her personality.

Sessions during this period began with a welcome song, and a verbal discussion of any issues or problems on Mary's mind. Then, based on this discussion, I would engage her in one of the following musical experiences:

1) Composing lyrics and music to a song. This was done to work on her irrational fears or beliefs.

2) Playing or singing pre-composed music in different ways, or with different interpretations. This helped Mary to gain some insight into her own traits and characteristics when making music and in other daily situations. It also helped her to see that there were different ways to perceive and interpret things.

3) Improvising with or without a verbal theme, and with or without the therapist. These experiences were aimed at making Mary aware of how the music changed with the various feelings she was trying to express.

4) Projective listening activities (e.g., storytelling). These were used to help her integrate cognitive and affective components, and personal needs and goals through her musical experiences.

5) Listening to and discussing several musical pieces and then putting them into a hierarchy according to personal preferences or some other characteristic. This activity was aimed at helping Mary to adapt to changes in the real world, and to recognize how her own perceptions and preferences influenced her orientation to the world around her.

After the musical experience came a period of feedback and review. If Mary produced a song, improvisation or performance, I would tape it, and then we would play it back and she would react to it. Following this, we would talk about how Mary's music or the way she went about making it related to herself and her daily life. Based on this, I would give Mary a homework assignment. Usually, this involved rehearsing the songs she had written, and then using them throughout the week to guide herself into more functional and adaptive behaviors. At the end of each session, we would summarize what we had accomplished and close with a good-bye song.

The songs that Mary composed during this stage provide good examples of the issues and problems she confronted during this period. The songs were originally written in Italian; English translations are given below. Some of these were set to existing tunes (e.g., "I Accept Myself" was set to the Scout's "Farewell" Song); others had melodies especially composed by Mary.

I DON'T WANT TO BECOME REASONABLE

I don't want to become reasonable,
    it's too exhausting;
It's more comfortable not to work at it,
    anyway, I do not have the ability;
It takes time, time, time.

I decide to make an effort,
I think it's more convenient to have a better life;
I go step by step to be sure:
Exhausting obligation becomes joyful,
    Joyful, joyful.

SPRINGTIME TEARS

These are life's tears that I feel in myself
    I feel in myself.
When I am happier than now, the smile will come
    and glow again.
Joy gets down into my heart,
    Life creates love.
The joy will come from pain;
    soon merriment will come again.
I'd like to do easy things,
    within the need for toil.
I can try hard so that I am happier
Joy gets down into my heart
    And life creates love.
Joy will come from pain;
    Soon merriment will come again.

I ACCEPT MYSELF

I don't accept myself
as I'm afraid that other people don't love me anymore.
I am unsatisfied
because I think that I am unable to do anything.
But why? But why do I want to suffer?

I can accept myself as I am;
I am a worthwhile person, too.

DISCUSSION AND CONCLUSIONS

If we analyze the whole therapeutic process, we can see how music therapy played a positive role from beginning to end: it permitted Mary to overcome her resistance to therapy and to the therapists; it motivated her to play an active role in her own process of change; it helped me to reach Mary on the nonverbal level, avoiding the negative effects of verbal therapy; at the same time, it helped to integrate the verbal and nonverbal aspects of her problem, so that Mary could transfer the musical insights (i.e. irrational beliefs) and skills (e.g., problem-solving) outside the therapy session into her daily life (e.g., self-care, home activities); it allowed Mary to have multisensory experiences which helped to integrate fragmented aspects of her personality; it worked well when combined with other expressive arts to give Mary physical boundaries, and to move her from one kind of symbolic representation to another; it enhanced long term memory functions which were very poor; it increased Mary's symbolic cognitive abilities; it was useful in focusing Mary's attention when she was confused; it helped to modify some of her stereotypic behaviors; it provided a noninvasive way to address her needs, preferences, and goals; it gave Mary joy and pleasure and motivated her to be more playful; it facilitated social interaction, and lessened her feelings of inferiority; it provided tangible products that rewarded her hard work; and finally it provided an opportunity for her to develop a sense of pride in herself, and especially when sharing her musical accomplishments with her parents.

The advantages of music therapy are further underlined by how it compared to previous treatment using a verbal psychoanalytic approach. In response to the verbal approach, Mary lost contact with reality, and her condition worsened. This did not occur within the music therapy, except when sessions were interrupted for some reason (i.e. summer holidays), or when I inappropriately evaluated Mary's readiness and introduced verbal interventions prematurely. Clearly, Mary had difficulty with a verbal approach, and whenever she was not ready to approach her problems at the verbal level, it was necessary to return to music therapy activities alone.

Throughout the various stages, Mary's music changed considerably, going from confused to ordered, and from being disengaged or disinterested in the musical process to recognizing how her own feelings and personality were reflected in it. Her participation was at first whimsical, later music was a means by which she could enter into a personal problem–solving process, either alone or with the therapist's help.

My evaluations of her progress in the area of adaptive behavior were later confirmed by objective observations made by her parents and by Mary herself. Also, her psychiatrist reduced her medication to a very minimal dose.

Mary's social and coping skills are now quite adequate, and permit her to be involved in more satisfactory relationships with others. She is also more self-reliant, and has even decided to attend a pottery school. She is able to do a little cooking, and she now enjoys taking part in parties, trips and various recreational activities. Her thinking follows more logical sequences, and this permits her to follow a conversation, story or movie, and to express her opinions and emotions more easily.

Although I have presented the treatment process as if it occured in four clearly defined stages; in actuality, sometimes a session would contain elements of one stage exclusively, and at other times, a session would contained elements of several stages. This would depend on how Mary's readiness changed from one week to the next. Thus, during each session it was possible to consider peripheral or central issues, more specific or general ones, and to use simpler to more complex procedures. It was also possible to use a technique for assessment purposes at one time, and then later for treatment and evaluation.

In some cases, the same technique (e.g., music combined with other expressive arts) was used at two different stages (e.g., first to develop particular cognitive functions [perception, memory], and then later to analyze thinking modalities (e.g., loosening of associations) or to learn a problem-solving skill. Moreover, techniques such as song-writing were useful not only during the therapy session itself (e.g., to express and overcome a depressive state), but also as a homework assignment (e.g., to rehearse more functional self-statements or to develop a new self-management skill).

It is important when working with individuals like Mary that the therapist be always present as a guide and/or partner. The therapist must always have a flexible attitude, and be ready to modify the planned program or session to meet any needs that arise unexpectedly or to accommodate any shifts in the person's readiness to forge ahead in the therapeutic process. I have also found that having assistants was very helpful, and in some cases, essential. They were particularly important when we would play out a story with many characters, as their personalities would help to teach Mary about the complexities of social interaction, and the many aspects of her own personality that she could call upon in various situations.

In conclusion, I believe that integrated music therapy achieved such good results with Mary because it is a nonverbal, multisensory, joyful approach. As a result of the various techniques, Mary is now more aware of herself in relation to the real world; she can integrate different aspects of herself; and she is better able to verbalize her needs, resolve conflicts, process information. Now she is discovering the meaning and purpose of her existence, and has begun hear a new melody of life: "I accept myself as I am ---I am a worthwhile person, too."

GLOSSARY

Delusion: A fixed, false belief. A delusion involves believing things that are not real, and are frequently persecutory, grandiose or somatic in nature.

Dysphoria: A mood state which causes discomfort (e.g., anxiety, depression).

Loosening of Associations: Disorganized thinking and speech.

Personal Construct System: A psychological concept developed by George Kelly (1955) to describe how a person construes the world, and organizes his/her constructs into themes which permit anticipation of future events, and prediction and control of interactions with other people.

Reconstructive Stage: A period or phase of clinical treatment aimed at producing cognitive, emotive, or behavioral changes needed to achieve a more integrated personality.

Rehabilitative Stage: A period or phase of clinical treatment principally planned to regain previous levels of cognitive functioning or reality adjustment.

Residual Schizophrenia: A type of schizophrenia in which there are: a history of schizophrenic episodes with psychosis prominent, a current clinical picture without any psychotic symptoms, and continuing evidence of illness, such as blunted or inappropriate affect, social withdrawal, eccentric behavior, illogical thinking, or loosening of associations (APA, 1987).

REFERENCES

American Psychiatric Association (APA) (1987). Diagnostic and Statistical Manual IIIR (DSM IIIR). Washington, DC: Authors.

Andreasen, N.C. (1985). The Broken Brain: The Biological Revolution in Psychiatry. New York: Harper & Row.

Ellis, A. (1962). Reason and Emotion in Psychotherapy. Secaucus, NJ: Lyle Stuart.

Kelly, G.A. (1955). The Psychology of Personal Constructs (Volumes I and II). New York: W.W. Norton.

Unkefer, R.F. (Ed.).(1990). Music Therapy in the Treatment of Adults with Mental Disorders: Theoretical Bases and Clinical Interventions. New York: Schirmer Books.

Group Improvisation Therapy: The Experience of One Man With Schizophrenia

HELEN ODELL MILLER, R. M. Th., B.A. Hons., M. Phil.
Music Therapist and Therapy Services Manager
Fulbourn Hospital, Fulbourn, Cambridge
Great Britain

Abstract. *This case describes the involvement in group therapy of Brian, a 40-year-old man with schizophrenia. A psychoanalytically informed approach is taken to group work using interactive musical improvisation and verbal discussion. Music therapy provided Brian with a way that he could gradually begin to relate more to people around him and the environment in general. The case outlines the struggle of long-term work with small changes gradually apparent, within an initially negative transference relationship fraught with criticism and conflict.*

ACKNOWLEDGEMENT

I would like to thank members of the group and Brian in particular for all I have learned. I would also like to express gratitude to my colleagues and supervisors with whom I have discussed this work.

SETTING AND APPROACH

Brian attends a day clinic for people with a variety of psychiatric problems associated with long-term mental illness. The clinic provides a broad program of individual and group treatments, including medical, social and psychotherapeutic services (i.e., music and art therapies; problem-solving; life skills; vocational rehabilitation, etc.). The staff forms a multidisciplinary team that operates a case management system. I attend the clinic once a week to run a music therapy group and liaise with the team.

Criteria for referral to the music therapy group are broad, and over the years, the staff have recognised increasingly the particular problems people have which the group can help. These problems are related to interpersonal and intrapersonal difficulties rather than diagnosis, although diagnosis is a consideration in assessment. Within the clinic, I have said to clients and staff that the group is for those who feel they can benefit by using music as a means towards coping with various problems, and who do not find verbal ways of doing this easy or appropriate.

Referrals are considered at any time, but the group is semi-closed in that no visitors are allowed, and membership is constant within this slow, ongoing referral system. That is, people cannot drop in, and for all new members, a degree of preparation by members already in the group is necessary. Assessment for participation in the group is by interview with me.

The group runs at the same time each week for one hour, with myself as sole music therapist. Current members of the group are:

DOROTHY: A 57-year-old woman with diagnoses of severe depression and self-mutilation, who has been in the group for 61 weeks. Reasons for referral by the charge nurse were: to provide long-term support and a place to deal with suicidal and lonely feelings through nonverbal media.

BRIAN: A 41-year-old man with diagnoses of *schizophrenia* and *personality disorder*. Reasons for referral by the psychologist were that he spends nearly all of his time on his own, hardly communicating in groups at all. He has also expressed an interest in the music therapy group, which he has never expressed for any other type of group.

PETER: A 31-year-old man with a diagnosis of schizophrenia, who has been in the group for 43 weeks. Reasons for referral by the social worker were that people do not understand him, and he does not know how to make them do so. Hopefully, through music he can express his feelings about the past, present and future.

ANTHEA: A 29-year-old woman with diagnoses of *hysteria, M.E. (Myalgicencephalomyelitis),* depression and personality disorder, who has been in the group for 15 weeks. Reasons for referral by the occupational therapist were to help her deal with expression of and understanding of feelings constructively, through a medium she finds acceptable.

STEPHEN: A 45-year-old man with a diagnosis of *manic depression,* who has been in the group for 20 weeks. Referred by the psychologist, psychiatrist and music therapist for the following reasons: Music therapy would be useful for containing anxiety he feels with others in a group, and expression of aggressive feelings. He also needs ongoing therapy to provide a secure place for him to be understood, while also understanding some of his depressive feelings. Hopefully, the group will prevent recurrent patterns of admissions, together with a whole discharge package (e.g., sheltered work).

Firm boundaries are kept for the group, and I do not see the clients intentionally outside of it. Contact with other staff in sheltered housing where some clients live happens if necessary, but with the client's knowledge.

THEORETICAL ORIENTATION

A detailed description of method and rationale for my approach to group work can be found in a published article (Odell, 1988). For purposes of this case, a summary of the main points will be given.

The group runs using a psychodynamic model, which can be described as "analytically informed music therapy." This approach involves live interactive methods using improvisation as the focus for making relationships with clients that may reflect other relationships in their lives, and thus enable an awareness of difficulties that may be taking place. A wide variety of instruments are available for the improvisations, including tuned and untuned percussion, violin and piano, all of which are set up in the music therapy room before the group begins.

It is important to recognise that the way clients improvise may reflect their current states, and can lead to an understanding of changes which may need to take place internally. Freud, and subsequently other dynamic therapists such as DeMare and Kreeger (1974), learned that catharsis is not enough. Lieberman, Yalom and Miles (1973) found that catharsis is not related to outcome, and that we must remember that often we cannot observe more intensely significant events. I make this point because I feel that some people misunderstand the music therapist's use of free improvisation, thinking that the aim is to encourage catharsis. I believe that the important element in this way of working is to help clients understand more about themselves, and gain insight through the music therapy improvisation group process. This process can often take time, and inner changes may not at first be apparent to client or therapist.

An intense experience of the here-and-now is provided by a music therapy group. Interactions are played out often within improvisations, and it is fundamental to this way of working that the therapist gets hold of this and does not avoid issues s/he perceives or hears. It is also important not to allow the activity of music-making to override the group therapy process in a way that would encourage defenses and avoidance of interpretation. I have heard music therapists in Britain dismiss interpretation and psychoanalytic concepts as too rooted in the past and not forward-looking towards therapeutic change. However, I would suggest that group music therapy is important. Approached in a confident way, free improvisation in a group provides an intense experience for *transference* and *countertransference* relationships to be dealt with between group members as well as with the therapist. In addition, feelings of members about the way others play and their degree of skill provide material which can be used by the music therapist to understand more about the group and its members.

I also believe that the parental role of the therapist is one to be used, particularly in terms of carefully offering or not offering one's own music. For example, I have found that in some cases, my harmonic input from the piano can inhibit clients from being able to work through their own problems. However, there are times when just the opposite is true and the basis for someone exploring a problem is that a musical dialogue with a supportive or more dominant role taken by the therapist is necessary. Supervision is essential for this kind of work.

I see my role as making sense of **whatever** material comes up in the music, and in other ways, in terms of the group members and therapist. For example, in his first group experience. Brian asked: "Is it teaching or playing?" Then he tried to get me to play piano to the group because I am the "expert." When I refused to play as he requested, he tried to teach one group member, Jane, to play a tune, as if she were his pupil. Thus, my refusal to take the role of "expert playing to the group" enabled him to interact with others, and to take on a controlling role himself. Afterwards, we looked at this in terms of something which he finds a need to do all the time. Later, he smoked, breaking one of the boundaries. He understood this in terms of "avoidance of discomfort." Finally, Brian allowed a group improvisation to develop, and curbed his urge to both smoke and control the group with his tunes. He felt pleased with himself, and surprised at what came out musically. Jane began talking of isolation, and Brian became more able to focus on his issues in relation to me and the group, because his music was understood. My theory is that if I had become the teacher or taken control, this could have kept the group in its paralysed beginning stage rather than allowing the group to begin its own process.

BACKGROUND INFORMATION

Brian was born in 1950 and is the second of three boys. Little has been learned from Brian about his early childhood, and he has always been reticent to discuss his family and personal history. What is known will be summarised here.

Brian was diagnosed with schizophenia in 1973. At the time he was living in the South West of England, where he was attending a university but failed to complete the degree. All three boys went to university. Brian's father was a major in the army who died of a stroke in 1981; his mother is 74 years old, and well. Owing to his father's profession, the family had lived in several different parts of the world. After his father left the army, Brian had three admissions to a psychiatric hospital. During these, his father was diagnosed first as having schizophrenia and later manic depression. After his father died in 1982, Brian moved East of England to be with his mother. There he had several admissions to a psychiatric hospital. He later followed his mother to the village where he lives now. When things did not work out living with his mother (owing to tension in their relationship), Brian moved to Sheltered Accommodations. Brian's elder brother also lives in the same area, and is married with three children. He is described as "successful." Brian's older brother died in a car accident in 1979 at the age of 23 years.

In 1988, while living in sheltered housing, Brian was referred to the clinic because of his isolated existence and need for further psychiatric understanding. Upon coming to the clinic, the psychologist found him to be verbally aggressive and hostile. He refused to have anything to do with anyone; he refused verbal treatment; and he did not participate generally in the clinic's programme, attending the newcomers group only sporadically. He eventually had to be given a single room in his house, and it was generally believed that Brian was unable to settle in groups.

Brian also seemed unable to make long-term aims or plans for his life. The referral stated that "his mental state seems to make him inaccessible to rational planning for the future."

Brian had shown an interest in the music therapy group, probably as a result of his ability to play the guitar and piano, rather than from a wish to explore himself in therapy. However, the main reasons for referring him to music therapy stemmed from a belief on the part of the psychologist and team that Brian may be more accessible to nonverbal media, and that this in turn may help him in his relationships with the outside world generally, and eventually allow him to return to work.

ASSESSMENT

My dilemma after the first assessment meeting with Brian was whether to involve him in the group or to take him for individual music therapy. The assessment session was with musical instruments: Brian immediatedly engaged himself in interacting musically with me, trying to instruct me what notes to play, and also becoming quite animated in a drum improvisation and a chordal, more structured guitar improvisation. Brian showed interest in who might be attending the group, and what he might gain from it.

The decision to accept him for group therapy was based on a notion that if he was to work on increasing his ability/wish to socialise in the world, it would be through music. I also felt strongly that a very regular therapy group with firm boundaries may help Brian feel able to interact with others, and realise something of his effect on others. It was therefore worth a period of assessment in the group.

In our initial contact, Brian presented as an angry, rather sulky man, with a capacity for being challenging and argumentative, juxtaposed with a sensitive musical expressive side that seemed to represent his wish for contact and togetherness. He was very reticent about acknowledging anything about his life and difficulties, but his energy to challenge, abuse and debate gave me some optimism for his beginning group music therapy

TREATMENT

Brian has been attending the music therapy group for two years. After an initial settling-in period, when he attended alternate sessions, Brian made a commitment to coming regularly on a weekly basis, and when unable to attend, letting the group know the reason.

Throughout his involvement in the music therapy group, Brian was not involved in any other formal therapy. He occasionally attended activity groups (e.g., creative writing), and he saw a psychiatrist regularly for consultation regarding his medication.

The two year period can be divided into three main phases. The first two were six months each in length, and the final was twelve months. Looking back, these periods seem to reflect different developments for Brian. The main features in Brian's therapy during each phase will be described, with some detailed examples of sessions.

Phase One: Testing and Establishing Himself

Brian presented a challenge to me from the very beginning: he constantly criticised the group, its members, and me. In the first few weeks, he was often monosyllabic, and seemed confused and sometimes thought-disordered. I felt that it was important to constantly interpret some of his behaviour, whilst remaining receptive and nonjudgmental. He was often angry, and this meant that I had to constantly reflect upon the feelings this conjured up in me, in order to understand him without driving him away or letting him abuse the group.

During the first six months of his attendance, the group itself was beginning, and Brian was part of this beginning process. Its membership included Dorothy, Brian, Peter, and three other individuals who attended sporadically, and were eventually discharged. Thus, the group was small, with a core of four members most of the time.

An important feature during this phase was the difference in Brian's behaviors when the group was larger, and when he and Dorothy were the only members present (which happened on occasion). On one occasion, he acknowledged that he preferred a smaller group, and on another, he stated that he would like to "have me to himself."

I have found that the best way for the group to function is to allow things to develop, and to provide musical structures at times when this seems appropriate. I provided such structure much more frequently in the first phase of the group process than in later ones, for at the beginning, the group was in the process of finding out about possibilities of using instruments, and some members could participate only with rhythmic or harmonic support from me. During the later phases, I played less because the group was able to improvise without so much involvement from me.

A description of three sessions follows, each showing Brian's progression from a rather rigid non-acceptance of his own part in the process to some acknowledgement of his integration into the group, and an ability to acknowledge others and himself within it.

SESSION 5. During this session, Brian was challenging throughout, criticizing everyone and their music. Eventually however, he allowed himself to "let go" on the metallphone in a free improvisation during which he seemed very absorbed in the music. After it had ended, Brian denied that the group had any therapeutic value, and then accused me of being a bad therapist because I would not "prescribe." I suggested to him that, even when I did musically provide structures (e.g., rhythmic blues chordal progression), he could not join in because it was not "right for him."

In this session, and throughout much of this phase, Brian seemed to want to destroy the group. It was also quite noticeable that he avoided disclosing anything about his life, at least until the 11th to 15th sessions.

SESSION 12. We began with a series of integrated improvisations on the pentatonic scale, all sounding as if they had no ending. Brian was quite critical of this afterwards, and joined in with loud cymbal crashes or loud chord solos on the piano. The more I commented on the fact that he seemed to be wanting to criticize, interrupt, and possibly to be "told off" like a child, the angrier he became. Following my strong instincts that he really needed to have his behaviour understood and contained, I further suggested that he acted as though he were disinterested in Dorothy or Stephen. An exchange followed, which seemed to be a turning point in therapy when Brian asked about Dorothy's family. A long interchange took place between Dorothy and Brian about their families. Brian talked for the first time about his father dying eight years previously; he also shared that his mother lives in the same area as he and that her job is in catering. Dorothy talked about her parents dying, and Brian became interested in Dorothy's father's job in a cement works. In this shared acknowledgement of their losses, the three group members seemed close to each other for the first time.

SESSION 13. Brian showed an interest in Dorothy when she arrived, and gave her instruments to play, showing some awareness of her condition for the first time. (Although no one had ever commented on it before, Dorothy has no fingers on one hand, and also has a wound on her upper arm where she stuck nails into it).

Brian seemed desperate for help, and asked me to help him get more sleeping tablets from his doctor. He actually agreed, in response to my suggestion, that perhaps in looking after Dorothy and pleading to me, he was showing that he wanted love and attention for himself. He commented on Dorothy being helpless, and she seemed pleased with all the attention. Then he asked Dorothy what she was doing for lunch "today" and "tomorrow."

In the improvisations, Brian played rich piano chords and also used drums and metallophone in an expressive way with Dorothy. It was significant that he did not need my support to do so.

SESSION 15. This was one of the sessions leading up to a summer break, during which Brian was going on a holiday for the first time with people in the sheltered house where he lived. This itself reflected a change in that he could contemplate being in a close-knit situation with others for an entire week.

Brian entered very interested in getting started. He seemed less angry and more gentle, yet able to express how he was feeling. He became very frustrated that my music was not exactly what he wanted. Several times he challenged me: "Can you play octaves? Your music is a bit thin." I purposely did not want to influence or intrude. Then Brian began his questioning of the value of the group: "We've had ten minutes and not done anything!" Then later, when I was trying to explore silence, he said: "Silence is noise."

Brian started drumming and then stopped to write down some dates in his diary concerning cancellations of the group. Dorothy accompanied throughout, and he paid little attention to her. Eventually, Brian was very willing to express himself and let go---after the awkward silence at the beginning, and after challenging me further: "What about taping some records and having a proper music therapy group?"

After the first improvisation (Brian on drums, Dorothy on xylophone, myself on piano), he said "it was fun, but still not quite good enough---your hands are too small." Dorothy, however, commented on how pleased she was that Brian was very involved in the improvising.

Near the end of the session, Brian asked Dorothy for the first time what was "wrong" with her arm. Dorothy replied that she had stuck nails in it. Brian seemed shocked and said in a thoughtful way: "You must have been very angry."

In this session, Brian showed more involvement than ever before, albeit in a challenging way: continually trying out pieces, wanting me to play in a certain way, etc. He agreed that he worried about not knowing what might happen next in the group. He seemed much more open. When I suggested that the group was feeling more in touch with each other, Brian agreed, but then added: "It's monotonous, and I'm trying to change things." His music was much more fluid and flexible, often within a structured rhythmic framework, but towards the end, he used drums and cymbals in a free dialogue improvisation with me.

SIX MONTH SUMMARY. During this period, Brian was able to gradually make a commitment, and attend more regularly. After three months, he attended every week, and would always let the group know if he could not come. This is of major importance, as Brian's previous history showed a difficulty in making relationships and keeping commitments. At first, he found it very difficult to take into account anyone else's needs. He did not even talk directly to other members of the group, apart from to me as the leader. He was very keen to control others, and his initial interactions with members of the group were commands or derogatory comments, such as "Your music sounds abominable!" Part of his wish to control others seemed to be manifest in a need to keep himself in control. He often became angry with me because I did not tell everyone excatly what to do. Often, when things became difficult, Brian would express a dire need to smoke, and because the group had established the boundary of not smoking, he would have to leave the group to do so. Gradually, with help, Brian began to acknowledge his need to challenge authority. He also became better able to relax and to allow himself to get to know others and even understand their needs. He began to stay for the entire hour.

As these changes occurred, they showed in his music. He became able to improvise more freely and to follow others--in addition to expressing himself through music which often had very loud, structured beating as its main feature. Previously, Brian had been dominant to the point of being often abusive to others, but as this became less frequent, he began to notice and listen to others more, allowing them the time to talk and play their own music. A turning point was when, in addition to feedback from others, Brian listened to a tape of the group improvising, and heard himself "drowning" other people's music. When he was angry, he often benefitted from being able to release some tension and aggression by playing loudly and freely in improvisations. It also seemed useful for Brian to receive feedback from others about how he made them feel when he was organising or criticizing them. He also benefitted from positive feedback from others about his musical skills on piano and percussion.

By the end of this period, the group had helped Brian integrate with others in a more positive way than before his referral. He was more sensitive and trusting of others. He seemed to feel more confident and "good" about himself, better able to organise his time, and more amenable to spending time with others. He seemed to benefit from the regular support and insight possible in the group, and had begun to make links for himself regarding his personal difficulties and how he might change. His psychotic traits seemed to be disappearing and his mental state seemed more settled.

Phase Two: Trusting or Not - In or Out

This phase showed Brian really grappling with whether or not he wanted to be close to others in the group and explore things further for himself.

He had his only admission to hospital in the middle of this phase. It did not last very long, and was more for the purpose of the psychiatrist monitoring him more closely rather than because everything in his life was breaking down. In fact, he continued to attend the group during his admission, coming to the clinic from the ward in a taxi. His group therapy seemed quite central to his fairly quick discharge.

After his discharge, he moved to a smaller sheltered housing situation run like a therapeutic community where his case manager and other team members felt he would fit in better. He is still settled there, and has remained more stable ever since this move.

Leading up to his admission, Brian did stop taking his medication and generally because confused. However he also used the group to deal with some of his feelings concerning relating closely to others. He went through a pattern of sitting in silence for whole sessions at a time when five members were present. He acknowledged that it was easier for him to relate to one or two people at once. Twice, when only he and Stephen were present, Brian said he wanted me to himself.

During this phase, he began to explore his relationships in more depth, and asked me more personal questions, such as: "What do you do on the weekends?", and "Can you come for a drink afterwards?". However, he did not seem ready to try to understand some of these desires, and would either play music in order to avoid talking, or not attend the group after a particularly insight-oriented session. It seemed difficult for him to acknowledge his wish for contact, and he appeared to run away whenever he moved nearer to understanding something. However, the fact that he continued to attend the group throughout this phase is significanat, and following many weeks of angry silence, he began using the instruments expressively again towards his discharge time.

He desperately wanted me to help him be discharged, and we agreed together that I would give my opinion in ward rounds, after discussing it with him beforehand. My opinion was that if he moved to the new housing, where there was more psychiatric follow-up, he was well enough to go at any time.

In fact, I had not really felt his admission to the hospital was essential in the first place, although in some ways he seemed to benefit from the overall attention he received. His admission also convinced him that he did not want to identify too much with long-term, institutionalised clients.

All of these issues were examined in the group towards the end of this six-month phase, as he was settling into the new community house. At this time, his music became more adventurous and expressive.

Phases Three: Hard Work

During this one-year phase, there were three new members in the group making six regular attendees. Brian's music because much more complex and intense, and he really became involved in the group. He began to mention people by name, show concern if they did not attend, and acknowledge how he hurt others by his criticisms. This seemed to be particularly possible with two new members, Stephen and Anthea, with whom he was constantly supporting or criticising.

The following two examples illustrate how Brian tried to deal with his competitive feelings towards others through interactions with Stephen and Anthea. He also tried to come to terms with the consequences of his criticisms towards women particularly. Overall, these examples show how much Brian was changing, now being able to consider his "place" in the group rather than angrily deny his involvement as he did in the past.

EXAMPLE 1. Near the end of this session, a fifth improvisation took place, with Brian very much leading on piano with strong chordal, rhythm patterns, and Stepehen beating loudly on drums as if competing with Brian. Peter and Anthea were rather lost in directionless playing. A dialogue followed:

Stephen: *I thought the last piece was OK.*

Brian: *I thought it came off quite well, but it carried on after I had finished.*

Stephen: *I stopped when you stopped.*

Brian: *Oh well, somebody didn't. Can't remember who was making the best accompaniment.*

Me: *It seemed quite important to you that people stopped when you did, Brian. I thought, Stephen, that you wanted to let Brian know that you think of him as a leader.*

Stephen: *Brian had finished his piece, so I stopped playing the drums.*

Me: *(Sensing much underlying anger between Stephen and Brian). It seemed, Stephen, that earlier in the group you felt at home in coming to your first group and being a leader too. (I later suggested that there was some competitive tension between them, which they both seemed to acknowledge).*

EXAMPLE 2. This session was four months later, and the first session after Brian and Peter had been on holiday together with a group from their house. They both seemed able to discuss it in the group, which was a new development. They also improvised a gentle melodic duet during which some intense listening and "give-and-take" took place.

The mood changed during the last improvisation, when all members played feely (Brian on piano, Peter on metallophone, Stephen on xylophone, Anthea on glockenspiel, Melissa on gato drum and Dorothy on maraccas). Brian suddenly shouted: "It would help if you told Anthea what notes to play!" The women all immediately stopped playing, and Anthea left the room. For the next 30 minutes, I tried to help the group understand what was happening.

Brian's comment and this session was significant in that, by the end, Brian had actually regretted pushing Anthea out. For the first time, I found my countertransference towards him had been useful in that somehow we were able to recognise together that he needs to be destructive and abusive. I tried to help him see something I had been feeling for a long time---that he needed to be this way to avoid the fear of being hurt himself, and that he desperately wanted to be looked after too. Since that time, a main focus of his work in the group has been to contain his rage, criticisms and denial of the benefits of therapy. It became clearer that his fear of being being hurt and avoidance of what others are feeling manifested themselves in Brian's attempts to squash many improvisations by the group. He did this by being critical of others, by suggesting or playing complex harmonies that others could not follow, and by denying the value of any music other than the precomposed pieces of his own choice. I am still convinced that at some level Brian has been hurt and needs repairing, but we have not explored this yet in any depth.

DISCUSSION AND CONCLUSIONS

Brian's history, and rather fixed schizophrenic disposition, may lead everyone connected with him to feel despair. He has not held down a job for twenty years, yet is intelligent and talented. He does not now exhibit particularly bizarre, psychotic behaviour (which was seen mostly while he was in hospital), but rather maintains a constant disposition of hatred towards the world and other people. He could be experienced as quite passive-aggressive at times.

In the entire two years, he has admitted only twice that he has any problems, and oftens states that he is forced into attending the group. The reality is that he has the ultimate choice, and has often brought himself along to insult me and others, week after week. So, of what value is the music therapy? Why are we all still meeting? The reasons are complex, but to summarise finally, I will briefly mention some essential points.

Brian's only motivation to relate to others in the last three years has appeared to have been through the group. Before attending it, he was reported never to speak to anyone in his home or at the clinic; likewise, he did not even venture into the drop-in room. He now interacts with others in the drop-in room, and joins in community life more in his house. I cannot be sure that this is related to his music therapy, but what I have experienced is Brian gradually realising over a long period of time, that his destructive instincts can be tolerated and perhaps understood.

Brian has also begun to trust and enjoy the freedom of improvising with others, and the music has served the function, I believe, of making a link between his internal, destructive paranoia of being "cut-off" and the way that others respond and react to him, which he has been forced to acknowledge and understand, and perhaps even want to understand. Yes, his prognosis overall is not hugely encouraging, but perhaps through constant trials and struggles to understand and contain his more psychotic and destructive instincts (partly through music providing a different way of communicating these things), he can interact more easily with the world.

Now he seems stable and quite relaxed, and last week, when a new member joined the group, he even acknowledged him by name. Two years ago, he sat for weeks without even using anyone's name, and not showing any wish to be anything other than critical and destructive. Last week, he did attack the new member initially with: "I don't know why you're here if you can't play anything." But then, after half an hour of improvising said: "Gosh, your drumming was really sensitive and I like it." He laughed when I ventured to suggest that perhaps he was able to welcome the newcomer after all.

There is probably still much to understand and grapple with, but this is long-term work. Brian has still not verbalized very much about himself, but he has communicated to me through his musical and nonverbal behaviour, and I have attempted to understand as much as possible. The constant weekly commitment, and sense of boundaries are important, as is the belief that something is changing.

What would be lost if therapy were to stop? Brian has a huge investment at present and hardly ever misses a session. His music is becoming more relaxed and less rigidly fixed. For someone like him, all these phenomena seem important in helping him maintain his present quality of life, and hopefully preventing him from admission to hospital and repeated breakdown, even if his capacity for insight and inner major change is small.

GLOSSARY

Countertransference: The therapist's unconscious reactions to the patient, especially to the patient's own transference.

Hysteria: A neurosis with principal features of emotional instability, repression, dissociation, physical symptoms, and vulnerability to suggestions.

Manic Depression: A severe mental illness causing repeated episodes of depression, mania (obsession, compulsion or exaggerated feeling for), or both. These episodes can be precipitated by upsetting events, but are out of proportion to the causes.

M.E. (Myalgicencephalomyelitis): A diagnosis which is fairly recent, often thought of as post-viral. There are disputes as to whether it is a psychosomatic disorder or a medical condition of muscular inflammation and other symptoms, producing lethargy and depression.

Personality Disorder: Severe maladjusted patterns of behaviour, deeply ingrained and lasting for many years. For the diagnosis to be made, these patterns cause suffering to the person, or others, or both.

Schizophrenia: A severe mental disorder thought to have a strong genetic component, but which can be brought on by stress. Characteristics include psychotic traits - loss of contact with reality, a disintegration of the process of thinking at times, delusions, and hallucinations. Social withdrawal can occur, and the patient often feels that his/her thoughts and actions are controlled or shared by others.

Transference: In analytic therapy, this involves the patient's unconscious wishes. Within the relationship with the therapist, "infantile prototypes re-emerge and are experienced with a strong sensation of immediacy" (Laplanche & Pontalis, 1973).

REFERENCES

DeMare, P. & Kreeger, L. (1974). Introduction to Group Treatment in Psychiatry. London: Butterworth and Company Ltd.

Laplanche, J., & Pontalis, J. (1973). The Language of Psychoanalysis. London: Hogarth Press.

Lieberman, M., Yalom, I., & Miles, M. (1973). Encounter Groups: First Facts. New York: Basic Books.

Odell, H. (1988). A music therapy approach in mental health. Psychology of Music, 16, 52-61.

Composition, Improvisation And Poetry In The Psychiatric Treatment Of A Forensic Patient

PHYLLIS BOONE, RMT-BC
Music Therapy Supervisor
Norristown State Hospital
Norristown, PA

Abstract: *This study describes music therapy with a male forensic patient diagnosed as paranoid schizophrenic with grandiose, religious, and persecutory delusions and suicidal ideation. Incarcerated for terroristic threats, the man used poetry, musical composition, and improvisation to express his inner conflicts and feelings.*

BACKGROUND INFORMATION

Michael was admitted to the forensic unit of a state psychiatric hospital in 1985 for the purpose of being evaluated for competency to stand trial. He had been charged with making terroristic threats.

Upon evaluation, he was diagnosed as *paranoid schizophrenic* with *grandiose, religious and persecutory delusions* and suicidal ideation. He believed himself to be the "Antichrist" and that his life was in danger. He was hearing voices that he believed to be demonic, claiming that Satan was directly responsible for many of the natural disasters that were occurring throughout the world. He was found incompetent to stand trial.

Michael grew up in a family that had a history of suicide attempts, both by his brother and his uncle. Michael, at age 15, also attempted suicide which resulted in his first hospitalization. At that time he was hearing voices that were telling him to kill himself. Prior to this attempt, he had told his family that he was homosexual, which not only exacerbated some already existing problems within the family, but also caused a deterioration in the relationship with his parents. His self-esteem suffered considerably as a result.

At the age of 21, Michael began to experiment in the occult and remembers hearing voices that were increasingly malevolent. He was unable to hold a job for more than several months, which culminated in an ultimatum from his father that he either get a job or leave home. At this time Michael expressed fears for his life because he was the "Antichrist" and believed that there was a plot to kill him. This resulted in a second brief hospitalization.

During the next two years, Michael began to experiment with drugs, and his parents asked him to leave home several times. His preoccupation with Satanic worship and his delusional thoughts intensified, and eventually culminated in his crime. Although the crime was one of threats rather than overt violence or assault, he did target children as his victims, and he demanded that certain political figures step down from office in order for he and Satan to take control.

Competency to stand trial depends upon whether an individual has the ability to "consult with defendant's lawyer with a reasonable degree of rational understanding and otherwise to assist in the defense, and whether the defendant has a rational as well as factual understanding of the proceedings" (American Bar Association, 1986, p. 167). Michael's paranoia prevented him from cooperating with his defense, and his delusions also confused his thinking in terms of understanding the possible consequences of his behavior as it related to the trial process.

As he was obviously unable to stand trial at that time, he was committed to a forensic unit of a state psychiatric hospital, where he was treated for a period of three years, and then re-evaluated. This time he met the criteria for competency to stand trial. The courts then found him

"Guilty but Mentally Ill," sentenced him to 15 years, applied the three years of treatment on the forensic unit towards the sentence, and then paroled him to the civil section of the same state hospital.

Although the courts cannot deny probation solely because of mental health status, they can condition probation on receiving the necessary therapeutic treatment (American Bar Association, 1986). A key factor, however, in determining parole eligibility is the assessed dangerousness of the individual. In Michael's case, this was particularly relevant to his legal disposition.

Michael presented as a very intelligent, withdrawn and seclusive individual. He seemed disinterested in participating in many of the therapeutic activities that were available to him (e.g., group therapy, occupational therapy, and gym sports). On the ward he interacted with only a few patients, and at times would talk with select staff. His appearance was disheveled, and at times he appeared preoccupied and depressed. He was articulate but it was difficult to engage him in conversation.

The one interest Michael did express was listening to music. Because of this, and the need for the team to observe him in some type of therapeutic group, he was referred to music therapy.

TREATMENT PROCESS

Phase One: Assessment through Group Participation

Upon referral to music therapy, Michael was placed in an ongoing group that I led once weekly for 60-90 minutes. Although many different techniques were utilized, improvisation proved to be the most valuable in assessing Michael's treatment needs.

When Michael began attending the group, he did so reluctantly, and following the encouragement of his psychiatrist and other members of his treatment team. He was aware that, in order to progress through the legal process, he needed to cooperate with treatment, which minimally required attending and participating in some groups. During this initial assessment period, his attendance was sporadic, his level of *resistance* was high, and his affect was blunted.

Despite these difficulties, Michael's intellect was intrigued by the song discussions and his interest stimulated by the variety and quality of the instruments used in improvisations. During song discussions, his grasp of metaphors was apparent. It quickly became obvious, however, that he was only able to *project* his own feelings onto the lyrics, and that he often used *intellectualization* to deal with issues that were poignant and pertinent to his problems. Since this was a *support group*, his egocentricity and guarded responses often kept him peripherally involved.

During improvisations, especially those that described feelings or specific relationships, he exhibited very fixed or rigid responses. Rhythm was the most dominant element, and was markedly *perseverative*. He most often chose non-melodic instruments, but with encouragement would use a xylophone. Because his rhythm was so fixed, his melodies lacked continuity, creativity, and the development of musical ideas. They consisted of short intervallic sequences that were also repeated perseveratively. His playing was loud, and he was seemingly unaware and unresponsive to others in both group and dyadic improvisations.

As he became less resistant verbally and interactionally, he began to express an impressive knowledge of popular music. He also began to bring tapes to the sessions that were relevant to the issues at hand for the group.

Two significant events occurred during this phase of treatment. The first was his announcement to the group that he was a poet, and that he would like to bring some of his poems to the group so that they could be set to music. When the time came however, he told the group that, on second thought, he did not want to share his poetry because of the type of material expressed. He then took the opportunity to request individual music therapy sessions for the purpose of setting his poems to music. He also requested than an intern (from England) work with him, because she was familiar with the type of music that he liked.

The second significant event shed more light on the hypothesis that Michael was unable, and not simply unwilling, to vary his music. Michael expressed a strong preference for *"New Wave"* and *"Punk"* music and used that preference to validate his perseverative style of improvising. On one occasion, Michael was asked to improvise in a random and subdued manner in order to convey a specific idea to the group, and after two attempts, showed that he was unable to do so. After the first attempt, he was asked to explain the task and he did so with ease. After the second attempt, Michael became suddenly and acutely aware of his inability, dropped the beaters, and refused to continue. He remained quiet and pensive for the rest of the session. Despite the efforts of the group and myself to talk about what happened, Michael's defenses had been challenged and he was off balance as a result.

Phase Two: Achieving Competency in Individual Therapy

Upon his request, Michael began receiving weekly, one-hour individual music therapy sessions with the English intern, in addition to the weekly group. At the time, his clinical status was unstable, and he was not yet competent to stand trial. Being on the forensic unit, therapy had to occur in close proximity to the day hall with very limited privacy or access to much of the equipment that could have enhanced this phase of his treatment. Despite this, Michael was motivated and anxious to share his poetry and to investigate the possibilities of adding music to his work.

One of the main goals of this phase was to enable Michael to musically release the anger and fear that he verbalized in his poetry. It was felt that adding the dimensions of sound would help to "unfreeze" these emotions, while also providing ways of "synthesizing the energies freed from repressive and defensive mechanisms and giving them a new direction through rehearsal of action in sound" (Priestley, 1975).

The following is one of the earliest poems that he set to music. The themes of violence and terror were common to his work during this phase.

THE PSYCHOPATH

look at all the dead men
see the bloody bodies
slaughter them like pigs
cut him open like a dog
bury him in sand
Let me be your boyfriend
tell me that you love me
                    (would you kill for me?)
I know something you don't know
I'm gonna get you
with a kitchen knife
better pray to Jesus

I am coming after you
they will tell me where you are
I will follow you home
You had better run
You had better hide
I know where you live
I know how you die.

Michael was at first very interested in sharing his poetry with the intern. He continued to be very concerned about the response that he would get because of the violent and sexual explicitness of the work. Once he was able to be sure that the focus of treatment was not to "clean up his act," he began to concentrate on the relationship, as well as the task of adding rhythm, ostinati and melodic sounds to his poems.

A very simple electronic keyboard along with some rhythm instruments of Michael's choice became his options for this process. The *compulsive* and perseverative nature of his music seemed to be paralleled in his poetry. He continued to relate his work to many New Wave and Punk artists who successfully validated his style.

This process evolved over a period of several months, and was relatively uneventful except for the slight but gradual improvement in his affect and appearance. Along with this improvement were some significant gains in his group participation. He often assumed a leadership role in group improvisation and was less guarded in his verbal responses. In one session, when asked to title a duet improvisation, he defiantly responded, "Orgasm."

Although Michael never announced his sexual preferences in the group, he began to openly discuss it in individual sessions and had begun to develop a relationship with another male patient on his ward. This interest in others was viewed as progress in terms of his treatment.

A strong relationship was also developing between Michael and the intern, as he continued to receive weekly individual sessions with her in addition to the group I led. This relationship was as significant to Michael's growth at this time as was the opportunity to musically release the emotional energies that drove his delusional and violent thoughts and repressed his self-deprecation and anger.

A nondirective approach (Wheeler, 1981) was taken in relating to Michael. In both individual and group sessions, we made no attempt to guide Michael in any direction, but rather accepted his musical and poetic material and ideas. It was this nonjudgemental environment that enabled Michael to invest himself in the relationships, and to explore aspects of himself that others had rejected in the past. It was important to build such strong relationships to enable him to proceed to trial, and because Michael would later put them to a test.

A significant event during this phase was a state-wide art contest that was taking place in the hospital. Michael wanted to enter, and asked me and the intern to help him create a set of audio tapes containing his music and a booklet with corresponding poems. During this time, he worked intently towards this goal, but in the process, he began voicing his delusions and then expecting the intern to validate them. It seemed as though he was testing us by asking to go beyond accepting his feelings and to become part of his delusional system. I counseled the intern in terms of responding to Michael's challenges. The ensuing conflict in the relationship was weathered only because of his goal to win the contest and the degree of trust and respect that had developed. The mutuality of musical interests and intellectual pursuit had been extremely important in the relationship.

The music that Michael created for the tapes had a strong pulse but lacked the development or formation of rhythm patterns. Meter and accents were quite strong. This was taken as an indication of his need to to sublimate unconscious drives. According to Bruscia (1987) "...meter exerts power and authority over the other components of rhythm and thereby provides a moral context for the discharge of instinctual energies (p. 432)." "The components of rhythm are usually considered as manifestations of instinctual energy. Thus, pulse, meter, subdivisions, rhythmic patterns, and accents are interpreted as symbolic derivations of the amount, direction and flow of instinctual energy or drives (p. 430)."

His music was almost completely devoid of melody and tonality. He chose to chant or whisper the lyrics. It was as though he was unable to "voice" his true feelings and wishes through pitch. Michael believed that tonality would somehow decrease the intensity of his work by adding another dimension. At this time he was dependent upon the intensity and his control of it.

The way he used (and did not use) his voice was also significant. According to Bruscia (1987), "timbre represents the identity of the player through his/her selection of medium, instrument, production techniques, and sound vocabulary. The voice reveals the invisible, inner self, externalizing it so that it is audible (p. 455)." Michael used his voice as if he was concealing his identity and avoiding self-disclosure.

Michael was able to achieve the necessary musical tension through his perseverative use of the musical elements. However, because of this, his music did not permit the *catharsis* that he needed, but which did occur later in his treatment.

Michael continued to improve and was more able to trust others and eventually participate with his defense. Although his delusions remained, he was able to discuss the consequences of his illegal act and proceed to trial. He was declared Guilty but Mentally Ill and was sentenced. Because of his mental illness, he returned to the forensic unit for continued treatment.

Michael won second prize in the state-wide art contest. During the process, he was feeling good about himself and his creative abilities; but he was extremely frustrated and confused about only winning second prize, which gave further evidence of his grandiosity.

From a therapeutic point of view, writing poetry had been a self-initiated activity, which though self-isolating in the past, had provided him the means of communicating with and relating to others. Moreover, with the addition of rhythm and music, his poems had become an outward expression of his pain and conflict. He had begun to look forward to the future and to discuss his plans after completing his sentence.

Soon after winning the contest, he was paroled and transferred to the civil section of the hospital. When faced with the opportunity to work and earn money, which he perceived to be the most expeditious way to earn privileges such as leaving the building and moving freely around the hospital grounds, he refused to continue with his individual music therapy sessions.

The transition from a forensic to a civil commitment is frequently difficult for many patients, because they expect an immediate increase in freedom which does not always occur. The amount of freedom allowed is dependent upon the patient's clinical status, the severity of the crime, the judge's restrictions on parole, and the hospital's transfer policy.

Though he had decided to discontinue music therapy, Michael did ask me to assist him in purchasing an electronic keyboard. His parents agreed to finance it, and he specifically requested that it feature an extensive rhythm section. When he received the keyboard, Michael assured everyone that he would continue to write and compose on his own.

Phase III: Repressed Feelings and Unresolved Conflicts

Over the next six months, Michael was enrolled in a vocational workshop, and had earned some degree of independence. Though he did visit the music therapy area for instruction in the use of his keyboard, attempts to get Michael to return to individual therapy were unsuccessful.

One day, while visiting the hospital canteen, Michael happened to meet another music therapy intern. After some brief introductions, Michael discovered that this young man had a great deal of electronic equipment, including some sophisticated recording equipment, all set up in a room in the music therapy area. The following day Michael made a formal request to return to individual music therapy sessions with the intern he had met. His request was clear in that he was anticipating access to this equipment.

After some discussion with the intern, I agreed that Michael could work with the intern under my supervision. Michael was attracted to this intern for different reasons, but mostly for his usefulness. As the intern's supervisor, I was concerned first for Michael as a patient, and second for this particular intern being a novice. Michael's manipulativeness, intensity, and sexuality were threatening to the intern; however, I decided that with close supervision, both Michael and the intern could progress.

Michael was thrilled with the capabilities of the synthesizer and the professional quality of the recordings. He began to experiment with recording separate tracks and mixing them, as well as using some special effects (e.g. "reverb" and "echo"). After several sessions, he announced his intention to record as many pieces as possible while the intern was available to him. He became *obsessive-compulsive* about this, and later declared that his intention was to become a recording star. He believed this would convince the judge that he should be released from the hospital.

His poetry continued to be violent and sexually explicit in nature. He was clear and decisive about the type of sounds and rhythm that he wanted. He quickly learned how to create a chilling effect. Although he was less perseverative and compulsive, both musically and poetically, the effect was no less powerful and provocative. The intern continued with the same approach that had been successful in the past. However, some very difficult *transference* and *countertransference* responses began to develop, and the relationship became quite dynamic. The intern's *homophobic* reactions and religious convictions were provoking judgmental responses and intense feelings related to his work with Michael. These responses in turn provoked defensive and retaliatory responses from Michael because of his unresolved conflicts with his family, primarily his father who was the disciplinarian.

Michael's poetry became increasingly morbid with graphic descriptions of brutal dismemberment and mutilation. The intern continued working with me on the transference and countertransference issues, and was communicating with Michael's psychiatrist about the violent nature of Michael's compositions. At this time there was a concurrent suspicion of possible drug usage by Michael. He was temporarily restricted and tested.

The psychiatrist eventually confronted Michael during a treatment team meeting about the violence in his work. She had read the intern's progress notes and was well informed. The intern was unable to attend that particular meeting, and Michael interpreted this to mean that he would no longer be permitted to compose with the intern. Michael was frantic, and shortly after this he presented "Lord of Slaughter" to the intern.

LORD OF SLAUGHTER

I hold you under water
bury the city under water
Give the world to the Mad Hatter
Give him the world on a silver platter

I hold you under water in the deep
the final resting place where you will sleep
Those so grim will surely reap
build me a castle that I can keep

Lord of murder, Lord of morter, Lord of slaughter,
Lord of order

I hold you under water
Bury the city under water
Hey, hey under water

He explained that this piece represented what he would like to do to everyone who had hurt him in the past, including his family. This was the first time he expressed the rage he felt towards his family.

The following months were clinically significant in that he became increasingly more willing and able to discuss his feelings, although discussing his crime, a hostage situation, remained extremely difficult and painful for him.

He had begun to add melody and tonality to his compositions, nevertheless, his first attempts to have them commercially recorded were rejected. Nearing the end of his training, the intern was beginning to make closure with his patients, and encouraged Michael to write a poem about their impending separation. Michael did so, but this piece was never set to music.

TOOTH DECAY

Tooth decay, tooth decay
learning the truth means
burning my soul away
throwing my youth away

I hope you will be the last one
not to know. I hope you can let
go. And let go of it without
falling below.
I need you not.
I must prepare myself for the loneliness
that was here before you came
and will be here again after you've left.
anguish and despair are there
and they are all around here.
all of hell wishes you well.
go, be on your way
and go away from me.
I need you not.

Michael explained that the metaphor represented his illness, which he often experienced as a decaying process. Michael expressed an interest in continuing with music therapy even though he knew that the equipment available to him would be much more primitive. He asked to work with another intern, rather than me. By this time, he was aware of my role in supervising previous therapy sessions with the intern, and judging by his distance and abruptness when interacting with me, was quite angry because of the difficulties and challenges he experienced.

Phase Four: Catharsis and Termination

The vicissitudes of Michael's illness continued to affect his creativity and participation. Another intern began working with Michael and was introduced as a bit of a composer as well. This intrigued Michael even though he found out that the intern's style was jazz keyboard and he did not write lyrics to his work. The intern eventually presented Michael with a piece he had written and challenged him to write lyrics for it. Because the piece was the complete antithesis of Michael's style, he was initially unable to do so.

One day, about four months into their work together, Michael came to his session extremely elated. He had written a love poem to the music which he called "Rainbows and Harmonies". He announced to me: "You'll never believe it, Phyllis! I wrote a love song." The intern's music provided parameters in terms of phrasing, tonality, tempo, and pulse within which Michael was finally able to risk exploring another aspect of himself. He was more able to be vulnerable. For the first time, Michael was accepting and working with a melody.

RAINBOWS AND HARMONIES

When I see you I see flowers
All the hours slip away
The price to pay seems meaningless
Oh, it feels so much like love

When I touch you I see showers
flowing from my eyes like tears
The sky rains down upon us
All the days melt into one

When I see you I see starlight
running through the night and day
The moon shines down upon us
as hand in hand we walk away

Rainbows and harmonies
so hard to see before
The clouds approaching beckon us
As we go off to war

The love in my heart
attacks from the start
time and time again
again...

He was anxious to make a recording of this song, and obviously believed it was a breakthrough in therapy. He wanted to play it for his psychiatrist as a demonstration of his clinical stability. Soon after this, he was diagnosed as being in *remission*, and discussions about possible discharge began. He made it clear that the love song was not for the intern, but was an expression of well being. He sang this song on the recording. The sound of his vocal production was almost falsetto and childlike in quality. He had some difficulty in matching pitches, but was very intent upon making decisions about the instrumentation and production of the piece. He made several revisions of this work, and eventually began to express difficulty in knowing what else he could do in his therapy sessions.

There was a lingering perseverative quality to his musical choices and a recurrence of an agitated quality to his rhythms and tempi. Michael began to learn photography and the use of computers. His treatment team agreed that he needed to demonstrate his ability to maintain and sustain a full schedule on a daily basis. This was very stressful for Michael, and he did so with a great deal of reluctance and resentment. He expressed that he was waking up angry in the morning because of his (perceived) loss of control over decision-making about his daily routine. He announced that he viewed music therapy as a *regression* and that he would no longer be involved. Since this was the one aspect of his life that he believed he could control (his creativity), he told the treatment team of his intention and they agreed.

Michael agreed to be involved in some of the preparations for this case presentation. When reviewing some of his earlier work, he said it was difficult for him to believe that he wrote some of it. He was very pleased with the prospect of this publication, because he believed that it was important for others to know the full dimension of his personality, which includes his intelligence and creativity.

DISCUSSION AND CONCLUSIONS

Some significant aspects of Michael's illness that relate to both his legal and clinical disposition were paramount to driving the treatment decisions throughout his incarceration and parole. His paranoia, violent fantasy life, history of drug abuse, and intense but repressed anger and self-deprecation were significant determinants in assessing his potential for violence to himself and others. His poetry was and remains a graphic and complex metaphor for his feelings about his illness and delusions, his sexuality, and his family. His music proved to be an additional diagnostic measure in that it finally was the salient feature reflecting significant repressed material for future treatment.

Michael's crime was one of desperation. Although he threatened violence, there was no violent act. When considering this along with his past suicide attempts, violent thoughts, and intense energy commitment in his music, even the most experienced clinician would have cause for concern. When Michael's lyrics changed, they were driven by the music created for him. Following "Rainbows and Harmonies" he attempted other similar pieces, but his music was in conflict with the poetic theme.

Some studies indicate that the potential for suicide may be even greater for those who threaten violence. Future dangerousness may be greater for self than for others in these patients (Kozol, Boucher, and Garofalo, 1972).

The addition of music to Michael's poems was especially important because of the energy that it helped to release. Had the goal been to continue improvisation without linking with his poetry, the depth of his experience would probably have been less meaningful. The intensity of his music and poetry paralleled his fixation on delusional thinking. His self-deprecation and fear drove the violent fantasies.

Consider the lines, "Cut him open like a dog, bury him in sand," and "I hold you under water in the deep, the final resting place where you will sleep." Although they are from two different poems and represent two separate phases in his treatment, both are indicative of Michael's attempts to rid himself of his pain and illness. What is especially significant and representative of the intensity of his delusions is the music. As one would suspect, the energy required to "cut" and to "hold" were graphically represented in his rhythms and choice of timbre, tempo, phrasing and volume.

"Tooth Decay" is especially interesting because of its double message and use of metaphor. Michael's separation from the intern who had a powerful effect on him, and the initial phase of letting go of his illness are depicted in many lines. His choice of music for this piece could have been particularly valuable in assessing his affect at the time.

Ironically, the last piece, "Rainbows and Harmonies," which seemed to have a cathartic effect on Michael, may have been a critical point in beginning to assess or predict dangerousness. Michael's attempts to repeat this success which revealed the remaining musical agitation, compulsiveness and rhythmic dominance, may represent some important issues that could be critical to his future success.

Hall (1984) and Monahan (1981) articulated several factors that form the basis for predicting dangerousness, including baseline, developmental, and reinforcing variables (e.g., demographic factors, personality and behavioral traits), and "triggering stimuli." What is most important here is that the most "potent internal triggers" are substance intoxication, command hallucinations, paranoid states and obsessive thoughts of revenge or violence.

With this in mind, the necessity for Michael to continue writing and composing is further substantiated. The goal of future treatment would be to encourage Michael to listen to some critical indicators in his music that could warn him of negative symptoms. Treatment may eventually begin to encourage more insight. Michael was guarded during verbal processing, and he used the task at hand to avoid confronting his issues.

Ironically, Michael's criminal act was probably the most influential factor in his achieving remission of his disease. The longevity of his treatment probably contributed to the degree of success that was achieved. The use of his creative expression was important, diagnostically in assisting him to achieve competency to proceed to trial, and clinically in forming the basis upon which he could sustain a meaningful and therapeutic relationship.

Finally, this process was significant in helping him to cast off his dependence on self-deprecation and delusions via his improved freedom of expression.

Delusional material is most significant clinically in terms of purpose or function for the patient, relationship to any paranoid or grandiose features of the illness, and the degree of the patient's ability to disguise or hide the symptoms. Even when Michael stopped talking about his delusions, they were obvious in his music and poetry. The intensity of his fear and anger represented in the music, coupled with the grandiosity, self-protection and clearly defined methods of conflict resolution that were identified in the poetry, presented a significant clinical picture with much information relative to his court commitment and assessed potential dangerousness.

Michael has again requested to work with a music therapist. This time he wants a bass player---but will settle for a guitarist!

GLOSSARY

Catharsis: A purification or purgation of the emotions primarily through art that brings release from tension or elimination of repressed traumatic material by bringing it to consciousness and affording it expression.

Compulsion: Repetitive, purposeful, and intentional behaviors that are performed in response to an obsession, or according to certain rules or in a stereotyped fashion.

Countertransference: Arousal of the therapist's repressed feelings by the patient; symbolic libidinal relationships, partly unconscious, of the psychoanalyst with the patient.

Delusions: In general, false beliefs: grandiose delusions are false beliefs of having inflated worth, power, knowledge, identity, or special relationships to a deity or famous person; religious delusions are false beliefs of having extraordinary powers, or religious identity; persecutory delusions are false beliefs of being malevolently treated in some way.

Falsetto: The male voice above its normal range. A special method of voice production that is frequently used by tenors to extend the upper limits of their range.

Forensic: Belonging to, used in, or suitable to courts of judicature.

Homophobic Reactions: A persistent fear of homosexuality, homosexuals, or situations involving them, which manifests itself in anxiety responses or avoidant behaviors.

Intellectualization: Ego defense mechanism by which the individual achieves some measure of insulation from emotional hurt by cutting off or distorting the emotional charge which normally accompanies hurtful situations.

New Wave: A general designation for the rock music played by numerous English and American bands since the late 1970's. The term is applied to a variety of styles whose direct antecedent was punk rock but whose forms and rhythms drive directly from the rock 'n' roll of the 1950's and 60's.

Obsession: Recurrent and persistent ideas, thoughts, impulses or images that are experienced, at least initially, as intrusive and senseless.

Paranoid Schizophrenic: A type of schizophrenia in which there is a preoccupation with one or more systematized delusions or with frequent auditory hallucinations related to a single theme, but none of the following: incoherence, marked loosening of associations, flat or grossly inappropriate affect, catatonic behavior, grossly disorganized behavior (APA, 1987).

Perseveration: Persistent continuation of a line of thought or activity once it is underway. Inappropriate repetition.

Projection: Ego defense mechanism in which the individual places the blame for his/her difficulties upon others or attributes to others his/her own unethical desires and impulses.

Punk Rock: A type of music that emerged as social protest among English and working class youths in the mid-1970's. It rejected rock's emphasis on technique and professionalism and relied upon sheer volume and rhythmic energy applied to rhythms and forms derived from rock 'n' roll of the early 1960's.

Regression: Ego defense mechanism in which the individual retreats to the use of less mature responses in attempting to cope with stress and maintain ego integrity.

Remission: When a person with a history of schizophrenia is free of all signs of the disturbance (whether on medication or not).

Repression: Ego defense mechanism by means of which dangerous desires and intolerable memories are kept out of consciousness.

Resistance: Tendency to maintain a symptom, undermine treatment, and/or prevent the uncovering of repressed material.

Sublimation: Ego defense mechanism which directs the energy of an impulse from its primitive aim to one that is ethically or culturally higher.

Support Group: A group of people with mutual problems or interests where the focus is on sharing feelings, experiences and concerns in order to benefit from one another's strengths and skills.

Transference: Identification, usually unconscious, of some person in the individual's immediate environment with some important person in his/her past life, i.e. a patient responding to his/her psychoanalyst.

REFERENCES

American Bar Association, Criminal Justice Standards Committee (1986). ABA Criminal Justice Mental Health Standards. Washington, D.C.

American Psychiatric Association (APA) (1987). Quick Reference to the Diagnostic Criteria From DSM-IIIR. Washington, DC: Authors.

Bruscia, K. (1987). Improvisational Models of Music Therapy. Springfield, IL: Charles C Thomas.

Coleman, J. (1964). Abnormal Psychology and Modern Life. Glenview, IL: Scott, Foresman and Co.

Hall, H. (1984). Predicting dangerousness for the courts. American Journal of Forensic Psychiatry, 5 (2), 77-96.

Kozol, H., Boucher, R., and Garofalo, R. (1972). The diagnosis and treatment of dangerousness. Crime and Delinquency, 18, 371-392.

Monahan, J. (1981). The clinical prediction of violent behavior. National Institute of Mental Health, DHHS Publication Number (ADM). Superintendent of Documents, Washington, D.C.

Priestley, M. (1975). Music Therapy In Action (Second edition). St. Louis: MMB Music.

Randel, D. (1986). The New Harvard Dictionary of Music. Cambridge, MA: Belknap Press.

Wheeler, B. (1981). The relationship between music therapy and theories of psychotherapy. The Journal of the American Association for Music Therapy, 1, 9-17.

Group Improvisation Therapy
For A Resistant Woman
With Bipolar Disorder - Manic

PAUL NOLAN, M.C.A.T., RMT-BC

Director of Music Therapy Education

Hahnemann University

Philadelphia, Pennsylvania

Abstract. *The elicitation of a chief complaint within a client's musical behavior can engender a cooperative therapeutic relationship, especially with a resistant client. Group music therapy helped Carla, a 27-year-old woman, to reduce resistant behavior and enter into a supportive relationship through which she acquired awareness and acknowledged elements of her illness. At discharge, she was able to focus less upon internal stimuli and more on external events. She appeared to generalize progress made in the group to outside situations.*

BACKGROUND INFORMATION

Carla, a 27-year-old black woman, was voluntarily hospitalized by her father because she had been unable to sleep for several days. This was her third psychiatric hospitalization in five years. Her admitting diagnosis for this admission was *Bipolar Disorder - Manic.*

Carla is the first born of two female siblings. She is single and lived alone for the past six months. She has been employed as a part-time cashier at a local supermarket for the past seven years. She reports that she is close with her father but has little contact with her mother. She states that she belongs to a religious group but did not specify other information about the group or of her participation.

First Hospitalization

Her first psychiatric admission occurred in 1981 for a six week period at a local psychiatric hospital. At that time she was brought to the hospital involuntarily by her father because, for two months prior to admission, she had been wandering the streets, not eating well, frequently absent from work, sleeping more than usual, and having frequent irrational outbursts at home in the context of increasing family problems. Carla claimed to have psychic powers and that she was being followed by customers from work. She denied alcohol use but admitted to marijuana use once or twice per day; she had also used cocaine, angel dust, and speed within the past year.

At the time of admission, she did not appear to demonstrate symptoms of Bipolar Disorder, however she reported that she could not concentrate and denied any other problems. She was diagnosed as *"Schizophreniform Psychosis* ---rule out *Drug Induced Psychosis."*

Following admission, her psychiatric condition seemed to clear up rather quickly. She then had a period of manic-like behavior and displayed irritable, inappropriate, excited, euphoric, laughing and hostile behavior. Anti-psychotic medication produced neurological side effects. A *Lithium* trial proved initially successful in eliminating psychotic symptoms, but before a psychiatric free plateau period could occur under medical supervision her insurance coverage ran out and she had to be discharged. Just before discharge it was noted that she began to develop alterations in blood chemistry relating to renal functioning which were abnormal. It was suspected that these changes were due to the Lithium, and it was discontinued. Upon discharge, Carla was diagnosed as having Bipolar Disorder-Manic, and *R/O Multiple Endocrine Adenopathy Syndrome* with a guarded prognosis. She was scheduled for follow-up appointments with an endocrine specialist and with a psychiatrist.

Second Hospitalization

Her second psychiatric admission occurred in 1984 and lasted just under two months at this present hospital. She appeared flambuoyantly dressed with a turban. She was observed to mumble aloud to herself, with *loose associations* and *flight of ideas*. She also appeared to be hallucinating. Her hospital course was characterized initially as uncooperative, agitated and delusional. Her course of treatment over the two month period vacillated between partial remission (reduced reports of hallucination, less delusional) and *decompensations*. She demonstrated side effects from *Haldol,* however when this was reduced there was a return of psychotic symptoms. Her laboratory data were normal and it was felt that Lithium treatments could begin. She exhibited no adverse blood chemistry reactions from this medication.

Carla's initial contact with this music therapist came during her second hospitalization. In fact, one of the unit treatments which Carla attended consistently was group music therapy. She was placed in a regularly meeting group which met three times per week.

Throughout her stay Carla exhibited no overt verbal manifestations of psychosis within the group sessions. However, her musical behavior generally seemed to show marginal reality-testing in relation to her use of the musical elements; i.e., poor sense of pulse and meter of the music in the group and little musical or verbal demonstration of awareness of her musical expressions in relation to others in the group. She was better able to organize her musical expressions and maintain some involvement with the group when she used simple percussion instruments. A primary goal was to increase her awareness of the musical structure and of her effect upon that structure. She was then able to work toward increasing the number of musical options available to her within group improvisations.

In other interpersonal matters, she was able to talk to the group about her anger and conflicts with the nursing staff, and stated that she felt safe to express herself in the group. She regularly attempted to "help" others in the group, but this was actually understood as a means of control and deflecting the focus away from herself. One example of this was her manner of diagnosing other group members and prescribing behavioral regimes for them. This was similar to her interpersonal behavior on the unit. By the end of her hospitalization, she became more organized in her musical expressions and was better able to lend musical support to the musical expressions of others.

Carla was discharged with a diagnosis of Bipolar Disorder - Manic and received Lithobid, Haldol, and Symmetrel to control side effects from the Haldol. Following discharge, she attended outpatient treatment with a psychiatrist from the hospital and took her anti-manic medication. She also was placed with a community mental health agency which specialized in re-entry to the community following hospitalization.

Within six months she discontinued all of these treatments. Although it is not clear why she discontinued going to her doctor and the agency, she discontinued the Lithobid medication because it made her feel "bloated and dehydrated."

Present Hospitalization

The present hospitalization, one year later, seemed to be precipitated by several factors. Carla was upset that her father lost his job because the industrial plant closed. She was unable to sleep well; she was becoming irritable at work and aggressive with the customers ("I would diagnose the ones who looked like they were on Haldol"). She was unable to attend work for several days.

She apparently was psychiatrically stable and off of all psychotropic medications until approximately two weeks prior to this hospitalization. She began to fast for religious reasons whereby she could not eat during daylight. This occurred one year following her last discharge.

Carla's admitting diagnosis was "Bipolar Disorder---rule out Organic Brief Psychotic Reaction, rule out Dehydration." The mental status exam upon admission included the following information:

> *"Young black female flambuoyantly dressed in red turban with a skirt with sparkles, bright blue painted fingernails, very euphoric and expansive manner. Mood was irritable with constricted affect. Flight of ideas present. Paranoid ideations. "No Haldol, no tricks please"... The client did have some ideas that she had special powers... Abstraction was intact. Insight and judgement poor. Could not state reason for admission or precipitating events."*

During her hospital stay she had changes in her electrocardiogram which seemed related to taking *Mellaril*, an anti-psychotic medication. This required a cardiology consultation and outpatient follow-up. She was also found to have a mild iron deficiency anemia and was given iron supplements with good response. She was resistant to multiple staff recommendations to continue her Lithobid due to her history of good response psychiatrically. She did take Mellaril 400 mg orally at bedtime.

Since there were no reports of psychological testing in the discharge summaries from previous hospitalizations, testing was ordered. The report is summarized as follows:

(1) Cognitive functioning: Carla is functioning in the Borderline range of intelligence although it appeared that she was functioning below her capacity. She scored best in areas of fund of knowledge and social judgement. Her worst scores were in areas of arithmetic, concentration, and verbal concept formation. It was indicated that she was impaired in her ability to focus her attention. (2) Emotional functioning: She presented as an "acutely and severely disturbed woman" who "if provoked, is petulant and angry." "Her reality testing is severely impaired and she is disorganized in her thinking." She is unable to defend against the intrusion of primary process thinking, uses regression, denial, splitting, and vacillates between the extremes of despair and grandiose euphorias. In short, Carla's ego functioning is severely impaired. She has a difficult time tolerating her angry feelings, in that she is highly fearful of the angry impulses which might be provoked. (3) Diagnostic impression: Carla's "functioning is consistent with the diagnosis of manic - depressive illness with underlining borderline personality disorder."

METHOD

Upon admission, all patients on the twenty bed unit are oriented by the psychiatry resident to the milieu services. These include music therapy (group and individual), family therapy (where indicated), activity groups (arts and crafts, current events and other discussion groups), community meeting, psychoeducational groups and relaxation training. The music therapist then meets with the client to describe music therapy and to schedule the initial session. The results of this meeting are communicated to the treatment team and initial goals are discussed based upon input from others concerning the client's projected length of stay, strengths and areas of immediate clinical concern.

Carla was not scheduled for the usual individual orientation to music therapy due to her involvement in music therapy with this therapist one year prior. Because she threatened to leave the hospital, it was thought that group music therapy should begin immediately to allow for the inherent supportive contact from the therapist and the group members, and because she enjoyed these groups during her prior admission. She remembered the music therapist and seemed to look forward to her first group.

Her group consisted of three other low-functioning clients and met three times per week for one hour at regularly scheduled times. The room was located across the hall from the nursing station, but was reasonable sound proofed, and contained a piano, stereo system, movable tables, closets for instruments and was approximately 15 x 20 feet in size. The room was also used for meals, community meeting, some of the activity groups and relaxation training.

Generally, musical experiences included various forms of live music making such as improvisation, song writing, singing with instrumental accompaniment and ensemble adaptations of popular and folk music. Carla was placed in a group in which improvisation methods were used exclusively.

In this group, the approach to improvisation was to use varying degrees of therapist or client suggested structure. Often, the improvisations began with one person who was responsible for the creation of a musical statement or mood. The group members and therapist would join in when each member felt that he or she could understand the opening musical expression and felt comfortable adding their instrument to the music. At the close of each piece the group often spoke about the musical experience or about their own thoughts from the music. The therapist could use this opportunity to assess issues such as the comfort level of each member, emotional responses which seemed to be elicited by the musical events, reality testing and the presence of other psychiatric concerns from the verbal content. The therapist would also use this "rehash" to assess group interpersonal functioning by asking the members what they were aware of during the music.

This information would provide data concerning the amount of structure needed for subsequent musical experiences and if any other changes are required. By evaluating the group statements concerning the musical and interpersonal events, the therapist could tune into his own involvement in terms of the awareness of his own feelings and their relation to technical decisions made. At times, tape recording the music was used to assist this process. Finally, all musical, verbal and other non-verbal behavior from the group members and the therapist provides information related to the evaluation of treatment progress.

The treatment orientation consisted of psychodynamic (with emphasis upon interpersonal theories) and humanistic approaches. Carla's group behaviors were understood as responses, rather than random occurrences, to here-and-now events. Yet the orientation allowed for an understanding that behind her resistance was a need for a declaration of self. This combination allowed for an understanding of Carla's behaviors in terms of her reliance upon the defense of denial, as manifested partly by her pervasive resistance to treatment, and her perceived need for acceptance by others. Since it was apparent that Carla enjoyed music therapy and seemed to benefit from supportive, positive acceptance, the orientation pointed to an approach which allowed for a flexible style, with emphasis on the constructive elements of group treatment without a great deal of limit setting (which she seemed to perceive as criticism).

Improvisation methods were employed so that Carla could freely use musical elements in a manner to establish her way of relating to others with few restrictions, supplied mostly by musical structures. Structured improvisation methods were primarily used with the degree of structure related to variables such as: the immediate level of functioning; topic and level of conversation prior to the use of music in each group; mood of individuals; overall level of energy; and so forth.

The initial goals from this approach were to provide a musical holding environment in which Carla could feel: (1) that her communication was accepted and understood within a musical context; and (2) that she was connected, to some degree, to the group. Eventually, it was hoped that she could begin to see that her musical expressions were related in some way to her feelings. Encompassing these goals were those which related to improved reality testing, and a decrease of her hostile resistance. These goals were constructed as a preliminary means through which to assess her response.

Confrontations by the therapist were avoided since this was often the response used by many other treatment personnel, to no avail, and because it was not congruent with the construction of a supportive environment. This approach was maintained throughout music therapy treatment based upon the evidence that Carla attended regularly with few absences. She had very poor attendance in all other groups.

TREATMENT PROCESS

Phase One

Carla's first three groups were marked by her attempts to counsel the other members. She attempted to clarify the treatment goals of each member. Verbally, she exhibited behavior which was suggestive of mania such as pressured speech and flight of ideas. These symptoms seemed to dominate her xylophone playing in that she chose rapid successions of notes with frequently changing motifs without a bridging of some common feature to connect the phrases. Generally, during this phase her melodic contour seemed to be shaped by which range on the instrument she happened to find herself, at which point it seemed that she would simply reverse direction. In response to this playing the therapist responded on piano with chordal accompaniment in an attempt to envelope the motifs, echoing rhythmic groupings but leaving space to convey the therapist's background role. In this manner the therapist attempted a response which communicated an "understanding" of the melodic statements without suggesting a specific direction which Carla had to follow.

During these interactions, Carla's musical behavior, although not clearly organized as a sequence of developing musical events, seemed to differ from her verbal interactions. For example, she would verbally direct others as she began an improvisation, at times in a hostile manner: "Wait until I get started before you come in and don't bug me like that again!"   Musically she was beginning to accept some feedback from group members in that she would occasionally reorient to the musical structure by reentering in the same pulse pattern of the person playing the drum and cymbal. By the end of this period she would at times repeat a rhythmic motif and follow a brief change of dynamics initiated by the therapist on piano. These behaviors seemed significant in how they differed from her hostile and controlling verbal interactions with her doctors and nursing staff. There were signs that she was less resistant and at least partially willing to have brief periods of mutual interaction.

Psychotic behaviors were still apparent within these first group sessions. She mumbled, apparently to herself, during her playing, was not able to recall events which transpired between group members, and continued to show virtually no insight into her condition. At this time she could only identify her inability to procure an out-of-hospital pass from her doctor as her only problem. She continued to refuse medical intervention other than a small dose of Mellaril at bedtime.

The goals in music therapy began to focus upon her conscious awareness of musical organization, i.e., to create and respond to musical ideas.

Phase Two

By the beginning of the fourth group session, Carla, although still locked in a power struggle with the staff, began to accept some suggestions from the therapist concerning her musical organization. It was apparent to the therapist that Carla was able to maintain a steady pulse in time with the group music when she played simple percussion instruments. Although she always chose the xylophone for improvisations which she was to lead, or begin, she would accept the suggestion to play maracas or snare drum with brushes when she was not leading the improvisation. Now she was able to accept the suggestion by the therapist to "try to maintain a steady beat so that Bob can locate the group rhythm on this piece." By the next session this suggestion expanded to "see if you can make sense of Bob's playing before you add your instrument."   Carla was able to take the therapist's suggestion to begin her own pieces on xylophone with one mallet so that the group and therapist could easily follow her ideas. This suggestion was meant to encourage Carla to begin her musical ideas simply and to reduce the possibility of an not being understood. Although Carla heard similar suggestions many times from the staff in terms of slowing her pace of speech the suggestions raised within a musical context seemed to be received by her without the usual resistance. The quality of her melodic statements seemed to begin to convey intentionally expressive qualities. She was also able to comment on the playing of other members in terms of hearing aspects of them differently than in verbal realms.

During her improvisations the therapist made more direct musical responses on piano in attempts to form antecedent-consequent dialogue. This change seemed to add length to musical interactions which the therapist understood as "musical thinking." This level of musical "dialogue" was only possible for brief periods in each improvisation.

Following some of the group improvisations either a group member or the therapist would suggest that we listen to the tape playback. Often we would hear Carla's mumbling in the background on the tape without verbal acknowledgment by the group. During the fifth session one member said, "Who is that talking?" Carla turned her attention to the tape when another member stated that it was Carla's voice and that she mumbled all the time when she played xylophone. Carla appeared slightly embarrassed and said that sometimes she had too many thoughts in her head at once, and it caused her to have concentration problems. This admission seemed to become a turning point in that the therapist understood this statement as her chief complaint. Also, the statement appeared as a manifestation of a symptom of mania known as" flight of ideas," and seemed to correspond to her frequent shifting of musical motifs and tempo in her xylophone playing.

Later that afternoon when Carla was brought into the treatment team meeting the usual power struggle occurred over why she was in the hospital. She again threatened to leave the hospital against medical advise. By this time the nursing staff was frustrated in their dealings with her. Their attempts to treat her were continually met with hostile resistance, and they fell into a series of verbal confrontations with her. The music therapist reminded Carla of her complaint voiced during the music therapy session concerning her problems with concentration. It was suggested to Carla that she may be able to improve her concentration through the treatments available on the unit. She agreed that she would stay a little longer to improve her concentration. She also agreed to a slight increase in her Mellaril but she continued to refuse Lithium medication.

Although there was now an established "chief complaint" in Carla's own words which corresponded with a diagnostic criterion for Bipolar Disorder-Manic, she was not remarkedly compliant with treatment. Although Carla was also felt to have an underlying *Borderline Personality Disorder*, the therapist chose to focus upon the problems stemming from her psychosis. This was decided because the psychotic symptoms were acute and responded to treatment in the past and left unattended they could become worse and pose a real threat to her safety. Also, the treatment for Borderline conditions usually requires a longer term and different approach than the treatment for acute psychotic disorders. The therapist attempted to observe and guard against high degrees of borderline manifestations but this was difficult to separate from the resistant behaviors that often accompany the denial found in psychosis.

Preparing for Discharge

With her discharge scheduled one week away, Carla attempted to maintain a pleasant mood and seemed preoccupied with her leaving the hospital. Nevertheless, she paid attention to verbal attempts by the therapist to focus her concentration on her xylophone playing (i.e., "See if you can follow the pattern of the drum while you play"). There was a noticeable decrease in her mumbling while playing and she could establish clear pulse-oriented rhythmic patterns with brief pauses which seemed to define phrases.

Although she was able to respond in an echo response to dynamic changes initiated by the therapist she did not show signs of accepting suggestions in areas of melodic contour or the repeating or extending of musical statements. When she accompanied the improvisations of other group members on the drum she seemed to demonstrate a somewhat higher level of functioning in that she could maintain a particular style of playing without erratic changes in tempo, dynamics, or out-of-time subdivisions of rhythm. She began to accept direction from the therapist to play with just one hand to simplify her organization. She also followed suggestions to try to listen to the xylophone and orient to the mood expressed by that person. This represented the peak of any cooperation she could offer within interpersonal realms while dealing with her symptoms. The therapist was able to join on piano with the pulse and rhythmic groupings of her drumming in these accompaniments. This imitation by the therapist was intended to reinforce the musical decisions and organizational boundaries created by Carla in her attempts to meaningfully add to the group music. The therapist made efforts not to anticipate her playing but to stay with it while also responding to the group as a whole. Carla's musical relation with the therapist seemed now to be able to tolerate some degree of direct synchrony, or moving in the same rhythmic direction together.

When Carla's discharge date arrived she was offered to decide the musical experience for the group. She elected to lead an improvisation on xylophone and told the two other group members to chose what they wanted to play. She asked that the therapist join in last on the piano. She offered no verbal instructions before playing but spoke clearly while she and the group played about her plans following discharge. Although her playing did not appear to contain the organizational elements which she demonstrated in the prior group her verbal content was clear. She did not say good-bye nor did she acknowledge the events from her stay in the hospital. The group and the therapist wished her well and expressed hope for her return to her job. The session closed with listening to recordings of group selected popular music with some general discussion.

Her discharge report notes that initial behaviors of threats to sign herself out of the hospital, hypomania, pressured speech, hostility, magical thinking, preoccupation with detail, poor concentration and possession of special powers improved during treatment. She was referred to a cardiologist and to a community mental health center. She refused to follow-up with her prior outpatient psychiatrist because he insisted that she take Lithium as a condition for treatment. Carla stated that she would continue taking Mellaril.

DISCUSSION AND CONCLUSIONS

Although Carla's treatment did not result in a "therapeutic triumph," in that all issues were solved, she seemed to make gains in areas which seemed important to her in an otherwise very difficult situation. Her involvement in the overall treatment process was extremely limited, unlike her prior hospitalization one year earlier. However she seemed to make a therapeutic connection within the music therapy group which may have provided some support to her during this trying episode in her life. It was believed that the group music therapy treatments were somewhat helpful to her based upon the evidence that she maintained a degree of regular involvement. This was not the case with any other group treatment. This also may have had to do with her prior involvement in music therapy which provided some familiarity for her of the process.

Her relationship with the music therapist changed in that the degree of resistance lessened. This also was not the case with her relationships with her doctors and with the nursing staff. It seems that the main ingredient which allowed for this change within music therapy was due to the method which encouraged acceptance and support of her expressions via musical processes. The improvisation style provided a combination of flexibility and structure which seemed to eliminate the need for her defensive resistance. Her symptoms and her health (her willingness to join in the music making process with others) were accepted within an environment which was intended to convey an attitude that what she expressed was worthy of a non-judgemental response. The musical responses by the therapist were intended to allow Carla to experience that she could be with others without limit setting restrictions, thus reducing her manipulating and splitting behaviors. This approach allowed her to evaluate and alter her own behaviors in terms of musical processes.

It seemed that she reduced her psychotic behaviors (responding to internal stimulation over external musical events) based upon feedback from others and from her own awareness that these behaviors detracted from her musical thinking and her ability to be with others in the group. The opportunity to isolate and express a chief complaint as a result of her own experiences in the music, rather than from the judgement of the treatment staff, seemed to provide a bridge whereby she could become involved in some aspect of the treatment process. This was evident in that Carla connected her problems of poor concentration in the music with her experiences outside of the group.

The use of music within group treatment provides for a here-and-now experience which is considered to be the heart of the inpatient group therapy process, and helps members to learn invaluable interpersonal skills such as: to communicate more clearly, to get closer to others and to become aware of personal mannerisms which push others away (Yalom, 1985). Within this approach Yalom suggests that the therapist attempt to emphasize the positive rather than the negative aspects of a defense. This may require that the therapist provide support in a direct fashion. The use of music within this group model, especially with severely regressed members, allows the therapist to help the client spot interpersonal problems and reinforce interpersonal strengths. The tendency of short-term inpatient group treatment to demand some concrete result often invites tension, resistance and splitting (Hannah, 1984). The improvisation method employed in this case allowed for the emergence of a realistic and realizable goal and provided a bridle for the therapist's negative countertransference responses which can occur when goals are enforced without the client's involvement.

The final evidence of the benefit of the music therapy group to Carla's experience was acquired by accident when the therapist encountered Carla months after discharge in a supermarket. Carla said that she was doing well and was maintaining employment. She also thanked the therapist and said that the music therapy experience was enjoyable for her. She wished the therapist well as she said good-bye.

GLOSSARY

Bipolar Disorder - Manic: A major mental illness. Typical symptoms of mania include pressured speech, motor hyperactivity, reduced need for sleep, flight of ideas, grandiosity, elation, poor judgement, aggressiveness, and possible hostility.

Borderline Personality Disorder: A pattern of maladaptive behavior typified by significant instability of mood, inconsistent and unpredictable behavioral changes, and serious conflict in self-image or identity recognition (Cameron & Rychlak, 1985).

Countertransference: The unconscious feelings of the therapist toward the client.

Decompensation: Collapse of defenses and regression of the personality in general.

Drug-Induced Psychosis: An organic mental disorder brought on by ingestion of drugs.

Flight of Ideas: A symptom found in mania when thoughts race erratically from one topic to another without transitions.

Haldol: A major tranquilizer for use mostly in the management of manifestations of psychotic disorders.

Lithobid: An anti-manic medication containing Lithium for oral administration.

Loose associations: The breakdown of the logical ability to connect persons, things, or ideas.

Mellaril: A high dose, low potency tranquilizer used in the management of psychotic symptoms.

Multiple Endocrine Adenopathy Syndrome: A syndrome involving enlargement or swelling of endocrine glands with possible results in changes of behavior.

Reality Testing: The ability to distinguish one's thoughts, feelings, and perceptions (internal reality) as separate from external reality.

Schizophreniform: A brief manifestation of schizophrenic symptoms lasting less than six months.

Symmetrel: An anti-parkinsonism medication used to eliminate side effects from some anti-psychotic medications, such as Haldol.

REFERENCES

Cameron,N., Rychlak,J. (1985). Personality and Psychopathology: A Dynamic Approach (Second Edition). Boston: Houghton Mifflin Company.

Hannah,S. (1984). Countertransference in inpatient group psychotherapy: implications for treatment. International Journal of Group Psychotherapy, 34 (2), 257-272.

Yalom,I.D. (1985). The Theory and Practice of Group Psychotherapy (Third Edition). New York: Basic Books.

Group Music Therapy In Acute Psychiatric Care: The Treatment Of A Depressed Woman Following Neurological Trauma

MARCIA MURPHY, M.A., CMT-BC

Independent Consultant

Sound Alternative Associates

New York, New York

Abstract. *Group music therapy was used in the interdisciplinary treatment of Fiona, a 43-year old woman hospitalized with severe depression following rehabilitation for neurological trauma. The acute psychiatric admission was based on a diagnosis of severe bipolar disorder with borderline features. The inability to cope with the discontinuity of her life had caused Fiona increasing anxiety and despair that was manifest in suicidal ideation necessitating hospitalization. Group experiences, including those in music therapy, provided Fiona not only with psychosocial support, but with greater insight into herself and the coping skills to face critical life change as her depression lifted.*

BACKGROUND INFORMATION

Fiona, a 43 year-old woman, appeared younger in years, and almost childlike when she arrived for her first therapeutic group in an acute psychiatric hospital unit. Diagnosed with a history of depression, Fiona had been hospitalized for psychiatric and medical treatment of a *Major Bipolar Affective Disorder* that was secondary to a *head trauma* which had left her partially paralyzed. Subsequent to this crisis, she had been hospitalized in a larger rehabilitation center to treat the physical and neuropsychological deficits following the sudden onset of a *subarachnoid hemorrhage.* The primary disability that resulted from this trauma was impaired ambulation and balance.

As she was adapting to her impaired mobility, she sustained a fall that caused multiple fractures. In her then prolonged recuperation and rehabilitation, her depression had become profound as she realized that she could no longer continue to maintain her independent living status, even with the help of home aides and visiting nurse services. Fiona was a withdrawn and sad individual on first impression.

Biopsychosocial Profile

Fiona had a complex set of psychiatric and medical problems that needed to be addressed in her hospitalization at an acute care facility. Given the interdisciplinary treatment available at the hospital, a biopsychosocial profile of the entire person is created upon admission.

PHYSIOLOGICAL ASPECTS. Fiona was admitted to the geripsychiatric unit due to her physical limitations and consequent need for more nursing care than the average psychiatric admission. Her history can be described in an overview of the factors that had so profoundly impacted her life. When she was 39 years old, Fiona was disabled by a subarachnoid hemorrhage that ultimately affected her motor control. Specifically, it limited her ability to walk and use her legs, and occasionally caused a slight loss of control in her hands and arms. She was able to use a wheelchair, and walk with a walker or with the assistance of one person.

After her initial hospitalization, Fiona had returned to her apartment with part-time nursing assistance. It was at this time that she suffered a further setback: an injurious fall which led to another hospitalization. By this time, her partial loss of motor functioning impaired her physical coordination.

PSYCHOLOGICAL ASPECTS. Fiona's cognitive functioning was not significantly impaired by the neurological trauma, but she could not remain in her demanding, responsible management position. Her concentration, ability to organize and communicate information under pressure, and to make management decisions had been affected. Her low frustration tolerance and mood swings were further liabilities to effective functioning in a large corporation. Fortunately, in Fiona's case, the intracranial hemorrhage had not been severe. The irritative and pressure effects had been located in the tissue where the cerebrospinal fluid passes near the motor pathways; however ramifications on the patient's emotional status could not be discounted (Walsh, 1978).

Fiona's personal history was marked by tragedy. In her early twenties, she broke her engagement to be married. Her ex-fiance had fatally shot Fiona's sister, mistaking her for Fiona. Fiona was treated for depression as a result of the tragedy which had affected the entire family.

Her father died several years afterwards, however. Her mother and brother moved to a community upstate. They were emotionally as well as physically remote. She had built an independent life as a self-supporting single person who held a responsible position. Now she was the recipient of a generous disability insurance income from her former employer. She had become more withdrawn and vegetative, although she had the support of her primary therapist (a clinical psychologist), a community social worker, and a regular team of nurses. However, she had made some suicidal gestures and it became necessary for Fiona to be admitted for acute psychiatric treatment.

SOCIAL ASPECTS. Perhaps the most devastating consequence of Fiona's disabling condition was the impact on her social life, in particular, the loss of some friends, and a social life that she had built around a career. Her life had changed drastically following the neurological trauma: from a full daily schedule and social life to the collapsed world of her apartment as a disabled person, dependent on others. Nurses, aides and homemakers were unable to motivate her.

She owned and maintained her own cooperative apartment. Following the trauma, the alternative to this type of life was an adult residence with rehabilitation facilities. Fiona was very outspoken about her resistance to such a move. She denied the need for this change.

Team Assessment

Team treatment objectives were for Fiona to be medically evaluated and supervised and to be engaged in the hospital's interdisciplinary group treatment program. A house psychiatrist was assigned to her upon admission, and Lithium was prescribed for treating the differential diagnosis of bipolar affective disorder. Fiona's moods varied from tearful resistiveness to hostile and disruptive outbursts.

In the first week on the unit, the treatment team had observed her depression, along with other behaviors that were typical of a *Borderline-type Personality*. Her behavior and attitude were self-defeating, and seemed to be a continuation of the emotional and psychosocial decline that had begun while she was living in her apartment.

Given her age, Fiona was an atypical patient on a geripsychiatric unit. The other patients were on average twice her age, and Fiona was understandably distressed. However, she made an effort to establish contact with several of the more alert and aware elderly that turned out to be beneficial to all involved. She adapted to the unit and initially was compliant with the team treatment plan.

Fiona was intelligent and well educated; she had retained her sense of humor and common sense. However, her manic-depressive mood swings were frequent and pronounced, and therefore interfered with treatment. When her mood swings were brought under control with medication, the depression remained. Often, she became tearful when talking about her reasons for wanting to live independently. In reality, this was no longer possible, yet she remained in denial, and refused to acknowledge a need for a major change in her living arrangements.

The borderline features of her personality emerged as she became overly manipulative, splitting staff (who is "good" and who is "bad" from day to day). She also sabotaged therapeutic alliances and threw periodic temper tantrums.

Fiona began to participate in therapeutic groups at the end of the first week of her hospitalization. It became evident after the second week that her mood swings were a way of protesting her hospitalization to her therapist, the inhouse psychiatrist, and treatment team. Her mood swings became more clearly defined, ranging from passive withdrawal to occasional disruptive outbursts in treatment group sessions. There were few sessions in which Fiona was so disruptive that she was either taken out of the group or she chose to leave. When she was not able to tolerate a group process or to complete an occupational therapy task, she would become sullen and withdraw into herself or wheel her chair to her room. She was not overtly noncompliant because she hoped to be discharged from the hospital much sooner than medically advised.

Fiona was referred to music therapy because she had an interest in music that was life-long. Music was part of her childhood and music listening was part of her initial recovery from the neurological trauma. Her adaptation to hospitalization was supported by music therapy interventions to which she responded positively. She had the ability to express herself verbally and in song. She was able to use music improvisation to express repressed feelings of rage and hurt in percussive instrument sound and vocal toning. The music experiences opened Fiona to facing the turning point in her treatment, that is, accepting the need for change and learning how to cope with the decision.

In addition to music therapy, Fiona received physical therapy, occupational therapy, dance therapy, art therapy and recreation, and each program was individually planned and implemented within the parameters of the unit's interdisciplinary treatment plan.

TREATMENT PROCESS

The music therapy sessions in which Fiona participated included large milieu or dayroom programs ("Sing-Out Groups"), closed listening sessions (no more than six patients), improvisation sessions for psychomotor coordination, and closed improvisation sessions for self expression, tension release, and exploration of control issues. During the three and one-half months that Fiona was on the unit, she was engaged in twenty-three music therapy sessions, most of which were in a group setting.

Establishing Trust

Fiona's primary nurse brought her to the first music therapy session in the dayroom, a "Sing Out Group." She appeared withdrawn and quiet, but as she remained in the group she seemed to know many songs from the "oldies" repertoire, either singing along or responding with limited body movement or facial expression. Although she appeared to be interested, she also appeared to be depressed. She acted bewildered and tearful, resistive to talking with staff except her nurse. She had remained in her private room and was taking her meals alone there.

The day after the first music therapy session, I made a point of inviting her to a morning energizing session with the support of her nurse. She responded positively, and came willingly to the group, although her participation was minimal. Fiona's energy level was low. During the session, I provided live music at the piano for breathing and stretching followed by movement from a chair position. As the session progressed, I observed that her level of alertness increased and she appeared brighter, smiling at times. In this type of open session, a forty-five minute group might actually last only fifteen or twenty minutes or the full time period, depending on the attention span and responsiveness of the group. If group members stopped responding or drifted in attention, I closed the group and talked with individuals from the group.

This session lasted a half hour, following which Fiona asked if she could play the piano. After I moved the piano to a corner of the dayroom, I helped her position her chair to face the keyboard. She picked out a few notes of a familiar song phrase and withdrew her hands as she could not complete the musical line. She seemed to be angry or annoyed, and so I asked her what she had been thinking about when she began to play. She responded easily that she had learned many songs from her father when she was a child. He had sung, accompanying himself on the piano.

St. Patrick's Day was the next day, and she had tried to play the opening line to "Danny Boy." She had taken piano lessons as a child, but had not become proficient in playing. What became evident in the conversation was her fond memories of her father, who had been deceased for over ten years. She mentioned that the old tunes and the Irish music were a comforting memory link to him.

Later that day I was able to include her in a small group for improvisation based on the image of the annual Fifth Avenue St. Patrick's Day parade to be held the next day. Since it would be a Saturday parade, there would be no music therapy group on a weekend day. I had brought portable percussion instruments and the group responded to creating parade/march scenarios for motor coordination and concentration, but most of all, for spontaneous and tension-releasing expression. Fiona became totally involved, laughing and singing with assurance and control. After a particularly enthusiastic rendition of "McNamara's Band," she commented, "This reminds me of the good times we had at home when we all made music."

Regression

The next week was the beginning of Fiona's regression into herself and acting out behavior that clearly indicated disdain for hospitalization. I brought her into a small, closed improvisation session for psychomotor stimulation and coordination. She discovered the slit drum (Gato), and she became intrigued with it for a brief time. Then she randomly hit the drum, with no apparent purpose or relevance to the progression of a pattern and cohesiveness toward which I had been leading the group. After several minutes of disorganized sound resulting from Fiona's self-absorbed, inattentive and random drumming, she joined the group with her drum sound. She refused to discuss her participation in the session following a playback of the improvisation sequence. She dismissed the group's feedback to her that her playing indicated a lack of involvement with the group and treatment itself.

A window of opportunity had opened with the drumming session, but she closed it as she refused participation in all her treatment groups into the following week. She exhibited behavior that was inappropriate at times, manic and disruptive, fitting the profile of patients diagnosed with bipolar affective disorder. The depressed moods seemed to be prolonged sulking periods. Her loud, aggressive acting out was childish and a cry for attention. However, she could not achieve her main objective: to be discharged to her apartment and to continue independent living.

Expression of Feeling

When I next saw Fiona in a group, she had agreed to come to a morning listening session for relaxation and imagery. After a brief systematic relaxation sequence with Halpern's "Spectrum Suite," the group listened to excerpts from classical symphonic music that was selected to elicit a sense of quiet, space and security.

Afterwards, we discussed the reactions of the participants. Familiar scenes from one's most recent or childhood home emerged in the ensuing discussion. Fiona talked about her childhood and how much she missed her father. She stated that she was ready to move ahead in the current treatment and that she wanted to close the door on the past.

After the session, she remained in the room and asked if she could play the slit drum. As she began to explore the sound, I selected a small hand drum to support her playing. What emerged was a total refutation of her reaction in the previous session. Holding and mirroring her mood became difficult as her drumming became more rapid and disorganized. She became more angry and strident, almost bashing the drum with the two mallets she gripped tightly in each hand. It was at this point that she paused and loudly announced, "This is my doctor's head." Fiona was clearly demonstrating her anger with the hospitalization and her frustration with the doctor, who was female. She began to cry after this outburst. I shifted the focus to her breath and voice, and we breathed and sighed in unison which seemed to calm her. The shift in energy seemed to be soothing to Fiona as she reached deep inside to release sound, breath, and repressed pain. The gentle sobbing had been transformed through sighs, sounds and focused breathing from the abdomen into a regular rhythmic pattern. Fiona then was able to acknowledge her sadness about the past, her anger about the current need for hospitalization and her fears about the future. The catharsis evolved because she expressed her feelings nonverbally. The words were too easy.

The following day, she was ready for the scheduled music therapy session which was a small, closed improvisation group. The instrument selection included metallophones. Fiona selected the pentatonic chime bars, and she appeared to be enchanted by the sound. One member of the group commented that it was the resonance of Fiona's instrument that made the predominant sound in the music ensemble. Although the group members were aware of Fiona's mood swings, they were not intimidated by her. One reason is that this group was composed of older women who assumed a motherly if not grandmotherly role with her. They gave her permission to express herself, and Fiona found cross-generational sharing and support to be quite a special ingredient. Fiona's relationship with women had become a critical part of her sessions with her doctor and were also discussed with her psychologist, a male.

In this music therapy session, the theme became change. Spring was in the air and Fiona was restless, bursting with energy. In the session, she had begun to listen to others as she played. In the closing improvisation, she was able to blend into the sound of the other instruments and thereby become the underlying solid support for the music. In the closing discussion,

Fiona maintained her denial about her own need for change; but she had expressed herself as a hurt child musically. The treatment challenge was identifying who she really was---angry woman or hurt child.

Although responsive in music therapy, Fiona's coping skills were maladaptive on the unit. She had recently upset several of her older peers. In the safe environment of the therapeutic group, she had disclosed her feelings. However, this proved to be a ploy to what she thought might lead to discharge. She had become angry, reverting to acting out with staff and patients as she avoided discussing her fears about her future. On top of her anxiety, she had experienced physical stress from the side effects of the Lithium treatment. The coping skills that the team had tried to support, construct or reinforce had been lost in a matter of days.

Developing Coping Skills

Fiona's ongoing psychotherapy was crucial for her resolution of unresolved emotional conflicts. The team was aware of her splitting tactics-- "good" staff versus "bad" staff, and male versus female. In team meetings, we discussed her denial.

After returning from a brief vacation, I observed a change in Fiona when she participated in the next improvisation. She had declined to join a larger dayroom music session in the morning for energizing before a community meeting. After our group time, she saw her psychologist for a session during the unit weekly community meeting.

After lunch, she joined the small music therapy session. Her tremors seemed more pronounced than I had ever seen. Fiona chose the slit drum, but she had difficulty using the mallets. She refused a hand drum offered by one of the group and asked the group to support her as she attempted to use the mallets with the slit drum one more time. She was able to maintain solid control and was supported by the percussive sounds of the group. As the group was about to close, she suddenly became irritable and negative, denying the feedback of the group, commenting on how direct and strong she had sounded in the music portion of the session. She then proceeded to pour out her anger about losing control of her body and her life. When she stopped speaking, she left the room with only slight signs of tremors but in an agitated and depressed state. She refused to talk with me afterwards.

Change in Medical Protocol

After the session, I asked Fiona's nurse about her. It was then I learned that the side effects of her medication were escalating. Fiona was experiencing involuntary movements and tremors, causing her increased anxiety and frustration. As a result, the psychiatrist had decided to change the medical protocol from psychotropic medication (Lithium) to

Electroconvulsive Therapy (ECT), scheduled to begin the end of the week.

In the team meeting the next day, her behavior was discussed. Fiona had continued to manipulate staff. The team agreed that she was not coping with the hospitalization, and that Lithium was producing intolerable side effects despite careful monitoring. The anxiety and depression for which Fiona had been hospitalized were not lifting, and it was generally agreed that a change in medical protocol was necessary.

At the beginning of her ECT, Fiona experienced temporary memory loss, poor attentional skills, and problems in motor coordination. She also was very lethargic immediately following the treatments. During the first week of ECT treatments Fiona attended only a few groups, and participated less consistently, however her mood was relatively stable. She even agreed to participate in her case conference.

As Fiona completed the prescribed course of ECT (9 treatments over 3 weeks), many of her problems with memory, attention, and motor coordination began to disappear. Her lethargy also began to dissipate.

Her involvement in music therapy became more active. She had learned to ask for and receive support from the group, musically and verbally. Fiona also selected instruments that were less intrusive in sound than drums. She alternately used the chime bars, maracas, and tambourine. She found that she had good motor control and the soft shaking of the tambourine reflected her search for quiet and peace within herself. She was more focused on the "here and now" group process, and she was able to address the relevant concerns about the transition in her life to which she had been previously so adamantly resistant.

The music therapy goals were adjusted to become two-pronged: to support her expression of the difficult feelings of anger and hurt, and also to reinforce her maintenance of psychomotor control. At the same time she was encouraged to express the spontaneous, fun-loving side of her personality as appropriate to the situation. With the change in treatment plan, her music therapy sessions supported Fiona's sense of autonomy in controlling emotional and physical responses as well as in controlling her life. The transition was a smooth one.

Discharge

As Fiona became medically stable, her depression lifted, and her mood stabilized. Plans for discharge were then begun by both the hospital social worker and the community social worker, who collaborated with Fiona to negotiate a difficult transition period. As Fiona became somewhat optimistic about the future, she also accepted the plan for a move to long-term care.

Before Fiona was discharged from the hospital, there was a brief gap in the music therapy treatment because of my absence. On my return, the remaining sessions were directed to her discharge and facing an unknown, new living situation.

Music therapy groups had been critical in allowing Fiona an opportunity for expression and in helping her gain insight about her behaviors. More important, these sessions had assisted her in building coping skills for maintaining control, both physical motoric strength and emotional stability, in order for her to plan for the future and to be able to make the major transition to a new living situation.

Fiona had learned to accept and acknowledge the emotional and physical setbacks in her life. She was able to talk more openly about her sadness and disappointment in the changes her disability had forced her to make. At the same time she was able to express hopes for a successful adjustment to the new life that was ahead of her, including her wish to have a relationship with a man. She had become more direct and honest in her treatment.

In music therapy group sessions, this was apparent in more direct musical expression and interplay with others in the group. She was able to find satisfaction and pleasure in the outcome of her improvisation and in her newly reinforced strength as a leader.

In the last music therapy session which was a free improvisation from which a theme of moving on emerged, I observed a transformed person in her presence and in her participation nonverbally. She was communicating and not demanding attention. In the closing processing of the music that had been created by the group, Fiona commented, "I can control it (body, moods, thoughts) if I want."

DISCUSSION AND CONCLUSIONS

Fiona was able to address the difficulty of coping with life as a disabled person as a result of this hospitalization. Her coping skills increased as she became more actively involved in her treatment planning, less resistive to the therapeutic process, and more committed to participating fully in the treatment groups. Fiona often became tearful after a music therapy improvisation session. She was an angry woman, hurt by emotional loss in the past, and handicapped by a neurological condition that was physically disabling and emotionally devastating. Through the support of the interdisciplinary treatment team, Fiona realized success and pleasure each day she participated in a therapeutic group, and as she responded to the medical treatment. Coping with the difficult transition from living without structure and supervision to a secure environment, and at the same time retaining a sense of autonomy about her life, was the issue that faced Fiona and to which she was resistant. This immediate issue was the main focus of treatment.

Music therapy sessions kept Fiona involved in the moment, as the focus was to create a musical outcome that can give satisfaction and immediate gratification. When Fiona was most aware and involved, she pursued several goals: to address the here-and-now, to control her contribution to the music making process, and to explore nonverbal ways to ask for and receive response.

When she was able to accept the positive feedback of the group members about her contribution to the group music, she was responding as well to the medical treatment. As Fiona's depression was lifting, she was able to move beyond playing, and stopped masking her real emotions and demanding attention. She also used the group process to reinforce and experience her increased control and strength. In fact, her self esteem was improved and she acted with conviction and confidence in every aspect of her participation on the unit.

Another important outcome of the treatment process, including the music therapy sessions, was Fiona's interaction with women. Those on the unit were chronologically peers of her own mother, and in some cases, her grandmother. Fiona's relationship with her female psychiatrist had been strained at best in the first month of treatment. As she accepted herself and her changed life, Fiona also was able to examine her relationship with her mother. She began to select group peers to have meals and socialize with her. The social worker was able to arrange a meeting with Fiona and her mother.

Fiona's brother had brought their mother to the hospital, and he himself had visited Fiona on several occasions since he had business in the city. It took the hospitalization and the effort of the hospital social worker in collaboration with Fiona's community social worker to schedule the family meeting. This signified a family reconciliation of differences that was a contributing factor to Fiona's acceptance of the move to long-term housing with rehabilitation.

The support Fiona received from members of the music therapy group was critical to her recovery and adjustment--recovery from a severe depression and adjustment to disability from neurological trauma. The group gave Fiona permission to express her feelings, but not to act out and regress to childish behavior; to cope with her anger and sadness in closed groups by either supporting her music or responding to her in discussion; and to provide her with ego supporting feedback that enabled her to acknowledge her capacity for control within the limitations of her disability.

All of the services, including the music therapy sessions, helped Fiona to learn to cope with hospitalization and to better cope with her losses. Her most recent loss of physical functioning became less devastating to her when her older group peers presented the reality of her relative youth and the time she had to take her life in a new direction faced with the change in living. The age disparity often played a part in Fiona's recovery drama that worked to her advantage. In return, Fiona was able to offer her respect, and thereby reinforce the strength shown by the older group members in coping with their respective need for continuous care. All were able to share their feelings about their lives and concerns about the future in music therapy groups and other groups on the unit.

In hospitalization and in wellness, most people need support from outside themselves in order to maintain their activity, productivity, or creative pursuits. Support groups offer a forum for reinforcing strengths and skills (Knox, 1977). The music therapy group became for Fiona an avenue to discharge from hospitalization because it was through this group that she could demonstrate her strength and leadership skills. All her positive group experiences in acute care enhanced Fiona's ability to cope and to acknowledge the talents and creative skills that she had shown as she adapted to an irreversible condition that had transformed her life.

GLOSSARY

Bipolar Affective Disorder: A disorder characterized by alternating episodes of depression and mania. Depression is an emotional state marked by lethargy, decreased appetite, disrupted sleep patterns, withdrawn and isolated behavior, sadness, and apprehension which then changes to mania. Mania is an emotional state characterized by intense but unfounded elation evidenced by talkativeness, flight of ideas, distractibility, grandiose plans and spurts of purposeless activity (Davison & Neale, 1978).

Borderline Personality Disorder: A disorder characterized by any five of the following symptoms: impulsivity or unpredictability in two potentially self-damaging areas (over-eating and physically self-damaging acts); inappropriate, intense anger or lack of control of anger, temper; affective instability: marked shifts from normal mood to depression, irritability, or anxiety, usually lasting a few hours and only rarely more than a few days, with a return to normal mood; physically self-damaging acts such as suicidal gestures or accidents; chronic feelings of emptiness or boredom; identity disturbances; and a pattern of unstable and intense interpersonal relationships. The symptoms are current and long-term rather than episodic, and lead to significant impairment in social or occupational functioning or subjective distress (APA, 1987). Fiona exhibited the first five of these symptoms.

Electroconvulsive Therapy (ECT): Treatment which produces a convulsion by passing electric current through the brain; useful in alleviating profound depression based on stimulation of neurotransmitters, affecting the neurological biochemistry.

Subarachnoid hemorrhage: Intracranial bleeding resulting in damage to brain tissue as well as irritating and creating pressure in the area through which the cerebrospinal fluid flows (Walsh, 1978).

REFERENCES

American Psychiatric Association (APA) (1987). Quick Reference to the Diagnostic Criteria from DSM IIIR. Washington, DC: Authors.

Davison, G.C. & Neale, John M. (1978). Abnormal Psychology. New York: John Wiley & Sons, 633-656.

Knox, A.B. (1977). Adult Development and Learning. San Francisco: Jossey-Bass, Inc.

Walsh, K.W. (1978). Neuropsychology, A Clinical Approach. Edinburgh: Churchill Livingstone, 87.

The Song-Writing Process:
A Woman's Struggle Against
Depression And Suicide

GEORGIA HUDSON SMITH, M.M., CMT-BC

Music Therapist/Addictions Counselor

Interim House

Philadelphia, PA

Abstract: *This study describes individual and group music therapy with a 27-year-old suicidal woman, dually diagnosed with Major Depressive Disorder and Borderline Personality Disorder. Through song writing, Jean found a creative way to share her thoughts and feelings while also developing positive self-regard. The creative process also helped to access unconscious material and unlock repressed memories that were important in gaining insight about herself.*

BACKGROUND INFORMATION

Jean was a white, obese, 27-year-old, single female when first admitted to a psychiatric hospital. Prior to admission, she was in the last phase of her training to become a nun. She had converted to Catholicism approximately 8 years earlier, and had entered the convent 6 years earlier. Jean felt that these decisions were a major source of conflict between herself and her Protestant parents.

The referral to the hospital came from a private psychiatrist due to several recent suicide gestures and depression. Jean subsequently had 3 hospitalizations over an 18 month period. With each admission she was placed in an open hall music therapy group for high-functioning, non-psychotic patients. She was also seen privately 2 times per week for individual music therapy for 8 months between her second and third hospitalizations.

During the months prior to her admission, Jean began to feel increasingly troubled and depressed. She identified several stressors: moving to a new convent house while attending a new college, conflicts with two other nuns in the house, and her brother's discharge from the Marines due to alcohol problems. She also felt constant disapproval from her father for becoming a nun. Approximately two weeks prior to admission when Jean was feeling troubled, she swallowed some windshield washer fluid. This was brought to the attention of her peers, and Jean was seen by a psychiatrist in private practice. Initially this was considered as impulsive, and Jean appeared to make a reasonable response to office treatment. However, prior to her second visit, Jean superficially slashed her wrist and, following her doctor's reevaluation, hospitalization was recommended.

Jean grew up in a rural setting, attending a small town consolidated school. Her father had been alcoholic as far back as she could remember, and, he had had numerous affairs when she was younger. Jean considered her father to be very harsh and negative in his relationship with her. She reported that her paternal grandfather was an alcoholic as well.

Jean described her mother as kind, and genuinely concerned that Jean be happy. Though her mother was passive toward the father's verbally abusive behavior, she would try to comfort and reassure Jean when the father was not present. Jean reported that her mother was physically abused as a child by her own father.

Jean's brother was 5 years younger, and had a severe drinking problem. He had been charged several times with "Driving While Intoxicated" and he had been involved in several life-threatening auto accidents. As he became older, Jean felt that he also became verbally abusive toward her.

During her first hospitalization, Jean characterized her childhood as fairly uneventful. She did well in school and had numerous friends. She reported dating and having normal peer relationships during her adolescents, despite always being troubled by her home life.

Jean began working after graduating from high school. She enjoyed a responsible position in an office, making good money, and, occasionally taking a course at a local community college. After saving her money, she moved into her own apartment, hoping to provide a healthy separation from the constant bickering at home.

A few months after Jean's emancipation at age 19, her mother showed up at her apartment, suitcase in hand, saying that she had left Jean's father. Jean let her move in. They lived together for almost a year. Jean worked hard to try to get her parents to reconcile, to no avail. She finally gave up the apartment, and she and her mother moved back home---she did not want the expense if she could not also have the freedom.

During the time Jean lived in her apartment, she had begun attending a local Catholic church. She found the worship comforting and peaceful. After returning home, she continued attending as a way to "get away" from the confusion and pain she experienced at home. During the first few months back home, Jean completed a catechism class, was baptized, and became a member of the Catholic church. Jean reported that her father threatened to disown her and engaged in hurtful verbal degradation. Within six months of returning home, Jean made a decision to become a nun, and began the process to enter a convent, which she did at age 21.

TREATMENT PROCESS

First Hospitalization

Jean was first hospitalized at the age of twenty-seven, six years after entering the convent. Her therapy focused on a growing awareness that she had difficulty in communicating her needs to others. She became hurt or resentful when her needs were not met, but tended to have excessive feelings of guilt or hyper-responsibility concerning the behavior of others. What Jean was able to initially identify was a sense of guilt and helplessness over her brother's "difficulties" in the military. She felt that if she had been a better sister, he would not have been discharged from the military.

As Jean's depression had deepened, she had begun questioning her decision to become a nun. During the early part of treatment, she further explored her sense of vocation, and decided she could continue with the help of counseling aimed at improving her communication skills. Her feelings were complicated when her order decided to terminate her religious training because of her suicide attempt. After further discussion with them, they modified their decision and extended her training period. Jean expressed relief to have another chance, but remained moderately anxious about her relationship with the sisters, fearing dismissal if she "messed up" again.

Jean had been placed in a music therapy group to promote improved communication skills through a creative, expressive media, and, to increase social interaction. The group met daily for one hour. Since the average stay of treatment at the hospital was 3-5 weeks, members were added at any time as space allowed, and generally, left the group at time of discharge. There was an almost constant flow of members in and out of the group, and music methods varied accordingly. The group most frequently operated on an individual-within-a-group basis, with brief periods of stability of membership allowing for true group dynamics to function.

Jean was initially quiet and withdrawn, refusing to participate in improvisation sessions, and passively participating in singing or listening exercises. She borrowed relaxation tapes to listen to in her room to help her sleep at night.

She remained fairly quiet throughout her four week tenure in the group, but her affect noticeably brightened. Eye contact became good, and peer interaction, though still limited, was more open and friendly.

After 30 days of treatment, due to apparent resolution of suicidal ideation, cessation of self-destructive behavior, and brightening of affect, the decision was made to discharge Jean.

Second Hospitalization

Jean appeared to do well after her discharge. She returned to the convent where she was doing her religious training and continued seeing a psychiatrist privately for four months. Then, she began to regress again, following a visit home, where she was once again confronted by the severity of her family's dysfunction. She grew increasingly depressed and irritable. She once again began to question whether she should continue her religious training. She was sleeping poorly at night and unable to concentrate or function well during the day. As her suicidal ideation increased, arrangements were made for her readmission. This time, she remained in the hospital for 4 1/2 months.

At Jean's request, she was placed in my music group once again; she felt safer exploring more difficult family history issues in light of the positive rapport we had developed in her previous hospitalization. Jean became more actively engaged in the group process this time. She found that song-writing was particularly helpful in expressing inner feelings that she had difficulty verbalizing. She also learned how to fantasize while listening to music in a relaxed state and then using the images to help her be more aware of unconscious forces and repressed memories that influenced her current behavior. The positive response of group members to Jean's songs also served to help her build a more positive self-image.

Approximately three weeks into treatment, the group did a series of song writing sessions where many childhood and family issues surfaced. Jean contributed actively, by generating ideas and putting the words into meters to fit the melodies; however throughgout these sessions, she did not personally identify with any of the issues raised.

One day after group ended, she asked if she could bring a song to the group that she had written. This was the first time she had indicated that she ever wrote her own songs. At the next session, in a very nervous, quiet voice, she sang the following song of her own.

> *Children's lives are precious and rare*
> *Treat them gently, handle them with care*
> *See their precious eyes, feel their gentle smile*
> *They're so young and there's so much they really want to know.*
>
> *Butterflies and worlds of "Let's pretend"*
> *Daddy's hand and joys that never end*
> *Some will never know the joys that life can show*
> *fear and pain and loneliness is all they'll ever know*
>
> *CHORUS:*
>> *Lives are precious things*
>> *Fragile like a tiny string*
>> *Just some love is all it takes*
>> *To start a life anew*
>
> *Little hearts are broken easily*
> *Little souls, when cut, will quickly bleed*
> *They must know they're loved, that somebody cares*
> *Otherwise they'll hide away and never take a chance.*
>
> *Beautiful is laughter ringing out*
> *Let them feel the feelings that they feel*
> *Let them dream their dreams; do not block the way*
> *Let us not destroy the hearts and souls of ones we love.*

The group responded positively, indicating that she had put into words many of their own feelings. They asked if she would permit them to make copies of the lyrics, and over the next few days the whole group worked together to learn the song. Jean still had not shared much of her personal motivation for writing the song, saying only that her father had been overly harsh and negative, and her mother highly passive and ineffectual throughout her childhood.

Jean began lingering in the room after the group had left, helping me clean-up and rearrange the room for the next group. Gradually over several weeks, she began to tell me bits and pieces of her story. She had a life-long pattern of keeping secrets that made it difficult for her to share her history. At this time she confided that in order to survive in her home, she had had to keep her thoughts to herself. The threat of emotional abandonment was real, as demonstrated by her father refusing to talk to her for months at a time if Jean displeased him. She reported being confined to her room at age 12 for an entire summer due to arguing with her father about a minor rule infraction at school. She ate all her meals alone in her room, only coming out to use the bathroom and occasional walks in the yard.

It took Jean a long time to trust staff and peers to not punish (or worse yet, shun) her if she displeased us. And she feared that sharing her childhood pain would bring on retribution by her family if they found out, and abandonment by staff and peers if we did not believe her. She was highly self-conscious about not "looking foolish" as demonstrated by her refusal to participate in any form of improvisation. She said that it felt "too open ended, with too many possibilities of failure."

Medically, Jean had begun experiencing marked ataxia, falling on several occasions, bruising her nose and eyes, and requiring wheel-chair transport to off-hall groups. During this time Jean became highly discouraged, and shared with the group that she was having renewed and intensified suicidal ideation. A variety of pharmacological combinations were tried over the coming weeks to reduce both depressive symptomatology and negative side effects.

In music group, her level of participation decreased and she often appeared very depressed, withdrawn and defeated. She insisted on attending group regularly, saying that it was one of the few places she had found acceptance and comfort. After several weeks of being "stuck" in this depressive state, she asked that we sing the song she had written. Jean then shared that she had begun having flashbacks to a time in her childhood when an older neighbor-boy had raped her and threatened her "with more of the same" if she told anyone. She was 7 years old at the time, and related how she tried to tell her mother, but that her mother rebuked her, saying that "good girls" don't talk about such things.

Jean said that she had not begun to remember the incident until about a week after she originally shared the song in group. She told us what strong feelings she had when the group had worked together to write songs and share their experiences with one another. As she tried to understand why she was reacting so strongly, and why she had written the particular song she wrote, her memory of the childhood incident had become conscious. She said that she experienced a lot of embarrassment and shame in telling the group, but felt she had held it in long enough. The group reassured her that the rape had not been her fault, and that she did not need to feel ashamed.

Suicidal ideation began to increase after this time of self-disclosure in group, and Jean engaged in several episodes of superficial wrist cutting. She also developed flu-like symptoms, but later told staff that she had taken a small bottle of aspirin to overdose. She was placed on eye contact supervision for several days as she continued to work through the sexual abuse memories in individual sessions with her doctor. She was not permitted to attend off-hall groups during this time, but the music group made a cassette recording of familiar songs we used in sessions, and gave it to her to listen to until she could return. She expressed deep gratitude for such a caring response.

During these months of hospitalization, Jean made the decision that the life of the convent was not right for her, and began to separate from the sisterhood. Notification from Rome of the official dissolution of her vows arrived at this time, further intensifying her regression. She repeatedly became immobilized by the fear generated from her memories, and the day-to-day decisions she needed to make to establish an independent life-style.

Jean had made plans to move in with a patient she had met at the hospital, and had arranged for a job after discharge. However, in the latter period of hospitalization, these plans fell through due to reasons beyond her control. She had no recourse but to move into a women's shelter in the city and begin looking for a job upon discharge. Jean's intense sense of hopelessness would appear to wax and wane, but finally, she began to stabilize. Due to her insight into the roots of her depression and low self-esteem, and her hard work to use stress-reduction strategies to manage her impulses, it was decided to prepare Jean for discharge.

Preparing for Discharge

Continued treatment with her psychology intern was arranged through the hospital's out-patient clinic. Jean's medication was to be monitored by the clinic's psychiatric resident. Jean also asked me to work with her post-discharge to help provide some stable transition to independent living, and to continue her expressive outlet through music to help defuse continued self-destructive tendencies. Her primary therapist and I quickly established a supportive working relationship to head off Jean's attempts to split. Our goal was to provide consistent treatment to best meet her needs for working through parental transference issues, and to nurture and support her while she mastered tasks of independent living.

Two weeks before her discharge, Jean experienced a high level of anxiety over leaving the safety of the hospital. She had experienced tremendous gratitude toward, and comfort from, the staff and peers who had supported her for the past four months. She seemed to be searching for a way to focus and express her feelings, so I suggested she try writing another song. Two days later she brought the following to group:

> *Deep within each of us*
> *Lies a special kind of place*
> *A place where love can root and grow*
> *And touch our very hearts and souls.*

No one finds this special place
By searching hunting on their own
For this place can not be found
It needs another's love to guide the way.

CHORUS:
>*You touched me*
>*You reached into my darkness*
>*You found me crushed and broken*
>*I turned away in fear and you didn't walk away,*
>*No, you stayed.*

The path is long and sometimes hard
There are many times I want to quit
Then I feel your love within my soul
That's when I find the courage to go on.

How can words express my gratitude
For the kindness that you've shown
If your love had not reached out to me
There's so much of me I would have missed.

The group once again affirmed her ability to put into song a similar sense of gratitude for the support they had felt and the increased sense of personal growth they had experienced in treatment. This time Jean was better able to share how the song expressed her feelings and had grown out of her experience.

Out Patient Treatment

Jean moved into a shelter and began the process of job hunting. She did volunteer work at the hospital, helping with evening recreation activities. It provided her with further staff contact, participation in group activities and a sense of contribution to the recovery of other patients.

We spent the first 3-4 weeks adding to her group song recording. She would choose 2-3 songs per session, practice them once or twice, record them, and then talk about why she wanted them included on her tape.

Jean quickly secured a job in a nursing home as an aide, but left after only a few days. She became discouraged by the hard physical labor required and the depressive surroundings. Shortly thereafter, she took a job with a family of two professional adults and 3 small children, doing house cleaning and child care. She initially experienced a lot of anxiety about whether they would like her. She would come into sessions anxious or in some way upset, but often unable to identify why.

Using New Age style music (her choice), we would do imaging exercises to help her explore, and hopefully identify, the source of her feelings. For several weeks her images included some type of ferocious dragon or mythical beast. She finally was able to identify this image as a symbol of her self-destructive impulses. She learned to gauge the seriousness of her impulsive thoughts according to the size and degree of danger felt in her imaging. When the "beast" began approaching equal size with her, she needed extra reinforcement in the form of phone calls, relaxation exercises, journal writing and/or other expressive activities. The strategy of sharing about her self-destructive feelings, but not permitting acting out, seemed to help manage her behavior well into the fourth month of her out-patient work.

Writing a Life Song

During one of our imaging sessions in the tenth week of treatment, I used the title track from David Lanz's "Cristofori's Dream." Jean had a very different experience, imaging scenes throughout her life, feeling sadness and hurt, as well as moments of hope and well-being. She described her images as giving her "little windows" into the future of "what might be." She was so moved by the music, she asked if I would play it again.

As the introduction led into the melody, she began quietly singing:

> *Storm clouds and darkness and fears*
> *Shadow the days of our lives*
> *Filled with long lonely hours*

I quickly began writing - she stopped the tape and rewound it, singing the lines again, then adding:

> *Days pass so quickly and yet*
> *Too many hours to think*
> *Of the sad regrets.*

She talked about how the housework part of her job afforded her too many hours to ruminate on past memories. She could have fun in the morning with the kids, but a sense of doom or hopelessness would override all the good feelings as she did laundry in the afternoon during their naps. Her fear of going out and about in a strange neighborhood also contributed to feelings of loneliness and isolation.

We closed the session by deciding to continue working on this song. Jean had been feeling a strong desire to write another song, but felt her melody ideas were too simplistic for what she wanted to express. She felt that "Cristofori's Dream" could become an expression of her own dream. For the next nine weeks, we spent one session a week talking, writing and processing until we had completed lyrics for the entire piece. The other session each week was used for singing, relaxation or imaging.

Stanza Two

Rainbows and moonbeams and sunshine and candlelight
All flicker softly
And gently they light up

The darkness which covers our dreams and our mem'ries
Of days in the sunlight,
Which guided our way through

The caves and the caverns - the labyrinth patterns,
The maze that we follow throughout
The days of our lives.

Jean had been feeling frustrated at how elusive the moments of hope were. She felt she was wandering through dark caves of hurtful memories that blocked her ability to feel gratitude for her current situation---living with a caring, concerned family, safe and warm, with two committed therapists and several good friends. She felt guilty for not feeling gratitude.

Stanza Three

Spiraling downward, we follow the child
Which can lead us to heights
Which we thought we'd forgotten.

The laughter and joy that we shared with a toy -
It was special and innocent -
Loving - forgiving.

Always afraid that the moments of peacefulness
Soon would be stolen
And smashed in an angry attack.

Jean began to realize how she did not trust "good" feelings because she was always vigilant to anticipate when "the attack" was going to come. Her relaxation exercises worked for the moment she was engaged in them, but the positive effects quickly dissipated as she began wondering when the punishment or negativity would begin. She began to have some insight about how that fear was a learned response from her childhood, due to her father's behavior.   As an adult, she knew on a cognitive level that she would not actually be punished for everything she enjoyed, but internally she still felt the fear of the child and anticipated the punishment anyway.

Stanza Four

> *Feeling afraid to let go*
> *Of all the pain and the sorrow I know*
> *Fearing that change just won't work out.*
>
> *I don't know how to believe*
> *In all I am or the things I can be.*
> *I just don't know...*

This was the first time Jean began to articulate her fear of "getting better." Her borderline personality features had been evident from the middle of her last hospitalization, but her narcissistic neediness and fear of abandonment seemed to move into uncharted territories at this point.   Her symbolic dragon began growing with no abatement.

Jean talked about her fear of the psychologist and me terminating treatment if she mastered independent, healthy living.   She recalled the death of a neighbor woman who had been particularly supportive throughout her childhood, and how difficult it had been for Jean to cope with that loss. She also recognized that at least part of her motivation for joining the convent was to surround herself with a stable resource of supportive people. Her emotional instability had escalated when her training forced her to move about, frequently changing the people closest to her.

Stanza Five

> *Just when I feel all the pain's been discovered*
> *Another new memory*
> *Sends me to depths of*
>
> *Despair and confusion well up all around me*
> *I feel I am drowning and sinking -*
> *I panic.*
>
> *The voices of Daddy -*
> *The silence of Mommy...*

Jean was tapping into her rage toward her parents and then increasing her self-destructive thoughts as an intense sense of guilt and disloyalty took over.   She also continued to experience fear that her primary therapist and I would terminate treatment. No amount of reassurance on our part helped to decrease her obsession with this fear. We began to work from the premise that she was projecting her desire to leave therapy onto us, caught in an internal battle between wanting to be free of self-destructive thoughts and behavior, but not wanting to mature and live independently.

Stanza Six

> *As each new day starts to dawn*
> *I want to look at the face of the sun -*
> *letting the dark drift away.*

> *I need to hear things anew -*
> *Try to believe in the things I can do*
> *No matter what those things may be -*
> *I have a right to be free...*

As Jean's primary therapist and I approached the idea of her internal conflict over treatment and what "getting well" symbolized for her, she was able to more consciously grapple with her fear of becoming a mature, independent adult. The locus of control was still external; the pain would "drift away," and it was the responsibility of others to tell her what she needed to hear.

Stanza Seven

> *Storm clouds and darkness and fears...*
> *Shadow the days of our lives...*

> *Out of the past will come voices which haunt me,*
> *And though they are strong,*
> *I can't let them beat me.*

Jean was beginning to recognize her need to identify negative inner messages and replace them with healthier ones. The locus of control was beginning to shift inward. As her cognitive understanding grew, unfortunately, so did her symbolic dragon - she was calling her primary therapist with increasing frequency, almost once a day, as self-destructive thoughts increased. It was during this time that she shared with us that her in-hospital fall attributed to ataxia had been a deliberate, self-destructive "accident."

We became increasingly concerned over Jean's ability to maintain independent living. She was clearly using her phone access to her primary therapist in a manipulative way, promising to not hurt herself if he would just talk to her for a while. We worked on additional back-up with the psychiatric resident following her for medication.

During the next month, we each took a week's vacation, and her employment family prepared for a four week vacation trip. There had also been increased stress at work with the birth of a fourth child.

Stanza Eight

> *Small seeds of hope that lie deep down inside me -*
> *I'll nurture and care for*
> *Until they have grown into*
>
> *Hopes, and the dreams that had long been forgotten-*
> *They struggle for life in the midst of suppression.*

Jean took a dramatic "flight into health" this week. She made many connections about how she was acting out her fear of independence by calling for more frequent support. Her phone calls dropped to twice per week. She made arrangements to meet a friend for dinner and a movie. She was appropriately assertive in asking her employers for some much needed time off. She shared openly about her fears that each of us would be traveling on our vacations, and how that brought up irrational fears that we would be injured or killed. She expressed relief that we were not taking the same week off, so that she would still have some continuity of treatment.

We planned to use our last week before my vacation to finish the song, and make a recording of it for her to keep.

Stanza Nine

> *A light in the darkness -*
> *A path through the troubles -*
> *I'll follow until I have reached*
> *The way of new life.*

Jean talked about the sense of loss she was experiencing as I prepared to leave on vacation. She also expressed relief that we had finished and recorded the song to help "hold her over" until I returned.

The week-end that my vacation began, Jean made an unplanned visit to see her parents (only the second visit since leaving the hospital). We had talked about how destructive her father's negativity was for her still fragile self-image. During this visit, she was able to ask him to stop putting her down, and she helped him cut paneling for a family room. She found that having a work project to share helped ease their time together, and at the end of the week-end, he thanked her for her help. These were big steps in their relationship.

The next week-end, she went to the convent alone to pick up the remainder of her belongings. She had not discussed either of these out-of-town trips with us prior to our vacations. In the meantime, she was helping her employer family pack and prepare to leave on their month's vacation.

The series of reminders of previous losses and of temporary vacation losses seemed to unravel any progress Jean had made. Her intense need for reassurance that we were not leaving her seemed at times to be a regression to a two-year old's fears around "object permanence." If we were not in sight, she was not emotionally convinced that we existed, although cognitively she knew we did.

When we both returned from vacation, the threats of self-injury took on renewed vigor. We tried to convince Jean to admit herself to the hospital in her catchment area, since she could no longer promise her own safety. As we worked to pursue legal avenues to have her committed for an evaluation, she put her face through a storm window and was rushed to the hospital for emergency treatment.

It seemed at the time to have been a cathartic experience, releasing repressed psychic energy. Jean was finally able to accept that we were not going to repeat childhood patterns of abandonment. She was also, for the first time, able to identify positive qualities in herself, strengths that she could use to help her continue to grow and heal. She successfully worked through several anxiety attacks without resorting to self-destructive behavior to relieve the tension. She felt she could use these experiences to say "no" to herself and utilize more healthy coping tools.

With understandable reservations, Jean's employer-family required tremendously restrictive "promises," creating an increased subservient situation for Jean. She decided to "house sit" alone for a friend in long-term residential treatment, and procured a job in a national department store's catalogue mail room.

Three weeks after her release from the hospital, her primary therapist and I held a joint session with Jean and her family. She had first suggested it to them in her visit home, and with her readmission to the hospital, her parents requested a session to help them understand Jean's continued suicide attempts. Their concept of emotional illness was similar to "getting over" the flu.

Jean was able to share the pain she experienced in not being supported by the family. The parents were able to share how hurt and frustrated they were hearing this; essentially, they felt their actions of providing food and shelter were ways to show support. They admitted that they did not know how to be supportive "with words." The parents also related some of their personal history. There was clearly multiple generations of alcohol addiction and physical abuse on both sides of Jean's family. They expressed interest in continuing to meet, and certainly used their first session in a surprisingly useful manner.

During Jean's first week of full-time employment, two weeks after the family session, she reported having been sexually molested on the way home late one night. We each had several extra sessions that week. Due to inconsistencies in her story, we were never certain about what, if anything, had actually happened. Jean became increasingly needy as additional vacation time for her primary therapist and I approached. The primary therapist was also beginning to suggest various options for their continued work once his residency ended at the hospital and he began private practice work.

As Jean's anxieties continued to escalate once again, we decided to set clearer boundaries, giving her the choice of working through her feelings without hurting herself, referring her to a psychiatrist for more support, or having her become part of a day treatment program for more support. We made it clear that we were willing to work with any outside support needed to ensure her safety.

Eight weeks after her emergency hospitalization, she once again went to her parents' home without notifying us or planning ahead with us. A week later she was rehospitalized, having taken an overdose of Trilifon. I had a joint session with her hospital therapist, outlining my desire to have her in a safe, structured program, as I could not assume sole responsibility for her treatment. Her out-patient primary therapist had also made it clear that he was concerned about continuing to work with her unless she was involved in a more structured program. Jean agreed to enroll in a day-treatment program, and would look into various options while I was away on vacation.

She remained in the hospital for 3 1/2 weeks after my return from vacation, primarily due to the slowness of making arrangements for her discharge. The seriousness of her suicide attempts disqualified her from various half-way house programs where she could have lived in a more supportive environment. We felt concerned that her fear of living alone would undermine any sense of support found in a day-program. She finally contacted the public mental health agency near her parents, deciding to move home, attend a day-program there until a bed became available in a half-way house in her home town.

Jean talked openly about the risk involved in living at home, but she felt strongly that there were few other viable options available. I regretfully agreed. We worked through closure as she prepared for discharge, reviewing the history of our time together, naming the strengths she had begun to discover and reframing the hurtful experiences as resources from which to learn.

We maintained contact over a six month period, with approximately once a month phone calls. She was briefly rehospitalized two more times before finally being placed in a half-way house. The program had a blackout period and she has not contacted me since.

DISCUSSION AND CONCLUSIONS

All of us who worked with Jean marvelled at her determination to put herself in potentially healing situations. She certainly had a strong desire to find a more satisfying way to live, and she desperately wanted to share that insight with her family. She showed great determination in trying to take suggestions, she was grateful when people put forth effort on her behalf, and she helped draw us in as willing co-workers in her healing journey. At times, her indomitable spirit led the primary therapist and me into *countertransference reactions*: we would use her willingness to work as an excuse for us to assume care-taking roles, when firmer boundaries would probably have been more useful.

It was through music that Jean was able to first experience her creativity, and to share her inner self with others. She described few moments of feeling fully human in her life until she shared her first song in the music therapy group. She felt empowered to release her "inner dragon," and hopefully, find a way to subdue it.

I do not know how significant the music experience will prove to be in Jean's life, probably because our time together ended long before any ultimate sense of healing or renewal was evident. Jean made copies of our music tapes so that she would not wear them out playing them over and over again. As she was preparing to move to the group home, she was making a fresh set to take with her.

Jean's primary therapist and I felt frustrated that better support systems were not available for her, especially when she needed safe transitions from out-patient to in-patient and more structured living situations. Cognitively Jean was too high functioning for typical long-term psychiatric day-program clients. And yet she clearly did not have the stability or autonomy necessary to live independently. We seemed to be trying to provide early infancy stability that Jean needed to develop trust and ego strength, and at the same time, we had to encourage Jean to become more autonomous and independent.

I felt both privileged to have been able to share in Jean's courageous journey, and frustrated at my personal and at society's limitations in providing adequate, healing care.

GLOSSARY

Borderline Personality Disorder: "The essential feature of this disorder is a pervasive pattern of instability of self-image, interpersonal relationships, and mood, beginning by early adulthood and present in a variety of contexts. A marked and persistent identity disturbance is almost invariably present. This is often pervasive, and is manifested by uncertainty about several life issues, such as self-image, sexual orientation, long-term goals or career choices, types of friends or lovers to have, or which values to adopt. The person often experiences this instability of self-image as chronic feelings of emptiness or boredom. Interpersonal relationships are usually unstable and intense, and may be characterized by alternation of the extremes of overidealization and devaluation. These people have difficulty tolerating being alone, and will make frantic efforts to avoid real or imagined abandonment... Recurrent suicidal threats, gestures, or behavior and other self-mutilating behavior (e.g., wrist-scratching) are common in the more severe forms of the disorder. This behavior may serve to manipulate others, may be a result of intense anger, or may counteract feelings of 'numbness' and depersonalization that arise during periods of extreme stress. Some conceptualize this disorder as a level of personality organization rather than as a specific Personality Disorder." (APA, 1987, p. 346).

Major Depressive Disorder: "One or more depressive episodes, and has never had a manic episode or hypomanic episode" (APA, 1987, p. 228).

Major Depressive Episode: "Dysphoric mood or loss of interest or pleasure in all or almost all usual activities and pastimes. The dysphoric mood is characterized by symptoms such as the following: depressed, sad, blue, hopeless, low, down in the dumps, irritable. The mood disturbance must be prominent and relatively persistent, but not necessarily the most dominant symptom, and does not include momentary shifts from one dysphoric mood to another dysphoric mood, e.g., anxiety to depression to anger such as seen in states of acute psychotic turmoil." (APA, 1987, p. 218)

REFERENCE

American Psychiatric Association (APA) (1987). Diagnostic and Statistic Manual of Mental Disorders - IIIR. Washington, DC: Authors.

Guided Imagery And Music (GIM) With A Dually Diagnosed Woman Having Multiple Addictions

EUGENIA PICKETT, M.A., L.C.S.W., AMI Fellow
Psychotherapist- Private Practice
Baltimore, Maryland

Abstract: This case describes how GIM helped a 35-year-old woman who had a dual diagnosis of major depression and addictions to food and alcohol. In the course of therapy, the woman identified and worked with various parts of her self, until she could coordinate and integrate their roles in her recovery process.

INTRODUCTION

Penny enters my office. Her eyes are downcast and she is mumbling, "I am drowning... invisible...empty." Her pain is alarming, yet it lets me know that she will probably accomplish important therapeutic work today. I smile as we sit down. As she looks at me, I see fear in her clear blue eyes and tension furrowing her brows. This 39-year-old, 295-pound woman is exceptionally well-dressed, and is groomed to perfection. I hand her the art materials and say, "Show me how you are feeling right now." As she reaches for the chalk box, I notice that her light perfume has carried a delicate sweet scent into the room.

With shaking hands, Penny picks up the purple chalk and draws vertical parallel bars descending from the top to midway down the paper. She reaches for the black chalk, and slowly colors in three large black areas, pressing hard and moving the chalk methodically up and down at the bottom of the paper. With a fiery red chalk, she then fills in the spaces between and around the black areas, and then colors all the remainder of the paper with yellow. Her drawing is tight and compartmentalized. "My addictions," she announces in a trembly belligerent voice; then tears fill her eyes as she says, "I am so trapped." I direct her to the recliner, cover her with a light blanket and suggest she focus on her breathing..."Allow each inbreath to take you more deeply into your feelings and your self... and each outbreath to assist you in relaxing...I am with you now and will stay here with you while you explore whatever you need to explore today."

I put on Pierne's "Concertstucke for Harp," and Penny embarks on the imagery portion of her session. As the music resonates with her emotional nature, tears begin streaming from her eyes, and she reaches out for my hand. This is our first intimate contact today. "I feel so far away from you," she says. I take her extended hand in one of mine and cradle her neck with the other. Encouraging her to be with her strong feelings, I again reassure her that I will remain by her side. As the music continues, she says, "I am so alone... always alone...alone...I feel myself lying here...heavy... ugly...fat...sad...behind a big wall...[she sighs]...the fat is my fault...if I didn't eat so much, I wouldn't feel like this."

This session is one of several which marked the beginning of Penny's shift toward recovery. Previously we had been working in traditional, verbal psychodynamic psychotherapy. And although she progressed in self-understanding, she had bouts of extreme depression, and her addictive process was essentially untouched. Her weight increased to almost 300 lbs. Penny had psychiatric and substance abuse problems, and was in need of simultaneous treatment for both. She was suffering from a recurring major depression in addition to food and alcohol addictions.

Dually diagnosed persons exhibit complex defenses of denial, and as a result are often very difficult to treat. The dual problems make them less amenable to conventional treatment approaches (Evans & Sullivan, 1990). Something more is needed. Beyond theory and method, they need to be engaged on an experiential level (Hornyak & Baker, 1989), and sometimes they need psychotropic medication.

It was not until she began working creatively that Penny began her recovery process. About Guided Imagery and Music, Penny says, "My problems were so deeply buried and well protected, that I used to be unable to release control and allow them to surface... The music relaxes me into almost a dream state and feelings deep within me rise to the surface... This therapy seems like it works from the inside out... Talk therapy used to work from the outside in."

THE THERAPEUTIC APPROACH

Imagery

Guided imagery can be systematically used to bring about changes in emotional health. Information from the past, and the affect associated with it can be used to make sense of obstacles to emotional health in the present. For example, when unresolved grief issues are creating relationship problems, asking a client to imagine placing a flower on a parent's grave usually elicits more emotion than talking about the death which may have occurred many years before. And once the affect is expressed, a person is able to get beyond the grief.

Pribram (1981) described thinking as a process of searching through holographic memory in an imaginative and emotional mode. Based on this, he proposed that problem-solving is a sequence of repeated searches through holographic memory in imaginative and emotional modes. These repeated searches help to generate additions to previous holographs while also providing opportunities to rehearse new ones, thereby creating new possibilities for solving a problem, and ways of evaluating them.

Systematic use of the imaginative process makes it possible to both assist in eliciting emotional response, and in generating resourceful behavior. Leuner (1984) encourages his patients to daydream on specific themes, and then guides them through their emotional responses to desirable changes in affect and attitude. He uses his technique in short-term psychanalytic psychotherapy, and claims that it changes both perception and behavior. An individual can both explore emotions and then imaginatively create or generate more adaptive behavior. Cameron-Bandler and Lebeau (1985, 1986) provide specific formulas for this process.

Music

Music animates the emotion below consciousness (Sessions, 1971). It reaches into the imaginative mind, beyond defense mechanisms, and accesses possibilities for self exploration, sometimes presenting emotions and moods that we have not felt before. One reason for the link between music and emotions is that they both unfold and reveal themselves through time. Zuckerkandl (1969) explained how there is "an interconnectedness between phrases, [wherein] each musical tone points beyond itself... We are auditively in the tone and... ahead to the next tone..." This means we are literally carried through our emotional experience by the movement of the music from moment to moment. Grof (1985) noted how this facilitates therapy: "Music creates a continuity and connection in the course of various states of consciousness," and when used in a therapeutic context, it "creates a continuous carrying wave that helps the subject move through difficult sequences and impasses" (p. 386).

Guided Imagery and Music

Guided Imagery and Music (GIM) as originated by Dr. Helen Bonny (1978a, 1978b, 1980) is a method of self-exploration in which classical music is used to access the imagination. The technique is sometimes referred to as music assisted psychotherapy (McDonald, 1986), because music is the medium used to interact with and therapeutically influence the imaginative process. When chosen appropriately, music---being itself simultaneously multidimensional---will evoke emotional response, activate the senses, impact physiologically on the body, and stimulate symbolic representation or imagery (Bonny, 1986). Music-facilitated imagery such as this brings therapeutic issues into focus, thus making it possible to both work with them and to generate adaptive solutions (Bonny 1978a). Clark and Keiser (1989) further state that GIM helps a person to strive towards wholeness by self-actualization in the imaginal realm. For this reason, outward therapeutic changes resulting from an inward journey often yield benefits beyond stated therapeutic goals.

Typical GIM sessions are 90 minutes in length. The beginning of each session includes a preliminary conversation, guided physical relaxation, focused concentration on an image relevant to the client's goals, and the selection of a taped music program. Each taped music program is carefully constructed for both musical contour and the various elements which contribute to it (Bonny, 1978b). The contour is designed to carry the listener into a deep emotional experience, and then deliver him/her safely back to the present; it begins at a baseline, builds to a peak, stabilizes and then returns to the original baseline. The musical variables within this form are pitch, tonality, rhythm, tempo, vocal and instrumental considerations and mood. Tapes for music sessions are selected on a session by session basis so as to match the mood and needs of the client. Once the music begins, the therapist encourages, comforts, and actively inquires into the client's imaginative process as it is occurring.

Advanced, specialized training in GIM is necessary to use the method professionally. Besides having the necessary knowledge and skills to use GIM, Bonny describes the trained GIM therapist as a good listener, empathic, self-confident, imaginative, and intuitive (1980).

BACKGROUND INFORMATION

Penny is a 35-year-old, divorced woman who is obese. She has been in treatment with me for five years. She and her 11-year-old son live with her parents. At the time she began treatment, Penny was afraid to be alone at night, and was sleeping in the same bed with her son. He was plagued by multiple allergies and a school phobia. She moved back home with her parents when she left an emotionally and sexually abusive marriage which lasted for five years. She was out of touch with her feelings, overeating, abusing drugs, and dependent on alcohol. She seemed unsocialized, and she did not know how to carry on a conversation about herself.

Her father is an alcoholic and a retired railroad worker, who according to Penny, was disappointed when she was born because he wanted a boy. He was hard on her. She said he cursed her, called her names, and tried constantly to make her rough and tough. In fact, she felt that she had not received even the slightest approval from her parents until she gave birth to the son they wanted her to be.

Her mother, who worked outside of the home as a secretary, did not protect Penny from her father's alcoholism, his roughness, or his abusive language. Penny remembers being jealous of her sister who she says was very smart, feminine and popular.

She remembers her peers ridiculing her from an early age, and although she has lived in the same city all her life, she has no friends except for the ones she has made since she has been in therapy. She did poorly in school, and until two years ago believed she was "stupid."

Her eating disorder began in adolescence. She says that after school she would frequently eat an entire loaf of bread with lunch meat, and then buy more food to replace it before her parents came home. As an adult she learned to binge and vomit, and at the time she began therapy, she was bulimic.

Penny missed a lot of school as a child and adolescent, due to multiple colds, allergies and asthma. When she began therapy, she was sick a lot. She was taking oral medication for hypertension, weekly allergy shots for asthma, and she had kidney stones. Her blood pressure is now normal, she no longer takes allergy shots, she has developed no more kidney stones and is rarely sick.

Penny was not sexually active until marriage. During the marriage, her ex-husband encouraged and enjoyed bondage and beating as part of their sexual experience. She says she enjoyed hurting him. She is attracted to women, but has never had a sexual relationship with one. She has been sexually inactive since the end of her marriage.

Penny has had no hospitalizations except for childbirth and no previous psychotherapy.

TREATMENT PROCESS - THE BEGINNING

Developing trust was a major issue for Penny in our early work. We focused on two things. The first was for her to learn how to carry on a conversation about herself with me, and regardless of whether it really mattered to me if she did. The second was for her to discover what a therapy relationship is all about and whether it would work for her. Sessions were difficult for us both, and contained long periods of time when neither of us said anything. I was more comfortable with the silences than her confrontations of me; she was more comfortable with her confrontations! Eventually we developed a therapeutic alliance.

Our next focus was on her parenting skills. Her son needed protection and care. He needed to have his own room and bed, and he needed to be going to school. She learned to set limits, for both herself and him, while also becoming a caretaker who could properly express both positive and negative feelings. She got him in his own bed and to his own therapist, and his school phobia subsided quickly.

Then Penny began her grief work---a process which continues today. She began dealing with the pain of losing her marriage, and she discovered how she used her addictive behaviors to control this pain. She voiced her realization quite clearly: "Alcohol and fat keep me safe." I expressed my concern about her weight and her drinking, and how they were affecting her health; it was clear she was on a slow suicide path with alcohol and food. At the time, I did not know that she was abusing her prescribed medications as well. She talked about her feelings of worthlessness and about there being "somebody in me who wants to be free." She began attending Alcoholic Anonymous (AA), and started the recovery process. In the months that followed, her misuse of minor tranquilizers, blood pressure medications, and randomly chosen "over the counter" drugs was exposed. As she "got clean," Penny became more frightened about exposure. Deeper feelings were closer to the surface. Being in recovery, she could not flee to her previous safety with alcohol and drugs. Being close to me began to feel dangerous. She was afraid most of the time. Her binge eating and purging skyrocketed.

It was at this point that we began to work with music and imagery. Her food addiction, which had been present all along, was more accessible because of her recovery process with alcohol and drugs. So we began working directly with the addictive process. As this work progressed a major depression recurred, and the physician with whom I work prescribed Prozac.

GIM TREATMENT PROCESS

The Wall

In our initial work with GIM, Penny was confronted by a very high and very thick black cement wall. She said, "It looks like a dam, and it keeps everyone out and holds all my secrets in... I dwell on the private side and allow no one in... Some others know parts of the private side, but only as much as I want them to know... I can be on the other side of the wall if I want." However, she spent all of her time isolated behind the wall, and was becoming lonelier and lonelier. Penny decided she wanted to remove the wall but was afraid of losing control if she did.

One day she said, "It has gotten too painful to maintain such a solid and tall wall." She had been drawing pictures and bringing them to therapy, and I noted a change in the wall's height. In her session, Penny tried adding a door, but then voiced her fears: "There will be no way to control the door once it is opened... My secrets will spill out and people will come in...I will lose my protection and won't be able to close the door." She decided to make the wall lower instead.

Eventually, Penny added doors with locks on her side. This was about the time she started making new friends. As subsequent GIM sessions dealt with making friends and being close to people, she added windows. Then the wall itself changed from black concrete to grey stones and mortar, with vines and flowers growing on it.

The Addict

In working with addictive behavior, the person I first see in my office is the one who wants to be more disciplined---the one who wants to recover from the addiction. The undisciplined part that overindulges with food, alcohol, or drugs, rarely presents for psychotherapy. Successful therapeutic work involves getting the addicted part of that person involved in the recovery process.

What follows is a transcript of one session with "The Addict" in Penny. I used a programmed tape entitled "Mostly Bach" which was created by Bonny (1978b). The music is very regular and structured. It is continuous, complex, and exalted in mood. The music helped to give Penny the energy and power needed to work productively with intense psychological material.

I started her with an induction that invited the part of her that is out of control and taking control with food, to come forward and to join me in the treatment room.   As Bach's "Passacaglia and Fugue in C Minor" began playing, Penny looked peaceful. Her breathing was deep and regular. Her eyes began moving underneath closed lids and she said, "I am outside in a park...There are many trees... The grass is green, light green like in the spring.. It feels good to be here...I feel good ... My body feels light."

I asked, "Is the part of you who is causing trouble with food around?" Penny's face changed to a deep frown, and holding her breath said: "Yes, and she is surrounded in darkness... dark gray." I reminded her to keep breathing evenly, and made a suggestion that the music could help her to meet and talk with this part who has been causing trouble. Then I suggested that Penny thank both herself and the "Other Part" for their willingness to communicate with one another.

During Bach's "Come Sweet Death," Penny made friends with her Other part, as I helped her to ask: "What do you do for me?   How are you helping me? What is your usefulness?" Penny continued a dialogue with that part of herself for some time.

Trying to clarify its positive intentions, the Other Part told her, "I help you to relax, and to feel comfort and love." I suggested that Penny and her Other Part together search for alternatives to eating which would fulfill the positive intentions of relaxation, comfort and love.

During Bach's orchestral "Partita," Penny and her Other Part came up with several alternatives. Penny should resume work on her crafts, garden and car. She and Other Part also reached an agreement to generate more alternatives as necessary, rather than to revert to out of control eating behavior.

During Bach's "Little Fugue in G Minor," Penny, with the help of her Other Part, began to explore and try out these alternatives. She saw herself creating ceramics and waxing her car, and she felt herself sorting packages of flower seeds for planting. I asked her, "Are you satisfied with what you have done so far? Do you have any concerns about doing this in the future?" She answered: "My Other Part is not satisfied because there is no plan to keep other people away. That's what binging does---it keeps people away." Penny continued: "When I was waxing the car a new friend dropped by, and my Other Part did not want to talk to her." I told Penny that she and her Other Part can make anything happen here, and that the music might be of help." She replied: "My Other Part and I are blended together, and we are telling my new friend that I need space to be by myself right now."

The Adagio movement of Brahms' "Violin Concerto" began playing and Penny said, "I have just finished waxing the car and I am going off by myself on a walk."   Towards the end of the movement, Penny returned home and decided to call her new friend on the telephone. She thanked the friend for understanding, and she told her that she was learning to say no, and that she would be asking for help too, because she had difficulty being close. Her new friend said that she had the same kinds of difficulties.

During the Largo of Bach's "Double Violin Concerto," Penny repeated the process of choosing more appropriate alternative behaviors.

The Talking Loaf Of Bread

How many times in your life have you spent an hour and a half talking with a loaf of bread? Probably never! And you would probably balk at spending the price of a therapy session to do it. Clients often joke about spending money to listen to music, beat pillows, talk to chairs, fight with dragons, or confront whatever arises in their imaginations. And their jokes always end with their talking about how it was actually useful to do so.

Hornyak and Baker (1989) stress engaging eating disordered clients on an experiential level, because the disorders have cognitive, somatic and body image components. Persons suffering with them are cut off from their internal experience. Experiential techniques facilitate body responses, affect and cognition in a process which claims and integrates their inner world.

A pivotal session for Penny's eating disorder is one where she literally spent most of the session expressing her feelings to and making an agreement with a loaf of bread. The programmed tape I used for this session is entitled "Positive Affect" (Bonny, 1978b). It is characterized by music with very similar tempos and provides the listener with both orchestral and choral support.

During Elgar's "Enigma Variation #8," Penny sets the stage for the session by setting an imagined table before her with white bread, salt, crackers, doughnuts, orange soda, alcohol and milk. She acknowledges that food is her friend, and after the full chords and expanding crescendos of the Variation #9, Penny chooses her most important friend---the white bread.

During the tender and tranquil vespers from Mozart's "Laudate Dominum," Penny talks lovingly to the bread in soft tones: "You are so soft...always there when I need you... so nice to touch...You taste so good... and, no matter how much of you I eat, I can always eat more... You make me feel so good...and can even put me to sleep." She picks up the bread lovingly, and as the soprano voice is heard, the bread speaks to Penny in very gentle tones: "I know why it is hard for you to give me up... I am here for you always... You have trouble breathing when you think about giving me up." At this point, I say "That feeling is grief... loss... You might let yourself experience it here...now... The music will help...I am with you."

Barber's "Adagio for Strings" begins, and Penny says to the bread: "You make up for not having friends." As the sustained melodic line of the music builds evenly to its second peak, a full emotional response is evoked, and Penny calls out, "It never hurt as bad then [when little] as it does now... This is so hard... Without you [bread] to keep my hurt down." I ask her: "Penny, right now, how are you feeling?" While the music repeats its crescendoes and diminuendos, high and deep, with waves of tension and release, Penny, with tears streaming down her cheeks says, "I hurt... and I have to cut back even more... This is so hard." I sympathize with and console her about her pain. Then I remind her that her food plan includes bread, and that she might think about what she can eat. She then says to the bread, " I must substitute you for whole wheat... and I don't like it... It makes me mad...and it hurts... But I want friends, and stuffing myself with food prevents me from having friends... So I am going to have to feel the hurt when it happens instead of stuffing it." As the music resolves, Penny says "good-bye" to the loaf of bread, and sighs deeply.

The "Offertory" from Gounod's "St. Cecilia's Mass" has a stabilizing effect on Penny, and her focus shifts from food to friendship. "There are people in my life I can trust, and open my heart to," she says. Then as the emotionally moving "Sanctus" begins, the orchestra, soloists and choirs identify themselves, and Penny begins to name her new friends: Paula, Joan, Betty---and me, her therapist.

The programmed tape concludes with the powerfully majestic "Death and Transfiguration" by Strauss, and Penny returns to a stabilized and restful state of mind.

The Dead Tree

Penny took a very big step into recovery when she stopped drinking alcohol and abusing medications. When she began her food plan, the depression she had been masking with substances became evident. It came and went in cycles, and she struggled with it on her own, with the support of weekly GIM sessions, group psychotherapy, and *12-step recovery* meetings.

After four months, Penny went into two very deep depressions which she tried to "eat her way out of." Despite working very hard in therapy, she could not control the depression. We discussed medication. She was afraid of abusing it. I brought up the possibility that appropriate antidepressants could allow her to engage in fuller recovery, and although medication would not do the work for her, it might help her to do it. She did not have to abuse the medication, but could learn to take it appropriately, just as she had learned to follow a food plan. She went for the evaluation for antidepressants and began taking Prozac.

The following session occurred about three weeks later. I used the programmed tape called "Death - Rebirth," created by Bonny (1978b). I chose it because Penny was in another cycle of grieving, and I was looking for musical selections to help her to complete the cycle, and perhaps start anew with the medication. The tape can be used to assist individuals in going through with the feelings aroused by grief.

Supported by the low, mournful tones and slow measured rhythms heard in "Siegfied's Funeral March" from Wagner's "Gotterdammerung," Penny revisited the house she had lived in with her ex-husband. It was a part of her life that she had not completely let go of, and as she approached the house she found herself walking to the back yard.

Then, while experiencing seventeen churning minutes of sad and pulsing, never resolving 5/4 meter, and the rising and falling, struggling motif in Rachmaninoff's "Isle of the Dead," Penny grappled with a dying tree which she found in the back yard. Her head hurt, her chest hurt. She sat with the tree, a very heavy tree. She struggled to prune away the dead wood. At times, when she wanted to give up, I would remind her: "I am with you, and I will stay with you in this process," and "The music will help carry you through whatever you need to do today." Shuddering as the piece was coming to a close, she said: "I have to take some of the tree with me, and leave some of it behind." I assured her, "You can take what you need... leave what you don't, and be able to sort the difference." Then she told me she was in a light, which she said, "feels like being in a bubble... It looks so soft...It feels so soft" as the piece finally ended.

The "Crucifixus" from Bach's "B Minor Mass" follows in a somewhat slower, more subdued and restful mood. She sat in the light with the pruned tree on one side of her and a stack of dead wood on the other. She asked me if she could "Stay here in the light" and I replied, "Yes." Then she said, "Wherever else on earth I go, I am going to sit under my tree."

"Der Abschied" from Mahler's "Song of the Earth" followed, and Penny started to sort through the dead wood. As the mood of the music changed, Penny said, "I don't have to be here alone... I will bring my friends... Paula, Joan and Betty... and you." And with the uplifted tones of the music, she became more uplifted and said: "I am not ugly... I am real pretty," and pointing to her chest, she said, "Special, joyful."

Judge, Nasty, Tender, Child, and Shame

As Penny put it, "Through my imagery work with music, I have been able to see how big and powerful my addictions had become... The work enabled me to separate the parts that make up my addictive nature... Once I could identify each part and [its] purpose or need, [it] became less powerful... Once the parts were revealed, no one of them alone was strong enough to activate my addictive process... [Now] the parts are currently working together to help with my recovery... each part through GIM has been able to surface... and to be respected and loved."

Penny's alienation from the world was a direct reflection of a deep internal alienation from herself. It took about three months of work to clarify this process, and in that time, Penny became aware of and learned to appreciate some of the fragmented parts of her ego which had been working at cross purposes. This process allowed her to relate in a caring manner both toward herself and toward the fragmented parts of her ego structure which were created by early neglect and trauma.

The various parts known as "Judge," "Nasty," "Tender," "Child" and "Shame" had been functioning in opposition to one another. The ego state work involved meeting them, finding out their trauma, consoling and respecting their presence, and then eliciting their aid in caring for Penny (Watkins & Watkins, 1990). She now understands them as the parts of her addictive process. When she begins to relapse into food, Penny rebounds quickly by using GIM to work with these parts of herself.

"Judge" was the angry part of Penny who turned out to be essential to Penny's intelligent functioning in the world. After she introduced herself and told her story, her judgementalness became less negative, allowing a positive critical intelligence to emerge. This critical intelligence has been exceedingly helpful to Penny when one of her parts was about to get her into trouble.

"Nasty" was the three-year old Penny who had been held down and smothered to sleep by her mother because she would not stay in bed at night. Nasty's healing was from asthma, and she was rather easily healed with warmth and a tender listening ear. Penny no longer needs to takes asthma medicine. Sometimes Nasty's job is to slow the therapy down to protect Penny from changing too fast.

"Tender" is the one who eats. She was always present as the target of mother's frustrations, and as a result developed multiple somatic problems and drug abuse. Tender used to be sick all the time. Now instead of taking drugs, she takes an antidepressant medication and bubble baths. When Penny is doing well, Tender often gets scared and begins to look for problems. The other parts have learned to console, cradle and nurture her. This is helping to transform her fear into the strength and courage to continue recovery.

"Child" thinks she is ugly as a girl and should have been a boy. She hated to wear tops on her bathing suits because then everyone knew she was a girl. Her daddy wanted a boy. She disappointed him. She spent this past summer being proud to wear bathing suits, thanks to Judge, Tender and Nasty. And she is getting better since she has learned to talk about her feelings.

"Shame" has been the last part to emerge, and is both boy and girl. It usually needs lots of encouragement to talk when something is on his/her mind. It remains confused about sexual preference right now, and needs some clarification. Its breathing is usually rapid and jerky. Shame has a lot of anxiety and suspects that a lot of pretending is going on about being healthy. I often assure Shame that relapses do occur, and the point is to rebound from them quickly. I also assure Shame that a large part of getting better is acting "as if" things are better. Shame says it was easier when things were "black and white," and that all this "gray" is confusing.

DISCUSSION AND CONCLUSIONS

Persons who are dually diagnosed are among the most difficult to treat; their dual problems make them more defended and less amenable to conventional treatment approaches. With Penny, conventional psychotherapy only took us so far into her psychology and her recovery. We did not touch the deeper stronghold that the addictive process had on her until we began the GIM work. It was only then that she began working directly with her food addiction and the overwhelming alienation she was experiencing from the world and from herself. It was with GIM that she directly confronted her feelings about early childhood rejection, deprivation and abuse. It was with GIM that she worked through ridicule by her peers and her husband. And only now, by virtue of having done this work and having been in recovery, has she been able to make friends with people who value her as an individual and with them develop relationships which meet her needs.

I think conventional psychotherapy probably would have viewed her as damaged, and the results might have been to expect less of her in therapy. Conventional therapies work rationally in an ordinary state of consciousness, and in a rational, ordinary state, she probably would have searched in panic and confusion for solutions to her overwhelming pain; in a creative state, the unconscious seems to bring solutions out of nowhere. Creative approaches call on fuller potentials than conscious process. With Penny, the conscious world of words is joined with the unconscious world of imagery, and in the interaction, I believe that she is able to simultaneously explore regions closed to one and open to the other. Music, as the medium, carries her through the process. It takes unecessary pressure off both Penny and me, and places responsibility on the creative process itself.

Therapy within a single modality (like words alone) can be limiting. It would be far more difficult to generate alternative behaviors from an addict, to talk with a loaf of bread about selecting a more appropriate diet, to sort learnings of the past from what needs to be grieved by pruning a dying tree, or to separate and converse with fragmented parts of an addictive nature. Interplay between several modalities like words, imagery and music, which involve the creative process, opens psychotherapy to a broader experience of human potential and healing.

GLOSSARY

Dual diagnosis: A substance abuse/dependency disorder, and a co-existing psychiatric disorder requiring simultaneous treatment.

12-step Program: Guidelines for recovering from alcoholism developed by the founders of Alcoholics Anonymous (AA).

REFERENCES

Alcoholics Anonymous. (1981). Twelve Steps, Twelve Traditions. New York: World Services.

Bonny, H. (1978a). Facilitating Guided Imagery and Music Sessions: Monograh #1. Salina, KS: Bonny Foundation.

Bonny, H. (1978b). The Role of Taped Music Programs in the GIM Process: Monograh #2. Salina, KS: Bonny Foundation.

Bonny, H. (1980). G.I.M. Therapy: Past, Present and Future Implications: Monograh #3. Salina, KS: Bonny Foundation.

Bonny, H. (1986). Music and healing. Music Therapy: Journal of the American Association for Music Therapy. 6A (1), 3-12.

Cameron-Bandler, L. (1985). Solutions. San Rafael, CA: Future Pace.

Cameron-Bandler, L., & Lebeau, M. (1986). The Emotional Hostage. San Rafael, CA: Future Pace.

Clark, M. F., & Keiser, L. H. (1989). Teaching Guided Imagery and Music: An Experiential-didactic Approach. Garrett Park, MD: Archedigm Publications.

Evans, K., & Sullivan J. M. (1990). Dual Diagnosis: Counseling the Mentally Ill Substance Abuser. New York: Guilford Press.

Grof, S. (1985). Beyond the Brain: Birth, Death and Transcendence in Psychotherapy. New York: State University of New York Press.

Hornyak, L. M., & Baker, E. K. (1989). Experiential Therapies for Eating Disorders. New York: Guilford Press.

Leuner, H. (1984). Guided Affective Imagery: Mental Imagery in Short-term Psychotherapy. New York: Thieme-Stratton.

McDonald, R. (1986). Healing Parasitic Infection Through the Partnership of Guided Imagery and Music and Applied Kinesiology. Unpublished paper. Salina KS: Bonny Foundation.

Pribram, K. H. (1981). Languages of the Brain: Experimental Paradoxes and Principles in Neuropsychology. New York: Brandon House.

Sessions, R. (1971). <u>The Musical Experience of Composer, Performer and Listener</u>. Princeton, NJ: Princeton University Press.

Watkins, J., & Watkins, H. (1990) Ego state therapy. Workshop at the Second Annual Eastern Regional Conference on Multiple Personality and Dissociation. Mt. Vernon Hospital, June 21-25.

Zuckerkandl, V. (1969). <u>Sound and Symbol: Music and the External World</u>. Princeton NJ: Princeton/Bollinger Paperbacks.

CASE THIRTY-FOUR

Group Music Therapy
For Women With
Multiple Personalities

C. JOHN DUEY, M.M., CMT-BC

Music Therapist

Northwestern Institute

Fort Washington, Pennsylvania

Abstract. *This case describes the use of songs, improvisation, and music imaging with an outpatient therapy group for 12 women with multiple personality disorders. During the 28-week period, the women confronted issues resulting from histories of sexual, physical and emotional abuse during childhood. Group goals were to develop trust, to promote sharing with others, and to express feelings. Special considerations for male therapists working with this population are noted.*

INTRODUCTION

Multiple Personality Disorder (MPD) began to gain attention and recognition in 1980 because of its acceptance as a diagnosis by the American Psychiatric Association (1987) and because of an increase in articles being published about the disorder (Ross, 1989). Since MPD is one of the newer disorders to be recognized in the mental health field, a brief description will be given here.

The criteria for multiple personality disorder given in the DSM III-R (APA, 1987) are: "The existence within the person of two or more distinct personalities or personality states (each with its own relatively enduring pattern of perceiving, relating to, and thinking about the environment and self). At least two of these personalities or personality states recurrently take full control of the person's behavior" (p. 272).

According to Braun and Sachs (1985), three factors are necessary for multiple personality disorder to develop: (1) predisposing factors - an individual's capacity to dissociate (i.e., to separate from or sever parts of one's self), as well as exposure to an inconsistently stressful environment; (2) a precipitating event - a traumatic event during childhood which required dissociation; and (3) perpetuating factors - repeated and unpredictable abuse that required further dissociation. Through repeated abuse, the dissociated memories become linked into separate personalities (or "alters") within the same individual system.

BACKGROUND INFORMATION

Group Membership

The outpatient group program described in this case was designed for women who: (1) met criteria for a diagnosis of multiple personality disorder or dissociative disorder, and (2) maintained involvement in individual therapy while participating in the group. The group consisted of 12 women, ranging in age from 25 to 47 years.

A core of four women joined the group within six weeks of its inception and remained active during the 28 week period described in this study. The other eight women joined the group at different times and remained in the program for an average of five weeks.

Group attendance and attrition were affected by a number of factors. Four of the women were experiencing difficulties that could not be safely handled by their primary therapist or the outpatient group and they were subsequently hospitalized. Three of those women attempted suicide either before or after being hospitalized. Two women dropped out of the group because of conflicts with work schedules or heavy work loads, and another woman could not keep up her long commute. One woman quit individual therapy as well as the out-patient group due to denial of her diagnosis, but came back to the group at the end of the 28 week period. Only one woman was asked to leave the group because of inappropriate behavior. She disrupted the group by trying to manipulate the therapist, tantrumming when she did not get the amount of attention she required, and verbally attacking another group member because of jealousy over an outside therapist. Braun (1986) notes the difficulties of including patients with borderline personality disorders in a group, and recommends screening out such patients.

Shared Problems

Child abuse has been found to be the cause of multiple personality disorder in 97% of the cases (Braun, 1990). And this certainly held true for the outpatient group. Based on the various forms of abuse experienced by the women in the outpatient group, the main thing they shared was a life history of trying to survive severe emotional and physical trauma during childhood.

It was difficult to get a complete history of the abuse experienced by each woman. Because of their dissociation or multiplicity, the women were often not fully aware of the frequency or severity of the abuse perpetrated upon them. Histories for this group were gathered by psychiatrists or primary therapists through various means, including sodium amytal sessions, hypnosis, interviews, and ongoing therapy. In some cases, memories of the most traumatic experiences were recovered at later stages of therapy.

In all cases it was found that the women were severely and repeatedly abused from an early age (two to five years). The abuse was most commonly sexual and incestuous involving fathers, stepfathers, brothers, and an uncle. Some of the women were also sexually abused outside of the family in places such as boarding schools, through satanic cult involvement, and in one case, involvement in a child pornography ring.

Other psychiatric disorders found in the group included: major depression, suicidal tendencies, self-injurious behavior (e.g., cutting and burning self), drug or alcohol abuse, and eating disorders (e.g., anorexia and bulimia). In addition, the women generally experienced difficulties as they worked through these problems---difficulties that affected their capacity to be self-sufficient and pursue career goals, as well as their ability to form and maintain satisfactory relationships with others.

During their involvement in the group, four women worked full time, two worked part time, and six were not able to work. One woman was married, two were separated, and nine were single.

METHOD

The outpatient group met for a three-hour session each week. The first

90 minutes were led by a social worker, after which the music therapist conducted a one-hour session. The remaining half-hour was co-led by both therapists and was devoted to reviewing and processing the entire morning session, and checking on the status of the group members. After every session, the music therapist and the social worker spent time discussing the group, identifying issues that emerged in their respective sessions, and planning for the following week.

A variety of music therapy methods were used, including: song association exercises, lyric discussion, song-writing, song dedications, poetry and short story writing, instrumental improvisation, and imaging to music and lyrics. Each of these methods served a different function in evoking and addressing issues.

TREATMENT PROCESS

At the time of this writing, the group had been together for over seven months. During those 28 weekly sessions, goals were varied. This study will focus on the work done with regard to three main goal areas within the music therapy sessions: developing trust, breaking the code of silence, and exploring feelings. What follows is a chronology of how the group developed with regard to each goal, and a description of the methods used.

Developing Trust

A major concern from the very beginning was to establish trust within the group so that therapy could proceed. As the group progressed, it became apparent that establishing trust was not just a hurdle for the group to overcome for the sake of it's own development, but was a fundamental issue in the growth and change of each individual. For all of these women, trust had been betrayed repeatedly throughout their childhood, not only by parents but also by other authority figures.

Group activities were therefore designed to allow the women to share information about themselves in a safe manner, while also encouraging interaction. Activities to encourage sharing included: comparing song preferences and associations, describing themselves in terms of song titles, bringing in songs to share with the group, imaging to music, and making up short stories. Activities for developing interaction and cohesion were: group instrumental improvisation, song writing, and group poetry writing.

During the first session, the therapist spent some time talking and getting to know the women in the group. Two songs were presented for discussion: "True Colors" by Cyndi Lauper and "Either Or Both" by Phoebe Snow. "True Colors" was chosen because of its themes of acceptance and love of self. The group was asked to respond to any word, phrase, idea, or feeling presented in the song. One woman picked up on the final lines: "So don't be afraid to let them show, your true colors; true colors are beautiful, like a rainbow." She saw the colors of the rainbow as representing the different alters in her system.

The second song, "Either Or Both," also contained a theme of acceptance, but it took the perspective of asking for acceptance of positive as well as negative aspects of self. In response to the song, the group talked about self-acceptance coming before acceptance by others. Many seemed to connect with the line in the song: "Sometimes these hands get so clumsy, that I drop things and people laugh. Sometimes these hands seem so graceful, I can see them signin' autographs."

During the second session, the group completed an adapted version of the "Personal Song History Questionnaire" (Bruscia, 1986), which requests 12 song associations (e.g., favorite song, love song, sad song, etc.). The manner in which the women filled out the questionnaire gave some indication of how they function psychologically. One woman expressed trouble connecting to music, had a fleeting memory of songs, and could only list titles to 5 of the 12 categories. This was consistent with her history of loosing large amounts of time, feeling fuzzy, and dissociating often.

Another group member talked about a very strong connection to music but had difficulty with naming a song that reminded her of each parent, and a song that reminded her of childhood. She continues to feel obligated to her family, despite being emotionally and physically abused by them.

Another woman expressed difficulty choosing between different titles being called out by many different "alters" (or different personalities). This woman has co-consciousness with some of her alters (i.e., awareness of more than one personality operating at once), and she also has some degree of control over switching executive control between alters. Executive control occurs when one of the multiple personalities becomes dominant, and thereby directs the person's behavior, feelings, etc..

During the third session, the issue of trust was raised by listening to "And So It Goes" by Billy Joel. The group talked about the vulnerability they experienced when trying to trust others, and the methods they use to establish trust. One woman asked very directly, "How do I tell the sheep from the wolves?"

During the eighth session, the group was asked to imagine a story involving action to go along with some instrumental music. Because of their propensity to dissociate, all tasks involving imagery were done without physical relaxation or inductions. The women were also kept seated, and not asked to close their eyes. Despite these conditions, their imagery was surprisingly rich and relevant to their inner experiences. The music used was "Mercury: the Winged Messenger" by Holst.

One woman described the image of two figure skaters on a frozen pond. When asked what perspective she had during the imagery, she said that she had become the marks being made on the ice by the skaters. The group talked about her sense of being under other people's control and feeling stuck or "frozen." That theme had emerged earlier during the fifth session, when she pictured herself as a handle on a wagon waiting to be pulled. (She was listening to "The Life Is a Red Wagon" by Jane Siberry).

During the ninth session, after listening to "Castle On a Cloud" by Andrew Lloyd Weber, the same woman found herself in "the catacombs" and was given the assignment of finding a way to get out of them. She eventually found her way out but once above ground, she put down her heavy load and was ambivalent about returning to the catacombs or continuing her climb up the slope.

Another safe method for the group to share information about themselves was used during the tenth session. A list of 180 song titles was culled from a list of popular songs from 1955 to 1985. The group was asked to find approximately ten song titles they connected with their feelings or experiences. After choosing the titles, each person in the group was asked to read each title and explain its significance. This activity enabled people to talk about feelings or experiences that might not have come up in any other context. Each song title had the potential to trigger a memory or feeling. The structure of the activity gave permission for each person to only share what they were comfortable telling the group.

Instrumental improvisation was introduced during the sixth session as a means of having some fun, looking at group dynamics, and developing group cohesion. The group was terrified of the instruments, and two women left the group as they saw the instruments arriving. One of the women who left later told us that her father was a musician, and that he made her play an instrument but then later would not allow her to play because she was not good enough. The other woman who left was abused in a child pornography ring, and she associated some types of music with her abuse.

Those who remained in the group were quite timid in their approach to the instruments. The group style of playing was quiet and conforming. It appeared that no one wanted to stand out from the rest of the group. As a result, the music became increasingly soft and monotonous and consisted of all rhythmic "grounds" (simple beats or repeated patterns) and no "figures" (distinct or differentiated patterns). One woman was frustrated because her child alters were excited with the opportunity to play, yet she was not having any fun. Another woman admitted that she had fun doing her own thing without attending to the rest of the group. A third woman complained that she felt pathetic sitting on the floor and playing instruments.

The group discussed and tried different methods of making changes in the music, such as splitting the group into contrasting sections and breaking out of the ongoing rhythm, but these attempts had minimal success. The experience of playing the instruments in the group was important for pointing out the group dynamics; on the other hand, it was not very enjoyable and did not contribute very much to group cohesion, at least in the beginning.

In subsequent attempts to build cohesion, imagery was found to be useful in unifying group improvisations. In the twentieth session, which is described more fully below, the group was asked to develop an image of something that was soothing or comforting. The women then shared various images and further elaborated on them until they formulated a strong, collective image that could be represented through musical improvisation. It was also useful to give the group an image of something they had all experienced (e.g., approaching storms) to guide their improvisations. Presenting these kinds of images as the focus for improvisation gave the group permission to explore and express a much wider range of emotions than they would have done with the instruments alone.

Song-writing was introduced during the thirteenth session but proved to be quite difficult for the group. The group had no trouble writing some humorous verses for a twelve bar blues, but they avoided singing the resulting song. Only one woman would sing along with the therapist, and after several attempts to increase group participation, a member of the group suggested that everyone simply hum a blues melody while the therapist played guitar. Afterward, the group discussed its resistance to the singing and reasons for it. The discussion revealed how singing connected to the emotional abuse the women had experienced as children. As children, they were all told in various manners that they could not sing and had to be quiet, or that they did not have any rhythm and could not dance, etc. And aside from this denegration of their abilities, many women had been forbidden to express their feelings in any way.

The group planned a party around the holidays for the sixteenth session, and they asked for games, music, and food. The therapist brought a singing game and some lyric sheets for popular songs from the sixties. Surprisingly, the entire group played the game and then proceeded to request songs for the group to sing together. The crucial difference between this session and the previous one where they resisted the singing seemed to be that, this time, the group asked to sing, whereas in the previous context, they were being expected to sing.

As the group developed more cohesiveness, an exercise was used in the nineteenth session to allow them to give more feedback to each other. Each person was asked to describe themselves in terms of a song on a record album. The songs on side A would be the internal characteristics that others may or may not be aware of; those on side B would be those characteristics that they try to portray to others or that they thought people perceived about them. After the group had a chance to share their song titles, they then gave feedback about the characteristics that people thought were internal or external. The exercise gave the group permission to give useful feedback and talk more directly about one another in a structured, protected situation.

A turning point in the group cohesiveness came during the twenty-second session, when the women worked together to write a group poem. The activity was structured so that one person would write a line and then leave only the last word of the line visible for the next person to continue. The group participated freely in the poetry writing, but began to complain about the background music. They also voiced concern about being judged on their poetic talents. By the time the poem had gone around the full circle and was read, the women began to criticize the different contributions--- exactly what they initially feared would happen.

As we analyzed what had happened in the process, the group came to some important insights. Everyone acknowledged how concerned they were with doing the task correctly. They expressed fear that they might have misunderstood the task and would be embarrassed when the poem was finally read to the group. There was concern over relating appropriately to the one visible word and over giving a good word for the next person to develop. They were concerned about exposing their creative talents to the group, and expressed discomfort with that vulnerability. The activity did not give them the control they needed to be comfortable.

From a group dynamics point of view, the group had also developed enough cohesiveness to confront and resist the therapist. Until that session, the group had cooperated as best they could with all of the activities presented. Now, it appeared that the group was finally expressing a transference reaction (i.e., relating to the therapist as if he were a person from the client's past). These circumstances seemed to bring out their unspoken suspicions that he was "just another male authority figure" who was making them uncomfortable by asking them to figuratively expose themselves and show their vulnerability. It was significant that the group was able to shift its focus from the task at hand, to their difficulty with trust and their transference with the therapist. In a sense, the group was saying that their feelings were more important than the expectations of others, and men in particular.

The social worker helped to process the transference reaction and to explore the issue of trust further. One woman was able to admit that her mistrust of the therapist had been ongoing, despite the fact that trust had never been broken. Further discussion pointed out that, paradoxically, it had taken her several months to build up enough trust to tell the therapist of her mistrust, and that the question was much broader: Could she trust anybody?

By the twenty-fifth session, the format had changed. It was no longer necessary or desirable for the therapist to be as directive as before. The women were now bringing in their own songs or ideas for the group to process. One woman brought in "Shattered" by Linda Rondstat; another brought a tape recording she made of "The Silver Boat" by Ann Adams, which is a fictional story about MPD. The group even discussed the possibility of creating musical accompaniments to stories.

Breaking the Code of Silence

Secrecy emerged as an issue that related both to trust and to the development of the group. Many women in the group kept their abusive experiences a secret, both out of shame and out of a desire to survive. In order for the group to begin to share their secrets, trust had to be built.

As children, there were severe consequences for telling "outsiders" what was going on behind closed doors. Those lessons of secrecy had been reinforced for years and internalized to the extent that some women had even developed alters who would retaliate through self-injurious behavior for too much disclosure.

Methods of working around the fear or consequences of telling secrets included using imagery and metaphor for expressing feelings, bringing issues to the group through song lyrics, and discussing songs containing themes of self-disclosure and secrecy. It was essential for the therapist to respect each individual's own pace for opening up and sharing with the group.

During the fourth session, the group was asked to listen to some instrumental music and write a short fantasy piece. The music was "Venus: The Bringer of Peace" by Holst. Two members of the group wrote very similar stories in which they were young and alone, near large bodies of water, in seemingly idyllic surroundings, but in imminent danger from some unknown source. Different aspects of the stories were discussed including isolation and generalized fear of the unknown.

"Fairy Tales" by Anita Baker was discussed in the sixth session. One woman related how her family kept up a perfect front for everyone to see, and that no one suspected the incest that was taking place. Another woman spoke of a couple in her family who seemed to have a perfect relationship, and she questioned how it could be so perfect. The group continued discussing the difference between appearances and reality.

The theme of keeping secrets was directly addressed in the seventeenth session by listening to "Code of Silence" by Billy Joel. One woman brought up the subject of her efforts to get information relating to her abuse and her abuser. She had an impending family reunion and was looking at strategies for sharing her diagnosis of MPD with relatives and getting information about her father who abused her. Another woman expressed frustration from trying to talk to her parents about her abuse and not being able to get any information or validation from them.

"Valley Vista" by Wendy and Lisa was introduced in the twenty-third session because of the imagery and ambiguity of the lyrics. The theme centered around returning to a home from the past and being ambivalent about going inside. The group was asked to talk about what the house represented to them and why there could be so much ambivalence about going inside. Two women kept their discussions on a concrete level, relating how when they return home they still feel obliged to meet parental expectations.

One woman spoke of learning to make decisions and gaining self-respect, but when returning home, being treated by her parents as if she could not make decisions and had no self-respect.

Exploring Feelings

Another central issue for the group was the dissociation of or compartmentalization of feelings into various alters. Painful or uncomfortable feelings were often dissociated or felt by some alters but not others. The powerful link between the music and lyrics enabled issues to be processed on an intellectual as well as affective level.

Through song discussion, the group was able to explore feelings with which they were not comfortable yet decrease dissociation or loss of control by keeping the person present through group interaction and support. When issues became too difficult, the therapist would intervene by maintaining a dialogue with the group member, asking her to describe the feelings and at times asking for eye contact. This dialogue and eye contact would often help to keep the person connected to her present feelings without dissociating.

A wish for "the good mother" was explored in the ninth session, and deep emotions were aroused. "Castle On A Cloud" by Andrew Lloyd Weber was played and discussed. The entire group was disturbed by the song. One woman found herself in "the catacombs," and another woman was thinking about her friend's suicide ten years ago. After spending some time discussing the song, another piece of music was played (Adagio from Bruch's Violin Concerto), and the group was asked to follow the music and find a way to a more comfortable or positive place before leaving the session. One woman imagined herself as a butterfly in the graveyard where her friend was buried and found herself flying to the car where her friend committed suicide. She rested on the vacuum cleaner hose connected to the exhaust pipe but could not look into the car. The group listened to her talk about her friend, her sense of guilt for not doing something when she had received hints, her long period of mourning, and her difficulty letting go. It was the first time that someone had shared such intense feelings with the group, and it was the first time that the group had an opportunity to support and comfort one another.

The other woman found her way out of the catacombs but expressed ambivalence about leaving that place. A third woman could not stay with the imagery at all, and thought about all the things she needed to do that day. The differences in how each woman responded brought to light how each of them had developed different ways to survive their feelings.

Loneliness was explored in the fifteenth session through the song, "The Sea and Me" by Eddie Brickell. First the group was asked to write down their responses to the song, then after replaying the song, they were asked to respond from another point of view---perhaps from another alter's point of view. This exercise was intended to acknowledge the existence of the other alters and to invite their input in a controlled manner (i.e., without giving full executive control to that alter). It also had the unexpected effect of allowing the person to be resistant to the song on one listening, and then be given the opportunity to respond differently on the second listening.

Discussion centered around the simplicity of the song and the central idea in the line "there's nobody here to mess it up for me... but man I wish I had a hand to hold." The group talked about isolation and one woman mentioned that she is becoming like her mother in her isolation, and that she does not like it and wants to break out of it. A related idea emerged in the third session when talking about finding a safe place. Someone in the group responded that being alone was not safe because of destructive alters that could emerge. All of the women in the group agreed that they never really felt safe---with or without people.

Anger was explored during an instrumental improvisation in the twentieth session. The group was doing a series of improvisations based on imagery they had developed (e.g., being on a tropical island, being stuck on the expressway, witnessing a thunderstorm come and go). In the process of creating thunder, one woman began playing the bongo drums with an intensity that was not the norm for the group of for herself. Afterwards, the group discussed the improvisation, and it became apparent that she had surprised herself with the intensity of her playing and then dissociated the rest of her playing. Issues of anger, ambivalence about the person toward whom the anger was directed, and fear of the loss of control if the anger were expressed had been discussed in the earlier session with the social worker. The therapist therefore asked the woman if she would like to continue exploring this anger with the instruments. She agreed and the therapist suggested that she reproduce the intensity for the anger from before, and then begin to experiment with losing control by going in and out of time with the group beat.

The group agreed to provide a strong and steady accompaniment and the therapist set up signals for the woman to leave and come back to the group rhythm. When signalled to let herself go, her playing became highly energized incorporating cross rhythms, punctuations, much syncopation and flurries of rhythmic patterns. As she appeared to be losing some control and was beginning to hurt her fingers, the therapist signalled her to join the group beat which she did very quickly. The exercise was then repeated, and after playing with the group for approximately 30-seconds, she again played with much intensity. This time, however, she did not need to be called back by the therapist. Afterwards, the group talked about how anger can be used as an energizer if it is recognized, and that it can be released in small amounts to test control.

Loss of innocence was brought up in the twenty-fifth session after listening to "Shattered" by Linda Rondstat. The woman who brought in the song described the way the song affected her and described one of her paintings that was inspired by the song. Another woman imagined a wall of denial between herself and her alters being slowly shattered. Another woman talked about the ways to fix the many parts of shattered glass (glue, tape etc.) and finally concluded that no matter how the parts were put together they would never be seamless---the glass would never be the same. She finished her thought with "It's just not fair." The group was silent as the impact of her very simple analogy was felt deeply.

DISCUSSION

The women have made slow but measurable progress in several areas, as a group and as individuals. As a group, they eventually developed enough trust and cohesion to challenge structures or activities given by the therapist, and to provide one another with feedback on their behaviors and feelings. The group also took a new level of responsibility when individuals began bringing in their own songs for exploration within the group. Their level of sharing with one another also increased as the code of silence was relaxed and increasingly more intense feelings were acknowledged.

As for individual progress, feedback from an outside therapist indicated that one of the group members was dissociating less during individual therapy. That same group member also began to make decisions and spend less time "talking in circles." One group member progressed from not being able to sit in the same room with the music therapist to sitting through part of the sessions to staying throughout the sessions (although she frequently dissociates or switches). Another group member who initially presented herself as very "together" was able to show more sides of herself to the group, and eventually get in touch with some of her child alters during the group sessions.

Being a male therapist presented myriad possibilities for counter-transference (i.e., personal reactions of therapists to clients and their transferences). The one that became most evident was the ongoing effort to represent a male figure who was caring and not abusive. This posed particular problems when women in the group experienced or dealt with painful feelings. It was difficult for the therapist to not quickly try to ease the pain or to make the group feel better. One way of doing this was to bring in songs that were uplifting or encouraging to use at the end of the session, with the hope that they would make the group feel better before leaving. Paradoxically, these seemingly "positive" songs often had the effect of depressing the group because the songs touched on their desperate need for love, security, comfort, etc..

Another paradox was that the women were being encouraged to trust the therapist and take risks, while also being made aware of their tendency to please and comply with authority figures. Hence, when the therapist presented a particularly challenging activity or raised a difficult issue, the women were placed in a double bind.

The need to take care of the group was also evident in the therapist's level of directiveness. Although the group, in fact, did need more structure and direction at the beginning, they grew less and less reliant on the therapist as time passed, until eventually they were confident enough to confront him regarding his directiveness and implicit expectations of them.

Music played a significant role with this group of women because of its ability to evoke and support imagery, metaphors, and feelings. Through imagery and metaphor, the women were able to creatively and safely explore very difficult issues stemming from their abuse. Through their affective responses to songs, they were able to acknowledge and work through some very painful feelings in the safety and support of the group.

REFERENCES

American Psychiatric Association (APA) (1987). Diagnostic And Statistical Manual of Mental Disorders (DSM III-R). Washington, DC: Authors.

Braun, B. G. (1990). Dissociative disorders as sequelae to incest. In R. P. Kluft (Ed.), Incest Related Syndromes of Adult Psychopathology. Washington, DC: American Psychiatric Press.

Braun, B. G. & Sachs, R. G. (1985). The development of multiple personality disorder: Predisposing, precipitating, and perpetuating factors. In R. P. Kluft (Ed.), Childhood Antecedents of Multiple Personality. Washington, DC: American Psychiatric Press.

Bruscia, K. (1986). Personal Song History Questionnaire. Unpublished manuscript. Philadelphia, PA: Temple University.

Ross, C. A. (1989). Multiple Personality Disorder: Diagnosis, Clinical Features, And Treatment. New York: John Wiley and Sons.

Unit Six

Case Studies with Adults
In Medical Treatment

Music Therapy
At Childbirth

DIANNE ALLISON, R.M.T., B.MUS.
Music Therapist - Private Practice
Melbourne, Australia.

Abstract. *This case study presents the application of music therapy in the antenatal, labour, delivery and postnatal phases of birthing by a 30-year-old primipara woman and her husband. The study outlines the antenatal preparation of music for their labour, and describes the musical, nonmusical and medical events of the labour and delivery. Postnatal follow-up through questionnaire and discussion with the couple is presented along with the conclusions as to the effectiveness of music therapy assisted labour with them.*

BACKGROUND INFORMATION

The subjects of this case study were a 30-year-old woman, Annie, and her 39-year-old husband, Rob, expecting their first child. Prior to her confinement, Annie was a clerk in the Accounts division of a National Communications Company, and Rob worked as a labourer for a Metropolitan Water Board. Their employment indicated them to be middle-income earners.

Annie and Rob were first made aware of the opportunity to use programmed music at 22 weeks gestation, when their obstetrician gave them a questionnaire designed by the author (hereafter called the therapist) as part of her post-graduate research project on the use of music in pain management during labor. The questionnaire sought information regarding the the couple's intention to use music and/or a support person in addition to the male partner, as well as their general expectations for the labour and delivery of the child. At this stage, Annie and Rob were given no details concerning the programmed music other than anecdotal information from their obstetrician. Their responses to the questionnaire indicated that they intended to use their own music rather than programmed music, and that they were not taking a second support person into the labour. Their expectations were for "active labour if possible in birthing unit but pain relief if necessary." Their preferred methods of pain relief were music, nitrous oxide (gas mask) and massage. They took the option to withhold their names from the therapist but did give the obstetrician's name.

The therapist was introduced to Annie and Rob at their antenatal class, when Annie was at 33 weeks gestation. During the class, the therapist discussed pain management in labour and briefly explained details about previous research findings on the use of music in labour. She also outlined the present research project. By the end of the class session, Annie and Rob changed their minds, deciding to utilize the programmed music being offered. After contacting the therapist, they arranged a private meeting with her.

MUSIC THERAPY ASSESSMENT

The first consultation was held at the therapist's home, a requisite of the research design, when Annie was at 35 weeks gestation. She appeared to be carrying the fetus quite low in utero and, as a result was more comfortable seated on the edge of the couch for most of the 90-minute consultation. Rob, on the other hand sank into the couch next to Annie and appeared very relaxed, resting one foot on the other knee. They were both dressed casually; Annie was in a maternity dress/T-shirt, her hair short and neat; Rob was in shorts, T-shirt and thongs with long shoulder-length hair. They were both relaxed but excited about the imminent birth of their first child.

The consultation was kept informal so as to engender in Annie and Rob a sense of trust in the therapist's professional advice regarding their music for labour, and to enable the therapist to gain an impression of their musical tastes and preferences through discussion about their life experiences. It was also essential to establish a rapport which was both appropriate and conducive to the therapist's attendance at the birth, should Annie and Rob so agree.

Annie's pregnancy had been planned and free of worry. She enjoyed excellent health, with Rob commenting that her health had been better during pregnancy than when not pregnant. (Annie was susceptible to headaches but had experienced none since becoming pregnant). An ultrasound was performed at 17 weeks gestation in order to determine an estimated due date for the birth, which was set at February, 1991. An obstetric visit at 30 weeks queried fetal growth with the suggestion that fetal size was "*small for date.*" Hospitalization was suggested at 32-34 weeks if no increase in size was detected, however, an Ultra-Sound at 36 weeks revealed fetal development to be within normal limits. This episode worried Annie and Rob, but they firmly believed the fetus to be healthy because Annie's health and weight gain had been normal.

Annie's and Rob's musical tastes and experiences were quite different. Annie had received formal piano lessons from her mother who was a music teacher; whilst Rob had received no formal music education as such. Neither of them actively pursued music as a leisure time activity, however both enjoyed listening to music. Annie's preferences were for classical instrumental and middle-of-the-road vocal music such as Elton John, Bette Midler and Lionel Ritchie. Rob, however enjoyed heavy rock music such as the Rolling Stones and The Who, explaining that the discrepancy in their preferred style was more likely to be a function of their age difference of 9 years rather than differences in their personalities. Rob was happy to have any of Annie's preferred music, assuming (quite correctly) that heavy rock music would have a limited role to play in their labour.

Following a detailed explanation by the therapist about music in labour, a music programme was designed to Annie and Rob's specifications. They had brought the required audio-cassettes for recording by the therapist with a "starter" tape being given to them at the conclusion of this first consultation.

The author's impression of this couple at the conclusion of the first consultation was that Rob was easy-going and satisfied that whatever music Annie chose was best for her and their baby in labour. He was positive toward the suggestion of the therapist's attendance at the birth, understanding that active birth may require maximum energy and effort from himself. To this end, he felt a second support who could focus on the music and its function in labour would likely benefit himself, and in turn Annie.

Annie was also relaxed about the labour. Her expectations of the labour and birth were "Looking forward to the birth - hoping for a natural birth if possible." She was slightly hesitant about the therapist's attendance at the birth. This was seen by the therapist, and later verified by Annie as an embodiment of "fear of the unknown" and fear of losing control in front of a stranger. This was not uncommon in primipara women. It was hoped that continued contact with Annie and reassurance and support by the therapist would alleviate this hesitancy.

METHOD

The design of this empirical case study was influenced by three main sources: four American projects researching the same area; the therapist's personal birth experiences; and a six-month pilot project conducted by the therapist prior to commencement of the research project.

Clark (1981), Codding (1982), Hanser, Larson and O'Connell (1983) and Winokur (1984) investigated the effectiveness of music in reducing pain, fear, and/or anxiety responses of women during childbirth. The present research follows a similar design to Winokur's with the use of individualized music programmes for women and their partners in the third trimester of pregnancy. Similarly, couples using these programmes were prepared by the therapist for their use during labour and delivery, with the therapist attending forty percent of these births.

This preparation was done in conjunction with the antenatal classes offered by the hospital where delivery was planned. Antenatal preparation and the actual approach and procedure of labour and delivery in Australia differs greatly from that in the U.S.A., where childbirth classes are usually Lamaze-based. The levels of breathing for stages of labour (i.e. shallow breathing, panting, etc.) have been all but phased out of Australian antenatal preparation, as has the notion of "coaching" women in labour. Similar to both is the aim to educate a woman and her partner in lay terms about the theories, physiology and psychology of childbirth with strategies for coping during labour. However, the greatest difference between the antenatal preparations is that women in Australia are being taught and encouraged to labour instinctively, trusting the process of labour coupled with the knowledge they have acquired from classes. The woman establishes her own natural breathing patterns in accordance with the stage of labour. Women will use different breathing patterns instinctively in labour without necessarily being made aware of them. Rather than "coaching" the woman, partners now take a nondirective, supportive role, trusting the process and supporting the here-and-now of the woman's labour experience. These differences are subtle but significant.

The research project used only *primipara* women. The four reasons are as follows. First, fear of the unknown and the shock of the intensity of contractions once labour is established can have negative effects on a labour and, hence, outcome. If a woman and her partner are not adequately prepared for the psychological and physical impact of labour, there may be a greater need for analgesic and/or anaesthetic pain relief. It is important to note that anaesthetic pain relief through an *epidural* greatly increases the likelihood of a forceps delivery and *episiotomy,* as effective bearing down on the fetus is made difficult by numbed pelvic and abdominal muscles.

Second, if physical and psychological trauma to both mother and child during childbirth can be avoided or at least minimized, the mother has a better chance of bonding and coping with a new routine, decreased amount of sleep and the learning of parentcrafts such as breast-feeding, nappy changing and bathing.

Third, a *multipara* woman will generally already have networked and acquired a support system of at least one other mother within her own community, whereas a primipara woman invariably must begin this networking at the same time as learning to cope with a major change of lifestyle. Continuity of care by the music therapist from the antenatal and labour and delivery period into the postnatal period can assist the assimilation back into the home and wider community.

Finally, multipara women often labour differently with the benefit of experience and hindsight, and as a result can have significantly reduced length of labour and, hence outcome.

A pilot project and the therapist's second childbirth, which took place 6 and 8 months prior to the commencement of the project, also helped to refine the design of the present treatment and research. The purpose of the pilot project was manifold: to test the incidence of active and drug-free labour, as experienced by the therapist, but in primipara women; to refine the recording of music; to determine preferred music styles of women; to refine a personalized clinical approach when attending a labour; and to determine whether specific types of music were more effective at given times in labour.

The pilot project was conducted over six months and was offered to primipara women delivering at the small private hospital at which the research was to be based. The therapist attended five births for experience but prepared music for seven women and discussed its use (no tapes given) with another thirteen. The refined results of this pilot project were employed in designing the methodology for Annie and Rob.

The Tapes

Annie and Rob provided eight blank 90-minute audiocassettes (TDK-D90), for the therapist to make the recordings. Ninety-minute cassettes were used because experience had shown that cassettes shorter in length did not allow optimum process to be achieved with the music; cassettes longer than 90 minutes in length often compromised the quality of the music.

Each tape was designed for a specific purpose, and was to be used during the weeks prior to delivery or during labour itself, as Annie and Rob deemed appropriate. Table 1, which appears at the end of this paper, gives details on the eight tapes comprising the individualized music programme for Annie and Rob. The cassettes were distributed to Annie either by mail or were picked up by her personally. Contact was maintained via telephone. Tapes numbers 6 and 7 were given to Annie and Rob at the final consultation.

The Hospital, Midwives And Obstetrician

Annie and Rob had booked a Family Birthing Unit (FBU) at a 100-bed private hospital 15 minutes drive from their home. The hospital, which had a reputation as being progressive for its encouragement of active labour with minimal intervention, offered two FBUs with bedroom, lounge, kitchenette and bathroom (one with a spa and shower). The decor was in co-ordinated pastel colours with the impression of a comfortable and spacious motel unit. Medical and resuscitation equipment was stored behind floor-to-ceiling pastel curtains at the head of the bed. Lighting was controlled by dimmer light switches and vertical blinds in each of the three rooms. The lounge offered a couch and two armchairs as well as a dining table, chairs and television. Fluids (water, juice, tea, coffee, ice) and snacks were stored within the kitchenette for immediate access.

One midwife was allocated per labouring woman to allow for continuity of care over an eight hour shift, and to decrease the number of people entering the room thus potentially affecting the labour process.

Observations (blood pressure, pulse and fetal heart rate) were monitored hourly in early stages of labour and half hourly once labour was established and progressing. Internal examinations were generally performed only when either dilatation was suspected to be complete or when there were contraindications, e.g., non-progressive labour, fetal distress (as detected via Fetal Heart Monitor or a show of *meconium* stained fluid), examination of position of fetus especially if in abnormal position, maternal distress and the likes.

Annie's obstetrician showed a positive and keen interest in the use of programmed music during delivery.

Final Consultation

The therapist met with Annie and Rob at their home at 39.5 weeks to complete antenatal preparation for using the music programme during labour and delivery. Annie returned two cassettes for minor alteration (i.e. changing two songs on Tapes 4 and 7). Other than this Annie had enjoyed all of the cassettes, and had listened regularly to the "Support - Relaxation" and "Pelvic Rocking - Vocal" cassettes.

Annie and Rob were excited and psychologically prepared to give birth and meet their baby. The baby's head had engaged in Annie's pelvis and was lying in normal cephalic position. Medical observations by Annie's obstetrician indicated that a normal labour was anticipated and imminent.

At the end of the consultation, Annie appeared to be more positive toward the therapist's attendance at the birth. However, the final decision was to be made once labour was established. The two revised tapes were to be returned to Annie 3 days later. Two and a half days after the therapist left them, Annie went into labour (39.5 weeks).

TREATMENT PROCESS

At Home

0200   *Spontaneous rupture of membranes (SROM)* occurs. Annie and Rob are excited; Rob is slightly anxious. Contractions increase from 15 minutes apart and mild to 3-4 minutes apart and moderate. Annie sleeps till 0700.

0845   Therapist is notified. Annie and Rob listen to "Pelvic Rocking-Instrumental" and "Contemporary Instrumental" until leaving home for hospital.

1045   Annie and Rob go to hospital. Therapist is asked to attend. Contractions are 3-4 minutes apart and moderate. Annie is distressed with side effects of onset of labour (i.e., shaking, vomiting, diarrhea). Amniotic fluid begins draining. Annie and Rob are unsure of what tape to play in the car.

At Hospital

1105   Annie is admitted to hospital, walks to Family Birthing Unit, and goes into warm bath which provides immediate relief. No music is played.

1205   Therapist arrives. Contractions are 3 minutes apart and moderate. Annie sits in bath with heels together and knees apart while Rob rubs her back. Annie feels relaxed in the bath and was conscious of different positions to facilitate the progress of labour. Annie listens to "Contemporary Instrumenta" as she is coping well and relaxed. This tape was also helpful to her for visualization in early established labour.

1225   Annie is talking between contractions, and inhales/exhales slowly during contractions. The therapist chooses "Pelvic Rocking - Vocal" as Annie has no signs of tiring and had energy. She felt peaceful and positive and wanted to maintain her general mood.

1230   *Mucous plug* from base of cervix came free while in the bath. New mid-wife comes on duty and introduces herself.

1243   There is a sudden increase in intensity of contractions, 2-3 minutes apart. Annie switches to "Flute/Harp tape." The nature of her contractions and mood changes. Vocal music is no longer suitable, as Annie needs something soothing and relaxing. Annie is managing the pain well so the therapist decides to save the "Support" tape for the next acceleration (speed/intensity) of contractions.

1255   Fetal Heart checked (recorded by therapist).

1305   Contractions are 2 minutes apart and strong. Annie has slight urge to push with contractions. Internal examination by Doctor showed cervix to be 8 cms dilated but with a thick *anterior lip*. Due to the lip, Annie was requested by Doctor not to push as damage to the cervix and moulding of fetal skull would likely result. Urges to push become stronger. Rob and Annie were surprised and pleased that 80% of dilatation had been completed. "Support" tape is chosen, as Annie requires all the assistance and support possible to control her natural urges to push. Music needed to offer her maximum relaxation to decrease any panic or anxiety and to help her rest/sleep between contractions. Volume of music is increased considerably by therapist so as to aggressively draw as much attention away from her pushing urges. Annie nodded her head in rhythm to three regularly sequenced beats in one particular piece of music. She was so relaxed that her head lowered closer to the bathwater with each repeat of these beats.

1330   Annie and Rob are alone in bathroom. Mood was peaceful and Annie was well-controlled, using "Support" tape and prayer to control the urge to push.

1355   Contractions are 2 minutes apart with stronger urges to push on alternate contractions. Fetal Heart rate is taken (recorded). Volume of the music is decreased on "Support" tape as Annie is controlling urges well.

1415   Contractions are further apart (3-4 minutes). Annie tries different positions in bath to encourage contractions but pressure to push increases with the change. She resumes sitting with heels together and knees apart. Annie is tiring and sleeping between contractions. She is shaking with the cold. "Pelvic Rocking - Instrumental" tape is used to encourage gentle movement and to increase alertness. Annie feels disappointed and unsure as to why contractions slowed down. Volume of music is decreased to provide quiet background, and to give Annie the option to use the music actively or just relax to it.

1450   Volume of music is decreased further so as to allow maximum relaxation while still offering support to move if desired.

1501   Annie is very relaxed, slow, and sleepy in bath. "Support" tape is used to encourage Annie to rest and get her sleep between contractions.

1505   Therapist asks Annie if music was suitable. After putting the "Pelvic-Rocking Instrumental" tape on it seemed a little too slow for the present mood. Annie requested "Contemporary Instrumental" after considering the question for about 15 seconds. Annie, Rob and therapist agreed this tape was more appropriate at this time.

1540   Contractions are 5 minutes apart but 2.5 minutes in duration (1 minute moderate pain/1 minute strong pain/30 seconds easing off). The labour appears to have slowed down considerably with contractions seemingly less effective. Annie is aware of slower pace.

1555   Annie gets out of bath to encourage movement, and thus contractions. Doctor arrives. Annie is comfortable standing with her back to Rob and swaying slightly to music.

1605   Annie gets onto bed. Internal examination by Doctor reveals cervix to be fully dilated and effaced. Mood of the room changes with Annie sitting on side of bed and rocking vigorously to music. Midwife asks which position will be used for delivery. Annie is full of renewed energy as she is able to push with her urges and becomes ready for delivery of their child. As Annie sits on the Birthing Stool ready for pushing stage of labour she says to therapist, "This is Van Morrison, isn't it?......the 'Pelvic-Rocking' tape."   Rob sat on a normal sized chair behind Annie on the birthing stool, supporting Annie under her armpits. With each contraction and push she would grasp Rob's fingers.   Annie whispered to Rob, "I don't think I can do this."   The therapist positioned a mirror in front of Annie so that she and Rob could witness the progress of their baby's journey.
        "Pelvic Rocking - Vocal" is used as it matches Annie's energy level without being overly loud and imposing. Annie speaks with the doctor, midwife, therapist and Rob between contractions. Thus, vocal music was appropriate.

1617   Annie is pushing effectively with each contraction. Doctor is lying on floor next to therapist at Annie's feet, observing progress. Annie and Rob rock side-to-side with the music between contractions. Doctor alludes to the music frequently. "Support" tape is used for delivery, as it was the most familiar to Annie and would, therefore be easier to attach to and focus on. Also, if so needed, as the head came onto view she is requested not to push, Annie would have a point of focus for restraining the urge.

1635   Rob changes positions with therapist so as to assist doctor with delivery of their baby. The therapist now sits behind Annie, allowing her to squeeze her fingers and push back onto her during contractions.

1650   Hindwaters of amniotic fluid break as head of baby crowns the perineum. Annie is asked not to push in order to allow perineal stretching. Therapist reminds Annie to focus on the rhythm of the music, which, at that time was appropriately matched to the shallow breathing required by Annie. The doctor encourages small pushes so as to minimize trauma to the perineal and vaginal area. Again, the music has moderately short phrasing which was suited to such short and regular pushing.

1654   Delivery of a live baby girl. The therapist places "Post-Natal" tape on 3 minutes after delivery. The last 20 minutes of labour and the delivery are recorded by therapist and continued post-natally until cassette is full.

1745   The therapist departs the birthing unit, having spoken to Annie and Rob about their immediate thoughts on the experience. Rob states repeatedly that he felt the music was what made the difference to both him and Annie. Annie felt that the music and the prayer together were the effective methods for restraining the urges to push. Both were surprised and very pleased at Annie's ability and strength to complete the labour without drugs for pain relief. The mood was one of pride and elation.

EVALUATION

More formal evaluation as to the effectiveness of music in pain management consisted of giving Annie a Post-Natal Questionnaire and interviewing the couple. The Post-Natal Questionnaire, completed at Day 3 after the birth revealed the following:

1) Annie described the degree of discomfort or pain experienced during labour and delivery as intense. This was level 6 on a 7 point scale which included: None, Very Mild, Mild, Strong, Very Strong, Intense and Extremely Intense.

2) When asked to rank order the effectiveness of various techniques she used in pain relief and management, Annie placed the music first and prayer second.

3) Annie stated that she felt that music was helpful to her during labour. The manner in which music was helpful was that it was a "means of relaxation, distraction for myself and Rob."

4) On a scale of 1-10, Annie rated her childbirth experience as "8" with regard to expectations and satisfaction. The three words Annie used to describe her feelings about her first childbirth experience were "peaceful, relaxed, and beautiful."

5) Annie stated that in retrospect she would "try to stay more relaxed in early stages at home and during internal examinations" for a future labour and delivery experience.

The interview with Annie and Rob post-natally focused on their labour and childbirth experience and how music was or was not incorporated into that experience. The interview took place on Day 7 after the birth, when they were both tired but still happy with the events surrounding the birth of their daughter. Annie said she was most aware of the "Support" tape during her labour. She felt that the tapes which she preferred i.e. "Support," "Contemporary Instrumental" and "Harp and Flute" were the ones she could focus on more readily. On the whole, Annie felt that the music gave her a focus. "I knew the music was there for me - it kept coming to me." Annie felt that she was more conscious of the music in hospital than at home, and at no time did the music or therapist irritate her. Annie felt that suggestions by the therapist as to management of contractions and discomfort were helpful (e.g. breathing/visualizing the music, and focusing on the music at strategic times).

Post-natally Annie still listened to all of her tapes, especially her "Support" tape which assisted with feeding and settling of the baby. Rob admitted to usually being a "bundle of nerves" with anything new, but he firmly believed the music helped him and Annie to relax. He was conscious of the music most of the time, but particularly when the "Support" and "Contemporary Instrumental" tapes were played. Annie and Rob both agreed that they would use music in a subsequent labour.

DISCUSSION AND CONCLUSIONS

The results of the present case study support showed music to be an effective means of pain management for Annie and Rob. Music and prayer were the two techniques used by Annie to control the pain, with music being rated as the most effective of the two. According to a Victorian Birthing Services Review in 1988, 29% of women (multipara and primipara combined) used no drugs or *TENS* units in their labour. Annie was one of those women.

There are many factors which can affect how a woman labours. One of the greatest influences is her physical and psychological approach to her pregnancy and childbirth experience. It cannot be understated that in their relaxed, flexible but committed approach to their childbirth preparation, Annie and Rob improved their chances of having the active, drug-free labour they had hoped for.

The format of this case study may be noticeably different from ones detailing music therapy with a disabled client. Annie and Rob in effect set their own aims for their childbirth experience, that is, active labour to facilitate the birth of their child and drug-free labour so as to minimize any trauma on Annie and the child during the labour process.

Because their aim was achieved, Annie and Rob naturally attributed some of that success to the programmed music. It is difficult to determine whether Annie would have managed her labour as positively without the music. Two main factors contributed to the effectiveness of the music with

Annie, which may not be present with other women. First, Annie already believed in the role of music, and had fully intended to use it during labour and delivery; hence, she expected the music to have a positive effect. Second, she used music as an integral part of her psychological preparation antenatally. Thus, an experimental test of the effectiveness of music would have to control for at least two variables: expectations regarding the effectiveness of music, and the use of music in antenatal preparation.

Another issue is that obstetric research is such that no one labour can be re-constructed or re-experienced. Hence, the events and outcome of a labour such as Annie and Rob's must be accepted as an entire unit---which is quite difficult to match with other couples for experimental purposes. From a clinical point of view, the most important points of discussion seem to be the role and appropriateness of the therapist and the music programme. Aside from all the positive comments, Annie did not fault any choices of music or professional decisions made by the therapist. She stated that at no time did the therapist or music irritate her during the labour. An interesting question, however, is whether music could have been used to greater advantage at various points in the labour, and if so, when.

As obstetricians will verify, hindsight is one of the most important aspects for learning about labour. Hindsight would benefit every primipara woman. However, hindsight of a previous labour is a luxury available only to multipara women---as well as obstetricians, midwives, and assisting therapists.

For this therapist, hindsight brought forth two insights. Firstly, without a doubt, Annie needed the therapist to be present earlier in the labour. The therapist would have used the "Support" and "Flute/Harp" tapes at home in order to calm Annie and to minimize the side effects of the labour (i.e. vomiting and diarrhea, which were causing her anxiety).

The second insight is more of a question with regard to the labour itself. For the final three hours of her labour Annie, due to incomplete cervical dilatation and effacement, had to suppress natural urges to push her baby down the birth canal and thus give birth. By suppressing that urge, Annie was actually causing contractions to regress (i.e. denying her natural urges). The contractions then became further apart. It is difficult to argue which type of music if any could have assisted Annie more effectively at this point. The fact that the therapist tried both active ("Pelvic Rocking-Instrumental") and relaxing ("Support") music as well as asking Annie which music she preferred at the time ("Contemporary Instrumental") meant that every opportunity was given to maximize the music's potential.

Obstetric procedure and outcome have many permutations and combinations and can be discussed ad infinitum. What is clear from this case study, is that Music Therapy-Assisted Labour was an effective pain management technique for Annie and Rob, and that it holds equal promise for other couples who are committed to a similar approach to the birthing process.

GLOSSARY

Active labour: Taking various positions and moving, usually in a vertical fashion, to facilitate the labour process

Anterior lip: Occurs when front of cervix is not thinned evenly, causing partial obstruction of the birth canal.

Cervix: Neck of the womb.

Contractions: Tightening and releasing of abdominal and lower back muscles which draw up the sides of the cervix, causing it to open; can be described as mild, moderate, or strong according to their effectiveness.

Dilatation: Spreading or widening of the cervix, which must reach 10 cms before a vaginal birth can occur.

Epidural: Place in the lower spine where a plastic catheter is inserted in order to inject anaesthetic for pain relief.

Episiotomy: Surgical enlargement of perineum via incision.

Hindwaters: Amniotic fluid which sits behind the fetal head.

Meconium: The first bowel movement of a fetus or neonate, which is usually black, like thick oil.

Mucous Plug: A mass of mucous which seals the cervix during pregnancy, and breaks loose before or during labour.

Multipara: Woman expecting her second or subsequent child.

Perineum: Skin area between the anus and genitals.

Primapara: Woman expecting her first child, having no previous labour.

Small for Dates: Fetus is suspected to be abnormally small for its gestation.

Spontaneous Rupture of Membranes (SROMS): The amniotic fluid surrounding the fetus in utero bursts.

TENS: Transcutaneous Electrical Nerve Stimulation: Two or four electrodes are strategically placed on the lower spine with a hand-held battery pack, and small shocks are administered to block pain messages to brain.

REFERENCES

Clark, M. (1980). An evaluation of music therapy-assisted labor. Unpublished master's thesis. University of Kansas.

Codding, P. (1982). An exploration of uses of music in the birthing process. Unpublished master's thesis. Florida State University.

Hanser, S., Larson, S., and O'Connell, A. (1983). The effect of music on relaxation of expectant mothers during labor. Journal of Music Therapy, 20 (2), 50-58.

Health Department of Victoria (1990). Having a Baby in Victoria: Final Report of the Ministerial Review of Birthing Services in Victoria. Melbourne: Author.

Winokur, M. (1984). The use of music as an audio-analgesia during childbirth. Unpublished master's thesis. Florida State University.

Table 1

INDIVIDUALIZED MUSIC-BIRTHING PROGRAMME

FOR ANNIE AND ROB

TAPE 1: SUPPORT - RELAXATION

Style: Instrumental music from Baroque and Classical periods.
Examples: Mascagni's "Intermezzo" from "Cavalleria Rusticana"
            Gluck's "Gavotte" from "Iphigenia in Aulis"
            Haydn's "Serenade"
            Rachmaninoff's "18th Variation" from "Rhapsody on a Theme of
                 Paganini"
Antenatal: Listen at least once per day from 36th week onwards to relax,
            and to develop an association of this music with relaxation.
            Use as **focus** while relaxing.
Labour: Listen when help, support or comfort is needed, and
            particularly when contractions increase in length of intensity.

TAPE 2: PELVIC ROCKING - INSTRUMENTAL

Style: Instrumental music from Classical Period.
Examples: Williams' "Fantasia on Greensleeves"
            Dvorak's slow movement from "New World Symphony"
            Mozart's "Menuet" from "Don Giovanni"
            Poncielli's "Dance of the Hours"
Antenatal: Listen to when active (e.g., driving, cooking, moving around).
            Learn to associate music with relaxing movement and activity.
Labour: Use during active, later stages of labour (i.e., when nonverbal
            but still active).

TAPE 3: SUPPORT - BACKGROUND 1

Style: Flute and Harp Pieces from Classical and Baroque periods.
Examples: Wagenseil's "Harp Concerto in G Major - Andante"
            Mozart's "Concerto for Flute, Harp and Orchestra in C Major"
Antenatal: Use as **background** music for relaxed activities, in addition to
            Tape 1.
Labour: Same as Tape 1.

Table 1 Continued

TAPE 4: PELVIC ROCKING - VOCAL

Style:	Popular vocal with strong movement implied in rhythm.
Examples:	Van Morrison: "Have I Told You Lately?"
	Chris DeBurgh: "Lady In Red"
	Louis Armstrong: "What A Wonderful World"
	Elton John: "I Need You To Turn To"
	Simply Red: "If You Don't Know Me By Know"
Antenatal:	Same as Tape 2.
Labour:	Same as Tape 2.

TAPE 5: POST-NATAL

Style:	Annie's favourite popular songs.
Examples:	Dan Fogelberg: "Longer"
	Harry Chapin: "I Let Time Go Lightly"
	Phil Collins: "Father to Son"
	Amy Grant: "Father's Eyes"
	Chris DeBurgh: "For Rosanna"
Antenatal:	To encourage singing to baby in utero and for breathing.
Labour:	To stimulate hormones if labour is slow to progress and to encourage deep breathing and body vibration.
Postnatal:	To affirm birth of baby.

TAPE 6 SUPPORT - BACKGROUND 2

Style:	Contemporary instrumental: Sound tracks and New Age.
Examples:	Fresh Aire: "Embers"
	Enya: "Watermark"
	Sky: "Hello"
	Mark Knopfler: "Irish Love from 'Cal'"
Antenatal:	Use as background music for whatever is desired (e.g., entertaining, housework, etc.).
Labour:	Use as alternate to support tapes, mainly for relaxing.

Table 1 Continued

TAPE 7: EARLY FIRST STAGE

Style: Popular vocal.
Examples: Van Morrison: "Bright Side of The Road"
             Wet Wet Wet: "Broke Away"
             Dire Straits: "Brothers in Arms"
             Eagles: "Best of My Love"
Antenatal: For times of increased physical activity or exercise.
Labour: Limited use during early labour.

TAPE 8: BLANK

Labour: During final 15 minutes of labour, record fetal heartbeat (via
             Sonicaid or Monitor) and conversations; record moment of
             birth, first sounds of baby, and conversations immediately after
             birth.

CASE THIRTY-SIX

Reclaiming A Positive Identity:
Music Therapy In The Aftermath
Of A Stroke

NANCY MCMASTER, MTA

Music Therapist in Private Practice

Professor of Music Therapy

Capilano College

Vancouver, B. C. Canada

Abstract: *This study describes how music therapy helped a forty-year old woman cope with the effects of a stroke. Through improvising, composing and singing, Vera grieved and protested what life had brought her, while also finding a way of validating the ability and strength that still lived inside her debilitated body.*

BACKGROUND INFORMATION

This is the story of Vera, a married woman in her early forties, and the mother of four children. Her life as a bright, vivacious, socially-active, ambitious, and philosophically-minded woman was cut short three years ago by a stroke or cerebrovascular accident (CVA). The CVA was precipitated by the rupture of an unsuspected tumor in her heart. She was left without the use of her right arm, dragging her right leg, drooling, with no speech, virtually no sight, and an undetermined cognitive impairment which affects her memory and body awareness. Extensive assessment indicated that little value would result from therapeutic intervention. A year after the accident, she was placed in a residence for seniors, where she had the support of a personal attendant and frequent contact with her children. This residence provided social, activity, and religious programs but no rehabilitation beyond maintenance of functioning.

Vera's husband arranged for her to have a daily personal attendant and frequent contact with her children. Visits from her husband were very stressful, as Vera did not understand why she could not live at home. Visits from friends decreased as they found it very difficult to accept Vera's condition and also very difficult to communicate with her. Vera's parents made daily phone calls and several trips each year from hundreds of miles away to offer their love, support and sympathy.

Vera's emotional response to this set of circumstances moved through a wide range: from devastation, hope and determination to despair, apathy, grief, and later to frustration and anger. Her movements have tended to be slow; her neck, shoulders and spine drooping; and her face almost blank, except for slightly raised eyebrows. Vera was generally preoccupied with the losses in her life, which she indicated by the frequent use of signs which she had created to refer to each one.

Vera tended to remain uninvolved in her day-to-day life, neither seeking nor responding with interest to anything except eating, listening to music, religious services and studies, and conversations which might contain solutions to her dilemma. When her interest was stirred by any one of these events: her spine and neck would straighten, she would cock her head, raise her eyebrows, make vocal sounds of interest; she would move quickly and confidently, even taking several steps unassisted; she would even strain, if necessary, to get a better access to what was interesting her, and then demand help, forcefully, if she could not get such access. But generally this keen interest would last no more than five minutes and then be forgotten, at which point her body would settle back into her more typical state.

Three years after Vera's CVA, her husband requested music therapy for her on a private contractual basis, outside of the residence. His hope was that music therapy would alleviate some of the bleakness in Vera's life.

The background information I was given about Vera gave me the impression that Vera and all of the people in her life viewed her situation as completely tragic and debilitating. Without having met her, I anticipated that Vera would have a need to mourn and protest her situation, and a need to develop a positive sense of her identity.

I was prepared to encourage equally, expressions of distress and enjoyment; to acknowledge and appreciate equally her limitations, challenges, abilities and efforts; and to give Vera many opportunities for choice and initiative so that her personality could shine through and be clearly acknowledged.

I did not know what Vera would initiate, comprehend, remember, or respond to musically. I was ready to design musical experiences according to her abilities, as they emerged---making some readily available to her, and others that would require some effort, as both types of experience can provide a sense of accomplishment.

My assessment of her abilities and needs was ongoing, as was my evaluation of her progress and the relevance of musical and nonmusical approaches.

TREATMENT PROCESS

First Meeting

As Vera entered the room and I greeted her, she left her attendant to walk over to me. She reached out to feel my face, then readily took my hand to go to the piano. When we were seated, Vera gestured to her attendant to tell me the details of Vera's situation. Vera listened attentively, nodding frequently. When Vera sobbed at one point, the attendant discouraged her, saying it did her no good to cry about it.

When I turned to begin to present to Vera how she and I could make music together, Vera did not understand and suddenly interrupted with a few loud smacks on the keyboard. I laughed in surprise and jumped in to join her on the bass with equal strength, setting a tonality and adding a bit of swing. Vera immediately started to stomp her foot and grin, continuing to play apparently random clusters of the white piano keys. (2 min.)

When asked if she would like more of the same or something different, Vera indicated a desire for something different, yet in the next few beginnings, Vera played the same types of clusters and stopped after a few seconds each time. When I moved into a very different sound---full, slow bass chords---Vera began to sob deeply. I put one hand on Vera's back, shifted into a gently rocking bass and began to improvise a lullaby without words, at which Vera instantly stopped crying, her face blank.

At my invitation, Vera joined in singing, her voice strong, very quick to sense where the improvised melody was going. After several minutes of that music, I shifted into an improvised waltz. Vera sang along with gusto and confidence, as if she knew the waltz. The attendant applauded enthusiastically when the waltz finished. Vera grinned.

The attendant was surprised to see such a normal musical interaction between Vera and me. Vera's disability had slipped into the background. The attendant also witnessed a different way of responding to Vera's grief.

Phase One: Musical Explorations

We set up a schedule so that I would see Vera for thirty-minute sessions every two weeks. In this phase, Vera and I began to discover her musical interests and abilities.

Vera learned the pentatonic scale (on the raised/black piano keys) very quickly, needing only one verbal reminder after a hand-over-hand introduction. She started with a short, somewhat cautious exploration. Later, this progressed to longer explorations of about two minutes. Vera was attentive, quiet, sometimes repeating one cluster for awhile, sensing good ending places. For this work, I matched her timing and volume, adding no musical direction beyond whatever Vera initiated. Vera tended to be moderate in both speed and volume.

I invited Vera to switch places with me to play the bass, suggesting she might like to play loudly. She spontaneously altered her hand position to play more strongly. During her first improvisation on the bass, Vera initiated an accelerando as well as a slow strong section. When asked if she likes to be loud, sometimes, Vera nodded affirmatively and giggled. Her second improvisation on the bass lasted for four minutes; it had a gentle quality. She initiated singing to the improvisation, although it had no constant tonality. Her third bass improvisation began very fast and loud, slowed and stopped abruptly, followed by a strong vocalization. When asked whether it was exciting, Vera shook her head to disagree. She nodded when I asked if it was scary. I suggested she could try playing more slowly, at which she began again, choosing her notes more deliberately, apparently seeking more preferable sounds, although still without any consistent tonality. Throughout, I continued to complement whatever she did, following her lead. Vera agreed when I commented that the bass seemed to move her.

I introduced some percussion instruments in this phase. Vera played a two-beat pattern (quarter-half) on the conga drum, when I played the waltz from our first session, and she held her own beat when I added more complex rhythms and syncopation on a second drum. Vera's drumming tended to be soft, even after verbal and hand-over-hand suggestions as to how to play more loudly. Together we did slide into some dynamic changes in speed and tempo, however. She frequently chose and/or welcomed the drum in the first phase of working together.

The sound of the temple blocks (a pitched series of hollow wooden bowls) evoked grins and laughter. After attentive exploration, Vera discovered where to place her mallet to hit each block, and we had an intense, syncopated rhythmic duo.

The attendant reported that Vera's absorption and responsiveness during the last three sessions had far exceeded that evoked by any other stimulus in Vera's life at this time.

Phase Two: Developing Musical Language

Thirty minute sessions became inadequate, and we started to go on for 45 minutes. Vera's improvisations were becoming increasingly tonal, more deliberately shaped. I was watching the pitches she played and choosing notes which would create chords, whenever I could. This resulted in a constantly changing tonality, and both Vera and I were always adjusting to try to fit together tonally. Vera tended to use parallel 4ths, 5ths or 6ths, interspersed with clusters, occasionally repeating one interval 5 to 10 times before moving on. She often sang spontaneously with these improvisations.

When I reinforced this new level of awareness and purpose with comments such as, "You were really listening, weren't you? You were choosing," Vera agreed emphatically, pleased.

While this work marked a significant development in Vera's concentration, it also tended to inhibit the flow of dynamic, emotional expression and enjoyment she had demonstrated in her first session. To facilitate access to that freer expression, I introduced several different ethnic idioms (Spanish, Middle Eastern and Eastern European) chosen for their combination of vitality, intensity and touch of melancholy. The harmonic accompaniment was provided in a variety of ways: by myself on guitar or piano, by Vera strumming as I chorded the guitar, or by Vera holding a simple bass pattern on the piano as I filled in the other harmonies. We would always sing improvised melodies as we played. These idioms often evoked whole-hearted singing, but not reliably. Vera usually continued with an idiom for several minutes before stopping.

I also began to explore a way for Vera and I to play a dance form of some kind. We evolved a polka, with me using a traditional bass pattern, and Vera in the treble playing parallel 6ths. This developed into a set composition with 2 sections: the first section going up to the first half of the C scale (to F) and returning to C: the second going down the entire scale. As soon as the form was set, Vera concentrated fully for over 10 minutes, sitting straighter and being much more vocally involved in response to my directions and comments. Any time I suggested that maybe she had worked hard enough, Vera disagreed strongly and gestured for more. Several times she laughed in a breathless, excited sort of sound, as we started yet another repetition of this very challenging work.

For several sessions, sustained work on one section would obliterate her memory of the other section, even if she had just worked on it previously.

Vera laughed when she realized this, but could not retain both sections at the same time. The approach I used in this work seemed to follow a fairly regular sequence: reminding Vera to listen carefully and then playing the sound of the section we were going to work on; moving her hand through the sequence, giving the verbal cues I would be using later; giving her verbal cues, with a slight touch when needed; giving her no cue, every once in a while, to notice her tendencies; calling out and stopping her at any mistake and beginning the whole sequence again; calling out a caution and a verbal cue, any time I saw her about to make a mistake; and later, calling out a caution with no verbal cue, for her to correct herself. This was accompanied by very active, enthusiastic encouragement and bit of clowning.

Towards the end of this phase, Vera's attendant started to talk about songs Vera used to know and like before her CVA. After listening for a few minutes, Vera suddenly sat very still, her hand to her mouth, obviously trying to remember a song so she could sing it. After about 20 seconds, I suggested we sing one of the songs, "Let It Be" by the Beatles, and we sang it together. Vera reached out her hand, wanting to play the song. I said I would try to work out an arrangement that she and I could play.

The attendant reported that Vera's concentration outside of the sessions was markedly improved. She could now stay awake and alert for up to one hour in situations of interest to her.

Phase Three: Music Reaching the Heart

Work on the polka continued well into this third phase. Vera was able to play both sections and, with practice, could play the whole piece through without any mistakes. Work on this piece usually lasted 10 minutes at a time.

Vera also worked on the arrangement I made of "Let It Be," involving only 2 parallel 6ths (C/E and B/D) for Vera and an octave bass for myself. I used the same basic approach outlined in Phase Two. Vera had to remember at each point in the song whether it was time to move her hand up or down the keyboard or to repeat the chord she was on. She would work eagerly on the song for 20 minutes at a stretch. With some persuasion, she would stop when her concentration began to fade. Later on in this phase, Vera started to work on "Hey Jude," another song by the Beatles, suddenly singing it in response to being asked what she would like to do next. Vera sang along patiently as I worked out an arrangement on the spot, giggling whenever I got stuck and had to find a different voicing. In "Hey Jude," Vera had to move stepwise between 3 parallel 6ths.

Vera's improvisations in this phase tended to be much more extensive than previously, often lasting for 5 minutes. They included a lot of simple scales, repeating each note in the scale using various rhythmic patterns (eg. 2 sets of triplets; combinations of 4 eighths and a quarter). Once in this session, when her mother had come to the session, Vera was obviously dissatisfied with a long improvisation she had done. When I asked if she was trying to make it beautiful, Vera nodded yes. I encouraged her to work at that challenge, given how good she felt when she succeeded. She tried again for several minutes, with similar results. She burst out laughing when I said I could see that she wanted to be a composer. When I said how ambitious I thought that was, she laughed again, pleased, and went at it again. She persisted for about 12 minutes, all together, before being ready to move on. I told her that one of the things about composing was that she might not like everything she tries. Vera received that with a "Hm." Vera's mother, meanwhile, had been enthusiastically appreciative of both Vera's music and her work, this being the first time she had seen Vera absorbed and creative since her CVA.

This phase was marked by several very emotional outbursts, as Vera's husband had recently arranged for a divorce. In one session, Vera stopped playing and gestured toward her eyes, crying. Her attendant called out, "Come on now, get on with it, that's a waste of time. Tell Nancy about your birthday party." After a rather labored conversation about the party, Vera gestured to her right arm, crying again. I began to sing a lament in the Middle Eastern idiom, using its minor, ornamented melodic style. Vera reached out to strum the guitar as I sang, tears running down her face. At a natural ending point, I asked Vera if she wanted more. She nodded.

I shifted slightly into a slow Flamenco strum with a similar melodic line, at which Vera began to stomp her foot and grin, but as soon as I began to sing, Vera began to sob deeply. I kept singing but stopped playing, to touch Vera's face and hold her hand. At the end of that session, after talking with the attendant, I told Vera that her crying was fine with me, though I might at times suggest that she move on into making music again. When I checked if that felt alright to her, Vera nodded and reached out to hold my hand for a moment. Soon after, when it was time to leave, Vera was not ready to go and remained sitting, her back turned to us, grinning widely.

In the same period, during a subsequent session, the attendant encouraged Vera to start playing, knowing that Vera was upset. Vera played one chord once, then stopped, turned to me and proceeded to vocalize and gesture, quite urgently, for about 2 minutes. When the attendant saw that Vera was making a sign referring to her husband, she called out "Don't worry about that." Vera persisted, wanting to "tell" me, somehow, about what was on her mind and heart. I listened and watched, silent except for some small sounds to let her know I was paying attention, and finally said "You have a lot of woes don't you?". Vera nodded, still trying to communicate. Then I said, "Well, given all of that, what would you like to do now with our time together?" Vera laughed and immediately reached out to the piano, playing a beautiful simple scale pattern of 6ths.

At the end of the session, Vera returned to the subject of her sight. It turned out that she wanted to know how long she would have to wait until she could see again.   I gathered that the doctors involved in Vera's assessments thought that she would never regain any sight, and I told Vera so.   She slumped a bit and simply said "Hm."   I acknowledged the challenge it was for Vera to live her life without regaining her sigh.   Then I played some well-known classical pieces for Vera (Brahms' "Lullaby" and Beethoven's "Moonlight Sonata").   She sang along, breaking down in the middle of the sonata and then singing again, through to the end.

Vera's mother had now seen glimpses of Vera's abilities, motivation and pleasure, and Vera's husband had been informed of her progress through monthly reports.   The attendant, far from being unsympathetic to Vera's distress, had witnessed hours of Vera's crying with no stopping or resolution. In music therapy, she was witnessing a new ability in Vera to express her grief deeply, and then move out of it into a lighter state.   She had begun to actively encourage Vera's emotional expression through the music.

Phase Four: A Quiet Period

There was a relatively quiet period, emotionally, when Vera worked on her song repertoire and the polka.   She also learned to play a waltz pattern. We had a few sessions where we sang a lullaby together, swaying side-by-side, with our shoulders touching.

Phase Five: Going Deeper with Music

We began to meet weekly for 45 minutes.   Work on the song material continued.   Vera added two new songs spontaneously.   She was becoming more vocal, taking much more initiative in directing the flow of the sessions.

Vera's improvisations had more freedom and flavor, sometimes jumping lightly over two-thirds of the keyboard with a laugh when it was over, sometimes more song-like, using only fragments of scales, sometimes dance-like, with Vera's leg jigging to her own music.

This was another very upsetting time in Vera's life, when her husband remarried.   In one session, Vera was looking particularly sad.   Her attendant encouraged her to get her feelings out on the piano, but Vera was not ready to do anything.   I began to play the lullaby we had swayed to in an earlier session and just kept repeating it for over five minutes, with Vera alternately singing and crying.   At the end of the music, Vera sobbed, sounding heartbroken.   I gave an audible sigh and asked, "Does it feel hard today?" Vera nodded.   "Some days are harder than others," I added.   Vera responded, "Mm!"   Then I asked if she wanted to continue singing.   She did.   I shifted into a new improvised waltz and we sang together.

One particular session best demonstrates this period.   When asked how she would like to begin, Vera played a burst of clusters very fast and forcefully, then slowed to a scale, using 6ths.   I simply said, "Hm!" and Vera launched into another short improvisation similar to the first. I sensed an emotional charge in Vera which was not yet released through the music and asked, "More?". Vera laughed. She nodded when I asked if I should join her. The sound was still somehow held back.

When we stopped, Vera pointed to her stomach, nodding when asked if she had pain there. She nodded again when I asked if there were any other feelings in there, nodding and vocalizing loudly when I asked if it was jealousy. I said, sympathetically, "Yuck! That's my least favorite emotion. You know why?" Vera gestured that she wanted to know. "Because it can be so consuming!" Vera responded, "Hm!"

I then suggested that Vera feel right down in that part of her body. With no further prompt, Vera immediately reached out and pounded the keyboard for about 4 seconds, began to sob and stopped a second, pounded again for a few seconds and stopped, racked by very deep sobbing. I put my hand on her back, encouraging her for a few moments and then began to play a deep octave bass, very slowly, and sang a heavy lament with a Slavic flavor. Vera started to sing with it, her voice wavering.

At its end, Vera reached out and landed on a chord which was the major version of the tonic. I immediately changed to the major and between us, Vera and I found a simple sequence of chords, using parallel 6ths, which suggested a feeling of comfort, and we proceeded to sing several variations of that music. This ended in a long held note, initiated by Vera and a downward vocal slide, initiated by me, which resulted in both of us laughing.

I then moved into teaching Vera a new waltz pattern which required her full concentration. After working on that for 5 minutes, Vera chose to practice her song material, working hard for another 30 minutes. At the end of that session, Vera's face was alert and glowing and she walked very erect. She thanked me enthusiastically when she said goodbye.

At the end of a later session, the attendant noticed Vera referring to her husband's marriage and said, "We're not talking about that any more". Vera looked blank. "What's past is past." Vera nodded emphatically in agreement with the attendant.

Towards the end of this phase, Vera had separate meetings with her ex-husband and with his new wife and seemed to feel deeply at peace with them and with her situation. This feeling was corroborated by Vera, when the attendant reported it to me. Anger and sadness came back several times, later, but not with the same gut-wrenching intensity: expressed more often through a growl or a symbolic kick, sometimes with a laugh and/or a dismissive wave and a choice to move into her more structured musical work.

Vera's husband decided to increase the amount of music therapy in each week in response to Vera's expressed desired, the attendant's recommendations and my reports. Sessions were increased to 90 minutes each week.

Phase Six: Developing A Musical Identity

Sessions in this period often began with solo improvisations by Vera in response to the invitation to play how she felt. These tended to begin very forcefully and atonally, with a freedom of emotional expression which would either lead into sobbing or shift into a more tonal framework. I would wait a moment as an improvisation ended, to see whether the impulse was really finished. When it didn't seem quite complete, I would only need to say "Hm" or "More?" for Vera to begin again, often with a laugh. At other times, she would pause to check if she wanted to play more and then give a dismissing wave of her hand, again often laughing. When the impulse had truly ended, Vera would often grin or settle back with a thoughtful "Hm". In this phase, Vera's attendant often encouraged her to play what she felt, to get it off her chest, as soon as Vera got to the piano, when she knew that Vera was upset. The attendant would call out, "That was good", when Vera had been particularly energetic and would chuckle, sometimes, when Vera indicated there was more to express.

Vera's major focus in this phase was on structured keyboard work. She was a very vocal, active and increasingly independent participant in this work. She had somehow, on her own, discovered how to go back to a place in a song which came just before an area she found difficult. She would catch her own mistakes and either correct them herself or take my reminders and then go over the trouble spot many times until she felt confident that she had learned it. This was rote learning, and often would not be retained when she started back at the beginning of the song. I coached her on the difference between endless repetition and memorization.
I began to see a noticeable difference in Vera's face and posture between when she was simply working hard and when she was focusing in a highly concentrated way. When I pointed out this difference to Vera, she could sometimes feel the difference.

The call for yet another repetition of a whole song or a fragment fell about equally between Vera and me. If she played a song perfectly but with hesitation, Vera would repeat it. If she played a song perfectly with no audible hesitation but did not feel confident, Vera would not be satisfied and would want to repeat it. If she played it perfectly, she would be thrilled, raising her fist in the air and squealing in triumph. Sometimes this would change into sobbing, after which Vera would stop and laugh, as if a bit surprised. I would comment on how exciting it was to see that her mind was working so well and she would agree strongly. And then she would want to play it perfectly again. As she could rarely sustain that much concentration, this often led to her desire to work longer at the same song. After one or two repetitions, I would suggest that it was time to move on and wait until the next session to work on that song. Vera would agree, reluctantly, and then move on to work on the next song with the same single-minded concentration.

In this phase, Vera and I began to have conversations about how we know things. When she would play a piece perfectly, I would ask, exclaiming, "How did you do that?!" Vera would laugh---as if so pleased with herself---and then shrug. She would disagree if I suggested that she knew the piece. So I would ask her who had just played the piece perfectly. Vera would hesitate, looking blank and then point to her chest.

We had some moments of hilarity when I would say, "Someone in there knows this song and someone doesn't." Vera burst out laughing at that statement. The suggestion that she might be wise to pay attention to the side of her that knows a song brought another gale of laughter. Gradually she came to acknowledge that she might know a song and even to recognize, sometimes, the feeling of knowing a piece.

During a few sessions in this period, Vera "talked" to me urgently (with the help of her attendant) about wanting to practice her songs at her residence, in between her sessions. She also worked hard one day to let me know that she was bored, in her week, and wanted to be learning things. The attendant said Vera had been thinking about it all week, and wanted the attendant to organize some solution. Shortly after, the attendant arranged for Vera to audit classes at a local college.

The attendant began to report that Vera was no longer so angry or preoccupied with her losses. Her facial expression, though still predominantly flat, was no longer so blank. While Vera continued to feel that her life was very hard (which in fact it was!), she would confirm at times that she felt happy or peaceful. Her readiness to express distress and then to let it go increased. She would laugh often and occasionally show that she was excited or even thrilled. She began to express appreciation for people more often than previously.

It was now common for friends, family and staff to hear stories of Vera's accomplishments and pleasure in music therapy sessions. In a case conference on Vera, the team agreed that everyone involved with Vera should come to terms with limitations in her situation and help her to focus on the positive aspects as well as the challenges of her life. Music therapy was identified as a major area of communication and satisfaction in Vera's life, and everyone recommended that it continue.

DISCUSSION AND CONCLUSIONS

Vera responded strongly to music therapy in the areas of emotional expression, self-image, and her ability to be absorbed by and appreciative of her environment.

Emotionally, Vera found the laments and lullabies to be both evocative and supportive of her grief. Occasionally, Vera and I were both taken by surprise when the music evoked a sudden shift from pleasure or a more neutral state into sobbing. More often, Vera's expressions of grief grew out of her preoccupations with the numerous losses in her life. The laments and lullabies provided her with tangible evidence that her grief was being accepted, understood, and honored by others.

Vera's protest found its expression in the free improvisation. She showed considerable abandonment in releasing her feelings through this medium, taking full advantage of my open invitations to play however she felt. Her discernment of whether she needed to continue became very acute.

There was also a nonmusical benefit within the music therapy relationship. The fact that I was not identified by either Vera or myself as having responsibility for altering the structure of her everyday life freed her emotional expression of any agenda other than to experience and deal with her feelings.

Vera's sense of a positive identity gradually blossomed over the course of these sessions. She invested an increasing attentiveness and care in her creative improvisational work. Much more dramatically, her absorption persistence, excitement and eventual exhilaration with the structured musical compositions gave rise to her sense of ability and pride.

Initially, Vera responded positively to my appreciation of her abilities and accomplishments, and agreed whenever I commented that she was working well or that her music was beautiful. As her excitement emerged, I increased the enthusiasm with which I encouraged and acknowledged her.

As well as applauding the quality of her work, I actively reinforced Vera's sense of herself by giving her many opportunities for choice, by finding ways to join in with her impulses and by telling her what I saw of her responses, tendencies and interests in a way that called for her to acknowledge them actively herself.

I believe that Vera's increased absorption in and appreciation of her world grew organically out of the validation she received in these sessions: validation of her emotional responses to her situation, validation of her ableness and perserverance, and validation of her ability to be seen and enjoyed in a deep exchange with another human being.

The music contributed a flexibility of structure, a natural meeting ground, an absorbing challenge and focus, and most importantly, the richness of its own beauty.

Rehabilitation Of Piano Performance Skills Following A Left Cerebral Vascular Accident

DENISE ERDONMEZ, M. Mus. RMT-BC,
Senior Lecturer in Music Therapy,
University of Melbourne,
Parkville, Victoria, Australia

Abstract. This case describes the rehabilitation of piano performance skills in a 54-year old man following a left cerebral vascular accident (CVA). The CVA rendered the client expressively dysphasic and dyslexic, although his ability to play from music notation was unimpaired. Due to paralysis of the right hand, rehabilitation was restricted to performance skills in the left hand only. Weekly music therapy sessions were provided over a 3 year period. Assessments taken at 18 month intervals showed improvement in rhythmic short-term memory, keyboard dexterity, and the ability to play music of increased complexity in key and rhythm. These results support current knowledge that the brain compensates for areas of impairment through involvement of new pathways and strategies.

BACKGROUND INFORMATION

John suffered a *Cerebral Vascular Accident (CVA) infarct* at the age of 54 years. A *Computerised Axial Tomography (or CAT scan)* confirmed the massive extent of damage to the left temporal and parietal lobes of the brain. John was rendered *aphasic (expressive type)* and *hemiplegic* on the right side of his body.

John's *pre-morbid* talents were quite impressive. He was a General Medical Practitioner with a busy practice; he spoke three foreign languages fluently (Latin, Italian, German); and he was a talented pianist and organist with a broad classical repertoire.

Ten months after suffering the CVA, John was referred for individual music therapy. Tests had been carried out by several professionals, and the results made available to the author.

The neurological tests revealed paralysis of the right arm and hand. This was his dominant side in that previously, John used his right hand for writing and all manual tasks. He had residual spasticity of the right leg which severely restricted his mobility. John also had left-right disorientation, and had lost half of the visual field in both eyes.

The speech pathology tests indicated an *expressive dysphasia*, as some speech had been regained. John could speak short phrases, characterised by literal and verbal *paraphasias* (incorrect substitution of consonant sounds in different words). He had lost knowledge of all three foreign languages. On processing auditory information, he could cope with only 3 units. He could read single words of several syllables, but not words of 3-4 letters such as "the" or "for."

Neuropsychological tests indicated that his I.Q. on the Weschler scale was 117. He was well orientated in time and place and could count backwards from 20 to 1. His short-term memory was tested on digit recall (reproducing a series of random numbers), and John showed a memory span of only 3 units (consistent with the speech pathology tests).

MUSIC THERAPY ASSESSMENT

Upon referral, the author administered the Botez-Wertheim (1959) tests for *amusia*. Although no normative data are available, the tests are classified according to the subject's musical training. There are 45 tests in the battery grouped under several sub-categories.

MELODIC AND HARMONIC ELEMENTS: John could vocally reproduce a series of individual notes with accurate pitch. He was also able to continue singing a known melody in AABA form when only part A was given, and recognise musical errors when played intentionally. He had difficulty differentiating major from minor chords and discerning the number of notes in a chord. He had considerable difficulty when asked to name notes in a music score, but could easily pick out the same notes on the keyboard. He also had difficulty playing a note when asked to do so by letter name. Recognition of intervals was totally beyond him: he could neither identify an interval, nor choose an answer if several options were put to him, e.g. "Is this a 3rd or a 5th?".

RHYTHMIC ELEMENTS: John had great difficulties with rhythmic tasks. He could identify the meter of a piece as duple or triple, but was unable to reproduce a rhythm either presented on a single note of the piano or as a melody---unless the pattern was less than 3 or 4 units in length. This finding was consistent with both the speech pathology and neuropsychology tests indicating a 3-unit memory span.

LEXIC ELEMENTS: When asked to play at sight a 12-bar melody in the key of G major with his left hand, John played with near accuracy, and made mistakes at a modulation point. Upon finishing the melody, he was able to identify the mistakes he made. He correctly translated the Italian terms (i.e., moderato, allegro) but said that the symbol "mf" meant "slow but loud and soft..then hit big!". He could not name the one sharp in the key signature, but correctly played it throughout the piece.

SINGING AND WHISTLING TESTS: John was able to sing a well-known melody from memory without cuing. He was unable however, to sing from memory a melody of 8 notes played once by the therapist. He could sing scales accurately from a given note, and was careful to differentiate the characteristic intervals of the scale.

SUMMARY: John was unable to name notes in a score or when played; he was also unable to play notes when given their letter names; he could, however, correctly interpret these symbols and play the correct notes on the keyboard when reading directly from the score. This is not a musical dyslexia as such since there is no impairment in his ability to read, but rather in his ability to associate a letter name with a note. This is similar to a nominal aphasia where the person experiences difficulty in finding a target word. In the music context, we could term this impaired skill an expressive nominal amusia. (See Glossary for other categories of amusia).

John has the ability to sing in tune and sight-read music notation remarkably well, given his dyslexia for written prose. Rhythmic skills show the greatest impairment: he cannot reproduce rhythms or melodic rhythms of more than 3 notes (units), or sing from memory short examples of more than 3 notes (units).

METHOD

Following the initial assessment of music skills, John commenced weekly individual music therapy sessions. The aims of the sessions were: to rehabilitate John's piano playing skills in his left hand; to extend his short term memory span for rhythmic and melodic phrases; to improve the rhythmic accuracy of his playing; and to extend the dexterity of his playing to include pieces of increasing difficulty.

Each music therapy session lasted 45 minutes. A central activity was to have John play the treble line of piano pieces with his left (unimpaired) hand, while the music therapist played the bass line with her left hand. Opportunities were also provided for practising rhythmic patterns, singing familiar songs, and for relearning music terminology.

During the week, John practised 1-2 hours per day of his own volition. He often selected new piano pieces, and therefore determined the pace of his own rehabilitation. Given John's level of intelligence, and his pre-morbid professional orientation, it was essential that his rehabilitation provide as many opportunities as possible for decision making, initiative and self-direction. Thus, each music therapy session commenced with work John had prepared, and ended with rhythmic exercises and other tasks planned by the music therapist.

TREATMENT PROCESS

Music therapy sessions were carried out over a three year period with a re-assessment after 18 months.

The First Eighteen Months

At the beginning of the first 18-month period, John played pieces in the simple keys of C and G major. The pieces were elementary, with simple melodic lines which he played with his left hand, and chordal accompaniment played by the therapist. While it is customary to mark piano scores with fingering, this numbering system could not be used with John because he became confused by the association of the numbers with the fingers of his hand. In addition, John played the treble line (which is written for the right hand) with his left hand. Frequently, the line of the music followed the natural line of the right hand over the keyboard, and playing this part in the left hand created additional problems of hand positioning. Despite the inappropriateness of conventional learning aides, the therapist devised a number of ways to assist John in mastering the pieces. For example, an 'X' was used to denote the thumb, so that in learning new fingering patterns the thumb was placed correctly and the other fingers fell into correct sequence. Dotted rhythms in the melodic line frequently had to be practised in a range of ways to assist the internalising of the pattern. John would be encouraged to tap out the rhythm on a single note of the piano, or clap it on his knee, or sing the rhythm to on a "la." It was essential to introduce new methods of practising the same material as John had very high expectations of himself and became discouraged very easily.

After 12 months of music therapy, John began to study the Bach two-

and three-part inventions, playing as much of each piece as possible with his left hand. These pieces were more difficult than the previous pieces in several ways: the melodic line often had unpredictable changes in pattern; the melodic contour was frequently interwoven and linear in concept, whereas the simple pieces had been more vertical in concept; there were more accidentals and modulation points; and there was greater demand for finger dexterity, particularly when scale passages written for the right hand were transferred to the left hand.

John showed remarkable perseverance in learning these pieces and his dexterity improved because of their contrapuntal nature. While the two-part inventions require playing one linear melody in the treble, the three-part inventions require the interweaving of two linear melodies, and consequently much greater finger independence, for the left hand.

It should be noted that John had learnt some of the inventions at a younger age, however, for all practical purposes, each piece had to be mastered anew since his left hand was learning the right hand part.

About this time, John took an interest in the art songs of Schubert and Schumann. He played the treble part of the accompaniment with his left hand, while the therapist filled in the bass part. The songs also provided an opportunity to sing the vocal line while playing the piano accompaniment. Often, singing these songs allowed John to ventilate some of his emotions, and afterwards he often tried to explain how frustrated he felt in coming to terms with his speech and motor impairments. At times, John showed lability in mood (as is characteristic of CVA clients), and he would weep during the playing of pieces and songs that were meaningful to him.

Re-assessment after 18 months

John was re-assessed on the Botez-Wertheim battery of tests after 18 months. On the rhythmic sub-tests (which are graded from 3-unit examples to 7-units), all examples except one, were reproduced accurately. A simple test of digit recall was also given, and John succeeded only on those patterns of 3-4 digits. His rhythmic memory had improved from a 3-unit span to a 7-unit span, however his memory recall for digits remained at 3 units. The advances made in rhythmic short-term memory did not generalise to digit recall, however it should be noted that rhythmic skills were consistently practised within the music therapy sessions, and digit recall was not.

Progress in Third Year of Program

John's motivation for practice and increased self-confidence became apparent in the third year of music therapy sessions. His interest in art songs developed further, and we studied song cycles in their entirety. He found books on the composer's life and wanted these read to him during music therapy sessions. He took an increasing interest in the development of certain motifs in one song, which he found in another song by the same composer in a later period.

His piano repertoire increased rapidly and he re-learnt the Beethoven Piano Sonata in G Major (Opus 79), and several of the Bach Preludes and Fugues. The span of his left hand developed to cover 10 notes, and this enabled him to play both treble and bass parts of some pieces with his one hand (e.g. Satie's "Gymnopedies").

At the end of the third year, we were playing contemporary pieces of complex rhythms and complex key signatures, including Scriabin's Etude in C# Minor (Opus 2 #1), and Hindemith's "1922 Suite for Klavier" (Opus 26). His practice schedule remained at 1-2 hours practice each day.

DISCUSSION AND CONCLUSIONS

Each of the aims of the music therapy program were achieved. The first aim was to rehabilitate John's piano performance skills in his left hand. At the commencement of the program he was playing simple pieces in uncomplicated keys. At the end of the program his confidence had increased markedly, and he was playing pieces written in difficult keys involving many accidentals.

The second aim of the music therapy program, to develop short term memory for rhythmic skills, was also met. The initial assessment indicated a 3-unit memory span for rhythmic tasks. The follow-up assessment 18 months later indicated an improvement to a 7-unit memory span, which is within acceptable or normal memory limits. The reason for this improvement may have been the consistent practise of rhythmic patterns within the music therapy session. Alternatively John may have developed or rehabilitated the ability to process rhythmic patterns in "chunks." Sloboda (1978) in a study of sight reading strategies in musicians suggests that patterns of more than 7 notes may be processed as gestalt patterns rather than separate units of information. The fact that John improved on rhythmic tasks (which were practised) but not on recall of digits (which were not practised) suggests that consistency of repetition is a major factor in successful rehabilitation of short-term memory skills.

The third aim of the music therapy program was to develop rhythmic accuracy in his piano-playing. At first, John experienced great difficulty with dotted or complex rhythms, but with creative approaches to learning and practicing them, John successfully regained the ability to accurately play complex rhythms, as was clearly demonstrated in the contemporary works of Hindemith that he mastered.

Several factors contributed to the success of the music therapy program. First, John was highly motivated. Moreover, his high level of intelligence and commitment to practice enabled him to succeed in mastering pieces of increasing difficulty. Second, given the massive extent of damage to the left hemisphere, particularly the parietal and temporal lobes, it is evident that John's brain effectively compensated for areas of damage, enabling him to learn new material accurately, which ordinarily requires analytical skills and logical thinking generally ascribed to intact left hemisphere function.

This achievement is all the more remarkable because John was playing right handed parts with the left hand. This required the anatomical design of the right hand to be accommodated by a left hand of reverse anatomical design. The changed fingering patterns necessitated considerable practice and therefore contributed to the rehabilitation of several motoric skills.

This case study has similarities to a study by Luria, Tsvetkova and Futer (1965) of a composer and professor at the Moscow Conservatory, who suffered a CVA which caused damage to the left temporal and parietal areas of the brain. He suffered aphasia and sensorimotor deficits of the right side of the body, however he continued to compose and many of his later works are in keys requiring excessive use of accidentals.

Other studies of musicians who have suffered brain impairment are sparsely reported in the literature, yet they provide valuable evidence for understanding how the brain processes music information. Different strategies are required for music tasks according to the musical ability and experience of the subjects, the processing strategy and the nature of the task.

It is evident in this case study that new pathways for memorising short rhythmic phrases can be developed, and that short term memory spans can be increased. New motoric skills can also be acquired (e.g., playing right-handed music with the left hand), and improvements can be made in speed and dexterity of performance. It is also possible to devise new strategies for deciphering music and for coping with the complexities of key signatures, accidentals and rhythms in contemporary music.

In terms of theoretical orientation, this case study describes a process of rehabiliation over a long period of time. The initial degree of impairment was severe and a music therapy approach was needed to encourage John in the slow advancement from simple pieces to complex. As John was highly self-critical, various approaches had to be taken to keep his self-esteem and confidence focussed on more positive aspects of the rehabilitative process. It was essential to stay "with him" when he skipped a measure, or a line of music, or if the rhythm was incorrect. Creative and spontaneous practice mechanisms needed to be offered by the therapist, so that inaccurate sections could be practised without a concomitant loss of confidence.

On many occasions during the singing and playing of art songs, John became emotionally upset. CVA patients with language impairments have immense difficulty in adequately expressing feelings of frustration and depression. In John's case, the lyrics of the various songs became clear projections of his feelings. One song cycle in particular (Schubert's

"Winterreise") was particularly helpful in dealing with issues of blame for the CVA. The song cycle expresses many aspects of human suffering: coldness, rejection and despair. The depth of emotion in these songs often reflected John's own suffering and enabled him to express it.

The client's wife expressed on many occasions how important the music therapy sessions were for his rehabilitation. Music became the focus of his life and gave him a purpose for his existence. Prior to the CVA, John had been a keen, amateur landscape painter. Following the paralysis of his right (dominant) hand, he taught himself to paint with his left hand, submitting his paintings to local competitions and winning prizes.

The success and extent of John's rehabilitation is attributable as much to his indomitable spirit to overcome adversity as to the efficacy of music as therapy.

GLOSSARY

Amusia: the loss of, or impairment to music function. Henschen (1920) identifies sub-categories of amusia as follows (Also see Benton, 1977):
1. Motor Impairment - Expressive Amusia
    a. Loss of the ability to sing (oral-expressive amusia)
    b. Loss of the ability to write musical notation (musical agraphia)
    c. Loss of the ability to play an instrument (instrumental amusia or musical apraxia)
2. Sensory Impairment - Receptive Amusia
    a. Loss of recognition of familiar melodies (amnesic amusia)
    b. Loss of the ability to read musical notation (musical alexia)
3. Musical deafness, including loss of recognition of familiar melodies.
4. Loss of ability to read musical notation.

Aphasia: A disorder of communication in which there is a complete loss of the ability to speak (expressive type) and/or comprehend speech (receptive type).

Cerebro-Vascular Accident (CVA): Commonly known as a "stroke," CVA occurs when there is a blockage of blood supply to the brain which causes damage to tissues of those areas deprived of oxygen. It may be caused by an embolus, hemmorhage or thrombus. Effects on the sufferer are determined both by the site of the blockage and the extent of the area involved" (Bright, 1989).

Computerised Axial Tomography (CAT scan): A method of imaging brain anatomy using different planes (vertical, horizontal) to detect damage.

Dysphasia: A disorder of communication in which there is impairment (but not complete loss of) the ability to speak (expressive type) or comprehend speech (receptive type).

Dyslexia: Impairment in the ability to read.

Infarct: Dead tissue as a result of lack of blood supply.

Hemiplegia: Paralysis or weakness of one side of the body. Following a CVA, the contralateral side of the body is affected.

Paraphasia: There are two types: (1) literal paraphasia, which is the transposition of consonant sounds from beginning or ending of words; and (2) verbal paraphasia - substitution of an inappropriate word when attempting to say a target word.

Pre-morbid: Before the onset of illness, disease or symptoms.

REFERENCES

Botez, M.I. & Wertheim, N. (1959). Expressive aphasia and amusia. Brain, 82, 186-202.

Bright, R (1989). Why Does That Happen? Discussions on Geriatric Care. Wahroonga, NSW: Music Therapy Enterprises.

Henschen, S. (1920). Klinische und anatomische Beitrage zur Pathologie des Gehirns (5): Ueber Aphasie, Amusie und Akalkulie. Stockholm: Nordiska Bokhandlen.

Benton, A. (1977). The amusias. In M. Critchley and R. Henson (Eds.), Music and the Brain - Studies in the Neurology of Music. London: William Heinemann Medical Books Limited.

Luria, A., Tsvetkova, L., & Futer, D. (1965). Aphasia in a composer. Journal of Neurological Science, 2, 288-292.

Sloboda, J. (1978). The psychology of music reading. Psychology of Music, 6 (2), 3-20.

Music Therapy For A Severely Regressed Person With A Probable Diagnosis Of Alzheimer's Disease

ALICIA ANN CLAIR, Ph. D., RMT-BC

Director of Music Therapy

The University of Kansas

Lawrence, Kansas

Research Consultant

Colmery-O'Neil Veterans Affairs Medical Center

Topeka, Kansas

Abstract: This study describes 15 months of weekly group music therapy with a 66-year-old, hospitalized man with symptoms of Alzheimer's disease. A treatment protocol was developed through videotaped analysis of sessions; it included structured vocal and instrumental activities. Observation and analysis of five categories of response in music therapy showed that his behaviors did not change significantly over an 11-week period, despite deteriorations in physical and cognitive capacities over the entire duration.

BACKGROUND INFORMATION

This case study was developed from a preliminary study of music therapy programming for *severely regressed* persons with a probable diagnosis of *Alzheimer's disease* (Clair & Bernstein, 1990). It is a study of a 66-year-old, Caucasian male who had been hospitalized at a Veterans Affairs Medical Center in the Midwest for a little more than three years. He was diagnosed with probable Alzheimer's Disease when he was 57 years old. At that time he was a carpenter, and he had been having difficulties reading blue prints and shop plans for about two to three years. He complained that he could not remember the names of people, even those he thought were familiar, and that he could not remember where he put things.

At the neurological exam his mood seemed depressed. His spontaneous speech was fluent but he paused to find words. He asked the same questions repeatedly. His memory deficit was marked, demonstrated by his inability to remember any of the three objects presented in the testing procedure. Questions concerning the diagnosis of other family members with Alzheimer's disease indicated that two nephews and one niece had been diagnosed with dementias of the Alzheimer's type on the maternal side of the family. The paternal side of the family apparently had no history of Alzheimer's Disease.

Mr. O left high school after two years to support his mother and siblings. He served in World War II in the European Theater. He was married for the first time to his current wife rather late. They had four children, one of whom was killed in a car accident. Three children, ages 18, 16 and 12 still reside in the home. Mrs. O works to support the family.

ASSESSMENT

Mr. O was referred to music therapy three years ago because he no longer had the cognitive capacities to participate in most other activities at the Center. In fact, the only form of therapeutic interventions he received were daily nursing care and a physical therapy stretch group which met three times weekly for 20 minutes. In the stretch group, Mr. O did not participate in response to verbal instructions and prompts. Any participation on his part was a result of physical assistance by staff members.

Observations on the hospital unit revealed that Mr. O was unresponsive, generally. He wandered the corridors and seemed agitated. He required a *geri chair* with a fixed tray to keep him seated during meals. Ocassionally, he was incontinent.

Mr. O had never been a musician, but at the first music therapy session, he came to sit on the piano bench with the music therapist. He sang along with her all the songs apparently familiar to him. These included patriotic songs and the state song.

Mr. O spoke in one-word responses when addressed directly. He was often confused as indicated by his requests for repeated instructions and statements.

Based on the initial session, Mr. O was placed in a small group with three other severely regressed men with dementia. The group met once weekly for thirty minutes with two music therapists.

Music therapy assessment was an ongoing concern. At the time, there was no basis from which to work since there was no known literature concerning music therapy in the treatment of severely regressed persons with Alzheimer's type *dementia.* The first task therefore was to establish a practice protocol which could be used with these patients. For this reason, all sessions during the first twelve months were video-taped and then analyzed to evaluate which activities yielded the most appropriate responses in the group.

Early sessions included singing, movement and rhythm playing activities. Mr. O and other group members responded less and less to the singing activities over time, and it was decided to exclude any sing-along activities with piano accompaniment. If singing occurred in later sessions, it was a spontaneous response.

Movement activities to recorded accompaniments of various types seemed similar to those activities used in the physical therapy stretch group. These were often met with resistance and a need for continual physical assistance. It was decided that only activities particular to the music therapy discipline would be used. Therefore, these kinds of movement activities were discontinued.

Rhythm playing was accompanied by tape recordings of popular big band music, by piano and also by acoustic guitar. This activity seemed to produce agitation in Mr. O, as evidenced by him getting out of his seat and wandering around the room, and facial expressions which seemed to show discomfort. Other group members had similar responses to both tape recorded and live piano accompaniments. It was therefore decided to do rhythm playing with acoustic guitar accompaniment and also without accompaniments.

TREATMENT PROCESS

Mr. O received music therapy for fifteen months through weekly 30-minute group sessions with three other men. The group met at the same time in the same place and in the same seating configuration each week. The music activities were led by two music therapists who used intermittent positive reinforcers throughout each session, such as: physical touch on the shoulder, arm or leg, smiles, facial expressions of pleasure, and quiet, verbal praise.

The protocol eventually developed for these sessions began with a song to greet the group members, calling each by name. This greeting was followed by selections of songs popular during the men's young adult years and some patriotic songs. All participants were encouraged to sing with both music therapists, while one of the music therapists accompanied the song on acoustic guitar. Mr. O responded with singing entire songs during his first year of treatment. Then, his singing began to decrease in duration until he sang just the phrases or choruses of songs during the second year. Even with less singing, Mr. O made eye contact with the music therapists and looked at other group members who were singing. His behavior indicated he was aware there were other persons present.

Following the singing portion of the session, each group participant was asked to choose one of two rhythm instruments presented. These instruments included professional caliber tambourines, hand drums, maracas and claves. After choosing an instrument, each group member was requested to imitate (one at a time) the music therapist's model of several, simple two- and three-beat rhythm patterns. They were then asked to play together as an ensemble. About half of the ensemble playing was accompanied with singing and acoustic guitar by one of the music therapists and the other half was unaccompanied.

Mr. O responded consistently on his rhythm instrument. He usually chose a hand drum or a maraca. He played throughout the ensemble portion of the session. He even learned to imitate rhythm patterns presented by the music therapist. His accurate imitations were limited to short beat patterns, but were consistently appropriate. When someone else in the group was imitating patterns, Mr. O looked at the instrument the individual was using. He seemed to watch intently when it was some else's turn to participate.

Following the rhythm ensemble portion, the session closed with a good-bye song composed by one of the music therapists. Each subject was told good-bye and reminded where and when the next session would be held. Mr. O responded by getting out of his chair and moving toward the door.

EVALUATION

Data Collection

Data were collected from the video tapes of 11 sessions which occurred in the last three months of the established protocol. To determine the behaviors for which to take data, the music therapists observed the video tapes. From these observations they grouped behaviors into categories and defined each in terms of specific criteria. Behavioral categories were as follows:

1) Communicating, including any verbal response;
2) Watching another group member or a music therapist participate or speak;
3) Singing alone or with the group, spontaneously or in imtation, including vocalizing or approximating a melodic contour, humming melodies, saying words, and/or singing words in the

song context;
4) Interacting with an instrument, along or with the group, spontaneously or in imitation, including holding an instrument, rubbing a drum head with a hand or a mallet, striking an instrument, strumming a stringed instrument, shaking a maraca or tambourine; and
5) Remaining seated without physical restraint.

Once the behavioral categories were defined, an independent observer was trained by the music therapists to take the data. The observer then watched each videotape as many times as necessary to get the durations of communicating, watching, singing, interacting with a musical instrument and sitting unrestrained. These data were checked periodically for reliability by requiring the observer to reexamine a session. *Reliability coefficients* ranged from .89 to .97, well within acceptable limits.

Because Mr. O was essentially a nonparticipant in any activities outside the music therapy session, no base line was taken. The structure of the music therapy sessions seemed to promote and encourage his participation.

Data Analysis

Durations for each of the five behavioral categories were obtained. These durations were then converted to proportions of time Mr. O participated in each of the behaviors during the course of the last 11 sessions. Figure 1 presents these proportions. It shows that he sat throughout most sessions and if he did wander, it was very brief and not frequent. The proportions of Mr. O's watching behaviors were up and down. While he watched throughout most of one session, he often was above 40% for the remainder of the sessions. For five of the sessions, he watched for better than 60% of the time. This watching behavior indicated an awareness of his environment which, according to other observations, he did not demonstrate outside the music therapy sessions.

Mr. O's instrumental participation was lower in proportion than his watching behavior. This is related to the amount of time allowed for instrumental playing as opposed to the opportunity to watch throughout the session.

The proportion of singing behaviors for Mr. O were the lowest of all the music participation activities in the sessions. He tended to not sing frequently or for long durations. The amount of time available for singing was about the same as it was for instrumental interaction. Yet, the singing was markedly less than the instrumental playing.

The least proportion of participation for the sessions were in the communication category. These proportions were low since Mr. O tended to be nonverbal in the sessions. Sometimes he answered a question directed at him with a one-word response. More often, he would say "What?" after a

Figure 1

PROFILE OF MR. O'S PARTICIPATION

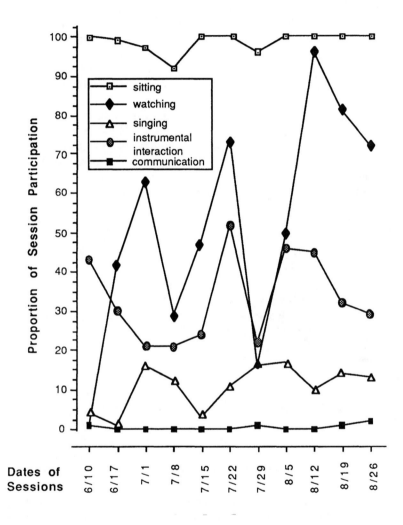

direction had been given, indicating that he was confused and did not understand what he was to do. He did not initiate conversations for the most part with any one in the group.

To determine if there were significant differences in the proportions of participation from the first three to the last three sessions in the 11-week period, a test for significance of proportion (Burning & Kintz, 1977) was computed. This test was calculated for each behavioral category. The test was also calculated between all possible pairs of behavioral categories to determine if the proportion of participation in one category was significantly different than the proportion of participation in the paired category.

The results for Mr. O were not significant for any behaviors over the 11-week period. This indicates his behaviors did not change significantly in any behavioral category. The implication is that Mr. O's behaviors in the session were maintained, though observations of him showed he had deteriorated in physical and cognitive capacities over the duration of the study.

The test for significance of proportion was calculated for all possible behavioral category pairs. The communication category was not included in the comparisons, however, since Mr. O's. communication levels were so low.

The results indicated that the following comparisons were not significant:

1) Watching and Instrumental Interaction
2) Watching and Singing
3) Singing and Instrumental Interaction
4) Sitting and Watching

There were significant differences, however, between the proportions of:

1) Sitting and Singing
2) Sitting and Instrumental Interaction.

These significant differences result from the high proportions of sitting in comparison to lower proportions of instrumental interaction and even lower proportions of singing in the sessions.

Current Status

Mr. O has begun his fourth year as a patient on the extended care unit of the Veteran's Affairs Medical Center. He continues to wander which, in an environment which is not secured, is a threat to his safety Therefore, he will remain on the hospital unit until he is no longer a wandering risk.

Much of the time on the unit Mr. O sits with his arms on his knees with his eyes cast down, looking apparently at the floor. He still feeds himself, but must be given one food type at a time so that he is not distracted. It is not known if he recognizes the music therapy staff who have worked with him for three years. He still seems to recognize his wife and children, though he can no longer speak with them.

Mr. O's small group music therapy sessions were discontinued about one year ago when the 15-month protocol study ended. He is now a passive participant in the unit-wide music therapy session which is held once weekly for 30-45 minutes for all 26 patients.

Though Mr. O no longer speaks he makes vocal responses which resemble a cry. Usually the "cry" is not accompanied by tears. This vocalization may be interpreted as discomfort, excitement, distress, frustration or any number of other emotional reactions. The vocal sounds Mr. O makes do not seem appreciably different from circumstance to circumstance.

During the unit sessions, Mr. O still reaches out to take a maraca when the music therapist offers it to him. After taking it, his usual response is to put it in his mouth immediately, as if it was a baby's rattle. When his hand is touched in an effort to remove the maraca from his mouth, he strongly insists on keeping it there by turning his body away from the music therapist and by crying out in apparent distress. When left unattended, Mr. O stays in the room for the duration of the music therapy session. While there, he turns his head to locate the sound source for music and makes eye contact with the music therapist. He occasionally cries out, but it is not known if this vocal response is an attempt to sing, an effort to speak or some other expression.

DISCUSSION AND CONCLUSIONS

Mr. O deteriorated physically and cognitively during the 15-month treatment program which began three years ago. Since that time he has continued in his deterioration. Even so he has maintained an interest in music and musical stimuli throughout the course of his hospitalization. He currently chooses to stay in the room with the music therapists during music activities, though he is free to leave. He does not participate at the level at which he once did, but he still has the capacities to respond to auditory stimulation. This response usually involves turning his head to locate a sound source and making eye contact with the music therapist. He also reaches for maracas, though he does not play them in traditional ways.

It is hoped that Mr. O's responses to music will continue throughout the course of his illness. Currently, it is the one stimulus, besides food, that attracts his attention. As his disease progresses and he becomes less functional and more isolated, Mr. O continues to have needs for sensory stimulation and contact with other people. Music provides these needs in very unique ways. It is through music that Mr. O can interact with others, and be aware that other people are around him. Music makes it possible for Mr. O to come out of his isolation, even if it is just for a short while. It is hoped that Mr. O will be responsive to music until the last stage of his disease is completed.

GLOSSARY

Alzheimer's Disease: This disease was first described by Alois Alzheimer, a German neurologist who lived from 1864-1915 (Dorlan's Illustrated Medical Dictionary, 1988, p. 54)). It is a progressive degenerative disease of unknown etiology, characterized by atropy throughout the cerebral cortex in which plaques (microscopic lesions) and neurofibrillary tangles (clumps of neurofibrils) develop. The first signs are slight memory disturbances or subtle changes in personality; there is progressive deterioration resulting in profound dementia over a course of 5 to 10 years. Onset may occur at any age (Dorlan's Illustrated Medical Dictionary, 1988, p.481).

Dementia: An organic mental disorder characterized by a general loss of intellectual abilities involving impairment of mental judgement and abstract thinking as well as changes in personality (Dorlan's Illustrated Medical Dictionary, 1988, p. 442).

Geri-chair: A straight-backed chair with arms designed for use with the aged. Usually the seat and back are padded and covered with a washable upholstery fabric. The chair has attached arm and foot rests. A removable tray which can be locked into place fits across the arms, and is large enough to hold a meal or materials for activities.

Reliability Coefficient: The extent to which a statistically derived measure (e.g., a mean or median) from a sample gives the same results upon repeated use under identical conditions (Dorlan's Illustrated Medical Dictionary, 1988, p. 1446). Reliability therefore refers to how consistent the scores are each time a measurement is made in a particular group or in an identical group when tested under the same conditions. A reliability coefficient is the result of the mathematical calculation of a formula which includes these measurements and which is designed to yield a result which indicates their consistency.

Severely Regressed: Regression is defined as a return to earlier, especially to infantile patterns of thoughts or behavior (Dorlan's Illustrated Medical Dictionary, 1988, p. 1444). Severely regressed in this case refers to the infantile type behaviors exhibited by Mr. O.

REFERENCES

Bruning, J. L., & Kintz, B. L. (1968). Computational Handbook of Statistics (2nd ed.). Glenview, IL: Scott, Foresman.

Clair, A. A. & Bernstein, B. (1990). A preliminary study of music therapy programming for severely regressed perosns with Alzheimer's-Type Dementia. The Journal of Applied Gerontology, 9, 299-309.

Taylor, E. (Managing Editor) (1988). Dorlan's Illustrated Medical Dictionary (27th Edition). Philadelphia: W. B. Saunders Company.

Embracing Life with AIDS: Psychotherapy through Guided Imagery and Music (GIM)

KENNETH E. BRUSCIA, Ph.D., CMT-BC
Professor of Music Therapy
Temple University
GIM Fellow: Private Practice
Philadelphia, PA

Abstract. *This case describes individual psychotherapy with Matt, a 26-year old man recently infected with the AIDS virus. In the eleven sessions, Guided Imagery and Music (GIM) was used as the main technique within a psychodynamic orientation. Through an intense process of imagery transformation, Matt gained insight into how traumatic events from his past prevented him from coping with the emotional challenges of living with AIDS. Ultimately, this led him to confront one of the most important questions of his life: Shall I live dead, or shall I die living?*

BACKGROUND INFORMATION

At the time we met, Matt was 26-years-old, and had been diagnosed as *HIV positive* just a few months earlier. I remember our first meeting quite vividly. When he shook my hand, I could feel him trembling. He was tall and gaunt, and had dark circles around his eyes. He looked scared and worried, and smoked one cigarette after another. When he smiled, he had to visibly work the muscles in his face. Sometimes I caught him looking at me to see if I was looking at him.

Matt complained of dizziness, tremors, nausea and fever, for which he was taking several different medications---in addition to AZT (an anti-viral drug for AIDS) and Xanax (a drug to control anxiety). He talked about his symptoms and medication needs in a very serious way, almost as if he needed me to know how much he was suffering, or how sick he was. Perhaps he was trying to tell me how much help he needed. I felt uneasy because, in fact, I was wondering if he really needed to take so many things, especially since many of his symptoms can be side-effects of Xanax (Schatzberg & Cole, 1986). I was also worried that he might be relying on drugs to fix (or numb) everything in his body and thereby relinquishing responsibility for his health to doctors and medicine.

Matt had stopped working, and in the last few months, had also stopped going out altogether. He was "petrified" of passing out on the street from dizzy spells, or having a full-blown anxiety attack with other people around. Apparently, he spent most of his time at home watching television, trying to distract himself from his ruminations and fears.

Matt told me that he had contracted *AIDS* through his work as a hemodialysis technician in a nearby hospital. He said that on several occasions he had stuck himself with an infected needle. As he told me these things, the tone of his voice became quite emphatic, even clipped. It sounded like he did not want me to assume that he had been promiscuous or that he used drugs. It upset me that he might worry about such a thing, so I tried not to change my facial expression or body language. I wondered if he had already experienced blame from others. I thought of all the people I know who justify their detachment from AIDS or their negligence of those who have it by simply saying, "They deserve it!" On the other hand, he himself may have feelings of guilt and shame. Maybe he feels he deserves it.

As Matt continued, I had to change my body position to let go of some of the tension building. Matt has been in a love relationship with the same man for six years. They live together, and Matt feels their relationship is quite strong. John is ten years older, and has a Ph.D. His results were negative on the HIV test. Right now they are having serious financial problems because John has just lost a high-paying job as a hospital administrator. To make matters worse, Matt's current insurance company refuses to cover his medical expenses. Matt changed jobs (and insurance companies) before being diagnosed, and now neither company will take financial responsibility. Matt has also been refused Social Security benefits and welfare. Understandably, his face was filled with anger and frustration.

Matt then shifted the conversation to his family. He has already told them all about his situation: that he is gay and that he is infected with the virus. I was relieved, for this is not always the case: many men like Matt face AIDS alone, without the support they need from loved ones. Matt is very close with his two sisters, and talked at great length about them and their children. Then becoming rather terse, Matt described his mother as a "dominating bitch," and said he has an ongoing battle with her. He then described his father as passive and uninvolved, and said no more.

I then asked him what he would like to accomplish in our work together. Matt replied:

> *I get these terrible images... I can see myself dead... It*
> *feels like I am falling backward into a deep black hole...*
> *I live in constant anxiety, dreading the minute that they*
> *will come back... When they don't go way, I go into*
> *complete panic... Sometimes I imagine John sitting beside*
> *me, and that helps to calm me... After the images go*
> *away, I get very depressed... I can't live like this.*

I was moved by what he said, realizing more each moment how desperate his cry for help was. I also realized that his trembling was more than a body symptom: his whole being was shaking.

I began to explain how *Guided Imagery and Music (GIM)* works: that after helping him to get relaxed and focused, I would put on a specially designed tape of music that would stimulate his imagination; that while listening, he might have body sensations, visions, feelings, memories, fantasies, or any variety of internal experiences; that while he was imaging, we would have an ongoing dialogue which I would transcribe for later reference; and that I would be with him throughout, helping him to explore his inner world in whatever way he wished. We talked about the possibility of his fearful image coming up, and that eventually he may need to confront it. Matt felt willing to take those risks, if someone was at his side.

TREATMENT PROCESS

Moving into Imagery

After preparing the space and making both of us as comfortable as possible (Matt lying on a floor mat, and me sitting beside him), I asked Matt to close his eyes and to start breathing deeply. I then led him through a relaxation induction that I created based on our previous discussions. It involved having Matt imagine a ball of light moving through his body and making each part feel "strong" and "alive."

I took this approach for several reasons. First, I was worried that closing his eyes and experiencing the darkness would trigger his fearful image of falling back into a black hole. Thus, focusing him on a light would help him to illuminate or move away from the darkness. Second, Matt expressed such fear over "falling dead," that I felt that he needed to perceive himself as strong (in control) and alive in order to relax more fully. Third, I purposely used a "see-feel" sequence in the induction (i.e., see the light, feel strong and alive), because in our previous discussions he had described his experiences in this way (i.e., seeing himself dead then immediately feeling himself falling backward). Following how someone sequences their sensory channels to process their experience helps to build rapport while also facilitating inductions to an altered state of consciousness (Grinder & Bandler, 1981).

I selected a GIM tape program that is commonly used for a first session. It consists of six musical selections (which are cited in italics below), lasting a total of 42 minutes. As each piece is quite different in instrumentation, mood and style, the tape has the potential to evoke many different imagery processes (visions, memories, fantasies, feelings); and since each piece is relatively short, the tape also allows the imager to move in and out of each image or process as desired. By encouraging the imager to explore different areas and layers of the imagination, the tape is useful for clinical assessment.

The Imagery Preview

Often GIM sessions present different chapters in the person's life, with the first session giving a preview of the entire story about to unfold. This was particularly true with Matt. Images from his first session set the stage, painted the scenery, and introduced the main characters of his life story. In the ten weekly sessions that followed, these same images returned, transformed, generated new stories, and clarified themselves continuously---as if they were speaking to Matt's psyche with insight and loving persistence.

Matt's began his story alone---stranded on an island. The opening sections of Ravel's ballet, "Daphnis and Chloe" set the scene. {Note to the reader: The italicized sections below are taken from session transcripts. Brackets have been used to enclose my interventions or observations, and titles of the music being heard. Ellipses have been used to indicate silence, passage of time, or irrelevant segments of the transcript.}

> *I am walking along a deserted beach...alone and stranded... I can see a huge rock ahead, blocking the shoreline...[Allegretto from Brahms' First Symphony begins]... I want to walk around it and get to the other*

*side... but I don't know how... [Take a good look
around]... [The "Gianicolo" from Respighi's "Pines of
Rome" begins]... Gulls are hovering over the edge of
the rock, way out in the water... I can't get around it in
the water... I have to walk inland... I'm climbing around
the rock... I see a cave that looks like a big black hole
in the ground... [How do you feel?]... I am scared...But
I'm OK---there are iron gates blocking the entrance... I
am walking past the cave entrance... I see an old dead
tree that has fallen to the ground... Its roots are all
sticking up... Its trunk has been burned and there is a
hole in it... [The "Sirenes" from Debussy's "Nocturnes" is
playing]... It's getting dark and starting to rain... I
don't think I can get around this rock... It seems
senseless to go on in the dark... I better go back to the
beach... I'm walking back... [How are you feeling?]...
Really frustrated... and anxious. I want to get off this
island, but for some reason, I can't... [Tschesnekoff's
"Salvation is Created" begins almost inaudibly] I'm back
on the beach... [How does it look now?] Over the water,
where the gulls were, I can see people dressed in black,
floating and hovering in the air... [Notice anything
else?]... I'm looking all around... Oh, my God... Two men
are coming to rescue me in a boat... I can't see their
faces, but one is dressed in red and the other in blue...
They're taking me to their boat... They don't have
faces... [Pachelbel's "Canon in D" begins]... I'm getting
in... we're leaving... I'm looking back at the beach... I
see a small child that we've left behind... and a huge
black bird is perched on the hill behind him, looking
down...We are reaching the mainland ... The blackbird has
followed us here, and is hovering over us... I'm going
home now, where I can be safe.*

As the tape ended, I helped Matt to return to waking consciousness. In
our discussion of the imaging experience afterwards, I encouraged him to
react to whatever affected him most, while also focusing him on aspects of
the experience that I felt were significant to his therapeutic process.

This session gave an incredibly accurate preview of Matt's process. In
the next seven sessions, he weaved in and out of the main images in this
session, and each time, the images transformed or moved his life story along.
What follows is a description of how Matt worked through these central
images (i.e., the black bird, the rain and the house, the island cave, and the
abandoned child), and as a result was resurrected to a life with AIDS.

The Black Bird

The black bird was a key image in the first session---one that had already begun some kind of active transformation process---from a gull, to hovering people dressed in black, to a huge blackbird with a foreboding and ominous presence. Matt felt threatened by the bird, yet he did not voice his fears, neither during nor after the imaging---as if it was too much for him at the time. Matt was also unable to identify what kind of bird it was. I allowed my own feelings to enter my awareness: I did not trust it with the child. I did not like it hovering and following---like a vulture insidiously waiting to devour a carcas. I was afraid of it.

Before the second session, I went through the transcript I had taken of Matt's imagery, and discovered that the bird appeared when Matt was confronted with an obstacle, when he felt powerless to escape, and when he left the child behind. My inquiry made me feel like I had begun to hover over the bird hovering over Matt, and I wondered why I felt it was important to do this. Does Matt need to be protected, or do I need to reassure myself that (like any good therapist) I could protect or rescue him? Will my rational understanding of the image somehow make it go away? Did I need protection from it?

The bird did not re-appear in Matt's imagery for several sessions, however it did arise quite prominently in his *mandala* drawings. In the first, he drew the bird quite representationally, flying beneath the sun. In subsequent portrayals, it changed positions and shapes. In the next drawing, it was so big that it created an eclipse of the sun; in another it was a large ground mass (like a black hole); and in the next, it turned into shadowy human figures on the edges of the mandala, with their backs towards the viewer.

Then, in the fourth session, the bird presented itself again in Matt's imagery. Bach's "Passacaglia and Fugue in C Minor" set the stage. Matt was walking along a path with the blueman and redman, when the bird appears and starts to follow them. As the melody in the bass repeats over and over, the bird circles and hovers around them, getting closer and closer with each increment in volume. The fugue begins, and relentlessly piles layers of fear and frustration on top of one another as the three men watch the bird hovering over them, arguing among themselves. A terrifying climax is inevitable, and as the chords crescendo to a crashing close, the blueman overcome by anger, shoots the bird to the ground.

A long silence ensues before Bach's "Come Sweet Death" begins---the music is now slow and desolate, and Matt sighs deeply, showing great consternation in his face, despite the relief evident in the rest of his body. When asked, he explains that he feels confused about why the blueman, who is his model of goodness, has killed the bird---rather than the redman (who Matt believes has an evil side). In the next piece (Bach's "Sarabande" from the "Partita in B Minor"), Matt questions the blueman, who refuses to explain himself other than to say: "One day you will understand." Matt's frustration with this evasiveness builds during Bach's "Little Fugue in G Minor" until all three men decide to leave. As they do, Matt has to pass by the dying bird. As he does, the bird tries to communicate to him, but is barely audible. Matt refuses to listen, and supported by the strong bass notes in the fugue, steps over it quickly, in contempt and disgust. In the final fortissimo chord of the fugue, a black snake sneaks away in the grass.

The slow movement of Brahms' "Violin Concerto" begins, and as the violin plays long, tender melodies over a soft orchestral accompaniment, Matt shares how he feels about the redman and blueman. Despite their differences, he loves and accepts them both. Then a wonderful transformation takes place during Bach's "Double Violin Concerto." Matt takes the blueman and redman by the hands and pulls them into himself, as if to unite them and to re-incorporate them into his own being. As he does this, the three merge to form a large green swirl. This integration takes place as the two violins (blueman and redman) play with orchestra (Matt) in perfect, harmonic counterpoint, each part barely distinguishable in timbre but clearly different in contribution.

Afterwards, Matt and I talked about what a relief it was to be rid of the bird. Matt felt like he had been successful in overcoming a menace that had tortured him for a long time. We talked about what menaces in Matt's life this bird might have represented, and how good it felt to triumph over them. We talked about the need to be strong to conquer the menaces of life, including AIDS. We also discussed how uniting the redman and blueman felt like he was literally "pulling himself together."

I was silently skeptical because of the black snake that appeared---I suspected that it was yet another transformation of the bird. The next week, Matt drew a mandala that had a huge black phallus penetrating the lower left part of the circle. In my thinking, the bird had transformed yet again, but I said nothing to Matt. He believed that the bird had really gone away, and in fact, it did not appear in his images for several sessions. Then, another mandala appeared with many black spots evenly scattered throughout the space. I could not help relate it to the previous drawing. It looked like the black phallus had exploded, and germinated enough spots to completely occupy the territory. The spots looked like sperm---the black sperm of the bird (or snake). Since AIDS can be transmitted through sperm, I further imagined that, in Matt's psyche, the bird was the carrier of AIDS, the 20th century black plague, and the black messenger of death.

In the fourth session, the bird re-appeared. Matt was sitting under a tree, as the Adagio from Marcello's Oboe Concerto edged him into feelings. The tree was alive, and its roots were in the ground, but it was very sad and lonely. Its branches were drooping downward, and there was a large hole in the trunk. It sounded like the tree he saw in the first session---before it had been uprooted from the ground. I wondered if Matt had gone back to an earlier time in childhood. He had.

> *I am wearing blue pants and a red shirt... an outfit I had when I was 8-years-old... The blackbird is back... It's perched on top of the tree... [The Adagio of Rodrigo's Concerto de Aranjuez begins]. The tree is trying to shake it off...but it can't. It's starting to rain... My throat is tickling... [Matt's body begins to writhe, and his voice gets constricted]. I am stuck on the ground... I feel caught... paralyzed... My arms and legs are so heavy I can't move... I am trying desperately to move... but I can't....[long silence during orchestra version of Bach's Prelude in E-flat Minor]... [What's happening now?]...I am down at the stream... washing myself... The bird has gone away.*

Matt's images came to a close peacefully, with the Romanze from Dvorak's Czech Suite---as if nothing had happened. I was shocked. What had transpired in those few moments of silence? Since it was not possible to pursue the matter within the imagery, I waited until Matt had regained consciousness, and then asked how he freed himself from the ground. Staring straight into my eyes with a stone face, Matt answered: "Sheer rage!" I noticed that he was trembling again. No more was said.

Strangely enough, the bird never reappeared in Matt's imagery. I took this as a sign that the full story, without symbolic or fictional characters, was ready to unfold. Often, images and symbols provide us with safe ways of dealing with very disturbing material, things that we repress and do not allow into consciousness. The bird had been very important to Matt because, as we shall see, it allowed him to work through very painful material in a gradual and ambiguous way, just as dreams do. The elusive nature of the image and its lack of reality as a "figment of his imagination" allowed Matt to deny or distort its true meaning at the earlier stages; however, every time it recurred, the bird further redefined itself, and in so doing began to gradually debunk each denial and distortion, until Matt was willing and able to admit and integrate into his consciousness what really transpired in that image and what the bird really signified.

This did not happen until a few sessions later. Several other recurring images had to develop sufficiently until Matt would be ready to recount the life events that he was trying so desperately to forget and confront at the same time.

The Rain and the House

Images of rain storms appeared in several of the early sessions. Rain is so ambiguous! It cleanses, muddies, and fertilizes. It can bring relief from a drought, or it can flood the landscape. It can pour down from black clouds or fall gently from grey skies, and when the sun follows, it can bring rainbows and pots of gold. It comes from above, as if the good and bad of it are sent to us from the heavens by God (Cirlot, 1971).

When Matt encountered rain, it was "stormy weather," and he frequently sought refuge in a house.   On the first occasion, Matt was walking along a country road, and passed by a white house that belonged to an elderly couple. Some time later Matt saw black swirls in the sky, and fearing that a storm was coming, ran back to the house for protection. Upon his return, he found that the windows and doors had been boarded up. Unable to go inside, Matt stood on the porch and waited until the dark clouds and rain had passed.

I remember this image so vividly. In my mind's eye, the house looked like the faces of his parents: with their eyes, ears and mouths completely covered. It was as if Matt were seeking the safety of his home, wanting to take refuge in the laps of his parents (the porch), but they had gone off somewhere and left him behind, at least in spirit. Their eyes had blinders on and they were unable to see the storm; their ears had been plugged, and they could not hear Matt's call for help; and most disturbing, their doors were closed, as if they were no longer willing or able to give him refuge from the storm. The image of Matt standing on the porch reminded me of the child who had been left behind on the island, unprotected from the bird.

Each time Matt saw a house in subsequent sessions, there was danger lurking. In the third session, he escaped another storm by running onto the same porch with his lover; in the fifth session, he passed a house before entering the island cave which had frightened him earlier. Again it was raining.

The Island Cave

Matt went to the same island in three of the initial five sessions. Islands are often isolated places where people go to withdraw (very much like Matt's apartment). They are also places of refuge from the ocean---or the deep, threatening waters of the unconscious (Jung, 1954). I felt that this was particularly relevant to Matt. He seemed to be struggling with whether he should allow certain material to emerge or to suppress it. Every time he went to the island he encountered some kind of threat, but then would leave before confronting it. His images on the island were full of fantasy and symbolism, with very few real-life people or events, suggesting that he could only deal with these images if their true meaning was disguised in some way. His repeated returns gave me the sense that he had some unfinished business to clear up there before he could leave it once and for all.

After the bird had been slain, Matt gained greater confidence in confronting images that frightened him. In the seventh session, he returned to the island and proceeded directly to the cave. This time Matt was accompanied by a man dressed in green (the swirl that merged the redman and blueman into Matt).

> *It's too dark to go in... I'm lighting a torch... We're inside... We're walking on a bridge over a huge cavern. At the bottom are deep craters... filled with bubbling black tar. I'm real uncomfortable in here... (What do you want to do?) I'm going to solve this once and for all... We're going back outside, to climb the hill over the roof of the cave. [With determination and a bit of anger in his voice, Matt says to the greenman]: "Let's dig a hole in the ground, and let sunlight into this f--king cave once and for all." We are digging... We've reached through the roof of the cave. I can see down into the cave. I want to go back inside now, and see what's inside. We're back where the hole in the roof is... I can see rays of sunlight coming down... There are tons of green powder everywhere... We are putting it in buckets and throwing it over the bridge... It's cooling down the tar... kind of deactivating it... We've won a battle.*

Afterwards, Matt was quite proud of himself. I told him how much I admired his courage and determination. He saw this session as a triumph over the big black hole that frightened him so, and therein his fear of death. I cautioned him that this image could still return, but that the important thing was that he had created his own "antidote" for it. We also explored what the greenman and the green powder might represent in terms of resources within himself. Matt concluded: "I have to care enough to do something about my problems."

For me, this was one of those split-level discussions therapists sometimes have. Outwardly, I was focused on helping Matt relate his experience and images to his life. Inwardly, I was focused on what implications these images had within the therapeutic process. I was struck with Matt's boldness in letting the sunlight flood the cave, and illuminate its contents. Was Matt readying himself to let the painful material into the light of day? What would emerge from the cave?

I agreed with Matt that the greenman was a part of himself---that part that wanted to help him---not only to pull himself together, but also to help bring something from his unconscious into the light. But I also realized that the greenman was an image of me as therapist. In Matt's positive *transference* towards me, he was beginning to see that I cared, and that through me, perhaps he could care and do something about himself. If there was a negative transference, Matt's concluding statement could have been a warning to me: "You have to care enough before I can do something about my problems."

Paradoxically, it is always scary for a therapist to gain this kind of trust or hope, even though it is a primary goal. I could not help think of all the greenmen in my life. I hoped that, for Matt's sake, I could be like the best of them---not the many that had let me down. I realized that this was a *countertransference* reaction that needed to be examined closely at another time; meanwhile, I had to refocus myself on Matt's needs in the here-and-now.

I often find that significant sessions such as this mark off stages within the therapeutic process, and that a review of what has been accomplished to date is very helpful in consolidating and integrating material that has been brought into consciousness. After we had finished discussing the specific details of the imagery in this session, I asked Matt if we could spend some time going over earlier sessions. To guide our discussion, we put all of his session transcripts and mandala drawings in chronological order, and then proceeded week by week. I asked him to summarize what each session and drawing meant in a few words, as I took notes. Upon finishing, we turned the individual statements into a brief narrative:

> *All of my troubles appear when I am alone---marooned on an island. I let the bird do his thing, as evil as it is, and I will face obstacle after obstacle until the nicest part of me reaches the breaking point. Before I do, I am consumed by fear, and I feel paralyzed to do anything about things, but then I become enraged and this gives me the power I need. There are different parts of me that take over at different times. The most frightening thing is when I stop caring and give up. If I really care---if I really want to live---then I can find the courage to work out my problems. Maybe the courage comes from rage over what life has brought me.*

As a result of this review, Matt and I both felt good about his progress. After the session, I realized that there was still one recurring image that Matt had not explored---the house.

The Abandoned Child

In the eighth session, the tar bubbled up and the full story of Matt's life was brought to light. It was a horrible tale of childhood---one that had made it necessary for him to create his images of the bird, the rain, the house, the island, and the cave.

Matt and I had decided to begin the session with a house as a focus or starting image. To prepare him, I asked him to concentrate on taking in-breaths that brought him inner strength, and releasing out-breaths that brought calmness. I then asked him to return to his favorite house from childhood. Matt began:

> *I am playing in the back yard... where I lived when I was six... I have on red pants and a blue shirt... Mom is calling me to go inside... Everyone has been packing... We're moving... Mom and Dad are leaving to take the last truckload... They have left me behind with Bruce, a friend of theirs... He's picking me up... I'm getting real nervous... He's holding me too tight.. [Matt's body tightens up so much that his trembling stops; his face reddens as if he cannot breathe] I wish he'd stop... Stop!...He's getting on top of me... crushing me... I can't move... I can't breathe... I can't even scream.*

He had been raped. I remember crying---realizing that he could not do so---not then, and for some reason, not now either. I also remember holding back the tears. Matt needed more than tears, he also needed someone strong who could support his rage, and help him survive this ordeal.

As soon as the rape scene ended, Matt's images were flooded with memories of violence and blood, all episodes that actually took place later in his life. He recalled: breaking the neighbor boy's arm with his bare hands (age 8); cleaning up the blood after his grandfather had a lung hemorrhage (age 12); being beaten by his pimp (age 15); killing a squirrel who had been hit by a car (age 18); and being struck by a car himself (age 21).

Afterwards, we talked very little. I said I was sorry for what Bruce had done to him. He said he still felt ashamed, because Bruce continued to rape him for several years. Apparently, his parents were completely oblivious. He admitted that most of the time, he controlled his anger over what had happened to him, but that occasionally it surfaced. When the session ended, I remember hating to say good-bye. I did not want our parting to feel like another abandonment. All I could think of was how he had been left alone that day in the empty house, and that later, he would be alone again in his apartment. He assured me he would be "fine."

As I drove home that night, Matt's images flooded my consciousness, coming together in streams: The hovering bird had descended upon an unsuspecting child who had been left behind, a child who was wearing red and blue. Then, while being held down and unable to move, the phallus was inserted. The rains came in storms of dirty sperm, and the house stood empty with no one to protect him. The family tree had been uprooted, and if it was to turn green again, someone would have to care. Matt was the island, alone then and now, for his secret would always set him apart. Yet he was surrounded by oceans of feelings that could flood him at any time. As with the cave, a part of him had fallen into a black hole and died, and the remains had been locked there with iron gates. In the aftermath came blood---blood that would be shed as sacrifice, blood that caused shame, and ultimately, blood that would become infected as a final punishment.

Resurrected: To Live or Die?

After this, Matt's images were quite different. None of the previous images recurred. The bird, the rain, the house, the island, and the cave had all given full voice to the horrors of his past life. The grief and rage of the child he had left behind were now in his awareness. Matt's life story had been told; it was up to date.

The irony of releasing the past is that, despite the relief that comes, the person is plummeted into the realities of the present---which for Matt, were as ugly as those in the past. The fact that he had AIDS came to the forefront of his consciousness, bringing increased anxiety. His symptoms seemed to worsen, and he became even more of a recluse. He took no consolation in the news from the doctor that his blood count was better than ever, and he ruminated over the progression of the disease. He seemed more frightened than ever, and his trembling was more pronounced. Even his imaging, which had been so easy and productive, was beginning to falter.

Though this seemed like Matt's bleakest hour, his imagery said otherwise. In the next (and final) three sessions, he had tremendously healing images---all related to the death and resurrection of Christ: Matt forgave his father for abandoning him and healed their relationship through a cross; his side was pierced with a harpoon, and he tried to wash it clean with water; and as he walked through the cemetery, Easter lilies bloomed over each grave.

Then came the turning point:

> *I am standing over my own grave...It's open, and I'm looking down at my body... I feel a man's presence behind me. I can only see his face. He's beautiful. His hands are on my shoulders now, and he is telling me to be strong...in a very fatherly and loving way... I feel love towards him, but I am afraid... He is telling me to go back into my body...to get into my body and live...But I'm afraid...how strange...I wonder if I am afraid of living or dying... He is repeating it again: "Go back into your*

body, and live!"... I feel unsteady... like I'm falling back...
I can't stand it anymore... I have to come out!

Suddenly (midway into the tape), Matt's eyes opened and he rose up, like he had just awakened from a terrible dream. Then, with seemingly no rhyme or reason, he blurted:

It's all so clear to me now:
Dizziness is not being held up...
Nausea is what I get instead of crying...
The knot in my stomach is when I lose myself...
Trembling is not having anything to hold onto...

This was the first time I saw Matt lose control of his emotions. And unlike anything that he had ever done before, he asked if I would hold him. I sat next to him, and as I put my arm around him, he rested his head on my chest and cried---very much like a child who needed to cry in the safety of his parent's embrace. I rocked him until his crying and trembling subsided, and then he said something I will never forget: "Living is more like falling into a black hole than dying is."

I was reminded of what Laing (1967) said about the human dread of nothingness: "We are afraid to approach the fathomless and bottomless groundlessness of everything. 'There's **nothing** to be afraid of' [is both] the ultimate reassurance and the ultimate terror" (p. 20). The relevance of an existentialist such as Laing made me realize that Matt had moved from an early life (or psychosexual) crisis to a full-blown existential (cognitive) one.

The Truth Sets Him Free

A few days later, Matt called me at home, and said that he needed to talk. After hemming around for several minutes, he told me that he had not been completely honest with me. For a long time, he had been abusing alcohol and his medications, and could not bring himself to tell me. I could hear in his voice how difficult this admission was for him, and despite my own feelings of shock, I tried to reassure him that his telling me was a significant turning point. I then asked him: "Why are you telling me now? What makes this secret so difficult for you to keep any longer?" In his reply, Matt's progress and the value of our work together was revealed: "Before it didn't make any difference. In the last session, I realized that I have been more dead than alive for a long time. If I'm going to try to live, I better do something about this now, before it's too late."

Matt checked into an in-patient unit of a local hospital for detoxification and treatment, where he stayed for nearly two months. After being discharged, he began regular follow-up treatment with his psychiatrist, and joined a weekly support group for alcoholics who are HIV infected.

Several months later, I called Matt. From what he said, it sounded as though he was back on the road of the living, taking full responsibility for himself. Before we ended our conversation, Matt thanked me and said: "You really helped me to take a look at myself, and to begin embracing the life I still have to live."

DISCUSSION AND CONCLUSIONS

Psychotherapy with Matt involved five dynamic elements: the imagery, the music, the mandalas, my personal perspectives, and our relationship as client and therapist. The roles of each are described below.

Role of Imagery

As implied throughout the case, imagery probably played the most significant role in Matt's treatment. Because they carry symbolic meanings and are by nature ambiguous, images provided Matt with the distance he needed to eventually integrate very threatening material into his awareness. As containers of feelings and the energy attached to them, images also helped Matt to acknowledge his despair, powerlessness and rage which had been buried deep inside since his childhood trauma.

Early in his work, Matt himself realized that his imagery provided symbolic vehicles for working through inner struggles. As we made progress, he also realized that transformations in his imagery provided symbolic representations of real interior changes taking place in his psyche.

Matt once commented that when new images appeared, it gave him an opportunity to discuss things about himself that he had never shared with anyone. Somehow his imaginary world brought forth reality, and presented it in terms that he could talk about with as much distance as he needed.

Images also bring time and timelessness into perspective. Because they are not limited to one time zone, they often reveal the links between different time periods. Thus, the stories that unfolded with each image allowed Matt to see the continuity of his own past, present, and future. Time made sense; sequels from the past became cycles of the present. The evil that the bird perpetrated on him in the past had planted the seeds of shame and guilt, which formed the basis of his present reaction to his AIDS diagnosis, which in turn spread the bird's blackness into an eclipse of his future. Matt realized he had given up on life a long time ago, and that rage was one of the few things left---even if it was suppressed.

Finally, images also instruct and inform the psyche by bringing forth the wisdom that already lies within the person. Matt's images helped him to find meaning in himself and to create meaning for his life. Perhaps, this newly discovered possibility---to find and make meaning out of the meaningless---had more significance for Matt than anything. His past was filled with pain and sorrow---which he suffered for no good reason; his present was filled with anxiety and fear, because of a disease that struck him---for no good reason; and now his life would prematurely come to an end---again for no good reason. What does it all mean? What is life really all about? Is it worth it? These are questions that haunted Matt.

In terms of process, imagery first served as an uncovering technique--- one well-suited for exploring secrets of the unconscious and past. But as Matt progressed in therapy, the past was uncovered, the experiences of the wounded child were revisited, and his unconscious scars were revealed. This allowed the images to move forward in time, and to focus Matt on current issues, and how these issues were residues from the past. At this point, Matt was ready to face the existential conflict that he was experiencing as a person living with AIDS: to live dead or die living.

Throughout this case, and in my discussion of the role of imagery, I have given a great deal of attention to the symbolic meaning and significance of Matt's imagery. I have done this, not because I believe that images always need to be interpreted, nor because this is common practice in GIM, for neither generalization is true. I have emphasized interpretation for several reasons peculiar to Matt's case. First, imagery was the main arena for action and change within Matt's therapeutic process. His progress was inextricably linked to and expressed within his images and transformations therein; it did not depend upon verbal interactions or our relationship, though these elements played important supporting roles. Second, Matt's images were primarily of the symbolic or metaphoric type: he did not often have purely sensory or affective types of images, or images that contained real-life people and places. Third, according to Wilber (1986), different pathologies characterize different developmental stages in the life span, and consequently call for different psychotherapeutic techniques and orientations. I believe that Matt was in the stage of personal development which is characterized by problems originating from the repression of unconscious conflicts from childhood. Unconscious material does not present itself to the psyche in a logical or direct way: rather it relies upon symbolism and ambiguity to make its entry into consciousness more acceptable. Thus, much of our work was geared toward gradually translating the symbolic language of Matt's unconscious into acceptable and decipherable terms, thereby moving him from pathologies steeped in the past to realities of the present.

Role of Music

The significance of music in Matt's case is quite basic: without it, his imagery (which was so central to his process) would not have been as rich, productive, or transformative. Matt was very susceptible to the various elements of music and to changes therein, and his images always related directly to what was happening in the music. In fact, Matt's images were so closely related to the music that I sometimes wondered whether they were dependent upon it. I find that when a person's imagery is "music-dependent," there are two potential problems in guiding, both of which I considered at various times in working with Matt. First, it gave me too much control over his images. I did not want to manipulate his process by selecting and changing the music in ways that would push his imaging in a particular direction. Second, it gave him an opportunity to resist the process. Sometimes, as he would approach an important experience within the imagery and the music changed, Matt would move away from the image to accommodate the music, thus avoiding something difficult or unpleasant that he may have been ready to confront. Other imagers are more "music-independent" and forge ahead with the imagery process they are undergoing, regardless of shifts or even drastic changes in the music.

Ironically, Matt did not respond to music very emotionally. When Matt had intense feelings, they arose from the images, which in turn were supported or amplified by the music---not vice-versa. I might even say that Matt resisted the emotional force of the music, and did not allow it to trigger any cathartic releases.

In contrast, the music helped me to stay emotionally involved and attuned to Matt's images. As suggested earlier, I often felt that I had to model the feeling responses that Matt denied himself.

Last but not least, the music helped to take Matt into deeper levels of consciousness, while also providing him with the supportive matrix he needed to do so.

The Mandalas

Matt thoroughly enjoyed drawing mandalas. From a therapeutic point of view, I found that they helped Matt in several ways. First, they helped him to contain threatening feelings aroused by the music and the imagery. Putting the images, shapes or colors into the confines of the circle provided boundaries for all the material that was escaping from his psyche; it also gave him the means by which he could exercise some control over the emotions attached to the material. Being a recognizable, archetypal form, the circle also afforded him some intellectual control over its contents, for after he was finished, he could take a good look at how everything fit together, and in doing so, he could see the "whole" of it.

From my point of view, the mandalas provided a framework or context for understanding Matt's imagery. And related to this, they helped me to recognize symbolic equivalents in his unconscious material. For example, he used black for several things in the mandalas which related directly to the black bird and its equivalents in the imagery (e.g., eclipse, dark clouds, phallus, seeds, black hole, snake, cave, grave, Bruce, etc.). These equivalences in the mandalas and images bring together seemingly unrelated unconscious material, and reveal symbolic themes or underlying processes operating in the psyche. For example, all of the black images or symbols used by Matt were either evil forces that penetrate (phallus, seeds, snake, Bruce) or empty spaces that are penetrated (black hole, cave, grave). Going one step further, the theme of penetration can be further understood by examining equivalences in the qualities and activities associated to it in the mandalas and imagery. Matt associated penetration to sexual exploitation, fertilization, infection, and burial.

Personal Perspectives

Throughout this case, I have kept the reader informed of my own personal thoughts and reactions to Matt and his imagery processes. I have even shared my projections, interpretations, and countertransference issues. I have done so because these personal perspectives are central to the way I work. For me, psychotherapy, regardless of mode and technique, is a process of travelling between three experiential spaces: the client's world, my own personal world, and my world as therapist.

I see the process as "lending" myself to the client---but not only myself as therapist, but also my personal self. Without going into every one of these spaces, psychotherapy is impossible: I cannot be fully present or empathic to the client without entering his/her world---however to do so, I must leave my own world as person or therapist to do so; I cannot react to the client authentically if I do not leave his/her world and return to my own personal world; and I cannot intervene therapeutically if I do not monitor my travels to both other worlds by seeking the expertise and skill found in my world as therapist. Of course, central to the ability to move between these worlds is the ability to have both fluid and firm boundaries, depending on what is required. A therapist must be able to leave him/herself, but also return at will.

These world travels are required regardless of method, technique or theoretical orientation: for who I am as person and therapist, and how I feel as person and therapist ultimately determine how I will use music, imagery, mandalas, verbal discussions, etc. Without me being fully human as both person and therapist, these are mere artefacts of therapy.

From an existential point of view, I can experience these worlds on three levels: (1) directly (i.e., through spontaneous and unmediated apprehension through the senses); (2) perceptively (i.e., through perceptual or affective classification of the experience, such as hot/cold, sad/happy, etc.); and (3) reflectively (i.e., through thoughtful analysis of relationships between experiences and worlds).

Thus, depending on which world and level of experience is relevant to the moment, I may experience any of the following:

THE CLIENT'S WORLD: Directly, perceptively or reflectively;
MY WORLD AS PERSON: Directly, perceptively or reflectively;
MY WORLD AS THERAPIST: Directly, perceptively or reflectively.
Of course, it is important to also acknowledge that the client has similar options as to which world and level of experience s/he will enter at any point in time.

Client-Therapist Relationship

Matt and I had what I considered a very positive relationship. At the most basic level, I liked him and he liked me. We enjoyed being with one another, and we were rarely at a loss of words. We also laughed a lot.

From a psychodynamic point of view, Matt had an essentially positive transference towards me through most of our work together. This was extremely important, and not always easy, given Matt's past experiences with men in my same age bracket. He resented his father for being weak, blind, and not protecting him from Bruce; and he hated Bruce for the unforgiveable crime of raping him. With this in mind, I had to be strong, reliable, present, kind, and nonsexual. I also took note of what he resented in his mother: she tried to dominate Matt in every way; yet because of her own oblivion, had no control over what Bruce was doing to him. I was careful therefore not to be directive, oblivious, or useless! I felt that it was important to avoid inviting or working through these negative transference issues with Matt because time was limited, and I felt that he desperately needed a positive male or father image. I was also certain that he could not meet the emotional challenges he had to face in our work together without unequivocal trust in me and the support that I would provide.

As for negative aspects of the transference, certainly Matt's concealments could be seen in this light. He had concealed his childhood "shames" from his own father until he was an adult, and similarly, he had hidden his adult "shames" from me until he was ready to terminate therapy. Ultimately, I suspect that the abruptness of our termination also had its origins in negative issues that were out of my awareness and therefore left unresolved. I have often wondered whether he "abandoned" me to punish his own father for abandoning him.

Unfinished Business

Matt's termination was timely yet premature. I missed the opportunity for us to achieve some kind of closure in our work. Given his decision to enter a residential treatment program, it was impossible for us to continue working together until after his discharge; and by that time, we were both in very different circumstances.

Had we continued, I feel that our work would have focused on two areas: dependency and the expression of feelings. My approach to his dependency issues would have been existential, emphasizing the importance of personal freedom, will, choice, and responsibility---this in contrast to a psychoanalytic approach focusing on dependency relationships and deficiencies in holding environments of the past. If a negative transference was present, I would stress the need to be "authentic" in our own here-and-now relationship rather than stuck in someone's else's from the past. Improvisational therapy would have been the method of choice, as it can explore these kinds of issues so directly, and especially within the context of authentic interpersonal relationships (Bruscia, 1987).

Matt did not express his feelings very freely. Even in the most intense GIM sessions, it was difficult for him to cry, lose his composure, or even raise his voice; yet it was quite obvious that he had very intense feelings that were suppressed. Here again, my approach would have been improvisational. I believe that Matt first needs to "sound" his feelings out with full use of his body, before he would be ready to release them fully in nonmusical ways. Once Matt became freer with musical self-expression, we could have resumed receptive methods of cathartic release, such as GIM.

POSTSCRIPT

Matt's case has truly been a source of wonderment to me: How indomitable must the human spirit be---that Matt has survived the ravages of so many rainstorms! How powerful must images be---that they healed Matt's deepest wounds and resurrected his life! What a gift of life music is---that it goes in and out of our deepest and most intimate spaces with such ease---resonating, soothing, and understanding the very fiber of our being. And how human a therapist has to be---to realize that it is not in our knowing or doing that we can help someone like Matt to move along his life path---but in our accepting and loving wherever he is.

GLOSSARY

HIV Positive: Presence of the Human Immunodeficiency Virus (or retrovirus) in the blood, causing an excessive increase in immune suppressor cells and a corresponding decrease in immune helper cells.

AIDS: Acquired Immune Deficiency Syndrome.

Guided Imagery and Music (GIM): Originated by Helen Bonny (1978), GIM is a method of psychotherapy, healing and self-actualization which involves spontaneous imaging to music in a relaxed state, while dialoguing with a guide. The practice of GIM requires special training.

Mandala: A drawing enclosed in large part within a circle.

Transference: Reactions client have towards therapists wherein the client relates the therapist as if the therapist were a significant person in the client's life, usually his/her parents. In a positive transference, the client projects positive feelings about the associated significant person onto the therapist/associated significant person; in a negative transference, the client projects negative feelings.

Countertransference: Traditionally, the therapist's reaction to the client's transference. The author's definition is: any conscious or unconscious reactions of therapists to clients which have their origins in the therapist's own personality or life experience. A positive countertransference takes place when the therapist uses these personal reactions to the therapeutic advantage of the client; a negative one takes place when the therapist is unaware of personal reactions towards the client, and because of this, puts the client at risk and endangers the therapeutic process.

REFERENCES

Bonny, H. (1978). Facilitating GIM Sessions. Salina, KS: Bonny Foundation.

Bruscia, K. (1987). Improvisational Models of Music Therapy. Springfield, IL: Charles C Thomas Publishers.

Cirlot, J. (1971). Dictionary of Symbols. (Second Edition). Translated from Spanish by Jack Sage. New York: Philosophical Library.

Grinder, J., and Bandler, R. (1981). Trance-formations. Moab, Utah: Real People Press.

Jung, G. (1954). The Practice of Psychotherapy. (Collected Works: Volume 16). New York: Pantheon Books.

Laing, R. (1967). The Politics of Experience. New York: Pantheon Books.

Schatzberg, A., & Cole, J. (1986). Manual of Clinical Psychopharmacology. Washington, DC: American Psychiatric Press.

Wilber, K. (1986). The Spectrum of Psychopathology. Treatment Modalities. In K. Wilber, J. Engler, and D. Brown (Eds.), Transformations of Consciousness. Boston: New Science Library - Shambhala.

Songs In Palliative Care:
A Spouse's Last Gift

JANE WHITTALL, B.M.T., M.T.A.
Music Therapist
Vancouver, B.C. Canada

Abstract: *This study describes music therapy with a 42-year-old woman with terminal cancer, who had her wedding on the palliative care unit. Through her choice of songs, she was able to gain insight into her own feelings during the dying process, and by listening to them, she worked through the pain of leaving her husband. A songbook and tape of these songs provided her husband with a last gift of her love.*

BACKGROUND INFORMATION

Claudette was a 42 year-old woman with a *metastatic* brain tumour that had been diagnosed eighteen months prior to her admission to the palliative care unit. As a result, she had a *transient left hemiplegia* and lacked the balance to sit in a chair unless she was well supported with pillows. In an effort to control her seizure activity and pain, she was on high doses of anticonvulsant medications (which caused drowsiness and made long visits impossible) as well as steroids (which caused edema, mood swings and increased appetite). She had had neurosurgery at the time of diagnosis to excise the tumour but it was too extensive. Her hemiplegia set in almost right after surgery. In the subsequent eighteen months, Claudette had remained at home and was relatively symptom-free, but was becoming increasingly troubled by seizures, pain and dysequilibrium prior to her admission.

Claudette's mother came to the hospital at least twice a week and appeared to have a close and supportive relationship with her daughter. Her father had died some time ago. She had been living with a man in common law for many years before she became ill, and decided to marry him as she was arranging her admission to palliative care.

Claudette appeared to be adapting well to her illness by developing an interest in activities that could be done in bed, maintaining her sociability, and focusing on those things that were important to her emotionally. She was seeing the art therapist regularly, but was not viewing these experiences as therapeutically oriented. She was concentrating on drawing for enjoyment. She was very articulate about her needs, though she did not dwell on her difficulties---almost to the point of denial.

Although there were no contraindications for music therapy, Claudette did tire very easily due to her progressive weakness, increased seizure activity and increased anticonvulsant medications. Music therapy sessions, therefore, were usually limited to twenty or thirty minutes twice a week. Claudette was referred to music therapy in a general way, mostly so that she could use music as an activity in bed and plan her wedding music.

TREATMENT PROCESS

Gaining Rapport

I became acquainted with Claudette in an informal way: by planning the music for her wedding together (the wedding was scheduled to take place three weeks after her admission to the hospital), and by providing her with a radio by her bedside. Although she enjoyed talking with me, she assured me that she had no areas of difficulty, and that her real interest in music was to listen to the radio and attend concerts for pleasure. I respected her request, always included her in concerts, and always stopped to chat on my way to see other patients in the hope of building a rapport with her. The wedding took place and was an extremely emotional event for everyone involved. This had been such a priority for Claudette that she became very fatigued afterwards for about one week. At this point, I wondered whether she would feel the need to process some feelings about being so ill, married, and admitted to palliative care.

When the excitement of the wedding had passed, I noticed that Claudette was beginning to ask me more about my role on the unit; she was also telling other patients about me. In the weeks following her wedding, she asked me if I had ever heard of a song called "Chapel of Love." She was glad to learn that I had, but she had asked very casually, and said that it was not really important. In fact, I was unable to find the song and might not have followed through on it, had she not continued to ask me about it on a number of occasions. At long last, I found the song. Its lyrics depict the innocent joy of love. Below is an excerpt:

CHAPEL OF LOVE

Spring is here, the sky is blue
Birds would sing if they knew
Today's the day we say, "I do"
And we'll never be lonely aagin

Because we're going to the chapel and we're
Gonna get married...

I made a tape of this song for Claudette and gave her a copy of the words. She designated it as her wedding song (even though it was not sung at her wedding), and began to play it over and over. She said it was a song of simple beauty, and that so was her wedding. She then asked the art therapist to help her to draw a "chapel of love" from the song in her diary.

Phase One

Claudette asked me if I could find another love song for her called "L'amour, C'est Etc." Again, she did not attach much importance to it, but told me it was a pretty song and she wanted me to hear it. She identified with several phrases in the lyrics. Among them were the following (translated from French):

LOVE IS ETC.

Love is like a bird - it travels great distances and falls
*   from great heights...*
Only when the sun does not rise will you know that you never
*   existed for me...*
Love is like a child - you give him everything and he leaves
*   when he is grown.*
Love is like the summer - we need autumn to miss it.

Again, I taped this song for her (following "Chapel of Love") and gave her a copy of the words. This time, we looked at the words together, and she pointed out to me the strong similes for love and the impact of the last line. "Love is like the summer - we need autumn to miss it." She focused more on the romantic content of the lyrics than on the implication that love is transient. She did, however, ask me for another copy of the words to give to her husband.

As we continued to talk and to develop a relationship, Claudette began to reflect on her relationship with her husband, its beginnings, and its importance to her life. She expressed interest in hearing what she called "their song," and asked me if I could find it for her. She remembered only the title ("L'été Indienne" or "Indian Summer") and main melody, but not the words. The verses with which she identified strongly were (translated from French):

INDIAN SUMMER

Today, I'm very far away from that autumn morning
It feels as if, were I there, I would think of you
Where are you? What are you doing? Do I still exist for you?
I'm looking at this wave, and, you see,
I, like it, am rolling backwards
I, like it, sleep on the sand and remember, I remember
The high tides, the sun, the happiness here by the sea
An eternity, a century, a year ago

I added this song to the tape and gave her a copy of the words. Claudette was surprised in listening to the song and in reading its lyrics to find such a nostalgic tone. She had remembered only the sense of commitment and romance. It was only upon reflection and discussion of the lyrics with me that she began to identify with the sense of loss and longing that is inherent in the song. She began to talk more about how things had changed since she became ill, and no longer assured me that everything was fine. She often cried while listening to this song, saying, "Isn't this ridiculous? It's only a song about someone else and here I am crying. Denis [her husband] tells me not to listen to these songs if they make me cry, but I want to."

I let her know that I had noticed a trend in the songs she had requested and asked her if she had. With encouragement and guidance, she was able to articulate that the songs reflected her recent life path and unexpressed feelings of loss, and she was relieved to find that other people had had similar feelings.

Phase Two

This new insight came at a time of many physiological changes caused by the disease process, and Claudette became more fatigued and weepy. She did, however, ask me to find another song to add to her tape and song book. Below are excerpts from the song that reveal the main theme (translated from French).

GOOD-BYE LOVERS

*I guess it's not always enough to love each other, because we
    weren't made to live together...
And now that you have to leave, we have a hundred thousand
    things to say
that are too close to our hearts - given such a short time...*

*We'll leave each other just like we loved each other
    Without thinking about tomorrow...
We'd forgotten something though
It's hard to say goodbye
And I know very well that sooner or later
    today, or tomorrow, maybe
I'll tell myself that all is not lost from this unfinished book
I'll make up a fairy tale, but I'm too old
And I wouldn't believe it...
A simple story like ours - one we'll never write
Come, little one, we must go, and leave our memories here
We'll go down together if you like*

Once again, Claudette knew the title and the melody, but did not know the words. When I presented them to her, she was astounded to see how related to death they were and asked "Why am I choosing such depressing death songs?" We talked about the possibility of her having an unconscious notion about the theme of these songs, and talked about speaking through

metaphors in song lyrics. I assured her of the progress she had made and of the wealth of her resource---MUSIC---in coping with her illness. She then said she had never been much of a talker, and wanted a way in which to include her husband in this process without upsetting him. It was at this point that I suggested making a booklet of all the songs in the order of her choice that could be left as a legacy for her husband as well as an accompanying tape. I emphasized the importance of her telling her husband about our sessions so that he would not find such a legacy to be depressing during his own grief process. I relied upon her to talk to him about these things, as her husband's visits almost never coincided with my time at the hospital.

By this time, Claudette was much weaker and I was not able to see her as often. However, she asked me for one more song whose title she knew and said it was a sad song. The following excerpts were taken from the end of the song, and give its main message:

HONEY, I MISS YOU

*...I came home unexpectedly and found her crying needlessly in
the middle of the day
And it was in the early spring when flowers bloom and robins
sing, she went away...
One day while I wasn't home, while she was there all alone,
the angels came
Now all I have is memories of Honey, and I wake up nights
and call her name
Now my life's an empty stage where Honey lived and Honey
played and love grew up*

*And Honey I miss you, and I'm being good
And I'd love to be with you, if only I could.*

Once again, Claudette was surprised at the death-specific theme of this song, how she came to choose it without consciously knowing the words, and how it reflected her recent process. This was the last song that was included in her legacy tape and song book. Until this point, she had been keeping her husband updated on our sessions and had prepared a song book for him with me.

Shortly after we worked with this song, Claudette had a severe seizure and was no longer lucid enough to process at this level. Although this occurred during her third month of hospitalization and she lived another three months, I left the hospital soon after this episode and, consequently, was not involved in her husband's bereavement process.

DISCUSSION AND CONCLUSIONS

Claudette's case points out several important factors to consider when working with the terminally ill. Many of us have come across countless references to the stages of dying, and, therefore, sometimes rely on our assessment of a particular stage instead of on the patient's appraisal of the situation. In this case, perhaps there was some denial; but it appears to have been a valuable coping mechanism for Claudette's emotional survival. This is why it is important to give the person space, and to take cues from him/her as to the content and depth of music therapy sessions. I believe that this respect is an essential element in gaining rapport and in establishing a relationship in which the therapist does very little other than support and encourage the patient. Working from a planned theoretical orientation, in this case, would have gotten in the way of my ability to give Claudette the space she needed. I would not have "been there" for her---I would have "done something" to her.

The selection of songs and their order reflects the process of moving from denial of emotional turmoil to the gradual identification of the main issues that were of concern to Claudette. This process also gave her insight about the opportunity to reach some emotional resolution about leaving her loved ones.

The making of a tape of these songs helped Claudette to slowly process this newly acquired insight (because she listened to the tape very often), and to provide her loved ones with a gift that would outlive her. This was perhaps one of the most personal gifts she had ever given, as it shared the inner emotional turmoil of her last days of living, as well as providing her loved ones with a legacy of her life. In the bereavement process, this might might serve as a *transitional object* for those who are grieving since it is a real presence of Claudette's personhood, yet it is also very soothing.

This process will, hopefully, live on in memory of Claudette, whose husband now has her legacy tape and song book.

GLOSSARY

Metastatic - Spreading.

Transient Hemiplegia: Paralysis on one side that comes and goes, in this case, because of pressure from the tumour on the spinal cord.

Transitional Object: An object that is treasured (often because of its association with loved ones) and therefore a source of comfort when separated from loved ones.

Life Review With A Palliative Care Patient

CHERYL BEGGS, B.A., M.T.A.

Nordoff Robbins Diploma in Music Therapy

B.A. Honors Music Education

Music Therapist in Private Practice

Past-President: Canadian Association for Music Therapy

Sarnia, Ontario: CANADA

Abstract.   This case describes the use of life review with an 86-year-old amateur violinist in palliative care. Given the patient's rich musical past, the life review process involved reviving his love for playing the violin, encouraging him to play his song repertoire for the therapist, his family and other patients, and eliciting personal memories through song reminiscence. A videotape was produced of a life review session, and a special musical evening with his family was held as he neared death.

BACKGROUND INFORMATION

At the time of this case, Mr. H was an eighty-six year old man in *palliative care*. He was born on June 25, 1889. He was married with five children, and served as patriarch and provider for his family. Mr. H's illness began in 1958 when he had a cancerous growth removed from his colon. Then in 1975, he was hospitalized for a prostate operation. Shortly before this time he had confided in his family that he had cancer of the prostate. In 1985, he entered the hospital because of a loss of bladder control. After this, he was primarily bedridden and unable to control bodily functions. He again entered the hospital in late January 1986 with the diagnosis of prostate cancer with metastasis.

It was at this time that he was referred to weekly music therapy sessions for the following goals: to promote independence, to increase acceptance of his limitations, and to encourage him to communicate musically.

A music therapy assessment designed by the author was conducted during the first session. It revealed that he was a native of Nova Scotia of English/Scottish descent and a member of the Church of Latter Day Saints. He had worked for Ford Motor Company before retirement. His family has been very supportive throughout his illness.

As for his musical background, Mr. H was a violinist who loved old time music. He had learned to play the fiddle when he was a teenager in Calgary, and as a country boy played it for amusement. In his mid-twenties, he put the violin on the shelf for a while, and did not touch it again for thirty-five years. Then in the late 1950's he went to a fiddle contest and decided to give it another try. He won a prize in the class of sixty-year-olds and over.

In the 1980's, after his wife had succumbed to Alzheimer's Disease, Mr. H made a practice of visiting the "old folks homes" around Windsor and playing for "the poor old souls," as he called them---many of whom were younger than he.

Since being hospitalized in January of 1986, Mr. H had regressed to the point of dependence on staff and family for his daily needs. He had essentially given up on himself and lost the will to live. It was decided that a caring humanistic approach was needed to encourage him to resume some responsibility for his life.

TREATMENT PROCESS

Music therapy was scheduled on a weekly individual basis with sessions lasting from 30 to 90 minutes. The sessions were held in a typical double room in a general hospital. Since Mr. H was clear in mind, and enjoyed talking about and playing music, the technique called *"life review"* was the logical choice of treatment method. It allows for a natural pairing of music and verbal discussion in exploring important life events. This combination also led to many creative musical experiences for both him and the therapist. The life review was accomplished through singing, playing, and listening to music that was important in Mr. H's life, and talking about any associations and memories that were triggered by the music.

Rediscovering the Violin

The first session began with Mr. H mistaking the music therapist for the dietician. He immediately began to complain about the hospital food. I proceeded to tell him that I was the music therapist, at which time he promptly pushed his food away and said: "Music is the best medicine." He then told me that he was a violinist, and asked if I could play the violin. I replied that piano and voice were my main instruments, but that I had played a little on stringed instruments. He then asked me to get his violin from the closet and tune it for him. I proceeded to do so (quite poorly), until he took the violin from me and began to tune it himself. This was an important step because he had done so little for himself in the past, and this was at least an attempt to begin regaining some control over his present situation. Mr. H was then encouraged to get out of bed to play, but he refused and instead played lying down with the bed raised.

Reactivation Through Music

During subsequent sessions, music played a role in encouraging Mr. H to get dressed and to use the wheelchair to come to music therapy. By this time, we had moved from his room to a larger space down the corridor to give him a change in environment. Playing the violin kept his mind alert, and he often commented that the more he played the more the titles of songs came back. Mr. H requested music therapy on a daily basis, but eventually accepted that sessions were only available on a weekly basis. Actually, this motivated him to find other ways of making music during the week. He soon began entertaining everyone with his playing, and was praised enthusiastically by other patients and the nursing staff. He also brought tapes of his own playing to listen to during his physiotherapy sessions.

In the music therapy sessions, Mr. H invited me to accompany him on the piano. He would select the songs (many of which were unknown to me), and before starting would tell me the key and chord progressions for the song. Sometimes he gave me tapes of his old band playing so I could learn the style of a song from listening. He took great pride in sharing these tapes with me, and would often say, "With all the letters beside your name, you'll have no trouble learning these songs. Psychologically, his playing increased his emotional well-being, while also promoting a sense of accomplishment and self-worth.

A Videotaped Life Review Session

By June of 1986, Mr. H was confined to bed, but despite intravenous tubes in his left arm and weakening muscles in his right arm, he continued to play the violin, bowing as best he could. He reported having some pain, but often refused pain medications in the morning, and he never complained of physical discomforts during music therapy sessions. Once he commented, "The only pain I have are tears of joy in my eyes when you come to seem me." He also reported that his pain and discomfort lessened by the end of music therapy sessions.

The musical life review was conducted on June 12, 1986. Mr. H agreed to have the session videotaped so that others could see the importance of music therapy. The life review was conducted by posing questions to Mr. H about his musical past. Questions were sequenced chronologically, beginning with songs Mr. H remembered from his childhood and youth, and then songs important during his adult years. We discussed the most significant musical works and styles, and his specific preferences. Mr. H also talked about what his life would have been without music. As we moved into the present, I asked him what the value of music had been in hospital. He replied that he would have felt weak and helpless.

Mr. H and I also played some of the music we discussed. The music selections ranged from old-time jigs, reels and waltzes to pre-1900 songs, spirituals and hymns.

The Final Stage

When it became increasingly obvious that Mr. H had little time left to live, a special evening was held in his honor by his family, a palliative care volunteer and myself. Mr. H played the violin, and his family sang while I accompanied on the piano. Mr. H's daughter also gave him a special tribute by singing "Somewhere My Love" from the film, "Dr. Zhivago." Mr. H had often played a tape for the therapist of his daughter singing this song. It was a very touching evening to hear such music coming from his hospital room.

Music therapy sessions drew to an end when Mr. H became too weak. When the final stage of dying came, the head nurse told me that I should say my goodbyes. I went to see Mr. H for the last time. We thanked one another for the times we had shared. Few words were needed. He died shortly thereafter, on September 25, 1986.

After his death, Mr. H's family donated a portable keyboard for use in music therapy. A gold plaque inscribed with "In memory of Mr. H" was placed prominently on the keyboard, and to this day serves as a constant reminder of our special relationship.

DISCUSSION

Music therapy provided Mr. H with an outlet for self-expression, while also motivating him to become more independent and to communicate with and relate to others. This also helped him to maintain feelings of dignity, self-accomplishment and self-worth. The music also facilitated reminiscence and evoked memories of significant events and people. The main factors contributing to these results were the strong and open relationships formed between the patient, his family, the palliative care team and the music therapist.

Music therapy also helped the family by giving them opportunities to share in Mr. H's music, and to have positive memories of him during the last few months of his life. These memories will be enhanced for years to come by the life review videotape documenting Mr. H's involvement in music throughout his life.

GLOSSARY

Life Review: A musical profile of a person, consisting of selections of music which have special meaning for the person at various stages during life.

Palliative Care: A program of active, compassionate care of the terminally ill aimed primarily at improving the quality of life. It is delivered by an interdisciplinary team that provides sensitive and skilled care to meet the physical, psychological and spiritual needs of both patient and family.

Music Therapy At The End Of A Life

JENNY A. MARTIN, M.A., CMT
Music Therapist
Calvary Hospital
Bronx, New York

Abstract: *This case describes music therapy with a woman dying of cancer and her family. Phases in the therapy process are described, and the techniques of "Song Choice" and "Life Review" are illustrated. Personal thoughts and feelings of the therapist are presented.*

INTRODUCTION

Dying is never easy, neither for the dying person nor their family. While it can be a very frightening experience, one which involves facing many painful changes, it can also be a time of warm, intimate sharing. Music therapy can play an integral role in this time of transition. Music, because of its capacity to give voice to the ineffable, its capacity to express beauty and pain simultaneously, and its ability to transport us to another time and place, provides the music therapist with a particularly well-suited tool with which to help dying patients and their families cope with the difficult challenges they face.

This case describes music therapy with a woman dying of cancer and her family. I will illustrate how various music therapy techniques are used, and I will share what it is like to do this kind of work from the therapist's perspective. Although music therapy with the terminally ill can be very brief, people approaching death can be open to others in a way that is most unusual It can be a singularly touching experience to enter so intimately into someone's life at the very end, and especially when joined by a lifelong friend----music.

BACKGROUND INFORMATION

Medical History

Sarah was admitted to Calvary Hospital with a diagnosis of breast cancer with *metastases* to the lungs, other breast, lymph nodes and skin. Calvary is a 200 bed hospital which provides *palliative care* to those with advanced cancer. Sarah had been diagnosed with breast cancer approximately two years previously. At the time of diagnosis, she had received radiation therapy, and four months later, she had a mastectomy which was followed by additional radiation therapy. She responded fairly well until a year later when she had a recurrence. Chemotherapy was attempted, but the tumors continued to grow, and Sarah started experiencing shortness of breath.

When she was admitted to Calvary she had a massive infiltrating right chest *lesion*, and *edema* of the right arm. She was experiencing intermittent pain, and had a fever secondary to infection in the chest lesion. She was increasingly lethargic and essentially bed-bound. The admitting physician also noted that Sarah was experiencing anxiety. He also documented that she did not want to be resuscitated, that a DNR (Do Not Resuscitate) order had been in effect at the previous hospital.

Sarah was receiving a variety of medications, including Morphine Sulphate (MS) for pain, antibiotics, Xanax for anxiety and oxygen to help with the shortness of breath.

Psychosocial History

At the time of admission Sarah, a Caucasian woman of the Protestant faith, was in her early fifties. She had three children, two sons and a daughter, all in their twenties. Her youngest son, who was living at home had a problem with substance abuse, and her daughter was described as having "multiple problems." Sarah's husband had died suddenly two years earlier. Within the last two years her brother had also died, thus she had experienced much grief in the recent past.

Her sister, Jane, in her early forties, was her primary means of support. Sarah's and Jane's relationship had gone through many significant changes. As they were growing up their mother (who was an addict) was unavailable to them, thus Sarah, being ten years older than Jane, took on the role of mother in many ways. In adulthood, Jane had become an alcoholic and Sarah had stepped in to help care for Jane's family. There had been a period of estrangement between the sisters, attributed to Jane's alcoholism. When Jane joined Alcoholics Anonymous and became sober, around the time of Sarah's diagnosis, the rift was bridged.

The Social Work admission note stated that Sarah was aware of both her diagnosis and her prognosis. The Social Worker also noted that Sarah was coping by using many facades to keep herself going, and that she expressed concern about not wanting to be a burden on her family. Sarah acknowledged having come to depend on her sister Jane.

TREATMENT PROCESS

Preparation

Sarah was referred for music therapy one week after she had been admitted to the hospital. She was referred by the Social Worker, the reason being that the "patient could benefit from additional support." The social worker also mentioned that Sarah was interested in making a tape for her children, and wondered if I could provide her with the necessary equipment.

Before going to see the patient I reviewed her medical chart in order to gain an understanding of her basic history. While all the patients at Calvary have advanced cancer, they vary greatly in terms of age, ethnicity and religious background, how recently they have been diagnosed as well as the course of the disease and treatment. All of these factors will influence a person's pattern of coping.

In addition to the above medical and psychosocial history, I looked for information regarding how the patient was adjusting to the hospital and any changes in her medical and/or psychosocial status since admission. The nurse's notes described her as "friendly and cooperative," and noted that she appeared "to be adjusting well." Three days after admission she had refused her Xanax and the routine Xanax had been discontinued as the physician noted her anxiety had lessened. She was receiving the oxygen continuously and had periodically been complaining of pain.

Introducing Music Therapy

When I first meet a patient I usually begin by explaining what, as a music therapist, I do at Calvary. This allows the patient to make an informed decision whether it is something they would want. When I entered Sarah's room (all of the rooms as Calvary are private rooms), I saw a rather large woman, lying in bed, the head of the bed raised, breathing with the help of an oxygen mask. I introduced myself and told her why I had come to see her, stating that the social worker had mentioned to me that she would like to have access to a tape recorder. Sarah answered that yes, she would. There were things that she would like to say to her children, and she was now too weak to write. I sensed that even speaking to me now was somewhat of a strain.

Sarah, while not exactly reserved, also struck me as someone who would need some time to get comfortable enough with someone to open up to them. I therefore decided that this first meeting would be relatively brief, focusing on the concrete task of operating the tape recorder. I showed her how it worked, and left it within reach of the bed so she would be able to use it if she felt strong enough.

Two days later I visited Sarah to see how she was doing and how things had gone with the tape recorder. She said that she had not yet tried to use it. She just had not felt up to it. I had the foreboding feeling that this was a task that, though important to her, might be left undone. Wanting to have something to base our interactions on other than the tape recorder which she might never have the strength to use, and feeling that Sarah could certainly benefit from music I introduced some other aspects of music therapy. I explained that much of what I did was to play guitar and sing for the patients, adding that some patients like to sing along, some want only to listen, others fall asleep while I play and that others simply are not interested in music. In my brief description of music therapy, I strive to get the idea across that our use of music is quite flexible, and that the music is available to patients to use in whatever way suits their needs at any particular time.

Most people have no experience with or understanding of music therapy; they have not chosen to come to music therapy. It is important to help them understand how it is different from entertainment, which is most people's experience of music, and to take away the pressure for them to respond in a certain way. Sarah liked the idea of my playing for her, but did not want any music at that time.

During the next week I stopped by to see Sarah several times, but she was sleeping each time. I chose not to wake her. Ten days after having left the tape player with Sarah, we had our first session. During this time she had gotten somewhat weaker, her arm was more swollen and in general she was experiencing more pain. Her sister Jane and a friend, Emily, were also present. There was a warm feeling in the room, I got the sense that these three women cared about and understood each other deeply.

Song Choice: The First Encounter

The music therapy technique I used during this session was "Song Choice," allowing the patient and her two visitors the opportunity to choose songs, which I then played. Song Choice on the surface can appear simple, yet when it is sensitively used, it can be a very rich therapeutic technique (See Bailey, 1984). It is often difficult for terminally ill patients and their families to recognize and express their feelings directly through words, yet they often choose songs in which the lyrics clearly express what they are experiencing. Whether this process is conscious or unconscious, it provides an excellent means of self-expression, which is important at this time. Often patients and families can be encouraged to discuss the themes and feelings presented in the song material.

Song Choice also provides an excellent means for patients and families to appropriately exercise control. This is important because terminally ill people have lost control over so many aspects of their lives. They can decide if they want to hear happy, sad, nostalgic, silly or sacred music. The feeling of being in control may also help them to have the courage to broach difficult topics. Song Choice is also a powerful assessment tool. As therapist, I am keenly aware of the kinds of songs which are chosen, as well as those which appear to be avoided. I also am sensitive to patient's reactions, both verbal and nonverbal, to the songs, both the music and the lyrics.

During this session Sarah asked to hear two songs, "Amazing Grace" and "Morning Has Broken," both religious songs. It was interesting because Sarah had not discussed religion very much up to this point, and there had been no mention of religion in the Social Worker's notes or conversation. Sometimes chart notes comment that patients' religious beliefs are a source of strength and/or comfort for patients. Jane asked for the last song, requesting "When Irish Eyes Are Smiling." My sense was that she wanted to finish on a lighter note.

The next session, again with the three women, took place one week later. Before going into Sarah's room, I reviewed her chart for information regarding changes in her condition and relevant psychosocial information. The nurse's notes documented that Sarah was complaining of increased pain, and that the lesion was worse. The Social Worker reported that Sarah was slowly opening up to her, and that Sarah spoke of how it is difficult for her to be in such a dependent, helpless situation, and that she feels that she has no control over anything.

I continued using music therapy in a similar fashion as in the first session, allowing Sarah, Jane and Emily to choose songs that they would like to hear, and discuss the feelings and memories evoked by these songs. I would periodically ask questions to help expand and clarify what they were feeling or expressing.

Towards the end of the session Jane asked to hear the song "Puff the Magic Dragon" (Lipton & Yarrow, 1965). This is an interesting song in that while it is a children's song filled with fantasy it also very vividly deals with the issue and feelings of loss. Puff is devastated by the loss of Jackie Paper:

PUFF THE MAGIC DRAGON - EXCERPT

His Head was bent in sorrow
Green scales fell like rain
Puff no longer went to play
Along the Cherry Lane

Without his lifelong friend
Puff could not be brave
So Puff that mighty dragon
Sadly slipped into his cave.

As I played this song, which starts off so cheerfully and then turns quite sad, I could feel the atmosphere in the room change as the song progressed. Jane, standing at the foot of Sarah's bed, was singing along with the song. Towards the end both she and Sarah were crying, as was Emily. After a period of gentle silence, I commented that that was quite a song. Jane started speaking of what the song meant to her, and why she thought that she may have chosen it. She acknowledged that when she first asked for it she had not remembered the ending. At the same time, she felt on some level that she must have known, and that she really had chosen it because it expresses how she will feel when Sarah is gone. She went on to say that one of the reasons the song is so meaningful is because it clearly depicts the different stages of Puff's and Jackie's relationship, and clearly demonstrates that it was because of the love and good times that Puff had shared with Jackie that he was so sad when Jackie was gone. She again related this to her and Sarah, acknowledging that it was because of the love that they shared that it was so hard for her to lose Sarah.

I left this session having a great deal of respect for both Sarah and Jane, as well as the music therapy process. I admired the way Jane was able to both identify and share her feelings about Sarah's impending death. I was also once more appreciative of the power of music to evoke and express difficult feelings.

Music Therapy Assessment

The procedure at Calvary is to write a music therapy assessment following the second music therapy session. In the assessment I examine the patients amenability to music therapy, as well as possibilities for various levels and kinds of participation. I describe the ways the patient has used the music thus far. I identify some of the needs of the patient that can be addressed in music therapy, as well as possible methods and techniques that could be used to meet these needs. I also write about any involvement in the sessions by family members. Following is the assessment I wrote for Sarah:

> Sarah is a XX year old woman with Cancer of the Breast with metastases to the lung. She experiences shortness of breath and her arm is quite swollen, thus she would not be a good candidate for music-making during sessions. She is very amenable to and appreciative of music. I have seen Sarah two times in music therapy along with her sister Jane and a friend. She participated through song choice, follow up discussion, and singing along some, to the extent that she was able given her shortness of breath. Sarah, her sister and friend openly express enjoyment of the music and use it as a springboard for discussion of a variety of topics, including memories and feelings regarding Sarah's illness and expected demise. Sarah is very open and articulate, and her sister is very supportive and communicative. Song Choice is a good means of self-expression for Sarah, sister, and friend; they consciously choose songs depending on what they need, choosing religious, happy and sad songs on different occasions. This also provides a sense of control. Sarah will mention her difficulties, but thus far has not wanted to discuss them in any detail. The treatment plan will be to see Sarah one to three times per week in music therapy until further modification. Interventions will focus on: (1) Facilitating self-expression via song choice and follow up discussion; (2) Diminishing anxiety through use of soothing, familiar music; (3) Facilitating communication with sister through use of song material; (4) Providing opportunities to appropriately exercise control via song choice; (5) Providing support to Sarah and sister through involvement in music therapy. The overall goal is to help Sarah and her sister adjust to Sarah's deteriorating condition.

Intimate Sharing

The next music therapy session took place five days later. This time I saw Sarah alone. I had decided that while continuing to have joint sessions with Sarah and Jane I also wanted to see Sarah privately a few times. This was because I had noticed that Sarah appeared reticent to discuss any of her difficulties, and felt that it might be easier for her to be more frank and open if Jane was not present. It is often easier for patients to delve into painful or frightening material when family members are not there. As Sarah appeared to have a need to keep up a facade for her family, I wanted to provide her with the opportunity to discuss some of her feelings and concerns when we were alone, when she did not have to protect her family.

Sarah's medical chart documented that she was experiencing increased shortness of breath, was using the oxygen continuously, and had increased pain accompanied by pressure on her chest. Her morphine dosage had been increased. There was greater edema in her arm and she had complained of feeling nauseous.

There was a give-and-take during this session: Sarah picked the first song and then insisted that I pick the next, and we rotated back and forth like this during the session. Although I generally encourage patients who are alert to choose all the songs, they often want me to choose some of my favorites also. Sometimes they feel that it is selfish for them to choose all the songs. With Sarah, I felt that a more likely interpretation of this was that, given the in-depth discussion of the significance behind the choice of songs which had taken place in previous sessions, Sarah felt that she was sharing a lot of herself through her song choices, and wanted the exposure to be a little more equal. The desire to know something about the therapist is not unusual, and I find that, in general with this population it is therapeutically beneficial for the therapist to disclose more about him/herself than is the norm in therapy.

Before starting the music I asked Sarah how she was doing. She told me how she had been feeling nauseous lately, and that the shortness of breath was getting worse. She was somewhat anxious and concerned about this, both because it is extremely unnerving not to be able to get one's breath, and because she interpreted these symptoms as a sign that the disease was progressing. After talking about these concerns I asked her if she would like to hear some music. The first song that Sarah asked to hear was "His Eye is on the Sparrow." This song is an encouraging spiritual, the chorus being: "His eye is on the sparrow and I know He watches me." While being hopeful, this song also discourages feelings of hopelessness or frustration because of the promise that God is watching. For Sarah it seemed like an interesting song choice in that it signified her need for hope in the face of her worsening symptoms, as well as the message that, on some level, maybe she should not be feeling what she was feeling. She seemed to have trouble taking care of herself and accepting that her feelings and needs were OK.

Sarah asked me to pick the next song. I decided to support her need for hope, and chose a song called "Song of Hope." This song speaks of how we can be overwhelmed by hardship and asks for help to come to a more positive place. I changed the words somewhat so as to be more appropriate to palliative care. The first verse, as I sing it at Calvary is:

SONG OF HOPE - EXCERPT

When the darkness overwhelms us
To dim our sight and mind
When all roads lead to confusion
And hope's impossible to find
Free our minds for dreaming
Of a time when pain shall ever cease
Free our eyes for vision
That leads us to the ways of peace.

The next song that Sarah asked for was "Raisins and Almonds," a Jewish lullaby describing a child being tucked into bed and sung to by his mother. When Sarah asked me to pick another song, I stayed with the theme of childhood and comfort, and sang a song called "Dolphins and Mermaids." This song presents nice images of dolphins and mermaids swimming in the sea, and also points out that our bodies and the various limitations are not as important as what we have inside us, our minds, and our hearts. I have found that imagery is often useful in relieving anxiety and thus diminishing the perception of pain.

The last song that Sarah asked to hear in this session was "Erie Canal." In this case, I did not have a clear understanding of the significance of this song for Sarah other than knowing that for many people the timelessness of folk songs seems to provide some sense of comfort.

When we were ending, I asked Sarah what the music sessions were like from her perspective. She spoke of how she had always enjoyed music, often felt very peaceful when listening to music. She said that she had never expected to find that enjoyment and source of peace here in the hospital. Recalling the sessions we had had with Jane and Emily, Sarah found that she was listening to the words of songs more now than ever, and that sharing the music with her sister and friend was very touching. She commented that she had never expected to depend on her sister as she was now, and that the music sessions somehow "took the edge off" of that. She described the music as "a real source of enjoyment." She also spoke of the comfort provided by the music and how the lullaby "Raisins and Almonds" made her think that some people might never have known what it was like to be tucked in.

The next session took place one week later. Sarah's general condition was about the same: she continued to be weak, with shortness of breath and her arm quite swollen. This session, like the previous one, was with Sarah alone. Again we went back and forth, Sarah picking one song and me choosing the next. Sarah asked to hear "Let There Be Peace on Earth," and "I've Just Seen a Face." I chose "I Believe" and "Perhaps Love." Sarah spoke somewhat more openly of the feelings and memories evoked by the music, as well as the changes she was going through in her relationships to others, these changes being precipitated by her worsening condition.

Sarah spoke of life when she and Jane were growing up. Since she had been like a mother to Jane in many ways, it was a struggle now to be so dependent on her. Speaking of her children, Sarah expressed concern about them, especially the younger two. At the same time, she was able to acknowledge that she had honestly done all that she could, and that it was time to trust and let go.

Sarah also spoke of how tiring visitors were. With gentle probing, she admitted that she felt the need to "keep up a front" with her family and friends. She did not want to bring them down with her. We discussed what a strain this was on her, and whether this was really how she wanted to spend what little energy she had. I asked her if Jane was aware of how she felt about this, and she acknowledged yes. While Sarah seemed to be able to see the other perspective, at the same time I got the impression that she felt the need to take care of others, and that this was one way she felt she could still do this. She had spent her whole life taking care of others, thus much of her self-concept was tied up in this role, and she needed a way to reinforce it. This was a source of frustration for Jane, yet it seemed important to Sarah.

Over the next two weeks, Sarah had music therapy three times, once alone and two times with Jane and Emily, as well as some other visitors. Her condition continued to deteriorate. As the shortness of breath became more acute, Sarah became more anxious. The Xanax was started again but then discontinued because Sarah said that it caused "bad dreams." She complained of greater pain, and her pain medication was increased. She was started on intravenous fluids because her oral intake was no longer adequate.

As Sarah's condition deteriorated her spirits also seemed to deteriorate. She admitted to feeling "down" and then "depressed" but did not want to talk about it. Earlier Sarah had told me that she had prepared herself emotionally for death, but she had not realized how difficult dying would be physically. She had not anticipated such pain and discomfort. It all seemed to be taking its toll on Sarah.

The music therapy sessions continued along the same general course. Jane and Emily started choosing more of the songs as Sarah became weaker. She would often close her eyes and listen during the music and she stopped singing along. Their pastor was often visiting and he also participated in the sessions. I played "Dolphins and Mermaids" which became a favorite of Jane's, and she asked for a copy of the words, which I gave her.

Dealing With Pain

Sarah's condition continued to deteriorate, and slightly less than two months after she had been admitted she was placed on the critical list. The physician's note stated that the patient "is markedly short of breath, receiving morphine and oxygen continuously." Her pain medication had again been increased.

Early that afternoon I went to see her; Jane had not yet arrived. Sarah was alert and responsive, though experiencing severe pain. I went out and told the nurse that Sarah was asking for pain medication. The doctor went in to see her. She had only recently received an injection of morphine, but clearly she was still suffering and the doctor gave her another.

I acknowledged Sarah's pain to her and explained that sometimes music could help, was she willing to give it a try? She said yes and I sat down to play, instructing Sarah to try and listen to the music. I chose not to improvise at that time, I wanted to provide greater structure and familiarity. Instead I played many of the songs which we had played over the past two months, gradually moving to more quiet, soothing music as the session progressed. I also gradually lengthened the phrases of the music after having coordinated the rhythm of the music with Sarah's breathing. Sarah, though still uncomfortable, appeared somewhat more relaxed at the end of the session.

This was an extremely difficult session for me. For some reason Sarah's pain and anxiety affected me deeply. Perhaps it was because I felt so helpless. It is difficult to witness someone in such acute distress, and as a professional, I felt that I was supposed to be able to help. While music could and did help, I wanted it to do more, to take away Sarah's pain and breathing difficulties. I began feeling uncomfortable and anxious myself. I also knew that for the music to be most beneficial it had to be steady and grounded yet flexible, which was certainly not how I was feeling. I wanted to provide a calm presence.

Being able to play the music helped. At first I focused on the music until I felt a little stronger, and then I was gradually able to focus more on Sarah and meet her in the music without losing my sense of groundedness.

I spoke with Jane later in the afternoon. She was concerned and anxious, but appeared to be coping well. She had worked hard at preparing herself for Sarah's death, and I agreed with the social worker that Jane seemed to have made peace with Sarah and was accepting of her impending death.

Life Review

The following day Sarah, though responsive, was sleeping for long intervals, and was described by one nurse as "slightly confused." She had also started to drift off during conversation. I went to her room, and found Jane, Emily and their pastor there. When asked, Jane and Emily both wanted me to stay and play some music. When working with someone who is dying, an important goal is to help someone to bring their life to a close. One way to do this is to encourage the patient to engage in the life review process, to look back over their life. Music because of its uncanny ability to evoke memories, can play a key role in this process. In this session, the music was used to stimulate a "life review" of the music therapy life which Sarah, Jane, Emily and I had shared. They chose many songs which we had done in the past and shared memories of previous sessions, including the joy and the sorrow which the music had evoked. I had not planned this, yet once started I encouraged it as I recognized it as a meaningful and fruitful way to spend what we expected to be our last session together.

That night Sarah's family stayed at the hospital, staying at her bedside. Sarah was lethargic but responsive, moaning at times. The next morning the physician's note read: "Anxiety and pain. Wants to die."

I spoke with Jane, listening and offering support. She also seemed ready for Sarah to die. I would not be at work for the next two days thus when we said good-bye we knew it might be for the last time. Sarah's condition continued to deteriorate over the next two days. She was poorly responsive, but she hung on. Her family stayed at her bedside.

Upon return to work I went to Sarah's room. Her youngest son, her daughter, her daughter's boyfriend and Jane were all in the room. They all looked a little ragged; it had been a long vigil. As a patient's condition deteriorates, the focus for psychosocial care often shifts from the patient to the family. I will often play music for a family that I have worked with when the death of the patient is imminent. While I had worked very closely with Jane, I had never met Sarah's children before. I did not want to intrude, yet I also felt that they all might benefit from a directive, supportive activity. This can be a very hard time for family members. They both want to and feel that they "should" be at the bedside of the dying person, yet often they feel that there is nothing that they can do. I offered to play some music, and Sarah's family all appeared quite relieved at the idea. Jane asked to hear "Dolphins and Mermaids" and stood at the foot of the bed as I played. After that song she left Sarah's room. I wondered about her relationship with Sarah's children, sensing that it might be somewhat strained. Sarah's son, daughter, and daughter's boyfriend chose the remainder of the songs. Most of them were spiritual or religious in nature and included: "Amazing Grace;" "Let There Be Peace on Earth;" "Rock of Ages;" and "Old Rugged Cross." The three of them seemed very young and somewhat lost, not knowing which songs to ask for, trying to do the "appropriate" thing. I wondered how they would do after Sarah had died. Many of the songs they asked for evoked memories from their childhood. I had the image of the rug being pulled out from underneath them, and that they were clutching at things to hold them up. I noticed and felt glad that the music provided a needed structure, along with some emotional and cognitive connections to their past. Still I left the room feeling sad for the family.

Sarah died at 2:00 that afternoon, surrounded by her family.

The next morning Jane called me and asked if I would be willing to sing at Sarah's funeral. It can be a strange experience to be so intimately involved with a family and then, not being present at the moment of death, you return to the floor and the patient and the family are gone. I welcomed the opportunity for closure and also to provide some continuity for Jane's sake. The Calvary staff had been very involved with her over the two months that Sarah had been a patient, and I was glad that we would be represented at the funeral.

Jane chose three songs for me to sing at the funeral. During the service the pastor introduced me and spoke of the meaningful role music therapy had played at the end of Sarah's life. The first song I sang was "Let There Be Peace on Earth," chosen because it exemplified Susan's spirit. Second was "Dolphins and Mermaids" which held such meaning for Jane. Last was "Amazing Grace" which speaks so deeply to so many. It was very moving, both painful and beautiful, to sing these songs at Sarah's funeral. It was a profound and meaningful experience for me to be there.

DISCUSSION AND CONCLUSIONS

I have come to believe that music therapy can help the terminally ill in two ways. First, it can be used to accomplish what we traditionally regard as "therapeutic" or "clinical" goals, (e.g., reduction of anxiety, strengthening of self-concept, and much of what was discussed in the assessment). Second, music can be a source of deep, meaningful interaction---between patients and families, patients and patients, and patients and myself.

Music therapy provided Sarah and Jane the opportunity to express themselves through the use of songs. At times the songs, such as "Puff the Magic Dragon," brought to awareness feelings and reactions which hitherto had been unconscious. Sarah and Jane both used the music as a springboard to discuss a variety of topics, including some that were quite difficult and painful. Other times the significance of the song choice remained unclear, and the value remained primarily in the expression.

How was this expression helpful? I will first look at the benefits from the sessions when I was working with Sarah alone. For Sarah it was difficult for her to state her needs, ask for help, and accept help from others. However she could do this, indirectly, through the song material. By choosing a song she could express either what she was feeling or needing. By my choosing to play songs which reflected what Sarah had expressed I could meet the need and let her know that I understood.

For Sarah and Jane together one result of this self-expression was enhanced communication and understanding between the two sisters, which, I believe, helped them to adjust to the changing roles in their relationship. The necessity for Sarah to move from the one who took care of others to the one who needed to be taken care of was a difficult change. One of the music therapy goals was to facilitate this adjustment, and I believe music therapy did play a beneficial role here. The music also helped enhance the feeling of closeness between Sarah and Jane. They shared many memories evoked by the music, experiences of childhood and their lives together. They also shared other thoughts and feelings they had experienced as they listened to the various songs.

The music also proved to be a real source of enjoyment for both Sarah and Jane. A terminal illness is difficult for both patients and families because it usually involves one difficult situation after another. An enjoyable experience provides a period of respite and can serve to "recharge the batteries" thus enabling the person to better deal with the next stressful situation. Sarah herself said the music helped to "take the edge off." As a pleasurable experience, it also provided the opportunity for Sarah and Jane to enjoy some of their remaining time together, which is not always easy in a hospital. This was important, as it could help Sarah to feel that it was not always a drain or imposition on Jane to come see her. These fun times also provided Jane with some wonderful, meaningful memories.

Just as an enjoyable experience can be a source of added strength for coping, so can a religious experience. It is common for people with a terminal illness to turn to their religions as a means of comfort and strength. Some people are more open and direct about expressing their spirituality than others. As Sarah did not address this topic directly, and I chose not to ask, I cannot know for certain whether the spiritual music provided comfort and strength. My sense was that Sarah's desire to hear religious music was indicative of her desire for spiritual support. I learned from Jane that Sarah had sung in her church choir, thus Sarah had a meaningful relationship to religious music.

Another goal I had with Sarah was to diminish her anxiety. Familiar music is helpful in doing this. A hospital room can be transformed from an unfamiliar environment to a familiar one through the use of music that the patient knows. In this general way, I believe the music therapy was effective in diminishing Sarah's anxiety, even if it did not take it away entirely. There were times when Sarah was anxious and in pain in spite of my intervention. While this does not mean that music therapy was a failure, this is a time when I wish it could have been more effective.

Jane clearly reached a good level of acceptance regarding Sarah's death, through hard work on her part with the help of music therapy, social work and other disciplines. Music therapy helped in this in the ways described above. In addition, the music played throughout Sarah's hospitalization at Calvary, as well as my playing at the funeral, provided a real sense of continuity through Sarah's physical deterioration and death. A death can be extremely disorienting, and some sort of continuity is crucial.

I was reassured that "meaningful interaction" had taken place when I received from Jane made it clear that it had occurred. Jane wrote: "

> *Words do not suffice in my telling what an integral, important part you played in Sarah's life and her death. Because of the wonderful memories we were able to build my loss is lessened. Your participation in the funeral helped me to close the circle on a wonderful part of loving Sarah, and I will ever be grateful.*

That is clear enough for me.

GLOSSARY

Edema: Abnormal retention of fluid, swelling.

Lesion: An open wound.

Metastases: The spread of the disease from its primary site to other parts of the body.

Palliative Care: Care which serves to alleviate the symptoms of a disease but does not strive for a cure. People usually receive palliative care when a cure is thought no longer possible.

REFERENCES

Bailey. L.M. (1984). The use of songs in music therapy with cancer patients and their families. Music Therapy, 4, 5-17.

Lipton, L., & Yarrow, P. (1963). Puff the Magic Dragon. Los Angeles: Pepamar Music, Warner Brothers.